SOCIOLOGY

SOCIOLOGY

SECOND EDITION

Erich Goode
State University of New York at Stony Brook

Prentice Hall
Englewood Cliffs, New Jersey 07632

Library of Congress Cataloging-in-Publication Data

Goode, Erich.
  Sociology.

  Bibliography: p. 571
  Includes index.
  1. Sociology.   I. Title.
HM51.G634   1988   301   87–35956
ISBN 0-13-821448-4

Editorial/production supervision: Virginia L. McCarthy
Interior design: Linda Conway
Cover design: Linda Conway
Photo research: Anita Duncan
Photo editor: Lorinda Morris-Nantz
Cover photo: Stan Wakefield
Manufacturing buyer: Raymond Keating

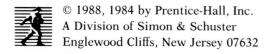

Printed in the United States of America
10 9 8 7 6 5 4 3 2 1

ISBN   0-13-821448-4

Prentice-Hall International (UK) Limited, *London*
Prentice-Hall of Australia Pty. Limited, *Sydney*
Prentice-Hall Canada Inc., *Toronto*
Prentice-Hall Hispanoamericana, S.A., *Mexico*
Prentice-Hall of India Private Limited, *New Delhi*
Prentice-Hall of Japan, Inc., *Tokyo*
Simon & Schuster Asia Pte. Ltd., *Singapore*
Editora Prentice-Hall do Brasil, Ltda., *Rio de Janeiro*

Chapter opening photo credits: Chapter 1—United Nations; Chapter 2—Ellis Herwig/Taurus Photos; Chapter 3—Guy Gillette/Photo Researchers; Chapter 4—Eastcott/Momatiuk/Photo Researchers; Chapter 5—Bill Bachman/Photo Researchers; Chapter 6—Lawrence Migdale/Photo Researchers; Chapter 8—Allen Green/Photo Researchers; Chapter 9—Ray Ellis/Photo Researchers; Chapter 10—Van Bucher/Photo Researchers; Chapter 11—David Frazier/The Stock Market; Chapter 12—Jerry Wachter/Photo Researchers; Chapter 13—Will McIntyre/Photo Researchers; Chapter 14—Stan Pantovic/Photo Researchers; Chapter 15—Lawrence Migdale/Photo Researchers; Chapter 16—Stan Wakefield; Chapter 17—Art Resource/Daniel Brody; Chapter 18—Don Carl Steffen/Photo Researchers; Chapter 19—Lawrence Migdale/Photo Researchers; Chapter 20—Greek National Tourist Association.

BRIEF CONTENTS

CONTENTS

8 DEVIANCE AND SOCIAL CONTROL *197*

PART THREE Inequality

9 SOCIAL STRATIFICATION *229*

10 RACIAL AND ETHNIC GROUPS *265*

11 WOMEN AND MEN *297*

12 AGING *321*

PART FOUR Institutions

13 MARRIAGE AND THE FAMILY *339*

14 RELIGION *367*

15 EDUCATION *395*

16 POLITICS *421*

17 THE ECONOMY *451*

PART FIVE Change

18 POPULATION AND URBANIZATION *475*

19 COLLECTIVE BEHAVIOR AND SOCIAL MOVEMENTS *505*

PREFACE

Recently, while having breakfast at a motel dining room, I overhead a conversation between a man I surmised to be a district manager of a fast-food chain and several men and women who were probably present and future operators of local outlets of this chain. The man was explaining how the corporation arrived at the decision to build an outlet in a specific location. Factors such as accessibility, traffic flow, density of the population, ethnic composition, per capita income, the location of nearby industry and offices, family composition—percent single, married, divorced, number of children, and so on—were discussed at that breakfast meeting. And I thought: These people are applying sociological variables and mechanisms in their work! How readily have the teachings of sociology been taken up and applied in the business world. I became aware of how practical the teachings of sociologists can be, how useful in the workaday world.

Unfortunately, the passions and prejudices of the social world too often overwhelm and nullify what we know as sociologists. As I write, the turmoil of the Howard Beach incident—three Black men were attacked and beaten by a mob of young whites; in escaping, one of the three was struck and killed by a car—is still very much with us. Sociologists often believe that they could contribute significantly to solving or ameliorating many social ills, if only others would listen. It seems a cruel irony that sociological ideas are now commonly used to turn a profit for the business world but not bring about intergroup harmony—ironic, because most sociologists would prefer to achieve the latter goal over the former.

Sociology touches on practically all aspects of our lives. No field explores so many facets of human existence. The 6 o'clock news on television is only one of the many things that remind us of the vast range of sociological investigation. News about the economy suggests how we are going to live in the months and years to come. A story about police brutality against Black people highlights the racial tension that troubles many communities across the nation. Distant wars flare up as a result of sociological forces—patriotism, exploitation, frustrated expectations, or the mass appeal of political leaders. Even sports news can yield evidence about the nature of our society. Everywhere we turn, sociological concepts stand ready to provide insights and explanations. Our relations with family and friends, our educations, the various jobs we do, our leisure activities, even the different ways we make love—everything from the most trivial and ordinary to the most momentous and sublime aspects of our lives—can be food for sociological thought. No other branch of learning can study and clarify such a broad spectrum of human existence.

The sociological umbrella is not only broad, but also exciting. Sociologists feel blessed to be working in such a captivating field. What other discipline permits us to investigate and learn about such social facts as crime and justice, marriage and divorce, wealth and poverty, and racial and sexual inequality, to name just a few? When people get together to discuss what interests them, what do they talk about? Their conversation revolves around themselves and other people—who they are and what they are doing. True, they do not quite approach the topic from a sociological point of view, but the subject itself is the same: social life. To ourselves, we are a source of unlimited fascination.

This partial list of topics sociologists study suggests a third characteristic of the field: It is personally relevant to our lives. It is concerned with forces, processes, and events that most of us have experienced first hand. Unlike some fields, sociology looks at the hustle and bustle of everyday life. We can see our own lives highlighted by sociological research. From childrearing to aging, we've lived through it, will do so in the future, know someone who has, or have an opinion on it. This real-world aspect of sociology adds immensely to its appeal.

Just as sociology is a way of thinking, it is also a subject matter. Thinking in a disciplined systematic fashion about the social world is a valuable skill. A sociology course can introduce you to a way of analyzing information that describes the nature of human life. When we encounter the results of the latest study on crime, divorce, the economy, population, or voting, we are forced to ask a basic question: How do we know it's true? Sociology provides tools to answer this question. Increasingly, the jobs that college graduates take deal with information. Sociology teaches you how to evaluate information, for assessing the accuracy of statements about the social world is a major feature of any sociology course. More than the information itself, this training can equip you for the job you will be seeking in the not-so-distant future.

Conveying the tumult and excitement of studying social life presents special problems for the instructor and for the author of an introductory textbook. Fascinating details must be harnessed to a more general structure, and the special relevance of basic concepts to our lives must be made clear. Such a venture demands discipline, balance, focus, and unflagging energy. I hope and believe that these qualities will be found in this book.

CHANGES IN THIS EDITION

I try to teach one section of introductory sociology each year, and some years, I have taught it more than once. Over the years, I have taught the course some twenty-five times to literally thousands of students. Each time I teach it, I learn more about what to say and how to say it. My students have taught me this, by reacting, questioning, challenging, asking for clarification, providing a stimulus to my thinking. What subjects do students find interesting? Which ones are boring? What's the best way to explain complex topics? How to present a controversial issue so that it teaches students about how the world works? How much detail is necessary to describe and analyze key areas of social life? I have found some answers to these and related questions from the feedback provided by the students in my introductory sociology courses.

The first edition of *Sociology* had the following primary goals. First, to provide a systematic over-

view of society; second, to present the various ideas, concepts, and approaches that sociologists use to study, understand, and interpret social life; third, to develop a critical faculty in students so that they can better think about how the social world works; fourth, to convey the intellectual excitement that studying sociology entails; and fifth, provide a foundation should the student wish to undertake later sociological inquiries, investigations, or courses. I have carried forth these objectives in the second edition of this book.

This edition of *Sociology* has been thoroughly revised. I have followed up on many suggestions from reviewers, colleagues, and students concerning what to add, modify, and take out. The essential approach and character of the book remained unchanged, however. Half the theme boxes in the new edition have been replaced with ones I believe to be livelier, more current, and more instructive. A score of new boxed inserts have been added to illustrate the discussions in the text. All statistical and strictly factual material has been reviewed and, where appropriate, updated. A large number of new sections have been added where their value was indicated. Where readers suggested gaps existed in the book, I have filled them in. Several chapters were substantially rewritten and restructured for a clearer presentation. Throughout, better examples were substituted for weaker ones; where ambiguity was the rule, I rewrote and clarified; recent trends and developments have been noted and described. These revisions have permitted me to write a better, and I hope, a more interesting textbook.

ORGANIZATION

Part I lays the groundwork for an introduction to the field by answering the fundamental question, "What is sociology?" In addition, it provides an overview of how sociologists gather and evaluate information about social life.

Part II introduces student to the basic concepts and ideas that guide sociological observation. What are the intellectual tools that sociologists use to investigate their special slice of the real world? What is it that sociologists focus on when they look at human behavior? This section of the book answers these questions.

Part III deals with the hierarchical side to social life—the ways in which people rank one another according to specific social characteristics. Inequality exists everywhere. Why? What is it based on? Does it have a future? This part of the book grapples with these questions.

Part IV examines the major social institutions—those guiding themes or areas that organize the details of social life in all societies.

Last, Part V investigates social dynamics—the ways, great and small, that social life changes over time and the impact that change has on our own lives.

FEATURES

Sociology is a tool for teaching and learning, not a summary of facts and opinions. To make it accurate, clear, and lively, we developed many special features:

Theme Boxes

Each chapter includes a box introduced by the theme, "What Do You Think?" These theme boxes deal with controversial issues like the usefulness of a nationwide census, bias in the criminal-justice system, and single motherhood by choice, to name just a few.

The "interactive" format of the theme boxes was designed to provoke reactions from students and to bring them directly and personally into the ideas and controversies of sociology.

Boxed Inserts

In addition, most chapters include more general boxed inserts illustrating such sociological ideas and issues as cultural integration, the significance of social labeling, and social interaction.

For the most part, I have adapted these boxed inserts from nonsociological sources, chiefly newspaper and magazine articles. Since the inserts themselves are adaptations rather than direct reprints, they not only present interesting and relevant material but also comment on its importance to sociology.

Readability

Sociology is lively and contemporary. Wherever possible, I used plain English rather than jargon; short and simple words rather than long and obscure words; and short and direct sentences rather than long and involved ones.

Every important point in the book is supported

by examples, many of them drawn from the lives of college students and all of them easy to understand. Each chapter is organized logically, and the coverage, though complete, is never too long or complex to be finished in a single reading. No effort has been spared to ensure that the information in *Sociology* is up-to-date and to cover all issues of current importance.

Theoretical Balance

Like the discipline it introduces, *Sociology's* theoretical outlook is flexible. The author of an introductory text has a moral and intellectual obligation to cover the whole field—theory included—not just a limited and too-opinionated segment of it. Functionalism, conflict theory, and symbolic interactionism receive more or less equal treatment here.

Much of today's sociology does not fit neatly into any of these categories, so I have introduced another one: "standard American sociology." Mainstream sociology is not a single outlook but a synthesis of several—a synthesis that aims to test "middle-level" (rather than all-embracing) theories shaped by the principle of value neutrality. These two ideas, value neutrality and middle-level theory, are fully explained in the text.

Cross-Cultural Materials

Although *Sociology* does focus on the United States, it presents much material from other countries and cultures, too. Contact with the rest of the world makes theories and abstractions come alive; shows us that our own ideas and institutions are not universal, inevitable, or "natural"; and gives us useful ideas about how people abroad deal with common problems of life.

Different foreign cultures have been particularly useful in making different points. The Soviet Union and South Africa both provide a useful political counterpoint to our own political system. For the chapter on economic institutions, I included a discussion of the Japanese economy, since it is now our most successful competitor. The experiences of Sweden and mainland China illuminate the relations between women and men in our own country. Of course, these are just three examples out of hundreds.

Summaries

Each chapter concludes with a brief, numbered, point-for-point summary that reviews its key ideas, generalizations, and facts.

Suggested Readings

Each chapter has a brief list of books that expand on the ideas or settings it explores. These lists were designed to help students research papers and pursue topics they find especially interesting.

Glossaries

All key terms in each chapter are highlighted in bold-face type in the text and defined in the margin. A glossary for the whole book follows the last chapter.

Photographs, Illustrations, Tables, and Graphs

Every illustration in *Sociology* informs and instructs the student by illuminating the text in a lively, often dramatic way.

SUPPLEMENTS

A Study Guide with Practice Tests, an Instructor's Resource Manual, and a Test Item File accompany the text.

The Study Guide with Practice Tests will help students review the important points of each chapter and understand the common themes of sociology as a discipline. Its self-test sections make it easy for students to evaluate their progress by checking their answers against the correct ones, placed in margin columns immediately beside the questions.

The Instructor's Resource Manual includes a detailed outline of each chapter; examples and illustrations for use in lectures; topics for papers, class discussions, and research projects; and a list of essay questions.

A separate Test Item File of objective questions comes both in book and computerized form.

ACKNOWLEDGMENTS

I have been extremely fortunate to have this book published by Prentice Hall. From its first stages to the last, *Sociology* has profited from skilled and painstaking attention at the hands of the editors and other publishing professionals who worked on it.

I owe a special debt to Prentice Hall sociology editors Bill Webber, who guided this edition through the months of its preparation, and Nancy Roberts, who guided it to its final publication. Louisa Hellegers and Virginia McCarthy labored ably to edit the copy and produce the book. Photographic research by Lori Morris and Anita Duncan proved to be invaluable. The behind-the-scenes administrative efforts of Susan Willig and John Isley will be forever appreciated. I am grateful, too, for the timely help of Kathleen Dorman, and for the technical assistance provided by Harold Cox (Indiana State University) in drafting the "Aging" chapter.

Thanks are due as well to Ray Keating, Prentice Hall's manufacturing buyer; to Linda Conway, who designed the book; to Bob Mony, the indexer; to Nancy Perkus, who typed the manuscript; and to Terri Peterson, social-sciences marketing manager of Prentice Hall's College Division.

The following fellow-teachers of sociology helped me a great deal by reviewing various chapters in manuscript:

- David Ashley
- Allan Mazur, *Syracuse University*
- Raghu Naath Singh, *East Texas State University*
- Edward Thibault
- J. D. Wemhaner, *Tulsa Junior College*
- Dale A. Lund, *University of Utah*
- Bruce A. Chadwick, *Brigham Young University*
- Stan L. Albrecht, *Brigham Young University*
- Patricia Harvey, *Colorado State University*
- LaVada Pepper, *Richard College*
- Rebecca Cramer, *Johnson County Community College*
- Richard R. Troiden, *Miami University*
- Richard M. Hessler, *University of Missouri—Columbia*
- Philip Berg, *University of Wisconsin—LaCrosse*
- Clyde W. Franklin, II, *Ohio State University*
- Barry Perlman, *Community College of Philadelphia*
- George T. Martin, Jr., *Montclair State College*
- George F. Stine, *Millersville University*
- Laura Kramer, *Montclair State College*
- Marshall J. Graney, *Wayne State University*
- Paul Luebke, *Univ. of North Carolina—Greensboro*
- Michael Hart, *Broward Community College*

Of course, any errors that may have slipped past them are my own responsibility.

I must also thank the countless friends and colleagues who helped me accomplish this revision, by providing direction, information, comments, criticism, and feedback. At the very least, they include: Patricia Roos, Norman Goodman, Andrea Tyree, Mark Granovetter, Linda Wicks, Lyle Hallowell, Stephen Cole, Kenneth Feldman, Michael Schwartz, Judith Tanur, Carol Marburger, my father, William J. Goode, and my wife, Barbara Weinstein.

E. G.
Port Jefferson, New York

SOCIOLOGY

chapter 1

WHAT IS SOCIOLOGY?

On November 17, 1978, a California Congressman named Leo Ryan—investigating rumors that former residents of his district were being systematically brainwashed, physically abused, and even murdered by cult followers in a jungle compound called Jonestown, in Guyana, South America—visited the commune and talked with its leader, Jim Jones. Embarking on a plane just after the visit on an airstrip in nearby Port Kaituma, Ryan's party was cut down by bullets exploding from the guns of angry cult members. Ryan, three news reporters, and another man were killed; ten others in the party were wounded.

Minutes later, at a crisis meeting in a building in the compound, Jones exhorted his flock to commit mass suicide as "the only way out." He claimed that the Guyanese Defense Force would come to Jonestown within the hour and torture and kill everyone in the cult. "Everyone has to die," Jones said. "If you love me as much as I love you, we must all die or be destroyed from the outside. . . . We must die with dignity." The few members who objected were shouted down by the crowd. "Bring the potion," Jones ordered, and a huge vat of grape-flavored Kool-Aid dosed with cyanide was dragged out and placed in front of the crowd. First, the poison was forced down the throats of the children; the adults then drank it from paper cups. Although guards stood by with automatic weapons, no one was killed trying to escape into the jungle. Only a few dozen members hid or escaped. The rest—the vast majority of Jones's flock—poisoned themselves or were forced by others to take the cyanide. In all, over 900 men, women, and children died at Jonestown (Kilduff & Javers, 1978; Krause et al., 1978). It had been the largest mass suicide since the Roman siege of the Judean fortress of Masada, almost 2,000 years ago.

Around the world, an explosion of shock and outrage greeted the news of the event. How could one man have wielded such power over so many people? Many observers assumed that the answer could be found in the unique features of the evil influence of Jones himself, or in some special personality defect on the part of his followers. Although the event was unusual, the processes that led up to it were not. The mass suicide at Jonestown can only be explained sociologically. First, the quality that Jones possessed was *charisma*: He generated the feeling on the part of others that he was exceptional, almost divinely inspired. Many other leaders have this quality and use it for good or evil. (We see how charisma works in the chapters on religion and politics.) Second, followers in the Jones cult were subject to the powerful and pervasive influence of the *group*—a process we examine throughout this book, particularly in the chapter on groups.

At least three well-known group processes operated at Jonestown—the same processes that operate in any group in which you and I have been members—*conformity, persuasion,* and *self-justification*. In this respect, the mass suicide that took place at Jonestown was not an aberration or a product of unique forces and dispositions (Osherow, 1984); it was an event that shares crucial qualities in common with all social life. Without understanding these specifically sociological concepts and processes, we would not adequately understand the Jonestown massacre. We would think of it as a totally unique event and fail to grasp its similarity with many events, some of them quite ordinary, taking place all over the world at this very moment.

If, for example, you are a sports fan, you are probably quite concerned with your favorite team's won-and-lost record. Does the best team always win? Is athletic ability the whole picture? Have you ever wondered about the so-called home advantage? Teams are more likely to win in their home cities than "on the road." A study of wins and losses in the National Basketball Association (1976–1977 season) showed that home teams won 68.5 percent of the time and that they won by an average margin of 4.4 points. During that season, not a single NBA team had a winning road record—not even the powerful divisional champions, like the Los Angeles Lakers and the Philadelphia 76ers. Teams that finished last in their divisions still managed to win nearly 60 percent of their home games (Watkins, 1978). Although during other seasons, championship teams may have winning records on the road, all teams win more games at home than away.

Why this strong, almost overwhelming advantage? Offhand, we might come up with several explanations. Officials may give an edge to the home team on their calls, not wishing to anger the crowd. A tough road schedule may leave athletes exhausted; home teams are more likely to be rested. Teams on the road are not as familiar with the visiting playing field, and so on. Two sociologists investigated the home advantage in sports (Schwartz & Barsky, 1977). They found that the factor of playing at home or away is as strong a predictor of a team's performance as the ability of its players. They also found that the home advantage is almost totally independent of fatigue and unfamiliarity with the playing area. The factor that seems to be most crucial in winning is the encouragement of the home team's fans. The home edge is least influential in sports where the playing field is large and the spectators are a considerable distance away from the players, as in football and baseball. The edge is most pronounced in sports where the playing area is relatively small and enclosed, and where the fans are close, as with basketball and hockey (Schwartz & Barsky, 1977).

Taking the analysis even further, Baumeister (1985) shows that even though home teams do have a significant edge during the course of an entire season, they tend to perform more poorly than visiting teams in the most crucial games. Whereas the "fan encouragement" factor operates overall, a "choke" factor appears to operate during important postseason championship series. For example, for all World Series, beginning in 1924 when today's scheduling system was established—and excluding four-game sweeps—the home team won the first two games 60 percent of the time. But for the final games (that is, game five, six, or seven,

The won-and-lost records of teams that play at home versus on the road clearly show a strong "home advantage." Sociologists argue that this can be traced to the home crowd's enthusiastic support of their favorite team.

Jim Amos/Photo Researchers

depending on how long the series lasted), home teams won less than half the time. For the twenty-six World Series that went to a full seven games, the home team won only 38.5 percent of the time. The same pattern prevailed in basketball. In the forty-one National Basketball Association playoff series between 1967 and 1982—again, excluding four-game sweeps—the home team won 70 percent of the first four games. But for final games, the home team's record was only 46.3 percent in the "won" column. And for seven-game series specifically, the home team won a dismal 38.5 percent of the time. Key performance indicators, such as fielding in baseball and foul shooting in basketball, decline significantly for the home team in the seventh and decisive game; the visiting team's performance in these areas remains unchanged (Baumeister, 1985, pp. 50–51). What is clear from the evidence is that home teams tend to "choke" in their most decisive and crucial games. The fans' vocal and spontaneous cheers encourage athletes to perform at the peak of their ability in less pressure-filled games. At the same time, when the championship is on the line, the same vocal encouragement creates an ironic "boomerang" effect. Players so powerfully identify with their fans' desire for them to win that they become self-conscious and self-aware to the point of performing less well on the playing field. Like the Jonestown suicide sect, players and home-team fans create a kind of *group*, with common goals, desires, and interests; they interact with one another in a positive, encouraging fashion. Yet, at times, especially under conditions filled with maximum tension, the intensity of their common efforts often frustrates their desires. It is not unusual for group membership to act in a negative fashion.

Sociology The systematic study of social life.

Although the Jonestown mass suicide fills us with horror, and sporting events with excitement, they share a crucial common feature: They are sociological events. All around us people are acting, reacting, interacting. The lives of some of these people are similar to our own, but some are very different. Sociologists attempt to enter social worlds to understand just what is going on. They attempt to look at worlds we know and are familiar with in a fresh, new way—and to look beyond what we know to get a glimpse at what may be unfamiliar, even alien to us. Social phenomena, both near and far, make up the sociologist's subject of investigation.

Sociology may be defined as the systematic study of social life. The focus of sociological attention is groups, which influence what individuals do and how they see the world. The People's Temple of Jonestown was such a group; membership in it influenced the behavior of members—even to the point that they willingly killed themselves. A team and its fans also form a kind of group, and belonging to it influences the athletic performance, for good and ill, of the members of that team.

We all have memberships in many groups. Our own special groups may comprise only two people—if we are part of a married couple, for example—or tens of thousands—if we work in an industrial corporation. Sociology is interested in the many ways that we belong to collectivities larger than ourselves and how this influences us. Some groups have an impact on us when we are in the presence of others—as when we cheer our home team on, or when a team responds by trying harder to win because of our encouragement. Other groups influence us even when we are alone: Away from home, the impact of our families can still be felt in all our actions, thoughts, and emotions. Whenever we are influenced by others, or take other people into account, sociologists take out their notebooks.

PATTERNS IN THE SOCIAL WORLD

When sociologists study the social world, they begin with certain basic assumptions. The first and most basic is that there is a pattern to the world, a certain degree of predictability. Our actions, thoughts, and emotions are not totally random or chaotic; they are to some extent orderly, structured in a systematic way. In the natural world, everyone takes such patterns for granted. We assume that the sun is going to rise in the morning and set at night; that a wet or icy surface will be more difficult to drive on than a dry one; that stones dropped out of buildings will fall to Earth. If we believed that events in the physical and natural world were totally random and without pattern, we would find it impossible to live, even for a single day.

The social world is full of patterns, too. Even people who scoff at the notion of social patterns and who grasp at exceptions to "disprove the rule" must act on the assumption that the social world is predictable. Do you really believe, for instance, that a friend you see on the street is as likely to say hello as to pull out a gun and shoot you? That sales clerks are as likely to give you all the money in their cash registers as to give you correct change? That the instructor of your sociology course is as likely to stand silent in front of the class for an hour as to lecture?

The fact is, we all learn the rules and regulations of "correct" behavior. We are surprised, even shocked, when someone violates these rules. Whether or not we admit it, we assume that the social world follows a pattern, and we act on that assumption. If we had absolutely no expectations about how others would act toward us, our lives would be just as insecure as the life of a person who has no notion of how the physical and natural worlds work.

Sociologists, like everyone who is reading this book, and like anyone else, all make assumptions and predictions about the social order. But there are differences, too. Sociologists do not take their assumptions and predictions for granted. They both state explicitly and systematically, and they test them with concrete evidence. They have rules for discovering and verifying social patterns. Sociologists attempt to study the social world, and not just to live in it.

Sociologists make few statements that apply to all human behavior. Most of the time, they try to identify and explain the differences among various categories or groups of people. Do rural dwellers, for instance, have more children than residents of cities (They do.) Are better-educated people more likely to vote in a presidential election than less well-educated people (Again, yes.) Are people more likely to violate a rule or a law if they see someone else doing so than if they don't (Yes, once again.) Social patterns can be discovered in differences among people and their circumstances, as well as in their similarities.

THE SOCIOLOGICAL IMAGINATION

The late C. Wright Mills called the special insight that sociologists must have to investigate the social world the **sociological imagination.** He was referring to the ability to locate an individual's life, and the lives of many individuals, in the larger scheme of things. Most of us tend to think we are unique. We have no clear idea how we are connected to larger groups. The sociological imagination is the quality of mind that permits an investigator to understand the subtle interplay between individual lives and their linkage in groups, categories, and other social phenomena. It is the ability to grasp the connection between biography and history. The sociological imagination is the ability to see where we, and everyone else, fit into the big picture, into the structure of society as a whole.

For example, married couples experiencing conflict will usually locate the blame for the conflict in their partners, themselves, or in the unique features of their relationships. But today, we live in a nation in which half of all marriages fail. The sociological imagination encourages us to look beyond the specific couples experiencing marital difficulty to the broader cultural and structural features of our society to understand the causes of this phenomenon (Mills, 1959, p. 9). Certainly these features, some of which we examine in Chapter 13, include a greater unwillingness to endure even a less-than-perfect marriage, a diminished expectation of marital permanence, the disappearance of the stigma that once adhered to being divorced, an increased feeling of individualism (which some commentators argue characterizes the current "me" generation), a decline in common values, an increase in the complexity of social life, the growing apart of many couples engaged in disparate enterprises,

Sociological imagination The ability to link specific details of individual lives with general structures of social life, to see where individuals fit into the "big picture."

and an increased likelihood that women partners are employed and are therefore less likely to be economically dependent. Although many couples can undoubtedly overcome these forces—after all, as many marriages succeed as fail—contemporary couples clearly face far more and far stronger sources of disruption than couples ever have in the past. Thus, their difficulty cannot be understood as a simple outgrowth of their individual and idiosyncratic characteristics. Rather, the causes must be located in the framework of contemporary society to understand why marriages today often unravel.

Every one of us has some unique qualities—that is, characteristics that make us unique. Mills referred to these as "personal" in nature. When only one person in a city of 100,000 is unemployed, that is a personal problem. In order to understand that problem and its cause, we must look at the nature of that particular individual: his or her character, personality, and skills—or the lack thereof. But in contemporary society, in which over 7 million workers are jobless (and in some neighborhoods, this is nearly half the labor force), unemployment is no longer simply a personal trouble. It has become a public issue as well, "and we may not hope to find its solution within the range of opportunities open to any one individual. The very structure of opportunities has collapsed. Both the correct statement of the problem and the range of possible solutions require us to consider the economic and political institutions of the society, and not merely the personal situation and character of a scatter of individuals" (Mills, 1959, p. 9).

The sociological imagination is the ability to see the interplay between private matters and public issues. It is, in short, a perspective enabling us to understand how social memberships influence individual life. It is not only a perspective that sociologists must have in order to understand the social world, it is also a valuable way of looking at the world that students may learn in a sociology course.

SOCIOLOGY AS A SCIENCE

You have just walked into a sociology course. Among the most difficult tasks your instructor now faces is to convince you that sociology is a science. When we think of "science," we think of people in white lab jackets pouring the bubbling contents of test tubes into beakers, peering through electron microscopes, or writing complex mathematical formulas. Behind that image is the idea that science must study the workings of the physical or natural world, matters with which most of us have no experience and about which we know almost nothing. By the lights of this image, social scientists—sociologists, anthropologists, psychologists, political scientists, and economists—are not "real" scientists, because they examine things with which we all have direct experience and about which we all know something.

What Is Science?

Sciences have five basic characteristics. First, they are empirical. Second, they are systematic. Third, they make statements that are falsifiable. Fourth, they make generalizations. And fifth, they attempt to explain the world.

An approach that is **empirical** is based on information obtained through our senses. The information must be seeable, hearable, feelable, tastable, or smellable—by anyone whose senses are intact. Is the information that lies behind the discipline of sociology empirical? Can you see it? Can others see it? If the answer is yes, we are in the world of the senses. If not, the information is not of the kind that scientists, as scientists, make. (Scientists are not always acting as scientists. When a nuclear physicist tells her husband, "I love you," she is not speaking as a scientist.) Some statements lie beyond experience—outside the reach of empirical evidence. They cannot be tested scientifically. Is a certain act moral or immoral? Does God exist? Is sociology worthwhile? Is a work of art beautiful or ugly? These are nonempirical questions. They are neither supported nor refuted by empirical evidence; they are outside the empirical realm altogether. The answers to them must be taken on faith, or they must be answered with kinds of evidence that a scientist would not accept as scientifically valid. Sociology, by contrast, is empirical. Sociologists collect evidence that involves real things that happen in the real world, a world that can be seen. Many different observers can test, and accept or refute, this evidence. Is sociology a science? Yes—because the information sociologists collect is based on the evidence of our five senses.

The second defining characteristic of all sciences is that they are **systematic** in their collection of evidence. This means that the information that scientists gather is not scattered, anecdotal, or hit-or-miss. Instead, it must be accumulated in a planful, disciplined fashion so that it is possible to determine whether a given statement is true or false. Scientists set forth a proposition or **hypothesis,** which they test with the relevant data, information, or evidence. Evidence must not be selected specifically to verify the hypothesis; it is scientifically improper to pick and choose one's cases to show that one is right. For instance, if one's hypothesis is that divorce causes juvenile delinquency, it is unscientific to focus only on delinquents from broken homes. One must investigate boys and girls from intact as well as broken homes to determine whether—or not—divorce has an impact on delinquency. To say that a science is systematic is to insist that its evidence be gathered methodically, according to a plan laid out in advance. Is sociology a science? Yes—because its data are collected in a systematic fashion.

A third defining characteristic of a science is that it must make statements that are **falsifiable.** A falsifiable statement is one that is capable of being supported or contradicted with the relevant evidence. Scientific statements have a special and almost unique characteristic: They are "designed to be proven *wrong*. Yes, wrong."

> The whole idea is to make statements that tell us how and why events occur and then try to show them to be wrong. This is done by collecting information or data on empirical events to see if things do indeed work as the theory says they should. If a theory stands intact after repeated assaults, then it is considered plausible and is accepted for the time being. . . . A theory is actually never proven; it can only be disproven. Tomorrow, someone might collect data to show that it is wrong, forcing us to reject or revise the theory. Yet, when theories stand the test of time—that is, repeated efforts to disprove them—then they become provisionally accepted as truth, as the way things are. This is the way all science works (Turner, 1985, p. 21).

On the other hand, if a statement cannot possibly be refuted or disproven with any conceivable kind of evidence, then it is not a scientific statement. Suppose a soothsayer predicts the end of the world in 1990. Let's say that time arrives and the predicted event does not come to

Empirical Pertaining to the five senses: something that can be seen, heard, felt, tasted, or smelled, and that can likewise be verified independently by others' senses.

Systematic Methodical, based on a plan, set up in such a way that valid comparisons can be made.

Hypothesis A statement set forth in advance of a study predicting the occurrence of a set of phenomena or proposing an explanation for facts that should be observed.

Falsifiable Capable of being supported or disproven by using the appropriate evidence. Falsifiable statements permit meaningful answers to two questions: "What facts would show that this assertion is true?" and "What facts would show that it is false?"

pass. The soothsayer might then claim that the world as we knew it previously ended in 1990, opening the way for a new order. In this case, the soothsayer's statements are not falsifiable: They are shielded from evidence, not exposed to it, as they should be. Unlike soothsayers, scientists construct statements that can be supported or refuted by evidence; they abandon rather than cling to clearly refuted statements. Is sociology a science? Yes—because it constructs falsifiable statements.

The fourth defining characteristic of a science is that it generalizes from facts. A specific fact applies only to one time and one place. "Ronald Reagan was elected president of the United States in 1984." That is a specific empirical fact. By itself, however, it has little or no scientific utility, for it describes only a single event, at a single moment in time. To put the issue another way, its informative value is low: It does not tell us very much. Certain statements tell us a great deal about many times and many places. A statement with a high informative value is a **generalization.** Here is an example: "The greater the agreement voters perceive between a candidate's views and their own, the more likely they are to vote for that candidate." This statement applies not only to the American presidential election of 1984 but to all elections, everywhere and at all times. A statement with high informative value tells us more about the world than a specific one, and it is more valuable to any scientific discipline (Zetterberg, 1966, pp. 79–80, 101–102). Is sociology a science? Yes—because its goal is to generalize from specific, concrete facts to make statements of high informative value.

The fifth and final characteristic of science is that it seeks to explain, or make **explanations** of, patterns and generalizations observed in the real world. Why are some stars red and others blue? What made the dinosaurs die out? What accounts for a high suicide rate in some groups and a low rate in others? Science provides answers for the question, "Why are things as they are?" The study of the world raises countless questions in the minds of inquisitive observers; science attempts to answer these questions. Scientific study represents a kind of intellectual problem solving. Is sociology a science? Yes—because it attempts to explain social phenomena, and it is not content simply to describe them.

Is a Science of Sociology Possible?

So far we've seen that sociology tries to describe and explain those things that we undertake collectively and the ways in which individuals are influenced by groups and by one another. We've seen that sociology is a specific and unique perspective of the world and that this social dimension of human activity is well worth investigating. And we've seen that the social world is to some extent predictable and that sociologists try to discover and explain its patterns.

Not everyone accepts these propositions. Some say that sociology is little more than glorified common sense. Of course, patterns exist in the social world. We all look for these patterns and act on them—but why study them? If they are what sociology is all about, then sociology is nothing more than the study of the obvious. Why spend a lifetime to reach conclusions that everyone's grandparents reached long ago?

A second, and related, objection is this: "I know everything there is to know about my life. I'm a man (or a woman) and nobody can tell me anything about sex or sex roles. I grew up in a family, and so a sociologist can't know any more than I do about that subject. I belong to a certain ethnic group, so I am an expert on it." This belief might be called the "automatic validity of the insider's view." Insiders look on themselves as instant experts.

Generalization A statement with broad application or relevance to phenomena that exist in a wide range of different times and places.

Explanation An account for why things are the way they are, or something is the way it is, that shows why something occurs or what causes it.

Third—and this objection is almost exactly the opposite of the first two—some people believe that everyone is absolutely unique, in all respects. Therefore, they claim, no one can make generalizations concerning human behavior. "I'm not part of a pattern!" as they often put it. "I'm not a statistic; I'm a person, an individual. You can't generalize about me!" They assume, in other words, that the premises of sociology rob them of their individuality.

Another objection has it that patterns and generalizations are not valid if there are many—or any—exceptions to the rule. Are generalizations really possible about a phenomenon so complex as social life?

Common Sense. It is widely believed that sociology is little more than a restatement of common sense. Sometimes, of course, this may be partly true, because many widely held beliefs are in fact correct. It would be cause for concern if the public were totally ignorant about all matters pertaining to itself! No field or discipline can be expected to undermine every bit of conventional wisdom.

But the findings of sociology often *do* contradict "common sense"— ideas that are widely believed to be true. In fact, it does just that so often, says one sociologist, that "the first wisdom of sociology is this— things are not what they seem" (Berger, 1963, p. 23). It is the job of the sociologist to look beyond what is taken for granted and widely accepted, to show how what is commonly believed may be erroneous.

Common sense, everyday wisdom, first-hand knowledge—all these are not always valid guides to reality because so many things cannot be understood by considering only the obvious or only what "seems reasonable." Let's take a look at one of the products of common sense: proverbs. If anything embodies common sense, it is the basic, everyday proverb. Proverbs seem to explain everything—and that is the whole problem. Why? Because they are completely contradictory! Proverbs can be shown to "prove" almost everything, because they say almost everything.

Say that you come across a couple in a happy, long-term, mutually satisfying relationship. The woman is calm, placid, and even tempered; the man is fiery and emotional. A proverb comes immediately to hand: "Opposites attract." However, you might just as easily meet a husband and wife who resemble each other in many ways and even look like brother and sister. If they are happy, you can invoke another proverb: "Birds of a feather flock together."

Likewise, when people rush off to do something, plan little or not at all, and botch the job we wisely say, "Look before you leap." If someone loses an opportunity through excessive caution, we are ready with "He who hesitates is lost." or perhaps, "Strike while the iron is hot."

If a couple is separated for a week and both partners begin to show interest in others, we say, "Out of sight, out of mind." But if they seem to miss each other, we say, "Absence makes the heart grow fonder."

Proverbs are a vast storehouse of common sense, but they are so contradictory that they have little or no value as descriptions of human behavior. Yet they are so old and so familiar that we tend to believe them. Sociologists attempt to move beyond common sense and conventional wisdom to find out what is really going on in the social world. Many sociological studies undermind common sense and conventional wisdom.

The Instant Expert. Many people regard themselves as experts on all the groups and social categories to which they belong. Marijuana smok-

WHAT DO YOU THINK?

Common Sense?

To demonstrate that sociology is not the science of common sense or the obvious, instructors often give their students "true-false" quizzes at the start of the course. I gave such a quiz to a recent introductory class. Imagine that the following six questions represent a "true-false" quiz. Take the quiz and find out how sharp your own "common sense" is. Are the following statements true or false?

1. Because people who have been divorced have already been disappointed in their previous marriages, they are less likely to marry in the future than someone (of the same age) who has never been married.

2. The higher someone's social class (measured by income, occupational prestige, and education), the higher the chances that that person drinks alcohol; the lower the social class, the lower the chances of drinking.

3. Of the four areas of the United States—the Northeast, the Midwest, the South, and the West—the *South* has the highest homicide, or murder, rate.

4. Despite what some liberals might say, male homosexuals are not "just like" heterosexuals except for their sex preferences; they are much more "promiscuous"—in other words, the average homosexual has had sex with more partners than the average heterosexual.

5. Taken as a whole, people who smoke marijuana are more likely to commit a wide range of nondrug-related crimes than people who do not smoke marijuana.

6. Because American Blacks are more economically disadvantaged than American whites, their suicide rate is much higher.

My class did not do very well on this quiz; in fact, only 48 per-

cent of the answers were correct—a shade worse than selecting answers at random. Let's look at the record.

1. *False.* At any given age, men and women who have been married and divorced are much more likely to remarry (to others, of course) than those who have never been married at all. Twenty-five percent of all divorced American men aged 25 to 44 remarried in 1977, and 14 percent of all divorced women of the same age. But of the people of the same age who had never been married, only 9 percent of the men and 8 percent of the women married for the first time in 1977 (Vital Statistics, 1979).

2. *True.* In a national study of drinking patterns, it turned out that more than half of all "lower" class respondents completely abstained from alcohol during the previous year,

ers typically believe that anyone must smoke "dope" to understand and write about it. Physicians typically believe that only other physicians have the right, or the ability, to judge physicians.

Fact: Not everyone who has first-hand experience of a thing or belongs to some social group necessarily has a valid overall grasp of it. Each of us has intimate experience of digestion, for example, but that does not make us experts on the subject. Not everyone who grew up in an Italian-American family has an adequate general understanding of his or her own ethnic group. There are different kinds of "knowing." Personal experience is one of them, but much knowledge lies wholly beyond it. We can look at social reality from the perspective of an "outsider," as well as that of an "insider."

Consider a few questions that might be wholly unanswered by the personal experience of an Italian-American household, however intimate but only one in five respondents who belonged to what was defined as the "upper" class (Armor, Polich, and Stambul, 1976, p. 54).

3. *True*. According to the annual statistics supplied by the Federal Bureau of Investigation (FBI), the South, year after year, has the highest murder rate in the United States. In 1985, for example, there were 7.9 murders for each 100,000 Americans in the population. The Northeast had a rate of 6, the Midwest 6, and the West, 8. The South's murder rate was ten. Of all the states with a rate above the national average, twelve out of eighteen were in the South.

4. *True*. Male homosexuals *do* have a strikingly greater number of sex partners than do heterosexuals, male or female. Female homosexuals do not, however; they tend on average to have sex with the same number of partners as female heterosexuals (Saghir & Robbins, 1973, pp. 59, 223; Bell & Weinberg, 1978, pp. 81–102). Is this good or bad? It is up to you, but this pattern has been found by every observer of homosexuality.

5. *True*. People who smoke marijuana do commit other crimes at a higher rate than people who do not smoke marijuana (B. D. Johnson, 1972, pp. 152 155). This finding does not mean that marijuana itself directly accounts for the difference—only that it exists.

6. *False*. In fact, the suicide rate of American Blacks is significantly below that of whites. Blacks as a group are economically more disadvantaged than whites, but suicide is not a simple product of poverty—or even misery! White males had a suicide rate of 19.4 per 100,000 in the population in 1982; Black males had a rate of 10.8. For women these rates were 5.8 for whites and 2.2 for Blacks (Statistical Abstract of the United States, 1986, p. 74).

How well did you do on this quiz? If this were an exam, would you have passed—that is did you get four or more correct? Did you receive an "A"—did you get all six correct? If the performance of my own class is a guide, the chances are, you probably would have done just as well if you had flipped a coin to find out the right answers. The fact is, sociology is a great deal more than an "elaboration of the obvious." It may be that "common sense" will help us figure out some social facts and relationships, but it may be of no use whatsoever with others. Simply being intelligent isn't enough; we must have the facts. Much of what we know about the social world comes to us only as a result of study and research. And this entails learning as much as we can about the discipline and the craft of sociology.

or extensive. What is the rate of intermarriage between Italian-Americans and other ethnic groups in the United States? Is it higher or lower than that of other racial and ethnic groups in this country—Jews, Blacks, Greeks, for example? What are some important consequences of church-going among Italian-Americans? Are highly educated Italian-Americans more or less likely to be observant Catholics than those who are less well educated? Have Italian-Americans assimilated into the middle-class mainstream? Are they a distinct, cohesive, ethnic enclave? How in this respect, do they compare with other ethnic groups?

We might ask many such questions and not only for Italian-Americans, but for every other group, too. Do you think that the members of these groups would be able to answer them more easily than outsiders? These questions call for systematic, concrete information that insiders usually do not have. The data needed to answer them must be searched out in many different places and in many ways. The minds and the feelings of insiders are not enough.

More than three-quarters of a century ago, the issue was summed up by one of the first and most influential of all sociologists, Max Weber, who wrote "One does not have to be Caesar in order to understand Caesar." In all likelihood Caesar did not understand a great many things about himself simply because he was himself, and he did not understand many other things because he was a man of his own times. The insight that every historical era has on its predecessors is what makes history possible. Of course, certain kinds of "knowing" come only from first-hand experience. But other kinds of "knowing"—the broader understanding of a phenomenon that links it with other aspects of social life—do not require insider knowledge, which may actually be a hindrance.

For some purposes the insider's view is vastly superior. For others, we may turn to the outsider. For still others, this distinction may be irrelevant. Finally, the claims of insiders and outsiders are complementary, not (at least in principle) competitive. Insiders may take "outsider" information and enrich it with their own experiences. Outsiders work with raw material supplied by insiders. What we might hope for is a kind of cross-fertilization, with one view enriching the other. In the words of sociologist Robert K. Merton, "Insiders and Outsiders in the domain of knowledge, unite. You have nothing to lose but your claims. You have a world of understanding to win" (Merton 1972 p. 44).

Are You Unique?   Every one of us is unique. You have an individuality that you must seek to express in your life and work. Does this make it impossible to generalize about social life? No. It is no contradiction to say that sociologists look for patterns and generalizations in social life

Are you unique? Many people who seem to stand out in a crowd actually share a great deal with the people around them. Part of a sociologist's job is to discover the similarities and differences that exist among the members of a society.

Ken Karp

and that they believe in and respect human individuality. You are like no one else on earth. But *in some ways*, to be frank about it, you are also a great deal like some other people. For certain purposes, human variation may be irrelevant. The precise contents of your breakfast, however odd, may be quite irrelevant if voting patterns are under study. Some of the things that make you unique may have no bearing on how you vote or whether you vote at all; when, or whether, you will get married; whether you will continue postgraduate education after you receive your bachelor's degree (or if you will receive a bachelor's degree at all); the likelihood of your getting arrested sometime in the next year; or your prospects of becoming a millionaire by the age of 30.

In sum: Yes, in the totality of everything you are, it is true, you are unique; there is no one quite like you in the whole world. And yes, again, in some ways, you do share important characteristics with some other people. How these characteristics influence our behavior is the basic subject matter of sociology.

Exceptions to the Rule. When sociologists discover a pattern in social life, they describe it in the form of a generalization. Let's take an example: "The higher a person's income, the more likely it is that he or she will vote Republican; the lower the income, the more likely it is that he or she will vote Democratic." On hearing this generalization—which is correct—one student thinks, "My Uncle Joe is a millionaire, and he always votes the straight Democratic ticket." Another says, "My Cousin Sally is really poor, and yet she votes Republican in every election." Do exceptions to the rule disprove generalizations? The sociologist's answer would be no. We will always find some exceptions to any rule concerning the social world. Of course, if exceptions are too numerous, the rule would not be valid, for they would not be exceptions; they would be the rule. Exceptions may sharpen the formulation of a rule, or they may specify the conditions under which the rule holds. But if a rule describes a majority of the cases being discussed, it is valid, regardless of scattered exceptions that we might dig up.

Sociological statements are probabilities; they are *not* certainties. Nothing in social life is certain except, so far, death. (Not even taxes!) Every rule, pattern, or generalization is a statement of probability or likelihood. Suppose we assert that every person who walks by a certain street corner wearing a skirt will be female. If a Scottish bagpipe band should come along our statement would be wrong. What we expressed as a certainty should have been expressed as a likelihood. Sociologists say that things are "more likely" or "less likely"—not that they are certain or impossible. To make the kinds of generalizations that will lead to interesting observations about society, you must learn to ignore the exceptions.

THE SOCIAL SCIENCES

Some of the sciences study the natural world; physics and biology are examples. The social sciences—sociology, anthropology, psychology, political science, and economics—study human behavior. Most colleges and universities have departments that offer courses in each field. This neat intellectual division of labor ignores a degree of overlap and mutual influence. Sociology, for instance, has been strongly influenced by all of the other social-science disciplines and has strongly influenced al! of them. Nonetheless, these somewhat arbitrary boundaries do serve to indicate differences in focus and emphasis.

Anthropology actually comprises four quite distinct subfields. Physical anthropology studies humans as biological organisms; it concentrates mainly on the evolution of humanity, *Homo sapiens*, from earlier primates, and on racial differences among the peoples of the world. Physical anthropology is more a natural than a social science. Archaeology, a second subfield, studies the physical remains of past cultures—such objects as pottery stone tablets, and arrowheads—and uses them to reconstruct an account of those cultures. Cultural anthropology is a subfield that deals mainly with cultures and societies that still exist. Cultural anthropologists typically study societies that do not have writing. In recent years, they have begun to study literate societies as well; this subfield thus increasingly resembles sociology. Linguistics, the study of languages and the structure of language, is another subfield of anthropology.

Psychology explores the workings of the mind—including problem solving, perception, learning, responses to stimuli, personality, and so on. Some psychologists, for whom psychology is a natural and not a social science, prefer to work with animals rather than humans. In general, psychologists focus on individual, not group, processes and influences. Of its subfields, the one that overlaps most heavily with sociology is social psychology, which investigates the influence of social situations on individual human behavior.

Political science studies political behavior—for example how people vote, how laws are passed, the differences among various forms of government, the causes of revolutions. In the past generation, political science has become more of an empirical and sociological discipline. In fact, a number of sociologists around the country teach in political science departments. So the two fields overlap heavily, and the dividing line between them grows steadily fuzzier.

Economics investigates the production and distribution of resources. What is the impact of taxes on the public's purchasing patterns? How do interest rates influence investment in factories and machinery? What is the impact of large multinational corporations on developing nations? These are the kinds of questions economists seek to answer. Of all the social sciences, economics makes the most extensive use of mathematics, yet it studies an aspect of human behavior—what people do with money, goods, and services—not impersonal forces totally beyond our will. Some observers believe that the economy is the most powerful and influential aspect of society.

THE HISTORY OF SOCIOLOGY

Although there has been philosophical speculation on the nature of society and social life at least as far back as ancient Greece, not until the 1800s did thinkers realize that the social world could actually be studied in a systematic, disciplined way. For the most part, the Greek philoso-

The Industrial Revolution seemed to create more problems than it solved, including child labor. The systematic, disciplined study of sociology grew out of an effort to make sense of the many problems brought about by the Industrial Revolution.

The Bettmann Archive, Inc.

phers were more concerned with the way things should be than with the way they actually were. They assumed that intelligent observers could learn about the nature of reality simply by thinking and talking with other intelligent observers about it. They held up an ideal of society and called upon it to conform to that ideal.

The 1700s are called the "Age of Enlightenment" or the "Age of Reason." Philosophers had by then decided that human beings were basically rational and that society was perfectable. The thinker's job was to uncover the universal laws of nature and simply apply them to social life, prodding society in the right direction. However, history quickly made these theories seem naive and outdated. Industrialization, an effort to improve and rationalize the manufacturing process, seemed to create more social problems than it solved. The Industrial Revolution, which began in the second half of the eighteenth century, transformed western Europe, forcing educated philosophers and social thinkers to reevaluate their views on the nature of society. Peasants, many of them forced off their land, left the countryside by the millions and migrated to the industrializing cities, to live in poverty and squalor. They worked in factories 16 hours a day, under extremely dangerous conditions, for low pay. Six-year-old children worked full workdays; workers were injured or killed by moving machine parts and received no compensation whatsoever. Unions were illegal and strikes were often crushed by the police.

How could these changes be explained by an "enlightenment" perspective? So many of the effects of industrialization seemed irrational, unexpected, a step backwards. It became clear that philosophers could not depend on reason alone to understand the social world. These new conditions demanded study. Partly as a response to these and related problems, sociology emerged as a means of studying them. In addition, the religious ferment in the centuries following the Reformation, which called into question the absolute truth of the Catholic church, and the discovery of non-Western cultures, which paved the way for a more relativistic approach to social reality, stimulated the emergence of sociology as a discipline. But the new perspective of sociology did not appear overnight; it germinated during centuries of thinking, studying, and writing. The first sociologists began writing in the early part of the 1800s.

Auguste Comte

The man who actually coined the term "sociology" was a French philosopher named Auguste Comte (1798–1857), who believed that the social world and the natural world obeyed the same rules. (Comte's original name for sociology was "social physics," but when he discovered that someone else had thought up that term, he abandoned it.) Whereas the ancient Greeks, and even the philosophers of the Enlightenment, had believed that thought and speculation are the basis of social thought, Comte stressed observation and study. Like the ancient Greeks, however, Comte regarded what "ought to be" as more important than what "is." Indeed, he hoped that the social laws he set out to discover would form the basis for a new social order—a kind of secular religion, with sociologists as high priests.

Comte developed what he called "the law of the three stages." Knowledge of any subject, he asserted, begins with the *theological* stage (superstition, magic, religion), progresses to the *metaphysical* stage (philosophical speculation), and, finally, emerges to the *positive* stage (or scientific explanations based on systematic empirical observation). Comte believed that all sciences progress through these three stages. He argued that mathematics, astronomy, and physics are the sciences whose subject matter is the most remote from human life and, hence, were the first to become truly scientific. Sociology, dealing with a subject matter intimately linked with human life, will be the last to do so. Although Comte urged the newly emerging discipline of sociology to practice the principles of science, he himself did not engage in any actual scientific research. "He was in too much of a hurry to finish his system" of outlining the new science of sociology. Instead, "Comte invoked some methodological principles that provided shortcuts to his goal" (Collins & Makowsky, 1984, p. 28).

Comte's principles may be divided into two parts—social statics and social dynamics. The most basic principle of his social statics is that parts of a whole cannot be understood in isolation, but must be grasped in context, in terms of their interconnections. A society provides an excellent example of this principle. Just as the organic body is made up of interconnected parts (the brain, lungs, liver, kidneys, etc.), every society, likewise, has its parts (the community, the state, the religious institution, the family), each with its own specific function to perform. Comte's theory of social dynamics dealt with change. Change, he argued, occurs in all societies in the same way and in the same sequence. By examining the most "advanced" society, we will know through what stages all other societies must pass. (Nineteenth-century France, naturally, represented the most highly evolved of all societies to Comte.) Comte also believed that all the features or spheres of society—for instance, the intellectual, the moral, and the political—progress in the same way and in the same direction. Today, no sociologist takes Comte's theories of social change very seriously, for change is an infinitely more complex matter than Comte could have dreamed.

Comte was an "ambiguous and Janus-faced" figure in the history of sociology (Coser, 1977, p. 41). He insisted that science be based on empirical fact, and yet he never conducted an empirical study himself. He equated progress with the decline of the influence of religion, and yet he founded a sect, the Religion of Humanity, and instituted himself as its Pope. And although his system of thought placed great emphasis on change, progress, and development—in much of his writing, he seemed to be a "flaming spirit who wished to provide a unified vision of the past and future" of humankind (Coser, 1977, p. 41)—at the same time, in some of his writing, he insisted on the preeminence of order and stability, "a fearful old man who counseled the Czar to tighten his censorship to prevent the emergence of subversive ideas" (Coser, 1977, p. 41). Nonetheless, as one observer comments, if Comte "was torn between the twin demands of order and progress," so, too, is the entire profession of sociology (Coser, 1977, p. 41).

Herbert Spencer

Herbert Spencer (1820–1903), an English philosopher, adopted many of Comte's insights, but without their religious trappings. Spencer's sociology was similar, in a sense, to Darwin's biology: Societies, like organisms, obey the law of evolution through "natural selection." (It was Spencer who invented the phrase "the survival of the fittest.") Societies, he thought, function very much like biological organisms. Both unite interrelated and interdependent parts, each with its own specific function. Spencer believed that the evolution of societies not only followed a pattern but also produced the best of all possible worlds. Any tampering with this natural process of evolution—through welfare programs, for instance—would permit the physically and mentally unfit to reproduce and populate the next generation. Therefore, thought Spencer, it would cause a gradual degeneration of society. Today, Herbert Spencer would in many ways be regarded as a political reactionary.

Karl Marx

Karl Marx (1818–1883) was the most influential social scientist who ever lived. His writings are the theoretical inspiration for governments that rule over a third of the world's population—although, incidentally, he viewed the withering away of government as a mark of true socialism. Marx was not exclusively a sociologist—his writings run the gamut of economics, history, political science, sociology, and philosophy—but he influenced many contemporary sociologists. A small band of American sociologists could be described as Marxists, and Marxism is much more influential among sociologists in other countries.

Marx was, above all, a student of **capitalism,** which he defined as an economic system in which the ownership of the means of production—like land and factories—are in private hands. Marx called the people who own them the bourgeoisie, or the capitalist class. The vast bulk of employed persons are members of the **proletariat:** They own only their ability to work and have no other source of income. Other classes—small shop owners, for instance—continue to exist but in time are swept into one or the other of the "modern" classes, which confront each other as openly competitive and thus hostile forces. Profit rates, moreover, have a long-term tendency to fall, and Marx argued that the capitalists would not be able to raise those rates by using more machinery. Therefore, they would have to exploit these workers more and more ruthlessly. These experiences would embitter the proletariat and force it into a class with common views and attitudes. At long last, the people would take destiny into their own hands, overthrow capitalism, and create a socialist revolution—or so Marx thought.

Marx believed that intellectuals like himself could act as "midwives," exposing the flaws of capitalism so it could more easily be overthrown by organized, militant workers, thereby helping to usher in the socialist revolution. In the past, Marx wrote, "philosophers have only interpreted

The early writings of Karl Marx were humanistic, even romantic, in orientation, while his more-often-quoted later works were more rigidly deterministic and dogmatic. Here, the young Marx expounds on his views.

Culver Pictures, Inc.

Capitalism An economic system in which the means of production and the ownership of wealth are in private hands.

Proletariat According to Marxist theory, the working class in a capitalist society; those who must sell their labor to live.

the world"; instead, he argued, the point "is to change it." Any honest analysis of social life in a capitalist economy must expose the system's flaws, or "contradictions." These contradictions doomed private ownership of industry.

For Marx, what "ought to be" and what "will be" were more or less identical. We see shortly how Karl Marx influenced one major present-day school of sociological theory.

Emile Durkheim

Comte, Spencer, and Marx can be considered the "founders" of sociology—the pioneers who created an intellectual discipline where none existed previously. Not one of them managed to secure anything like a job teaching or practicing sociology; they were simply writers. Emile Durkheim (1858–1917), a French rabbi's son, was the first person to receive an actual professorship in sociology. Of all the early sociologists, Durkheim has had the greatest continuing impact on American sociology. Like Comte and Spencer, but not Marx, Durkheim stressed the way the individual members of a society are bound together by their common interests and attitudes. According to him, societies are above all characterized by unity and cohesion. Even individual differences, he thought, produced cohesion by making everyone dependent on everyone else.

Durkheim rejected biological, climatic, and psychological explanations for social behavior, and he insisted on a distinctly sociological level to explain social facts. He stressed seeing society as a force above and beyond the isolated individual; society's rules become internalized, or "present within the individual." Like his predecessors, Durkheim believed that a thorough understanding of society would make it a more reasonable, happier, and saner place in which to live. In other words, Durkheim—like Comte, Spencer, and Marx—believed that studying society would represent a step toward improving it. Durkheim's most notable contribution to sociology was the way he integrated his theories with his research methods. More effectively than any observer of society before him, Durkheim made extensive and extremely sophisticated use of statistics to test his hypotheses. For instance, in his classic study, *Suicide*, Durkheim calculated the precise suicide rates of men and women; of the married and the unmarried; of Protestants, Catholics, and Jews; of every European nation; of every province within certain nations; of different professions; and so on. Using these data, Durkheim fashioned a theory of why people commit suicide based on social integration. Contemporary researchers are strongly influenced by Durkheim's research methods.

Max Weber

Ill health prevented Max Weber (1864–1920) from teaching most of the time, but he wrote many learned and brilliant volumes on a variety of sociological topics, including religion; bureaucracy; class, status, and power; law; and research methods. Even today, Weber remains a towering, awe-inspiring intellectual figure. His work, more than that of any other early sociologist, resists easy summary, because it is so rich, complex, and wide-ranging. Practically alone among the early sociologists, he stressed the differences, rather than the similarities, between the natural and the social sciences. With all sociologists, he believed that societies are full of patterns and predictable events but held that what makes sociology distinct is the subjective *meaning* that things in the social world have for individuals. Our understanding of natural phenomena (physical, chemical, biological) is purely an external or intellectual understanding. We do not reach into our own experiences to help us understand the movement of the stars. Our understanding of social behavior, by contrast, places us inside the minds and emotions of those people whose behavior we are trying to understand, because we too have minds and emotions.

Weber differed from the other early sociologists in two other crucial respects, as well. On the one hand, he argued that the sociologist must give an objective, or value-free, analysis of society, but that, on the other, the sociologist's conviction that a topic is important enough to study can never be strictly objective. Other early sociologists claimed that their interests were objectively important, not just interesting to them as individuals holding opinions. Yet Weber turns out to be the most objective of the early sociologists. We may choose to study something because of our private values, but the *way* we study it must be scientific and objective. Unlike Marx, or even Comte, Spencer, and Durkheim, Weber believed that a scientific understanding of society was totally removed from morality, ideology, and political views. Knowing what *is*, in other words, does not automatically tell us what *ought* to be. Although he did not make the extensive use of statistics that Durkheim did, Weber was, in many ways, the most accomplished and contemporary of the early sociological figures.

THE DEVELOPMENT OF SOCIOLOGY IN AMERICA

Sociology emerged in the United States a generation or two later than it did in Europe. By the 1890s, however, the fledgling discipline of sociology had given rise to an academic department at a major university, the University of Chicago, and an important scientific journal, *The American Journal of Sociology*. Sociology had arrived in America.

For almost half a century, until the coming of World War II, the University of Chicago remained the most influential center of sociological work in this country. The early Chicago sociologists focused on many of the same social problems that had earlier launched sociology in Europe. Using the city of Chicago as a natural laboratory, they studied such topics as slum neighborhoods, juvenile delinquency, drug addiction, race and ethnic relations, and mental illness. These early Chicago researchers disliked what they saw and wanted to reform it. Yet one of their major contributions to the dicipline was their empiricism—their insistence on viewing society under real-life conditions. To find out what society is like, the Chicago sociologists insisted, you must get out into the streets and get your hands dirty. They rejected "armchair" research, conducted without contact with the real world.

By the 1940s, this kind of problem-oriented research had ceased to be the dominant trend in American sociology. From its reformist beginnings, the discipline was trying to establish itself as a "pure science." Many sociologists came to believe that it is more important to contribute to knowledge for its own sake than to try to solve such practical problems as crime and poverty. This "pure science" approach moved in two separate directions. One developed more precise and sophisticated research methods. Throughout the 1940s and 1950s, American sociologists devised increasingly scientific sampling techniques, valid and reliable means of constructing questionnaires, and powerful statistical formulas for analyzing the data they gathered. Data gathering became a major focus in American sociology. The second approach was called "Grand Theory" (Mills, 1959, pp. 25–49). Harvard University's sociology department was founded in the early 1930s. On its original faculty was an instructor, Talcott Parsons, who received his graduate training in Germany. Parsons generated a theory of society that conceived of all societies as a kind of balanced state, or equilibrium (Parsons, 1951). This theory came to be known as structural-functionalism or, more simply, as functionalism. Parsons's theory is quite abstract and attempts to explain all social behavior, everywhere and throughout history, with a single model. This style of abstract theorizing is no longer fashionable, but Parsons influenced a generation of graduate students who eventually taught at other universities and became very influential themselves.

These two trends—the shift toward data gathering and abstract theorizing—characterized American sociology in the period during and just after World War II. They were the two most influential and dominant modes in the field at that time. A "minor" mode also developed, called radical, or conflict, sociology. In its earliest years, this perspective was represented almost solely by the writings of a single sociologist, C. Wright Mills, who was profoundly influenced by the work of Karl Marx. Mills wanted to trace the sources and consequences of the unequal distribution of power in American society. During an extremely conservative period of our history, when most sociologists viewed this country as harmonious, cohesive, and truly democratic, Mills said it was dominated by a small, self-interested "power elite" (Mills, 1956). Mills's work later gave birth to a whole generation of conflict theorists.

MAJOR SOCIOLOGICAL THEORIES

"Theory" has a bad name among many Americans. It seems to mean "wild speculations," as opposed to facts. To most people, saying that a certain statement is "just a theory" makes it plain wrong.

The truth is that we all use theories, every day. A **theory** is a general explanation for a range of phenomena. Theories try to explain the world and, within limits, to predict the future. Whereas empirical study tells us "what," theories tell us "why." But scientists use the term in a more restricted sense—not to explain specific events, such as John F. Kennedy's assassination, but to explain more general classes of events, like "Why did organisms evolve?," "How did the universe originate?," and "What makes for political revolutions?"

"Theory" is also used in a broader, looser way. In this sense, a theory is a **paradigm,** an overall conception of how the world works. A paradigm is a perspective, a way of looking at things. Sociology has several such perspectives, not just one; it is a multiple-paradigm discipline (Ritzer, 1975), broken up into a number of competing schools of thought. Each school embraces a somewhat different conception of the social world and how it works. These various sociological theories do not always

Theory A general approach, a perspective, a paradigm; an explanation for a general class of phenomena, such as Darwin's theory of natural selection.

Paradigm A model of how the world works; a theory or perspective.

■ **TABLE 1–1 Key Propositions of Leading Contemporary Social Theories**

Functionalism	*Conflict Theory*
Society as a whole is composed of inter-related, mutually dependent parts; these parts work together to maintain stability within society.	Clashes among groups within a society are routine; social life is a continuous power struggle.
Societies develop institutions that are adaptive and that ensure survival.	Resources are differentially distributed in all societies.
Social phenomena should be examined in terms of their consequences.	Social arrangements benefit some groups at the expense of other groups and those on top organize society to maintain their position.
Dysfunctional activities or institutions threaten the capacity of a society to survive; such activities or institutions tend to be controlled or eliminated.	Almost every action helps some segment of society while it harms others.

Symbolic Interactionism	
Individuals attempt to understand the *meaning* of social interaction.	To interpret an act, individuals must understand the interpretations of those whose behavior they want to understand.
The meaning of an act is not inherent in the act itself; meaning is highly flexible and variable.	Emphasis is on the concrete situations that influence behavior; personal traits are less important in explaining behavior.

directly contradict one another; often, they just look at different aspects of the world, different classes of facts. They complement rather than contradict one another. Different sociological explanations of the same problems tend to differ in emphasis or focus, not to clash directly. These theories differ in a number of important ways (see Table 1–1 above). One of the most important of these differences is the social scale they examine.

Some sociologists prefer to study social relations on a small scale, at the level of person-to-person encounters. Their theories, which direct us to examine face-to-face relations between individuals or categories of individuals, are called **micro-level theories.** Other sociologists prefer the "big picture." They examine the relations among structures and social institutions, not among individuals. These theories are called **macro-level theories.** On this level, a sociologist might ask, "How does a society's economic structure influence the content of its education?" Note that micro does not mean "specific," nor macro, "general." Generalizations are just as possible on the micro as on the macro level. (We see how in the sections describing the actual theories.) But this distinction is one of the most fundamental in theoretical sociology.

According to most observers, there are three basic theories, approaches, or traditions within sociology: functionalism, which is significantly influenced by Emile Durkheim; conflict theory, which derives from the writings of Karl Marx; and symbolic interactionism, or simply interactionism, which began in the thinking of George Herbert Mead and Max Weber (Collins, 1985b, 1985c). Although individual sociologists do not necessarily proclaim exclusive and undying loyalty to one or another of these traditions, much sociological writing is influenced more by one than the others.

Micro-level theory A perspective that examines social relations on a small scale, at the level of person-to-person encounters.

Macro-level theory A perspective that examines the "big picture," society on a structural and institutional level, rather than at the individual level.

Functionalism A sociological perspective that stresses stability, cohesion, consensus, and the impact of behavior and custom on society as a whole.

Functionalist theory argues that every basic social institution has a "function" to perform for the whole of society. Religion, for example, integrates the community and contributes to society's stability and well-being. Here, Italian-American Catholics celebrate the feast of St. Anthony.

John Bova/Photo Researchers

Dysfunction Something that has a detrimental effect on society as a whole.

Latent function Consequences of social actions or customs the members of a society are unaware of and may not desire.

Manifest function Consequences of social actions or customs the members of a society know about and usually desire.

Functionalism

As was evident in the work of Herbert Spencer, twentieth-century **functionalism** does not adopt such a literal analogy between organisms and society, but it has kept the idea of society as a whole comprising interrelated, mutually dependent parts. Each part has a "function" to perform for the whole, and each part is intimately and intricately connected to the others, like a jigsaw puzzle. Education's function is to transmit knowledge to the young; religion's function is to satisfy a hunger for definite answers to troubling questions about the unknown; and so on. Each function represents a contribution to society as a whole. Every part of society, every institution, fills a need. If each part did not play its role, society would not survive. Over the millennia, the centuries, the decades, and the years, all societies have groped unconsciously—but effectively—to solve their most basic problems by developing institutions that are adaptive, that ensure survival. Societies that have not solved such vital problems have simply died out.

Functionalists argue that social phenomena should be examined mainly in terms of their consequences—their contribution (or the lack of one) to social stability. Functionalists often find that customs, behavior, and institutions that on the surface appear to be mistaken, harmful, or unjust actually serve useful purposes. For instance, functionalists have argued that prostitution helps to maintain the traditional patriarchal family (Davis, 1937). Bossism and political corruption serve social functions by personalizing and humanizing the political process to groups that have no other kind of access to government (Merton, 1968, pp. 125–136). Even conflict, if it is not over deep or fundamental issues, may actually function to "knit society together" by preventing the emergence of conflict over a single explosive issue (Coser, 1956).

Of course, functionalists do not argue that all activities or institutions have a beneficial impact on a society. Some actually threaten it. Functionalists describe such activities and institutions as **dysfunctional. A dysfunction** diminishes the capacity of a society to survive or adapt. Romantic love, for example, can disrupt all kinds of social and economic arrangements. From this point of view it is dysfunctional. As a result, it has always been tightly controlled, either by efforts to prohibit it as a basis for marriage or by making sure that only the "proper" partners fall in love in the first place (W. J. Goode, 1959). Activities or institutions that are actually or potentially dysfunctional tend to be controlled, banned, or eliminated; those that are positively functional for society tend to be encouraged, and they survive over time.

Sometimes the functions and consequences of an action or an institution will be neither clear nor intentional. Those that are not are called **latent functions;** those that are both are called **manifest functions.** Functionalists separate the motives of people who engage in certain actions from the consequences of those actions. The best intentions can sometimes produce disastrous results—and once in a while, evil intentions can have beneficial consequences. Moreover, people may not even be aware of the positive or negative results of their actions, even when they occur. For instance, Durkheim argued, one of the consequences of the greater religious diversity and individualism that accompanied Protestantism was a less cohesive, less tightly knit community of believers. A latent function of this individualism, in turn, was a higher suicide rate among Protestants than among Catholics and Jews (Durkheim, 1951, pp. 159–160). No one planned things this way. Indeed, aside from sociologists, very few individuals even recognize that one consequence of increased religious freedom is a higher suicide rate. At the same time, such unintended, unrecognized, or latent consequences of certain actions or institutions are common—and intriguing to functionalist sociologists.

Functionalism was the dominant perspective in American sociology during the 1940s and 1950s. Even into the early 1960s, several introductory sociology textbooks adopted an exclusively functionalist perspective (H. Johnson, 1960; Bredemeier & Stephenson, 1964). No such books exist today. In the 1970s, a dwindling number of American sociologists adopted the functionalist perspective, and at least one observer (W. J. Goode, 1973) argued that no contemporary sociologists identify themselves as functionalists. This is no longer true; in the 1980s functionalism (in its reborn guise of "neofunctionalism") has made a comeback (Alexander, 1985). At the same time, functionalism is currently more often written about—and criticized—than actually adopted.

Conflict Theory

Functionalists emphasized the stable aspects of society, the contributions that certain activities or customs make to a society's cohesion and well-being. Even conflict, they argued, can promote cohesion if it is not over deep and fundamental values or issues. Functionalists argued that most people agree about the most important things, so theirs is also called the **consensus perspective.** By contrast, conflict theorists think that fundamental and potentially disruptive clashes among social groups are routine, perhaps inevitable. In all societies that have ever existed, conflict theorists argue, some members have more resources than others: more power, more prestige, more wealth. Those who are on top will attempt to ensure that they continue to monopolize these resources; they try to make their privileges seem natural and good for society as a whole, including those at the bottom. In other words, those who are on top of society organize society to keep themselves on top. Conflict need not erupt into outright violence. In fact, if privileged groups succeed in convincing underprivileged ones that they should be happy with their lots in life, overt force is not needed to maintain social stability. Consensus and agreement on basic values may be a sign of exploitation, not of a fair and just society.

Consensus perspective The view that most members of society agree on the most important values and issues; it is regarded as an aspect of functionalism.

Conflict theorists argue that basic social institutions operate to benefit some members or segments of society at the expense of others. Unemployment, they hold, prevails because some industries profit from it.

Herman Kokojan/Black Star

Conflict theory A sociological perspective arguing that exploitation and coercion dominate social relations among groups in society.

According to **conflict theory** social arrangements typically benefit some groups at the expense of others. The powerful seek to uphold their power and coerce the powerless, and the powerless resist if they can. By these lights, few if any social actions or institutions benefit society as a whole. Actions and institutions can be "functional" only from the point of view of particular groups (Collins, 1975). Who profits? Who loses out? These are questions we must always be asking, say the conflict theorists.

Some key sources of conflict in any society are class, race, and sex. For instance, feminist sociologists argue that men have greater access to power and wealth than women do, and that the relations between the sexes are at bottom relations of conflict—indeed, the most fundamental of conflicts—not cooperation. Two observers call that conflict "the longest war" (Tavris & Wade, 1984). Our economy, for instance, benefits from the fact that many women work in the home as homemakers, for little or no pay. A functionalist would say that "women's work" contributes to the society as a whole. A feminist sociologist would say that it contributes to male supremacy. Conflict theorists see social life as a continual power struggle that certain groups win and others lose. Each group in society has different interests, and each has different resources for protecting or maximizing them.

Marxism A sociological perspective arguing that economic conflict between social classes is the most important dimension or factor to examine in capitalist society.

The most detailed, comprehensive, and celebrated variety of conflict theory is called **Marxism,** which is important both for the history of sociology and as a source of inspiration for many contemporary sociologists. Marxism is a distinctive outlook, in many ways quite unlike even the other varieties of conflict theory, for it stresses economic conflict above all others.

Symbolic Interactionism

We see two men kissing. Many of us think, "Aha! Homosexuals!" Symbolic interactionists do not make such assumptions. They attempt to understand the meaning that kissing has to the two men and to others in their environment. Perhaps the act takes place in a society, such as France or Italy, where kissing does not necessarily have a sexual connotation. How do others react to the sight of these two men kissing? Do they treat them as homosexuals? And how do the men in turn respond to this treatment, whatever it may be? The act may be essentially the same in different societies, but its meaning can be vastly different. The meaning of the act is not inherent in the act itself; it is imposed by individuals who engage in it or witness it. Meaning is highly flexible and variable from person to person, society to society, and situation to situation. To interpret an act, we must understand those whose behavior we wish to understand.

Interactionism See **Symbolic interactionism.**

Symbolic interactionism A perspective within sociology that stresses the meaning phenomena have for individuals and groups, the interaction that takes place among individuals, and the ways in which people interpret things in the world.

Symbolic interactionism, or simply **interactionism,** whose most influential theoretical founders were Max Weber and George Herbert Mead (1863–1931), is a major perspective within present-day sociology. Weber introduced the idea of *Verstehen*: interpretive understanding, or using one's own experience to grasp a social phenomenon. This is the interactionists' guiding principle. Another idea, introduced by Mead, is that people often act as their intimates expect them to act.

Today's symbolic interactionists are guided by "three simple premises" (Blumer, 1969, p. 2). First, we act on the basis of the meaning we attribute to any course of action. One person, for example, may go off to fight a war because refusal to fight symbolizes, or means, cowardice—

Symbolic interactionists view meaning as a central sociological concept. In some social circles military participation is defined as necessary, even desirable. The members of other social circles view fighting in a war as immoral, an evil to be resisted.

United Nations

U.S. Army Photograph

and, consequently, shame and dishonor. A second person may refuse to fight, and may become a conscientious objector instead. To that individual, any kind of killing means, or symbolizes, murder.

A second premise of symbolic interactionism is that meaning grows out of social interactions we have with our fellow human beings. The friends of the first person just described equate fighting with bravery and patriotism, and the refusal to fight with cowardice and treason. The individual, too, adopts these views. The second person, in contrast, was friendly with pacifists and thus became a pacifist, too.

Third, symbolic interactionism stresses the interpretative process. In other words, people do not mechanically accept everything others

What Can I *Do* with a Sociology Major? The Job Market for Sociologists

Sociologists are employed mainly in two economic sectors: *academic* and *applied*. Academic jobs involve teaching, research, and administration at the college and university level. Today, in the United States, about 10,000 to 12,000 sociologists are employed full-time in the academic sector, and about 3,000 to 4,000 work part-time. This represents roughly seven out of every ten jobs held by sociologists. The rest, about 6,000 to 7,000, are employed in the applied sector, working for government at all levels, for nonprofit organizations, and for industry.

The Bureau of Labor Statistics projected changes in employment and anticipated the number of sociologists who would be employed in 1990, based on supply and demand. The number of academic jobs for sociologists who wish to teach and do research at the college and university level will remain more or less constant until 1990, which means that the number of new sociology professors entering the profession will roughly match the number of retirements and deaths. Another way of saying this is that there will be no growth in this sector (although there will inevitably be small year-to-year fluctuations). Unlike the academic sector, however, the applied sector is a growth market. The Bureau of Labor Statistics estimated that the number of jobs for sociologists in the applied sector will increase between 1980 and 1990 by about 25 percent (Manderscheid & Greenwald, 1983).

For an academic career, studying at the graduate level after college is an absolute must, and receiving a Ph.D. degree (or a doctor of philosophy in sociology) is strongly recommended. A Ph.D. generally requires four to six years of full-time graduate study, including courses, qualifying or comprehensive exams, a master's degree, language exams, and a dissertation—typically, a book-length study or monograph on a specialized topic.

The American Sociological Association summarizes the prospects in an academic career in the following words:

> Sociology is a rewarding field to convey to others. It combines the importance of social relevance with the rigor or a scientific discipline. It includes a broad range of subject matter, since all forms of social behavior are potential objects of sociological study. Sociology is not only being taught to future sociologists and to undergraduate students as part of their liberal arts or vocational education, but is also included in the programs of many professions, such as law, education, medicine, engineering, social work, nursing, etc. In addition to the standard college and university courses, sociology courses are popular with adult and continuing education programs and are increasingly prominent in the nation's high schools.
>
> Teaching sociology is not the same in every setting. It is one thing to give a general introduction to a class of high school students and quite another to give a specialized course to college seniors. Both of these differ with leading an advanced research seminar for graduate students who are well along toward the Ph.D. In each case there are rewards and frustrations. For many persons, teaching seems a desirable occupation which provides considerable job security and the satisfaction of providing knowledge and stimulation to students who respond with respect and appreciation. But if this is teaching at its best, there are moments when even the best teachers are disappointed. It is not easy to communicate material to students of unequal and uneven capacities. Invariably, some students will be more turned

tell them; they continually reevaluate their knowledge and experience. The person who went off to war might interpret the situation differently if asked to fight against relatives, friends, or neighbors. Warfare will have a totally different meaning in this case. Our second individual may see warfare as the equivalent of murder; if an enemy were to threaten everything he or she cherished, he or she too might reexamine his or her attitudes. Everyone actively creates meaning; no one is a passive receptacle of meaning receiving it like a jug receives milk.

Interactionists emphasize the concrete situations that influence our behavior. After all, in different contexts, the same person will react in different ways. The other perspectives assume that once we have identified an individual's basic characteristics—young or old, male or female, on than others. And no matter how much work the teacher puts into a particular presentation, there is always a student who not only keeps looking at his or her watch, but actually listens to see if it is running!

Teaching is one of the two most common career options within sociology and research is the other. Note, however, that there is not necessarily a choice *between* teaching and research. Many teaching positions, particularly in universities, require research activities. . . . It is certainly true that publishing scholarly articles or books is the foremost route to job security, promotion and salary increases in most universities. But this applies to only a relatively small number of faculty members in those settings where original scholarship is highly prized and supported. In other schools, there is much less pressure to publish (American Sociological Association, 1977, pp. 10–11).

Sociologists who work in the applied sector are employed by state, local, and federal government, nonprofit organizations, or business firms. Most of what sociologists do in this sector deals with people or with information. Clearly, for the latter, facility with computers is called for. Sociologists in the applied sector work, for example, as criminologists (see Chapter 8), urban planners and demographers (see Chapter 18), marriage counselors (see Chapter 13), gerontologists (see Chapter 12), statisticians (see Chapter 2), minority consultants (see Chapter 10), and personnel directors. Some specific jobs in which applied sociologists are engaged include:

- collecting and analyzing data
- evaluating firms' organization and productivity

- conducting market research
- managing and administering programs
- planning and evaluating programs
- conducting cost-benefit analysis
- conducting public opinion polls
- acting as representatives for publishers
- dealing with personnel.

In addition, a large number of sociology majors who receive B.A.s do not become professional sociologists, but instead continue on to graduate or professional schools and receive advanced degrees, not in sociology itself, but in such related fields as social work or social welfare, criminology, urban planning, hospital administration, business administration, counseling and guidance, labor and industrial relations, and law—in other words, in *people-oriented* fields. Sociology majors who do not continue their educations beyond college and look for work only with bachelor's degrees are prepared for the job market in the valuable, general way that all college-educated individuals are who have studied diligently: they have developed critical judgment and habits of mind that make them good candidates for learning on the job. In addition, a sociology major offers two important qualities to the prospective job seeker: the ability to gather and assess information and sensitivity to the human factor—that is, to how people act, see, think, and feel in social situations.

Sources: American Sociological Association, 1977; Wilson & Selvin, 1980; Manderscheid & Greenwald, 1983.

Black or white, and so on—we can predict that person's behavior accurately. In contrast, interactionists emphasize that a person's traits are less important in explaining behavior than the situations in which people find themselves. Who could possibly have predicted the Jonestown mass suicide simply from an understanding of the characteristics of the cult members themselves? Can anyone doubt that a young person is far more likely to experiment with a drug for the first time among friends in a familiar, comfortable setting than among strangers in an unfamiliar, uncomfortable setting? Experiment after experiment has shown that people report seeing things they do not see, because companions claim to have seen those things (Sherif, 1936; Asch, 1951, 1956). Experiments even show that in certain circumstances ordinary people are willing to subject others to pain—for example, throw acid in their faces—and grasp live rattlesnakes (Orne & Evans, 1965). This "situational" factor—our willingness to act unpredictably—especially fascinates symbolic interactionists.

Interactionists also stress what they call "the looking-glass self." How we see ourselves, they think, is partly a result of how others see us, especially people we regard as important, initimate, or significant. To a certain extent, we all try to see ourselves in the eyes of others, and this "looking-glass self" is what we find there, or what we think we find. It does not dictate everything we do, but it is always there, and we are always checking it out. Our minds are filled with a constant dialogue between ourselves and others. Do our actions measure up to the way we see ourselves—our self-images? Do they measure up to the way others see us and the way we would like others to see us? According to interactionists, these questions determine much of our behavior.

Standard American Sociology

Much of the writing and research in contemporary American sociology—perhaps most of it—cannot be located in any one of these theoretical schools. It does not assume a clearly recognizable theoretical stance and is almost as distinctive for what it is *not* as for what it *is*. The tradition that was once functionalism has permeated the sociological "mainstream" and no longer remains a separate theory. Yet this mainstream clearly is not functionalist; it is not at all concerned with any of the central issues that functionalism struggled with decades ago. Nor has mainstream American sociology embraced symbolic interactionism, although insights from it have been absorbed into much sociological writing, implicitly or explicitly. And the sociological mainstream has not embraced conflict theory, although some of the less extreme ideas of conflict theory have become widely accepted. In other words, "mainstream" sociology has gathered to itself bits and pieces from many theories and created a kind of perspective from this synthesis. This perspective can be called standard American sociology (Mullins, 1973, pp. 39–74).

Middle-range theory The view that constructing grand, all-inclusive, abstract theories is not productive, and that studying delimited or specific aspects and issues in society is.

Standard American sociology generates hypotheses and tests **middle-range theories.** It abandons grand theories representing "all-inclusive systematic efforts to develop a unified theory that will explain all the observed uniformities of social behavior, social organization and social change" (Merton, 1968, p. 39). Most sociologists attack delimited aspects of the social world—like the causes of social mobility and successful marriages and the effects of imprisonment. They generalize, to be sure, but grand schemes that explain everything anyone wants to know about the social world with a single hypothesis no longer appear in mainstream sociology. The functionalist question "How is social order possible?" has come to be seen as too general, too sweeping. "What accounts for the sweep of history—what is the cause of social change?" is likewise seen by "mainstream" sociologists as too general to be answered.

Most contemporary sociologists are concerned with how theories and hypotheses can be tested rigorously and empirically. But their conception of "empirical" data differs from that of symbolic interactionists and conflict theorists. Most sociologists are comfortable, by and large, only with highly quantitative information: facts that are precise; statistical; capable of being presented in the form of charts, tables, and graphs. They would argue that the data must be collected from large, representative samples of respondents. Mainstream sociologists are suspicious of any other types of sociological information. (The next chapter says more about the different styles of sociological research methods.)

Standard American sociology searches for cause-and-effect explanations. In this sense, it is positivistic in orientation: It tends to adopt the natural science model as the proper way to think about and study the social world. And like natural scientists, practitioners of standard American sociology argue that objectivity is crucial, even necessary, when studying the real world. They hold that it is possible, though difficult, to practice an "objective," **value-free** sociology. They agree with French statesman and diplomat Talleyrand, who said: "I do not say it is good; I do not say it is bad; I say it is the way it is."

Value-free Free of bias, value judgments, or personal opinions. Some sociologists argue that this stance is necessary to engage in any science, whereas others argue that all approaches to studying the world are inevitably based on values.

Conclusions

These theories are not mere names and ideas to memorize and then drop or stash away. Recall them in the chapters that follow, for each of them can be applied to, and can illuminate, every sociological phenomenon we examine. Each theory has something to offer; each has strengths as well as drawbacks. Some sociological subjects are analyzed most fruitfully by means of one perspective; a different subject is best explained by a different perspective. Overall, no theory is best or most valid; each theory is adequate for some issues, but not others. No single theoretical perspective dominates this book.

SUMMARY

1. Sociology is the systematic study of social life. Sociologists are especially concerned with studying group influences on individual behavior.

2. Events that occur in the world can often be understood with a grasp of key sociological concepts.

3. All sociological study begins with the assumption that there is a pattern to the social world, a certain predictability to the way things happen.

4. In order to think sociologically, it is necessary to adopt the sociological imagination, or the ability to understand the lives of specific individuals in terms of their location in the structure of society.

5. The central characteristics of any science are that it is empirical, it is systematic, it makes statements that are falsifiable, it makes generalizations, and it seeks to explain the way things are. To the extent that sociology possesses these five characteristics, it is a science.

6. Some critics of sociological thinking argue that sociology is little more than common sense. The fact that most people are unaware of much that takes place in the social world shows that this argument is false.

7. Many critics of sociology assume that because they are members of several social groups, they are "instant experts" on those groups. However, insiders are not aware of many crucial features of the groups to which they belong, and they are not knowledgeable about where their own groups stand in relation to others.

8. Many people believe that the sociologist's effort to generalize about social life is misplaced, because we are all unique. The fact is, our individuality is often irrelevant to the similarities we share with others.

9. Some people believe that exceptions to a rule disprove that rule. In fact, sociologists do not make absolute statements that have no exceptions; sociologists' statements are based on probabilities, not certainties.

10. Sociology is a social science. The social world is also studied by anthropologists, psychologists, political scientists, and economists. Each field studies a certain slice of human behavior from a particular slant or point of view.

11. Sociology emerged in Europe as a distinct perspective in the 1800s, partly as an effort to explain the Industrial Revolution. Some of the field's early theorists include Auguste Comte, Herbert Spencer, Karl Marx, Emile Durkheim, and Max Weber.

12. In the United States, sociology became an academic discipline late in the nineteenth century; it developed into a multiple-paradigm discipline. Within sociology, three major schools, or paradigms, may be delineated: functionalism, conflict theory, and symbolic interactionism. A fourth, standard American sociology, takes bits and pieces from these three.

13. Functionalism stresses stability, cohesion, and consensus.

14. Conflict theory stresses coercion, exploitation, and struggle. Marxism is the most comprehensive and well-known of all varieties of conflict theory; it stresses the central importance of economic conflict above all others.

15. Symbolic interactionism stresses meaning, interaction, and interpretation. It is concerned with situational influences and the role that others play in influencing our behavior.

16. Standard American sociology attempts to synthesize elements from these theories, avoids high-level abstractions, is empirical, makes use of quantitative or statistical information, seeks cause-and-effect explanations, and attempts a "value-free" stance.

SUGGESTED READINGS

American Sociological Association, *Careers in Sociology*. Washington, D.C.: ASA, 1977.
   What can you do with a degree in sociology? This pamphlet answers the question. Unfortunately, it is a bit out of date. It should, therefore, be supplemented with: Ronald W. Manderscheid and Mathew Greenwald, "Trends in Employment of Sociologists," in Howard E. Freeman et al. (eds.), *Applied Sociology*. San Francisco: Jossey-Bass, 1983, pp. 51–63.

Pauline Bart and Linda Frankel, *The Student Sociologist's Handbook* (4th ed.). New York: Random House, 1986; and Leonard Becker, Jr., and Clair Gustafson, *Encounter with Sociology: The Term Paper* (2nd ed.). San Francisco: Boyd & Fraser, 1976.
   Two books that inform students how to gather research materials that they can use to write papers for sociology courses.

Peter L. Berger, *Invitation to Sociology: A Humanistic Perspective*. Garden City, New York: Doubleday Anchor, 1963.

An insightful description of the nature of sociological thinking. What is the sociological perspective or "slant"? Berger provides an answer. This is one of my all-time favorite books in the field.

Randall Collins, *Three Sociological Traditions*. New York: Oxford University Press, 1985, and Collins (ed.), *Three Sociological Traditions*. New York: Oxford University Press, 1985.
Two books, one written by the author and the other a selection of readings, on the history of sociological theory, organized into "three sociological traditions."

Randall Collins and Michael Makowsky, *The Discovery of Society* (3rd ed.). New York: Random House, 1984.
A stimulating introduction to the emergence of sociology in the nineteenth century.

Lewis A. Coser, *Masters of Sociological Thought* (2nd ed.). New York: Harcourt Brace Jovanovich, 1977.
Probably the best discussion of the history of sociological theory in existence. A true sociological analysis, in that Coser deals with those features of the theorists' lives—cultural, social, biographical—that are related to their writings.

Anthony Giddens, *Sociology: A Brief But Critical Introduction* (2nd ed.). New York: Harcourt Brace Jovanovich, 1986.
A lively and forceful discussion of the task and approach of sociology from the point of view of a major conflict theorist. Giddens argues that sociology must be linked with social criticism.

Erving Goffman, *Interaction Ritual*. Garden City, New York: Doubleday Anchor, 1967.
Intriguing essays on "face-to-face behavior" written by a major interaction theorist on such topics as deference and demeanor, embarrassment, and "where the action is."

Elliott Krause, *Why Study Sociology?* New York: Random House, 1980.
A book on "thinking sociologically" about a number of issues: "discovering yourself," understanding relationships, finding work, joining a community, and acting politically. What does sociology have to say about these issues? This book may provide the answer.

Jonathan H. Turner, *Sociology: A Student Handbook*. New York: Random House, 1985.
A very brief discussion of some central sociological concerns, such as how we know abut phenomena, culture, the social being, disorder, and the structure of society.

chapter 2

SOCIAL RESEARCH

Every scientific discipline has devised ways of studying the world. Chemists conduct laboratory experiments; biologists peer through microscopes, dissect frogs, and breed fruit flies; psychologists run rats through mazes, wire people to machines that monitor their heartbeats, and administer Thematic Apperception Tests.

Like these other disciplines, sociology also has its own special research methods; I describe them in this chapter. The important point to remember about the methods of scientific research is that learning a subject and learning how to do research go hand in hand. It is impossible to know a great deal about a discipline unless one knows how its practitioners gather information. This chapter explains just how sociologists go about gathering theirs.

The word "research" sounds dry, dull, academic, and altogether removed from the real world. It brings to mind images of white-coated scientists jotting complex and incomprehensible mathematical formulas on blackboards and of scholars poring over dusty, obscure volumes. In reality, some of the most exciting moments of a scholar's life are spent engaged in research. Most sociologists love asking people questions about their lives, discovering things that no one has written before, and writing articles and books that stir up controversy.

There is probably a bit of the "Peeping Tom" in every sociologist, for behind every closed door, the sociologist will "anticipate some new facet of human life not yet perceived and understood" (Berger, 1963, p. 19). Social research is not only exciting in itself but it is also the avenue to social knowledge. Social research is "where the action is" in sociology. It is how sociologists, along with other scholars, earn their reputations, advance within the profession, get promoted, receive grants and fellowships, and are invited to give speeches all over the world.

Finally, social research, for the most part, is relevant to the practical, everyday concerns of the real world. It deals with life-and-blood issues like racism, crime, marriage and the family, divorce, poverty, war, and politics. Through what other discipline could you study so many fascinating topics?

THE SCIENTIFIC METHOD

Sociology studies the way our various group memberships influence human behavior. To undertake such studies, we must first gather facts, for sociology is a factual (or empirical) discipline. The things we study must be observable through the senses and verifiable through the senses of other observers. Facts are not as easy to observe as you might suppose. You must be prepared—among other things—with the fundamentals of scientific method. Anyone who claims to be engaged in science must accept certain specific processes, and follow them.

Scientific method does not mean just equipment: test tubes, electron microscopes, and computers. Science begins with thought, insight, imagination. Above all, science means systematic and rigorous thinking about the real world. And, in order to think seriously about how the world works, it is necessary to become acquainted with certain key scientific ideas; these include concepts, operationalization, variables, correlation, and controls.

Concepts

The dictionary tells us that a concept is "a general notion or idea." Both scientific and ordinary, everyday thinking are based on the use of concepts. Every time we use a word, a term, we are using a concept. Every noun, verb, and adjective is a concept. By using concepts, we draw a mental boundary around those things we intend to include within their scope. Even such commonplace words as "dog" and "table" are concepts, because they point, not to "this dog" or "that table," but to dogs and tables in general. People cannot communicate without sharing a common body of concepts and attaching about the same definitions to them.

Concepts like "dog" and "table" are not in themselves concrete, but the things to which they refer—this dog, that table—are. Sociologists mainly deal with concepts like "prestige," "cohesion," "love," and "conflict." They are less tangible and more complex and abstract than are concepts that refer to physical objects. You would have little difficulty deciding whether or not a given object is a chair, but does John love Mary? It is often hard to say, yet if you have ever experienced love you will not doubt its existence. This uncertainty is just one of the reasons why indicators (see the next paragraph) are so important in social research.

Operationalization

Because we cannot touch or smell so many social concepts, we need signs to inform us of their presence. Indicators tell us about, measure, or point to concepts that are somewhat removed from our senses. Say that two football fans argue about who should be regarded as a greater quarterback. One fan insists that it is Joe Namath; the other, Fran Tarkenton. They shout back and forth and get nowhere. Finally, one of them says, "Look, why don't we decide exactly what we mean when we use the term 'great quarterback.'" The two fans agree that a quarterback, above all, must be able to pass accurately. They decide that the percentage of "passes completed" (which should be high) and the percentage of "passes intercepted" (which should be low) would make a fairly good measure of a quarterback's skill. By consulting the record book, they discover that Tarkenton completed 57 percent of his passes and was intercepted only 4 percent of the time. Namath, however, completed 50 percent of his passes and was intercepted 6 percent of the time he threw the ball.

These two football fans have constructed specific indicators to measure a concept. The concept is "great quarterback"; the indicators are "passes completed" and "passes intercepted." Unless the Namath fan comes up with additional indicators or successfully challenges these two, the Tarkenton fan is right. This process—measuring a concept with a specific indicator—is called **operationalization.**

Sociological concepts, too, must be measured and indicated, or operationalized. Sociologists try to move beyond vague feelings about the social world and to make precise and specific assessments of it.

Some concepts are fairly easy to measure—sex, for instance, or age. Most concepts are more complex and thus more difficult to measure then sex and age. Social class, for example, is made up of different elements and strands. Sociologists have devised a scale called the Occupational Prestige Rating Scale, which measures the amount of prestige the public accords to different occupations. Each occupation has been assigned a "score," based on many studies that have measured the degree of prestige most people attach to each occupation. If you ask someone, "What is your occupation?," and he or she replies, "airline pilot," you can assign the occupation an exact score, 86 points out of 100. This score is a concrete indicator for the general concept occupational prestige, which is itself only one strand of the even more general concept of social class. (We discuss the Prestige Rating Scale in Chapter 9.)

To use a sociological concept, you must know what form it takes in the real world, so that you and other observers can see it, measure it, and discuss it in much the same way. Whenever you read the findings of a study—in a newspaper article or on television, for instance—you ask yourself how the important concepts in the study were measured. What were used as indicators for the key concepts? You might read, "Half the population suffers from stress." What is "stress"? How was it measured? Or, you might read, "The crime rate is highest in poorest groups." How was crime defined? What concrete indicators were used to measure it? Even concepts that are relatively straightforward, like income, have to be indicated in specific ways: by answers to interview questions, through tax records, or from statements by employers, and so on.

Variables

Sociologists are particularly concerned about concepts that vary from one person, time, or society to another. A concept that varies is called, quite simply, a **variable.** A variable is a concept that assumes different forms or appearances in different individuals, at different times, or in different societies. All scientists deal with variables.

Temperature, for instance, is one such variable. One day, it is 70°F, and the next day it hits 85°. If everywhere and at all times in the universe it was 70°F, no scientist would employ the concept of temperature, because it would not be a variable. It is important just because it does vary and because other things vary when it does. Likewise, indicators of social concepts measure variables. When we measure the concept

Operationalization The process of measuring a concept with a specific indicator.

Variable A concept that varies or changes from one person, time, situation, or society to another.

Sociologists are interested in relationships among key variables. There is, for instance, a positive relationship between degree of education and voting in elections: The more educated you are, the more likely you are to vote.

Mimi Forsyth/Monkmeyer Press

"income," we know that it varies a great deal, that there are interesting differences between rich and poor. Sociologists therefore study income as a variable. On the other hand, if everyone in the world earned exactly the same income, sociologists would not investigate the impact of income on other things. In this case, income would not be a variable.

Luckily for sociologists, almost all traits and characteristics are variables. Some people, some families, some cities, and some societies are rich, while some are poor; some people are men, others, women; some are young, others, old. Each of these traits—income, sex, and age—is a variable. Sociologists are interested in the relationships among variables. Often, as one variable changes, others do, too. For instance, there is a relationship between cigarette smoking and a wide range of diseases, especially cancer. There is also a relationship between degree of education and willingness to vote in elections: The more educated you are, the more likely you are to vote. Of course, there will always be some exceptions to the rule (see Chapter 1). Not every well-educated person votes; not every poorly educated person does not. When sociologists make generalizations describing the relationship between two variables, they know that not every individual case will fit. But if enough cases fit, the generalization is valid.

Correlation

Studying relationships between social variables—like education and voting—is one important goal of sociological research. Such relationships can be summarized in the form of a **correlation**—a formal, statistical measure of the strength of the relationship between two variables. A **positive correlation** states that as one variable increases, so too does the other; and that as one variable decreases, so too does the other. A **negative correlation** means that as one variable increases, the other decreases. A perfect positive correlation between two variables is expressed by the coefficient 1.0; a perfect negative correlation is −1.0. In social life, correlations are almost never this strong, however. Generally, the greater the percentage difference between categories within the independent variable with regard to the dependent the stronger the relationship between these two variables. A fairly strong positive correlation

Correlation A formal statistical way of measuring the strength of the relationship between two variables. A **positive correlation** exists when a variable moves in one direction and another variable moves the same way; a **negative correlation** means that as one variable increases, the other decreases.

TABLE 2–1 Lifetime Prevalence of Six Types of Drugs by Sex, American High School Seniors, 1984

Sex	Marijuana	LSD	PCP	Cocaine	Heroin	Alcohol	N
Male	57.9	9.6	6.8	18.7	1.5	92.9	7,600
Female	51.3	5.9	3.1	12.8	1.0	92.2	7,800

Note: Lifetime prevalence is defined as use at least once in the respondent's life.

Source: Lloyd D. Johnston, Patrick M. O'Malley, and Jerald G. Bachman, University of Michigan, Institute for Social Research, Use of Licit and Illicit Drugs by America's High School Students, 1975–1984. *Washington, D.C.: U.S. Government Printing Office, 1985, p. 25.*

measures at 0.6 or higher; a moderate one, at about 0.2 or 0.3; and a weak one, 0.1. When two variables are not related in any way—when they do not vary together at all—sociologists say that the correlation between them is zero.

The simplest and most basic tool for describing the association between two variables is a two-variable table (see box on page 39). In a simple, clear-cut fashion, this shows exactly how two things are related and the strength of that relationship. It does not say *why* the two variables are related—only that a relationship exists between them. Note the accompanying two-variable table presenting the relationship between sex, on the one hand, and drug use, on the other. Table 2–1 shows that there is a relationship between sex and drug use: Male high school seniors are more likely to use a number of different illegal drugs than are female high school seniors. For some of these drugs, the relationship is fairly strong, and for others, it is weak or nonexistent. Twice as many of the young men in the study have at least tried the drug PCP (6.8 percent) than have the young women (3.1 percent). On the other hand, the study's males are almost exactly as likely to have used alcohol once or more (92.9 percent) as are the study's females (92.2 percent). Had there been no difference in these figures—if the same percentage of males and females had used these drugs—we would have said that there is no relationship between sex and drug use. However, looking at the figures, it appears clear that there is a relationship: that males are more likely to use several different types of drugs than are females. This does not mean that all males use drugs and no female does—only that there is a difference in the percentage of males and females using drugs.

Dependent and Independent Variables

One sociologist hangs out on a street corner and interviews juvenile delinquents. Another tabulates answers to questionnaires and presents these findings in the form of complex statistics and formulas. Both are engaged in social research, but their goals are different. Descriptive and explanatory studies are the two basic types of social research (Cole, 1980, pp. 25–31). For sociologists who engage in descriptive studies, facts are ends in themselves. Descriptive research aims to discover and establish facts, to describe social reality. What is the college drug scene like today? In which countries of the world are hunger and malnutrition most severe? Research of this sort is descriptive because it tries to establish the facts. As a general rule, descriptive studies are crucial when very little is known about a certain aspect of social reality. When facts have been gathered and more is known, explanatory studies become important; now, scientists want to explain what has been described.

For many sociologists, describing facts and establishing relationships among variables is only a step toward a second and more ambitious goal. Explanatory studies take social research a step further. They are concerned with what actually causes the observed relationships. Table 2–1 is descriptive, not explanatory. It does not explain the relationship but only tells us that it exists. To answer the question "Why?," we need additional information.

Dependent variable The factor on which an effect is posited or may be observed; in the design or analysis of a study, the variable that is a candidate for a given effect.

Independent variable One factor that influences or has an effect on a second factor (the "dependent" variable).

In order to know the true cause-and-effect relationship between two variables, it is necessary to establish which is the **dependent variable** and which is the **independent variable.** A dependent variable is the effect, the variable that is influenced by the cause. The independent variable is the cause, the variable that produces the effect. For instance, ordinary street crimes are more likely to take place at night. In this case, the independent variable is the time of day, and the dependent variable is the crime rate. Obviously, the crime rate cannot determine or influence whether it is day or night—but the time of day can and does influence the crime rate.

The relationship between the independent variable (IV) and the dependent variable (DV) can be diagrammed as follows: IV——→ DV, with the arrow's representing the direction of influence or causality. The relationship between the time of day (T) and the crime rate (C) can also be represented the same way: T——→ C, with time of day's influencing or causing the crime rate.

In many two-variable relationships, neither one directly causes the other. Both may be the result of another variable, which influences them both. Many variables are related, or correlated, and untangling the causal direction is an extremely delicate and complex business. Simple associations can be misleading, even if the facts are gathered skillfully. It is very simple to identify falsely the cause of a relationship. A fundamental fallacy is confusing a correlation with causality. Two variables may be related, but there may be no direct causal connection between them.

For instance, a simple two-variable relationship can be shown between the presence of storks in an area and that area's birth rate: The more storks, the more newborn babies; the fewer storks, the fewer newborn babies (Cole, 1980, pp. 45–49). The relationship is real—but what does it mean? What causes it? We know that there is no direct causal connection between the presence of storks in an area and its birth rate. What is the origin of this relationship? Reason supplies the answer: Storks tend to live in rural areas, and the birth rate is higher in rural areas than in cities. There are fewer storks in urban areas, and fewer births. Storks do not deliver babies; the true causal factor here is the urban or rural character of an area.

Controls

As this example shows, to move beyond simple two-variable relationships (or correlations) to a more convincing level of analysis, we must apply **controls**. We have all heard the expression, "other things being equal." Often, two variables are related, but the nature of that relationship is obscured by the fact that other variables are related to them both. In real life, "other things" are almost never equal. Controls make them so.

Control A relevant variable in a study that is held constant to determine causal relationships between other variables.

To find out if a two-variable relationship is truly causal, we must hold the other relevant variables constant. We try to nullify their influence and see whether, and to what extent, our original variables relate

How to Read a Table

Tables convey a great deal of precise information fairly compactly, in a small number of words and numbers. Being able to read a table is a form of literacy; dismissing tables as "just a bunch of statistics" condemns you to a form of ignorance. Most tables are easy to read if you follow step-by-step rules.

1. *Determine the source.* The data in Table 2–1 were collected by a research team at the Institute for Social Research, which is located at the University of Michigan. This tells us that the source is a reliable one. Furthermore, the table was taken from a publication of the United States government, which means that, in all likelihood, the study that produced the table was federally funded, another indication that the data are worth paying attention to. In contrast, if information showing, for example, that cigarette smoking is harmless were collected by a cigarette company, we might very well not trust it.

2. *Identify the variables.* On what variables is the table based? In this case, two variables: sex and drug use among American high school seniors in 1984. This is explained in the title of the table. Sex is self-explanatory: We all know what is meant when a table compares males with females. The second variable, "lifetime prevalence," is a little more complicated, and a note at the bottom of the table explains what it means: The respondent was asked if he or she has used any of the drugs mentioned once or more during his or her lifetime.

3. *Determine how the figures are computed.* Some figures are presented in the form of total numbers, such as the population of the nation's cities. Some contain rates, such as the murder rate of different states. In Table 2–1, the figures are presented in the form of *percentages*: the percentage of males and females who have used the drugs listed at least once. We see that 57.9 percent of the males in the study have used marijuana and that 51.3 percent of the females have done so. For each drug, we can make the same comparison by reading across the rows in the table.

4. *Decide which is the dependent and which the independent variable.* If there is a cause-and-effect direction, find out which way it goes. For instance, in Table 2–1, it is clear that sex is the independent variable and drug use, the dependent variable. Whether a person is male or female can influence his or her drug use, but drug use cannot determine or influence a person's sex.

5. *Examine the total number of individuals in the table.* Unfortunately, not all tables contain the total number on which the figures are based. But many do. Obviously, it makes a great deal of difference whether a table is based on twenty individuals or 20,000. In Table 2–1, the study is based on 7,600 males and 7,800 females. The large size of this sample gives us a degree of confidence in the study's results.

6. *See if the variables are related and, if so, how strongly.* What do the data say? Is there some direction or pattern? In Table 2–1, the pattern is fairly clear: Males are more likely to use drugs than are females. A second generalization seems warranted as well: For some drugs, the sex difference is large, whereas for other drugs, it is small or nonexistent. Males are twice as likely to use PCP as women; one and a half times as likely to use LSD, cocaine, and heroin; and about six percentage points more likely to use marijuana. For the one legal drug in the table, alcohol, the difference is too small to be meaningful. If the percentage differences are substantial, the chances are they are significant, and a pattern can be found.

7. *Draw conclusions.* What do the patterns tell us? What do our generalizations point to with respect to a cause-and-effect relationship? Why are men more likely to use drugs than women? Men are probably more likely to use drugs than women because something about men increases their drug use, and something about women diminishes theirs. What do you think these things are? The information contained in a table allows the readers to raise and possibly answer important questions about social life.

to one another in a cause-and-effect fashion. For instance, if an area is rural, it tends to have a high birth rate, storks or no storks; if it is urban, its birth rate is low, again, storks or no storks. By analyzing statistics from many rural and urban areas, we can see that the presence of storks really has no effect at all on the birth rate. The control represents a kind of equalization factor, neutralizing the possible influence of certain key variables, so that we can see how the other variables respond.

Let's take another example. We know that smokers are more likely to contract cancer than nonsmokers. And the more you smoke, the more you increase that terrible likelihood. Is this relationship actually causal in nature? Or is it due to other factors? In order to answer this question, we would have to control the other variables. It is possible, for instance, that the personalities of people who smoke would make them more likely to get cancer even if they did not smoke. Perhaps people who live in areas with pollutants in the air smoke and are therefore more likely to contract cancer. What a causal study would attempt to do is rule out the effect of all these other variables by controlling them and then comparing the relationship between smoking and cancer among people with similar characteristics or in areas with similar levels of pollution.

SOCIAL RESEARCH

Social research is an exciting, yet difficult, enterprise. The strengths—and limitations—of sociological methods are to some degree unique. Sociologists, inescapably, are human beings engaged in studying other human beings. This fact creates certain problems for them—problems that natural scientists do not have. Stars and earthquakes are not altered when we study them, nor do the scientists who study them have to free themselves from attitudes and preconceptions they have learned from earliest infancy. But human beings do not passively sit by and allow sociologists to examine their behavior; they change it when they know it is being studied. And the scholarly investigator may be full of biases and preconceptions that are misleading. Human behavior *can* be studied, but sociologists must use their imaginations to devise methods that solve two problems: first, that they are studying men and women who often react to the way that they are being studied and, second, that researchers are usually part of the society they seek to understand.

Methodology A systematic, scientific research technique that is used to study a phenomenon.

Sociological research is guided by specific rules, called **methodology,** or research methods. They tell the researcher how to gather information about the social world and how to draw valid conclusions from this information. Sociologists use many research methods, each of which has its own strengths and reveals a slightly different glimpse of the social world. There are two main styles (or modes) of social research. In the "active" mode, sociologists directly generate information by asking questions or observing behavior. Unless sociologists ask these questions or make these observations, the information would not exist.

The second basic style (or mode) of sociological research is using already-available or existing sources of information. A sociologist who examines newspaper articles to see how the press treats juvenile delinquency would be making use of such a source—the newspaper articles themselves. Other sociologists have put the findings of the 1980 United

States Census on computer tape and analyzed them, hoping to discover new insights about the population of the United States. Gigantic quantities of information already exist, waiting to be used for sociological purposes. The challenge is to use it to clarify the mysteries of social life.

There are three basic types of active social research: (1) surveys; (2) participant-observation; and (3) experiments. In addition, a fourth type possesses features of both surveys and participant-observation: the in-depth, unstandardized interview. Two of these methods are regarded as **quantitative** research techniques: surveys and experiments; quantitative information researchers gather can be expressed in the form of numbers and statistics. Two of these methods are **qualitative** research techniques: participant-observation and the in-depth interview; qualitative information gathered cannot be expressed in the form of numbers and statistics. Like everything else in social life, however, these categories are not perfectly air-tight.

Survey Methods

A **survey** is a research effort in which the researcher or an assistant puts direct, formal, structured questions to a sample of respondents, whose answers are tabulated in a quantitative or statistical fashion. The questions asked in a survey call for fairly clear-cut answers: "Did you vote in the last election? If so, for whom did you vote?" Or "What is your marital status? Single__; Married__; Separated__; Divorced__; Widowed__." Surveys are conducted by means of three principle techniques: face-to-face *interviews*, telephone interviews, and *questionnaires*. In an interview, the sociologist or an assistant asks the questions, either face-to-face or over the telephone. In contrast, questionnaires are sent or distributed to people who write down their answers directly on the questionnaires themselves. The persons in whose behavior or opinions the researcher is interested are called **respondents.** Interviews and questionnaires have essentially the same purpose.

Interviews and Questionnaires.
Generally, questionnaires are useful when specific, clear-cut, and simple information is wanted. There should be little or no doubt about the meaning of the questions or the answers, and the number of possible answers should be small. Interviews are better when detail and nuance are crucial, and where give-and-take is needed to draw accurate answers from reluctant or absent-minded respondents. In short, it may be said that "the limitations of each method may be offset by the strengths of the other" (Chadwick, Bahr, & Albrecht, 1984, p. 139).

Questionnaires, however, are much less expensive and time-consuming to conduct than interviews. Interviewers must be hired and trained, and then sent out to track down and talk to hundreds, perhaps thousands, of respondents. A complete questionnaire survey, based on 1,000 respondents, can be conducted for a few hundred dollars; the same study, based on interviews, may cost as much as $100,000. On the basis of economy, the questionnaire clearly yields the maximum amount of data per research dollar spent (Chadwick et al., 1984, p. 137).

Whenever a researcher is interested in tabulating the respondents' answers in quantitative or statistical form, the questions must be fairly structured or closed-ended. With a closed format, the researcher requires the respondents to choose from among a series of alternatives, as with the preceding sample questions on voting and marital status. On the

Quantitative Capable of being measured or expressed in precise, statistical terms, such as in the form of a percentage or an arithmetic ratio.

Qualitative Having the characteristic of being inexact, and thus relying on information that is subjective and illustrative rather than definitive; being incapable of being measured precisely.

Survey A set of research techniques that entails drawing a fairly large sample, asking specific questions, and analyzing the data obtained in a rigorous, quantitative fashion.

Respondent The individual who is interviewed or who fills out a questionnaire in a survey.

Survey research is the most commonly used sociological research technique. It entails asking a sample of respondents questions, either in the form of a printed questionnaire or, as here, in an interview.

Mimi Forsyth/Monkmeyer Press

Open-ended question A question that does not require that the respondent choose among forced alternatives, but that can be answered in a free-flowing, detailed fashion.

other hand, the more unstructured or **open-ended** the questions—that is, the more the respondents answer in their own words—the more difficult it is to reduce the answers to a statistical format. (One research technique—in-depth qualitative interviews—is not, strictly speaking, survey research at all; we discuss it in another section.) Questionnaires, which respondents fill out themselves, are almost always highly structured and closed-ended. Interviews in survey research, however, range from highly structured to moderately structured. Researchers can ask for a bit more detail in interview situations, because respondents are more comfortable with speaking than writing, and thus usually give more elaborate answers.

Another advantage of interviews is that an interviewer can make sure that a respondent understands a question. Also, a sensitive interviewer can often feel when a respondent is not telling the truth and may be able to frame a question in a way that will make the respondent more truthful. Interviews are full of give-and-take. The interviewer can ask for clarification, more detail, or examples. No such dialogue is possible in a questionnaire.

But interviews may suffer from so-called interviewer effects, or interviewer bias. Studies show that the characteristics of the interviewer often influence the way respondents answer certain questions. For instance, early surveys found that Blacks who were interviewed by Blacks gave more militant, and probably more truthful, answers to questions pertaining to race than Blacks who were interviewed by whites. In general, when the interviewer and the respondent share characteristics—especially the most important ones, like sex and race—the answers will be the most truthful and revealing. Researchers therefore attempt to match the characteristics of interviewers and respondents. With a questionnaire, of course, there is no interviewer to create a bias.

Researchers disagree about whether the questionnaire or the interview is the superior technique to elicit honest or valid answers to questions about sensitive topics, such as drug use and abortion or to questions about "deviant" behavior. Some researchers (Wiseman, 1972; Sudman & Bradburn, 1982) argue that the questionnaire is better, because it is a more anonymous technique. Respondents can give answers more freely, without fear of embarrassment or reprisal. In contrast, other researchers (Mangione, Hingson, & Barrett, 1982) claim that interviews yield a higher proportion of "extreme" answers to questions about sensitive or socially disapproved behavior or attitudes. From this, they conclude that the answers are more valid.

The truth is that questionnaires and interviews are much more alike than different. Both are tools for conducting survey research, the best way of amassing data that can readily be obtained by asking direct questions. For getting at such basic information as age, occupation, education, religion, politics, and so on, surveys are the only way of doing social research.

Sample A group of individuals chosen from a population to be studied in social research.

Sampling.   Survey methods use many respondents, often thousands of them. Such data, therefore, can be subjected to sophisticated statistical tests, including causal analysis: the study of cause-and-effect relationships among variables. To make this kind of analysis meaningful, sociologists must make sure that the people who respond to their surveys are typical of the larger groups they wish to study. That larger group or category—commonly referred to as a *universe* or *population*—could be all the dentists in the United States, all disciples of the Reverend Sun Myung Moon, all married couples living in Pittsburgh, or all criminal suspects arrested in New York City in 1987. The part of this universe that actually responds to a survey is called the **sample.** Unless the universe is very small—such as all Black Jews living in Ann Arbor, Michigan, for instance—or the study is huge—like the United States Census—we simply cannot consider the entire universe. Most of the time, we need to examine samples. If a sample does not typify the universe, if it differs from the population in important ways, it may not accurately reflect, or represent, the universe. A sample that does not reflect the universe from which it is drawn is called an **unrepresentative,** or **biased, sample.** But, of course, sociologists try to make their samples as **unbiased,** or **representative,** as possible.

When social research was first conducted, the problems of sampling were poorly understood. Researchers assumed that large samples were always representative. The classic instance of this fallacy was a poll conducted in 1936 by a magazine called the *Literary Digest.* From the early years of this century, the *Digest* had been attempting to predict the outcome of presidential elections by sending questionnaires to people whose names were drawn from such sources as magazine subscription lists, telephone books, and automobile registrations. In 1936, over 2 million Americans answered the poll, and they said—overwhelmingly—that they were going to vote for Alfred Landon, the Republican, not for President Franklin D. Roosevelt, the Democrat. The *Digest* predicted a landslide victory for Landon.

The prediction was dead wrong, of course; Roosevelt won by the largest margin in American history. How could the poll have been so far off? The people who responded to the survey were probably not lying; no doubt most of them actually did vote for Landon. And the sample was huge; very, very few studies today question 2 million people about anything. So what went wrong? The universe or population the *Literary Digest* wanted to study was the entire American electorate. And the 2 million respondents simply did not represent a cross-section of the American voters. In other words, the *Digest's* sample was biased, or unrepresentative. And the reason was that in 1936, anyone who could afford a telephone or a car was fairly well-to-do, compared with the average American, and affluent voters went heavily Republican.

Another poll conducted in 1936 was carried out by a man named George Gallup. The Gallup Poll was based on a much smaller sample of the electorate than the *Digest's,* but it included a representative, unbiased cross-section of American voters: rich people and poor, voters with and without phones, with and without cars, Democrats and Republicans. And Gallup predicted the Roosevelt victory that actually occurred. In short, size alone does not make a sample representative. Choosing a sample carefully and intelligently is far more important than including a large number of people in it. A carefully selected sample of only 1,000 people can be a fairly accurate cross-section of our population. Within a margin of a couple of percentage points, we can expect that their opinions will reflect the opinions of the electorate. Of course, in a very close election—decided by only one or two percentage points—a poll may tell the researcher that the election is "too close to call."

Putting together a representative sample of any particular universe requires thought and planning. For instance, you might choose a sample of the undergraduates at your college by writing down every student's name on a slip of paper, putting all the slips into a bowl, mixing them up thoroughly, and selecting one-tenth of the names. If you compared that sample with the undergraduate body as a whole, they would probably be very much alike in many important characteristics: age, sex,

Unrepresentative sample A group of individuals selected for study whose characteristics do not reflect those of the population from which they were drawn.

Biased sample A sample of a population drawn in such a way that every individual does not have an equal chance of appearing in the sample.

Unbiased sample A sample that was drawn in such a way that every individual or unit in the population has an equal chance of appearing in it. As a result of such a selection technique, it is to be expected that these individuals reflect the characteristics of the population from which they were drawn.

Representative sample A group of individuals chosen to be studied who reflect the characteristics of the population from which they were drawn.

What's Average—Mode, Mean, or Median?

Four people are in a room: One is a 10-year-old child, two are 20-year-old college students, and one is a 70-year-old grandparent. What is the average age of the people in this room? The term "average" is widely used in a loose and imprecise fashion. Technically, there are three distinctly different kinds of averages.

The *mode* is the number that appears most frequently. There are more 20 year olds in this room than individuals of any other age, so the modal age is 20.

The *mean* is the arithmetic average, what most people refer to when they use the term "average." The mean is computed by adding up all the figures and then dividing the total by the number of cases or individuals. The mean age of the individuals in this room is 30, even though three out of four of the room's occupants are under that age. The problem with using the mean to measure the average is just that: A small number of extreme cases can influence the mean very strongly and distort our idea of what the population or the sample really looks like. If only one millionaire lives in a small town, the mean can make its residents seem very wealthy even if most of them are poor.

The *median* is the figure that falls exactly in the middle, with an equal number of cases above and below it. In this room, 20 is the median age, because one person is younger and one older than 20. The median is used by sociologists more often than the mean because it is not subject to distortion by a few very large figures.

Probability sampling A technique of choosing individuals to study by using a random device. In order to generate a true probability sample, each person in the targeted universe must have an equal chance of being selected.

Interval sampling Selecting individuals to study on the basis of their appearance in a sequence—for instance, choosing every tenth name in a telephone book or interviewing every twentieth person entering a building.

Nonprobability sampling A technique of selecting individuals to study that does not use a random device.

Quota sampling A sampling technique based on achieving a certain percentage of respondents with certain characteristics in the sample— for instance, half women and half men.

religion, race, and so on. By doing this, you would be **probability sampling**—that is, generating a probability sample, in which each person in the target universe or population has an equal chance of being chosen.

Another way of sampling a population or universe is **interval sampling.** Suppose, for example, you wished to draw a 10 percent interval sample of all the names in a telephone book. Step one would be to randomly select a number between 1 and 10; let's say we select the number 5. Step two is to select the person in the phone book whose name corresponds to this number—in this case, the fifth name in the book. And step three is to choose every tenth name following the first one throughout the entire book.

Interval sampling is actually quite an effective way of obtaining a representative sample of a population, as long as your listing is complete. Note, however, that even today, taking names from a telephone book does not yield a representative sample of our entire population—only of households that have phones and are listed. If your universe consisted of all the people, with or without telephones, in a given area, the telephone book will not yield a probability sample.

Nonprobability sampling generates nonprobability samples, in which anyone's chances of appearing are not calculable. **Quota sampling** is a common nonprobability sampling technique. In fact, firms that conduct regular public opinion polls and report their results in newspapers and magazines, like the Gallup, Harris, and Roper organizations, often use quota sampling. Researchers begin drawing a quota sample by examining a distribution of the relevant characteristics of the target population. On this basis, they then target a predetermined number of interviews with respondents possessing these characteristics. The most common characteristics on which such quotas are set are gender, age, geographical region, marital status, education, race, and income (Chadwick et al., 1984, p. 67). Interviewers are sent out to fill quotas based on specific percentages in those categories. For instance, a quota sample that aims to be nationally representative might target its sample to be 48 percent male and 52 percent female; 60 to 65 percent married; 20 percent single, 5 to 10 percent divorced, and 5 to 10 percent widowed; and so on. Of course, if the information on which the quotas are based is inaccurate, certain segments in the population will be overrepresented or underrepresented. Also, when interviewers cannot contact a certain individual with specific characteristics, they find another. This introduces another bias: People who are easy to contact are sociologically different from those who are difficult to contact. Nonetheless, even though quota samples are nonprobability samples, "if they are done systematically and attention is paid to the problems of availability and the potential bias it introduces, they may provide generalizable results" (Chadwick et al., 1984, p. 67).

How would you go about studying people who practice yoga, people who own unregistered handguns, or men who live in a city's "skid row" district? Some universes cannot be studied with traditional sampling methods, because no listing of their members exists anywhere. Because we know nothing about the nature of such a universe, we cannot draw a probability sample from it. One common nonprobability sampling technique used by sociologists in such instances is called **snowball sampling.** The sociologist gets in touch with several people who share a certain characteristic or engage in a certain form of behavior that the sociologist wishes to study. After they have been interviewed, they are asked to supply the names of similar people. Eventually, the sample "snowballs" into a fairly large number of people. This is a somewhat more informal and less rigorous method than probability sampling, and it usually produces a biased sample. But relatively hidden, inaccessible groups can sometimes be studied only by using this technique. Experts agree that data based on snowball samples can be used for certain limited purposes, such as developing hypotheses or generating suggestions about the nature of the real world. But they also agree that such studies cannot be used to draw definitive conclusions. To generalize from a snowball sample, methodologists argue, is a risky proposition indeed.

Snowball sampling A technique of selecting respondents by beginning with a few that the researcher knows to possess a certain characteristic (for instance, vegetarians); then, after interviewing them, asking each to supply a few names of others with the same characteristic; and, finally, continuing this process until the sample has "snowballed" into an acceptable size.

In-Depth Qualitative Interviews

In-depth qualitative interviews are quite different from interviews conducted by sociologists who engage in survey research. The most important difference is that the interview schedules used by survey researchers are **standardized**—that is, each respondent is asked the same set of questions. These are also called **structured interviews.** In contrast, in-depth interview schedules are **unstandardized:** The interviewer only has a rough guide to the questions to ask, a list of the topics to be covered. Such interviews are also known as **unstructured interviews.** These interviews are much like conversations: spontaneous and free-flowing. Much of such an interview is emergent—that is, what questions the interviewer asks often occurs to him or her during the process of the actual interview itself. In contrast, the questions asked in an interview conducted for a survey are always preordained.

An in-depth qualitative interview might thus include a question like, "Tell me about your relations with your father and mother when you were growing up." A formal interview schedule and a questionnaire would ask the question in a much more structured fashion instead: "In your grade school years, were your relations with your father: mostly positive__; mixed or neutral__; mostly negative? Were your relations at the same time with your mother: mostly positive__; mixed or neu-

In-depth qualitative interview See **Unstructured interview.**

Standardized interview schedule See **Structured interview.**

Structured interview An interview in which the interviewer asks specific questions, with a limited number of possible answers, in a predetermined order.

Unstandardized interview schedule See **Unstructured interview.**

Unstructured interview An interview that is open-ended and free-flowing and that permits the respondent flexibility and detail in his or her answers.

tral__; mostly negative__?" A qualitative interview permits respondents to answer the questions in their own terms, to discuss what is important and relevant to them, rather than what may be of interest only to the researcher. A survey researcher is seeking fairly specific information to test one or several fairly specific hypotheses. A researcher who makes use of in-depth qualitative interviews is seeking much broader, looser, less definite information.

One purpose of in-depth interviews as a sociological research method is *exploratory*: This technique is used when very little is known about a certain group or phenomenon. In such a case, survey interviews and questionnaires can be constructed only when the researcher knows enough about the population under study to ask meaningful and relevant questions. For instance, if a sociologist wished to do a study about hired killers or "hit men," it would be unwise to start with a standardized, formal interview schedule. Not enough is known about the lives of hit men to begin research on them by asking the same specific questions to a sample of representative professional killers. It is necessary to select a small number and ask them to talk in detail about themselves and their work. Only then can the sociologist learn enough to ask more specific questions. If the sociologist were to ask a hit man a question he considered stupid or ill-informed, he might decide that the sociologist is not worth talking to and terminate the interview. In short, then, the in-depth qualitative interview is a good means of gathering a great deal of detailed information on a few representatives of a group about whom little is known.

In-depth interview studies may also be conducted when full-scale surveys are inadvisable because the researcher wishes to know a great deal of detailed information about a very small population. This is especially the case if the population is an elite group that is difficult to interview because of the many demands on its members' time. For instance, one sociologist (Zuckerman, 1977) conducted interviews with forty-one Nobel Prize-winning scientists. The Nobel Prize is the most prestigious honor in science and represents "the supreme symbol of excellence in science." When the study was conducted, only seventy-two Nobel laureates were living in the United States. The researcher decided that "the standard pattern of interviewing was inappropriate" for this top elite: It interfered with rapport and inhibited detailed, elaborate answers. The scientists "resented being encased in the straightjacket of entirely standardized questions." Some questions—for instance, those about collaboration with other scientists—were relevant to certain respondents but not others; thus, "the attempt to make the interviews strictly comparable by the use of fixed questions was abandoned" (Zuckerman, 1977, p. 267).

Much the same technique would be followed with other elite samples, such as Catholic cardinals, high-level business executives, movie stars, successful popular musicians, and best-selling novelists. In-depth interviews of such individuals are often recorded on tape, to preserve the precise wording of the respondents. This permits retrieving exact word-for-word quotes and allows the researchers to capture the respondents' detailed elaborations. Because in-depth interviews rely on illustrative quotes, for most quotes, it is necessary to record the respondents' exact wording. Moreover, unlike for survey questions, the way a respondent expresses an answer in a qualitative interview is extremely important—in fact, it is actually part of the respondent's answer. And, lastly, during an in-depth interview, the full attention of the interviewer can be focused on what is being said rather than on writing it all down. Closer attention is likely to yield more accurate and more detailed answers.

The unstructured, in-depth interview is often used to supplement several of the other research methods discussed previously. Many surveys making use of formal interviews also include sections that ask some or all respondents open-ended qualitative questions. And nearly all participant observation studies include in-depth interviews of a number of informants.

Participant-Observation

Some kinds of behavior can only be studied by direct, first-hand, face-to-face, natural observation. Imagine conducting not just one interview for each respondent, but many. Imagine that these interviews are very much like ordinary conversations: spontaneous, free-flowing, informal. Imagine too that you not only converse with the people you are studying—who are called **informants**—but that you do just about everything else with them as well: go bowling, play cards, attend weddings, visit families, go drinking—everything. *Participant-observation* thrusts researchers right into the behavior they are studying. They examine the human race in its "natural habitat," observing behavior as it takes place, more or less around the clock, over a period of many months or even years. The researcher takes notes daily and acquires a huge mass of information, called field notes. There is no need to rely on a single question, or even several questions, to clarify any particular point, as there usually is with surveys.

Informant In participant-observation or field methods, an individual who supplies information to the researcher; an insider in the social setting that is being observed.

Sociologists and anthropologists sometimes "go native," or adopt the way of life of those they study. Anthropologist F. H. Cushing devoted two years of his life to becoming a member of the Zuni warrior organization, the Priests of the Bow.

Smithsonian Institution National Anthropological Archives Bureau of American Ethnology Collection

WHAT DO YOU THINK?

A Sociologist Protects the Identity of His Informants

During the summer of 1982, Mario Brajuha, a Yugoslavian immigrant who was a graduate student in sociology, began working in a restaurant as a waiter. Mario had been employed in the restaurant business for nearly fifteen years and knew it intimately. As a result, he decided to write his doctoral dissertation on the subject. In this way, he combined research with a paying job. Mario was, in short, a participant-observer engaged in studying the restaurant business from the inside.

In March, 1983, a fire of suspicious origin destroyed the restaurant. After a preliminary investigation, the county Fire Marshall suspected arson. The District Attorney's office believed that the owners had arranged to have the building torched so that they could collect the insurance money. Two detectives, learning of Mario's research, contacted him and requested to see "any and all notes, records, log, diary pertaining to . . . any restaurant." Mario refused, arguing that he could not turn over his field notes to them because he promised to protect the identity of the informants he talked to and observed.

The principle of **privileged communication** or **confidentiality**—the right not to reveal incriminating statements made by clients, confessors, and informants—extends to physicians, lawyers, and priests. In some states, a "shield" law partially protects journalists from having

Mario Brajuha was conducting participant observation research working as a waiter when the restaurant for which he worked burned to the ground. He protected the information he collected from county and federal prosecutors, even though some of his employers may have committed a crime. Do you agree that what he did was right?

Erich Goode

to reveal the sources of potentially incriminating stories, although a number of reporters have had to go to jail to protect the identity of their sources. At present, sociologists have no such rights. Mario's refusal to hand over his field notes was not a product of his idiosyncratic stubbornness. Rather, he simply expressed a nearly universally accepted principle in social research: Never endanger your informants. No one should get into trouble as a result of giving you information. Make sure that the identity of your informants is protected. After all, if you had not promised them anonymity, they

would not have revealed incriminating facts about themselves. Therefore, you have no right to reveal their names to anyone.

Naturally, the two detectives who approached Mario had no interest in researcher-informant confidentiality. They simply wanted to acquire information relating to possible crimes in any way they could, within the law. The detectives handed Mario a subpoena that demanded his appearance in court and the release of all his written materials. Though Mario was not a suspect in the investigation, the District Attorney's office believed that entries in his notes could lead authorities to the suspected arsonists. Mario decided that he had to protect himself by hiring a lawyer.

Mario began by contacting a university attorney, who advised him to "tell them everything and maybe they will let you off the hook." That was the last thing Mario wanted to hear. Because he had very little money, Mario sought the services of a pro bono lawyer—that is, one willing to work for free, "for the public good." Dozens of firms turned down the case. As things stood, Mario faced a choice between going to jail and surrendering his field notes, a grim prospect.

The day before Mario's requested grand jury appearance, a New York lawyer named Simon Wynn finally agreed to accept the case on a pro bono basis. Wynn argued that the First Amendment implies a kind of "shield," protecting privileged or secret communication by those engaged in disseminating knowledge to the public. Having to give up his field notes, Mario's lawyer argued, would imperil that communication.

In September, 1983, the judge decided against Mario's case. The appeal, decided in December, resulted in a nine-month stay or delay of the subpoena. Unfortunately, two days later, a federal District Attorney issued a subpoena almost identical to the county one that was stayed. Attorney Wynn continued to support Mario on the county case, but he had to find a new lawyer for the federal case.

Mario's prospects seemed bleak until New York University law professor James Cohen and all his legal interns agreed to take on the federal case. Cohen's job was to build a case on First Amendment grounds, with the resultant recognition that a researcher had the right to privileged or secret communication with informants.

In April, 1984, a federal judge rendered his decision: He quashed the subpoena, concluding that "serious scholars are entitled to no less protection than journalists." This seeming victory was short-lived, however. The District Attorney's office appealed the decision, and, in December, 1984, a circuit court judge remanded the case back for additional evidence on Mario's scholarly qualifications, his research activities, and his claim to confidentiality. In the spring of 1985, nearly two years after the suspicious fire, the Suf-

folk County District Attorney's office withdrew its subpoena. Mario's legal troubles were over. Further litigation was unlikely, because during the course of Mario's case, the two principal targets of the investigation had died.

Ironically, Mario's refusal to give up his field notes to the authorities may have had an unintended impact on the very individuals he sought to protect: his informants. Because the investigation was based on suspected arson, the insurance company refused to pay the owners' claim. Consequently, the owners could not rebuild the restaurant. As a result, the employees who worked for the restaurant were either unemployed or had to seek work in less desirable, less remunerative jobs. Far from appreciating his efforts, the restaurant's former employees, its owners, and their financial partners deeply resented Mario's stubbornness. They felt that Mario's refusal to turn over his field notes was based on trivial, academic, and esoteric notions. As a result, after being a trusted insider for so long, Mario became an outsider, a "problem person," a persona non grata. Moreover, because he found himself shunned socially within the restaurant business, he found it extremely difficult to get another waiting job during the period of time he defended his case.

The two-year litigation process took a tremendous toll on Mario's personal and professional life. Mario is married and has two small children. His wife felt that he was neglecting the family, which generated resentments and

arguments. Although legal counsel was contributed free, much of the family's financial resources were expended on the trial, adding to the strain. Friends, fellow graduate students, and faculty began to resent Mario's voracious obsession with the case. They felt that he had become engulfed in the role of litigant. In turn, Mario began to feel betrayed by their inability or unwillingness to be as supportive to him as he needed them to be. The "pressures of the case pushed faculty, friend and family relationships to a breaking point." Fighting the case also cost Mario two years of his professional life. He was unable to conduct his research on the restaurant business during the entire time.

At long last, when the end of the case secured the confidentiality of the field notes and Mario was free of legal threat, renewed support and a slow return to active research and scholarly activity commenced. And with that came a gradual return to normal relationships, roles and identities. . . . Mario started taking notes on the case itself as a tangential research involvement. . . . No longer a litigant, Mario was eventually able to return to normal research activity and is back on the trail toward the Ph.D. (Brajuha & Hallowell, 1986).

Do you think that Mario should have protected the identity of his informants? Should he have spent two years of his life fighting this legal battle? Was it worth it? What do you think?

Source: Based on Brajuha and Hallowell, 1986, pp. 454–478; and Brajuha, 1983, p. 79.

Privileged communication. See **Confidentiality.**

Confidentiality The principle that certain information given to a researcher should not be' revealed, especially if it is likely to harm the informant in any way. It applies most directly and specifically to ensuring the informant's anonymity and protecting his or her identity—that is, making sure that no one can link up any of the behavior described or opinions expressed in a published work with a specific individual.

Participant-observer A sociological researcher who studies human behavior either by taking part in the activities of the informants or subjects under study or by witnessing those activities in a naturalistic way.

Case study The observation of a single individual, group, organization, community, and so on, to highlight general features of social life.

Experiment A research method that puts randomly assigned subjects into carefully designed situations, studies their reactions, and determines the impact of specific variables on their behavior.

The **participant-observer** also profits from the richness of this mode of research. Any idea or hypothesis may be confirmed and reconfirmed with many different indicators, questions, and facts. You don't have to rely on a single question in a single interview or questionnaire. "In general, multiple observations convince us that our conclusion is not based on some momentary or fleeting expression of the people we study, subject to ephemeral and unusual circumstances" (Becker, 1970, pp. 53–54).

The informant in the field faces the sociologist in many different situations: at home, on the street, at work, with friends and relatives, and so on. This makes it "difficult for people to tell a coherent lie and even more difficult for them to act on it. Because they are unwilling to be caught in a lie or an incoherence, they eventually reveal their true beliefs" (Becker, 1970, p. 54). Of course, informants can and do lie to participant-observers, just as husbands and wives can and do lie to each other. But the more you know about someone, the harder it is for that person to lie to you.

Another advantage of participant-observation is that it maximizes the chances that what the researcher sees and hears will reflect real-life behavior and beliefs. All other research techniques are several steps removed from behavior itself. By going into the streets, into factories, into homes—into the lives of informants—sociologists remove many of the barriers between what they want to know and what they can observe. More than in any other research technique, participant-observation gives access to the insider's point of view, while the sociologists' training and objective points of view supply the outsider's perspective.

Field work has a number of drawbacks, as well. One such drawback is that it forces us to rely on the **case study.** If you examine only one street gang or only one factory, how do you know what gangs or factories are like in general? How can you be sure that the group, scene, community, or organization you study is typical? Answer: You cannot. Participant-observation does not employ formal sampling procedures, so all the problems of nonprobability sampling are problems of participant-observation; the problem of representativeness is more severe for participant-observation than it is for any other research method. You can never really know if what you have seen is a cross-section of the whole picture or merely a very narrow and unusual slice of it.

Second, field work tends to yield qualitative rather than quantitative data. Qualitative data cannot be measured precisely; quantitative data can. Usually, the results of field work cannot be worked up into numbers or statistical tables. Data from questionnaires and formal interviews can be standardized, and the results can then be analyzed quantitatively.

Participant-observation also cannot resolve questions of cause and effect. In general, it suits description better than explanation. Participant-observers are not able to answer the question "Why?" definitively. They are, however, able to accurately describe the details of a particular social setting.

Experiments

Let's suppose you want to test a theory like, "The greater the reward for high performance on a test, the greater the tendency for subjects to resort to cheating." You might try to test it by designing and carrying out an **experiment.** The experiment might, for example, have volunteers engage in certain kinds of activities or tasks in an experimental setting. (In experiments, the people whose behavior is being studied are usually called **subjects.**) This research technique is still much more common among psychologists than among sociologists, but many sociologists use it.

To test the theory about cheating, you could administer an exam testing your subjects' understanding of certain difficult words. The room in which the exam is given would have several dictionaries, which the subjects would be told not to use. Two separate groups would take the exam, at different times. The **experimental group** would be told beforehand that everyone achieving a certain score on the test would receive $25. The **control group** would not be so informed. The researcher running the experiment would not be present in the room when these exams are given but would be in the next room, viewing the subjects through a one-way mirror. Every time a subject looked up a word in the dictionary, the offense would be recorded as cheating. The amount of cheating in the experimental group would be compared with that in the control group, and the theory would be either confirmed or refuted by the results. Some experiments, of course, are much more dramatic and raise serious moral problems.

Laboratory Experiments. In the early 1960s, a psychologist named Stanley Milgram placed subjects in front of a "shock machine," a panel with levers. Milgram told each subject to read pairs of words to a person who was supposed to memorize the second word in the pairs. This person, who sat in a chair connected to the "shock machine," was supposed to be the subject of the experiment but was really an actor in cahoots with Milgram. When the actor-subject made a mistake, the real subjects were instructed to punish him by giving him an electrical shock. (The "shock machine" was phony, too, by the way.) Over the course of the experiment, the intensity of the shock supposedly delivered by the real subjects to the actor increased. Also, the actor (whom experimenters call an "accomplice") made mistakes intentionally, thus creating the situation in which the real subjects were expected to shock him. Milgram wanted to find out how compliant people are—how obediently they would follow the experimenter's orders, whatever they might be.

The first shocks were fairly mild. The real subjects were then instructed to increase the level of shock, and the accomplice's reactions grew increasingly dramatic. He screamed for mercy, begged the real subjects to stop the experiment, pounded the table, and kicked the wall. Eventually, he did not respond at all and appeared, indeed, to be dead. The screaming and passing out were just an act, of course.

About half the subjects in the experiment continued to shock the actor—or thought they did—right up to the end, to the apparent death of the accomplice. Milgram concluded, "A substantial proportion of people do what they are told to do, irrespective of the content of the act and without limitations of conscience, so long as they perceive that the command comes from a legitimate authority." This study, argued the author, showed that many people will inflict "inhumane treatment at the direction of malevolent authority" (Milgram, 1974, p. 189).

One drawback of such experiments is the possibility that people may not behave in real life the way they will behave in an artificial, laboratory setting. In another experiment (Orne & Evans, 1965), a researcher successfully ordered subjects to reach into cages and grasp live rattlesnakes, to put their hands in beakers of acid that had dissolved coins before their eyes, and to throw beakers of acid into the experimenter's face. (These events were all rigged, of course.) If these same people behave as imprudently in the ordinary course of events, how do they stay alive?

Subjects Individuals in an experiment whose behavior is studied.

Experimental group A category of individuals in an experiment who receive an experimental condition or treatment so that its effect may be observed.

Control group A category of individuals in an experiment who do not receive the experimental treatment, but who are exactly like the "experimental group" in every other crucial respect.

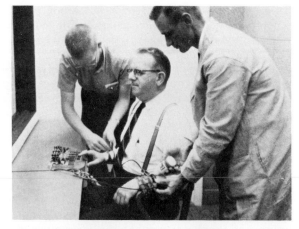
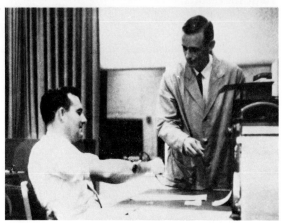
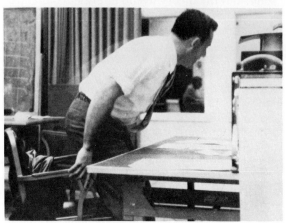

The laboratory experiment is used by some sociologists as a means of studying the social world. Psychologist Stanley Milgram investigated the question of compliance by ordering his subjects to do something that, ordinarily, they would refuse to do—shock someone to death.

© 1965 by Stanley Milgram. From the film Obedience, *distributed by the New York University film library.*

Hawthorne effect The impact research has on the people studied, resulting from their awareness of being studied; it is usually regarded as a distortion of experimental findings.

It appears, as several observers put it, that "subjects in an experiment will do practically anything they are asked [to do]. Although there must be limits to this kind of compliance, no one has yet reported them" (Freedman, Carlsmith, and Sears, 1970, p. 395).

The Limits of Experiments.   If experiments are to tell us a great deal about behavior in the real world, they will have to be more naturalistic, for laboratory experiments tend to be highly "obtrusive" (Webb, Campbell, Schwartz, and Sechrest, 1966). Of all sociological research techniques, experiments make their subjects most conscious that they are subjects of observation—and the results of the study are most influenced by this fact. The classic "Hawthorne" experiments of 1920s and 1930s highlighted this problem (Roethelsberger & Dickson, 1939). The management of the Western Electric Company called in a team of industrial psychologists to improve the productivity of the Hawthorne plant's workers. The researchers manipulated every variable they could think of: coffee breaks, lighting, salaries, lunch hours. Throughout the experiment, productivity rose steadily. Even when the researchers dimmed the lights, productivity rose; when they brightened the lights, productivity rose. Everyone involved in the study was puzzled until the researchers finally realized that the higher productivity resulted, not from the experimental conditions, but from the workers' awareness that they were being studied. Even today, the impact of obtrusive research methods on a study is called the **Hawthorne effect.**

An early experimental study, the Hawthorne experiment, showed that subjects often react to being in a study even more than to the experimental conditions themselves. In this photograph, Hawthorne-experiment subjects have been assigned numbers.

Courtesy Western Electric

These problems do not condemn the experimental method in sociology. Like all methods of sociological research, the experimental method has both weaknesses and strengths. Its weakness is its obtrusiveness and artificiality. Its strength is its conformity to the research model of natural science. Experimental conditions can be precisely controlled to isolate the influence of key factors and eliminate the influence of irrelevant ones. If two groups are similar in every way except the experimental condition, any differences observed in their behavior must be caused by the experimental condition.

Field Experiments. The problem of "obtrusiveness" has to a large degree been overcome by so-called field experiments—those conducted not in laboratories but in real-life, natural conditions. The subject should not be aware of the researcher's presence. Two sociologists rigged up the following field experiment: An accomplice would shoplift goods in a store, in plain view of customers, who were the experimenter's unsuspecting subjects. (The store's employees and management knew about the experiment.) Two researchers stood nearby and pretended to be store employees. Half of the team of "shoplifters" wore soiled, patched jeans, scuffed shoes without socks, and long, dirty, unkempt hair. The other half were clean, neatly dressed, and well groomed. The researchers expected the customers would report the messy looking shoplifters far more often than the respectable looking ones, and this is what actually happened (Steffensmeier & Terry, 1973).

Such field experiments can tell us a great deal about behavior in natural conditions. But the use of deception in social research has become an increasingly touchy and controversial issue. Is it really fair to study people scientifically without their consent or even knowledge? Sensitivity to this issue has reached the administrators and officials who provide financial support for social research. Many "deceptive" experiments approved a few years ago cannot receive public funds today. Paradoxically, the very beauty and power of the field experiment—the fact that subjects do not know that they are taking part in a study and, therefore, act naturally—is just what has undermined it. Such field experiments may require some degree of deception. As a result, the future of this line of research may be in doubt.

■ **TABLE 2–2 The Advantages and Disadvantages of Active Social Research Methods**

	Advantages	*Disadvantages*
Survey Method— The Questionnaire	Low cost. Maximizes impersonality and anonymity. No interviewer effect. Good for clear-cut answers to unambiguous questions.	Writing out responses can be burdensome, which inhibits detailed answers. Lack of give-and-take communication can lead to a loss of clarity in both questions and answers. Both the questionnaire as a whole and the answers called for must be fairly brief.
Survey Method— The Interview	Dialogue between interviewer and respondent facilitates understanding of both questions and answers. Give-and-take permits greater length, detail, nuance, and subtlety of both questions and answers.	Interviewer's presence can influence responses. Time-consuming and costly.
In-Depth Qualitative Interview	Great flexibility. Excellent as a preliminary study when little is presently known. Maximizes depth, detail, complexity in respondents' answers.	No strict comparability in wording of questions from one respondent to another. Usually based on nonprobability sample; hence, has problems with representation and generalizability. Technique necessitates skilled, sensitive, knowledgeable interviewer. Number of respondents small; cannot determine causability.
Participant-Observation	Generates a great deal of detailed information. Uses data from a variety of indicators. Maximizes the chances that what the researcher sees is real life. Comes as close as possible to the "insider's" view.	Problems with generalizing results due to reliance on the case study. Data collected are descriptive and do not usually lend themselves to precise measurement. Cannot address questions of cause and effect.
Laboratory Experiments	Controlled experimental conditions allow conformity to the research model of natural science.	Behavior observed may be artificial due to a laboratory setting.
Field Experiments	Can observe behavior under natural, real-life conditions.	Ethically questionable due to intentional deception.

The Use of Available Sources

One sociologist reads comic books for common themes they might contain. Another digs into dusty birth and marriage records dating back a century or more. A third analyzes a computer tape from the United States Census. Some sociologists make use of information that is already available in the public record. Much information is collected and filed by government agencies.

One process by which information is accumulated and recorded is called a **registration:** the continuous official record of social facts; marriage and divorce statistics; crime statistics (sent every year to Washington, D.C., by local police departments); and every other kind of official statistic known to the human mind.

A somewhat different use of available sources is called **secondary analysis:** the use of raw data already collected by active researchers. This research is then analyzed in a somewhat different way. The results of many surveys have been incompletely—or, for that matter, poorly—analyzed, and other surveys have been undertaken for nonsociological purposes. In such cases, a sociologist might get hold of the study's punched cards, or computer tapes, or completed interview schedules, or filled-out questionnaires, and then look anew at the facts and their meaning. Of all secondary analysis sources, the most important is the United States Census. The United States and other governments spend billions of dollars to collect data about their citizens. Sociologists pore over these studies to discover striking, novel, or revealing patterns that other researchers have overlooked. Private organizations, too—churches, for instance—collect data on their memberships. Sometimes, a sociologist conducts a secondary analysis of another sociologist's study!

Content analysis—the systematic examination of cultural material that exists in some physical, often documentary form—is another research technique that uses available sources of information. Such materials might be lurking in advertisements, newspaper stories, novels, photographs, films, biographies. taped conversations, letters, even garbage—any document created by human beings. Sociologists have analyzed suicide notes, to find out why people kill themselves (Jacobs, 1970); biographies in popular magazines, to see if the kinds of heroes people admire change over time (Lowenthal, 1961, pp. 109–136); popular songs, to look at shifts in the courtship patterns of adolescents (Carey, 1969); advertisements, to see if men and women are presented differently in them (Goffman, 1979); and children's picture books, to compare the treatment of little boys and little girls (Weitzman, Eifler, Hokada, and Ross, 1972).

Research Methods: Conclusions

Which is the best method of studying the social world? Which yields the most accurate answers to any sociological question? There is no one "best" technique. The best way of studying social reality varies from phenomenon to phenomenon, and from question to question. You must know what you are studying and what you want to know about it. Before you choose a research method, you must choose a research problem. Some questions can be answered in one way only; others must be answered in quite different ways.

It would not be possible, for instance, to do a participant-observation study of any social phenomenon that involved large numbers of cases and required highly precise measurements, such as income distribution in the United States. But it would be foolish to study the social lives of professional killers by means of the formal questionnaire.

Registration A continuous official record of social facts.

Secondary analysis The use of material or information that was not collected by the researcher originally, such as census data.

Content analysis The systematic examination of cultural material that already exists in a physical, often documentary form—such as photographs, short stories, news, advertising, love letters, comic books, even garbage—to draw conclusions about social life.

The largest and most expensive of all social-research efforts is the United States Census, conducted every 10 years. Sociologists make extensive use of census data; some do secondary analysis of this information to uncover new facts about American society.

Catherine Ursillo/Photo Researchers

Social life is best studied by several different methods. When you combine several techniques in one study, making use of different kinds of data, you can have much more confidence in your findings than you would have if you relied on a single technique. Using several research modes is called **triangulation:** getting a "fix" on social reality by making use of different types of information, each with its own strengths and flaws. Through such "multiple confirmation," you assure yourself and your audience that your conclusions can be trusted (Webb et al., 1966, pp. 3, 5).

Triangulation A method of confirmation using several research methods or indicators to get a "fix" on social reality.

SOCIAL RESEARCH: A COOKBOOK

Almost all social research, whatever method it may use, follows a pretty standardized pattern, or model. From the first sprouting of an idea, it proceeds step-by-step to the writing and publishing of the results. These procedures are neither secret nor very much out of the ordinary. In fact, they can be followed by students writing sociology papers or by anyone who thinks and writes systematically and seriously about the nature of the real world.

1. *Choose an area to study*. Some sociologists are fascinated by race relations; others, by life in the armed forces. Some sociologists, too, have studied particular areas for personal reasons; others, because they believe that those areas—by providing "strategic research sites"—reveal general sociological processes.

2. *Select a topic within this area*. The next step is to select a specific topic within that area—an angle, a slant, a research "problem." If race relations is your area of study, you might choose as a topic income differences between Black and white families. With the broad area of the military, you might study basic training.

3. *Construct an hypothesis*. Social research is far more than measurement and simple fact gathering. No social or natural scientist simply begins gathering facts without a preconceived idea of where they will lead. It is necessary to formulate an **hypothesis** before conducting the study itself. An hypothesis is a proposition, stated clearly and usually in a single sentence, predicting a relationship between two or more variables (Hoover, 1984, p. 31ff). An hypothesis is a supposition that serves as a starting point for the proposed research. For instance, our hypothesis might be: "Income differences between Black and white families have remained stable over the past two decades in the United States." Or: "Women military recruits are more likely to drop out of basic training than are men recruits." It is important that the hypothesis be empirically testable; if not, it is not a true scientific hypothesis. To put it another way, to be meaningful, an hypothesis must have **falsifiability:** We should know in advance what kind of evidence would verify it, and what kind would make it false. An hypothesis that is not potentially falsifiable is not scientifically meaningful. For instance, most astrological statements are not falsifiable and are therefore scientifically meaningless. The statement "You will experience ups and downs in the years to come" applies to everyone; there is no way of refuting or confirming it in any individual case.

Hypothesis A statement set forth in advance of a study predicting the occurrence of a set of phenomena or proposing an explanation for facts that should be observed.

Falsifiability A quality that all scientific statements must have: the capability of being disconfirmed or disproved if relevant data are collected.

Lastly, we must emphasize that scientists do not simply dream up hypotheses, nor do hypotheses drop out of the sky. Rather, hypotheses grow out of a general notion or *theory* concerning how the world works. Thus, our hypotheses about the Black-white income gap and female drop outs in basic training might have grown out of a commitment to the conflict perspective. Hypotheses are guided by theory; they also provide evidence supporting or questioning a given theoretical approach. Theory and research are not clearly separable entities, but are densely interwoven into one another.

4. *Survey the literature.* Once you have an area, a topic, and an hypothesis, try to learn what other researchers have discovered and thought about them. Perhaps your prediction has already been proved or refuted. You would want to know this before undertaking your study. Perhaps someone has discovered interesting facts that would allow you to sharpen or focus or redirect your hypothesis.

5. *Choose a research method.* Sociologists must choose among the methods of social research and decide which method or combination of methods most adequately tests the hypothesis. Perhaps, for instance, data drawn from the United States Census would best answer questions about income distribution.

6. *Gather the data.* Each research method rests on techniques for gathering information. With survey research, you must get the best possible sample, and word your questions quite carefully. Participant-observation puts a premium on personal sensitivity, establishing rapport, and empathy. Experiments must be designed to minimize obtrusiveness. Researchers making use of available sources of information must be certain that their information can test their hypotheses adequately. Each research technique has its own special problems and strengths, and researchers must be aware of them.

7. *Analyze the data.* The facts do not "speak for themselves." Analysis, or interpretation, of data is one of the most difficult steps in research. The data should indeed tell us whether our hypothesis is correct, but data rarely point in a single direction; usually, they speak with many voices. You must read them correctly and determine whether your original hypothesis has been verified or refuted. Two researchers can look at exactly the same findings and draw quite different conclusions from them by focusing on different aspects of the factual record. For instance, a study might reveal that Black families have earned only slightly more than half the income of white families, and that this gap has persisted since 1945. Relative to whites, the income of Blacks has not improved in recent years. But, in absolute dollars, both Black and white incomes have risen since the end of World War II. Both facts are important. But to interpret them you must decide which one tells you more about what you are studying.

8. *Explain the results.* "Why?" Explanations attempt to answer this question. They help us understand why the facts turned out as they did and not in some other way. They answer the questions, "What caused this to happen?" and, "Why are things as they are?"

For an explanation to be valid, you must not only provide facts on its behalf, but you must also eliminate competing explanations of those facts. For instance, you might show that women do indeed drop out of basic training more than men do. But why? One explanation might be that the army is dominated by men and that male officers discourage female soldiers. This might very well be a valid explanation, but to confirm it, you would have to disprove other explanations.

The Correctability of Science

However fully a model may or may not be carried out, the most important consequence of sound research methods is correctability. No scientific statement can be regarded as holy writ, eternal and unchangeable. Science thrives on new discoveries, controversy, and debate. The world is under constant scientific observation and exploration, and former truths are challenged daily. Through inquiry and empirical investigation, the human race makes discoveries, accepts them, and uses them to verify general explanations. But inquiry and investigation can proclaim the truth and expose falsehood only when scientists follow rigorous, systematic research procedures that enable others to follow in their paths.

ETHICS IN SOCIAL RESEARCH

Either directly or indirectly, all research raises questions of right and wrong, good and evil. Even natural scientists cannot escape the ethical implications of their work. Ethical considerations enter into the research enterprise in at least three major ways: First, the scientist's justification for engaging in a certain line of research must rest on ethical, not scientific, arguments. Second, the consequences of scientific research often have ethical implications that demand to be considered. Third, all scientific research must deal with the issue of how research should be conducted.

Science: A Choice between Values

Why be a scientist? Science strives to be objective, yet the value of science cannot be determined objectively. The belief that it and any particular scientific undertaking are worthwhile rests on unprovable assumptions. Believing them is an act of faith. Is it more valuable to humanity to study the mating habits of an obscure species of tropical frog or to discover new ways to feed the hungry? This is an ethical, not a scientific, question. Scientists who pursue their own research have already answered such questions implicitly by devoting their efforts to studies that may enrich human life only by increasing our store of knowledge. The basic premise of science is a belief that knowledge is good (see Chapter 1). But science is hardly cheap; by pursuing it, we neglect other worthwhile goals. The very fact of science raises ethical questions and demands ethical answers.

Research and Ethics: Choosing Sides

How much responsibility do scientists have for the results of their research? Do they have the right to engage in research that may be dangerous to human life? Can they legitimately take the attitude that what others do with their work is none of their business? For example, the atom bomb, which was developed during World War II, contributed much to science, but it also placed the human race in dread peril. How do scientists resolve dilemmas like these? Science will not provide an answer. That answer must be sought in the subjective realm of values, morality, and ethics.

Even more than physics, sociology has practical consequences. In the 1960s, the United States Army paid millions of dollars to a team of social scientists who studied the causes of revolutions in South America. The Army intended the study (called "Project Camelot") to help prevent revolutions from taking place. Is it ethical for a sociologist to participate in a study whose aim is to help suppress revolutions against governments that many Americans consider repressive? On which side is the sociologist—that of the government in power or that of the revolutionists? Does the sociologist have to be on anyone's side, or can research on a politically charged issue be conducted objectively (Horowitz, 1967)?

Whether the sociologists who took part in Project Camelot supported the government or its enemies, it should have been clear to them that involvement in such a study always entails taking sides. By participating in the research, a sociologist either supports certain aims or says, in effect: "Although I do not support these aims, I regard this study as more important than any real-world consequences it might have." This is an ethical choice, not a scientific one.

Social research can be very expensive. Typically, the organizations that can support it are rich and powerful. Often they try to use the research to promote some practical benefit to themselves, to advance their own special interests. Sociological research is not only more available to organizations that can afford to support it but also tends to entrench their power even more firmly. What would sociology be like if the poor and the powerless could support as much social research as the wealthy and the powerful do (Nicholaus, 1969)? Should sociologists think about the ways in which their sources of funding may influence their research? Does the social scientist have a responsibility to do research for groups that cannot afford to pay, to ensure that we as a nation have a well-rounded picture of social reality? These are difficult questions. They remind us how delicately intertwined the practice of social research is with moral, ideological, and ethical issues (Becker, 1967).

Human Rights in Social Research

The third ethical issue that sociologists must inevitably confront in their research concerns the manner in which they conduct it. Respondents, informants, and subjects are human beings, with rights and feelings. Researchers must not abuse the people they study. When respondents reveal intimate and possibly damaging facts about themselves to researchers, they have an ethical right to privacy, confidentiality, and anonymity. Sociologists should not disclose information that would help others trace embarrassing information to those who gave it. The subjects of experiments must not be placed in any physical danger, or humiliated, or psychologically abused in any way. If deception is used, the subject should be "debriefed"—told about the experiment after it is over. It is worth mentioning that some sociologists believe that any deception at all is unethical. A researcher's respondents, informants, or subjects should not be exploited through the sociologist's position of authority.

More than a decade ago, a sociologist named Laud Humphreys studied homosexual encounters in public restrooms as a participant-observer (Humphreys, 1970). Although Humphreys acted as a lookout, to warn these men of approaching police and other intruders, he never told them that they were being studied. Many sociologists felt that this omission was not ethical, because sociologists have an obligation to tell their informants that they are conducting research. Humphreys not only failed to say anything about his research, but he also recorded the license plates of cars parked near public urinals and obtained the drivers' home addresses. A year later, he interviewed them, pretending to be participating in a routine public health survey. This deception, too, was condemned by many sociologists, and the study generated heat as well as light. Humphreys himself later (1975) admitted that he should have told his informants that he was studying them, although if he had done so, a number of them would probably have refused to participate.

Ethical questions have no clear-cut answers. What seems right to one researcher will be condemned as unethical by another. No sociologist can possibly lay down the law in this area for all the others. Every self-respecting sociologist follows certain broad guidelines; some, but not others, follow more specific "dos" and don'ts." At any rate, social researchers are becoming more sophisticated about questions of values, ethics, ideology, and morality. It is no longer possible to pretend that they do not exist.

SUMMARY

1. Like all scientific disciplines, sociology follows the scientific method.
2. Sociological research, like all scientific research, is empirical, based on the study of things that can be shown to exist.
3. A major building block of all thinking is the concept: "a general notion or idea."
4. Concepts are measured or made known by indicators. Devising indicators and measuring them is called operationalization.
5. Concepts whose concrete appearance varies in different individuals, societies, or times are called variables.
6. Sociologists are very interested in the relationships among certain variables.
7. A formal way of measuring a relationship between two variables is called a correlation.
8. Descriptive studies are concerned only with gathering facts, including relationships among variables. Explanatory studies attempt to explain these facts and relationships.
9. A variable that causes an effect on another one is called an independent variable. The variable on which the effect is observed is called the dependent variable.
10. To establish a valid cause-and-effect relationship between two variables, it is necessary to introduce controls into the study.
11. Sociologists have devised a number of specific research methods to study social reality.
12. Studies that make use of formal interviews or questionnaires are called survey methods.

13. When using survey methods, the researcher must pay careful attention to sampling, or selecting individuals to study.

14. Another major research technique, the in-depth qualitative interview, is less structured than survey methods, but more structured than the technique called participant-observation.

15. Participant-observation permits sociologists to study people in their ordinary, everyday settings.

16. Experiments test formal hypotheses by having subjects engage in certain activities or tasks, in specific stipulated settings.

17. Some sociologists use information that already exists—available sources. Examples of this research technique are the registration, secondary analysis, and content analysis.

18. Overall, no single research technique is superior to any other. Each has its own strengths, drawbacks, and limitations. Some techniques are more appropriate for certain types of studies than others. Perhaps the best way to conduct research is to combine several methods and get a more complete picture of social reality.

19. Social research is a standardized, step-by-step process that can be spelled out in detail.

20. Sociologists must understand the ethical problems that must be addressed in social research.

SUGGESTED READINGS

Earl Babbie, *The Practice of Social Research* (4th ed.). Belmont, California: Wadsworth, 1986.
The bestselling textbook on sociological research methods. Takes the reader from philosophical underpinnings, through sampling and research design, types of research techniques, and analysis, to discussion of "the ethics and politics of social research." For a thorough, detailed treatment of the subject, this is the volume to consult.

Stephen Cole, *The Sociological Method* (3rd ed.). Chicago: Rand McNally, 1980.
Provides a clear description of how sociologists conduct social research; especially strong on surveys.

Irwin Deutscher, *What We Say/What We Do*. Glenville, Illinois: Scott, Foresman, 1973.
Explores the discrepancy between what people say in an interview and what they do in real life—and how to get around this research problem.

Kenneth R. Hoover, *The Elements of Social Scientific Thinking* (3rd ed.). New York: St. Martin's Press, 1984.
A clearly written, easy-to-understand initiation into how social scientists do their research. What is a concept? A variable? How are hypotheses tested? An excellent place to begin reading about the subject.

Darrell Huff, *How to Lie with Statistics*. New York: Norton, 1954.
My all-time favorite among books on research methods; exposes common fallacies in using (and misusing) information and pseudoinformation. Entertaining, even hilarious at times.

John Lofland and Lyn H. Lofland, *Analyzing Social Settings: A Guide to Qualitative Observation and Analysis*. Belmont, California: Wadsworth, 1984.
A guide that explains how to collect, examine, and analyze qualitative information for social behavior. Deals with such topics as aspects of qualitative social research, using personal biographies, handling the issue of ethics, overcoming informants' fear of disclosure, access to the research site, and so on.

Arthur B. Shostak (ed.), *Our Sociological Eye: Personal Essays on Society and Culture*. Port Washington, New York: Alfred, 1977.
How do sociologists feel about the research they conduct? How do the people they study feel about it? The authors of this book discuss their personal relationships to their research.

Judith M. Tanur et al. (eds.), *Statistics: A Guide to the Unknown* (2nd ed.). San Francisco: Holden-Day, 1978.
Do speed limits reduce traffic accidents? Is an intentional walk good strategy in a baseball game? Does the size of a police force reduce crime? Can people control when they die? The authors of the essays in this book discuss strategies for gathering information to answer these and many other such questions.

Stephen J. Taylor and Robert Boydon, *Introduction to Qualitative Research Methods: A Phenomenological Approach to the Social Sciences* (2nd ed.). New York: Wiley, 1984.
Discusses the "soft" research methods, especially participant-observation, the use of personal documents (like letters, journals, diaries, accounts, etc.), and unstructured, in-depth interviews. Part Two of the book explains how to write up one's findings once the data and information are gathered.

Eugene J. Webb, Donald T. Campbell, Richard D. Schwartz, and Lee Sechrest, *Unobtrusive Measures: Nonreactive Research in the Social Sciences*. Chicago: Rand McNally, 1966.
How to study something without influencing what one sees. An entertaining and informative account of "unobtrusive measures" in social science research, such as noting the wear and tear of floor tiles in front of a museum exhibit to measure its popularity, or counting the number of liquor bottles in a town's garbage to measure liquor consumption.

chapter 3

CULTURE

In Spain, men kill bulls for sport; in America, in the boxing ring, man fights man; and in Indonesia, men pit one rooster against another in mortal combat. In Iran, women appear in public clothed from head to toe; on the Riviera, women walk about clad only in tiny bikinis. The Mbuti Pygmies of Central Africa's Ituri rain forest hunt antelope with nets; the Eskimos hunt seals with rifles. Each of these customs and practices is but one small segment of a much larger whole. Each is the product of a specific and distinct **culture.**

WHAT IS CULTURE?

Most people use the word "culture" to refer to what is more precisely called "high" culture—Beethoven quartets, Chinese porcelain, fine cooking, rare wines, fashionable clothing, Shakespeare's sonnets, and so on. Sociologists, however, use the word in a much broader sense, to mean all of the learned and shared ideas and products of a society. It includes beliefs, values, politics, customs, rules and regulations, morality, law, social institutions, art, language, and material objects—in fact, everything people have done or created together, shared with one another, and transmitted to one another from one generation to the next. Baseball is no less a part of our culture than Beethoven. Soap opera qualifies as much as grand opera. Just for starters, culture determines or influences what you eat, how you make love, the clothes you wear, whom and when you marry, what type of family life you will lead, how many children you will have (and how you will raise them), what you do for fun, how you earn a living, and what your moral attitudes are. Culture can, in fact, be said to represent a people's total way of life.

Sociologists define culture as all of the learned and shared ideas and products of a society. Although some features of every culture are shared with other cultures, many are unique. Here, Egyptian girls learn how to sew in a Koranic school.

United Nations

Culture All of the learned and shared products of a society.

Cultures Are Learned

Instincts do not dictate specific customs or forms of behavior. We do not instinctively speak English or Arabic, or develop a preference for beef or pork. Each custom or behavior must be taught, and each must be learned. Genetic "programming" makes wasps build nests and spiders, webs, but human instincts, if they exist at all, are very weak; so weak that they cannot determine such specific forms of behavior. Human cultures, in fact, play in our lives the role that instincts play among animals. Nearly everything that we do is the product of a learning process. Human infants are born into one society and grow up to learn

Cultures are learned; cultural traditions are passed down from one generation to the next. In Mexico, on an island in Lake Patzcuaro, an Indian family makes fishnets. The father, a fisherman, is teaching his children a basic element of culture.

Porterfield Chickering/Photo Researchers

and practice its customs and its culture. If you take the same infant and put him or her into a different society, you will get a different human being. The process of learning a specific culture is called **enculturation.** A broader, more general term, which refers to all learning, is socialization. (See Chapter 6.)

Enculturation The process of learning a specific culture.

Cultures Are Shared

A second basic characteristic of all cultures is that they are shared by a collectivity of people. A restaurant serving only pork dishes would go out of business in Islamic countries, where pork is prohibited by religion. A widespread preference (or dislike) for certain types of food is one feature of a culture. Note that this does not mean the sum of individual, or personal, preferences. People in Islamic countries do not, as individuals, dislike pork; they learn that their societies dislike it, that it is forbidden. This prohibition, and all other aspects of culture, bring the members of this society together.

When we meet other members of our own society, we assume that they will share certain basic features of our culture. We assume they will speak English; know the fundamentals of arithmetic; think of storms and wind as natural phenomena, and not as manifestations of gods or spirits. We assume they will know how to cross the street without getting hit by cars; open cans of soda; and buy newspapers. When we meet people who cannot do these things, we assume that they come from another society. And we are right—by its very nature, a culture is shared by the members of a given society.

The Symbolic Quality of Culture

Culture is absolutely unique to humans. All humans possess a culture, and no animal species has one. Some animals have what could most aptly be described as a _proto_-culture, a very different thing. During the 1960s, scientists observed Japanese monkeys in their natural habitat. The researchers gave the monkeys food—mainly wheat and potatoes—by placing it in a location near the seashore, so they could observe the monkeys more easily. Because the wheat was placed in piles on the beach, grains of wheat got mixed with sand. The monkeys spent hours painstakingly separating the two by hand, so that they could eat the wheat. One day, something truly remarkable happened: A young female monkey scooped up a handful of the mixture, dipped it into the water, and, while she watched the wheat float on the surface, she let the grains of sand sink. When all of the sand had dropped to the bottom, she grabbed and ate the wheat. The other monkeys observed the new technique and soon adopted it. A tradition had been created, one that passed from one monkey to another by being taught and learned (Kawai, 1965; Menzel, 1966). The new technique had one feature of a true culture: It was learned. But it was not an aspect of a true culture. What made it a piece of a proto-culture and not a true culture was its lack of symbolism. The Japanese monkeys washed their wheat in response to a direct, immediate need, much as they do everything else. They could not embody this act in a **symbol.**

A symbol is anything that represents something else. The symbol has an existence independent of what it represents; the connection is created by the human mind, by culture, and not by the characteristics of the thing itself. Wheat washing among monkeys does not symbolize or represent anything else: It is simply another way of separating the

Symbol One thing that stands for another, whose meaning is arbitrary and imposed by the human mind.

A symbol's meaning is not direct or obvious. The distinctive feature of being human is the ability to create symbols. All cultures are symbolic. A flag is a symbol for a country, a symbol that has been created by the human mind.

Herbert Lanks/Monkmeyer Press

Sign One thing that stands for another, the meaning of which is direct, obvious, and nonsymbolic.

wheat from the sand. Animals do not create symbols, nor, unless humans intervene, do animals use them. But humans do, and this is a major feature that marks humans off from animals. A flag is a symbol for a country. The cross is a symbol of Christianity; the Star of David, a symbol of Judaism; the crescent moon and the star, a symbol for Islam. A candy-striped barber's pole outside a building symbolizes the fact that a barbershop is within.

Language is a system of symbols. Words mean what they mean simply because the people who speak a language agree that they do. For instance, there is no direct or intrinsic connection between the English word "book" and the actual physical object for which it stands. The word symbolizes the thing solely because we have found that we need symbols of this kind to communicate, and we share a language that designates the meaning of certain words.

Animals do interpret **signs,** however (Becker, 1962, pp. 22ff): direct indications in the real world whose meanings are obvious and innate. A sign is representational; its meaning, given within the phenomenon itself, is not consensual. Dark clouds signify rain; a dog's growl signifies unfriendliness; smoke signifies fire. The connection between a thing and its sign is direct. In contrast, a symbol's meaning is not obvious or direct. It has been created by the human mind; it is assigned by mutual agreement; and it is learned. No animal possesses the ability to create symbols. It can be said, in fact, that the distinctive feature of being human is the ability to create them (Farb, 1980, p. 63).

All this is important because a repertoire of signs is very limited and very rigid. If, tomorrow, a new phenomenon appears, we can quickly invent a word for it, discuss it, and master it. Consider the poor monkey! The wretched animal cannot free itself from those signs that come ready to hand in the external world and in its own genetic makeup. It is the slave of these accidents, for it lacks the intelligence to create symbols and transcend its immediate surroundings.

BIOLOGY AND CULTURE

The members of the human race do not make very impressive physical specimens. Porpoises can outswim us, lions can outfight us, and antelopes can outjump us. Why, then, don't porpoises, lions, and antelopes rule the world? Because the human anatomy, for all its deficiencies, serves its purpose: Human beings do most things rather poorly when compared with those animals specialized to do them, but we are equipped to do many more things than those other animals. Specialized animals can perform only a narrow range of actions; the behavioral range of human beings is very broad. Porpoises cannot venture onto land; lions cannot thread needles; and antelopes cannot climb trees or pile large rocks on top of each other. Human beings have, and by far, the vastest behavioral repertoire of any animal that has ever existed.

A second remarkable feature of our anatomy is our massive and complex brain. A few species do have brains as large as ours—for example, the porpoise, though most of its brain is devoted to navigation. The human brain is distinctive, however, less by virtue of its size than by virtue of its function: thinking and reasoning. The brains of most animals oversee specific functions, like balance, smell, and sight. But most of the human brain is not committed to any special task or function. This lack of specialization makes culture not only possible but absolutely essential, for as the brain grows in size and power, the importance of instinct diminishes in proportion.

The third anatomical feature characteristic of the human animal, and shared only by the great apes (like the gorilla and the chimpanzee), is the opposable thumb—a thumb that can touch the tips of every finger on the same hand. By this means, we can get a secure but sensitive grip on objects large and small. The flippers of the porpoise, the paws of the lion, and the hooves of the antelope are all highly adapted, each to its own specific function but to none other. An opposable thumb makes the human hand an extremely versatile and adaptable organ, capable of a wide range of activities, especially picking up and holding things.

These three characteristics—our unspecialized anatomy, the size of our brain and its reasoning power, and our opposable thumb—have permitted us to conceive, invent, and use tools. These tools help us adapt to our environment in the same way that the anatomy of an animal helps it to adapt to its environment. Cheetahs pull down their prey with fangs and claws; the Zulu, a tribe in Africa, forge spears to do the job. Sharks gobble up fish by slashing away with their mighty jaws and sharp teeth; the Polynesians, in the Pacific, haul in schools of fish with nets. These tools are vastly superior to the natural, biological tools of animals because we do not have to carry them around on our bodies, because we can invent and use different tools for different tasks, and because we can steadily improve them and make them more effective (Farb, 1980).

Ants cannot suddenly resolve to build square anthills, nor lions to become vegetarians. But human beings can decide to build structures of every conceivable description and to eat an astounding variety of foods. We have drives—urges that can stimulate a broad category of actions—but few if any instincts. We are "driven" to eat, to drink, to engage in sex, and perhaps also to love, seek affection, and protect ourselves from death and mutilation. If we were not, we would die, individually or collectively. But our ways of satisfying these drives vary a good deal from culture to culture and time to time. Drives make certain broad kinds of activities possible for us, but they do not dictate the form they take. For an account of this enormous variability, we must turn to culture.

Because our instincts are too feeble and shallow to protect us or to ensure our survival, culture is absolutely crucial to the human species. We rely on it almost completely. Culture tells us how to survive in certain environments: where to find food, how to build shelter, how to make clothing, and how to deal with sickness and disease. None of these activities derive from instinct; we must be taught them.

Centuries ago, philosophers speculated about the so-called state of nature—the absence of culture. We now know that "there is no such thing as human nature independent of culture." Without culture, human beings "would be unworkable monstrosities with very few useful instincts, fewer recognizable sentiments, and no intellect: mental basket cases." Culture makes us human, for we are "incomplete or unfinished animals who complete or finish ourselves through culture" (Geertz, 1973, p. 49).

Sociobiology

Sociobiology The theory that human behavior, like physical characteristics and animal behavior, is acquired through biological inheritance, as a result of natural selection.

Sociobiology is a modern form of the theory that human behavior is inherited through the genes, much as physical characteristics and animal behavior are. Sociobiologists believe that evolution promotes the selective inheritance of certain forms of behavior because they are adaptive for the organism and the species. These forms of behavior "become genetically encoded in a species if they contribute to the fitness [i.e., the reproductive success] of those individuals" that have them (van den Berghe, 1978, p. 20). For instance, in certain environments, a small and weak, but fast, animal has a better chance of surviving than a slow one. In such a species, those individuals that are a little quicker than the others will survive in greater numbers, and they will pass their speed on to their offsprings and to later generations. In time, the entire species becomes faster and faster.

Natural selection The survival and perpetuation of favorable characteristics in biological organisms.

Sociobiologists regard human behavior, like animal behavior, as the end product of **natural selection.** According to them, some social customs are adaptive, whereas others are not. Those that are pass the test of time and are passed on through the genes from parent to child. They do not have to be learned through the process of socialization but are "encoded" in individuals at birth. Customs dictating that men should be dominant over women, that parents should care for their children, and so on, have survived because societies that adopted them survived more readily than those that did not. Eventually, they developed into instincts, inherited through the genes.

At present, this theory remains sheer speculation; its proponents have never even suggested just how it could possibly be supported—or refuted—by any kind of evidence. They present us with a mere string of analogies, metaphors, and parallels between animal and human behavior. A good deal of evidence creates severe problems for sociobiologists. First, much of the behavior that sociobiologists regard as universal is, in fact, practiced only in certain places at certain times. For instance, the idea that we should behave more altruistically toward genetically close relatives than to others is far from universal in human societies: Infanticide—the killing of children shortly after birth—has been very common. Besides, who are our relatives? The answer is a product of culture, not of genes. Sociobiology, in other words, is flawed by the bias of its **enthnocentrism:** its tendency to universalize the values and customs of our own society.

Sociobiology ignores what is most significant about human behavior—its diversity—and focuses instead on its universals, and imposing a genetic explanation on them. Sociobiologists do not dismiss the importance of culture. But they minimize the importance of cultural differences among different societies. In reality, the constants in human behavior are so few, and the variation is so vast, that sociobiologists may be said to be looking through the wrong end of the telescope.

Ethnocentrism Viewing another culture from the perspective of one's own.

BUILDING BLOCKS OF CULTURE

A concept as broad as culture, which includes the total way of life of all the peoples living on Earth, obviously comprises a number of separate but interconnected features, or "building blocks." The broadest and least specific building blocks of any culture are its values. Values are those things that a culture regards as morally good and bad. Culture is made up of a second aspect, too—beliefs: what a given society regards as true or false. Christians, Jews, and Moslems believe that "God exists"; Soviet communists do not. A third building block is the instructions a culture gives to its members about correct and incorrect behavior: its norms. Norms tell people what they should and should not do. "Drive on the right-hand side of the road" is a norm. The fourth building block that all cultures have (and partly consist of) is material artifacts, the objects that the members of a society manufacture and use. The fifth and last building block of culture is language: a system of words and word structures, or grammar.

Values

Values are notions of what a particular culture regards as good or bad, desirable or undesirable. Usually, they are quite broad and abstract and do not dictate specific kinds of behavior in concrete situations. Different cultures stress different (and even opposing) values, and, in the long run, conceptions of right and wrong influence behavior.

For instance, American society tends to uphold such values as activism, achievement, success, material affluence, practicality, progress, self-reliance, and optimism (Williams, 1970). In many other societies, these values do not carry the same weight, and, in still others, they are regarded with hostility. To take one case, Chinese culture upholds conformity, cooperation, and community well-being. This difference in values has created differences in behavior that are immediately obvious to any observer.

Values Notions of what is regarded as good or bad, desirable or undesirable.

Of course, societies give some of their values mere lip service. In the United States, we claim to believe in humanitarianism, individualism, equality, and democracy. But in this country (as everywhere else), people often say one thing and do another, and so we see much elitism, conformity, special privilege, expediency, and "copping out" among Americans. A sociologist usually needs to see a society's values in action to grasp their true meaning and importance.

Even within a single society, different values may contradict one another. Honesty is a positive value in many cultures, but so too is survival. Who would not tell a lie to save his or her own life? Some values are difficult to act on because, in doing so, we are forced to violate others. Nearly everyone values friendship, but pursuing economic success may entail moving away from and severing close ties with our friends.

Beliefs

The **beliefs** held by the members of a society are the second building block of its culture. Beliefs are cultural conventions about what is true or false: descriptions or assumptions about the world and our place in it. Values are broad notions of good and bad; beliefs are more specific and, in form at least, factual in appearance. (Of course, this appearance may be deceptive.) "Democracy is good" is a value of American society. "Democracy is the best way to run a government" is a belief; it contains assumptions about the correct way to run a government in the real world. Most people in a given society assume that their beliefs are rational, reasonable, and so firmly grounded in common sense and reality that it would be perverse to believe anything else.

Any conceivable area of life can generate beliefs. Some are true, some are false, and some are "nonfalsifiable": They cannot be proved or disproved (see Chapter 1). Sociologists are less concerned with the correctness of a belief than with the role it plays in a culture and the lives of its people.

Beliefs Cultural conventions about what is true or false.

Every culture holds certain values as desirable. Achievement and success are basic American values—stressed more heavily here than in many other societies. Receiving an Academy Award is a widely coveted achievement, while college graduation is seen by many as a step on the way to a successful career.

UPI/Bettmann Newsphotos; Mimi Forsyth/Monkmeyer Press

As you look from one culture to another, and from one period of time to another, you find beliefs of almost every conceivable kind, and not a few that may seem to be inconceivable. In ancient India, for example, a respectable man or woman would have believed that "many gods exist," not that "God exists." Until 200 years ago, democracy was almost everywhere regarded as a form of anarchy, and monarchy was regarded as the only form of government suited to a complex society. Much of what we hold dear, members of other societies reject; and much of what some cultures hold dear, we reject.

Norms

Norms—a society's rules of right and wrong behavior—are the third building block of culture. Norms dictate appropriate standards of conduct. They tell people in a culture what they should and should not do. Norms rest on the assumption that if you are caught violating them, you will be punished in some way. Such a system of punishment and reward is called **social control.** All of the ways in which people can be punished for violating norms, or rewarded for following them, are called **social sanctions.**

Consider an example: At 11 o'clock on a Saturday night John decides that he wants to go out with Mary, a fellow student in his introductory course in sociology. He walks to her dormitory room and knocks on her door. As it happens, she is not doing anything very special. And she likes John and had actually hoped that he would ask her out. But she is also a bit insulted at the manner of his request. Politely, she tells John to get lost—not quite in those words. Had Mary accepted a spontaneous date with John, her friends might have said she was being "too available." In many societies Mary's behavior would seem crazy; they do not have our elaborate system of planning dates days in advance and prefer to arrange such matters more spontaneously.

Just about all societies tolerate a certain amount of nonconformity. Norms like these—which do not raise strong emotions, are almost optional, and call only for very mild criticism of the transgressor—are called **folkways.** Try wearing one green sock and one brown one. While talking to a friend, prop up your feet on a desk, so that your mismatched socks show. One of our society's folkways is the wearing of socks that match in color. If you don't follow that norm, a mild rebuke is the worst thing that might happen to you.

Mores are norms that are held quite strongly. When they are violated, we are outraged, and we think of those who violate them as criminal, insane, or depraved. Disobeying mores is serious business and calls for severe punishment: "snubbing," vicious gossip, public ridicule, divorce, the loss of friendship, exile, arrest, beating, being fired from a job, or getting expelled from college. Dominant American mores call on us not to assault anyone without provocation, to be sexually faithful to spouses, to get jobs, to restrict sexual contacts to persons of the opposite sex, and so on. The Ten Commandments provide a fairly good (though not complete) list of the mores of Western culture. Sociologists call behavior that calls for strong negative sanctions *deviance.* Someone who habitually violates mores is called a **deviant** (see Chapter 8).

Some norms are **prescriptive:** They dictate, in a positive sense, what people ought to do—"Honor thy father and mother," for example. Other norms are **proscriptive:** They say what people ought not to do—"Thou shalt not kill." Some norms apply only to certain people or to certain

Norms Instructions telling the members of a society what is correct and incorrect behavior; rules about what people should and should not do.

Social control All of the social efforts to discourage deviant behavior and the mechanisms designed to ensure conformity to norms, rules, and laws.

Social sanctions Rewards or punishments called for in a culture for engaging, or not engaging, in certain actions.

Folkways Norms that are not strongly held, are regarded as almost optional, and call for only mild chastisement of the transgressor.

Mores The norms that are regarded as important, the violation of which brings strong punishment to the offender.

Deviant Having the characteristics of violating the norms of a culture.

Prescriptive norms Rules telling the members of a culture what they *should* do.

Proscriptive norms Rules telling members of a culture what they should *not* do.

situations. A 12-year-old girl who is caught driving a car will be arrested, because, in our society, norms regulate who can and who cannot drive. The norm of not talking during your sociology class does not apply most other times—for instance, if you are talking with a friend in the student union. Other norms seem to apply to almost everyone and in all times and places. "Thou shalt not kill" does not specifically exempt certain categories of people. Most societies do, however, permit some people to kill others, though only in strictly defined circumstances.

Keep in mind, too, that norms represent ideals, not actual behavior. We do not always do what society says we should. Who has not violated some norm or other? Norms, however strong, do not have the compelling quality of physical laws; they may even be broken quite often. Remember the distinction between a society's *ideal culture*—its norms—and its *real culture*—the actual behavior of its members.

People who violate norms are punished in one of two ways: formally or informally. Some norms are made into law, and violators can be arrested and imprisoned. Punishment is meted out by the state government and has an official, formal status. Police, courts, jails, and prisons are called agents of **formal social control.** If you sell a kilo of cocaine, murder your father and mother, or rob a liquor store, you can be punished in this way, because these are violations of a formal legal code. Other norms are not crystallized into law; violating them only brings forth unofficial, informal, interpersonal punishment. Cheating at cards, joining an unconventional religious "cult," or espousing revolutionary political doctrines will not, usually, get you arrested; it will, however, create hostility against you—one form of *in*formal social control.

Material Artifacts

Material artifacts are the fourth building block of culture. These are the physical objects that the members of a society design, make, use, and share. Artifacts stem not only from a society's technology but also from its values, beliefs, and norms. They reflect a "world view," an *ethos*. Cultures with traditions of scientific inquiry and receptiveness to intellectual change are much more likely to generate inventions than are societies that reject empirical study and change.

Formal social control The imposition of sanctions on offenders by agents and agencies that have been empowered by society to enforce the law; includes the police, the courts, and the prisons.

Material artifacts Physical objects created and shared by the members of a society.

Many material artifacts originate in one culture, cross cultural lines, and are used elsewhere. Skyscrapers were first built in New York and Chicago, and later appeared in all large cities the world over. Here, we see the present-day skyline of Tokyo, Japan.

Tadanori Saito/Photo Researchers

Of course, material objects can and do cross cultural lines: Sky-scrapers, for instance, originated in New York and Chicago and then spread to all the large cities of the world. Physical objects are created because they express a society's cultural values or answer its needs, and they spread to other cultures for the same reasons. Material items do not move from one culture to another unless they have meaning in the lives of people in the adopting culture.

A society that adopts material items from another society may use them or think about them very differently. Among the Eskimos, the rifle is a tool for survival, because the Eskimos use their rifles to hunt for food: seals, walruses, and polar bears. For most of today's Americans, rifles are mere recreational devices, like baseball bats, backpacks, and novels. In both cultures, the material item itself is identical; its use and meaning, however, vary a good deal.

Material artifacts often react back upon culture in general and influence what people think and do. Think of all the ways in which the automobile has changed every society that has adopted it; or the effect of the printing press upon the spread and sheer quantity of knowledge. The ideas and the behavior of any society's members, and its material artifacts, meet in a two-way street. They mutually influence one another—often in unexpected ways.

Language

Language is the fifth crucial aspect or building block of culture. If you have ever played a game of "charades," you know that a word that might take a second to pronounce might require two minutes, or more, to communicate through gestures. Language is thus a quick, precise, efficient, and flexible means of communication. In fact, there is no other way of communicating complex ideas. Language does more than just make communicating easier. It actually makes conceivable some ideas that would otherwise be inconceivable. Philosophy, science, and literature could not exist without it.

The Sapir-Whorf Hypothesis. Many people think that different languages express pretty much the same ideas and describe the same objects, using different words. Considered this way, language is simply a series of labels attached to various things, with rules (called syntax) for uniting them in intelligible sentences. Words, in this view, passively reflect the real world. Some contemporary social scientists think that language plays a more active role in shaping our thoughts. In fact, many observers feel that actually language channels the thinking of its speakers along certain lines and blocks off other lines of thinking—a theory that is sometimes referred to as the **Sapir-Whorf hypothesis,** after its originators (Sapir, 1929; Whorf, 1956). Their theory is also called the **linguistic relativity hypothesis:** Languages, like cultures, approach the world in different and largely incompatible ways. Languages do not represent reality in a neutral fashion. Instead, the language people speak shapes their perception of reality, and so, in a sense, the reality itself is different. "The worlds in which different societies live are distinct worlds, not merely worlds with different labels attached" (Sapir, 1949; p. 162).

Edward Sapir was a linguist and an anthropologist of Native American tribes. Benjamin Whorf was an employee of an insurance company and a student of Native American languages. He argued that a language forces its speakers to notice certain aspects of the real world and to ignore others, and that this pattern influences their behavior. In his

Sapir-Whorf hypothesis The theory that language profoundly shapes thought and action.

Linguistic relativity hypothesis See **Sapir-Whorf hypothesis.**

WHAT DO YOU THINK?

Language and Culture in America: Black and White

Are the various groups, categories, and subcultures in American society converging or separating culturally? Are their members becoming more alike or different in their values and beliefs? Is the United States becoming more homogenized or heterogeneous on the cultural dimension? More specifically, are Blacks and whites coming together or apart culturally?

A common assumption in recent years has been that mass communication, especially television, is bringing about cultural unity through a common socialization process (see Chapter 6). The fact that Blacks and whites are exposed to essentially the same television programs and much the same news all over the country, some argue, inevitably leads to cultural convergence.

Some linguists study dialects in an effort to determine what their differences tell us about cultural differences among their

speakers. A dialect is a variety of a spoken language with certain features of vocabulary, grammar, and pronunciation that differ from other varieties. In the United States, dialects are based on region (for instance, Southerners speak a slightly different dialect than New Englanders), social class and education (a longshoreman speaks a slightly different dialect than a college professor), and race. Sociologists, anthropologists, and linguists argue that language and culture are intimately related. Language is an aspect of culture, and it influences the way the members of a society think and act. In turn, language is a reflection or indicator of cultural differences among groups.

A team of linguists at the University of Pennsylvania is busy studying the dialects spoken by Blacks and whites, and it has concluded that the differences are growing, not diminishing. The "Black English vernacular," or

the dialect spoken by urban Blacks, is steadily growing apart from what linguists call "standard English," or the dialect spoken by radio and television announcers. (In addition, local regional white dialects are also diverging from both standard English and the Black vernacular, so that all racial and regional subcultures are becoming more disparate, at least from the point of view of language.) Dr. William Labov, director of the research, stated: "There is evidence that, far from getting more similar, the Black vernacular is going its own way. . . . It's a healthy, living form of language. But separate development is only made possible by separate living."

Wendell Harris, who is Black and who grew up in an area of Philadelphia that was studied, is a member of the Pennsylvania research team. A number of the Philadelphians whose speech was studied were friends, acquain-

work, Whorf often investigated insurance claims resulting from fire damage. He believed that the English language actually caused some fires. Some fires are set off by people who light matches near empty gasoline drums. The English word "empty" implies that the drums contained nothing at all and were therefore safe. In actuality, "empty" drums are far more dangerous than those filled with gasoline because, far from being truly empty, they contain inflammable and explosive fumes and gases. A language that did not treat such drums as "empty" might promote greater caution in their presence. Indeed, Sapir and Whorf believed that the ways we can and cannot think, and the experiences we can and cannot have, are determined culturally, through language.

Margaret Mead found that the Arapesh, a tribe living in New Guinea, did not have a particular word for any number past two. Three was tances, and relatives of Professor Harris's. "The results of our analyses show a Black English vernacular that's more remote from other dialects than has been reported before. . . . We also believe that Philadelphia reflects a national trend in the Black community towards continued linguistic divergence. The differences appear to us to be increasing." Dr. Labov added: "People's speech behavior . . . is not influenced by the remote communication of the mass media." The relative-to-relative and friend-to-friend socialization process is much more potent in teaching the young to speak a certain way, Dr. Labov explained.

A large number of educated Blacks, especially those who come into frequent contact with whites, switch back and forth between Black and white dialects, depending on the situation. And a growing number of middle-class Blacks speak standard English, although often with a Black accent. But the absolute number of speakers of the Black vernacular is growing, the research team believes. Still,

the researchers were surprised to find how little language contact existed between Blacks and whites. Throughout much of Philadelphia, many Blacks never speak to a white person before the age of 6, when they enter school; many whites never speak to a Black person at all. Most Black Philadelphians, like urban Blacks in all American cities, live in increasingly segregated neighborhoods. "The more we study," Dr. Labov declared, "the more it shows the signs of Black people developing" all of the basic features of their own dialect.

Cultural and linguistic differences, by themselves, should not represent a problem to anyone, if such differences were mutually accepted and respected by interacting members of different subcultures. One problem with the linguistic divergence under study, however, is that when urban Black children enter the school system, they are judged on their ability to speak standard English. "We're looking at this as a danger signal that our society is being

split more and more," Dr. Labov said, "and we're not ruling out the possibility that it is contributing to the failure of Black children to learn to read. How much a little child has to do to translate." Moreover, although white children who speak a class and regional dialect are also judged according to the yardstick of standard white English, the depth of "misunderstanding" between Blacks and whites is greater than it is for members of the various white subcultures.

The research team did not suggest a remedy to the problem of linguistic divergence. What should be done about it, if anything? Should white teachers and other professionals who interact with urban Blacks be required to become acquainted with the Black vernacular and treat it as an acceptable alternative way of speaking? Or should urban Black children be forced to become fluent in standard English? What do you think?

Source: Stevens, 1985, p. A14; and Labov and Harris, 1983.

---

expressed as "two and one." The word "dog" was used for four. Beyond that, the Arapesh made use of combinations—seven, for instance, was "one dog and two and one." So cumbersome is this system that, above a certain number, quantities must be expressed as "a lot" (Geertz, 1973, p. 60). Can you imagine complex mathematical formulas making use of this system? You cannot. The Arapesh do not make mathematical calculations with words that are different from ours: They think in an altogether different, nonmathematical way. Their language closes off certain lines of thinking.

Although all social scientists today agree that language can influence the way we think and look at the world, most feel that Sapir and Whorf carried their argument too far. The Eskimo language has over twenty words for different kinds of snow—one for drifting snow, one for hard-packed snow, and so on. The English language only has one such word, and a second—"slush"—that is closely related to it. Certainly, the Eskimo vocabulary reflects a preoccupation with snow. Yet even without a specific word for "drifting snow," we can distinguish this kind of snow from all others and form a phrase that expresses our meaning. The lack of a specific term does not prevent us from observing a reality in the external world.

Two psychologists (Heider & Oliver, 1972) studied the members of the Dani, a tribe in western New Guinea, to test the Sapir-Whorf hypothesis. The Dani language only has two words for all the colors in the spectrum: One refers to all the dark, cool colors; the other, to all the bright, warm colors. In this study, the color perceptions of the Dani were compared with those of American college students. The two groups, the study found, were equally capable of distinguishing different colors from one another. The fact that we have hundreds of words for different colors and hues, and that the Dani have only two, does not mean that our color perception is very different from theirs. Language is certainly a crucial aspect of culture, as Margaret Mead's example of the Arapesh shows, but its influence may be less pervasive than the Sapir-Whorf hypothesis would imply.

VIEWING CULTURES

Looking at cultures the world over, sociologists observe a number of crucial and inescapable facts. First, the differences among cultures are enormous; the variation from one culture to another should strike us forcibly. Even things that are regarded as concrete and tangibly real, like time and space, are conceived and treated in radically different ways in different societies.

Second, the variety of the world's cultures forces us, in viewing them, to adopt the perspective of cultural relativism. We must, in other words, look upon cultures as they look on themselves: on the basis of their own beliefs and assumptions, in terms that make sense to their own members. We must abandon the ethnocentric view that our own culture is the standard by which all others should be measured.

Third, despite the considerable cross-cultural variation, some cultural universals—customs or practices—appear to be present in all societies. Even so, these are only broad, not specific, universals. Cultures do have certain practices in common, but they carry them out in their own special ways.

Fourth, each culture is, to a large measure, "integrated." This cultural integration refers to the elements or aspects of a culture's "fitting together" and being consistent with one another. Cultures are integrated on the individual level, because the members of every culture share basic attitudes and practices. They are also integrated on the institutional level, because major social institutions tend to be consistent with one another.

Finally, in every culture, some individuals and groups do not share all the values, beliefs, or norms of the majority. Those groups that are "just different" from the dominant culture in some ways are called subcultures. Countercultures are those that are actually in direct opposition to the surrounding culture.

Cultural Variation

When students read about the cultures of other peoples, they are usually impressed by exotic and unusual customs: eating grubworms, instead of cheeseburgers, let us say, or sleeping on thin bamboo mats instead of mattresses and box springs. Students tend to see the cultures of other peoples as grab bags of peculiar customs—odds and ends that can be collected and observed, much like curios and antiques. They view these customs as colorful, but basically unimportant features of other peoples' lives, worn like elaborate, flamboyant costumes that can be taken off, revealing a fundamental humanity. We come to think of such customs merely as different ways of doing basically the same things that all people do: eat, sleep, marry, live, love, die.

This is a mistaken view. Culture is not worn like a garment, to be put on or taken off as occasion demands. It is not a collection of assorted and peculiar customs, to be admired and marveled at like a string of brightly colored beads. Culture is more like a medium, a surrounding fluid, in which people live: It is a total environment. Culture touches all aspects of our lives, determining the way we think and the nature of our experiences at every moment of our lives, creating within us every detail of what we perceive as reality. There is, of course, such a thing as individuality; not all the members of any culture are exactly alike. But the ways in which we express our individuality lie within the range of what a society considers meaningful. Even the insane express their mental illnesses in ways that are distinct to their culture.

Time and Space. Let's consider something as basic and obvious as time, and the way it is perceived and interpreted. An hour is an hour, you might say, whether you are in New York or in Nairobi. From a cultural point of view, you would be wrong. The clock may measure the passage of time in the same way everywhere, but time is a symbol that conveys different meanings to the members of different societies. Compared with members of other societies, North Americans have precise notions of time. If you are forty-five minutes late for an appointment, the person you are meeting will probably regard you as inconsiderate. However, throughout most of the world, lateness of only forty-five minutes is not a sign of disrespect. In other cultures, Americans who are concerned about such matters are regarded as silly and overpunctual. The passage of exactly the same length of time, forty-five minutes, symbolizes (or means) totally different things in different cultures (Hall, 1959, p. 18),

Likewise, cultures symbolize space in different ways. Space, like time, is symbolic; people communicate messages to one another by making symbolic use of space and time. Therefore, the same physical distance, like the passage of the same period of time, may be interpreted differently from one society to another. For instance, to North Americans, two feet or more between speakers is a comfortable distance. Latins regard this distance as too cold and impersonal and prefer to speak to one another at a much closer range. The same distance—a foot or so—that in Latin America implies an ordinary conversation, in the United States would imply either intimacy or hostility. An American would feel very uncomfortable speaking to someone at a distance of only a foot unless there was something special about the conversation or the relationship. When a North American and a Latin speak to each other, the American tends to inch backward, and the Latin to step forward, each to arrive at a comfortable speaking distance. Unless each understands how the other's culture symbolizes space, their attempts to communicate will be clumsy (Hall, 1959).

Culture is not a collection of assorted and peculiar customs to be admired and marvelled at like a string of brightly colored beads. Culture is more like a total environment in which people live; it touches all aspects of our lives.

Kay Miller/Woodfin Camp & Associates

Conceptions of Time as an Aspect of Culture

Recently, an American professor, Robert Levine, journeyed to South America to spend a year as a visiting professor at a medium-sized Brazilian university. During his first day on the job, walking toward his 10 o'clock class, Professor Levine noticed a clock as he strolled by. It said 10:20. He ran to the classroom only to find it empty. Frantically, he asked a passerby the time; the answer was 9:45. Incredulously, Levine asked another, and the reply was 9:55. A clock in a nearby office said 3:15. Finally, he found out the right time and got to his class by 10. Many of the students in the class arrived after 10, and several did so after 10:30. A few showed up close to 11, and two, after 11. All wore casual smiles that seemed to say, relax, everything's fine. None seemed concerned about being late. The class lasted until 12, and yet, only a few students left when it was officially over. A large number of students were still asking questions and waiting for answers at 12:30. When several kicked off their shoes and appeared to be settling in, Levine decided to beg off and make his exit. Apparently staying late had no more significance for these students than did arriving late.

As a result of this experience, Levine decided to study the cultural sense of time in several societies. In his first study, he started by asking his Brazilian students questions about time; later, he asked his California students the same questions. Brazilians defined lateness for lunch as thirty-three minutes after the appointed time, on the average. California students indicated an average of nineteen minutes. When asked how many minutes before the appointed time that they would regard someone as early, the Brazilians answered an average of fifty-four minutes. The California students averaged twenty-four minutes. Brazilian students were less likely to attribute being late to a lack of caring for the other party than were the California students. The Brazilians also regarded being consistently late as a sign of success; someone who possesses high status is expected to arrive significantly later than someone who is of lower rank. This belief was not common in the United States.

Levine's second study entailed checking how the residents of different societies actually behaved with respect to time by using three basic indicators: the accuracy of bank clocks, the speed with which pedestrians walked along a sidewalk, and the amount of time it took a post office clerk to sell one stamp. Levine examined these indicators in two cities in each country—the nation's largest and one medium-sized city. Of the six societies selected—Japan, the United States, England, Italy, Taiwan, and Indonesia—Japan's citizens had the most accurate sense of time and moved at the quickest pace. Japan's clocks were an average of only thirty seconds too fast or too slow. Indonesian clocks were the least accurate; they were off by an average of over three minutes.

Walking speeds bore out the fact that the Japanese made the most of time. Clocking over 100 pedestrians walking alone down a main downtown street during business hours on a day with fair weather, Levine found that the Japanese walked 100 feet in an average of 20.7 seconds. The English were second, at 21.6 seconds, and the Americans clocked in third, walking the 100 feet in 22.5 seconds. The Indonesians again were last, at 27.2 seconds. As we might expect, people walked faster in a nation's largest city than in a smaller one. The Japanese postal clerks were the fastest at selling a stamp—an average of twenty-five seconds—and the Italians were last, at forty-seven seconds.

Even though time is an individual matter, it is a cultural matter, as well. We all learn to move at a certain pace from the people around us; we take our cues from them. We learn how much lateness will upset them and how little lateness will not. Others will be surprised when we are upset at their being a certain number of minutes late, and they will be apologetic at our being upset when they are late by a greater number of minutes. Even though each one of us may have our own special, unique sense of time, we acquire it within a specific cultural setting. A sense of time is a component of culture. Each society teaches its members its own distinctive pace and tempo.

Source: Levine and Wolff, 1985, pp. 28–35.

Cultural Relativism

When members of one society come into contact with those of another, each group usually acts and thinks with the perspectives and the assumptions of its own culture. Communication is often superficial, hostile, or absent. "It is easy for people to feel that their way of life is natural and God-given" (Spradley & McCurdy, 1977, p. 4). Much of the time, we regard foreigners as uncivilized, irrational, immoral, wrong-headed, or just plain stupid. When European explorers came into contact with the peoples of Africa, Asia, and America, in the seventeenth and eighteenth centuries, they tried to make them more like Europeans—by force, when necessary. Early Christian missionaries, for example, attempted to force Polynesians to wear clothing that fully covered their bodies because they regarded nudity as immoral. Ethnocentrism, as we discussed previously, is the tendency to judge the beliefs, values, and behavior of one culture by the standards of another; it is the mistaken view that a particular culture is the center of the universe, and that all others are, in varying degrees, inferior or wrong. Ethnocentrism was behind the racist nineteenth-century view called the "White man's burden," which held that Europeans had an obligation to militarily conquer non-European peoples, steal their land, convert them to Christianity, and teach them the virtues of a Western way of life. Ethnocentrism is behind the view that Mexico, Central America, and the Caribbean region make up "America's backyard" and that they should be forced to accept political and economic arrangements in the best interests of the United States government, however much it may hurt local residents. Ethnocentrism is a fallacy and has no place in sociology.

Various cultures symbolize space in different ways. Space is symbolic: People communicate messages to one another by making symbolic use of space. What does the space between these two people tell you about their relationship?

Richard Hutchings/Photo Researchers

Cultural relativism Viewing cultures on the basis of their own beliefs and assumptions.

Today, sociologists and anthropologists try instead to understand each culture on its own terms. This **cultural relativism,** the opposite of ethnocentrism, is the idea that we must understand the values, beliefs, customs, and behavior of all societies through their own perspectives, not ours. Today's sociologists and anthropologists do not denounce Polynesian nudity but try to see how it grows out of, and contributes to, Polynesian culture as a whole. Even beliefs and practices that might strike us as cruel, oppressive, or bizarre may have a legitimate place in another society.

Cultural relativism does not demand that we give up our own beliefs or attitudes, only that we recognize that other people are different, have a right to be different, and are not inferior just because they are different. Cultural relativism insists merely that we try to see how a belief, a custom, a form of behavior fits in with a society's broader cultural patterns. To do so, we must see these beliefs, customs, and acts as the members of the society we are studying see them. We may not like a certain custom, but we would be remarkably unobservant if we failed to notice it and the reasons for it.

Cultural Universals

Cultural universal A custom or practice that is common to all societies.

Some features of societies are similar across culture lines. Cultural universals are customs or practices that are common to all societies. Religion is a cultural universal. It attempts to answer questions of ultimate meaning.

United Nations

Some features of societies are similar, if not identical, everywhere. **Cultural universals** are customs or practices that are common to all societies. Because human beings are biological animals inhabiting a particular physical environment, they all must engage in certain activities to survive. Cultures everywhere must have ways of feeding and sheltering their members, teaching and caring for their young, healing their sick, and so on. Activities that contribute to the physical survival of human beings are a universal aspect of cultures everywhere.

In addition, social life imposes certain restrictions on the forms that cultures take. Religion is a cultural universal, in large part because the human mind, being intellectually inquisitive, asks and, to the best of its ability, answers questions about ultimate "meaning." The family exists, in some sense, everywhere, partly because it provides an effective way of caring for and teaching the young, and partly because human beings need to feel a sense of security and continuity in the most crucial areas of collective life. The incest taboo (see Chapter 13) is in some sense universal, for it promotes social harmony—and thus better care of the young—in society's most basic social institution, the family.

Of course, each of these cultural universals takes a distinctive and unique form in all societies. For instance, the ban on incest is found everywhere, but different societies treat different relatives as "off limits," maritally and sexually. In some societies, the definition of incest embraces sex with half the population; in others, the ban is limited to a few close relatives. Likewise, all societies care for the sick. But some cultures do so by making use of hospitals and modern medicine, whereas others employ magic, herbs, and chants. When considering cultural universals, we should notice the differences, as well as the similarities.

Cultural Integration

"Like an individual," a culture "is a more or less consistent pattern of thought and action" (Benedict, 1934, p. 46). Its aspects are to a great degree in harmony with one another. This **cultural integration** does not drive all contradictions out of the world's many cultures. But the more serious the contradiction, the greater the pressure for social and cultural change to resolve it.

Cultural Integration: The Individual Level

The Jones family lives in a house on the main street of a small American city. Sally Smith and Bob Weiss live together next door. Although the members of the two households are neighbors, there are many differences between them. Mr. Jones is an executive at an aircraft company. Mrs. Jones, a full-time homemaker and mother, is not gainfully employed. (The Joneses have two children.) Sally and Bob, in contrast, have lived together for two years but are not officially married. They both work—Sally as a lawyer, Bob as a teacher at a community college. They share all the housework 50-50. They think of themselves as married but they have decided that they will never have children.

The two households look very different. Mrs. Jones always works very hard to keep their house looking clean and neat. Sally and Bob's house has a casual, lived-in appearance. Foot-high piles of newspapers are stacked against one wall; large swirls of dust accumulate in the corners; and the bed is never quite made.

Although the two households have about the same amount of income, the total value of Sally and Bob's two cars—both more than ten years old—is a few hundred dollars. The Jones's two late-model cars together cost most of a year's salary. The Jones's front lawn is green and neatly trimmed. Sally and Bob's lawn is a wild meadow, with weeds flourishing everywhere. Sally and Bob call it a "weed garden."

The two families are not openly hostile, yet they avoid each other. Both households feel that they have nothing in common. The Joneses resent the appearance of the "weed garden." The Jones children make fun of their neighbors' old broken-down cars. The senior Joneses, besides, are not at all sure they like living next door to an unmarried couple, especially with their own children nearing adolescence. As for Sally and Bob, they regard Mr. and Mrs. Jones as hopelessly "square" and old-fashioned. They feel as superior to the Joneses as the Joneses feel to them.

Culturally, Sally and Bob and Mr. and Mrs. Jones seem to inhabit totally different worlds that happen to be next door to each other. In fact, this is far from true. Sally and Bob on the one hand, and the Joneses, on the other, belong to the same culture: They all speak English; eat with knife, fork, and spoon; kiss while making love; read the morning newspaper; watch TV; pay their bills by check; invite friends over for dinner; sleep at night between two sheets on a bed; and basically share identical notions of time, space, social obligations, love, friendship, cause and effect, logic, evidence, justice, and, generally, how the world works.

Consider, too, all the things that the Joneses, on the one hand, and Sally and Bob, on the other, don't do—and that people in some cultures do do. They don't hunt, kill, and eat monkeys; scar their bodies to make themselves look more attractive; marry their cousins; take more than one husband or wife; sacrifice animals in religious ceremonies; paint their bodies white when relatives die; chop off fingers at the knuckle from time to time; eat rotten meat; starve themselves for days on end to induce visionary trances; or resort to black magic when other people have things that they want.

Consider, too, a few differences between the two households that are really similarities. Sally and Bob are political liberals; the Joneses, political conservatives. But they all vote at election time; believe in democracy; oppose fascism, communism, monarchy, dictatorship in general, and anarchy. The Joneses are observant Lutherans who attend church weekly; Sally is a lapsed Catholic and Bob, a nonobservant Jew. But all have a common (and rather vague) understanding of God, and none of them believes in polytheism, magic, satanism, or reincarnation. When they are sick, they all see physicians, not witch doctors. Sally and Bob own an expensive Nikon camera and take "arty" photographs, which they display on their walls; the Joneses use a Brownie Instamatic to take traditional snapshots of their children and each other. But none of them believes that a photograph will steal a person's soul or regards the camera as the devil's tool.

In short, the Joneses, and Sally and Bob, all share a common culture—and it is your culture, too.

Cultures are integrated on two distinct levels: individual and institutional. On the individual level, members of a given culture tend to share its most important, or "core," beliefs, values, and practices. The more basic they are, the more widely shared they will be. Anyone can see how American culture differs from that of other countries. But many

Cultural integration The consistency of the various aspects of a culture.

of us resist the idea that all Americans share a common culture, that our culture is integrated on the individual level. Looking at your next-door neighbors, you may notice the differences, not the similarities— *Rolling Stone* or the *National Enquirer*, marijuana or the martini. Yet the similarities are there, and they are striking. Even people with very different beliefs and customs share a basic common culture.

The institutional level of cultural integration reflects the fact that the values, the beliefs, and the norms of all a society's major institutions are compatible with one another. The "pieces" of a culture fit together, much like a jigsaw puzzle. No culture is a jumble of random ideas or beliefs. Imagine a sixty-story building without an elevator, or a country with 100 million cars but no roads or streets suitable for driving. A bad fit between one aspect of culture and another is equally unlikely. For instance, religion tends to support the institution of the family ("honor thy father and mother"); the family tends to support religion ("the family that prays together stays together").

Contradictions do sometimes exist among the various aspects of a given culture, but they tend to be over interpretations, not general princi-ples. The more serious the contradiction, the greater the pressure to resolve it by changing some aspect of a culture. For instance, the fact that over half of all American women work for a living clashes with male domination of the family. In all likelihood, working women will continue to create pressures to promote sexual equality.

Subcultures

In every society, some people do not fully share certain aspects of the dominant culture and hold instead to an alternative point of view. Indi-vidual beliefs, values, norms, and actions always vary to some extent, of course. In a small, relatively simple and homogeneous society, these variations, most of the time, are purely individual; a few people, here and there, do not quite fit in. When a society is large and complex, individual differences harden into group differences. A **subculture** is a group or category of people whose members share certain values, beliefs, norms, and customs that differ somewhat from those of the majority. In addition, the members of a subculture tend to associate with one another more frequently and more intimately than they do with mem-bers of other groups or categories of people. Subcultures basically belong to the dominant, majority culture and accept its more essential (or "core") aspects, but they differ from it in less fundamental ways.

The most readily identifiable types of subcultures are those based on racial, ethnic, and religious differences. Here, beliefs, values, and norms pass from one generation to the next. For example, in many na-tions, groups of people whose ancestors migrated from other areas have maintained family traditions that differ from those of the cultural main-stream. In New York City, for instance, Puerto Ricans constitute a dis-tinct subculture, with their own food, music, and personal style. By and large, New York's Puerto Ricans coexist peacefully with the city's many other subcultures. But sometimes cultural differences based on race, religion, or ethnicity generate open conflict, even warfare—as the bloody struggles between Catholics and Protestants in Northern Ireland, Muslims and Christians in Lebanon, and Hindus and Sikhs in India attest.

Subcultures are not limited to religious and ethnic groups. They have also formed around illegal drug use, unconventional sexual practices and preferences, imprisonment, alcoholism, extreme political views, membership in "outlaw" motorcycle gangs, and prostitution. The mem-

Subculture Groups or categories of people whose beliefs, norms, and values differ somewhat from those of the majority.

Members of a subculture share certain values, beliefs, norms, and customs that differ somewhat from those of the majority. At the same time, subcultures belong to the larger cultural entity. Here, a Puerto Rican Cub Scout watches a parade honoring Hispanic ethnicity.

Terry Rosenberg

bers of these various groups engage in behavior, hold beliefs, and accept norms that are different from those of the "mainstream" culture. Sociologists call subcultures based on unconventional and widely condemned behavior or beliefs **deviant subcultures** (see Chapter 8).

   The majority does not consider most subcultures "bad" or immoral, just different. Many subcultures, for instance, form around quite legal and respectable occupations with special conditions, making those people who work in them different from others. Part of being a college professor involves learning a specific and distinct way of life—a subculture—that even most college students know little about. You must dress in a certain way, talk in a certain way, and think in a certain way. Physicians, too, have a recognizable, distinct subculture, with its own values ("keeping up with the latest medical advances is a good thing"), beliefs ("laypeople know next to nothing about medicine"), norms ("don't work with an incompetent colleague"), even vocabulary (a

Deviant subculture A subculture based on unconventional and widely condemned bahavior and beliefs.

"crock" is a patient with complaints but no illness). Most occupations generate subcultures. Some, such as that of physicians, have a very strong influence on their members; others are weak, almost nonexistent. (Is there a true dishwasher subculture? Probably not.)

Some of the most important subcultures in complex societies, like our own, form around age groups. In small, tribal societies, fathers typically teach their sons how to stalk and kill wild game. Peasant fathers usually teach their sons how to plow, plant, and harvest. In such societies, mothers, too, generally pass on traditions of weaving, food gathering, and cooking. In Western societies, the family has lost many such functions, which are performed by an age-segregated school system. Consequently, young people develop an adolescent subculture, with its own values, beliefs, norms, and behavior (Coleman, 1961). (See Chapter 15).

Countercultures

Counterculture Groups that have made a conscious effort to reject some of the basic beliefs, values, and norms of the majority.

Unlike subcultures, **countercultures** make a point of not belonging to the larger culture. Countercultures make a conscious attempt to reject some of the basic beliefs, values, and norms of the majority (Yinger, 1960, 1982). The youth movement of the 1960s—including the "hippies," who chose to "turn on, tune in, and drop out," and the political revolutionaries, who chose to "fight the system"—rejected many fundamental American values and practices: material success, competition, conformity, and obedience to law. Remnants of the 1960s counterculture exist to this day. The many experiments in communal living that sprang up across the country were another type of counterculture. Some were based on conventional religious views, others had a political focus, and still others were based on opposition to our dominant sexual and family customs. Countercultures tend to be smaller and more unstable than subcultures, and they usually attract more hostility from the majority culture.

SUMMARY

1. Physically, the human animal is capable of a wide range of activities; this contrasts with other animals, which are usually adapted for specific activities and environments. Human beings also have large brains capable of generalized thinking, opposable thumbs, and lastly, weak instincts that do not dictate specific forms of behavior. These four biological features permit—indeed, decree—culture.

2. Culture can be defined as "all of the learned and shared ideas and products of a society"; it represents the total way of life of a people.

3. Different cultures around the world must be studied in "relativistic" or unbiased fashion. Sociologists must always be careful to avoid ethnocentrism: judging the beliefs, values, and behavior of one culture by the standards of another.

4. All true cultures are symbolic by nature; the meanings we assign to things in the world are not derived from their own intrinsic nature but imposed by human thought.

5. Throughout the world, cultures vary considerably from one another. Growing up in one culture opens up many experiences and perceptions and closes off others.

6. A culture tends to be unified through common beliefs and behavior, and the compatibility of its many aspects or elements.

7. One basic "building block" of culture is values—notions of good and bad.

8. A second aspect, or building block, of culture is beliefs about truth and falsity.

9. A third is that all cultures have norms—standards of behavior that members are expected to follow.

10. The fourth building block that all cultures make and use is material artifacts, or physical objects.

11. A fifth and final building block of culture is language, a system of words and word structures.

12. Large, complex societies tend to include one or more subcultures, groups or categories of people whose beliefs, norms, and values differ somewhat from those of the majority. Two of the most important such subcultures in contemporary industrial society are those formed by age and by social class. Countercultures are groups that are in direct opposition to the surrounding culture.

SUGGESTED READINGS

Ruth Benedict, *Patterns of Culture*. Boston: Houghton Mifflin, 1934; and many subsequent reprintings.
Still the best discussion of cultural integration that has ever been written; a classic.

Peter Farb, *Humankind*. New York: Bantam Books, 1980.
A fascinating and well-written account of what makes humans distinct, our culture included. The subtitle of the book is: "What We Know about Ourselves. Where We Come From and Where We Are Headed. Why We Behave the Way We Do."

Joel Garreau, *The Nine Nations of North America*. New York: Avon, 1981.
The author redraws the map to create nine "nations," or societies, within North America: New England, The Foundry, Quebec, Dixie, The Islands, Breadbasket, MexAmerica, The Empty Quarter, and Ectopia. Each of these regions has its own unique flavor, culture, economy, and history. "These nations look different, feel different, and sound different from each other, and few of their boundaries match the political lines drawn on current maps . . . when you're from one, and you're in it, you know you're home." Controversial, provocative, interesting.

Clifford Geertz, *The Interpretation of Cultures*. New York: Basic Books, 1973; and Clifford Geertz, *Local Knowledge: Further Essays in Interpretive Anthropology*. New York: Basic Books, 1983.
Two collections of beautifully written, insightful essays on culture. Understanding culture, Geertz holds, involves interpreting the meaning systems of a people—or engaging in "thick description."

John Langston Gwaltney, *Drylongso: A Self-Portrait of Black America*. New York: Vintage Books, 1981.
Forty-two detailed interviews with members of the "core Black culture." ("Drylongso" means ordinary.) Many students will find this book a revelation.

Edward T. Hall, *The Dance of Life: The Other Dimension of Time*. Garden City, New York: Doubleday Anchor, 1983.
A fascinating account of how different societies approach, define, perceive, and experience time. Hall argues that time is not a universal; instead, there are different *kinds* of time: biological, personal, physical, metaphysical, and so on. Cultures also use time in different ways. For instance, "polychronic" time is non-Western: A number of different things can go on at the same time, appointments are far from sacred and frequently broken, and involvement of people and completion of transactions are stressed. "Monochronic" time is Western and especially North American time: Only one thing takes place at a time, schedules are adhered to precisely and are rarely broken, even if the transaction is not completed. This book explores these and other facets of the cultural dimension of time.

Arnold Mitchell, *The Nine American Life-Styles: Who We Are and Where We're Going*. New York: Warner Books, 1984.
An examination of different "American life-styles" or subcultures—including the "need-driven" groups, "inner-directed" groups, "outer-directed" groups, and the "integrated" life-style. The author's approach has had a grat deal of influence on market research—that is, strategies for selling specific products to the public. Unlike the Garreau book, which is geographically based, Mitchell's approach focuses on socioeconomic status.

J. Milton Yinger, *Subcultures: The Promise and the Peril of a World Turned Upside Down*. New York: Free Press, 1982.
Explores a great variety of countercultures—in art, ethics, politics, religion, the family, sex, and education.

Mark Zborowski, *People in Pain*. San Francisco: Jossey-Bass, 1969.
An anthropological study of subcultural differences that characterize how members of different ethnic groups express pain in medical emergencies.

chapter 4

SOCIAL STRUCTURE

No man is an island, entire of itself", said the English poet and preacher John Donne; neither, we might add, is any woman. Every one of us is connected, in countless ways, with countless other people. These bonds we share with others are not haphazard, or random, but patterned and predictable. Through the process of socialization, we learn rules, or norms, that tell us how to act with others. Our acceptance of these norms makes behavior predictable. Our interaction with others, and their interaction with us, are shaped by a set of unspoken, taken-for-granted agreements about the way members of our society should act toward one another. We step into social settings and abide by agreements that were made long before we were born, agreements that will remain long after we have died. We cannot walk into a store in the United States and hand a sales clerk Turkish or Bulgarian or Sudanese money, because sales clerks have been taught to accept only United States currency. An eighth grader cannot walk up to the teacher and announce, "OK, now I'm taking over this class!" Both the teacher and the student understand that the "rules of the game" make such an agreement impossible.

To put it another way, the teacher and the student, and the clerk and the customer, all operate within a specific **social structure,** which sociologists define as a network of interconnected, normatively governed social relationships in a society. Social structures exist because the members of each society learn its rules and, by following them, create a web of social relationships. Social structure is just a fancy way of saying that people are tied to one another through specific social bonds, bonds that vary from society to society. These bonds create or make up a huge, informal organization—one that has a stable, enduring quality and is not likely to change radically overnight. Eighth-grade students do not suddenly become teachers, and sales clerks in the United States do not suddenly reject American currency in favor of Turkish money; nor do stores suddenly become schools, or vice versa. All the parties in each of these social structures know the general rules regarding what they should and should not do. These rules give rise to mutual expectations, and these in turn create and maintain social structure.

The linkages among the people of a society are not limited to concrete relationships between specific interacting individuals. The

Social structure A network of interconnected, normatively governed social relationships in a society.

sales clerk is tied not only to one customer but to many; not only to actual customers but to potential customers; not only to customers in general but to the store's supervisors, managers, and other sales clerks. All these relationships are governed by rules and norms that make on-the-job behavior fairly predictable. The clerk's supervisors, to take the linkages a step higher, will be connected to an accountant, with a higher-level manager, with suppliers, and with delivery personnel. If the store is part of a chain of stores, this pattern may be duplicated throughout the country. All these stores are linked together in a huge network—a social structure. Moreover, a sales clerk is not only a sales clerk but also (perhaps) a college student, a Catholic, a registered Democrat, a member of a specific family, and so on. And every individual with whom this specific sales clerk relates in each of these contexts is also related to many other individuals in those and other contexts. In other words, an invisible web links everyone in society to everyone else. This web—the sum total of all of the patterned, normatively governed relationships in a society—constitutes a social structure.

For instance, the American system of education includes more than just individual teachers instructing classes with individual students. It also includes networks of relationships that reach into each community and across the nation. It has hierarchies, specialized units to perform different functions, mechanisms for getting students into one end of the "tube" (nursery school and kindergarten) and out the other (graduate and professional schools). It has mechanisms as well for recruiting and retiring teachers, paying the staff, and maintaining the buildings that house it. Publishing, too, has a social organization. Authors write and submit manuscripts; editors on one level read them and decide whether to publish them; editors on another level prepare them for publication; typesetters, printers, and binders produce the physical books; truck drivers transport them to warehouses and bookstores; booksellers sell them; and finally, one hopes, customers buy and read them. Neither of these social structures, education or publishing, could be maintained simply as the added-up actions of isolated individuals. What creates a social structure is the coordination and organization of individuals through positions and norms.

As an analogy with social structure, think of a mosaic, a picture or a design made up of small, flat stones arranged in a certain pattern. The mosaic is not just a bunch of tiles, for each tile has a specific physical relationship to all the others. If the same tiles had been randomly thrown on the ground, they would not have formed a mosaic. What creates the structure we call a mosaic is the pattern, the arrangement, the relation of the tiles to one another (Denisoff & Wahrman, 1979, pp. 78–91). Likewise, the people in a society have a certain relationship with one another, and this relationship generates what sociologists call a social structure. There are many types of social relationships—legal, economic, familial, emotional, and intellectual, to name a few. The web of many such links, arrangements or relationships constitutes a social structure and, ultimately, a society.

Some kind of social structure exists in almost every context that involves social interaction. Rarely do we relate to another person as an isolated individual with another isolated individual, with no expectations about how to behave. Typically, we have such expectations, and our behavior is tied down or "anchored" to them. We constantly enter and leave specific settings, situations, or contexts, and within each one of them, certain kinds of behavior are expected and not expected. A school is one such social context; so is a store. We do not expect buying and selling to be the chief activities in a school, nor do we expect to teach or study in stores. Every day, we all interact within many such social contexts—a family, a neighborhood, a legal code, sporting events, friendships, romantic involvements, and so on. In each, we are surrounded by a "structure" of rules, regulations, norms, and mutual expectations.

LEVELS OF SOCIAL STRUCTURE

People are linked to one another in a social structure on two different levels. The first is the **micro level,** on which two or more individuals occupying certain positions interact face to face. A specific teacher in a classroom, an individual clerk with a customer—this is the micro level of social structure. Remember, when sociologists refer to a social structure, they do not refer only to face-to-face interaction between two or more individuals, but to interaction based on mutual expectations, on social bonds, on predictability. In fact, this predictability exists even when the interacting individuals don't know one another; each can guess how the other will act by his or her location in the social structure. When you interact with someone with whom you share no social bonds, you have no idea how that person will behave, for you are not linked through social structure even at the micro level.

Micro level of social structure
The organization of society at the interpersonal level at which individuals, occupying specific positions, interact with one another.

The Macro Level

The **macro level** of social structure is the sum of all the micro-level social relations. We examine the macro level to understand "how it all hangs together." Whereas a micro-level study would examine systematic relationships of clerks to clerks, clerks to customers, and clerks to supervisors, a macro-level study would examine the social and organizational structure of an entire financial enterprise—the store clerks who work for it, up to the president and the chief executive officer—and the way

Macro level of social structure
The organization of society at the organizational and institutionalized level, above the level of interacting individuals.

The microlevel of social structure operates when two or more individuals, occupying certain positions, interact face-to-face. Here, a supervisor explains the details of a job to a worker.

Will McIntyre/Photo Researchers

WHAT DO YOU THINK?

False Identity

On the evening of December 5, 1980, Michael Halberstam, a prominent Washington, D.C. cardiologist, went into the living room of his house and found a burglar. Halberstam lunged at the man, who shot him twice in the chest. Although seriously wounded, Halberstam was able to get into his car and drive to a nearby hospital. On the way, he spotted the man who had shot him; swerving his car, he managed to hit the burglar, although he did not injure him seriously. Dr. Halberstam died on the operating table an hour later. The burglar was caught by the police. After fingerprinting the man, they found he was a prison escapee named Bernard Charles Welch, Jr., age 40, a fugitive for more than six years.

It turns out that Welch had lived with a common-law wife (see Chapter 13) and three children in an expensive house, complete with indoor swimming pool, in an exclusive suburb of Washington. The couple also owned an equally expensive summer home in Minnesota. He was known by his neighbors as "Norman Hamilton." Even his wife didn't know his true identity—nor, apparently, his profession. Everyone assumed that "Norman Hamilton" bought and sold stocks and real estate. One neighbor said that "he acted and looked like a millionaire." In fact, Welch's true profession was burglary. After he was apprehended, more than $4 million in loot was found in his basement, all stolen during the previous four months (Morgenthau et al., 1980). Welch was convicted of murder and sentenced to 143 years in prison. In May, 1984, he escaped, and in August, 1985, he was recaptured. The tale of his identities during this period has not yet been told.

Welch, like millions of Americans, had been living under an assumed identity. These people have concluded their existence in one social structure and entered another. Who are they? Several million are illegal aliens. As many as 2 million are runaway children. Many are trying to evade felony charges (see Chapter 8). Tens of thousands of husbands have taken up new identities to escape alimony and child-support payments. Not all of these denizens of the social underground have constructed totally new identities, but a substantial proportion of them have.

How? Leaving one social structure and entering another is not just a matter of geographical mobility. Social structures are "sticky": They are difficult to leave and difficult to enter afresh. Many people who live underground, like Welch, get official documents, such as birth certificates, driver's licenses, and voter-registration cards, designating them as another person. Fake identification is surprisingly easy to obtain (Gunn, 1977). It has also been illegal, since the False Identification Crime Control Act was signed into law in 1982. The escapee need only locate the name of a dead person of the same sex, race, and approximate age, and write away for his or her birth certificate. (More than 10 million

---

it relates to other organizations and enterprises. The macro level begins when individuals—acting as incumbents of certain positions—cease to be the focus of attention and we look at the "big picture." The micro level is concerned with the way teachers relate to students; the macro level, with the way educational organizations across the country make up a common enterprise, with common rules, expectations, and purposes. In fact, the macro level aims at entities existing on an even higher, broader plane, as well—to show how institutions are linked together to form a whole society. Let us begin by discussing social structure at the micro level.

copies of birth certificates are issued in the United States each year.) This birth certificate becomes what is called a "breeder document," generating other kinds of identification. The appropriately pseudonymous author of the pamphlet, *The Paper Trip: The How and Whys of Getting False IDs*, a bestseller for Eden Press (Hopwood, 1983), claims that anyone can assume virtually any official identity, without having to resort to counterfeit documents (Lyons, 1980).

Assuming a false identify can be thought of as a kind of "social-structure suicide" and "social-structure rebirth." One researcher interviewed twenty-five men who had staged disappearances, to make it appear that they had committed suicide, and then took up new identities elsewhere (Weitzman, 1970, 1981). Interviews were also conducted with the missing persons' families, insurance-company employees, workers at a family-location service, private detectives, and police and court officials. These social suicides were "rationally calculated, carefully planned, and staged as a performance" (Weitzman, 1981, p.

17). First, these men abandoned their identity kits—the items that maintain a personal "front," such as personal belongings, clothes, grooming aids, a pipe, and so on. The failure of these men to take along their customary identity kits was "indicative of their symbolic leave-taking. . . . As they were no longer going to be the same people, they no longer needed things that belonged to those persons' identities" (Weitzmen, 1981, p. 18).

These men also left behind the "tools of their trade." The teachers and professors left their educations, degrees, and credentials—barring futures in their previous professions. The businessmen did not take letters of credit necessary for reestablishing themselves elsewhere. One physician left his medical license, diploma, and certification, making it impossible for him to practice medicine in another community. Two men left without their union cards, "effectively cutting themselves off from using the skills they had as well as from any seniority they had accumulated" (Weitzman, 1981, p. 18).

Third, they left behind all other official documents that locate and certify one in a social structure: "birth certificates, driver's licenses, draft cards or army release papers, Social Security cards, library cards, business cards, personal checks, and many personal-identification papers that we accumulate to function in society. Thus, they abandoned their official identities as well as their personal and occupational ones" (Weitzman, 1981, p. 18). In their new social structures, they had to generate such documents anew to reaffirm their new identities.

Perhaps "the most significant possession abandoned by the social suicides is something less concrete: their names. With their names they left behind the sum total of their social selves. Thus they symbolically destroyed their social selves as well as their physical selves." On the day that they disappeared, it would not be an exaggeration to say that "they did, in fact, cease to exist" (Weitzman, p. 18).

The Micro Level: One Example

A workplace is obviously a kind of social structure. Every occupation has built into it a set of expectations, demands, and constraints. Consider the social structure of one occupational setting—the receiving room of a large department store in an East Coast suburb. Such a setting typifies the micro level of social structure. A chain-link fence divides the receiving area into two sections. On one side, comprising about a third of the room, about twenty women employees price merchandise that is small, valuable, easily stolen, and easily mislaid. This area is called the "security cage" or "the cage." In the main area on the other side of the fence, also called "the line," about thirty women price the bulkier, less easily misplaced merchandise. To walk into the cage, you must first walk into the receiving room, go through the main area (or line), stop at the security gate, and be buzzed in by someone who is already inside. There is only a small amount of mobility between the cage and the line. Generally, a woman who begins working in the cage remains there as long as she works in the receiving department, and a woman who begins working on the line usually stays there, too. Originally, employees were selected for these two areas totally by chance. The work of the women in the receiving department is presided over by two female supervisors, who walk back and forth from the main area to the security cage, and two male managers, who do the same. The supervisors' principal responsibility is the receiving department itself. The managers have other responsibilities, as well.

The two areas are completely different in every conceivable respect. Of the chain-link fence that divides them, one employee said: "That's not a fence—it's a border between two different countries!" The managers hover over the women working in the cage, while they supervise the women "on line" casually, almost superficially. The managers rarely criticize or even comment on women in the main area, but if an ordinary conversation takes place in the security cage, the manager will say: "What's going on here? Shut up and get back to work. Pay attention to what you're doing—you're costing us money!" The women in the cage become socialized into the rules of their job in a week or so, and almost never question them.

The women in the security cage are extremely serious, almost severe, on the job. They are sober, quiet, thorough, and exacting in their work. They never use strong language. (The raciest exclamation heard in the cage was, "Oh, sugar!") On the line, in contrast, the work area is usually sloppy. Paper, even food, lies around on the floor and on merchandise boxes. There is usually at least one radio blaring.

In the larger part of the room, about twenty "boys" (ages ranging from 18 to 30) "hump" the merchandise; in other words, they move it in and out of the room. Because the quantity of the merchandise processed in the cage is relatively small, they are less likely to enter it than to enter in the main area, where they are friendly, even flirtatious, with the women. Their interaction has an overtly sexual air. Touching, pinching, and "horsing around" are common activities, and the women do not discourage them. But when one of these young men goes into the security cage, he is serious, uncomfortable, sullen, red-faced, seemingly intimidated. One of the newer "boys," who had yet to learn the rules of the receiving room, once tickled a woman in the cage. One of the women there said, coldly and dryly, "If it isn't Mr. Macho!" Added another woman, "He's got some hell of a nerve, coming in here, touching us." The young man retreated from the cage in a state of embarrassment.

The differences in the demeanor of these two groups of women do not carry over into the off-hours, however. During breaks and lunchtime, they socialize with one another, without regard for which part of the receiving room they work in. Their everyday, after-working hours personalities emerge: Some of the women who work in the security cage turn out to be outgoing and boisterous, and some of the women who work on the line are shy and withdrawn. Whatever these women may be like on the outside, "once you hit the door to the receiving room [the author was told] you act the way you're supposed to in your own area."

In the receiving room, very little interaction takes place across the fence barrier. When interaction does occur, it seems to generate a certain mutual distaste. One day, an unusually large quantity of merchandise was brought into the security cage. All the women from the line had to come into the cage to help price the items. The women from the main area "took over" the cage, continuing to act in a loud and boisterous manner; the regular staff of the security cage moved to an area blocked off by piled-up boxes and worked by themselves, behind the boxes. They became even quieter than usual, crouching down closer to the merchandise as they priced it.

This was a unique event, and it lasted for about four hours. Both groups of women talked about the incident for a week afterward. "Wasn't it just awful when the women on the line came into the cage!" So the women in the security area told one another. "It was horrible! They were so loud, I couldn't hear myself think or even work! What a terrible experience!" The women on the line, breaking the informal rule against talking across the fence, severely heckled the women in the cage. "Couldn't take it, huh? What's the matter—too much noise for you?" For about a week, when a woman from the cage walked out of the receiving room to take a break, the women from the main area of the room would "get on her case." "That's right," they would taunt, "go get a cup of cocoa to soothe your shattered nerves!" Or "Go to the ladies' room and lie down, honey—you need it after what you've been through." After about a week, the taunts died down, and the receiving room reverted back to its normal routine.[*]

The receiving department is a social structure—a unit of stable behavior that its participants are expected to follow. People who violate these expectations and behave inappropriately are critized or punished. ("Isn't it Mr. Macho!" or "Shut up and get back to work!") The ways in which the staff of the receiving room behaves—the ways in which its members interact with one another—cannot be explained by the characteristics of the specific individuals who work there. This behavior, this interaction, is a structural characteristic of this work site. People who enter it simultaneously enter a social structure of demands and expectations no less real and no less binding than the physical structure of the receiving room itself.

BUILDING BLOCKS OF SOCIAL STRUCTURE

Every social structure is made up of several basic "building blocks," or components (Turner, 1981, pp. 111–116). Sociologists often use the metaphor of a building to explain the concept of social structure. Every building rests on a foundation and has walls, supports, a roof, and floors; all of these components are united in a single physical structure. In the same way, people in societies have organized relationships with one another and are tied to one another by mutual expectations. The basic components that fuse the members of a society into a social structure are statuses, roles, and institutions.

[*] I would like to thank Ms. Joanne Preissler, an employee of this store, for supplying me with this description. For more detailed accounts of similar group interactions, see Homans (1950).

Being a woman is an ascribed status: It is something one is born into. Being a physician is partly achieved and partly ascribed: Having intelligence, a good memory, and the right parents help, but one must work hard to achieve the job.

Michal Heron/Monkmeyer Press

Status

Status A normatively governed position in a society.

Most people use the word **status** to refer to someone's prestige or lack of it. Sociologists, however, also use the term to refer to a position in society—any position at all, formal or informal, official or unofficial. Sex, or gender (male or female), is a status; so too are "student," "trumpet player," "American citizen," "brother," "aunt," "writer," "friend," and "lover." No one occupies one and only one status. We all have a number of statuses at the same time. Sociologists call all of the statuses that any one individual occupies at any one time a **status set.** This combination of statuses has more influence on each individual's behavior than any one status does.

Status set All of the positions occupied by a single individual.

As Shakespeare wrote, "Some are born great, some achieve greatness, and others have greatness thrust upon them." We are born with certain statutes: the so-called **ascribed statuses.** The status of son or daughter, for instance, is ascribed, and so too is sex, or gender: Each of us is born male or female, and unless we undergo sex-change operations, we are pretty much stuck with that sex for life.

Ascribed status A position to which one is assigned through no effort of one's own.

Other statuses are the fruit of our own efforts; we get into them because we have done something. These are called **achieved** or **acquired statuses.** "Registered Democrat" is an achieved status, for example. So are "convicted felon" and "ex-convict." The line between achieved and ascribed statuses is not always clear-cut. You might, for instance, become a physician if you had sufficient intelligence and powers of memory (party achieved and partly ascribed); if your parents had enough money and the right occupations and connections (ascribed); and if your grades are good enough (achieved). Some statuses, in other words, display or are produced by a mixture of achieved and ascribed characteristics.

Achieved status A position that is acquired or attained through one's own efforts.

Acquired status See **Achieved status.**

Master status The position that is central to an individual's life and that determines or influences other positions and statuses.

Not all statuses have equal importance for the individual. A very important status is called a **master status;** this determines or influences many other positions and statuses in its holder's life. Being wealthy or poor is one such master status; it influences your education, marital partner, family size, taste, lifestyle, residence, health—even how long you will live. But some statuses—like being a tennis player—do not influence or determine other ones very much.

Emergent status A position that grows, spontaneously out of the special relations that some people have with one another.

Emergent statuses grow almost spontaneously out of the special relations that some people have with one another. They simply "emerge." In a group of friends, one person might be designated as the "clown," another as the "gossip," a third as the "daredevil," and a fourth as the "brain." These statuses have no legal standing; they will not appear on any official records. They are tags, labels, informal titles that are attached to certain people because they are, or have done, certain things. In time, the person who bears the label may grow into it, to conform to the expectations of his or her friends.

Role

A man and woman decide to get married. They discuss their future. The man talks about what *their* apartment will look like. The woman draws back. "Hey," she says, "who says we're going to live together?" The man's face registers astonishment and deep disappointment. "Married couples always live together," he objects. In our society, one of the norms of being married is living together; to do or expect otherwise is to violate a very widespread expectation, for the role of a husband or wife is to live with one's spouse. Sociologists define the term **role** as the sum of all the expectations attached to a certain status in society. You *occupy* a status; you *play* a role (Linton, 1936, p. 114). Role is the behavior that others expect from us because we fill a given position or occupy a given status. Certain norms cluster around or attach themselves to certain statuses. In the role of a brother or a sister, you are expected to be loving, supportive, and loyal. In the role of a college teacher, you are expected to attend class, to give interesting and informative lectures, to be fair in grading, to be present during office hours, and to advise students. Each status carries a set of normative expectations setting forth the duties of those who occupy it. A role is very much like a part in a play. If you are supposed to play the role of Hamlet, the audience and your fellow actors will be confused if you recite lines from *Romeo and Juliet*.

Status Set of One Individual

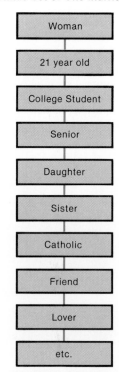

Role The normative expectations attached to a specific position.

Many statuses are relational: They imply a certain kind of relationship with another status occupant. For instance, the status "priest" implies social interaction of a certain kind with parishoners.
Mimi Forsyth/Monkmeyer Press

Performed role What someone who occupies a specific position actually does; may conflict with the expectations or demands of the role itself.

Role is therefore a normative concept: It is what you are expected to do, not what you actually do. When you stray too far from the expectations of others, you will usually be criticized, punished, and brought back into line, for you will have failed to live up to a role's demands. Sociologists call what people actually do in a position or status a **performed role.** This concept underscores the fact that there may be a certain disparity between what our positions demand and what we actually do in real life.

Roles rarely demand highly specific, precisely spelled-out, robot-like behavior. To put it another way, statuses vary as to the specificity of their role demands. Although the demands of some roles are fairly specific, we must not be careful to turn their occupants into automatons. Consider a surgeon performing an operation, for instance: The list of dos and don'ts is detailed and specific, but each surgeon has his or her own distinctive style of performing operations. At the other extreme are statuses whose role demands are extremely flexible, almost vague. What is expected of a friend is not nearly so precisely spelled out as what is expected of a surgeon. Still, we know that our friends expect us to do certain things, and not to do others, by virtue of our friendship role. We are supposed to be loyal to friends, help them when they are in need, see them from time to time, and so on. There is, in fact, a vast range or zone of acceptable behavior that friends may display and still be regarded by others as fulfilling the demands or expectations of what a friend is supposed to do. Although roles are sets of normative expectations attached to statuses, they typically define *ranges* of expected behavior, rather than precise enumerations of highly specific actions.

Role set All of the normative expectations attached to a position whose occupant interacts with a number of complementary statuses.

A concept that makes use of both role and status is called a **role set** (Merton, 1957, 1968, pp. 41–45). Many statuses are "relational" in character—one implies another. They are two halves of a relationship: Brother–sister would be one example; husband–wife, another. In baseball you can't have a pitcher without a catcher; and there can't be one neighbor without another. Each half of the relationship must interact with the other half according to certain rules and regulations—that is, norms. Professor–student is an example of a status pair that implies a normatively governed role relationship. One of the norms that make up the professor–student role holds that it is unethical for a student to bribe a professor and for a professor to accept a bribe. Professors interact with other professors, too, and that relationship is also governed by norms—for instance, the norm that prohibits professors, and others, from plagiarizing someone else's writing. Professors also have role relationships with administrators, librarians, union representatives, and, sometimes, parents of students. Each of these role relationships is governed by a set of norms. What appears to be one status (professor) is actually linked with other statuses. Those who occupy the position of professor really occupy half of a *series* of status pairs: professor–student, professor–administrator, and so on. All of the status pairs implied by a given position, and the rules and regulations of all these status pairs, make up a role set.

All those who interact with professors hold certain normative expectations about them, and the professors hold certain normative expectations in turn. But these expectations may be different for each role relationship. For instance, students expect professors to be friendly but not very intimate toward them. The professor–professor role relationship is characterized by norms permitting much greater informality and intimacy. Thus, the norms governing the role relationship between the various states pairs may be quite different—in some cases, actually conflicting.

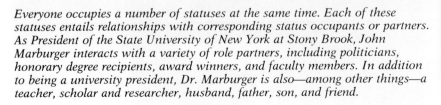

Everyone occupies a number of statuses at the same time. Each of these statuses entails relationships with corresponding status occupants or partners. As President of the State University of New York at Stony Brook, John Marburger interacts with a variety of role partners, including politicians, honorary degree recipients, award winners, and faculty members. In addition to being a university president, Dr. Marburger is also—among other things—a teacher, scholar and researcher, husband, father, son, and friend.

The Role Set of a Professor

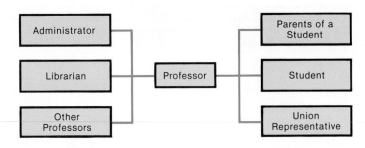

This may create certain problems for the occupants. For instance, a professor may be pressured by students to be an easy grader and by the administration and colleagues not to contribute to "grade inflation" by giving too many As. The pressures that a status occupant faces from different sets of role partners is called **role strain.**

Some conflicts result, not from playing the same role with different people, but from playing different roles entirely. These are status-set problems rather then role-set problems. Sociologists call this **role conflict.** The norms surrounding our different statuses usually conflict to some degree. As a result, all of us experience conflicting demands and expectations from different people occupying different statuses. Professors, for example, expect students to study hard and master their courses. Friends, however, often expect college students to socialize, "hang out,"

Role strain Contradictions among the many demands attached to a single status.

Role conflict A contradiction between the demands of two different positions that someone occupies at the same time.

Sociologists define a social institution as all the norms, statuses, and roles centered around a particular need, theme, or activity. The family is a major social institution, found in all societies and cultures of the world.

Spencer Grant/Taurus Photos

and "party." Playing the role of student may to some degree conflict with playing the role of friend. Some roles are thought to be so full of unavoidable conflict that they require complete separation. For instance, the Catholic church forces priests to devote their full loyalty to God and their flocks by preventing those who fill the role of "priest" from filling the roles of "husband" and "father."

Mutual Obligations.   Role obligations are not always met, but they usually are. Most students study enough to pass their courses; most parents care for their children; most friends respond to the duties and pleasures of friendship. The majority of us do what we are supposed to do—what others expect us to do—most of the time. When we do not, our role partners notice and, usually, make us aware that they wish we would live up to their expectations. In other words, social relations are fairly orderly, predictable, and patterned. This cannot be explained solely by "social pressure." Most of us want to please others. We've been taught that it is wrong to let people down, especially people we care for. Besides, many role relations are based on reciprocity and exchange: If we fail to meet our own role obligations, our partners may not bother to meet theirs. Some social relations, in other words, "work" because of mutual obligations (Homans, 1961; Blau, 1964; W. J. Goode, 1978).

Social relations work for another reason, too: We usually regard the roles we play as good in themselves, independent of pleasing our role partners. These two forces—the desire to live up to the expectations of others and the desire to do right—unite to make most of us conformists.

The significance of status and role, however, cannot be regarded as automatic or inherent. Though we all occupy a series of statuses, and therefore are likely to be faced with role demands from others as a result, we do not take our respective roles equally seriously. Just because roles and statuses exist does not mean that they have the same meaning to all who play or occupy them. Two individuals may both be students, but one may do all the assignments conscientiously, study long hours, receive straight As, and expect to progress from college to graduate or professional training—in short, one may take the role demand of student extremely seriously. The second, in contrast may rarely attend class, often miss exams, fail to hand in papers, receive many incompletes and Fs, and expect to drop out of school in the near future. For the second student, clearly, the role of student is not especially important. Thus, in addition to looking at the objective nature of roles and statuses—their significance to society at large, the normative demands occupants typically face in them—we must consider their *subjective* significance, as well. The *salience* of roles varies from one individual to another. For some individuals, a given role may be extremely salient or significant. But that same role may be far less so for another individual. Although we can specify the average or overall level of importance of statuses and roles in a society, we must remember that there is some variation in this regard.

Institutions

Role and status are the smallest, or most micro-level, building blocks in a social structure. They apply to the positions and norms occupied or followed by specific people or categories of people. A higher, macro-level, building block of social structure is the **institution.** Sociologists define a social institution as all the norms, statuses, and roles centered around a particular need, theme, or activity.

Institution All the norms, statuses, and roles centered around a particular need, theme, or activity.

Some institutions are so broad in scope that they touch the lives of almost all members of a society. Some address such basic issues or needs that they are just about universal. Sociologists refer to these as the *major* social institutions: the family, religion, politics, economics, and education (see Part IV). The family is the social institution that is specifically devoted to caring for and raising children. Religion comprises beliefs, roles, and practices relative to sacred matters. The political institution is concerned with power and order. The economy is a means of developing and allocating resources, especially goods and services. Last, education is the organized transmission of knowledge. All societies have each of these five social institutions, and nearly all members of every society are exposed to each of them. This is why they are regarded as the "major" social institutions.

The term "institution" is also used more loosely, to refer to other organized sets of statuses, roles, and activities centered around particular themes or social needs. These are not nearly as universal or pervasive as the major institutions. Examples include sports, law, science, and the military. They have much less impact and scope than the major social institutions do, although they are important.

Institutional Consistency.   Within any society, all institutions tend to be more or less consistent with one another. The values, beliefs, and norms of any institution are usually compatible with those of others. For instance, American educational institutions characteristically support existing political arrangements; in turn, state and local governments uphold the educational system by allocating funds to support it. A majority of American families participate in some form of religious worship; religion, in turn, bids us to "Honor thy father and mother." If the values, norms, and beliefs set forth by one institution clashed with those of another, the members of a society would be subjected to intolerable strains and their relations with one another would be filled with hostility and conflict. For instance, a majority of married women are employed today; as we might expect, "bringing home the bacon" gives a woman a certain amount of power in her marital relationship. At the same time, most women, and men, have grown up being taught that men should exercise power over women. Here, we have a contradiction between values that arise in two different social institutions. Such contradictions exist in every society. Typically, however, social change resolves the most glaring of such contradictions, and eventually brings conflicting values, beliefs, and norms into line with one another. Major social changes in one institution usually create or facilitate changes in others.

SOCIETIES

Society The people who live in a given area and share a common culture.

To many people, **"society"** means "high" society—the small group of wealthy, prominent, and fashionable people. Among sociologists, however, the term has a much broader meaning: the sum of all the people who live in a given geographical area and who share a common culture. Society is an even higher-level entity than any institution, for it comprises all the smaller building blocks of social structure: statuses, roles, and institutions.

Societies are not always equivalent to countries or nation-states. Most Americans have enough in common to make "American society" a reality. But in some countries, members of two or more distinctly different—even hostile—cultures live side by side. They may not share any basic features of culture—not even a common language. In the Philippine rain forest, for instance, live the Tasaday, a tiny band of nomadic people. Until recently, the Tasaday had no contact with members of any other culture, spoke a language that no other Filipinos understood, and had their own, distinct culture (Nance, 1975). They lived in the Philippine nation-state but did not belong to Filipino society.

There are, and always have been, thousands of different, specific societies. Their cultures have embraced sharply divergent values, beliefs, and norms; their members have practiced distinct customs and forms of behavior. Despite this startling diversity, at least one dimension of culture can be used to divide all societies among a few distinct types: the nature of the society's economic base, its **mode of production.** Although we must consider the manner in which a society secures food and manufactures goods to be important, however, we should not fall into the trap of **economic determinism.** The economy is only one among a number of many important factors influencing the characteristics of a society. At the same time, economic changes are strongly associated with changes in the other dimensions of social life.

During almost the entire course of the millions of years of human existence on Earth, societies have fed their members by means of a single technological strategy—hunting and gathering—which entails killing wild game and gathering wild plant food. For tens of thousands of years, human societies have also grown food casually to feed their members; continuous, intensive farming began only some 10,000 to 15,000 years ago. Societies based on simple growing techniques are called horticultural societies. Around 4000 B.C., the invention of the plow dramatically increased the productiveness of food growing in what became known as agrarian societies. The most recent period of history, in which industrialization became the dominant economic strategy, emerged in the 1700s. It is possible that the United States, which has the most productive economy in the world, is developing into a postindustrial society—that is, one whose work force is mostly employed in service occupations.

Mode of production The way a society generates food and other economic goods.

Economic determinism A perspective that argues that material factors play the central role in influencing social phenomena, especially social change.

Hunting and Gathering Societies

For roughly 99 percent of human history—until some 10,000 to 15,000 years ago—societies fed their members almost entirely by killing game and foraging for wild vegetables, fruits, nuts, and edible roots. Today, only a tiny handful of societies are based primarily on this technology. **Hunting and gathering societies** require huge tracts of land to support their members—roughly one square mile for each individual. (One exception is societies based mainly on fishing.) Because wild food resources are dispersed, and, if animal, mobile, societies that rely on them must move periodically to feed themselves. This has three major consequences: First, the populations of hunting and gathering societies tend to be quite small. They are typically made up of several bands, each with a few dozen members, scattered around several thousand square miles of territory. Second, hunting and gathering societies must be **nomadic;** they do not generally form settled communities. Third, the members of these societies do not make or own much in the way of material possessions, because carrying them around would be a burden. No true wealth exists in this type of society.

Hunting and gathering society A society that feeds its members primarily by foraging for food in the wild.

Nomadic Having no fixed residence, moving around from time to time.

Hunting and gathering is the least productive economic technique of feeding the members of a society. Such societies do not accumulate a large economic surplus, and have little in the way of material possessions.

Lee, Anthro-Photo File

Hunting and gathering societies thus tend to be fairly simple in a number of ways that largely result from their economic and technological simplicity. Because possessions are few, nobody is rich. The concepts of "rich" and "poor" just do not exist. Social distinctions are very simple. One member is marked off from another solely by sex, age, and kinship. Otherwise, everyone in such a society has very much the same level of possessions, power, and prestige. Even the chief usually has little power over his band, and the chieftainship is "usually no more than a part-time specialty" (Lenski, 1966, p. 100). Everybody does pretty much the same thing. There is no true division of labor, no occupational specialization. No one performs any economic activity but getting and preparing food, making clothes, building shelter, and making a few simple tools. Formal government is absent; political institutions exist in only the most primitive and simple forms. Warfare is rare, and armies do not exist.

Until the 1960s, the prevailing view in anthropology and archaeology was that hunting and gathering peoples worked full-time at feeding themselves, had barely enough to eat, depended on a precarious, unreliable food source, and often starved during lean times. In the past generation or so, evidence has been accumulating that challenges this view. Studies among hunting and gathering peoples indicate that they do not have to work very hard for their food supply, and that they have reliable, abundant, and varied sources of food, enjoy a remarkably adequate diet, are selective in the many foods available to them, and very rarely do without enough to eat (Cohen, 1977; pp. 27–33). For instance, the !Kung Bushmen of South Africa (Lee, 1968, 1979) have eighty-five species of edible food plants available to them, including twenty-nine species of fruits, berries, and melons and thirty species of roots and bulbs; of the fifty-four local edible species of animals, only seventeen are hunted regularly. The !Kung diet is well in excess of the recommended daily allowance in calories and protein. Indeed, the !Kung are a healthy people living on a healthful diet. Searching for and cooking food requires an average of some two hours per day. Both the old and the unmarried young are excluded from having to work, and so the labor is performed by only two-thirds of the society. In short, the !Kung, like most hunting and gathering peoples, eat well and do not have to work very hard to do so (Lee, 1968, 1979).

The Transition to Agriculture

Humans have always had an intimate relationship with the plant and the animal worlds. Hunters and gatherers did not wander aimlessly about the countryside. Rather, they stopped in areas of abundant food supply. Moreover, their actions often influenced the growth of plants and game. Replanting seeds that they gathered, irrigating areas whose wild plants would profit from it, protecting the seeds from partly harvested crops, avoiding the overfishing of certain streams so that the local fish will not be depleted and the next year's catch, nonexistent—these and other techniques have been used by hunting and gathering societies to maximize their food supply (Cohen, 1977 pp. 20–23). The step from such strategies to intensive farming is a short one.

The semidomestication of certain plant and animal species took place millenia before agriculture was adopted as a primary economic activity. Thus, agriculture was not devised suddenly and dramatically at a single point in time and then adopted thereafter by everyone who subsequently learned about it. Human societies have known about growing food since early times, and the casual cultivation of crops was practiced in conjunction with hunting and gathering. The energy that was put into this casual cultivation was minimal: A handful of seeds was tossed onto the earth and inspected months later on a trek through the area. A few plants were cultivated in a clearing and harvested months or even years later. (Such practices are termed "incipient agriculture" by Braidwood, 1975.) Casual, primitive agriculture thus "seeped in" over a period of many thousands of years, and many hunting and gathering peoples supplemented their diets with semidomesticated crops.

Independently, more or less simultaneously, and in a number of different areas of the world—in the Middle East, in Southeast Asia, in Africa, in China, and in Central and South America—slightly over 10,000 years ago, the leap from hunting and gathering combined with casual agriculture to intensive, more or less full-time agriculture was made. What was dramatic was not the discovery of agriculture; growing plants from seeds was neither a unique or revolutionary event nor a difficult or complex idea. What was revolutionary was the adoption of agriculture as a primary economic strategy:

> The most striking fact about early agriculture . . . is precisely that it is such a universal event. Slightly more than 10,000 years ago, virtually all men [and women] lived on wild foods. By 2,000 years ago, the overwhelming majority of people lived by farming. In the four million year history of *Homo sapiens*, the spread of agriculture was accomplished in about 8,000 years. . . . [Thus,]

the problem is not just to account for the beginnings of agriculture, but to account for the fact that so many human populations made this economic transition in so short a time (Cohen, 1977, p. 5).

Evidence suggests that early, full-time agriculture was very inefficient as an economic strategy—in fact, considerably less labor-efficient than the hunting and gathering technology (Granovetter, 1979, pp. 494–495, 1982). In the early stages of agriculture, it took more person-hours of work to feed a society by growing food than by harvesting it in nature's wilds. It is also possible that in the early stages of agriculture, growing food did not provide a more adequate diet than hunting and gathering. And, moreover, crops may very well have been less reliable as a food source than wild game and plants, because nomads have geographical mobility and can bypass adverse local climatic conditions.

Why, then, was hunting and gathering so widely abandoned and agriculture adopted? The issue of the origin of agriculture is controversial, and at least a half-dozen theories for it have been proposed (Redman 1978, pp. 93–103). Certainly a multifactor approach is necessary to explain it (Redman, 1978, pp. 103–112). Many experts (Boserup, 1965; Cohen, 1977; pp. 14–15) argue that population increases occurred throughout prehistory, and that, by 11,000 to 12,000 years ago, hunters and gatherers probably reached the point of population pressure. Evidence suggests that the available wild food did become increasingly depleted in many parts of the world and that increasingly unpalatable foods had to be consumed. Eventually, intensive, full-time cultivation became the only solution to the problem of feeding the growing population. Even though early agriculture was less *labor efficient* than hunting and gathering, it was nonetheless more efficient from the point of view of land. Growing food produces a greater number of edible calories per unit of land than hunting and gathering does. As a result, it can support a larger, denser population. Agriculture came to be practiced, many

When a society adopted agriculture, a number of significant transformations began to take place. In this Amazon jungle community, the people farm, fish, forage for vegetables, and hunt wild game.

Erich Goode

experts believe, only when population pressure necessitated it (Cohen, 1977, p. 15).

Horticultural Societies

The earliest technology for growing food was extremely primitive. At first, a digging stick was used to poke a hole in the ground and deposit a seed. Centuries later, a hoe was devised to dig up and turn over the soil so that seeds could be planted somewhat deeper. A technology based on the digging stick is called simple horticulture, and one based on the hoe is called advanced horticulture; the **horticultural societies** who used them are called, respectively, **simple horticultural societies** and **advanced horticultural societies.**

The introduction of agriculture took place over the course of many centuries. Its impact has been described as revolutionary, but this is true only over the long run. One of the most significant changes associated with agriculture was the formation of settled communities. Even this, though, was a gradual rather than a sudden change. There is, for example, evidence that some advanced hunting and gathering societies began to form settled communities before they adopted agriculture as a way of life (Redman, 1978, pp. 71–82). At the same time, simple horticultural societies tended not to form completely permanent settled communities. In many areas, even primitive horticultural farming methods depleted the nutrients in the soil over the course of several seasons. Consequently, new plots had to be sought out. Many simple horticultural societies relied on the "slash and burn" method: Trees were cleared by being chopped down, and shrubs, bushes, and underbrush were cleared by being burned. The ashes remained on the ground to provide nutrients for the soil. A crop was then grown in this location for several years, until this soil, too, was exhausted. At that point, the members of the society moved on to another location.

Thus, even though some hunters and gatherers formed settled communities, and many simple horticulturists were seminomadic, agriculture and the formation of villages were closely associated. With improved farming techniques and more productive harvests, larger populations could be supported. Horticultural societies had much larger populations than did hunting and gathering societies. The largest hunting and gathering societies were made up of no more than a few dozen members. In contrast, a large, successful horticultural community might house tens of thousands of people, and an entire advanced horticultural society could have as many as a million members. Consequently, another accompaniment of agriculture was a more detailed and elaborate **division of labor.** As work became more complicated, it also became more diverse. In hunting and gathering societies, very little specialization existed. Moreover, what specialization did exist was extremely simple and primitive: Men hunted large game, and women gathered wild vegetal foods, cooked, and raised and cared for children. In contrast, in village agricultural life, people began to specialize in dozens of different economic activities—making pottery; carrying out religious, magical, and ceremonial functions; weaving; and fashioning tools, buildings, weapons, sculpture, carvings, musical instruments, trophies, and masks, for example.

As material culture proliferated, possessing material goods became more important than it had been in hunting and gathering days. Some members of society were now much wealthier, others much poorer. Inequality was born and permitted (or perhaps encouraged) the emergence of **offices:** full-time positions that confer prestige and power on their

Horticultural society A society whose economy is based primarily on using the hoe or the digging stick as an agricultural method.

Simple horticultural society An agricultural society whose principal implement for growing food is the digging stick.

Advanced horticultural society An agricultural society that uses the hoe as a farming implement.

Divison of labor The specialization of roles, activities, and work functions involved in production within society or a bureaucracy.

Offices Full-time positions that confer prestige and power on their incumbents.

incumbents. Formal government made its appearance, with its chiefs, kings, emperors, ministers, and priests—persons designated, elected, or born to handle (and mishandle) affairs of state. Over the years, many appointive and elective offices came to be inherited—automatically passed on within families, from one generation to the next. True social classes came into being—groups of people with distinctly different levels of wealth or prestige, who passed those levels on to their children. Perhaps just as important, some societies waged warfare against others and attempted to absorb them into larger political entities—empires. Such conquests greatly expanded the size of horticultural societies and produced rules of awesome power and, sometimes, awesome wickedness.

Agrarian Societies

After its initial appearance, the most important invention in the history of agriculture was the fashioning and use of the plow, which occurred about 4000 B.C. Because plows dig deeper into the soil than digging sticks and hoes, they permit fuller use of the earth's nutrients. In fertile areas, a given plot of land could now be cultivated year after year almost indefinitely, and it could yield food in far greater abundance than it had before the plow's invention. Plow-based economies became even more efficient when domesticated animals, instead of humans, were trained to pull the plows. By comparison with all earlier societies, the economic surplus of these **agrarian societies** was enormous.

Agrarian societies An agricultural society in which the primary method of production is the plow.

The physical space occupied by some agrarian societies increased enormously, too. Such examples as ancient Rome, Egypt, and China show that agrarianism also permitted enormous increases in population—up to several million people. Just as important, agrarianism promoted the emergence of cities: large concentrations of people in one community. Because city dwellers, by and large, do not grow food, the phenomenon of the city rests on the accumulation of a large economic surplus outside it. The city dwellers managed to buy and live off this surplus by exchanging their nonagricultural occupational skills for it. The number of these nonagricultural occupational skills continued to grow. Artists, blacksmiths, stonemasons, weavers, scribes, and hundreds of other specialists enriched society's material culture—a flowering that brought forth the Egyptian pyramids, the Great Wall of China, and the cathedral of Notre Dame, to name just a few things.

Power and Wealth.   All great agrarian societies were conquest states, which began as small territorial entities and grew larger by waging war against other territories and absorbing them. Economic surplus and wealth produced increasingly deadly weapons of war and full-time military specialists to wage it. Less affluent neighboring societies, which could not support powerful armies, were conquered and dragged into the growing empires.

As these societies adapted themselves to a more or less continuous state of war, or rumors of war, the powers of the ruler expanded. The king, emperor, sultan, or czar seized absolute power over his subjects. Despotism reached its peak with agrarianism; the actions of such Roman emperors as Caligula (who granted a high office of state to his horse) bear eloquent testimony to the-life-and-death powers assumed by the rulers of agrarian societies.

The economic gap between the rich and the poor also reached its peak in agrarian societies. The royal family alone generally controlled about half the total economic surplus (Lenski, 1966, pp. 210–219). In ancient Rome, one emperor's family owned some 20,000 personal slaves. English kings in the 1300s had incomes equal to thirty times those of their richest nobles, or the combined incomes of about 24,000 field laborers. True social classes were firmly entrenched in agrarian societies: Families passed on their wealth, prestige, and power—or their poverty, unimportance, and impotence—to their children, generation after generation. Mobility from one social class to another was minimal. The transition to a true monetary economy, in which all goods are exchanged for money, took place during this period. In intensified social inequalities because monetary wealth is more easily controlled and monopolized by a central power than is agricultural wealth.

Up to and including this point in history, wealth and inequality marched hand in hand. The richer a society grew, the more unequal it became. A few families controlled the bulk of a society's riches; the mass of the population benefited little or not at all from the growth of the surplus. The next step in society's technology changed this.

Industrial Societies

Industrialization began in England in the 1700s and spread out across the whole world. Of course, even today, some societies are more industrialized than others. In many societies, most of the work force remains in the agricultural sector, in others—those that are thoroughly industrialized—fewer than one worker in ten is still on the farm.

What is industrialization? Its basic features are the following: (1) the replacement of tools operated by hand or pulled by animals with power-driven machines; (2) the organization of the workplace into large productive units, or factories; (3) the creation of highly specialized jobs and activities; (4) the use of interchangeable parts in machinery and in the products of industry (see Chapter 17). Industrialization proved to be a very efficient means of producing—and adding to—the economic surplus, whose growth hastened many processes that had started during agrarianism (though it reversed certain other trends). The average size of industrial societies increased. (Even today, however, the two largest societies in the world, China and India, have basically agricultural economies.) Above all, industrialization encouraged the growth of cities, which grew larger in population (and often in size) and accounted for an increasingly large proportion of the people in all industrialized societies.

Wealth, Prestige, and Power. Among the more revolutionary transformations industrialization brought about was a more equal distribution of wealth, prestige, and power than had been possible under agrarianism. Industrialization reversed the centuries-long tradition of increasing inequality. In no mature industrial economy could a single family control anything remotely like half of a society's surplus wealth. Industrialization therefore produced a large middle class—the first in human history. Manual laborers began to live much more comfortably than they had before. In short, industrialization in effect redistributed society's wealth and income. Movement up and down the class ladder—social mobility—occurred far more frequently than it had in agrarian times, so that members of an industrial society were less likely to be "stuck" in the social class of their parents than were members of an agrarian society. Inequality exists even today, of course, but it is a far less extreme inequality than had prevailed before the coming of industry. The distribution of power, too, became far more equitable than it had formerly been.

The Decline of Traditionalism.   Industrial countries needed workers trained in technical skills. Governments now set out to provide these skills by expanding their educational systems. Literacy became almost universal—a social revolution whose consequences, already vast, may only be in their earliest stages. Urbanization, social and geographical mobility, and higher levels of general affluence weakened the hold of many traditional institutions on the society as a whole and on its individual members. The two institutions most profoundly weakened by these trends were the family and organized religion. Industrialization tended to weaken the ties that parents and other kinship groups exerted over individuals. Many customs, like arranged marriages, disappeared because elders no longer controlled the lives of young people. Even day-to-day contact with close relatives fell sharply, because people tended to live away from their places of birth. Young people became more independent now than they had been. Religion was no longer at the center of the intellectual stage, and people had the choice of belonging or not belonging to any religious body. They could believe or not believe anything at all. Religious leaders lost the political power they once had.

The Postindustrial Society

As an advanced industrial economy becomes increasingly productive and efficient, a decreasing proportion of its labor market is engaged in manufacturing. Increasingly, manufacturing is sent to be done abroad, in countries where wages are lower; at the same time, jobs expand in the **service sector of the economy**—that is, workers who deal with people or with knowledge rather than work with their hands. Thus, in a postindustrial economy, the number of lawyers, bus drivers, physicians, sales personnel, teachers, bookkeepers, accountants, computer programmers, clerks, and so on, outweighs the number of factory workers. In the world today, the United States is perhaps the only society with a postindustrial economy. In many ways, a **postindustrial society** is as different from an industrial society as the latter is from a society based mainly on agriculture. (The impact of the postindustrial economy is so important that we discuss it in more detail in Chapters 17 and 20.)

Service sector of the economy Economic activities that use products to perform a service—like teaching, flying an airplane, banking, providing legal assistance, and so on. Service activities do *not* involve extracting raw materials from the earth (like fishing, farming, and mining), which is called the primary sector, and they do *not* involve manufacturing or turning raw materials into products, which is called the secondary sector.

Postindustrial society A society whose work force is located mainly in the service sector of the economy.

THE PROBLEM OF ORDER

More than three centuries ago, an English philosopher named Thomas Hobbes (1588–1679) published a book that was and has remained controversial: *Leviathan*. In it, he posed and tried to answer a problem that is still relevant: How is social order possible? After all, as Hobbes himself points out, the weakest person in the world can buy a gun and kill the strongest person in the world. By and large, however, this does not happen. Why? This question has come to be known as the "Hobbesian problem of order" (Parsons, 1951, pp. 118–119).

Hobbes argued that all people are selfish by nature and seek to fulfill their desires—at the expense of others, if need be—through force and fraud. By and large, all human beings want the same things: power, wealth, and glory. There is just not enough of those things to go around, so conflict is inevitable. Below the surface, society is "war of all against all."

If these tendencies flourished without restraint, human life would become, as Hobbes put it, "nasty, brutish, and short." Why doesn't this happen? Hobbes argued that society does not collapse into a state of open internal war, because rational human beings calculate that if they are free to do whatever they want, so too is everyone else. As a result, no one could count on keeping anything. Out of self-protection, we all willingly give up our freedom to use force and fraud, to obtain long-term security from the force and fraud of others. In the long run, we can better and more effectively satisfy our selfish acquisitive desires by giving up our absolute (but essentially useless) rights and handing them over to a central government strong enough to ensure law and order. But we give up those rights solely to gratify our selfish desires all the more completely, not because we regard government control as good in itself. Human beings, according to Hobbes, have no impulse to sociability; we accept social restraints because we are rational and because we have no choice in the matter. We always feel these restraints as restraints, not as bonds of union with other human beings. To Hobbes, the heart of social order is repression, albeit a repression that can be rationally understood and accepted.

Sociologists, too, are concerned with the problem of order, though they find Hobbes' answer to it mistaken. Today, we believe that order does not grow out of nothing but self-interested calculation. Sociologists recognize that societies are relatively stable and orderly because the people in them are linked together in a social structure of mutual expectations and obligations. Large, complex societies are made up of people who have many statuses, and many role relationships with many partners. Each role relationship links every person with society in a different way, and each link contributes to social stability. Your status as a student snares you into relationships with other students, with teachers, with the school administration, and so on. Your status as a member of a family links you with your relatives, to whom you have stable and ongoing obligations. Nowhere can you act as a totally selfish, calculating individual. Everywhere your role partners expect you to act in certain ways, and almost everywhere, almost all of us do act in those ways. We do so, in part, to please these partners or at least to try to satisfy their expectations. Why do we want to please them? One reason is that we want them to think well of us: We care about their opinions of us. Second, our relations with them are reciprocal; we know that if we let them down, they can let us down, too. Society is made up of vast networks of role and status reciprocities, which make for a certain order and stability.

Karl Marx (see Chapter 1) added that when the members of a society do not share mutual obligations and expectations, the society will experience conflict. If a large segment of a society has no stake in the social order—if, indeed, it has a stake in overturning that social order—society will not be stable. Societies that give each individual many links with role partners throughout the social structure tend to be stable; societies where individuals have few such links tend to be unstable. In Marx's scheme, a factory worker and a factory owner have very little in common, except for the fact that the worker is being exploited by the owner. Inevitably, Marx argued, this must lead to revolution.

SUMMARY

1. Sociologists define social structure as a network of interconnected, normative social relations in a society.

2. Social structure exists on both a "micro," or face-to-face level, and a "macro," or organizational, institutional, or societal level.

3. Status is one basic building block in the social structure; a status is simply a position in society.

4. Statuses can be achieved or ascribed—or a mixture of the two.

5. All of the statuses that one person occupies at a given time make up what sociologists call a status set.

6. A very important status, which determines or influences a number of others, is called a master status.

7. Statuses usually imply rules and regulations, or norms, which dictate what their occupants should do.

8. Sociologists refer to a role as all the normative expectations attached to a certain status in society.

9. All of the statuses with which the occupant of one status routinely interacts, plus the norms surrounding the relationship of each status pair, make up what sociologists call a role set.

10. Status sets and role sets may result in conflicting expectations from interacting partners; when this takes place within a given status set, it is called role conflict; when this takes place within a given role set, it is called role strain.

11. Sociologists define a social institution as all the norms, statuses, and roles centered around a particular need, theme, or activity. The most important of these are the major social institutions: the family, religion, politics, education, and the economy.

12. A society is all the individuals who live in a given geographical area and who share a common culture.

13. Societies can be arranged along a dimension of technological efficiency; this feature influences nearly all the other basic characteristics of a society.

14. Hunting and gathering is the least efficient and productive method of obtaining food. Hunting and gathering societies tend to be small, nomadic, and relatively egalitarian. Their material cultures have few physical artifacts.

15. Horticulture, or gardening with a digging stick or a hoe, represents an early form of agriculture. Societies based on this type of technology tend to be larger, to be materially wealthier, and to have more inequality, as well as a more extensive division of labor, than hunting and gathering societies. In addition, full-time offices that carry with them a measure of status and power, inherited social classes, settled communities, and warfare and military conquest all make their appearance at this stage.

16. Agrarian societies are those based on the technology of farming with a plow, which is more productive and efficient than using a digging stick or a hoe. Agrarian societies tend to be very large,

with major urban centers; they grew in size as a result of military conquests of smaller societies. Of all societies, the gap between rich and poor is greatest in agrarian societies.

17. Industrialization was the next step in increasing technological efficiency and productivity. Income and power are far more equitably distributed in industrialized societies than in agrarian societies. In addition, education is available to nearly all members of the society, and traditional institutions, like the family and religion, lose much of their hold on members.

18. A postindustrial society is one in which a majority of the labor force is employed in the service sector.

19. Seeing a society as a kind of structure enables us to answer the basic sociological question, "How is social order possible?" This perspective tends to focus on society's more orderly features.

SUGGESTED READINGS

Diane L. Barthel, *Amana: From Pietist Sect to American Community*. Lincoln: University of Nebraska Press, 1984.
An historical study of the social structure of the Amana Colony, which began as a religious community of pious, fundamentalist believers and, as a result of secularization and economic forces, gave up its communal ways and "undertook a dramatic effort to catch up with the modern world." The temptations of modern life stimulated a transformation that reduced the role of the church to mere symbolism. Eventually, the community became a corporation, which now holds most of the political power.

Howard S. Becker, *Art Worlds*. Berkeley: University of California Press, 1982.
A study of the network of individuals, roles, and statuses—artists, suppliers of materials, dealers, critics, authors and writers, and fellow artists—who make up the art world. Adopts a symbolic interactionist approach to study social structure; looks at art as "collective activity."

Lewis A. Coser, *Greedy Institutions: Patterns of Undivided Commitment*. New York: Free Press, 1974.
Some statuses and roles demand a much greater commitment than others do. In fact, with some, the commitment is total: The institution attempts to "devour" the entire person and to minimize all outside commitments. This book explores such "greedy" institutions and their occupants, who include the court eunuch in ancient Egypt and a number of Asian societies centuries ago, royal mistresses, Jesuit priests, Leninists and other revolutionaries, court

Jews in seventeenth- and eighteenth-century Germany, domestic servants, housewives, and adherents of religious sects. An excellent historical study employing key ideas relating to social structure.

Lewis A. Coser, Charles Kadushin, and Walter W. Powell, *Books: The Culture and Commerce of Publishing*. New York: Basic Books, 1982; and Walter W. Powell, *Getting into Print*. Chicago: University of Chicago Press, 1985.
Two studies of the social organization of the publishing industry. These books discuss patterned social relations between authors, agents, editors, marketing people, reviewers, and book distributors.

Kai T. Erikson, *Everything in Its Path: Destruction of Community in the Buffalo Creek Flood*. New York: Simon & Schuster, 1976.
A sensitive and moving report of the impact of a disaster on a community's social organization.

Gerhard Lenski and Jean Lenski, *Human Societies: An Introduction to Macrosociology* (5th ed.). New York: McGraw-Hill, 1987.
A detailed exposition on the evolution of society, from hunting and gathering to industrial. The Lenskis' position has become controversial.

Colin M. Turnbull, *The Mountain People*. New York: Simon & Schuster, 1972.
An anthropologist's study of an African tribe, the Ik. A frightening account of what happened to one society's structure of social relations when its economic base was destroyed.

chapter 5

SOCIAL INTERACTION

E very minute of the day, every one of us is engaged in one of a wide range of activities—attending a sociology class, taking a friend's photograph, changing a lightbulb, daydreaming. Some of these activities take place in solitude, some in the presence of other people. When we act out behavior with others present, they react to us and what we do, and this influences our further behavior. Sociologists define **social interaction** as the process of people's acting toward or responding to other people.

Even when we are not in the presence of others, we are often influenced by them. Alone, we adjust our behavior to satisfy certain people's expectations, demands, or desires. Children who withdraw their hands from cookie jars for fear of their mother's reactions on discovering the missing cookies, and students who spend extra hours working on assignments to please their instructors, are engaged in social interaction, even though they are alone when they act. Whenever people take one another into account in what they do, they are engaged in some kind of social interaction.

In Chapter 1, we made the crucial distinction between the micro and macro levels of social relations. For the most part, social interaction is a micro-level concept that takes place on the small-scale, person-to-person level. When we picture interaction taking place, it is between specific individuals, or individuals in specific positions. Thus, social scientists who study interaction examine behavior that is usually face to face, up-close, and interpersonal. They study how people talk to one another (Goffman, 1981), what happens when two people make eye contact and stare at one another (Collins, 1983), what drug use is like among adolescent peers (Glassner and Loughlin, 1986), how some people manage to exercise influence over others (Cialdini, 1984), and what clues people give off when they tell lies to others (Ekman, 1985). The micro level exists when person A does something, person B responds to that act, and A, in turn, responds to B's act; it also exists when A and B, or a number of individuals, act in response to what C, or a number of individuals, does. Sociologists call this action-reaction sequence social interaction.

The idea of **social structure** (see Chapter 4) assumes a certain level of stability and even rigidity in society. People step into statuses

Social interaction The process of individuals' acting toward, responding to, or taking into account other people.

Social structure A network of interconnected, normatively governed social relationships in a society. The organized, stable relations that the many role partners, groups, and organizations have with one another, by acting out their role demands and mutual expectations.

and tend to play their roles more or less faithfully. When two people interact with each other in conformity with their roles and status obligations, they generate a stable social order. People, however, never interact with one another solely on the basis of the positions they occupy or the roles they play. All interaction is a give-and-take process. One individual does or says a specific thing, and another individual responds to that particular thing. People never act out their parts mechanically or automatically. They always vary a bit from the norms spelled out by their statuses and roles, so interaction introduces a certain spontaneous, creative, free-flowing, dynamic element into social life. Our reactions to others are always slightly unpredictable.

Two people standing face to face thus never quite know what to expect from one another. Knowing their social characteristics (such as gender, age, social class, ethnicity) will give each a great deal of information about the possible actions of the other, but it is only a start. Knowing the statuses the other occupies—teacher, student, sales clerk, customer, physician, patient, and so on—will give each a great deal more predictability, but, again, not enough to enable either to know with certainty what the other will do. First, each must know how the other defines and perceives his or her respective characteristics and roles: What meaning do they have for each individual? One person may consider adolescence as a time for carefree indolence, a period of freedom without responsibility, an extension of childhood but with adult freedoms. Another may regard adolescence as the first step in a career—a time for studying, getting high grades, and winning awards and fellowships. Simply because both are teenagers does not mean that they will react the same way to an invitation to a "beer blast." Two police officers with a totally different view of what it means to be a cop—one, as a way of making a great deal of money, however illegal, and the second, as a means of serving the public—are very unlikely to react in the same way when offered a huge bribe. The status police officer is the same no matter who occupies it, and the role demands on all its occupants are the same. Still, two occupants may interpret the job in very different ways, and their behavior as occupants of that status will therefore also differ.

Likewise, the setting or situation in which actors are located will influence how they will act. Even the most corrupt police officer acts more honestly when being observed by a superior. And even an extremely studious teenager is likely to become more irresponsible, carefree, and boisterous among beer-drinking peers at a party than at a meeting of parents and teachers. The point is that interpretations and situations make individuals' behavior somewhat unpredictable, even if we know a great deal about their social characteristics and statuses.

MEANING

For relations with others to be social in nature, the interacting parties need common ground. They must agree on the meaning of their actions, gestures, or words; otherwise, communication among them will be problematic or impossible. Of course, certain actions or words are hard

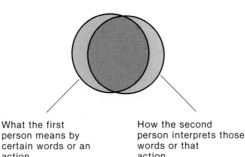

What the first person means by certain words or an action

How the second person interprets those words or that action

to misunderstand. If the government of one country drops a bomb on another country, the gesture cannot be interpreted as a friendly one. "Please close the front door." is almost always quite clear. My meaning and your interpretation of it will be more or less identical; the two will overlap almost perfectly. In the case illustrated above, the two (or more) interacting parties would share a common understanding. Certain words or gestures would mean the same things to them. Much social interaction, however, is problematic.

Interpreting Meaning

In Chapter 6, we see that taking the role of the "other" is probably the most crucial process in learning a society's culture. That process involves seeing the world from the perspective of another person. Sympathetic insight of this kind is called **empathy:** the ability to interpret or understand how another person thinks and feels. Empathy is the ability to stand in another person's shoes. Empathy is crucial not only in the process of socialization but also in everyday life, when we interact with others. We may and often do make incorrect assessments of other people's intentions or meanings.

We try to interpret what someone means by something in many ways. One is by the cues that person gives off: actions, gestures, and words. The same action, gesture, or comment often means different things in different situations. A smile, for example, might mean any one of the following things: "Hello," "You seem like a nice person—I'd like to get to know you better," "I agree with what you say," "Excuse me," "No thanks," "That's just about the dumbest thing I've ever heard, but I don't feel like arguing with you," or "Good-bye."

Imagine that you are looking at someone who is looking back at you; suddenly, one of that person's eyes blinks. What does it mean? Was it simply an involuntary blink, with no message for you at all? Was it a wink, a flirtatious invitation to further, and more intimate, interaction? In other words, you must interpret the blink. And, you attempt to give it the same meaning the blinker did (Geertz, 1973, pp. 6–7). This is true of all social action. The process of interpreting the meaning of the actions of others is both extremely complex and never-ending. What others mean by what they do, and how we interpret what they mean when they do something, lies at the heart of all social interaction. It is always possible for one person to misinterpret another's meaning. The overlap in the way they understand that thing will then be slight or nonexistent, shown in figure on page 116. In social interaction, communication takes place only when the meaning of an action overlaps with the meaning that others attach to it.

Empathy The ability to understand or interpret how another person thinks or feels.

The Role of Expectations in Social Interaction

The two most crucial qualities of social interaction are its *dynamic* and its *dialectical* characters. Although all interaction takes place within certain limitations, interaction is not like a stage play, enacted faithfully and rigidly from beginning to end from a prepared script; it is, instead, a flowing, spontaneous, slightly unpredictable activity. In addition, it is a two-way street, a give-and-take: Person A influences what person B says and does and, likewise, B's reaction influences A's counterreaction.

This basic principle is beautifully illustrated by a field of social psychology called *attribution theory* (Harvey and Weary, 1985). Attribution theory investigates the process by which people make judgments about the actions, motives, and traits of others. How do we "read" or perceive what others are doing or saying? How do we know, or come to think we know, about the characteristics of others? How do we infer what someone else is doing and why? When someone says or does something, how do we process this information? "How do we come to know the motives and traits of those around us?" (Jones, 1986, p. 41).

It is well known that our expectancies of others shape how we interpret their words or actions. We see in others what we expect to find. If we are already ill disposed toward someone else, what he or she does will tend to confirm that original image. If, on the other hand, we feel favorably about someone, we usually see good in what he or she says or does.

What is not as well known is that we may actually *elicit* in others the very behavior that confirms our expectancies about them. Our expectancies of them leads to our acting a certain way with them; this

in turn results in their behaving a certain way; their behavior in turn verifies our original view of them, and we hold it all the more strongly as a result. There is, in other words, *real behavioral evidence* that confirms our original hypothesis about them—actual, not imaginary, behavior confirming what we originally thought. We think ill of someone; we act toward him or her in a nasty fashion—abusive, insulting, hostile; he or she reacts by being correspondingly nasty to us; we arrive at the conclusion that we were right all along: That person is indeed a nasty person and deserves to be treated as we treated him or her. Indeed, this progression was the thesis of Robert K. Merton's classic paper, "The Self-Fulfilling Prophecy": "The self-fulfilling prophecy is, in the beginning, a *false* definition of the situation evoking a new behavior which makes the originally false conception come *true*. The specious validity of the self-fulfilling prophecy perpetuates a reign of error. For the prophet will cite the actual course of events as proof that he was right from the very beginning" (Merton, 1957, p. 423).

In an experiment, a group of teachers were told that some of their students (randomly chosen) would "bloom" academically in the months to come. The lofty expectations that the teachers had of these students led to their special treatment of them. These students, in turn, responded by performing significantly better academically than the students who were not so designated (Rosenthal and Jacobson, 1968).

In another experiment, fifty-one male college students were asked to become acquainted with female

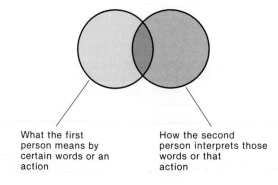

What the first person means by certain words or an action

How the second person interprets those words or that action

undergraduates on the telephone. One group was shown a photograph of an extremely attractive young woman; a second group was shown a photograph of a young woman who, by conventional standards, would have been considered plain. (The pictures were, of course, randomly assigned, and bore no relation to their actual telephone partners.) All the telephone conversations were taped, and the female side of the conversation was played back to a group of "judges." Consistently, the telephone partners of the women who were allegedly more attractive were judged to be more poised, self-confident, outgoing, and sociable than were those who were talking to the young men who thought their partners were plain (Snyder, Tanke, and Berscheid, 1977). The males' original views of these young women as attractive led them to actually *become* more desirable as potential dates—*even though this image was completely unfounded.*

What is so remarkable about this process is that behavioral confirmation occurs even when the perceiver knows the other person's behavior was elicited by his or her own behavior. If we act friendly toward another person, and he or she responds by acting friendly in return, we assume that he or she has a generally friendly disposition. If we are told, yes, but the reason why he or she acts friendly to you is that you acted friendly toward him or her originally, we tend to respond, "Yes, I know, but I *still* think she's a friendly person." Attributional theorists call this tendency the *correspondence bias:* Behavior is generally considered to reflect a certain type of person, rather than to emerge out of situational constraints. We are more likely to say that friendly behavior reflects a friendly disposition than we are to say that friendly behavior grows out of the demands of a situation that calls for it. (Situations that call for acting friendly include those in which someone is trying to influence us in some way, for instance, to sell us something, or to get us to vote for a certain candidate.) We discount the influence of the situation and assume the behavior is reflective of the kind of person who would do such a thing—in many cases, a fallacious way of reasoning. We often take behavior at face value and overattribute personal significance to it. Even if there are situational constraints on an individual to act in a certain way, even if those constraints are extreme, and *even if we ourselves created those constraints*, we tend to assume that the individual's behavior reflects a general, underlying, stable personality disposition. We tend *not* to think that the individual was not wholly free to act, that his or her behavior reflected the demands of the immediate situation.

The major lesson to be learned from examining social interaction is that all of us select and actively transform the social reality we confront. Often, this means that we are likely to confirm erroneous expectancies. It also means that, again, "we should be especially cautious about inferring stable dispositions from observed behavior" (Jones, 1986, p. 46).

Source: Jones, 1986, pp. 41–46.

Nonverbal Communication

Interaction is thus a form of communication, and it is always based on a kind of language. Sometimes this "language" takes the form of words, as when one person says to another, "I love you." Often, as with a blink or a smile, the language is nonverbal. There are many forms of **nonverbal communication,** by which we send information, or cues, to other people about what we think or feel, but we do not send this information directly, with words. Some forms of nonverbal communication may be more expressive than words—a clenched fist, for example. We can also use our tone of voice to say something that is very different from the literal meaning of our words. Facial expressions, too, nonverbally convey a

Nonverbal communication
Conveying messages through means other than words.

Most people gesture when they speak. Some gestures, like this one, emphasize a point being made by the speaker. Such gestures are examples of "body language," a way of communicating by using our bodies and faces.

Chester Higgins, Jr./Photo Researcher

Body language A type of nonverbal communication that conveys messages by means of our facial expressions and how we stand, walk, or gesticulate with our hands.

wide range of emotions. Kinesics, or the way we move our bodies, likewise conveys messages without words. A walk, for instance, may seem to invite a seduction. Even variations in the size of the pupil of the eye may convey information to a keen observer; enlarged pupils often mean sexual excitement and arousal.

Much of nonverbal communication is **body language.** By means of our facial expressions, and how we stand, walk, or gesticulate with our hands, we convey certain messages to others. Body language may be conscious or nonconscious, intentional or unintentional. Most of the messages we convey are intentional: A kiss signifies the affection we feel for someone; a frown indicates our displeasure. We are aware of the meaning that these nonverbal gestures have to others, and this is one reason why we use them. However, some nonverbal cues or gestures operate on a nonconscious, unintended level: We may "tell" other people something without realizing it. For instance, a student may communicate boredom during a lecture by drumming his or her fingers on the arm of a chair.

Nonverbal Gestures.   Some forms of nonverbal communication are universal or nearly so. For instance, certain facial expressions are most common in almost all cultures around the world and mean more or less the same thing everywhere. In one experiment, a large number of people were photographed while responding to a request that they display six basic emotions: sadness, anger, disgust, fear, surprise, and happiness. The photographs were then shown to members of a wide variety of different nations and cultures. Agreement among members of societies about which emotion was depicted in any photograph was extremely high, in most cases over 90 percent (Ekman, 1978). Some people display the emotions they feel; others mask them. And different things will arouse different emotions in different people. But the facial expressions that convey emotions are almost universally recognizable.

At the same time, many—perhaps most—nonverbal gestures are highly variable in meaning from one society to another. Nonverbal communication is a feature of cultures everywhere. It is learned in the same way that a language is learned. We learn to "talk" with our bodies and faces in the same way we learn to say certain words. The same gesture, however, often conveys different messages in different societies. When you interpret another person's nonverbal cues, the chance of being wrong about their meaning increases as cultural distance increases (Hall, 1977, p. 76). In Sicily, if a man holds up his hand in front of someone, with the index and little fingers pointing up and the others clenched in a semifist, it is a gesture of contempt. The first man is telling the second that his wife is unfaithful to him—one of the most serious of insults. At the University of Texas, exactly the same gesture is used by the fans of the school's football and basketball teams to declare a bond of solidarity with other Texas fans.

Likewise, raising the eyebrows means "yes" among the Polynesians and "no" among the Greeks. Almost everywhere friends greet one another with raised eyebrows, but not in Japan, where it is considered indecent. In many countries, people say "yes" by nodding their heads, and "no" by shaking their heads from side to side. The people of Sri Lanka, however, have two ways of saying yes: the usual way, and a second, used when a person agrees to do something—swaying the head in slow sideways movements, a gesture that would be interpreted as "no" elsewhere (Eibl-Eibesfeldt, 1972, pp. 299–300). Flashing two fingers in a "V" sign in Greece means "go to hell"; in England, during World War II, it meant "victory"; at present, it is an obscene gesture in England (Morris, 1977, pp. 200–201); in the United States during the 1960s, it meant "peace." In each time or place, the gesture is identical or nearly so, yet the meanings are extraordinarily different, often totally opposed. Clearly, these gestures and their meanings are cultural products.

Staring or gazing at someone is a form of nonverbal communication. But what does it communicate? Cultures around the world have different rules regarding "eye contact." In some cultures, it is not considered polite for people who are conversing to maintain a great deal of eye contact. Typically, people in these cultures will glance at one another

Some forms of nonverbal communication are universal, or nearly so. Certain facial expressions are common in almost all cultures around the world, and mean more or less the same thing everywhere. It is difficult to misinterpret the meaning of a smile.

Marcello Bertinetti/Photo Researcher

quickly and look away while speaking. This is true of Navaho Indians, northern Europeans, and East Asians. Other cultures, in contrast, maintain strong eye contact among speakers; this is characteristic of southern Europeans, Arabs, and Latin Americans. When the members of a high eye-contact culture interact with those of a low eye-contact culture, they feel ignored and rejected. Likewise, members of the low eye-contact culture feel that people from high eye-contact cultures are too familiar and intimate (Argyle, 1981).

A number of books have been published that claim that the reader can unlock the secrets of body language by using simple formulas to interpret certain gestures (Fast, 1970; Nierenberg & Calero, 1971). Presumably, you can go to a party and discover which of the people there might want to date you; talk to used car dealers and determine whether they are honest; play poker and know who is bluffing—simply by understanding nonverbal communication. Actually, body language is very complicated. There is a great deal of variation, not only from culture to culture but also from individual to individual, regarding what specific gestures, facial expressions, or physical postures mean. For instance, someone sitting with crossed legs is not necessarily saying, consciously or unconsciously, "Watch out, buster," or "Keep away from me"; nor do spread legs always mean "I'm available," or "Please come over here and talk to me." To a certain degree, every individual has his or her own private system of nonverbal communication, a distinct and personal body language. For instance, even when happy, Jane might smile less than many people in her society; John, however, might smile a great deal more, whatever his state of mind. On a given day, both are smiling: What does it mean? We have to know Jane and John. Some gestures have a personal, and not an exclusively cultural, meaning.

The same gestures and cues not only mean different things in different cultures and to different individuals, but they also mean different things in different situations, settings, and contexts. People define certain body movements, gestures, and facial expressions as appropriate or inappropriate for certain circumstances. If professors at parties were to speak to friends in the same loud, formal tones of voice they use in large lecture classes, they would be thought pompous, insensitive, and odd. But if these same professors were to come to class with drinks in hand, laughing a great deal, throwing their arms around everyone in class, and holding their faces only inches away from students, their students would think them very odd, to say the least. Yet most professors do engage in both forms of behavior—in appropriate settings—and are not condemned for it. Gestures are always associated with specific social or physical surroundings or contexts, which determine their meanings and their interpretations by others.

Proxemics The use of social physical space to communicate social messages.

Proxemics.   Where you sit or stand in relation to someone else communicates a great deal about your relationship with that person. **Proxemics** is the use of social and personal space in the process of communication (Hall, 1969, p. 1). But, as with body language generally, different cultures and different individuals use space to communicate somewhat differently. As a general rule, the closer two people are to one another physically, the more intimate their relationship is. To put things a bit differently, physical closeness symbolizes or indicates personal intimacy. Of course, people are sometimes forced to stand close to one another, as on crowded buses or trains, and this crowding does not indicate anything about the closeness of their relationships. Occasionally, extreme anger forces the contending parties very close to each other—as when a base-

Cultures vary with regard to the distance interacting parties stand from one another. In North America, a distance of less than two feet indicates or communicates either intimacy or hostility. Here, an angry manager contests a baseball umpire's call.

UPI/Bettmann Newsphotos

ball player contests an umpire's call. Sometimes, however, physical positioning can be a "proxemic cue," one that communicates the nature of a relationship, a mood, or an emotion. For instance, intimates are more likely to sit next to one another at tables, whereas strangers are more likely to sit opposite one another.

As with eye contact, different cultures convey nonverbal messages through distance or closeness. The cultures whose members make strong eye contact with one another are also physical-contact cultures. Individuals typically stand close, often actually touching. Likewise, noneye-contact cultures also tend to be noncontact cultures as well (Argyle, 1981). North Americans tend to keep a fair distance between one another, unless they are intimate. Latin Americans, however, prefer to stand close to one another. The distance between two people, therefore, has different meanings in North and Latin American cultures. The distance Latins use for ordinary conversations would indicate intimacy or hostility in the United States; this distance makes North Americans uncomfortable. An anthropologist who studied the meaning of proxemics in different cultures says, "I have observed an American backing up the entire length of a long corridor while a foreigner whom he considers pushy tries to catch up with him. This scene has been enacted thousands and thousands of times—one person trying to increase the distance in order to be at ease, while the other tries to decrease it for the same reason, neither one being aware of what was going on" (Hall, 1959, pp. 160–161).

Most people in every culture have a fairly strong sense of how close they will allow others, especially strangers, to come. In one experiment, subjects who were seated in a library were approached by an "intruder" who sat next to them, six inches to one foot away. This invasion of personal space created feelings of anxiety. Within ten minutes, half of the subjects got up and left. (Only 10 percent of the "noninvaded" subjects left during the same period of time.) Even those who stayed used a variety of techniques to protect their sense of space. They turned their backs to the "invader," leaned away, or blocked the intervening space with an elbow (Felipe & Sommer, 1969). Not everyone deals with space in the same way, however. As a rule, <u>women stand and sit closer to</u>

Most people have a strong sense of how close they will allow others, particularly strangers, to come to them. They feel "invaded" if others are too close. Here, people in a park settle into little clusters.

United Nations

one another than men do. Women also tolerate and accept much smaller distances between themselves and others, both men and women, than men do. The same distances make men uncomfortable. Of course, intimate male-female pairs tend to keep the smallest physical distance (Patterson, 1978). Clearly, distance is another nonverbal cue that tells us a great deal about the nature of relationships among people. Like a gesture, distance is a message, a form of communication.

ROLES AND SOCIAL INTERACTION

Status A normatively governed position in a society.

Role The normative expectations attached to a specific position.

Interaction takes place between two or more individuals. Every individual occupies a number of positions, or **statuses.** Every status calls for a set of norms that, taken together, constitute a **role.** (We examined these concepts in detail in Chapter 4.) Statuses and roles imply a certain stability in social life, because their content is known in advance. In contrast, interaction introduces a dynamic, free-flowing element in social life because we can never know in advance how two people will relate to each other, regardless of what their respective statuses and roles may be. How does the process of social interaction modify the nature of role relationships? Let's see.

No interaction is completely "role-free"—in other words, no one relates to anyone else without considering the social positions of both sides. We all fill these positions, usually act in conformity with their role obligations, and live up to the expectations attached to them by others. Yet in the give-and-take of social interaction, roles often take a back seat. The content of a role—the norms that must be observed to fill it—cannot determine precisely how we behave with our role partners.

Two people may occupy the same position or status but interpret their role obligations somewhat differently. The dynamic, fluid, give-and-take quality of social interaction forces us to interpret our roles, not to fill them up passively. Indeed, sometimes we or our "role partners" do not follow the norms attached to a role, and sometimes we fail to measure up to its demands.

Entering Role Relationships

Before our interaction can be guided by the appropriate norms, we must first decide that we are entering a certain "role relationship." Of course, some roles are established instantly because they have an "official" character. By the very act of enrolling in an introductory course in sociology, you have established a student-teacher role relationship governed by specific norms. Not all roles have this official character. How, for instance, do you decide that another person is a "friend?" Suppose someone reproaches you for failing to meet the obligations of friendship by refusing to grant a $10 loan. You might reply, "Hey, who said we were friends?" What one person thought was a clear-cut role relationship, another saw as nonrelationship. Interaction makes each interpretation clear.

In short, it isn't always clear-cut whether one is even in a certain role relationship. A relationship that one person regards as obvious and clearly established may be considered by the other as problematic or nonexistent. The nature of the relationship, and how both parties define it, is established during the course of social interaction.

Moreover, we are never completely socialized into the normative demands of statuses when we first occupy them. What happens when we adopt new, unfamiliar roles? How do we act on our very first date? On the first day of a new job? When we enter a new course and the material, as well as the expectations of the instructor, are unknown to us? Much of what we learn in the early stages of taking on new roles entails being able to determine what is regarded as appropriate and inappropriate behavior. Again, just because we occupy a given status and agree to play a certain role does not mean that what we do in its early stages can be predicted from the formal, normative demands of that status and role. In order to understand what people do in situations such as these, it is necessary to familiarize ourselves with the dynamics of the interaction process.

Altercasting.   Because interaction is a two-way street, our role partners must acknowledge not only that we occupy a certain status but also that this status has some importance to them. Consider the case of two hypothetical assistant professors of sociology, one a man, the other, a woman. In this case, the man regards the woman chiefly as a colleague and fellow sociologist. But the woman regards the man chiefly as a sex object. Which role is "activated?" Which one is regarded as most important? That must be resolved through the process of interaction. Simply because they occupy specific positions in relation to one another does not mean that their partners will honor them. This question cannot be resolved by examining the content of the norms alone. It arises out of a face-to-face, give-and-take confrontation with the status occupants involved.

When we create identities for, or assign roles to, our role partners, who do not acknowledge these roles or regard them as important, sociolo-

WHAT DO YOU THINK?

Street Remarks

Norms—rules that tell us how to relate to others—govern social interaction. These norms may be broken, even often, but nearly all members of a society are aware of them, even when they are violated.

Some actions may be unacceptable in certain situations, or with certain partners, but acceptable elsewhere, or with other people. One such norm, especially in large urban areas, is "civil inattention" between strangers in public (Goffman, 1963b, pp. 83–88; 1971, pp. 304, 331). When two people pass on the street, they accord each other only a passing glance, enough to acknowledge the other's existence but not enough to establish a relationship. Breaches of civil inattention are an infraction of the norms, a kind of deviant behavior.

When are the norms of civil inattention violated, and under what circumstances? Civil inattention may be breached legitimately if you ask for assistance, pay attention to an unusual event—a unicyclist's riding by, for example—or possess characteristics strikingly similar to those of the other person—say, identical clothing. A "badge" or an item that announces a characteristic that the public feels free to comment on may also invite violations of civil inattention—a jogging outfit, or a T-shirt with a certain message, for instance. Under most circumstances, however, the rules of civil inattention do indeed apply.

Yet violations occur. One analysis (Gardner, 1980) argues that nearly always, these breaches—frequently in the form of street remarks—are initiated by men against women. Many men regard women as legitimate targets of social contact; women, therefore, are "liable to receive street remarks at will," and consequently "are subjected to a free and evaluative commentary by men" (Gardner, 1980, p. 333). Many women find such remarks offensive, or at least intrusive. Yet many of the men who make these remarks are not aware that women regard them as offensive. In fact, not *all* such remarks are offensive, either in intent or in the eyes of some women. Yet to enjoy even an inoffensive, complimentary street remark, a woman must temporarily ignore the fact that it can only be made because the rules of our society permit men to be more aggressive than women (Gardner, 1980, p. 337).

Some women regard street remarks as verbal assaults, almost a form of rape. A young woman sees a man holding a map roll down his car window; he seems lost. She approaches the car in response to his "Hey! Hey there!" and he mutters obscenities to her (Gardner, 1980, p. 342). Two men make remarks to a passing

---

Altercasting In social interaction, as a result of our own needs, our creating identities for or assigning roles to others who do not acknowledge these roles or regard them as important.

gists say that we are **altercasting** (Weinstein & Deutschberger, 1963): attending solely to our own needs and goals. When men, for example, look upon women—whether they are professors, college students, Playboy centerfolds, or professional athletes—primarily as sex objects, these men are altercasting. This process involves suppressing certain personal or status characteristics and overemphasizing or even manufacturing others. A short story by Philip Roth, "Defender of the Faith" (1963), depicts a struggle between two World War II soldiers in the United States Army: Grossbart, a private in basic training, and Marx, his commanding sergeant, a combat veteran. Both soldiers are Jewish, and Grossbart attempts to use this bond to secure special favors from Marx, who refuses. Grossbart, in short, employed the technique of altercasting. As this example shows, it doesn't always achieve the desired results.

woman; when she does not reply, one says contemptuously, "Miss Snot" (p. 343). A man follows a woman for two blocks yelling at her at full volume, inquiring, with the use of a choice obscenity, how she is (p. 345). Even remarks that appear to be compliments may escalate into unwanted requests or demands, or even insults or abuse. Indeed, many seeming compliments are not compliments at all, but parodies of compliments (p. 344). A man says "You're beautiful" to a young woman on a New York street, then follows her down the block repeating his evaluation every few seconds. Many supposed compliments are evaluations of parts of a woman's body. Still other compliments are thinly veiled verbal insults (p. 340).

Women must often deal with offensive street remarks from male strangers. What should they do? Some adopt an assertive, confrontational response. Many women find that this more often than not produces a higher level of verbal abuse. Such a response

"constitutes a ratification of the interchange" (p. 346). Moreover, women are rarely trained or willing to carry such a response to its potential conclusion—a fight.

Some react by "blocking" or "repressing" the offending remark and its initiator, by looking away, pretending that nothing happened, or becoming preoccupied with a different activity, such as smoking. Other women deal with street remarks by avoiding the places where they are most likely to occur, or activities that are most likely to generate such remarks from men, such as riding a bicycle.

Taken together, and taken in the volume in which they may occur in large cities, street remarks . . . help to explain why some women reasonably regard the city streets with what seems to others paranoia: a constant series of announcements of female status always seems a possibility. Although women are often dis-

turbed by street remarks. . .the ways they report dealing with these remarks reinforce traditional definitions of the male as chivalrous and the woman as manipulative. Even if women respond, they are still in a position that is more subject to breaches of public order than is a man's. Men do find street remarks unobjectionable, for the most part, or consider them the woman's just deserts, and this highlights that their positive function for the male—a socialization effort that tests his ability to receive rejection—can involve as much risk as their function for the female, which is to learn to accept criticism in a properly passive way (Gardner, 1980, p. 350).

Source: Gardner, 1980, pp. 328–356; Bernard and Schlaffer, 1983, pp. 172–175.

Negotiating Role Obligations

Even after a given role relationship is established between two interacting parties, the exact conditions must be negotiated. Real-life roles tend to be defined vaguely. One's obligations and those of one's partners are subject to compromise, personal peculiarities, and bargaining. Even when the norms spell out fairly clear-cut behavior, we tend to "jockey" for advantage, to make our partners contribute more to a relationship and ourselves, less. Students, for example, will "sound out" a professor to find out how little they can do and still receive the grade they want. Bosses attempt to extract more work from their employees, and employees try to evade work. Each partner's contribution must be established in the give-and-take interaction between them. The outer limits of role relationships are negotiable, and role partners test one another to establish these limits. Only by understanding the nature of social interaction and how it works can we find out how roles operate in real life, in action.

A crucial element in these negotiations is the extent of each role partner's commitment to the other and to the role. One partner may have a greater stake in both and would stand to lose more if the relationship were discontinued, so this person will contribute more to its continuation and tolerate a lower level of performance from the partner. It is said, for instance, that in love, one partner loves, the other partner lets himself or herself *be* loved. A husband who is more in love with his wife than his wife is with him will have to try harder to make the relationship work and make more compromises and sacrifices. This pattern could not have been predicted by examining the formal content of the role of husband or wife. It must be seen in the unfolding of an actual relationship, through the process of social interaction.

Social Interaction and Deviant Behavior

In the give-and-take of social interaction, people eventually find out if they are—or are not—equally committed to their own role and status obligations (W. J. Goode, 1960b). Many people assume that, simply by occupying a certain status, a person automatically accepts its demands and expectations. Often this is not the case. Through the process of interaction, you sometimes find out that your role partner is not committed to the norms. For instance, two corporate executives may find out, over cocktails, that each is a socialist. Two weightlifters may reveal to each other that they are homosexuals. Two members of a church choir may find out that they both smoke marijuana. How does this mutual revelation occur? What gives social interaction the power to expose deviant behavior and even to stimulate it?

The dynamic, give-and-take quality of interaction makes it a process of continuous disclosure. One person's response to the other is rarely predictable in detail. Every response opens up a range of possibilities. One individual may flirt with the world of deviation by engaging in small, tentative steps. **Exploratory gestures**—actions that are slightly, but not seriously, deviant—permit either of the two role partners to stick his or her neck out a little and to retreat if the other objects to them.

> My exploratory gesture functions as a cue to you; your exploratory gesture is a cue to me. By a casual, semi-serious, non-committal or tangential remark I may stick my neck out just a little way, but I will quickly withdraw it unless you, by some sign of affirmation, stick *yours* out. I will permit myself to become progressively committed but only as others, by some visible sign, become likewise committed. . . . Each actor may contribute something directly to the growing product, but he may also contribute indirectly by encouraging others to advance, inducing them to retreat, and suggesting new avenues to be explored (Cohen, 1955, pp. 60–61).

Juvenile delinquency is a good example of the way people sometimes use interaction to explore deviancy. Suppose one boy engages in a slightly deviant act, like stealing a candy bar. A second may then encourage the first by voicing words of approval and by stealing a more valuable item, like a pair of sneakers. The two may spur each other on by their mutual encouragement, and they may eventually steal a car—not something that either boy would have done on his own. Such an act comes as a result of the exploratory process: engaging in slightly deviant ac-

Exploratory gesture An action that individuals enact in order to determine others' reaction to it, to test whether they may move even further in a particular direction.

tions, being rewarded for them by the other person, and going on to further and more serious deviancy.

SOCIAL INTERACTION: A CREATIVE PROCESS

Interaction influences human behavior in ways that such concepts as "role" and "status" cannot fully explain because, despite the strength of norms, many partners establish personal relations that move beyond socially acceptable limits. Social interaction has an emergent, fleeting quality that roles and statuses, which are more stable and solid, do not have. Social structure is quite distinct from the specific individuals who occupy positions within it. If the president of the United States dies in office, the office of the presidency remains and must be filled. The United States government is thus a social structure. In contrast, social interaction is a process, not a structure; it is something that happens, not something that exists. Consequently, it is subject to a great deal more change and reinterpretation than social structure is. This quite spontaneous, dynamic quality makes unconventional, rule-breaking, or deviant behavior not only possible but commonplace.

In short, we do not know everything there is to know about the way people relate to one another simply by knowing their statuses and their roles. These "structural" factors cannot explain crucial aspects of social life. For a fuller picture, we need to examine interaction—which focuses on spontaneity and process—rather than structure. Social interaction is a creative process that helps explain how role obligations are interpreted, how role partners negotiate their rights and obligations, and how deviant behavior emerges.

The Presentation of Self

The way we see ourselves depends to a great extent on how we think others see us. It is extremely difficult to maintain a certain self-image when no one around you accepts it. If your teachers, friends, and parents call you "stupid," it isn't easy to imagine that you are another Einstein. Yet other people's images of us are to some degree under our control. Most of us try to present favorable images of ourselves to others. Much social interaction, then, involves managing impressions that others will receive of us by suppressing certain unfavorable traits and stressing favorable ones. In short, life in society can be thought of as a kind of play in which each of us is an actor. Every one of us is always on stage, always in performance (Goffman, 1959).

In nearly all social interaction, there is an element of **impression management** (Goffman, 1959, pp. 208–237). This means that we stage or present ourselves to others in ways that tend to be favorable to our interests or images. We behave in public in ways that are different from the ways we act in private, totally unobserved by others. And we act in ways that are not entirely spontaneous; there is a certain degree of calculation and artifice in our public presentations and demeanors. We project contrived images of ourselves to others, usually without being aware of it. Most of us will comb our hair, wash our faces, select reasonably clean and acceptable clothing, and make sure we are properly but-

Impression management Presenting a public image of oneself to others, one that is, one thinks, more favorable than the image that would be obtained as a result of viewing one's private self.

Most of us engage in a "presentation of self"—managing impressions that others will receive of us by suppressing unfavorable facts and stressing favorable ones. We are often "on stage," in a kind of performance.
Allen Green/Photo Researchers

toned and zipped up in the appropriate places before going out in public. When interacting with others, we tend to obey certain rules of decorum; we try not to belch, emit flatulence, or pick our noses in public. We do not say absolutely anything that comes to mind. Rather, we are likely to say things that make us appear to be as sane, reasonable, worthy of respect as possible. We resent people's walking into our houses or rooms without knocking because that does not allow us enough time to prepare a proper image of ourselves and our quarters. We want to have a chance to eliminate the impression of a negative character that we allow to appear in private. We would resent anyone's reading our diaries, journals, or letters, or poking around in our drawers or closets, because that represents an intrusion into a private territory that has not been properly arranged for public exposure and sanitized of unfavorable indicators of who we are.

Of course, most people know the rules of social interaction very well. They conspire in the game of impression management, and "voluntarily stay away from regions into which they have not been invited" (Goffman, 1959, p. 229). Thus, for example, we always, or nearly always, knock on someone else's door before entering: We help the other person in the performance of impression management. Moreover, when we are in the company of others with whom we wish to maintain smooth social relations, we do not let on that we are aware of the artificial and managed nature of the impressions they are projecting to us. Any breach of this rule of etiquette is a tear in the social curtain; it "creates a scene" (Goffman, 1959, p. 210). In the course of polite social interaction, we do not, for example, remind a friend that she has a father who is an alcoholic, nor another that his mother resides in a mental institution. It disrupts or discredits the management of the impression that they have as respectable folk, worthy of our respect and esteem. To drop such reminders creates embarrassment and disturbs sociable social interaction. As a general rule, individuals attempt to protect the performances that others are putting on and the images they present. Revealing information that discredits the performances or images of their friends is considered a sign of disloyalty to the individuals or to their mutual group membership. One does not, for instance, gossip maliciously about an intimate to someone to whom that person is less close. If one does, one's friends will be critical of the action. One also does not reveal an intimate secret to a child for fear he or she will blurt it out to strangers.

In most interaction, discretion and tact are guiding principles for the parties involved. People who act in a tactless manner are criticized and may be socially shunned. They have violated the rules of polite social interaction. What they say or do is too revealing, too truthful: They have exposed the less-than-desirable reality behind the socially acceptable public image. They have violated one of the cardinal rules of social interaction: Create a good image to others and allow others to do the same. They have, in short, violated the rule of impression management.

Not everything we do will be evaluated favorably by the people with whom we interact. Even the hardest working students goof off from time to time; the most learned professors are inevitably ignorant of certain matters; and the most cautious and law-abiding citizens occasionally break the law. Our actions combine laziness and industry, intelligence and stupidity, good and evil. Only by looking at everything we do can we make accurate judgments about who we are and what we do overall. Yet no one actually sees the overall picture. Others always see bits and pieces of us and pass judgments based upon them. As a result, we try to expose those pieces that cast the most favorable light on us, our acts, and our intentions. This is called **information control:** making sure that others see our best side and not our worst side. Every one of us practices some form of information control. Consider a few examples:

> **Information control**
> Manipulating the presentation of facts about oneself to others to one's own advantage.

- Physicians who line the walls of their offices with framed or laminated diplomas and medical certificates;
- Students who plead with professors for higher grades by claiming to have received As in all their other courses;
- Married men and women who "cruise" singles bars with their wedding bands hidden in their pockets or purses;
- Professors who wear Phi Beta Kappa keys, jiggling them noisily in the middle of lectures;
- Heroin addicts who wear long-sleeved shirts, even in the hottest weather, to hide needle marks ("tracks") on their arms;
- Friends or acquaintances who "name-drop," or mention that they know celebrities.

Often this presentation of self is accomplished not by a single individual but by a group of individuals who are involved in a collective **presentation of self.** For instance, a restaurant's management might wish to make its customers believe that it is an elegant place. In this case, the **performance team** will be the restaurant's whole staff. The employees, especially those most visible to the customers, will be instructed in how to convey this impression. Coarse talk and slovenly dress will be discouraged; graceful movements, courtesy, and sensitivity to the customers' needs, stressed. Of course, the members of the performance team need not be taken in by the "act" at all—they know it is a performance; only the customers do not. The restaurant may be divided into regions: a **front region,** the area where the performance of respectability is played out in full view of the customers, and the **back region** (or **backstage**), hidden from the customers' view, where the performance is not neces-

> **Presentation of self** Conveying a certain image of ourselves to others in a conscious, intentional fashion.
>
> **Performance team** A group of individuals engaged in a collective presentation of self.
>
> **Front region** An area where the role performance of an individual or a performance team is visible to a given audience.
>
> **Back region** An area where role performance is hidden from the view of a given audience.
>
> **Backstage** See **Back region.**

sary. In the back region, the staff members do not have to perform, and they can "let it all hang out" (Goffman, 1959, pp. 106–140).

Role Commitment and Role Distance

Social life does not consist solely of false fronts. Some kinds of social interaction engage you more superficially and call for a more inauthentic presentation of self. Other activities and roles bring out more of "the real you." This is always a matter of degree; to some degree we all play roles and manage impressions. Some of us do it more than others do. And some situations call for more inauthenticity than others do. But there is always a measure of play acting in what we do and the impressions we contrive to create. Some athletes are highly competitive; they are not faking it when they perform on the playing field. Still, they are more competitive in some situations than in others—for instance, playing before a home-town crowd, while the coach is watching every move, during a playoff game, when their contracts are up for renewal, and so on. Many husbands and wives genuinely love each other and are affectionate in private as well as in public. And yet, there are times when one partner may not feel like expressing affection, but does so anyway, for fear of offending his or her spouse. Some degree of presentation of self is involved in practically all social interaction, especially when the interaction is tied to a social role. Some social roles call for a greater degree of commitment; they are embraced more enthusiastically. These reflect, to a greater degree, our private identities. Different individuals, likewise, throw themselves into the same role in varying degrees. For instance, some waiters and waitresses really are gracious: The "front" they present overlaps a great deal with their true selves. Still, the overlap is never perfect, and such factors as anticipating the tip, preserving the good name of the restaurant, keeping their jobs, and wanting to appear helpful and attentive always play a role in their behavior toward customers. Most waiters are involved in a fairly elaborate presentation of self to their customers. When one refuses to "play the game," remaining authentically surly and impolite, the chances are that his or her career as a waiter or waitress is likely to be brief.

Role distance Enacting the demands of a role with distance and detachment.

When people play roles that are inauthentic, they do so with a certain detachment. **Role distance** refers to playing roles in this detached way; it implies a kind of "wedge between the individual and his role, between doing and being" (Goffman, 1961b, p. 108). It is an announcement—public or private—that says, "This is not my true self; this isn't the real me." Identification with the role is low, and interaction with others is likely to be superficial and insignificant. Such distancing mechanisms prevent full identification with a role. Usually, roles that demand performances before large numbers of role partners—like those of waiters, teachers, and lawyers—produce a degree of role distance.

Audience Individuals with whom an individual, or a group of individuals, interact, and who witness and react to their behavior, especially role behavior.

Sociologists call those who witness the enactment of a role an **audience.** To a waiter, customers are the audience, for they witness the waiter's attempts to play the role. To a teacher, students make up an audience. Every one of us is both a performer of a role and an audience to the performances of others—our role partners. Typically, the audience accepts role performances as real. Most audiences are not aware of the "role distance," or the gap between the public and the private (or "true") selves of their role partners. Most interacting parties—friends, acquaintances, husbands and wives, colleagues at work—would feel shocked and betrayed if they were fully aware of their role partners' full range of attitudes and behavior toward them. We all occasionally say unflattering things about even our closest and dearest friends—things we would not want them to hear. By presenting a performance to others, we are not being insincere; we are ensuring smooth social relations. If our role partners saw the behavior and words we hide from them, they would feel that we are less friendly toward them behind their backs than we appear to be, face to face. Controlling the information they receive about us minimizes the potential conflicts in our interaction with them. Full disclosure in social relations would make interaction too abrasive and full of conflict.

ETHNOMETHODOLOGY

Interaction can be examined in a number of different ways. **Ethnomethodology** is the perspective that studies how interacting parties construct and learn to share definitions of reality in everyday life. Many of the things we do are based on assumptions we never examine or question. According to ethnomethodology, unspoken, unacknowledged understandings hold a society together (Garfinkel, 1967). We all make sense out of the events in our lives by working out explanations that fill in the gaps. Ethnomethodology attempts to uncover the process by which we try to make our lives meaningful. It strips away the "Of course!" that pervades social life and, in particular, interaction. Ethnomethodology is a perspective that forces us to examine what all of us take for granted.

Imagine that an ethnomethodologist asked you how you would explain crossing a street to a Martian. Most of us might say, "Just check to see if any cars are coming, and, if there aren't, cross." But what if our Martian asks, "Do we still cross the street if an earthquake hits the area?" We would reply by saying, "Of course not! If an earthquake hits the street you will have more important things to worry about than crossing or not crossing it." In other words, we follow certain rules implicitly; we adhere to them fairly closely, without being fully aware of their influence. They make up what are called **background understandings.** If the Martian were to ask, "What if we suddenly spotted our best friend on our side of the street, would we cross then?" You might respond, "Of course not. You stay and talk to the friend." The fact that no member of our own society would ever ask such questions shows how deeply embedded these rules are. They do not have to be explained, because we all know what they are. And yet many of our background understandings are not shared by members of other societies.

One ethnomethodologist (Garfinkel, 1967, pp. 25, 38–39) asked his students to write down ordinary, naturalistic conversations between a husband and a wife. One student presented a conversation in which the husband informed his wife that "Dana succeeded in putting a penny in a parking meter without being picked up." This statement might not make sense to an outside observer, especially one who is neither married nor a parent. Husbands and wives often communicate in a kind of shorthand; they know what the other means without spelling everything out. A different student, who had grown up in a poor neighborhood, interpreted this statement as follows: Dana was able to make the parking

Ethnomethodology A perspective within sociology that investigates how interacting parties come to share definitions of reality in everyday life.

Background understandings In ethnomethodology, assumptions we make about social rules that are rarely spelled out explicitly.

Face-to-face contact among intimates generally maintains and strengthens group membership. Routine and seemingly trivial interaction can have important consequences.

Junebug Clark/Photo Researchers

meter work by inserting a penny, instead of a dime, and wasn't caught by the police. What the husband really meant was that Dana, a 4-year-old boy, who had always had to be picked up to insert a coin into the parking meter, had grown tall enough to put it in by reaching up. With our intimates, we can make certain "background assumptions" about what they understand; they can "read between the lines." When people with whom we interact do not share these understandings, we are forced to become aware of them, and in doing so we often find out how we came to make them in the first place.

Ethnomethodologists believe that the best way of revealing these implicit understandings is to violate them and see how others react. One ethnomethodologist, Harold Garfinkel, asks his students to conduct experiments in which they make numerous normative violations: addressing their parents with formal titles, like "Mr." and "Mrs."; eating with their hands at the dinner table; attempting to haggle over the price of an item in a supermarket or a department store; asking "What do you mean?" in response to simple statements or greetings from others. In one experiment, someone told one of Garfinkel's students, "I had a flat tire." The student/experimenter responded by asking, "What do you mean, you had a flat tire?" Because we all share the same understanding of what having a flat tire is, the subject of the experiment became annoyed and flustered. He responded, "What do you mean, 'What do you mean?!' A flat tire is a flat tire. That is what I mean. Nothing special. What a crazy question!" (Garfinkel, 1967, p. 42). Another dialogue went like this:

SUBJECT: How are you?

EXPERIMENTER: How am I in regard to what? My health, my finances, my school work, my peace of mind, my . . .

SUBJECT: Look! I was just trying to be polite. Frankly, I don't give a damn how you are (Garfinkel, 1967, p. 44).

In these cases, the experimenters pretend that they do not share a common understanding of the world with the subjects. The subjects become irritated and frustrated, because these understandings seem so basic and obvious. These experiments reveal how delicately tied together are our relations with others, how necessary are these unspoken assumptions for orderly interaction. Ethnomethodologists argue that more traditional sociologists share many of these hidden assumptions, without sufficiently questioning or revealing them. For ethnomethodologists, the central task of sociology is to study the process by which members of a society construct meaning and rules.

EXCHANGE THEORY

Another perspective on social interaction is *exchange theory*. Exchange theorists argue that interacting parties maximize their self-interests. Two people related to each other because they both get something out of their relationship. Obviously, not all people can help others to the same degree, and we cannot always get from others just what we want. For one thing, we may not be able to offer them enough and, in any case, others are trying to do unto us what we are trying to do unto them—get as much as we can, and give as little as we can. In order to do so, we must bargain, and negotiate—in short, make exchanges with others. Exchange theorists predict who will have what kind of relationship with whom and what the conditions of those relationships will be.

For instance, we learn as we grow up that we should want to date physically attractive people—the more attractive, the better. It is a social "reward" to date an attractive partner. Obviously, not everyone can date the most physically attractive partner in his or her social environment. Why should he or she want to date us? What do *we* have to exchange? *Our* physical appearance, too, is evaluated, and constitutes a "reward" for potential dates. Every one of us commands a certain "price" on the dating "market," in relation to the competition. This price depends partly on our looks and partly on such other socially valued characteristics as our money, occupational prospects, and so on. Unattractive people may wish to date attractive ones, but such a date is not as rewarding to the latter.

Because we can all reward others in different ways, however, we can trade off different characteristics, behavior, or rewards. When we find discrepancies in the attractiveness of dating partners, we usually find other traits exchanged in place of good looks. An attractive woman may date a less attractive man who is very wealthy, for example. An intelligent woman may date a less intelligent man who happens to be a great lover. Exchange theory argues that the sum total of the value of the characteristics of dating partners will balance out, all things considered. So far, what we have can be considered a "fair exchange." Each partner commands roughly the same "market value," even though in some characteristics, one will be higher and the other lower.

Exchange theorists also address themselves to "unequal" exchanges. One "more desirable" partner can sometimes date a "less desirable" partner, one who commands a lower "price" on the dating market. In this case, according to exchange theory, the more desirable partner will have less interest in maintaining the relationship than will the less desirable partner. The less desirable partner must "pay," or exchange, more to maintain the relationship with the more desirable one. This means that the more desirable partner has the upper hand in the relationship and can extract more rewards from the less desirable one. Being with someone less desirable is, of course, less rewarding for the more desirable partner, but this can be made up if the less desirable partner gives up more rewards. For instance, a woman who is considered less desirable than a certain man may be able to date that man, but only if she yields readily to him sexually. And a less desirable man may be able to date a more desirable woman, but only if he spends more money on her, tolerates less sexual access, or is extremely indulgent of her faults (Waller, 1937; Edwards, 1969; Laws and Schwartz, 1977, pp. 104–116). Of course, dating is not the only type of social interaction examined by exchange theorists; they contend that this bargaining with social rewards characterizes all social relationships (Homans, 1961; Blau, 1964).

THREE CASE STUDIES

Social interaction is a fundamental social process that has been examined closely by many sociological researchers. Among many other things, they have analyzed intimate, face-to-face contacts among skid row alcoholics (Wiseman, 1970); members of a religious sect (J. Lofland, 1966); homosexuals looking for "pick ups" (Delph, 1978); adherents of a "flying saucer" cult (Buckner, 1971); police detectives (Sanders, 1977); and female impersonators (Newton, 1972). They have looked at social interaction in cities (L. Lofland, 1973); prisons (Irwin, 1980); nudist camps (Weinberg, 1970) and nude beaches (Douglas and Rasmussen, 1977); and mental institutions (Goffman, 1961a). Every study of the social interaction within specific groups at particular times and places tells us something about interaction in general. Even unusual and atypical individuals relate to one another in ways that reveal universal features of social interaction. Yet every interactional setting also has unique roles and norms. The three studies of face-to-face interaction that follow have been selected to show the similarities and differences between routine, everyday life interaction and the way people relate to one another in specific settings. How do people manage to move in and out of concrete settings, interacting with one another by observing (and, sometimes, ignoring) norms that are both general and specific at the same time?

Women as Police Officers

The police constitute an extremely cohesive, peer-oriented fraternity, whose members stick together both on and off the job. The police are also a paramilitary body, with strongly defined and quite traditional attitudes about masculinity. Most police officers believe that policing is a "man's work." During the past decade or two, the number of women police officers has increased significantly in the United States. How do police*men* react to the introduction of police*women* into what has traditionally been an all-male work setting?

What are the relevant norms? On the one hand, one norm makes all officers colleagues—that is, people who must be treated as professional equals. On the other, many policemen believe that women are inferior, especially as officers in police departments. How do the men on the beat resolve this dilemma? And how do the women on the beat deal with these reactions?

To answer these questions, sociologist Susan Martin (1978) joined the Washington, D.C., Metropolitan Police Reserve Corps, a volunteer citizens' organization, where she received training, wore a uniform, and patrolled a beat with regular officers. She interviewed more than fifty police officers, half men and half women. Almost without exception, the men interacted with the female officers primarily on the basis of their gender—which these men regarded as inherently subordinate. In a number of ways, they attempted to "keep them in their places."

One such technique involved verbal cues. Women were frequently referred to as "ladies," "broads," or "girls." A "lady" is expected to be dainty, demure, and proper. She is protected and, at the same time, dominated by men, who expect her to act within her "lady-like" role. "Broads" are also denied full control over their own lives. Seen primarily as sexual objects, they are not taken seriously in any other way; and when they try to assert themselves as full human beings, men ridicule them. The term "girl" implies frivolity and irresponsibility—a lack of power and independence. The policemen's use of language reminds the female police officers that their male colleagues regard them as inferior, and this, in fact, keeps them in an inferior position.

Joking and verbal putdowns are two other techniques of keeping women in their place. When the researcher, on duty in a scout car with a male officer, banged her knee on the car radio and, as a result suffered a large bruise, her partner asked, "What did you do, dear, break a fingernail?" (Martin, 1978, p. 52). In another case, a male and female officer were assigned for a tour of duty together. Throughout this tour, the man repeatedly told his partner to walk three paces behind him. He thought this joke so funny that he told it to his fellow male officers.

Nonverbal messages also helped the men to deny their female colleagues' right to be treated as equals. The policemen often put their arms around the policewomen with whom they worked; they also kissed, nibbled, and made passes at them, and lit cigarettes and opened doors for them. One female officer had just made an arrest. In the station, in full view of the prisoner and other officers, a male officer walked in and kissed her on the back of the neck. His kiss reminded her and the man she arrested that even though she had police powers, she was still "just a woman."

In such a "difficult interactional environment," a female police officer must assert her right to be treated as a colleague and not a sex object. The women want to be thought of as "just another officer," but the men resist. Some of the policewomen respond to the treatment of their male colleagues by ignoring it and trying to do the best job they can. They fear retaliation by their superiors who, by and large, support the men. Others attempt to "fight back." One male officer greeted a policewoman with, "Hey, baby, how ya doing?" She asked, "Are you talking to me?" He answered in the affirmative. She then said, "You don't know me that well. When I tell you my name is 'baby' and I ask you to address me that way, o.k. Until then my name is Officer—." This woman acquired the reputation of being "stuck up." Another woman explained, "If I'm unfriendly I get labeled a snob . . . which you can't be. If I'm friendly some of them think, 'she's looking at me.' If I act as I generally am

Most women police officers must do their jobs in a difficult interactional environment. Male officers typically hold a traditional view of what is a "woman's place," and rarely treat women as full equals or colleagues.

Steve Kagan

[warm and friendly] there are some who figure 'she's an easy catch.' What you have to do is catch it on the first remark and let them know where they stand. If you laugh it off, it doesn't do any good. . . . They take it as encouragement" (Martin, 1978, p. 57).

The author concludes that the policewoman's problems relating to her male colleagues are not specific to police settings. Male-female interaction on the job is determined by the relative positions of men and women in American society. Only when our culture as a whole moves in the direction of greater sexual equality will female officers be treated as equals on the job (Martin, 1978, 1980).

The Singles Bar

A sociologist and a senior sociology major investigated the singles-bar scene in New York City. They focused on the interaction taking place in these bars, where men and women go to meet people of the opposite sex (Allon and Fishel, 1977, 1979). Despite the growing acceptability of singles bars, something of a stigma is still attached to them. A generation ago, this stigma stemmed from the bars' air of disrepute, even deviance. Today's stigma—being considered a loser—is different. Presumably, people who go to bars for companionship do not have any other means of finding it. Bargoers, therefore, go out of their way to tell each other that they are not dependent on singles bars for meeting new people. These men and women wish to project a confident, secure, and slightly aloof image.

As one man put it, "Everyone knows why you're here: You want to meet people. But at the same time no one wants to seem overanxious. You have to be very cool about it and the tougher I act as a guy, the cooler people think I am. Besides, I really don't need to be here: I know lots of people. I just happened not to be doing anything tonight, so I thought I would drop by for a few laughs." A woman expressed the same sentiment this way: "I do want to meet new men to go out with, but I don't want them to think I'm hard-up for a date. I try not to seem too excited if a guy asks for my number or asks to take me out. I want him to think he's only one of many even if he's not. Keeps them on their toes, too. Guys can be real smart-asses, especially if they think you really want them" (Allon and Fishel, 1977, p. 17).

This aloofness created interaction that made both parties defensive, inauthenic, lacking in spontaneity, and anxious; both felt pressured and strained about faking an image they hoped would win them approval. Bargoers were putting on a front, interacting *to* and *at* each other—but not always with each other (Allon and Fishel, 1977, p. 19). At the same time they had to demonstrate to the people to whom they were speaking that they were interested (if they were, of course). These conflicting desires forced the two parties back and forth between role distance (acting aloof) and role commitment (acting interested in the other person). There is, in other words, a tension between "alienation" and "sociability." This tension made interaction ambivalent and tentative.

Every person in these singles bars was checking out the available "action"—sizing up and sounding out potential partners. Men and women judged potential partners by different criteria. Although both were looking for physically attractive partners, this was more important to the men. The women were more concerned with having long-term relationships. When a woman met a man, she attempted to find out if he was a "good prospect." She was looking for a man with a steady, well-paying job and feared starting a relationship with a man who did

Patrons in a disco usually put on a front to one another, making real intimacy very difficult.
Louis Goldman/Photo Researchers

not have a steady job or a decent salary. Such a man, she reasoned, was not capable of starting a family in the near future. The men, in contrast, were far more concerned with the present, with having a good time in the short run. They tended to focus primarily on the women's looks. After that, the main things they wanted to find out were whether the women they were talking with lived alone and where they lived.

This tendency to look around for the "best" available partner colored the interaction between men and women in bars. The possibility that there might have been a more desirable partner in the bar, coupled with the desire not to appear too overeager, produced interaction marked by continual shifts of attention. A man or woman might be talking to person one, looking at person two, touching the arm of person three, and thinking about person four. Stares around the bar tended to wander rather than focus on any one man or woman.

Looking and being looked at can be thought of as "nonverbal sales and purchase of bodies" (Allon and Fishel, 1979, p. 137). Glances assess the "value" of a potential partner's physical attractiveness. Bar patrons "size up" and "put a price on" a face and a body. Their own bodies, and the bodies of others, were "pieces of objective territory" (Allon and Fishel, 1979, p. 137) to be observed and meticulously evaluated. They were very conscious of one another's looks—including body size and proportions, body parts, faces, hair, and clothing. Of course, you evaluate how others look while your own looks are being evaluated by them. So most bargoers were working hard at the art of impression management— to "sell" themselves, to "come across successfully"; others worked hard at being "bought."

The patrons of singles bars may appear to be sad, lonely, desperate people. To some extent, they are. They work very hard to "make it" with other people—and to deny that they are doing so. They become "frantic achievers" in human relationships. The authors of the study feared that sincerity and generosity were giving way to phoniness and cynicism. They felt that perhaps they, too, had fallen into the trap of "pasting on false smiles," offering insincere compliments to others, and avoiding real intimacy and commitment by talking with as many different people as they could. "As we tried so hard to be sociable and make points with others in the bars, did not our alienation, our out-of-touchness with ourselves and others, show up all the more blatantly?" (Allon and Fishel, 1977, p. 24). But the very fact that insincerity was such a successful social tactic in these bars implies that it was acceptable to some and unnoticed by others.

Poker as Social Interaction

The setting is Gardena, California. Playing poker for money is not only legal here, it also seems to be the town's major industry. Eight players are sitting around a green felt-covered table; in front of each player is a pile of poker chips; some of them are large, and some, very small. The players represent both sexes and a wide range of ages, races, and manners of dress. Two of the players are tourists and have rarely played the game before, two are professionals who have spent a large portion of their lives making a serious study of the game, and four are regular but less-than-frequent players.

Betty and Jack, the tourists, have lost hundreds of dollars after only two or three hours of play. They have very few chips in front of them, and they are ready to quit. Their explanation for their poor performance is that they ran into a streak of bad luck. "You can't win with lousy cards," Jack sighs. Betty agrees. Over the course of the evening, when they were dealt a hand, they studied it intently. If it was good, they became visibly excited, began fingering their chips, and asked, "Whose turn is it to bet?" Their play is *egocentric*—that is, focused entirely on their own hand, unconcerned with the hands of their opponents. They fail to recognize that "poker is perhaps the ultimate game of human interaction" (Hayano, 1984, p. xiv). In truth, to win, it is not necessary to have a good hand. You can win with a bad hand and lose with a good one. All that is necessary is that you have a better hand than your opponents when the hands are declared.

Sally and Fred are the professionals. They barely glance at their cards when they are dealt. Poker, they realize, operates according to the "minimax" principle: Minimize your losses and maximize your wins. This means folding your hand early when you know your opponents have better hands and convincing them to stay in and bet heavily against you when you have a better hand. But how do they do this? How do Sally and Fred know when their hands are better or worse than their opponents'? Poor and average players telegraph their hands to their opponents; one need only read their body language to be able to read their hands. A telegraph (or "tell" to players) is an unintentional, involuntarily sent signal that reveals information about a player's hand or what the player intends to do. Examples of "tells" include using a nervous, strained, quavering voice; talking compulsively or loudly; questioning whose turn it is to bet or how much the betting limit is; adopting an overly attentive posture; coughing; straightening one's back; grabbing a stack of chips; holding one's hands in a tight, rigid position; flicking cards impatiently; and so on.

> The classic, most obvious tells are positive or negative affect displays, such as when amateurs smile, touch their noses, sit up straight when they are ready to bet a strong hand, or slump down when they have a losing hand.

Tells are also indicated by overly strong or hesitant betting movements, general attentiveness, an increase in talking, gaze direction, posture corrections . . ., and an overall interest in the hand in play and the size of the pot. These cues are common tells which amateur players frequently display, and which are easily recognized by experienced players. With startling accuracy professionals can ascertain what the exact hand value of an opposing player is by considering his movements in relation to opening or calling position, the number of cards drawn, the player's betting or checking decision, his emotional condition, and whether he is winning or losing. Amateurs, literally, are "read" (Hayano, 1980, p. 114).

Reading a "tell," however, is a difficult proposition; the message is there only to the experienced player. A few players, like Betty and Jack, are so obvious in their signals that they send messages with practically every hand to all but the most inexperienced players. Most players are not quite so obvious, and reading their gestures takes more skill.

At best, only about 5 percent of all the poker players in casinos and card clubs take a serious interest in the study of tells, because it is an extremely difficult and time-consuming task that requires many hours of total concentration in every playing session. . . . [However,] the very best players, the consistent winners . . . carefully observe and analyze the behavior of others, search for patterns between behavior and how certain hands are played and then make their own decisions based on their observations. This elaborate skill alone gives them quite an advantage. Some authorities estimate the professional poker's edge from studying others to be as high as 20 percent over their less skilled tablemates. In monetary terms, avoiding bad calls while eliciting calls from opponents can produce net differences of thousands of dollars per month for the regular high-stakes player (Hayano, 1979, p. 20).

At the same time that expert players read "tells" given off by other players, many also project false "tells"—that is, they deliberately send signals that communicate something that isn't true, but that is, in fact, a tactfully constructed lie. For example, a player may say "Raise!" out of turn, thus convincing some of the other players that he or she has an unusually powerful hand and causing them to drop out. Or a player might deliberately cough when bluffing. "The opponent, hopefully astute enough, soon recognizes this pattern of coughing and bluffing. In a crucial hand of the game when the stakes are raised, the deceiver coughs again, but this time he is not bluffing and so wins a wallet-breaking pot from his confused opponent" (Hayano, 1980, p. 117).

Some expert players may send out deliberate "anti-tells," which are "movements which appear to be tells but are displayed according to some random pattern unknown to observers. A player may gesticulate wildly or talk loudly according to a plan known only to himself. Opponents, as decoders, then have a difficult time unraveling this seemingly random relationship between behavior and the quality of a player's poker hand" (Hayano, 1980, p. 117).

By climbing to the top of the competitive pyramid, the best poker players have shown themselves to be among the most observant students of human behavior. Through the control of verbal and nonverbal messages, they can interpret, deceive and often financially destroy their less skillful opponents. How does one attain these skills or become a better poker player? . . . In the end, the thousands of hours at the poker table the experienced player has accumulated, in observing many kinds of players under varied conditions and stakes, is the touchstone. For the amateur or beginning player who cannot distinguish lies from truths, or tells from tricks, the teachers are there in almost every card club and casino. Unfortunately, in most cases, the lessons are quite costly (Hayano, 1979, p. 22).

The game of poker parallels everyday life. We are rarely completely candid about our intentions. We all deceive in varying ways and to varying degrees, presenting ourselves as smarter (or dumber), more—or less—virtuous, deserving, or desirable than we know we are. We protect ourselves from the reactions of others, trying not to reveal too much—for instance, by not letting on that we care about someone else when we do, or by pretending that we care more than we do. Our actions, whether intentionally or unintentionally, are geared toward eliciting a certain kind of reaction from others. And often, we project behavioral "tells" that the expert reader of social interaction can pick up and act on. In short, "Students of communication and deception have much to learn from people whose professions demand that they be skilled in manipulating others by feigning truths and disguising lies. Surely the study of human behavior does not lie solely within the laboratories and field settings of academic social scientists" (Hayano, 1979, p. 22). Bluffing, "bullying, and lying are not confined to poker tables. Our understanding of what professional poker players do over the cardroom table may very well be significant in detecting deception and distorted structures of communication in everyday life" (Hayano, 1980, p. 119; see also Hayano, 1982).

SOCIAL INFLUENCE

If two people tell you contradictory stories, which one do you believe? If two politicians are running for office, which one gets your vote? With dozens of brands of each product on the market—soft drinks, paper towels, cars, cough remedies, computers, television sets—which one do you purchase? If two charities compete for the same $20 bill in your wallet, to which do you contribute?

Most of us imagine ourselves to be hard-headed, rational, evidence-demanding creatures. We believe the argument using the most valid evidence and the most compelling logic; we vote for the best available candidate; we buy the best product for the price; we contribute to the worthiest charity.

In reality, however, if we are at all like other people, our rationality will be strongly tempered by distinctly irrational forces. Practically every study that has ever been conducted on social influence has shown that our decisions are not an unambiguous reflection of the rationality we so boldly proclaim. Our compliance in social interaction with others is often a thoughtless, almost automatic response to forces of which we may not be entirely aware, whose influence we would probably deny if asked about them.

An experiment conducted by psychologist Ellen Langer (1978) showed that people will agree to do favors for others if reasons are given, even if the reasons are meaningless. When Langer approached people waiting in line to use a copy machine and asked, "Excuse me, I have five pages. May I use the copy machine?," only 60 percent complied. When she supplied a reason, the results were strikingly different. When she asked, "Excuse me, I have five pages. May I use the copy machine because I'm in a rush?," 94 percent complied with the request. Fair enough, you might say; the request is reasonable, and perhaps those who let her ahead were not in so much of a rush. The justification, "because I'm in a rush" seemed to be a valid reason for others to let her cut ahead in line. But Langer showed that it was not the reasonableness of the request that led to the higher level of compliance in the second case than in the first. Rather, the simple use of the word "because" was the key to compliance. When Langer tried cutting in line by asking, "Excuse me, I have five pages. May I use the copy machine because I have to make some copies?," she received 93 percent compliance, almost exactly the same as when she used a rational-sounding excuse. This makes no sense at all; *of course*, she wanted to make some copies—why else would she be using a copy machine? *Everyone* waiting in line wanted to make copies. The simple use of the word "because" influenced nearly everyone to comply mindlessly with the request.

At this very moment, thousands of advertisers, market researchers, campaign managers and workers, consultants to charities—"compliance practitioners"—are trying to figure out a way of influencing you to purchase a certain product, vote for a certain candidate, and contribute to a certain charity. Compliance practitioners make use of six basic principles to influence your decisions: reciprocity, consistency, social proof, liking, authority, and scarcity (Cialdini, 1984). Although you may not be aware of it, each one of these principles has a subtle but powerful effect on what you believe and feel and how you act.

The principle of *reciprocity* dictates that we feel an obligation to repay someone who has given something to or done something for us. (The Portuguese word for "thank you" is *obrigado*, or *obrigada*, if the speaker is female, which means "I am obliged.") Followers of the Krishna sect make use of this principle when they solicit contributions for their religion. By giving a potential donor a flower, even if it is unwanted, they increase the likelihood of a forthcoming donation. This tactic has worn thin with many people who, knowing how and why it works, avoid Krishnas wherever they spot them. But even this avoidance strategy shows the strength of the rule, because very few, even those negatively disposed to begin with, and even if they are aware of being manipulated, can accept the "gift" without feeling the need to reciprocate.

When walking through the streets of San Juan a few years ago, my wife and I were approached by a woman who offered us a free breakfast at an expensive hotel the next morning. We showed up at the appointed hour, along with eleven other couples; each couple was seated at a table with a man. After the breakfast, we were shown a film, and then we listened to a talk extolling the excellent investment opportunity presented by purchasing land in Florida from the corporation sponsoring the breakfast. After the film and the speech, the man at the table attempted to talk us into buying land from his firm. It was a classic "hard sell," and he was an extremely effective, persuasive salesman, but we simply were not interested, and we resisted to the bitter end. His sales pitch was interrupted four times by an announcement that yet another couple had made a purchase of a plot of land in Florida; the announcement was greeted by applause from the twelve sales representatives. The rate of success of this venture—four sales out of a total target population of only twelve couples, simply pulled in off the street—was extraordinarily high. (Assuming that there were no "shills" in the bunch, which may or may not have been true.) Why were four couples willing to part with thousands of dollars to purchase land sight unseen, whose value they couldn't even remotely estimate? The answer, astonishing as it might sound, lay in the reciprocity principle: They felt obliged to the corporation for giving them a free breakfast! The breakfast, delicious as it was, probably cost the corporation at most $10 per couple; on the other hand, the land the four couples purchased cost thousands. This disparity should strike us as glaring. Yet, such is the beauty of the reciprocity principle: It takes us far beyond the boundaries of rationality and logic.

The second principle, *commitment* (or *consistency*), states that, once we have committed ourselves to a certain line of action, we tend to defend that decision. Moreover, the greater the effort we make to follow that line of action, the more that we value, support, and defend that decision and that line of action. For instance, bettors at a horse race are more strongly convinced that their choice is right after making their bets than before (Knox and Inkster, 1968). "Once a stand has been taken, the need for consistency pressured these people to bring what they felt and believed into line with what they had already done" (Cialdini, 1984, p. 67). The principle of consistency operates in the classic "foot-in-the-door" technique: A salesperson gets a potential customer to agree to make a small commitment, then increasingly larger ones; eventually, the customer agrees to quite substantial requests.

In an experiment, two social psychologists approached homeowners with a truly preposterous request: to agree to have huge billboards placed on their front lawns bearing the sign, "Drive Carefully." To give them an idea of how their properties would look with the billboards on them, the researchers showed them a photograph of an attractive house nearly completely obscured by just such a sign. Naturally, the great majority (83 percent) refused the request. A different group of homeowners, however, was highly compliant: 76 percent said that they would allow the sign to be placed on their front lawns. What was different about the second group? Why would they have agreed to such a bizarre request? Two weeks before being approached about the sign, each homeowner in the second category had been asked to display a tiny, three-inch-square sign that read, "Be a Safe Driver" in a window in the house. As a result, these homeowners developed self-images that included seeing themselves as concerned with public safety and welfare. The original small commitment led to self-images that were consistent with cooperating with good causes—and with agreeing to the second, much larger request (Freedman and Fraser, 1966).

The consistency principle works best when someone has made a public declaration of a given position, in the form of a statement or an act. "Whenever one takes a stand that is visible to others, there arises a drive to maintain that stand in order to *look* like a consistent person" (Cialdini, 1984, p. 87). Weight-loss and quit-smoking clinics make use of this principle by having clients state their intentions in public. Some even go so far as to require their clients to write down their goals and show them to as many friends, relatives, coworkers, and neighbors as possible. A classic experiment investigated the influence of this principle (Deutsch and Gerard, 1955). Three groups of students were shown a set of lines and asked to estimate their length. The students in one group had to commit themselves publicly to their judgments by writing them down, signing their names, and turning them into the experimenter. Students in the second group were asked to write estimates down in private on a Magic Writing Pad, which they then erased by lifting the pad's plastic cover. And students in the third group simply kept their estimates in their heads. All three groups were then supplied with new information suggesting that their original estimates were wrong, and they were given the opportunity to revise them. The students who kept their original estimates in their heads were the most likely to revise them in light of the new information. The students who had written the original estimates down privately on the Magic Writing Pads were somewhat more loyal to their original estimates and somewhat less likely to revise them in view of the new and more accurate information. But the students who had committed themselves to their original positions publicly by writing them down and handing them in, along with their names, were the most committed to these estimates and the least likely to revise them. "Public commitment had hardened them into the most stubborn of all." In short, "we are truest to our decisions if we have bound ourselves to them publicly" (Cialdini, 1984, p. 89).

The principle of *social proof* dictates that we are more likely to do or believe something if we see others doing or believing the same thing. Hardly anyone admits to liking "canned laughter" on a television comedy show. Why, then, do television executives use it? Are they stupid, foolish, ignorant, or are they, for some mysterious reason, ideologically committed to canned laughter? It works: That's why they use it. Consistently, audiences rate TV comedy shows with canned laughter more favorably, and actually laugh more often, harder, and longer at them, than shows without this artificial device. (This generalization holds most strongly for poor jokes and weak material.) We are most likely to turn to others or be influenced by them to the extent that we are uncertain about something; the more sure we are of something, the less strongly the principle of social proof works.

Social proof operates most strongly to the extent that the others we observe doing something are much like ourselves. One experiment (Hornstein et al., 1968) placed a number of wallets on the sidewalk in various locations around Manhattan; each one contained $2 in cash, a small check, and information about the wallet's owner. In addition, it contained a letter making it clear that it had been lost previously. The first finder explained in the letter that he had found the wallet and was happy to be of assistance to the wallet's owner, and he intended to return it. The wallet was wrapped in an envelope addressed to its owner. Two different sets of letters were enclosed in the wallets—one in standard English and the second in broken English, written by an individual who described himself as a recently arrived immigrant. The researchers made the reasonable assumption that most of the finders of the wallets would be Americans and would identify more closely with the writer of the letter written in standard English than the one in broken English. In fact, only 33 percent of the wallets that were in envelopes that contained the broken-English letters were returned, but twice as many (70 percent) that contained the standard-English message were returned. "These results suggest an important qualification of the principle of social proof. We will use the actions of others to decide on proper behavior for ourselves, *especially when we view those others as similar to ourselves*" (Cialdini, 1984, p. 142).

Liking is another principle of social influence: The more favorably we feel toward someone the more likely it is that we will be influenced by that person. Once again, the principle extends to similarity as well: We tend to like people who are similar to ourselves, and we therefore tend to be influenced by them, as well. In addition, we tend to like people who say positive things about us; we are "suckers for flattery," and we are therefore more likely to be influenced by them. But this varies by sophistication: More sophisticated individuals are more likely to be influenced by a mixture of flattery and criticism—with, however, flattery predominating. If the criticism comes first and the flattery last, the message works best; "we are fondest of evaluators who allow us to walk away experiencing the aftertaste of flattery's butter and the echo of its music" (Cialdini, 1984, p. 173). As with every one of these principles of social influence, we tend to underestimate the extent to which liking, similarity, and flattery influence us and our actions.

The liking principle has a number of fascinating implications. The good and bad things people associate with us, however valid or invalid the connection, influence how they feel about us. We all know the fate of the imperial messenger in ancient Persia who brought news of military defeats: He was slain. Had that same messenger brought news of victory on the battlefield, he would have been treated as a hero and been offered wine, food, and women of his choice. The poor messenger had nothing to do with Persia's victory or defeat; he just reported the news, he didn't make it. In Shakespeare's words: "The nature of bad news infects the teller." (And, likewise, good news imparts the teller with a positive aura.) In this way, too, are weather forecasters blamed for bad weather. Compliance professionals are aware of this principle, and try to establish a connection between their products and the things they know we'll like, such as lavish houses in the suburbs, expensive cars in our garages, and affluent, elegant lifestyles. Politicians, too, invoke this principle when they talk about the American flag, mom, and apple pie.

So powerfully does the liking principle work that people tend to strive to create a link between themselves and positively valued things and to sever links between themselves and negatively valued things—even if they had no hand in either. "An innocent association with either good or bad things will influence how people feel about us" (Lott and Lott, 1965; Cialdini, 1984, p. 185). For instance, we feel personally involved in the exploits of our favorite teams; if they win, we are elated, and if they lose, we are distressed. What fans actually wish to show is that they are *better* than fans of the opposing teams. The teams symbolize the fans themselves; when they win, the fans win, and when they lose, the fans lose in a very personal way. The fans' self-image is at stake, quite literally. When their teams win, they say, "*We* won." But when they lose, they say, "*They* lost" (Cialdini, 1984, pp. 191–199). Citizens of each country on Earth tend to follow this same principle: Any criticism of their nation represents an attack launched against themselves personally. Such feelings have touched off riots, wars, coups, and revolutions.

Authority is a fifth principle of social influence. As we saw in the Stanley Milgram experiment (see Chapter 2), subjects complied with the requests of a researcher, regardless of how bizarre they were, because of his authority. An extraordinarily high rate of incorrect prescriptions are written for medications by physicians in hospitals: the wrong dosage, the wrong combination of medications, even the wrong drug. And yet, nurses, pharmacists, and patients almost never question these mistakes because of the authority of the attending physicians (Cohen and Davis, 1981). Often, we even react to the *symbols* of authority, such as a respectable-looking, silver-haired, middle-aged actor selling us something on television.

Experiments back up the power of the authority principle. A jaywalker dressed in a pinstriped suit and tie was three and a half times more likely to be followed by pedestrians across the street against a red light than was a man dressed in a work shirt and trousers (Lefkowitz et al., 1955). People were over twice as likely to comply with a request to pick up discarded trash if the requester wore a uniform (92 percent) than if he wore ordinary street clothes (42 percent). Moreover, when college students were asked to guess the level of compliance such a request would elicit, they were fairly accurate with respect to the man in street clothes (50 percent versus the actual 42 percent), but were very far off for the man in uniform (63 percent versus the actual 92 percent). Once again, we tend to underestimate the power of authority in influencing what we do.

Scarcity, a sixth principle of social influence, often determines what we think, say, or do: "Opportunities seem more valuable to us when their availability is limited" (Cialdini, 1984, p. 230). Advertisers make use of this principle by announcing that they have only "a limited supply," that the "sale ends Sunday," that this is the customers' "last chance to save," that "time is running out—and so is inventory." An experiment asking subjects to rate the price and taste of cookies showed that they were most positive about those cookies that seemed to be in short supply (they were presented in a jar containing only two cookies) than those that seemed to be abundant (the jar contained ten cookies). Moreover, when the ten-cookie jar was *shown* to the subjects, but then taken away and replaced with a two-cookie jar, the subjects' ratings were significantly higher than if they were presented with the two-cookie jar initially (Worchel et al., 1975). In other words, "The drop from abundance to scarcity produced a decidedly more positive reaction to the cookies than did constant scarcity" (Cialdini, 1984, p. 249). Most highly rated of all the cookies presented to the subjects were those that became less available because, it was explained, other subjects wanted more of them. "Not only do we want the same item when it is scarce, we want it most when we are in competition for it" (Cialdini, 1984, p. 251).

Are we creatures of these six principles of social influence? Do we slavishly follow them, mindless robots unable to control our lives or choose the direction our social interaction takes? Are we condemned by forces of which we are ignorant and even unaware? Are we going to be eternally manipulated by the machinations of those who do understand these principles: used car dealers, politicians, fund raisers, advertisers, TV executives, perhaps even sociology professors? The answer is that once we are aware of these principles and understand how they act on us, the chances are that we will take steps to minimize their influence over us. We have choices in social interaction, but we are free to maximize those choices only when we are fully informed about what is going on.

SUMMARY

1. Social interaction introduces a dynamic, slightly unpredictable quality into social life.

2. Our expectations of others with whom we interact will influence how they act, even if those expectations are initially false.

3. Nearly all human behavior is social in nature; it is relational: All people take one another into account when they act.

4. In order for behavior to be social, some degree of common understanding is necessary; interacting parties must mean the same thing with their words and gestures when they attempt to communicate with one another.

5. Much interaction is nonverbal in nature.

6. Although roles are based on norms dictating what people who occupy specific statuses must do, these rules are not iron-clad; in the course of interaction, these rules are tested, reinterpreted, subtly transformed.

7. Interaction may help us understand whether or not we want to enter a certain role relationship in the first place.

8. Interaction may also lay bare the process of altercasting, or the process in which one role partner imposes on another a role that he or she does not accept or care about.

9. Role obligations may be negotiated; during the course of interaction, parties "sound out" one another to determine just how much each expects the others to fulfill their role obligations.

10. People attempt to present images to others that are mostly favorable and to suppress qualities that are unfavorable. This comprises the art of "impression management."

11. Sometimes impression management is conducted by "teams" that attempt to present a positive collective image to an audience.

12. Some roles are more completely embraced than others; actors keep a certain role distance from roles that they embrace less completely, acknowledging that the roles do not embody their "true" selves.

13. Ethnomethodology studies interaction by examining the process by which people arrive at certain assumptions about the social world.

14. One perspective that examines interaction is exchange theory, which views relations in terms of bargaining and negotiating for social rewards.

15. Many studies of social interaction have been conducted; three of them illuminate the concepts explained in this chapter: women as police officers, the singles bar, and the poker game.

16. Social influence takes place in social interaction; six factors in influence are: reciprocity, commitment, social proof, liking, authority, and scarcity.

SUGGESTED READINGS

Natalie Allon, *Urban Life Styles*. Dubuque, Iowa: William C. Brown, 1979.
A disclosure of social relations and interaction within three "modern urban life settings": group dieting, health spas, and singles bars. Each setting is an attempt to authenticate the participant's self-image, yet each entails a certain measure of insincerity. How is this dilemma resolved?

Elliot Aronson, *The Social Animal* (4th ed.). New York: W. H. Freeman, 1984; and Elliot Aronson (ed.), *Readings about the Social Animal*. New York: W. H. Freeman, 1984.
An engagingly written, insightful examination of the subject of social psychology through specific topics, including conformity, mass communication, self-justification, aggression, prejudice, interpersonal attraction, and interpersonal communication and sen-

sitivity. One volume is the basic text, and the other is an anthology of readings.

Erving Goffman, *Forms of Talk*. Philadelphia: University of Pennsylvania Press, 1981.
Goffman studies talk as a form of social interaction.

Erving Goffman, *The Presentation of Self in Everyday Life*. Garden City, New York: Doubleday Anchor, 1959.
How do we present ourselves to others in social interaction? This book is the classic statement on impression management in social interaction.

Erving Goffman, *Relations in Public*: *Micro-Studies of the Public Order*. New York: Basic Books, 1971.
Rules govern our behavior in public. We are unaware of most of them; we take them for granted. Goffman explores the public "social order" wherein such rules may be uncovered.

Thomas M. Kando, *Social Interaction*. St. Louis: Mosby, 1977. A textbook covering the most important aspects and manifestations of social interaction; adopts a "humanistic" approach.

Lyn H. Lofland, *A World of Strangers*: *Order and Action in Urban Spaces*. New York: Basic Books, 1973.
How does city life influence social interaction in public? What "skills" do urbanites develop to survive and thrive in the city? Knowing very little about one another, how do city dwellers "code" one another to determine how to relate to one another? This book answers these questions.

Esther Newton, *Mother Camp*: *Female Impersonators in America*. Englewood Cliffs, New Jersey: Prentice-Hall, 1972.
A study of professional "drag queens" or female impersonators. Men present a "front" of themselves to an audience, pretending to be women. How do they accomplish this feat? How do audiences respond to their act? And how do female impersonators relate to one another? This fascinating book explains.

chapter **6**

SOCIALIZATION

Human infants are totally helpless, totally dependent on adults. Hours after birth, a newborn pony can walk—unsteadily, to be sure. A three-month-old chimpanzee is far more intelligent, alert, and inquisitive than a three-month-old human baby. Reptiles are totally self-sufficient after hatching from their eggs: but without adult care, human infants would perish in even the least harsh environment. This period of helpless dependency is called *infantilization* (Becker, 1962, p. 4), and it lasts longer in human beings than in any other animal species.

As a general rule, the more intelligent the animal, the longer it will be dependent on its parents. After all, the more intelligent the animal, the fewer instincts it has and the more it must rely on learning to survive. The greater the need for learning, the more time nature must allow for it. Hence, infantilization.

Social scientists call learning *socialization*—the process of coming to understand and live in a culture or subculture. The dictionary's main definition of the verb "to socialize" is "to make fit for human companionship." That definition comes very close to what sociologists mean by the process of socialization, the process we all pass through to become members of a society, a group, a subculture. Socialization is the process through which we acquire the values; beliefs; norms; and physical, mental, and social skills that make us human.

THE EFFECTS OF EXTREME ISOLATION

All socialization involves learning from specific agents, including parents. What happens to an infant if parents are absent? One way to find out might be to study infants who grew up without adult contact.

Intelligent animals are emotional creatures who hunger for warmth and affection. Of all animals, human beings are the most emotional, but this hunger also characterizes monkeys and apes to a lesser

In order to become human, infants need human contact. Children raised in total isolation cannot develop their innate capacity to walk, talk, or even focus their eyes. Socialization is a deeply face-to-face, interactional affair.

Bill Binzen/Photo Researchers

Infantilization The period of helpless dependency of infants on their parents.

Socialization The process of learning: especially refers to acquiring the values, attitudes, roles, and identities taught by our culture.

degree. In a classic set of experiments, Harry Harlow, a psychologist, isolated infant monkeys at birth from their mothers. He provided the infants with two substitute "mothers": one built of wire mesh and rigged up with a bottle containing milk; the other, covered with soft terry cloth but without any bottle. The infant monkeys consistently preferred to cling to the soft, terry-cloth "mother" rather than to the "mother" who dispensed food but was hard and stiff. Physical contact with a warm, soft object seems to be more important to growing infants than food itself.

Harlow also raised to adulthood a number of monkeys kept totally isolated from all contact with other monkeys, including their parents. When finally placed in the company of normal monkeys, these experimental animals were either listless and apathetic or hostile and fearful. They were not interested in, or able to mate with, monkeys of the opposite sex. The females among them were artificially impregnated and turned out to be negligent and even abusive mothers who refused to care for their offspring. Monkeys obviously need social contact to grow up to become normal adults (Harlow, 1958; Harlow and Harlow, 1965).

Human beings need intimate physical contact even more strongly than monkeys do, and human beings are even less able than monkeys to grow up normally without direct contact with parents or other agents of socialization. Unhappily, there have been cases documenting this: children who were kept alive in attics, basements, or back rooms by parents who did not hold, talk to, or interact with them in any way (usually, because they were illegitimate). These children, in other words, did not grow up experiencing the satisfaction of meaningful human contact. When they were discovered by the authorities, these children were even more handicapped than the monkeys in Harlow's experiments. They could not recognize sounds, walk, talk, or even focus their eyes to see things. They were totally inert, passive, and emotionless and did little more than urinate and defecate. They were less like human beings than like vegetables.

From the age of 20 months until she was more than 13 years old, Genie was kept by her father in the back room of a house, tied into a harness placed in a wire mesh cage. Only when her father fed her (barely

The "Wild Child" of Aveyron

In 1799 three hunters found a boy of about 11 or 12 years old at the edge of a vast forest in a part of France called Aveyron. The boy, completely naked, could only make animal-like noises, shuffled about on all fours, was "disgustingly dirty," and "insensible" to sounds and to smell. He "swayed back and forth ceaselessly like certain animals in the menagerie," and "bit and scratched" anyone who approached him. He was "indifferent to everything and attentive to nothing." Opening doors and "climbing upon a chair to get the food that has been raised out of reach of his hand" were beyond him. It was clear that this boy, this "wild child," was living "a completely animal existence" (Itard, 1962, pp. 4,6,8).

At first, the boy was paraded around Paris as a freak. One of those who saw him was a young physician named Jean-Marc-Gaspard Itard, who worked at the National Institute for the Deaf and Dumb. The director of that institute believed that the wild child should be placed in Itard's care. For five years Itard attempted to train the child, whom he named Victor, in the rudiments of French culture. He wrote two reports on his efforts, the first in 1801, the second in 1806. At the outset, Itard was optimistic: "Here is a subnormal boy who has lacked civilizing experience. If I give him this experience he will become normal." All he lacked was ordinary social contacts, "an essential part of the training of a normal civilized person."

Even after five years of devoted effort, the boy did not become fully human. His vocabulary never went beyond a half-dozen words (including the French words for "milk" and for "Oh God!"); he always walked in a shuffle combined with a trot; he never interacted "normally" with anyone; and he never advanced beyond the mental age of 2 or 3. Was the boy already retarded when he was abandoned? How old was he when he was left to survive on his own? We don't know. What we do know is that (in Itard's words) only "in the heart of society" can men and women attain their "natural destiny." Itard was wrong when he optimistically assumed that "environment could accomplish everything." Socialization, in order to work, must take place at a crucial time in the child's life. Time is an essential factor here: If certain things are not learned early, they will never be learned.

enough to keep her alive) or beat her with a wooden stick for making sounds did she have human contact. When she was discovered, Genie was "unsocialized, primitive, hardly human" (Curtiss, 1977). Except for high-pitched whimpers, she could say nothing. Shuffling from side to side, she walked only with difficulty. She was incontinent. From time to time, Genie flung herself into rages, flailing about, scratching, spitting, frantically rubbing her face, and attempting to hurt herself.

What does this dreadful case show? Just this: More than any other animal, human beings need one another to function properly, or at all. Human contact makes us human. We must learn, or be socialized, to do the things that our anatomy makes possible, like walking, talking, and even seeing. Human beings do not spontaneously do any of these things; we do them only when, as infants, we receive instruction from adult agents of socialization. For centuries, philosophers debated whether or not society's influence was corrupting or beneficial, whether "natural" men and women, raised in isolation from society, would be innocent and virtuous or "nasty, brutish," and short-lived. Today we know that a so-called natural man and woman would be distinctly unnatural—unable to perform even the simplest organic functions. The earlier in life an infant may be isolated from human contact, the longer that isolation lasts, the more extreme and complete it is, and the less human that child will be. Such infants will never grow up to be fully human.

NATURE OR NURTURE?

Nature versus nurture The debate between the view that biology determines human behavior and the view that environment largely does.

To what extent do heredity, on the one hand, and learning, on the other, control human behavior? This is the so-called **nature-versus-nurture** question. "Nature" is shorthand for the human organism's inborn biological features: our anatomy, organs, hormones, instincts, genes, chromosomes, and the like. "Nurture" includes whatever we learn or acquire through the process of socialization: environmental factors. For a century and a half or more, the advocates of the "nature" and the "nurture" positions have been debating each other. One side argues that biological factors determine human behavior; the other, that environment and learning do.

Charles Darwin gave the "nature" position a big boost in 1859, by publishing his book *On the Origin of Species*. If biological evolution was the key to animal behavior, why shouldn't the same be true for human behavior? During the nineteenth century, many thinkers believed that our actions are largely determined by instincts, which are inborn and unchanging. According to this theory, human beings form communities because we have a "herding" instinct; women bear and raise children because of the "maternal" instinct; wars are fought because of our "aggressive," or "killer," instinct; and so on.

The extreme "nature" outlook dominated the field into the twentieth century. The pendulum swung in the opposite direction largely as the result of the work of two researchers: Ivan Pavlov, a Russian physiologist, and John Watson, an American psychologist. Pavlov showed that even animal behavior is strongly influenced by learning by teaching dogs to salivate at the sound of a ringing bell. If salivation is strictly instinctual, then it should occur only in direct response to food. But Pavlov created learned, or *conditioned*, responses in animals by teaching them to associate the bell with food, so that they salivated when they heard the bell ring, whether or not food was actually present. Because humans are vastly more intelligent than dogs, our behavior should be governed much more by learning and far less by inborn biological factors.

Behaviorism A theory in psychology that argues that learning or socialization accounts for nearly all animal and human behavior.

Tabula rasa The view that, at birth, human beings are a "blank slate" onto which anything may be written; usually associated with the extreme "nurture" position of early behaviorists.

Conditioning Learning as a result of reward and punishment.

John Watson extended this basic insight into a nurture-oriented perspective that came to be called **behaviorism**. He argued that humans are almost infinitely changeable and can learn to be or do almost anything. Socialization, Watson believed, determines everything, for human beings have no instincts. This was called the **tabula rasa** view—that people are much like "blank slates" on which just about anything can be written. "Give me a dozen healthy infants," wrote Watson, "and my own specified world to bring them up in and I'll guarantee to take any one at random and train him to become any type of specialist I might select—doctor, lawyer, artist, merchant-chief and, yes, even beggar-man and thief, regardless of his talents, penchants, tendencies, abilities, vocations, and race of his ancestors" (Watson, 1925, p. 82). That behaviorist tradition has been carried on to this day in the work of B. F. Skinner, a behaviorist psychologist. Skinner (1971) argues that all socialization takes place through **conditioning**, learning by rewards and punishments. Organisms, including human beings, passively react to events in the environment. When we are rewarded for doing something, we tend to repeat it; if we are punished, we usually stop.

Most contemporary social researchers now agree that both the extreme "nature" and "nurture" positions are wrong. Biology and environment should not be conceived as two distinct and separate entities. It is far more fruitful to view them as intermingling and influencing each other. Human behavior is never a question of biology *or* environment—"nature" *versus* "nurture." Each factor is an inseparable element of the other; they "blend" together. Our natural, inborn characteristics make possible certain forms of behavior; our biological makeup certainly underlies many human activities. The fact that humans have vocal cords and sharks do not, a biological trait, means that we can sing operas and that they cannot. The fact that humans are warm-blooded makes skin-to-skin contact especially pleasurable and thus creates in us a need for physical affection. These physical traits make certain human actions—like singing or being affectionate—possible, but our environment, through socialization, activates this potential.

Biological characteristics not only make possible human behavior but also set limits upon it. Our potential abilities are immense, so immense that they are almost uncharted. We are only just beginning to understand our limits. But there are limits, nevertheless. Customs and behavior do vary a great deal throughout the world, but human behavior exhibits certain patterns, and biological factors partly explain them. Customs are not totally random, nor can cultures socialize their offspring any way they choose. No society can require its members to totally abstain from food, or to murder one another routinely, or to ignore the need of infants to be picked up and held. Once again, does this mean that "nature" or "nurture" is more important? No—it means that separating them is a futile exercise.

GROWING UP: THE DEVELOPMENT OF THE CHILD

Human behavior is overwhelmingly the result of learning or socialization, but learning takes place within specific, inherited channels. What we are capable of learning and when and how we can learn it are all to a great degree aspects of our biological, animal nature. Children's mental development, for example, goes hand in hand with their physical development. Children learn different things at different times, through a developmental sequence that progresses from infancy to adolescence. This maturation process has been described and analyzed by a number of social scientists.

George Herbert Mead: The Self

Piaget's work on the moral development of the child, discussed a few pages ahead, points to, but does not fully explore, the central role of social interaction in the process of socialization (see Chapter 5). The importance of social interaction was explored by George Herbert Mead (1863–1931), a philosopher and social psychologist who was the "founder" of social interactionism (see Chapter 1). A central concept in Mead's perspective was what he called the **self**, each individual's notion of his or her identity. People generally "verify" a certain identity by

Self The notion that each individual has of his or her own identity.

acting in a way that does so. If someone responds to the question, "Who am I?," with the answer, "I am an honest person," that person will find it hard to live with acts of theft. Mead argued that this self—this consistent image that makes each individual distinct from every other individual—is acquired during the process of socialization, through interaction with other human beings. In fact, according to Mead, learning is possible only as a result of the crucial process he called **taking the role of the other**.

Unlike Piaget, Mead did not specify more or less precise ages at which specific stages of socialization take place. He did, however, stress the crucial importance of communication and with it, of language. Mead strongly implied that socialization during the months and years when children do not yet speak a language (the **preverbal stage**) differs radically from socialization after they begin to speak (the **verbal stage**). All human beings, Mead stressed, interact with one another by interpreting the meaning of one another's behavior. No tool for learning what the members of a society mean is more efficient and effective than language. Consequently, Mead thought, the learning process of the preverbal stage is quite "rudimentary." Mead himself focused on the verbal stage, which he subdivided into two separate periods: the play stage and the game stage.

The Play Stage. In the **play stage**, a young child acts out imaginary roles, one at a time, and pretends to be a mail carrier, a mother, a doctor, a shopkeeper, and so on. This stage is crucial, because in it the child learns to take the role of the "other"—learns, that is, to see the world from the perspective of other people. Role-playing children act out a series of activities, each representing a separate role that is connected to the next one in the series. A child may, for instance, play at being a doctor and then a patient, or a shopkeeper and then a customer.

Taking the role of the other Seeing the world through the eyes of another person.

Preverbal stage In Mead's theory, the period during which children do not yet talk.

Verbal stage In Mead's theory, the period of childhood that begins with speech.

Play stage In Mead's theory, the period during which children act out imaginary roles, one at a time; facilitates taking the role of the other.

In the "play stage" suggested by George Herbert Mead, the child acts out imaginary roles, one at a time. For example, the child may pretend to be a mail carrier, a mother, a shopkeeper, or a doctor, enabling him or her to take the role of the other.

Alice Kandell/Photo Researchers

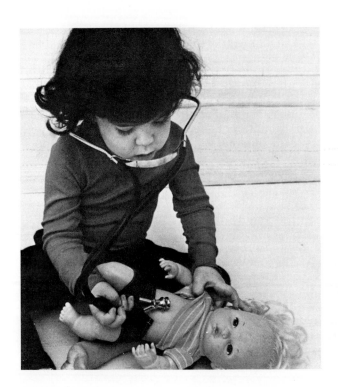

For the first time, the child tries to experience what it is like to view himself or herself as an object in the eyes of others. After all, the child who plays at being a doctor must imagine how a doctor's actions seem to patients, and the child-as-patient must try to imagine the doctor's feelings.

The Game Stage. Mead did not specify at what age a normal child will progress to the next level—the **game stage**. Children in this stage must integrate their actions into a network of organized activities. Instead of playing one role at a time, they learn how their actions reflect an ongoing balance among the many relationships that we all carry on at all times. Mead used baseball to illustrate this process. Let's suppose that one batter is out and that runners are on first and on third. The shortstop snares a sharply hit grounder and then has to consider the following: (1) Will he catch the runner going from third with a throw to home plate? (2) If not, will he be able to start a double play by forcing the runner going to second? (3) If not, will he be able to throw out the batter? While considering these choices, the shortstop must keep in mind the number of outs (the runner on third can score if he reaches home), the score, the speed of the different runners, his faith in the fielding ability of his teammates, and so on. In sum, he must coordinate his actions with the workings of the team as a whole. To play an organized game, like baseball, a child must abandon "one role at a time" thinking and form an overall sense of how each part relates to the whole and of how all the parts function simultaneously.

Baseball is a typical example of the kind of activity that generates adult thinking processes. By taking part in organized activities, children learn that a community is more than the sum of its unrelated parts. They learn that the community collectively expects them to learn and fulfill their role in it. The perspective of the community as a thing larger than the sum of isolated individuals is what Mead called the **generalized other**. Children come to view their behavior in relation to abstract rules and regulations, rather than to the expectations of one person at a time. Out of many individual expectations, each child abstracts standards and creates a more or less consistent image of society's rules. For sociologists, the development of this generalized other is the central feature of the process of socialization.

Mead held that this process is never complete. Even after the generalized other has developed through interaction with agents of socialization, it lacks complete control over the child. Mead conceived of the self as the product of two separate forces. The "me" is that part of the self that has been successfully socialized. It is the individual united with the generalized other, through the process of socialization; it is the social self—that part of every one of us that accepts the norms of culture, of conventional society. The other side of the self, to Mead, was the "I": the spontaneous, impulsive, inconventional, nonconformist, individualist, and selfish side of each individual. The "me" never fully controls the "I"; no one is ever completely socialized by society, though most of us, most of the time, do conform to what it expects of us.

Charles Horton Cooley: The Looking-Glass Self

Charles Horton Cooley (1864–1929) was Mead's contemporary, and each greatly influenced the other's thinking. Like Mead, Cooley believed that social interaction is the basis of the socialization process. Cooley considered the individual and society to be parts of a whole, not separate

Game stage In Mead's theory, the period of life when children learn to integrate their actions into a network of organized activities (such as in a baseball or football game), and they adopt the view of how all the parts relate to the whole.

Generalized other The perspective of the many individuals in the community, taken as a whole.

Looking-glass self The term Cooley used to explain the images we have of ourselves through the eyes of others.

Significant others Those individuals who are emotionally important to a person.

According to Charles Horton Cooley, the individual is linked to the social world chiefly through the looking-glass self. We all continually see ourselves in a kind of mirror—the mirror provided by others who react to us and our behavior.

Richard Frieman/Photo Researchers

entities. In Cooley's theory, each individual is linked to the social world chiefly through the **looking-glass self**. We all continually see ourselves in a kind of mirror—the mirror provided by the members of society who react to us and our behavior. Cooley thus held that we see ourselves as others see us. Through this social "looking-glass," we learn that we are intelligent or stupid, attractive or ugly, charming or abrasive. The self—how we see ourselves—is created and recreated through contact with the judgments of others and the incorporation of those judgments into our own self-images. Who we are to ourselves, Cooley argued, is a social product, a result of "feedback" from the way others see us.

Of course, the judgments of some people in our lives count a great deal more than the judgment of others. Cooley regarded the impact of the family as fundamental. The members of our families, like our close friends, are **significant others**: the people whose judgments of us are the most important and influential of all. The lingering influence of significant others helps explain how we can sometimes maintain positive self-images at times when many people look down on us, or negative self-images when many people think well of us.

A looking-glass is a simple and dramatic metaphor for the way society's image of us gets incorporated into our own self-images. But it is a bit too mechanistic and simple. After all, we do not see ourselves through the eyes of others quite as literally as we see ourselves in an actual mirror. Our notions of how others see us may not be quite accurate, and we may also be evaluated differently by different people. We do not derive from society, or even from significant others, a single, consistent, looking-glass self. One person thinks you are smart; another, that you are dumb. Whose image should you accept? In fact, you can "pick and choose" the image you feel most comfortable with and try to ignore or discount the others. Still, what others think of you is no

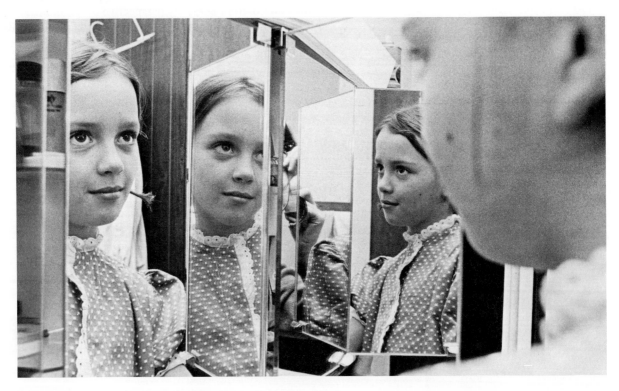

doubt very important in making your self-image and, as a result, who you are and what you do. Perhaps it is the very foundation of the process of socialization.

Sigmund Freud: The Psychoanalytic Theory of Childhood

Sigmund Freud (1865–1939) was a Viennese physician who founded the psychiatric school known as **psychoanalysis**. Psychoanalytic theory holds that repressed (or **unconscious**) childhood experiences and sexual drives largely shape each individual's personality and behavior. Whereas Cooley and Mead believed that society and the individual are basically in harmony with each other, Freud argued quite the contrary—that the two are continually at war. Every infant is born with strong aggressive and sexual drives or "instincts" (Freud used the term loosely). In his view, the process of socialization chiefly aims to subdue these destructive and "libidinous" (sexual) impulses. Although Freud argues that the social order would be impossible without this taming process, too-severe repression of these drives might lead to neurosis. So, the process of socialization must balance the needs of the individual against those of society. This balancing often fails to occur, and that is why we have so many neurotics.

Freud divided the personality into three components. The **id** represents the most primitive and selfish component of the personality; it demands fulfillment of the drives. Freud considered the id to be the embodiment of biological and instinctive nature. Through the process of socialization, the child acquires a second component of the personality: the **superego** or conscience. The superego represents the internalized voice of society, its resounding "no" to the demands of the id and to the calculations of the last component of the personality—the **ego**. The ego's specific field is reality. It attempts to mediate between the selfish but destructive demands of the id and the high-minded but unrealistic moral demands of the superego. To put it another way, it tries to satisfy the id but in a way that is socially acceptable—that satisfies the superego. The need to reconcile the id and the superego—and the impossibility of doing so—is a major theme in Freud's writing.

Criticisms of Freud's Theories. Freud's concepts, ideas, and theories have influenced a few sociologists. During the past decade or two, however, Freud's work has been much criticized, by sociologists among others. In order to be scientific, sociologists claim, a theory must be "falsifiable," and, according to them, psychoanalysis does not pass that test because Freudians tend to treat intellectual opposition to their views as a manifestation of "resistance." Second, many sociologists argue that Freud's theories are culture-bound. Freud made very little use of anthropological evidence, which shows that many of the things that Freud regarded as universal—anxiety about sex and toilet training, for instance—apply only to certain societies at certain times.

Many of Freud's assertions about behavior in Western society are doubtful, as well. Freud's view of sex roles has recently come under particularly strong criticism. His theories are far more influential in psychology than in sociology.

Jean Piaget: Cognitive Development

Infants learn to think and act like adults, but they do so at their own pace, in a more or less orderly sequence that cannot be rushed. For the most part, children cannot proceed to a higher, more difficult stage until

Psychoanalysis A theory in psychology, originated by Freud, which holds that repressed childhood experiences and sexual drives largely shape each individual's personality and behavior.

Unconscious According to psychoanalytic theory, the repressed, submerged portion of mental life of which one is not aware, but which determines behavior nonetheless.

Id In Freud's theory of psychoanalysis, the aggressive, sexual side of the personality that demands gratification, often at the expense of others.

Superego In Freud's theory of psychoanalysis, that part of the personality that represents the conscience, or society's view of right and wrong.

Ego Freud's term for that part of the personality that tries to reconcile our selfish, destructive side with our conscience, or socialized side.

DENNIS the MENACE

**"But how come you're buyin' Grandpa
a present for *Father's* Day?"**

*Very young children are able to
grasp their own relationships to
others, but not the relationships of
others to one another. To "Dennis
the Menace," Grandpa is
exclusively a grandfather, because
he has that relationship with him.*
*DENNIS THE MENACE® used by
permission of Hank Ketcham and ©
by Field Enterprises, Inc.*

they have successfully completed an earlier, easier one. Each stage can
be regarded as a kind of "milestone," representing a qualitatively separate stage, not a mere phase that gradually shades off into the next
phase. Many social scientists believe that this staging process results
from the growing child's biological maturation. Jean Piaget (1896–1980),
a Swiss psychologist, spent over half a century studying the way children
think and learn (1954, 1960, 1965a, 1965b, 1970). He isolated four stages
in the cognitive development of children.

Sensorimotor stage In Piaget's
theory of the cognitive
development of the child,
beginning at birth and lasting
until the age of 18 months to 2
years, when the child's central
and overwhelming concern is
making physical contact with the
world and navigating through it.

The Sensorimotor Stage.   Piaget called the first stage the **sensorimotor
stage**. It begins at birth and ends, roughly, at 18 months to 2 years of
age. At this point, infants' central and overwhelming interest is to make
physical contact with the world and to navigate through it. Sensory
perceptions and motor activity dominate the life of the infants, who do
not distinguish between themselves and anyone else—or anything else,
for that matter. Infants literally regard themselves as the center of the
universe. Cause and effect have yet to solidify in their infantile minds.
Infants also do not understand the notion of **object permanence**: If an
infant leaves a room, the objects in it cease to exist—"out of sight, out
of mind." If objects are covered up, the infants act as if the objects
have disappeared from the face of the Earth.

Object permanence The
realization that things still exist
even when they are not in sight.

Preoperational stage In Piaget's
theory of the cognitive
development of the child, the
period lasting from about 18
months to 7 years old, when
children grasp the idea of
objective permanence, and cause
and effect, but remain
egocentric, unable to adopt the
perspectives of others.

The Preoperational Stage.   The second stage stretches from about 18
months to the age of 7 or so. Piaget calls this the **preoperational stage**.
Children now grasp the idea of object permanence, and they develop a
more accurate, but still primitive, notion of cause and effect. They begin
to see their bodies as separate and distinct from other people and objects.
But they are still egocentric, unable to adopt the points of view of other
people. For instance, children of 3 or 4 cannot correctly identify the
right or the left side of a person facing them, because when asked to
do so, they identify *their own* right or left side, not that of the other

person. Four- or 5-year-old children are able to explain their relatives' relationships to them—but not their relationships to their relatives. A 4 year old who is asked, "Do you have a brother?," may reply, "Yes, and his name is Jim." But when the same 4 year old is asked, "Does Jim have a brother?," the answer is, "No." To answer "yes" would require the 4 year old to see the world from the perspective of another person—a brother (Phillips, 1969).

Preoperational children also cannot understand (or accurately estimate) such things as volume, number, speed, or weight. They always think that larger objects are heavier than smaller ones—that a pound of sponge rubber, for instance, is heavier (because it is larger) than two pounds of iron. If an adult pours a quantity of water from a tall, thin glass into a short, squat one, preoperational children think that the second glass has less water than the first because they judge quantity on the basis of water levels. ("Taller" means "bigger" and thus "more" to them.) The idea that the volume of water is independent of the glass containing it is foreign to preoperational children. Indeed, children under the age of 7 have great difficulty understanding the whole idea that objects keep the same volume or number, regardless of arrangement or shape—an idea that Piaget called the *principle of conservation.*

A child's thinking at this stage is also marked by "teleology": the belief that everything has an end or a purpose. Children have a naive confidence that the world, including the natural world, operates according to a wise plan. When a child was asked by Piaget why there were two mountains looming above the Swiss city of Geneva, he replied that the higher one was for big people to climb and the lower one was "for children." Children at this stage believe that the whole world—including natural and inanimate objects—thinks and acts just as they do. Their special brand of teleology is a tendency to project their own thinking processes to everyone and everything.

The Concrete Operational Stage. The third, or **concrete operational stage**, lasts from age 7 to 12 or so. Intellectual development now grows swiftly. Children learn to take the role of "the other." Yet abstract concepts, like love and death, are still beyond the grasp of the concrete operational child. Before the age of about 12, children can get insight into abstract concepts only through concrete references to the material world. For instance, a 10-year-old child who is asked, "What is love?," might reply, "Love is when you hug and kiss Mommy and Daddy and you feel good inside."

The Formal Operational Stage. Only in the final, or **formal operational stage**—after the age of 12—can adolescents begin to think abstractly, without specific references to the concrete world. An adolescent can imagine loving someone who may not even exist, or conceive of death without having known anyone who has died. At this stage, young people can think seriously and intelligently about general theories. They can discuss questions of morality. They can perform complex mathematical operations. They can follow the rules of logic. They can understand and embrace ideologies. These thought processes transcend direct, everyday experience.

Piaget argued that this four-stage sequence of increasing maturation is universal and fixed the world over. He also insisted that the whole process has a biological foundation. Three year olds cannot possibly think like 12 year olds. Only with biological maturity can real cognitive development occur.

Concrete operational stage In Piaget's theory of cognitive development, the period of life from age 7 to about 12, when concepts like speed, volume, number, and weight are understood, and the child can take the role of the other; abstract concepts, like love and death, are grasped only by means of specific references to the concrete world.

Formal operational stage In Piaget's theory of cognitive development, the period of life after the age of 12, when the adolescent begins to think abstractly, without specific references to the concrete world.

Jean Piaget: Moral Development

Piaget studied the child's moral as well as cognitive development. He argued that notions of right and wrong develop in a fashion roughly parallel to notions of truth and falsity. But moral development is slower, more gradual, and less divided into separate steps. At birth, according to Piaget, children are totally "locked into egocentrism." Everything in the world exists solely for their sake, and they grasp and understand little beyond their own immediate needs. Children at this stage cannot learn the difference between right and wrong. Rules imposed by parents frustrate and annoy them because they cannot take the role of another person and see the world through that person's eyes or distinguish between their own needs and the needs of others. Children do not think it inconsiderate or selfish to pester sick parents to play with them; after all, *they* aren't sick!

Morality of constraint In Piaget's theory of the moral development of the child, the view of rules as absolutes, imposed from above, to be rigidly obeyed; takes place between the ages of 2 and 7.

The Morality of Constraint.   At some point between the ages of 2 and 7, rules become internalized as absolutes, imposed from above, to be rigidly obeyed. They take on an almost sacred and inviolable status. Piaget called this the **morality of constraint**: an acceptance of commands imposed by authority. Children learn that it is wrong to cross the street against a red light, even if no cars are coming, or even if a street has been blocked off to vehicular traffic. Young children believe, in Piaget's words, that "a fault should automatically bring its own punishment." Knives, children under the age of 8 believe, will cut children who are forbidden to use them. Young children believe, too, that punishment should be proportional to the damage done, regardless of the transgressor's intention. Accidentally knocking over a tray and breaking ten cups is more serious in their eyes, and thus worthy of more severe punishment, than knocking over and breaking only one cup while deliberately stealing forbidden cookies from a cookie jar. Oddly enough, however, young children do not consistently obey these rules; to such children it is enough to believe in the rule.

The Morality of Cooperation.   By the age of 8, the idea that disobedience automatically leads to punishment begins to erode in the face of empirical evidence. Children learn that punishment must take into account the motives and responsibility of wrongdoers, and not only the consequences of their misdeeds. Right and wrong become more subtle and less certain. Somewhere between the ages of 8 and 10, children cease to believe that the rules are handed down from on high—and that they are eternal and unchangeable. The morality of constraint gives way to a **morality of cooperation.** As a result of contact with peers—the give-and-take among playmates in games—children discover that rules are made by human beings for human purposes. If you dislike a rule, you may be able to change it. Compromise, negotiation, and concession now become the basis for rule making. And for that very reason, children at last discover that rules should be obeyed, and not venerated.

Morality of cooperation In Piaget's theory, the view that rules are rarely absolute, but are for the purpose of human betterment; comes about through negotiation in the peer group, by age 8 or 10.

AGENTS OF SOCIALIZATION

The socialization of each human being takes place in specific settings. Representatives of society teach growing children the ways and beliefs of the cultures or subcultures to which they belong. These representatives are called **agents of socialization;** the most important such agents are the family, the peer group, the school, and the mass media. These agents do not always teach a consistent set of actions or ideas; what children learn from each may be different or even contradictory. Because the methods and the impact of each agent is so different, we discuss each one separately.

The Family

Some things truly are universal. In every society and throughout history, the family has been the first—as well as the most important and fundamental—agent of socialization during a child's earliest years. Without exaggeration, we might call the family both the foundation and the cornerstone of societies everywhere, for it passes on a society's culture from one generation to the next. Regardless of what may happen to any child later in life, life first unfolds in the bosom of the family (see Chapter 13).

We commonly read that young people in Western society by nature rebel against their parents. In fact, such rebellion is far from typical. Generational continuity is far more common than generational conflict. In general, parents strongly influence the ideas and behavior of their children, even in our own society. When children grow up, they tend to be far more like their parents than like other adults. If your parents are politically conservative, when you reach adulthood the chances are that you too will be conservative; and if your parents are liberal, you stand a high likelihood of becoming liberal (Dawson and Prewitt, 1969, pp. 105 ff; Niemi, 1973, pp. 125–129). Religious parents tend to raise religious children; irreligious parents tend to raise irreligious children. Like any generalization, generalizations about parental influence do not always hold true; but parental influence comes early, and it is profound and often decisive.

To very young children, parents seem to be all-knowing, all-powerful, the source of all things, good and bad. Their authority, even when it is questioned, is overwhelming. Infants are physically and emotionally dependent on their parents and can only resist them by throwing temper tantrums. To infants, parents are big and strong; the infants must literally "look up to" them. Parents can physically restrain infants from doing almost anything. Parents seem to know so much that, later on, chidren are shocked when they discover that they do not know everything. Wise or foolish, to infants, parents are "the law."

Parents are also a source of gratification. They feed their infants when hungry; comfort them when hurt; play games with them; provide companionship for them; and dispense gifts, attention, sympathy, and nurturance to them. Most important of all, parents give their infants their first experiences with love and affection—the two most powerful and effective resources for socializing children. Genuine intimacy is the most important gift parents can bestow on growing children.

Of course, a great deal of parental socialization is unintended. Parents do not always teach their children straightforwardly, and sometimes they "teach" lessons they had meant to discredit. Parents may preach to their children about the evils of smoking and drinking, for example, but if they themselves smoke and drink too much, they will probably socialize their children into the same practices. Children take their lessons from life.

Physical punishments, too, usually have unintended effects. When children are physically punished, they learn that "the use of violence is a proper mode of behavior. . . . It is impossible to use corporal punish-

Agents of socialization
Individuals or institutions that teach the culture of a society—including its attitudes, values, and norms.

The earliest and most basic of all agents of socialization is the family; parents strongly influence the ideas and behavior of their children. Here, a mother teaches her four-year-old son to dress himself.

Bill Binzen/Photo Researchers

WHAT DO YOU THINK?

"Oldthink" and "Newthink" on Childrearing

What's the best way to raise a child? Does permissiveness work best, or laying down strict rules and regulations? Should parents treat children as equals or let them know who's the boss? For quite some time, parents have been given advice on this subject by experts. This advice has changed over the years as psychologists and psychiatrists have discarded old theories and embraced new ones. The advice now given to parents differs significantly from the advice given a decade or two ago—so much so that some refer to "oldthink" and "newthink" on the subject of childrearing (Baumgold, 1982).

Oldthink on what to do when babies cry was to discourage picking them up; that, it was thought, only rewards their crying and spoils them, and this creates serious problems later on. Newthink points to studies showing that children do not become spoiled or more demanding of attention if they are picked up when they cry. In fact, the reverse is true: Responsiveness "actually *reduces* the amount of attention-seeking behavior." Children need mental and physical stimulation, positive emotion, and responsiveness. When a baby asks for something, there should be a response (Baumgold, 1982, p. 34).

On the subject of toilet training, oldthink was to wait until 18 months or even longer. Early toilet training would lead to neurosis and problem behavior. Newthink

rejects this notion. In fact, research shows that waiting too long may lead to problems. For instance, one classic form of problem behavior, bed wetting, is more likely to occur among children who were toilet trained after 18 months than among those who were trained before then (Baumbold, 1982, p. 35).

Oldthink, partly derived from Sigmund Freud's psychoanalytic theories, held that parents should not appear in front of their children nude: This might erotically stimulate the child. Nor should children observe their parents' having sex, for such a "primal scene" might cause many serious psychological problems.

Newthink on these subjects rejects Freud's ideas as fanciful. Contemporary mainstream opinion in psychology holds that if parents are natural about nudity, it is taken as natural by the children. Explains Anke Ehrhardt, professor of clinical psychology in the Department of Psychiatry at Columbia College of Physicians and Surgeons: "It is a sexual myth that children exposed to their parents nude together, or having sexual intercourse, will be affected." In fact, many observers now feel, something of the reverse of what was commonly believed actually holds true. According to Dr. Ehrhardt, "It can be good for the child to have some sense of the erotic life of his parents. . . ." If parents are affectionate, the children will learn to be affectionate,

too (cited in Baumgold, 1982, p. 36).

Oldthink on child care held that mothers should stay with their children full-time for at least the first three years. Children need the mothers' constant care, attention, and stimulation; surrogate care retarded the child's emotional, social, and intellectual development.

Newthink finds that high-quality child care can be as beneficial to the children's development as constant maternal care, acording to Gail Wasserman, a research scientist with the New York State Psychiatric Institute. The crucial factor, experts now believe, is that the care should be both consistent and long term. Working mothers do not have to feel guilty about having caretakers provide relationships once felt to be the exclusive domain of the mother. Of course, some quality contact with the children is a must. Still, parenting "is a continual letting go," Dr. Wasserman explains. "A good parent teaches the child to leave" (cited in Baumgold, 1982, p. 37).

Old theories on childrearing die hard. All of these new theories "are supported by research, but none should be taken as gospel. Parents must make their own decisions, consult their pediatricians, their books, and experts, and, above all, know their children" (Baumgold, 1982, p. 34). What do you think?

To the very young child, parents seem all-wise and all-powerful. Parents are a source of gratification: They feed the child when it is hungry, comfort it when it is hurt, provide companionship, attention, nurturance, love and affection.

WHO Photo by E. Schwab

ment on a child without simultaneously teaching that the deliberate infliction of pain as a form of persuasion and a means of gaining ascendancy over others is legitimate" (Van Stolk, 1972, p. 115).

The Peer Group

Parents attempt to socialize their children directly, deliberately, and intentionally. Socialization by peers—friends, playmates, schoolmates, and (later in life) business associates—almost always occurs indirectly and unintentionally. Parental authority over children is automatic. But peers have more voluntary, more equal, more give-and-take relations with one another. We must earn our influence over our peers; we cannot claim it as a birthright. Although our families impacts come early in our lives, our peer groups influence us in ways that are probably more pervasive and touch on more aspects of our lives. In American society, by the time children enter school, they have spent twice as much time with their peers as with their parents—because they prefer the company of their peers (Bronfenbrenner, 1970). In the supermarkets, at the parks, and on the streets, you can see that children's attention is riveted upon other children, not on adults. Peers are a much more potent force in the lives of children than adults in general are.

Peers are thus a strong socializing agent for a child; the older the child, the stronger the influence. The peer group's egalitarianism probably has a great deal to do with this power. Being told by a parent to do something "just because I said so" cannot have as much impact on a child as negotiating a deal through mutual consent and common interest.

The School

Schools are similar in at least one respect to the family: Their efforts to socialize children are intentional and deliberate. Like parents, teachers have automatic authority over children. Formal education in the strict sense—the curriculum of reading, writing, arithmetic, and the rest—is only a part of the socialization that takes place in our schools. There is also a more or less "hidden curriculum" on the educational agenda.

The first part of the hidden curriculum, and the one most openly acknowledged by educators, consists of social skills: consideration for others, unselfishness, being on time, neatness, cleanliness, and deportment. (Obviously, the children may or may not learn these things.) Second, children are taught to obey authority. Schools are miniature versions of the many hierarchical organizations that children encounter later in life, and their teachers very much resemble future authority figures. Children learn that some people give orders and others must follow them, and that the same people who give orders in some settings must follow them in others, and vice versa. And, of course, school children get a great deal of practical experience in the art of taking—and evading—orders. The third and, probably, least openly acknowledged part of the educational agenda is the inculcation of an ideology: teaching society's conscious political, social, and economic beliefs. For the most part, schools are middle-class institutions. Patriotism and citizenship are unquestioned in most schools, and they are implicitly woven into much of the curriculum. The school day often starts with the pledge of allegiance to the flag of the United States, and classroom exercises and reading materials often affirm conventional values—such as the traditional sex roles of men and women and the "naturalness" of the existing distribution of wealth, prestige, and power. Finally, schools teach children not to "rock the boat." Things are changing, of course—nonsexist children's texts, for instance, are far more common today than they were a decade ago—but most schoolteachers consider themselves to be affirmers of our traditional culture, not its critics.

The Mass Media

Mass media The means of communication that are one-sided and reach very large numbers of the public.

On a typical evening, more than 80 million Americans are separately engaged in exactly the same activity: watching TV. And 30 million of them may be watching the same program. Like the other **mass media,** television is a one-sided communication process that takes place entirely without face-to-face contact. The mass media give; the public receives. Books, newspapers, and magazines make up the so-called print media; radio and television, the broadcast media; and records, movies, and video cassettes, the electronic media. The public can "talk back" only indirectly—by either buying or not buying a record, for example, or by writing letters to the editor. Because the mass public is so large—it consists, for the most popular TV shows, of tens of millions of people— the mass media's products are highly standardized. If a TV show or a film is too specialized in its appeal, its audience will be small—too small, in all likelihood, to cover its costs. Generally, the larger the audience, the more standardized the medium. Television, with by far the largest audience, is also by far the most uniform in content.

About 98 percent of all American families have at least one television set, which (in the average home) is turned on for about six and a half hours a day. Typical American children spend more time in front of television sets than in any classroom. But do they learn from TV? Not everything, for they do not believe everything they see on the small screen. How, then, does TV act as an agent of socialization?

Clearly, TV gives us a very unreal sense of what the world is like. In an analysis of 1,500 TV programs containing about 18,000 characters,

Experts regard the mass media, particularly television, as a powerful agent of socialization. Television, a one-sided form of communication, takes place without face-to-face contact. Viewers typically watch television passively.

Michal Heron/Monkmeyer Press

men outnumbered women by a ratio of 3 to 1, and characters over the age of 65 made up only 2 percent of the total (as opposed to 11 percent in the real world). Yet crime is "about 10 times as frequent [on TV] as in the real world, and an average of five acts of violence per hour (four times that many in children's programs!) victimize more than half of all leading characters each week" (Gerbner, 1980, pp. 1, 6).

The Impact of the Mass Media. Sociologists have conducted thousands of studies focusing on the process of socialization by the mass media, and television is no doubt the most intensively studied of all. These studies have given sociologists many insights into the impact of the mass media.

First, people—children included—have great ability (and inclination) to ignore, resist, or misunderstand the messages thrust at them by the mass media. Indeed, some mass media campaigns actually produce a "boomerang effect," a response opposite to the one intended by the sender of the message (Merton, 1968, pp. 571–578).

Second, the mass media have a much greater impact on the relatively simple and more superficial aspects of our lives than on the deep-seated and fundamental ones. A television commercial may cause you to switch your brand of toilet paper but not, in all likelihood, your religion.

Third, the mass media have their greatest impact on those aspects of life least known and understood by the public. They are much less likely to influence attitudes or behavior in areas in which the public has experience and knowledge. If you have actually used two brands of the same product and clearly prefer one over the other, no amount of advertising will change your mind.

Fourth, the mass media reflect attitudes more than they influence them. Societies that do not regard women as the equals of men and treat women as inferior are quite likely to produce sexist movies and television shows. If the mass media in such a society were suddenly to change—to adopt nonsexist attitudes—the public might well continue to resist them. Such a transformation is not likely, in any case. The money lies in following, not in leading.

Last, the media are more likely to reinforce existing attitudes and behavior than to change them. People pay more attention to messages that repeat what they already believe; they walk away from those messages more convinced than ever. People who did not believe a message in the first place are much less likely to be influenced by it.

SOCIALIZATION AFTER CHILDHOOD

Socialization does not end at any particular age; it is a lifelong process. In fact, one of the more important types of socialization involves learning to grow older—that is, socialization into the life cycle. Just as we must learn to become human as infants, we must also learn to become, in turn, children, adolescents, young adults, middle-aged adults, and old people. You might assume that growing into each stage of life is simply a matter of maturing biologically—a "natural" process pure and simple. Not so. In reality, growing older is in large part a process of learning and accepting a culturally approved sequence of roles, each appropriate at a particular stage. We all know elderly men and women who act or dress in ways that more befit their grandchildren; people commonly think such people should "act their age." Children, too, are socialized to behave in increasingly adult ways by being told, "You're not babies any more." Children thus learn what others expect and require of them as they ease into the stages of the life cycle. We do not necessarily *mature* as we *become older*; maturity is taught and learned.

Transitions in the Life Cycle

The behavior that societies consider appropriate to any particular stage of life is in large part a cultural, not a biological, creation. For one thing, societies do not draw the lines between different stages at the same points. Age is partly a relative matter. Preindustrial societies lack the concept of "adolescence"; in them, a 16 or 17 year old is in every way an adult—a married man or woman, a parent, and a full-time economic provider. The transition from childhood to adulthood is not gradual, as it is in modern societies, but sudden; it often takes place at the end of a dramatic ritual or ceremony called a "rite of passage." In contrast, our society has no such rite into manhood or womanhood, which we attain gradually, in stages. The closest such rite we have is high school graduation. Still, most 18-year-old high school graduates retain the most crucial aspect of adolescence—economic dependence—and so cannot be regarded as true adults. In fact, adolescence lasts much longer in the United States than anywhere else, often stretching perilously close to the age of 30—which many societies regard as rather an old age.

Each society, though, regards certain roles and activities as uniquely appropriate (within that society) to each stage of the life cycle. Each stage must be learned as you get there. In our society, most people learn to drive a car at adolescence; to train for an occupation, and find out what it means to be a husband or wife and a parent, during young adulthood; to progress through a career in mature adulthood; and to cope with the loss of one's spouse or retirement in old age. For the most part, these socialization processes begin only when you actually enter the new stage and assume its responsibilities. You can never be fully prepared to assume a new role until you begin to play it. Socialization entails "on-the-job" training.

Adolescent Socialization

Adolescence does not exist in preindustrial societies, where children quite suddenly become adults. Industrial societies created this stage because they needed a highly trained and educated labor force. Because education lasts longer in our society, we have a huge number of physically mature high school and college students whom society regards as too young to earn their own livings, marry, or raise children. Most parents also feel extremely uncomfortable if their children have sexual relations at this age. Adolescents are physical but not social adults, social but not physical children. This in-between stage inevitably generates conflict and inner turmoil.

In a number of specific ways, the socialization of adolescence is different from that of the other stages of the life cycle. More than any other stage, adolescence is a bridge between specific life orientations. Childhood is a period of dependence; adulthood, of independence, autonomy, and responsibility. Adolescence teaches children to bridge the gap—to learn how to assume adult independence and adult responsibilities. At the same time, parents typically deny adolescents adult rights and adult

A great deal of socialization takes place during adolescence, often by the peer group. Adolescents form a kind of subculture, to some degree removed from adult values. Adolescence serves to bridge the gap between childhood and adult responsibility and independence.

Burk Uzzle

privileges. Another key aspect of adolescence is that it spans the gap between desire and reality. Life is hard, filled with disappointments and broken dreams. Adolescents must learn to be realistic about what they can and cannot attain. They must learn—perhaps for the first time— that "you can't always get what you want," or even what you need. Are you the next Nancy Lieberman, "Magic" Johnson, or Larry Bird? Or will you be cut from the high school basketball team? Adolescents dream about dating movie stars and rock performers, but the realities of dating typically teach them the difference between the world of fantasy and the world of reality.

The socialization of adolescence helps children bridge another gap, as well—between the present and the future. For preadolescents, the future is a vague, shadowy kingdom. Ten year olds want the world, and they want it *now*! Adolescents learn to postpone their desires and to work toward them. When 10 year olds say, "I want to be a doctor when I grow up," they are partly fantasizing. When 16 year olds say the same thing, they have usually given some thought to the many years of medical school and the long nights of internship and residency required.

During adolescence, children learn to stop toying with many vague choices and to start making concrete, long-term ones. Adolescents learn, for the first time, that many of the choices they make cannot be easily "taken back." They begin to realize that choosing one road sometimes means *not* choosing another. Perhaps they will hear a story about a slightly older person who dropped out of school, or got married, or became pregnant—and is now waiting on tables or pumping gas. Adolescents start to cope with the unpleasant but real fact that from now on, much of what happens is "for keeps."

Like it or not, adolescents learn to assume adult responsibilities and burdens, rights and privileges, and to bridge the gap between childhood and adulthood, dependence and independence. In many ways, adolescence prepares young people for the adult roles they will play for the next fifty or sixty years of their lives.

Adult Socialization

Early socialization makes later socialization both easier and more difficult. Some of the roles we take on as adults grow out of childhood roles, but other do not (Brim, 1966). Growing up in families helps prepare us for having families of our own. But being unmarried does not adequately prepare us for being married. Besides, social change makes much of what we learn as children obsolete. Newly defined roles demand new kinds of behavior, which must be learned. For instance, women who grew up in the 1940s, 1950s, and even the 1960s learned that they should quit work, get married, and devote themselves full-time to raising families. Today, 50 percent of all adult women work, and about 40 percent of all marriages end in divorce. What most women learned when they grew up about appropriate behavior for married women did not adequately socialize them in today's realities. Much adult socialization is actually a form of **resocialization**: "forgetting" what we have learned earlier and learning new kinds of appropriate behavior.

The two most important roles that are learned during adulthood deal with work and marriage (including parenting). Each occupation has its own demands and expectations, and beginners must start by learning them. In some job settings, workers receive conscious, formal training. In modern bureaucracies, for instance, rules and norms are

Resocialization The process of "forgetting" what we have learned earlier and learning new attitudes, values, and behaviors.

concrete and detailed. The workers learn when to take lunch breaks, how to address the boss, what to wear on the job, who may use the coffee machine and who may not, and so on.

Of all occupations, the one that requires the most drastic and exacting socialization process may be service in the armed forces. Basic training is resocialization in its purest form. The military attempts to break down civilian attitudes, behavior, and self-images, and to replace them with the attitudes, behavior, and self-images of soldiers or sailors. Of all civilian values, the military makes the strongest efforts to eradicate the sense of individualism and autonomy. Recruits are socialized to abandon this sense and to replace it with a new value: obedience to authority. They give up the clothes that reflect their personal tastes and put on standard uniforms, the same as all other recruits wear. Their role behavior should be as standardized as their uniforms. Recruits learn to be neat at all times, to salute officers, to follow orders, and to be addressed as "private" or "sailor," not by their own names. Much adult socialization, like basic training, attempts to replace old values, attitudes, and beliefs with new ones that are more appropriate to newly acquired statuses or roles.

Socialization into the marital and parental roles might seem to be straightforward and uncomplicated, because almost every one of us was raised within a family and had parents to provide models for the roles of husband or wife, father or mother. Yet the divorce rate in the United States—40 percent—reveals that many couples are not prepared for marriage. And the alienation that commonly divides parents and children, particularly in the latter's teenage years, may indicate that socialization into the parental role is hardly as "natural" as we might think.

For one thing, taking your own parents as role models for marital behavior may hurt more than it helps, especially because marriage has changed so much in recent years. What was appropriate a generation or so ago, when your parents probably got married, may not be appropriate today. Besides, your own husband or wife may be quite unlike your father or mother in crucial ways; and, in any case, each spouse has a separate set of parents, so taking parents as models would really mean trying to "marry" both sets, who may be wholly different from each other. Many parents may also provide a "negative role model": If you are lucky, you may avoid some of their mistakes.

Socialization into marriage is and probably will remain accidental, superficial, and limited. It is one of those roles that you learn largely by actually playing it. In many ways socialization into being a husband or wife only begins with the wedding ceremony, so marriage will remain a social trouble spot for some time to come. Remember, too, that marriage is among the most ancient and widespread of all social institutions and that the vast majority of adults have been and are married. As an institution, it has its troubles, but it also has powerful and persistent sources of strength.

Becoming a Parent. Socialization into parenthood is no less difficult than learning to be a husband or a wife. There is at least one major difference between them, however: Children are forever. You can end a bad marriage, but you cannot "take back" a child. The birth of a child powerfully and inevitably transforms a marriage. For the first year or so, the child dominates the household. The work is not shared equally, however, for even today, most marriages are fairly traditional with respect to child care: The wife and mother does most of it. She often comes to resent her husband's limited cooperation; he, in turn, may resent the attention and affection she gives the child. Both parents are

Socialization into certain roles is incomplete or discontinuous. Much of what we learn about the marital role takes place only after marriage. This frequently results in disharmony and, in four out of ten marriages, divorce.

Margot Granitsas/Photo Researchers

far less free than they had been before the "little bundle of joy" was born. There can be no more going out on a moment's notice. Sometimes, there can be no going out at all, for raising a child is expensive and always more difficult than either parent had expected. Parenthood is a role that you only begin to play when it happens to you. Very few young parents are prepared for it in any way, and when a child comes, some parents sink, others swim.

Becoming Elderly.   Our population is aging. In 1970, the median age of all Americans was 28. In 1980, it was 30. By the year 2000, it will be 36; and by the year 2010, more than 38. More than a tenth of our population had reached 65 or older by 1980, and more than 5 million Americans reached old age from 1970 to 1980 (see Chapter 12).

Despite this trend, we as a people and a society remain almost uniquely obsessed with youth. In many societies—China, for example—the elderly have great social honor and nearly monopolize political power at the top. But in the United States, the elderly are forced out of their jobs, made poor and useless, and left to die in institutions.

Old age surprises most people who reach it. Very few of us are prepared for it through prior socialization. In fact, the most substantial discontinuity in the entire lifelong socialization process is the one that divides middle from old age. In part, this discontinuity was created by industrialism, which had (and has) less use for the elderly than preindustrial societies. In preindustrial societies, the elderly continue to function in all phases of social life: the economy, family, religion, politics, and education. In our society, however, most of the elderly cease to play functionally significant, meaningful, and central roles and are forced into marginal, almost meaningless ones. From economic self-sufficiency, they are driven into poverty and economic dependency. Widowhood turns husbands and wives into solitary, lonely men and women. Chronic illness becomes steadily more frequent and serious, as do medical bills. By and large, it is not a pretty picture. Depression, mental illness, and suicide are far more common among old people than among the young and middle aged—and far more common in industrial than in preindustrial societies.

THE OVERSOCIALIZED CONCEPTION OF MAN AND WOMAN

Oversocialized conception of man and woman The view that human beings are wholly a product of socialization and that they believe everything they have been taught.

Men and women do not soak up a society's culture as a sponge soaks up water. The idea that human beings are a pure product of socialization—that we believe everything we have been taught by parents, peers, the educational system, and the mass media—is called the **oversocialized conception of man and woman** (Wrong, 1961). In actuality, we are never fully socialized. Do you recall George Herbert Mead's distinction between the "me"—the socialized side of the self, and the "I"—the spontaneous, impulsive, individualistic side? The "me" never fully dominates the "I," so we are and remain unpredictable, original, and independent.

There are at least six different reasons why socialization is always incomplete. First, the human mind is imaginative, creative, and infinitely inventive. Every one of us can think of a reason for not doing something that we've been taught to believe right—a reason to think that it might actually be wrong in some larger sense or in the long run.

Second, we are all subject to contradictory needs and desires. There is always some tension between what we really want to do and what others tell us we should do. The expectations of others often conflict with what we feel is best for ourselves.

Third, no society has a fully "integrated" culture (see Chapter 3). At times, we may all be expected to act in contradictory ways. We learn norms of thrift but also the norms of personal grooming and dressing, which may lead us to spend much money on clothes, haircuts, and makeup. We are socialized into the work and success ethic but also into feeling an obligation to spend time with family and friends. Two different people may make equally valid and legitimate demands on our time, and we may find that we cannot satisfy them both. Socialization cannot provide a route out of each and every conflict.

Fourth, we may also encounter totally novel situations, for which socialization has not prepared us—for instance, the proper way to address an Arab sheik or to talk a friend out of committing suicide. Imagination and creativity bridge the gap between what we learn from culture and the novel demands that culture sometimes makes upon us.

Fifth, even the most thoroughly socialized people see themselves differently in different social contexts. On the job, a professor may be formal, proper, and impersonal, even to colleagues. The same professor, in a bar at night with a group of intimate friends, might be warm, informal, and perhaps even silly. The "self" is always slightly elusive and undefinable because in reality we all comprise a number of different selves. Spontaneity and unpredictability are inherent features of human conduct.

Last, socialization can never impose a uniform interpretation upon the complexity of the real world. Socialization rarely provides us with a precise blueprint for all situations at all times. As the facts change, we must change our responses to them. We all know, for instance, that we should help friends in need. But what is a friend? And how much must you sacrifice? Your life? Your honor? Are you ever justified in deciding that a friend is "beyond help"? Socialization can never provide complete answers to any of these questions. You must feel your way through the baffling complexity of the world.

In short, socialization does not produce human "products" as a factory produces identical typewriters or hammers. We are not products. We may observe the rules of society, but we do so creatively, not blindly, and sometimes we do not do so at all. Socialization never completely stamps out the rebellious side of human nature.

SUMMARY

1. "Socialization" is the process of learning a culture or a subculture. It is how we acquire the values; beliefs; norms; and physical, mental, and social skills that make us human.

2. Of all animals, human infants have the longest period of helplessness and dependency on adults and are therefore uniquely sensitive to their parents' influence.

3. Infants need meaningful human contact to "become" human. This is clearly demonstrated by the case of children reared without such contact, who do not and cannot become fully human.

4. It is futile to consider "nature" (biological factors) and "nurture" (environmental factors, or learning) as completely distinct influences upon human behavior, or to stress one or the other of them. Both are essential, and they are so intertwined that they cannot be neatly separated.

5. Philosopher George Herbert Mead distinguished between "play"—taking one role at a time—and "games"—adopting the perspective of all the players in a game, understanding how all the parts (of society) relate to the whole. Both are key elements in the socialization process, necessary stages in children's discovery of the role of the "other." But the "game" stage teaches children to recognize and obey the "generalized other," society as a whole, as opposed to particular individuals.

6. Charles Horton Cooley, a contemporary of Mead, argued that the emergence of the "looking-glass self"—the ability to see oneself as others see one—is the most important ingredient in socialization.

7. Sigmund Freud developed a theory of socialization that is, in many ways, unacceptable to contemporary sociologists. Whereas Cooley and Mead regarded individuals as harmonious parts of society, Freud believed that society's demands on individuals often make them neurotic or worse. Freud believed that we all have a primitive, selfish side (the "id")—which demands satisfaction—and a conscience (the "superego")—which imposes the roles of the social order. The id and the superego are always at war with each other. The ego attempts to mediate between the selfish, destructive demands of the id and the unrealistic moral demands of the superego.

8. The biological factor strongly influences the learning process. Psychologist Jean Piaget isolated four separate, sequential stages in children's intellectual, or cognitive, development: the sensorimotor stage, the preoperational stage, the concrete operational stage, and the formal operational stage. Each represents an intellectual advance over the previous stage—a growth in cognitive reasoning power. Piaget argued that this developmental process is biologically determined.

9. Piaget also argued that the moral development of the children parallels their cognitive development. As children interact with peers, they become less self-centered and adopt a "morality of cooperation."

10. The most influential agents of socialization are the family, the peer group, the school, and the mass media.

11. Adolescent socialization represents a transition, or "bridge," between childhood and adulthood.

12. Adulthood socializes us for two main roles: work and marriage (as well as the parental role). However, most of this socialization occurs *after* we assume the role in question.

13. Likewise, socialization into old age does not really start until old age begins. In this society, the transition from mature adulthood into old age is marked by serious discontinuities in the

socialization process: The elderly are forced out of their jobs into poverty and economic dependency; they are driven into meaningless roles; they learn to suffer from loneliness, and physical and mental illness.

14. Socialization is a lifelong process that ends only with death.

15. No one in any society is ever "fully" socialized. Every one of us keeps a spontaneous, "unsocialized" side.

SUGGESTED READINGS

Susan Curtiss, *Genie: A Psycholinguistic Study of a Modern-Day "Wild Child."* New York: Academic Press, 1977.
A case study of a girl who was kept in isolation for twelve years. A team of psychologists attempted to socialize her, after her discovery in 1970, but were only minimally successful; she never developed beyond the mental age of four, and she now lives in an institution.

Frederick Elkin and Gerald Handel, *The Child and Society: The Process of Socialization* (4th ed.). New York: Random House, 1984.
A brief, readable, introductory account of childhood socialization from a sociological perspective. Especially good in the chapters entitled "Socialization and Subcultural Patterns" (which examines class, residence, and ethnic variations) and "Sex and Socialization."

Carol Gilligan, *In a Different Voice: Psychological Theory and Women's Development*. Cambridge, Massachusetts: Harvard University Press, 1982.
Contests a number of current theories of human development, which it considers to be male-centered and sexist. A feminist analysis of the socialization process.

Janice E. Hale, *Black Children: Their Roots, Culture, and Learning Styles*. Provo, Utah: Brigham Young University, 1982.
A controversial book that argues that the Black subculture in America is still powerfully influenced by African culture, and that the socialization process Black children experience reflects this fact.

Robert M. Liebert, Joyce N. Sprafkin, and Emily S. Davidson, *The Early Window: Effects of Television on Children and Youth* (2nd ed.).

New York: Pergamon Press, 1982; and Jerome L. Singer and Dorothy G. Singer, *Television, Imagination and Aggression: A Study of Preschoolers*. Hillsdale, New Jersey: Lawrence Erlbaum Associates, 1981.
Two books by teams of social psychologists on television's socializing impact on children. Recent research on the media, especially television, suggest that their impact is not as innocuous as had been thought previously—that they may, in fact, be hazardous to children's lives. These books present evidence on this question.

Mary Ann Spencer Pulaski, *Understanding Piaget: An Introduction to Children's Cognitive Development* (2nd ed.). New York: Harper & Row, 1980.
A clear, straightforward summary of Piaget's theory of the cognitive development of the child.

Irving Rosow, *Socialization to Old Age*. Berkeley: University of California Press, 1974.
How do the elderly learn how to "act their age"? This does not happen automatically; it takes place as a result of the socialization process. This book presents an overview of this process.

Lenore J. Weitzman, *Sex Role Socialization*. Palo Alto, California: Mayfield, 1979.
How do infants become boys or girls? This book discusses how we learn the "appropriate" sex-linked behavior and attitudes.

Thomas Rhys Williams, *Socialization*. Englewood Cliffs, New Jersey: Prentice-Hall, 1983.
An anthropologist's view of the socialization process.

chapter 7

GROUPS

You share certain characteristics with almost all of the people you know. With Jane, you may share an interest in playing chess; you both belong to the same chess club, which meets every Wednesday night. You and John work at the same part-time job in the library, reshelving books. Sally, who lives in the dormitory across from yours, has red hair—as you do. Both you and your sociology professor are left-handed. Some of these common characteristics bring you close to others; some do not. Red hair and left-handedness do not generate special bonds among individuals; red-haired or left-handed people have no strong "we" feeling. In contrast, belonging to a juvenile gang, being a member of a family, holding a membership in a fraternity or sorority, or playing on a school basketball team do bring you closer to others. Some characteristics, in other words, act as the basis for building **social groups.**

To a sociologist, a group is a collectivity of two or more individuals who have the following characteristics in common: First, they share a common *identity*, a sense of belonging, a "consciousness of kind." They not only perceive themselves as forming, but they also tend to be perceived by others as forming, a distinguishable entity. A Hell's Angels motorcycle chapter, for instance, has a name, an identifying insignia, which is usually sewn onto a jacket, and a clear-cut identity: its members know the other members, and all strongly identify with the group and their membership in it. In addition, this membership is highly important to nonmembers, who see someone primarily as a member of this group. A second crucial characteristic of groups is that their members possess an awareness of common goals or interests. For instance, the common goal or interest of a delinquent gang might be to control the relevant action in its neighborhood and to keep other gangs out, or to be "the biggest and the baddest"—and the most feared—gang in town. Third, a group endures over time. Groups tend not to be "fly-by-night" operations that disappear with the rising of the morning sun. Groups typically have some measure of stability, though they need not be permanent. Fourth, groups tend to generate a set of norms that govern the behavior of members—norms that are to a degree special and distinct to themselves. For instance, a norm that developed within the Peoples Temple, a religious cult, was "Never contradict or argue

175

Social group A collectivity of people who interact with one another, share a common identity, and adhere to a special and distinct set of norms.

with Rev. Jim Jones" (Mills, 1979; Nugent, 1979). Members who violated this norm were punished harshly. The norm in one office might be "Arrive at work at 9 o'clock sharp," whereas in another office, it might be "Never show up for work before 10."

A fifth major characteristic of groups is that their members interact more frequently with each other than they do with nonmembers. One clue to whether a given characteristic generates a group or not is social interaction. For instance, it is unlikely that left-handed people interact with one another more frequently than they do with right-handed people, relative to their numbers in the population. (In addition, their identity as "lefties" is minimal, and there are no special norms dictating that they should behave differently from "righties.") In short, left-handedness is not usually a characteristic that generates a group. Most sociologists would pick interaction as the most crucial group characteristic, because it is the glue of social life. Collectivities whose members do not interact usually have less interest for sociologists than those whose members do interact. But although interaction is a necessary ingredient of a group, it is not by itself sufficient. In certain social relationships—between bosses and workers, for instance, or, sometimes, professors and students—interaction may lack intimacy. And people can be physically separated and still interact, indirectly, through letters and telephone conversations. Even so, interaction—especially face-to-face interaction—is almost always the key ingredient in creating and maintaining groups. There is something inherently powerful about the immediate presence of other human beings—about looking into their eyes, touching their arms, talking to them, sharing adventures together—and this something generates a "we" feeling. Even though the media, especially television, have increased the strength of ties between people who do not interact on a face-to-face basis, such ties cannot substitute for physical proximity. For the most part, absence does *not* make the heart grow fonder.

CATEGORIES, POTENTIAL GROUPS, AND AGGREGATES

"Groupness" is a matter of degree. There are strong groups and weak ones. Members of some groups interact frequently and intimately, have little contact with nonmembers, and identify powerfully with their groups and their social and moral codes, which in some cases may be quite distinctive and demanding. For instance, certain fundamentalist religious sects, like the Amish and the Hutterites (Kephart, 1987) are strong groups, and so too are the local chapters of the Hell's Angels motorcycle gang (Thompson, 1967), Gypsy bands (Maas, 1976), and the Mafia (Ianni, 1973). As examples of weak groups, consider the residents of most college dormitories and apartment buildings, the students in the same college class, and the residents of a typical American suburb.

At no precise point can we say, "Aha! Behold a group!" "Groupness" cannot be measured with precision. Nonetheless, it can be observed, to one extent or another, in different collectivities. You might almost say that a kind of "social skin" surrounds the members of all groups, an invisible boundary that holds them together and also holds them somewhat apart from nonmembers.

Statistical Categories

In contrast to groups, **statistical categories** comprise people who share a given characteristic—any characteristic, whether or not it creates a group out of those who share it. Men and women make up statistical categories, as do Blacks and whites, Protestants, Catholics, and Jews. So do all Americans who live in cities with more than a million inhabitants, everyone who commutes more than twenty miles to work, and the employees of the federal government. Likewise, redheads and left-handed people each make up a statistical category. Although these are often loosely called groups by sociologists, proper usage would neccessitate excluding them. It is clear that members of categories do not necessarily share important social bonds; some do, most do not. In any case, categories are typically so huge that those who belong to them cannot possibly interact as a group. Individual redheads can have relations only with a few other individual redheads.

Statistical category A collectivity of individuals who share a given characteristic, regardless of whether it creates a true group out of those who share it.

Potential Groups

All the residents of San Francisco make up a collectivity too large and too diverse to form an actual group. Clearly, they are no more than a statistical category. But if a dozen people from San Francisco moved to a small town in Mississippi, their common past, to say nothing of the social difficulties they might have with the locals, would probably forge them into a group. When a category might serve as the basis of a group that does not yet exist, we might call it a **potential group.**

For instance, racial categories in the United States are made up of so many individuals that they cannot be considered real groups. Obviously, all the Blacks or all the whites in the United States are too numerous to interact with one another. However, all the Blacks—or all the whites (if in the minority)—attending a certain college probably qualify as potential groups. As likely as not, they would eventually "hang out" with one another more frequently than with members of other racial categories, share a common identity, and expect one another to do certain things that they would not expect of others. They possess what the early sociologist Franklin Giddings called "consciousness of kind." In short, statistical categories like race can form the basis of group membership. Yet in themselves, they are too large and too diverse to be called true groups. Of course, many categories, like left-handedness and red hair, never generate true groups.

Potential group A collectivity of people who possess characteristics that might serve as the basis for future group formation.

Aggregates

Another type of collectivity that sometimes resembles a real group is what sociologists call an **aggregate**: a bunch of people who happen to be in the same place at the same time. An example of an aggregate is all the people in New York's Times Square at 12 o'clock midnight on January 1, 1984. Obviously, this assemblage would not be a group in the sociological sense—that is, the people possess no identity or "consciousness of kind," their interaction is fleeting or nonexistent rather than frequent and enduring, their contact is superficial, not intimate, and their presence in Times Square entails no special code or subculture. Thus, they are an aggregate, not a sociological group. Once in a while, members of a certain aggregate may undergo a common experience that turns them into a group. For instance, people held hostage may

Aggregate A bunch of people who happen to be in the same place at the same time, but who share no special bond.

WHAT DO YOU THINK?

Brazilian Samba Schools

Carnival is a period of festivity in many Catholic countries around the world. Its roots extend back to the fertility rites of pre-Christian pagan Egypt, Greece, and Rome. Today, it is customarily celebrated just before Lent; more specifically, it begins the weekend before Ash Wednesday and ends on the first day of Lent, Ash Wednesday itself. In the United States, it is celebrated only in New Orleans, in the form of Mardi Gras ("fat Tuesday" or Shrove Tuesday), and in certain communities in urban centers with substantial numbers of Caribbean residents.

In Brazil, carnival (spelled *carnaval*) is celebrated enthusiastically with festivities, parties, dances, and parades in a general atmosphere of gaiety, revelry, spontaneity, and fun. A major part of every Brazilian *carnaval* is the *desfile*, or parade, with processionists in elaborate costumes and a percussion section, or *bateria*. Although many parades take place more or less spontaneously, with very little organization or planning, the most visible, popular, and spectacular are those that are organized and administered by the samba clubs or "schools" (called *escolas de samba*). And nowhere are the samba clubs more visible, popular, and spectacular than in Rio de Janeiro. Of these, the class 1-A samba schools represent the best of the breed, the cream of the crop; they are the "big league" of Brazilian samba schools. In 1986, there were fifteen 1-A samba schools in Rio.

During two days of *carnaval*, from 8 P.M. until almost 8 o'clock the next morning on two consecutive nights, the class 1-A *escolas de samba* hold their procession in Rio's "Sambadrome" (built in 1983), a huge, more than quarter-mile-long stadium, packed with hundreds of thousands of cheering, singing spectators. Each year, every school writes a song especially for *carnaval* that year. These songs are commercially released months before the *carnaval* date, so the words are familiar to the Brazilian public; for those who do not know a song, fans are released with the words of the songs printed on the back.

One by one, each school is announced over the public address system, in Portuguese, Spanish, and English. In turn, the percussionists, some 300 strong for each school, pound out the beat of their schools' theme songs. Then the songs themselves are sung by all the members of the schools, more than a thousand members for each school. Then the members parade along the runway of the stadium. The maximum time allotted for each club is eighty minutes, from beginning to end. Paraders are located in a section or *bloco*, which marches together; each section has its own costumes and coordinators. The movements of the paraders and the sections must be coordinated, of course; they may not simply "do their own thing" randomly. At the same time, they do not march in a synchronized fashion, as marchers do in American parades. More prop-

erly, they "boogie" down the runway in a more or less coordinated fashion. Each club depicts a theme, different each year: the seven deadly sins, soccer through history, a pro-Brazilian, anti-American nationalism, "if you're poor, you'd better be smart," and so on.

The parade is a contest, and each club is judged on its performance; ten items are evaluated by a panel of judges selected by city officials. To be awarded champion of the year is a stupendous honor, comparable to winning the World Series or the Superbowl in the United States. In addition, each year, the lowest-ranking club is knocked out of its 1-A bracket, and the best of the lesser schools is elevated to 1-A ranking. The entire, nearly twenty-four hour parade is televised all over the country to millions of viewers.

The costumes and floats are fabulously elaborate and extremely expensive. In 1986, one samba school spent nearly half a million dollars on its floats; that doesn't count the money that members paid out of their own pockets on their costumes, often the equivalent of a month's salary for a poor member. Each school receives a sum from the government, which covers only a portion of its cost. Most of the cost is contributed by wealthy members or financial backers; the principal patrons are *bicheiros*, a slang term for men who run the illegal lottery.

Every member of each 1-A samba school marches in Rio's parade in the Sambadrome. Indeed,

The Brazilian samba clubs (or "schools") are a type of group; their members maintain group loyalty, identity, and interaction, and group norms and special activities characterize each club. Some sociologists emphasize their positive contributions, while others insist that they are frivolous and, for poor Brazilians, counterproductive.

Erich Goode

one major reason to belong to such a club and participate in its other activities is to parade. The samba schools have all of the characteristics of groups: Each has a strong identity, its members are recognized by nonmembers as belonging to a particular club, its identity is relevant and important to all concerned, its members interact with one another more frequently and more intimately than they do with outsiders, and are bound to a certain code or pattern of behavior, mainly, although not exclusively, centering around preparation for and participation

in the yearly, all-important parades.

Samba clubs have their headquarters in the poorer neighborhoods of Rio. (Two, however, are located outside the city proper.) Many of the paraders are extremely poor; most are Black. Given the tremendous cost of the parade each year, both to the club as a whole and to each specific member, some observers have argued that the yearly parades are wasteful and profligate. More important, some say, is that *carnaval* generally and the parades specifically are a "Roman circus," an elaborate spectacle that acts to draw attention away from Brazil's serious problems—especially its poverty and extremely unequal income and wealth distribution. Consequently, some believe, *carnaval* may actually retard or help prevent progressive changes that might otherwise take place. The attention poor people focus on *carnaval* could be used to exert pressure on the powers that be to transform Brazilian society into a better place to live.

One fascinating feature of *carnaval* bears directly on this point: the *inversion of social roles*. Men often dress as women (though women rarely dress as men), and, in fact, women are "the center of the *carnaval* world"; Blacks usually play the more central roles in the parades, whereas whites play a more marginal, secondary role; and rich and poor may actually switch roles—for instance, a wealthy man may play a derelict or clown, while his servant may be queen for a day. Consequently, *carnaval* permits the poor to play out fantasies that, for the play act-

ing, are less likely to take place in real life; it permits the poor to "let off steam," to act haughty and regal for a few hours or a few days, instead of taking realistic steps to enact social change. In addition, the rich feel better and less guilty about oppressing the poor. When the confetti of *carnaval* is swept away, the poor are still poor and powerless, and the rich are still oppressing and exploiting them.

A second perspective toward *carnaval* is that it represents a legitimate outlet for the creative, artistic, and cultural expression of the Brazilian masses generally, and the members of samba schools specifically, that would not otherwise exist. The parades represent a kind of popular or even folk art carried to a fever-pitch intensity, engaging every Brazilian in once-a-year excitement. The floats and costumes are imaginative and daring. The dances and the parades represent stimulating popular drama. In addition, since the military regime stepped down in 1985, *carnaval* has begun to give vent to political expression. For instance, in 1986, the Rio 1-A *escolas de samba* in the Sambadrome poked fun at Brazilian mores, United States imperialism, the Brazilian tax office, multinational corporations, and poverty in Brazil.

Is *carnaval* a kind of "opiate of the masses," as Marx claimed religion was, or is it a legitimate expression of the artistic impulse of the Brazilian masses? What do you think?

SOURCES: Da Matta, *Universo do Carnaval: Imagens e Reflexões*, 1981; Da Matta, *O Que Faz O Brasil*, 1984, pp. 65–78.

become friendly with one another after their ordeal and form a group. But ordinarily, the members of an aggregate, such as a crowd, do interact with one another in face-to-face contact, but in a manner so superficial that it does not forge any kind of bond.

IN-GROUPS AND OUT-GROUPS

Belonging to one group sometimes entails *not* belonging to certain others, because some group memberships are mutually exclusive: If you belong to one, you automatically cannot belong to the other. If you are a member of a local Democratic club, you cannot, ordinarily belong to its Republican counterpart. Members of the New York Yankees can't play for the Boston Red Sox. Members of the Pagan motorcycle club automatically cannot ride with the Savage Skulls. Not all group memberships are mutually exclusive, but many are. Sociologists refer to groups whose members feel themselves to be separate from, or even in opposition to, other groups as **in-groups.** In-groups imply **out-groups**—those that are seen as separate from and outside the in-groups. An in-group comprises everyone who is regarded as "we" or "us," whereas an out-group comprises whoever is looked upon as "they" or "them."

Clearly, one person's in-group is another's out-group. Many groups are formed and maintained through conflict: "them against us." To all "jocks," nonathletes, or individuals who are not fans of their team, make up the out-group; to the campus "druggies," anyone who rejects mind-altering substances; to the "Greeks," nonfraternity and nonsorority students; to evangelical Christians, anyone who has not been "born again."

A competitive out-group usually increases the cohesion of the in-group (Coser, 1956). For instance, sharp athletic rivalries heighten the fans' senses of partisanship and the players' athletic performances. Opposition to one group often strengthens an individual's feeling of union with another one. In-group feeling is partly created and usually enhanced by out-groups. But do not push this notion of in-groups and out-groups too far: People can and do have positive feelings toward groups to which they do not belong.

In-group A collectivity of people whose members feel themselves to be separate from, even in opposition to, other groups.

Out-group A collectivity of individuals (not necessarily a true sociological group) to whom in-group members feel themselves to be opposed.

REFERENCE GROUPS

Our places in the world depend in part on how we view ourselves. This, in turn, depends on which groups we use as our standards of comparison. **Reference groups** are groups we use to evaluate ourselves—who we are and what we do. Interestingly, reference groups are not always membership groups: A person may belong to one group but use another one as the basis for evaluation and identification. For instance, a 30-year-old junior executive in a large corporation may earn $60,000 a year—considerably more than his friends and peers. But he may still consider himself something of a failure because his reference group consists of

Reference group A collectivity of individuals to which we may or may not belong, but which we use as a standard to evaluate ourselves.

Understanding an individual's reference group is a key to understanding his or her behavior. Some medical and dental students take established professionals as their reference group, while some see other students in this capacity

Paul Conklin/Monkmeyer Press

the corporation's executive vice-presidents, who each earn over $500,000 a year. Consider another case: A novelist takes little pride in her success, though she makes a living solely by writing (which is very, very rare), always gets favorable reviews, and is admired by a circle of friends and readers. Why isn't she pleased with her accomplishments? Because she aspires to join the ranks of Joyce Carol Oates, Saul Bellow, and Dorris Lessing: internationally acclaimed, prize-winning, best-selling novelists. She does not take her local success very seriously because her reference group consists of writers who are not merely successful, but successful on a grand scale.

Many students, during their years in college, shift their reference groups from people they knew in high school and in their neighborhoods back home to those they encounter in college. For instance, suppose it is something of a "big deal" among their high school friends simply to attend college. Once in college, they may realize that, for the highest-ranking social cliques, attending college is taken for granted, and academic excellence is highly prized. During our lifetimes, we typically pick up and drop reference groups. But again, not all are necessarily groups to which we personally belong. We can also measure our successes or failures by the achievements of members of groups to which we do not belong.

When it comes to individual cases, however, reference groups are usually membership groups, because our personal standards usually come from the people we know best and feel closest to. A classic study of the United States armed forces in World War II (Stouffer, Suchman, DeVinney, Star, and Williams, 1949) found that men who were in the Air Force—which had an objectively high rate of promotion—were significantly less satisfied with their promotions than were men in the Military Police—whose actual rate of promotion was very low. These Air Force people used the specific units to which they belonged as a basis of comparison (Merton, 1957, pp. 236–237); because so many members of these units got promotions, those who did felt no special sense of accomplishment.

Whether or not you belong to your reference groups, they influence your attitudes and behavior. Our junior executive will be influenced by the higher-ups because he identifies with and aspires to join them. Our modestly successful writer will be more interested in the themes and techniques that interest her "models" than in themes and techniques that might interest her readers. Graduate, medical, and law school students who take established professionals as their reference group are powerfully influenced by their professors and other eminent professionals. Students whose reference group is other students will be more insulated from this professional influence.

HOW GROUPS FUNCTION

A rock band whose records have sold millions of copies disbands, and each member forms a new group. One street gang holds a meeting and decides to invade the "turf" of another. A commune whose members worship an Indian guru expels an erring member.

These are groups in action. Most of us think that people engage in certain kinds of behavior out of conviction. Sometimes, of course, they do. But—and this is a key sociological insight—independent of individual convictions and characteristics, the nature of a group itself profoundly influences the behavior of its members. For instance, a group composed of thirty members will behave quite differently from one made up of only three. Groups function because of forces and processes that are powerful—often more powerful than individuals—yet not always obvious. Let's look at some of these forces and processes.

Size

The size of a group greatly influences the kinds of social relations that take place within it. It is hard to maintain close, intimate, emotional, personal relations with a very large number of individuals. Take a social party, for instance. As the number of guests increases, the party begins to break up into separate clusters of individuals. Only in a small gathering—up to six or seven people—can everyone talk to everyone else in a genuine conversation. Why? Simple: As the number of people increases, the number of possible, and separate, social interactions and relations increases even more rapidly. Look at the figure to the right. In a two-person group, a **dyad,** only one social interaction or relationship is possible—that between person A and person B. But when the group's size increases to three, a **triad,** three relationships are possible—between A and B, between A and C, and between B and C. In this case, adding just one member triples the number of a group's potential relationships. With four members, six one-on-one relationships are possible.

Actually, the _kinds_ of possible relationships increase even more dramatically than the number with an increase in group size. So far, we have considered only one-on-one relationships and interactions. When a group is larger than two members, alliances become possible. In a

Dyad A two-person group.

Triad A three-person group.

three-person group, for example, A and B might join together against C, or B and C against A, or A and C against B—in addition to the one-on-one relationships. And in a four-member group, three-against-one alliances become possible, too.

It is easy to see that, as a group's size increases, the group must break down into subgroups to sustain the members' feelings of shared

Group size makes a difference in how members interact with one another. A two-person group (a "dyad") has only one possible one-on-one relationship, while a three-person group (a "triad") has three, as well as three two-on-one coalitions.

Lenore Weber/Taurus Photos

Joseph Nettis/Photo Researchers

Group Size and Number of Possible One-on-One Relationships

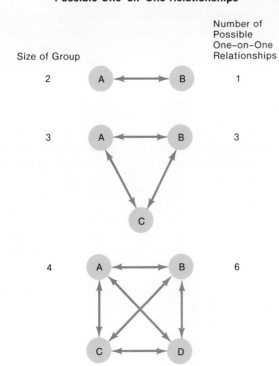

intimacy. In large groups, relations among group members become too complex and overwhelming for the members to remain close and personal with one another.

Leaders

The members of most informal groups would deny they had a real leader. Particularly in two-person groups (such as married couples), the members usually insist that "we're equal" in power and influence. But there are better ways of determining a group leader than asking its members. One is to see who has the most frequent and profound influence on what the group does. Leaders need not be chosen in a formal, explicit way. Most often, they emerge gradually and "spontaneously."

In the early stages of most groups, one person functions as a leader in all respects. Over time, groups generally acquire two distinctly different types of leaders: instrumental and expressive (Bales, 1951; Bales & Slater, 1955). Some members are leaders because they can coordinate the activities of others and help them pursue specific goals, such as deciding on the group's best course of action in specific situations. These **instrumental leaders** (also called "task leaders") are practical and may exert their leadership by giving orders, which they expect others to follow. In contrast, **expressive** (or "socio-emotional") **leaders** generate and sustain a sense of group solidarity, togetherness, and harmony. They crack jokes, pay compliments to others, keep conversations going, and mock people who do not belong to the group. It is easy to see why instrumental and expressive leaders are usually different people: Those who give orders are less likely to remain popular or well liked.

In the traditional American family, the husband and father most often played the instrumental role: He gave explicit, direct orders; made the major decisions; and "brought home the bacon." The wife and mother typically played the expressive role, providing emotional warmth, encouragement, and security (Parsons and Bales, 1955). Over the course of the past generation, these traditional, stereotyped roles have progressively broken down. Increasingly, husbands and wives are taking those family roles that reflect their own talents and personalities, not expectations they inherited from their parents and their parents' parents.

Leadership Styles.   Leaders typically display distinct styles of leadership. Three such styles have been isolated: authoritarian, democratic, and laissez-faire. An authoritarian leader rules simply by giving orders and expecting them to be obeyed: "Yours is not to question why, yours is but to do—or die." A democratic leader seeks to forge agreement within the group, through discussion and give-and-take interaction. A laissez-faire leader adopts a "hands off," live-and-let-live approach to the group, and makes no direct attempt to coordinate or organize its members.

In most groups, laissez-faire leaders are the least effective kind for getting things done, because most groups need at least some direction and guidance. The other two leadership styles may be more or less effective in specific situations. In wartime, it would be rather unwise for a lieutenant who leads a platoon to let all the soldiers decide whether to go out on a mission. When decisions must be made quickly and decisively, authoritarian leadership works best. But in most situations, followers do not want to be simply commanded; in western society at least, they want to participate in the group's decision-making processes

Instrumental leader Someone who leads by coordinating the activities of group members so they can rationally pursue specific goals.

Expressive leader Someone who leads by generating and sustaining a sense of solidarity, togetherness, and harmony.

and influence them. Leaders must learn to follow as much as they lead. Democratic leadership is most effective when members are comfortable with true give-and-take.

CONFORMITY

Most Americans think of themselves as "rugged individualists," non-conformists who refuse to "knuckle under" to group pressure, inner-directed souls who speak out against injustice, misconduct, and error. We express our opinions, we would assert, even if they are unpopular, even if they get us into trouble. If something happens before our very eyes, we agree with the baseball umpire's dictum: "I call 'em as I see 'em!" Yet one of the most remarkable facts about social life is the extent to which other people—particularly those who belong to the same groups to which we belong—influence what we do, feel, think, and are, particularly when we are actually in their presence. Alone, in private settings, we often act quite differently.

Perhaps there are exceptions to the influence of groups. But the remarkable thing is that this influence operates even in groups whose members are not close. Even when we know that something is clearly wrong, we often "go along" with the group. Of course, if we aren't sure what we feel about something, the group's judgment will have much more influence on us than it would if we had strong opinions of our own. But even when the group accepts something we know to be wrong, we may very well be influenced by its judgment.

A now-classic study of group influence was conducted by social psychologist Solomon Asch (1951, 1955, 1956). The subjects were told that they were taking part in an experiment on "visual judgment." Two cards were displayed; one showed a line of a certain length, and the second depicted three lines, one of which was the same length as the line on the first card. The lengths of the other two lines were strikingly different (see the figure below). The subjects were asked to identify which line on the second card was as long as the line on the first card. The subjects were placed in groups whose average size was eight, all but one of whom were "confederates" of the researchers. In accordance with instructions, the confederates one by one declared that line 1 on Card 2 was exactly as long as the line on Card 1, even though they were clearly of different lengths. The subject usually sat in the next-to-last seat and had to react to this epidemic of incorrect sense perception. "Were his eyes deceiving him? Had all of the rest of the group gone crazy? Did they have a different angle?" The subject may not have cared when the first or second confederates "gave an obviously incorrect answer, but after hearing six prior respondents agree on a choice that appeared very obviously incorrect, the naive subject was faced with a dilemma" (Albrecht, Thomas, and Chadwick, 1980, p. 136).

Nearly every one of us would say that we would not yield to such pressure. We would also predict that just about no one else would either. These experiments were conducted under a wide range of circumstances: The experimenters varied a number of factors, such as the difference of the length of the lines, the number of confederates who gave obviously wrong answers, and so on. But only one-quarter of all the subjects "were

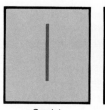

Card 1

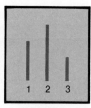

Card 2

completely independent and never agreed with the erroneous judgments of the majority" (Asch, 1955, p. 33). Tallying all of the subjects, 37 percent ended up agreeing with the false judgments of the group. When the subjects were asked to judge the length of the lines alone, away from the influence of the group, they made errors only 1 percent of the time. Clearly, when an individual's private perceptions—and, by extension, attitudes, feelings, and behavior, as well—clash with those of a group, the individual is likely to be influenced by the group's judgment and perhaps succumb to it, no matter how false it might seem. When the experiments included a few confederates who gave correct judgments, the subjects' error rate dropped to only 5 percent, instead of the 37 percent rate when the subjects were faced wth unanimous error on the confederates' part. Clearly, then, a unified group judgment is more difficult to oppose than a divided one.

Remember, these experiments dealt with simple cognitive perception—judgments given in a clear-cut situation. Most of what people do, think, and feel is not nearly so clear-cut. The stuff of group life is not based on simple perceptual judgments but on much more subtle, ambiguous, complex, and less easily demonstrable judgments and evaluations: religious and political beliefs, tastes in music and clothes, use or abstinence from drugs, and so on. In such areas of life, the group—particularly when composed of people who are intimate and emotionally close with one another—exerts its greatest powers over the individual.

PRIMARY AND SECONDARY GROUPS

Primary group Group based on informal, intimate, personal social relationships.

Secondary group Collectivity whose members relate to one another formally and impersonally.

Clearly, there are different kinds of groups. A married couple constitutes a group; so do the employees of General Motors. A street gang is a group; so are all the soldiers in the United States Army. How can we characterize differences among groups? No dimension captures more crucial differences than the primary-secondary distinction. **Primary groups** are based on informal, intimate, and personal social relations. **Secondary groups** are just the opposite; their members tend to relate to one another formally and more impersonally.

Group relations are "more or less" primary, not absolutely so, and "more or less" secondary. Still, it is easy to distinguish between the interaction of a primary group, like a family, and the interaction of a secondary group, like a business corporation. Body language in the two

In a secondary group, members relate to one another in a formal, restrained fashion, keeping emotional expression to a minimum. Here, secondary group members try to relax in an informal setting.

Susan McCartney/Photo Researchers

▨ TABLE 7–1 Relationships in Primary and Secondary Groups

In a primary *group, relations between members are*:	*In a* secondary *group, relations between members are*:
1. Emotional, intimate	1. Emotionally neutral
2. Diffuse, broad in scope, extensive	2. Narrow, segmental, specific
3. Particularistic; members relate to one another as individuals	3. Universalistic; members relate to one another as categories
4. Characterized by face-to-face interaction	4. Characterized by both face-to-face interaction and indirect communication
5. Valued as ends in themselves and of intrinsic value	5. Practical, expedient, purposive, and instrumental
6. Characterized by a flexible interpretation of rules	6. Characterized by a relatively close adherence to rules
7. Informal	7. Formal

Source: Derived from Talcott Parsons, The Social System. *New York: Free Press, 1951, pp. 57–58, 101–105; and William J. Goode,* Principles of Sociology. *New York: McGraw-Hill, 1977, pp. 187–198.*

settings will differ: Family members may lie on couches or on the floor; workers in an office always stand, or they sit up straight in chairs. Hugging and kissing is common in a family and rare in an office. Secrets are often revealed to family members and often concealed from fellow workers and managers. Laughing and crying are likely to be accepted, even encouraged, in families, and discouraged in corporate settings.

Emotional Intensity

Above all, primary groups permit or encourage emotion among members. They comprise circles of intimates who are allowed to "let their hair down" and "be themselves," to laugh and cry with one another, and to reveal themselves on the closest and most personal level. Psychologists use a term, "affect," to designate emotion. Affect includes those feelings that touch us most deeply: love, fear, rage, sorrow, joy. Primary-

In a primary group, relations among members are informal, intimate, diffuse, and characterized by face-to-face interaction. They are valued as ends in themselves. The expression of emotion is not only accepted, but encouraged.

Richard Hutchings/Photo Researchers

group relations are "affective,"—that is, emotional—because emotions are most readily expressed when we are with the people who are closest to us. Secondary-group relations, in contrast, are affectively neutral, because it is not appropriate for secondary-group members to express strong emotions toward one another.

Imagine walking into the office of a professor who teaches a 500-student course in which you are enrolled. Suddenly, suppose she declares her deepest love—or hatred—for you. You feel anxious, bewildered, extremely uncomfortable; this just "isn't done." Suppose, in contrast, that your closest friend suddenly became emotionally distant, cold, reserved, and unexpressive. Surely you would feel puzzled, hurt, distressed, and rejected. Of course, some people are by nature more emotional, others less so, but in primary groups everyone tends to be more emotional than in secondary groups.

Scope

Primary groups engage, encompass, and activate much broader segments of our personalities than secondary groups do. If a corporation wishes to hire a civil engineer to build a bridge, it matters little whether the engineer prefers Barry Manilow or Claudio Monteverdi, funny purple hats or tasteful beige ones. The important thing is the engineer's engineering skills. But among primary-group members, personal taste *is* relevant. In fact, these preferences may bring individuals together in the first place, because people sometimes use seemingly small things to represent larger points of common interest. To put it another way, the more secondary a group is, the more narrow the range of characteristics that members consider important in their group relations. Primary groups, in contrast, are diffuse—almost everything about their members is relevant. But selecting civil engineers on any basis but their ability to build bridges would be not only unwise but ludicrous. Organizations that build bridges are secondary groups; circles of friends are primary groups.

Particularism and Universalism

In a primary group, we not only relate to the total person but we also interact on the basis of special, already-established relationships. We do not set up universal standards—which apply equally to everyone, across the board—and then inform a primary-group member: "I've decided, on the basis of objective criteria, that I would be better off with someone else as a friend." Primary-group relations are "particularistic," based on special bonds with particular people, bonds that do not rest on objective measurements of a person's accomplishments, achievements, or performance. A "universalistic" relationship subjects everyone to the same standards, regardless of our personal ties to them. If a professor gives a student an A out of sheer friendship, he or she acts on a particularistic basis. If the same professor gives another student an A because that student has done well on a test graded according to criteria applied to all students, he or she acts on a universalistic basis. As a general rule, people in primary groups act in a particularistic way; they do things for and with one another because special relationships have already been established—as brothers, sisters, friends, neighbors, fellow-parishioners, or what have you. People in secondary groups act in a more universalistic sort of way: Abstract, formal, objective, universally applied criteria are more likely to guide their choices of what to do, and with whom. Neither way of acting is "better"; each is appropriate for a different kind of group relations.

Interaction

As we discussed earlier, it is very hard to maintain intimate, primary-group relations through letters, phone calls, messages—without direct contact, in other words. For a limited time, it can be done; but in the long run, intimacy requires face-to-face interaction, the rich soil in which intimacy grows. The physical presence of our intimates nourishes our emotions for them.

However, in secondary groups, communication among members can be of either type: face-to-face or indirect. Much secondary-group interaction takes the form of memos, phone calls, letters, announcements, and messages. After all, it would be wasteful to send an actual person to inform, individually, each worker in a factory every time management made a decision. In most cases, indirect contact works just as well. The lower the level of emotions within a group, and the more secondary it is, the less direct contact it needs to conduct its affairs.

Aims

People in secondary groups come together for specific purposes. Otherwise, what would be the point of associating with people for whom we have little emotional feeling? We interact with others in formal settings to achieve some practical goal: to make money, to save the lives of baby seals, to elect a senator, to find a cure for cancer, to receive a college degree, to prevent a nuclear holocaust, to achieve everlasting salvation in heaven, to assist earthquake victims. Secondary-group relations are not ends in themselves; they are means to an end.

Primary-group relations are just the opposite. We do not "hang out" with people we care about simply because we know they can help us in some practical way. Typically, the relationship has intrinsic value for those who participate in it: It is sought and sustained for its own sake. If we thought that our friends associated with us chiefly for hard-headed, practical reasons—to advance their careers, get higher grades in a course, or enjoy occasional free meals—our feelings toward them would grow colder and less genuine. Of course, friends do help each other in quite practical ways, but these are not the chief reasons for friendship. We are supposed to stick by our pals "through thick and thin"—not to associate with them only when they can help us and abandon them when they cannot.

Rules and Regulations

The closer we are to the members of a group, the more freedom, or leeway, we are likely to allow them in behavior; the more we accept behavior that strays from the general social norms; and the more our relations with them will tend to be unique, not tightly governed by rules and regulations. Most of us do not feel that we must observe the rules of etiquette and decorum rigidly when eating among intimates. But when we dine with secondary-group members, we are acutely aware of the need to "do the right thing" at all times. We make more of an effort not to eat with our hands, for instance, or not to talk with our mouths full or to reach across the table to grab second helpings. When we interact with members of a secondary group, our behavior is dominated by rules and regulations; norms hold us together, not intimacies or emotions. We are not likely to accept it when clerks shortchange us, when unfamiliar colleagues scratch our cars, or when students living on the floor above us party until 5 in the morning. But with primary-group members, most of us not only tolerate a great deal of rule-breaking behavior but even "explain" or "excuse" it to others: "Fred always shouts when he talks politics," we might warn a less-than-intimate acquaintance, to win for Fred an exemption from the ordinary rules of garden-variety social interaction.

FORMAL ORGANIZATIONS

Formal organization A group that has been deliberately created to achieve specific sets of goals and whose members' activities are systematically integrated to achieve them.

Rationality The deliberate setting of goals and the development of means designed to achieve them.

Bureaucracy A type of formal organization that is large and hierarchical and that forms the basis of an occupation and career for its employees.

A **formal organization** is a very special kind of group—the most secondary of all secondary groups. All the characteristics of secondary groups apply most strongly to formal organizations. Here is the land of emotional neutrality and narrow, universal rules.

What is a formal organization? To sociologists, it is a group that has been deliberately created to achieve specific sets of goals and whose members' activities are systematically integrated to achieve them. The hallmarks of the formal organization are a high degree of **rationality,** the deliberate setting of goals and the development of means designed to achieve them, and a high degree of organization or coordination among its members, usually achieved by an elaborate hierarchical structure in which it is always clear who can give orders to whom.

Nearly all of the formal organizations sociologists study are **bureaucracies.** Of all formal organizations, bureaucracies are the most formal, the most rational, the most hierarchical. They provide occupations and careers for their employees. Some formal organizations are not bureaucracies—for instance, voluntary associations, like Parent Teacher Associations: They are not large, have no hierarchies, and do not provide jobs and careers. For all practical purposes, however, the two terms—bureaucracy and formal organization—are interchangeable.

Bureaucracies existed thousands of years ago, in ancient China, Egypt, Africa, and Babylonia. Nonetheless, the word "bureaucracy" has a distinctly offensive ring: To many of us, it is almost a dirty word. Probably our first mental association with it is "red tape," waste, and inefficiency. Many things that informal groups could accomplish simply and easily—for instance, replacing a leaky roof atop a tribal meeting hall in a tiny African village—often take months or years when entrusted to bureaucracies. But only bureaucracies can run large organizations.

Weber's Model

The earliest—and, even today, most influential—description and theoretical analysis of formal organization was drawn by the great German sociologist Max Weber (1864–1920), whose ideas we touched on briefly in Chapter 1. Weber (1946, pp, 196–244; 1968, pp. 956–958) described bureaucracy with what he called the "machine model": the idea that bureaucracy is to social relations what the machine is to physical objects—practical, efficient, rational. Bureaucracies, as Weber described them, are set up to achieve specific goals or purposes—unlike primary groups, which arise spontaneously, in an unplanned, casual fashion. A bureaucracy's members have assigned tasks that are highly specialized. Each employee performs a very narrow range of activities and functions. A factory worker might spend seven hours a day, five days a week, fifty weeks a year attaching a particular bolt to a car fender. An office worker might do nothing but handle customer complaints. In bureaucracies, the principle of **division of labor** is carried to its furthest extreme.

Bureaucracies assign members to specific tasks, and promote them solely by testing their professional competence. Personal and particularistic criteria have nothing to do with promotion—only ability. Social relations within the organization are highly impersonal: cool, detached, affectively neutral. The members are ranked in a hierarchy of power and authority—a formal chain of command—so it is always quite clear who has authority over whom, who gives orders and who must take them. In other words, a bureaucracy is based on a network of superiors and subordinates. The mutual relations of all employees can be expressed in the form of an organizational chart.

Authority within the organization is attached to offices, not to individuals. An individual who occupies a given position has authority only as the occupant of that position, not as a result of any personal qualities he or she might have. Moreover, he or she has authority only in working hours and only in strictly limited ways. Being a boss doesn't mean that you can legitimately ask your subordinates to shine your shoes or change your baby's diapers. You have only job-related authority, even on the job.

Weber's characterization of the bureaucracy was written early in the twentieth century. It intended to sharply distinguish the bureaucracy from more informal types of social organization, like primary groups. Weber thus deliberately exaggerated the distinctive features of the bureaucracy. These features make up what he called an **ideal type** or **model**. In other words, not all formal organizations have all the characteristics Weber described. In fact, no bureaucracy conforms precisely to this model. Weber did not mean to imply that any organization that did not possess each and every one of these characteristics was not a bureaucracy. He meant only that the more an organization conformed to the model, the more it could be regarded as a bureaucracy. Some organizations are more bureaucratic than others, as you have no doubt found out for yourself.

A Contemporary Perspective

How accurately does Weber's early model depict contemporary, real-life bureaucracies? Most sociologists agree that it is quite useful as a starting point. But empirical research into the workings and structure of real bureaucracies have led sociologists to modify Weber's pioneering effort.

First of all, the "formal" features of a bureaucracy help determine what its members do, but other factors are at work, too. Informal social structures—which evolve within bureaucracies in an unplanned sort of way—often have more impact on the behavior of bureaucrats than the formal social structures, such as explicit duties and tasks, lines of authority, and rules and regulations. Sergeants may have more personal influence over the soldiers in their platoons than their commanding officers do. Company rules may require each worker to be as productive as possible, but few companies can enforce such rules: Workers informally and collectively arrive at their own, usually less demanding, output

Division of labor The specialization of roles, activities, and work functions involved in production within a society or a bureaucracy.

Ideal type The characterization of a phenomenon in a slightly exaggerated form to highlight its distinctive features.

Model See **Ideal type**.

levels (Homans, 1950, pp. 60–64). One researcher described one section of a certain factory (called "the bank wiring room") as follows:

> Whether or not the men were expected to behave as described, the fact was that they did not. They had a clear idea of a proper day's work. . . . The wiremen in the room felt . . . that no more work than this should be turned out. . . . They tended to work hard in the morning, until the completion of a day's work was in sight, and then to take it easy in the afternoon as quitting time approached. . . . If a man did turn out more than was thought proper, or if he worked too fast, he was exposed to merciless ridicule. . . . And ridicule was not the only penalty a nonconformist had to suffer. A game calling "binging" was played . . . [in which] a man walked up to another man and hit him as hard as he could on the upper arm—"binged" him. . . . Binging was . . . used as a penalty. A man who was thought to be working too fast . . . might be binged (Homans, 1950, pp. 60–61).

Manifest and Latent Goals. One good example of the importance of informal aspects of bureaucracy is the frequent conflict between ostensible, publicly declared, or **manifest goals,** on the one hand, and goals that may be inferred from the actual efforts of the bureaucrats, the **latent goals.** For instance, certain charities are supposed to assist the public welfare by fighting disease or discrimination or by promoting research, the arts, or brotherhood. Some of these charities, however, spend most of their contributions on fund raising and executive salaries, not on their stated goals (Bakal, 1979).

The Bureaucratic Personality. Weber also failed to anticipate the emergence of the so-called **bureaucratic personality** (Merton, 1957, pp. 123–124, 195–206). Emphasizing rules for their own sake, as bureaucrats tend to do, leads to a sort of "ritualism"—a tendency to forget about the goals that the rules were designed to promote and to stick to the rules at whatever cost, even if doing so destroys those very goals (Merton, 1957, pp. 149–153). The emphasis on rules and regulations makes for a built-in inflexibility, an inability to adapt. When conditions change, bureaucracies often make inappropriate responses, or (more inappropriate still) no responses at all. Strict rule following—in Merton's term, "ritualism"—is a "displacement of sentiments from goals onto means" (Merton, 1957, p. 201). It can undermine an organization's very reasons for existence.

Bureaucracies and Dehumanization. Weber also failed to see the dehumanizing aspects of the bureaucratic organization. He did not take into account the possibility that intense specialization, rigid rules, a strict hierarchy, and an impersonal work setting might give many bureaucrats a feeling of alienation, which in turn produces low morale, inefficiency, and, often, feelings of depression. One worker, a spot welder in a Ford plant in Chicago, says of his job:

> I stand in one spot, about two- or three-feet area, all night. The only time a person stops is when the line stops. We do about thirty-two jobs per car, per unit. Forty-eight units an hour, eight hours a day. Thirty-two times forty-eight times eight. Figure it out. That's how many times I push that button. . . . Repetition is such that if you were to think about the job itself, you'd slowly go out of your mind. . . . I don't understand how come more guys don't flip. Because you're nothing more than a machine when you hit this type of thing. They give better care to that machine than they will to you. . . . And you *know* this. Somehow you get the feeling that the machine is better than you are (cited in Terkel, 1975, pp. 221–222, 223).

Manifest goal The stated, widely recognized purpose for a group, organization, social institution, or action.

Latent goal An unacknowledged end toward which a group, an organization, a society, or any social arrangement is directed or that it manages to achieve.

Bureaucratic personality An individual who emphasizes rules for their own sake and forgets about the goals that the rules were designed to promote.

Clearly, such a job can be done by robots, which is one reason why robots are increasingly being used in modern factories.

Weber's failure to emphasize the workings of *informal* group processes within bureaucracies, and to recognize the demoralization and inefficiency that often flourish within it, do restrict the usefulness of his model. Even so, they do not make it altogether invalid. After all, formal organizations—and only formal organizations—can build cities, bridges, and roads; conduct warfare; communicate across continents; explore the vast uncharted universe; educate millions of students of all ages every year; pass and enforce laws; and budget billions of dollars to support programs that influence every aspect of our lives. Some of the most important social and cultural activities demand planning, organization, coordination, division of labor, hierarchy, and a certain degree of impersonality. At the same time, when we fail to remember that a bureaucracy is not a machine but a group of human beings organized in a certain way, we fail to understand entirely its most fundamental workings. Every formal organization is an assemblage of people with diverse motives for participation; different, yet distinctly human, needs and expectations; and unique reactions to this highly regimented setting. Above all, sociology studies the human factor, and the human factor is at work within bureaucracies, just as it is in every other aspect of social life.

GROUPS IN MODERN LIFE

Human beings are social beings. It is not enough to work at a job, earn a salary, live in a house or apartment, vote in elections, and watch television. We also need intimacy, closeness, the personal touch in our social relations. Much of our participation in groups—regardless of their stated goals—serves the end of engaging us in interactions that are primary in nature. People who are cut off from primary groups and the intimacy these create tend to live shorter, more psychologically troubled, unhappier lives than people who are involved with primary groups do, and they are more destructive, both to themselves and to others. Human beings seem to have a strong need for intimacy.

In small, rural villages, people automatically belong to groups that are close, intimate, and primary in nature. As societies grow in size, the amount of formal, impersonal contact among their members tends to grow, too. In contemporary society, many of these primary groups have either broken down completely or disappeared into the nooks and crannies of society. Intimacy, once an automatic result of living in a human community, must now be achieved. In every urban area, groups cater to this need that people have to be close to one another: "singles" clubs, yoga classes, local bars, discussion groups, escort services, and advice columns, just to name a few.

These groups and activities do not always achieve the desired results. Some merely permit an odious new breed of entrepreneurs to profit by exploiting a vulnerable public. And not all their members are searching for truly intimate contact. Those who are looking for it will often be disappointed. The search continues.

Intimacy can still be found in many associations and activities; most people do manage to connect with others. Over 90 percent of all Americans eventually marry, and a married couple is the most intimate of all primary groups. Marriage is so popular that divorced men and women are even more likely to get married (again) than people who have never been married. Even in the most impersonal work settings, informal networks and groups spring up and flourish amid the desert of bureaucracy. By appealing to this need for intimacy, some "new" religions (see Chapter 14) have replaced the many primary groups individuals ordinarily join with a single, all-embracing group. Many voluntary associations (like political, hiking, birdwatching, or chess clubs) do create meaningful friendships and other primary-group ties among their members. The more active you are in such clubs, organizations, and groups, the more likely you are to enjoy the satisfactions of intimacy. Despite all obstacles, people do manage to retain their primary ties to one another, even in modern society.

SUMMARY

1. Some human characteristics form the basis for creating groups, whereas others do not.

2. Sociologically, a group possesses three basic traits or attributes: It is made up of people who interact with one another frequently and intimately, share a common identity or "we" feeling, and expect one another to adhere to a special and distinct set of norms.

3. Statistical categories are made up of people who share a given characteristic, whether or not it creates a group out of those who share it.

4. Potential groups are made up of collectivities whose members share a basis for belonging to a group, but who have not yet come together to form one.

5. Aggregates are made up of people who are in the same place at the same time, but who do not share a common bond—and therefore do not form a group.

6. Belonging to some particular groups entails competing with and opposing other groups. In this case, the group to which a person may belong is the "in-group"; the group in opposition is the "out-group."

7. Many people evaluate themselves not only on the basis of the standards of the groups to which they belong, but also according to the standards of groups to which they do not belong; these groups are called reference groups.

8. The way people behave in groups is not a simple function of their personal feelings or beliefs. A number of characteristics of the group itself influences how the group members behave.

9. Group size strongly influences social relations among members of a group; for instance, the larger the group, the more difficult it is for members to maintain intimate social relations with one another.

10. In many groups, leaders emerge. Typically, they specialize into instrumental (goal-directed) and expressive (group- and member-

directed) leaders, usually two different people. Leadership styles may be authoritarian, democratic, or laissez-faire.

11. Most people are powerfully influenced by "peer pressure" or group influence. Group membership is a powerful agent in influencing all of our behavior and attitudes.

12. A primary group is one in which relations between members are emotional, diffuse, particularistic, characterized by face-to-face interaction, and intrinsically rewarding. Primary groups permit latitude in interpreting rules and norms.

13. A secondary group is one in which relations between members are emotionally neutral, segmental, universalistic, and characterized by face-to-face and indirect communication and fairly close adherence to rules.

14. A formal organization is a group that has been formed to achieve a specific set of goals and whose members' activities have been systematically integrated to promote those goals.

15. Although bureaucracies have been characterized historically as rational and highly efficient, some "irrational" features characterize them: informal group processes that may subvert the organization's goals, the emergence of ritualism, and a sense of alienation that many members feel.

16. In modern society, a number of groups have sprung up to answer the need that many individuals have for intimacy; some are successful in achieving this goal.

SUGGESTED READINGS

Tom Douglas, *Groups: Understanding People Gathered Together*. London: Tavistock, 1983.
In this discussion, the author locates key processes that operate in the dynamics of all groups, both those that arise spontaneously ("natural" groups) and those that are specifically created. In addition, the author argues that "natural" groups have some qualities that are special to themselves—qualities that can often be successfully injected into "created" groups to make them more effective.

Edward Gross and Amitai Etzioni, *Organizations in Society*. Englewood Cliffs, New Jersey: Prentice-Hall, 1985.
An introduction to the theories and research in the study of complex organizations. This is probably the best place to start in an investigation of the field.

George C. Homans, *The Human Group*. New York: Harcourt Brace, 1950.
A clearly written, sensitive analysis of the dynamics of interaction in the group setting. This book is timeless—a classic.

Rosabeth Moss Kanter, *Men and Women of the Corporation*. New York: Basic Books, 1977.
A sociological analysis of the organization of work and the distribution of power in the bureaucracy. Argues for decentralization, increasing the power of workers, and decreasing the numbers of layers in management.

William M. Kephart, *Extraordinary Groups: The Sociology of Unconven-*
tional Life-Styles (3rd ed.). New York: St. Martin's Press, 1987.
A description and sociological analysis of several unusual, unconventional groups, both contemporary and historical, including the Gypsies, the Oneida Community, the Father Divine Movement, the Mormons, and the Shakers.

Joseph Luft, *Group Processes: An Introduction to Group Dynamics* (3rd ed.). Palo Alto, California: Mayfield, 1984.
An explication of how group interaction can be facilitated. Especially strong on practical applications. Uses concept such as "the Johari Window" and "the Zucchini Connection" to help students grasp group processes and problems.

Theodore M. Mills, *The Sociology of Small Groups* (2nd ed.). Englewood Cliffs, New Jersey: Prentice-Hall, 1984.
A brief overview of small groups from a sociological perspective.

Benjamin Zablocki, *Alienation and Charisma: A Study of Contemporary American Communes*. New York: Free Press, 1980.
A detailed yet intriguing research report on one special type of group: the commune. How do communal members handle the problems of living together? What about love and sex, autonomy, inequality, vulnerability? Who leaves and who stays? This book explores these issues in a variety of different types of communes: Christian, Eastern-religious, political, alternative-family, and so on.

chapter 8

DEVIANCE AND SOCIAL CONTROL

Now and throughout history, all human societies everywhere in the world have set and enforced rules or *norms*. Rules and regulations do not exist only in formal organizations; they can be found everywhere. As we cast our sociological gaze up and down the annals of time, across the world's nations and societies, we notice that rules and norms differ, and so do the nature and severity of the punishments for violating them. *But rules themselves are universal, and so too is their enforcement.*

What would happen if anyone could do anything to anyone else, with no constraints whatsoever—if there were no punishments at all for murder, rape, robbery, and other harmful acts? No such society could endure for long; it would collapse into a state of "war of all against all." Punishing wrongdoing and rewarding appropriate behavior—a process sociologists call **social control**—is obviously necessary to keep the members of a society cooperating on a day-to-day basis and to prevent them from endangering one another's lives. Everyone in a position of authority whose job it is to oversee the behavior of others—judges, police officers, religious leaders, teachers, psychiatrists—is engaged in the business of social control. Social order requires social control. No lengthy explanation seems necessary to justify this observation; it appeals to common sense.

Oddly enough, however, relatively few norms are designed to protect members of society from injurious and predatory actions. Most norms discourage behavior that directly harms no one. Norms are *symbolic*. They protect an overall vision of the way society has determined people ought to behave, whether or not that vision really affects the physical well-being of society's members. In other words, society's norms are not, for the most part, "rational"—that is, meant to achieve specific objectives. They embody principles that are simply considered to be right, regardless of what they do for society. Obviously, some norms, like "Thou shalt not kill," do protect society from harm, but they are in the minority. No one would be physically injured if we were all to wear our clothes backwards, to speak every word twice, or to eat steak by grabbing it with our hands and tearing at it with our teeth. However, if we did these things our behavior would elicit disapproval, and that disapproval would be conveyed to us.

Social control All of the social efforts to discourage deviant behavior and the mechanisms designed to ensure conformity to norms, rules, and laws.

WHAT IS DEVIANCE?

Sociologists call rule-breaking activities "deviance" or "deviant behavior." But there are different kinds of norms and rules. Some norms are routinely violated; their violation troubles no one, yet the norms continue to exist. "Don't walk across the street against a red light" is a rule that may be ignored without consequences—unless a car happens to be coming. Violating this rule cannot really be regarded as deviant. No one will think the less of you, nor do anything to you, if you walk across the street against a red light.

In addition, behavior must be examined in context. Some acts may be regarded with disfavor in the abstract, but not in all situations. For instance, almost all of us regard stealing as bad, a violation of the rules— deviant behavior, in short. But what if stealing is the only way to save the life of a starving baby? The act might seem less deviant if we knew more about the situation that provokes it.

In the view of many sociologists, deviance is best defined reactively. To know what is and is not deviant, they would say, you must see what happens to someone who engages in an act observed by others. How do these other people react; what do they do to the person who engages

Deviance is behavior that offends some members of a society and elicits social disapproval, sometimes even hostility, from them. Sociologists call the people who observe, evaluate, and react to deviance an audience.

Gregory Heisler

in the act? Do they react with praise or delight, or with ridicule, condemnation, or punishment? In order to know what qualifies as deviant behavior, we must conduct a series of mental experiments. Imagine dozens of acts being undertaken in different situations by different people. How, for instance, would your roommate react if you stole his or her stereo? How would your mother react if she saw you injecting heroin? Or your father, if he walked into your bedroom and found you kissing someone of your own sex? If the answer to these questions could only be "in a negative, condemnatory fashion," the behavior is truly deviant.

Sociologists define **deviance** as behavior that offends some people in a society and moves them to disapprove of, condemn, or punish the actor. In a nutshell, it is behavior that is likely to get you into trouble (E. Goode, 1984, p. 17). This definition does not imply that the **actor,** the person who enacts the behavior, deserves to be punished, only that punishment is likely if the behavior comes to light. Nor does the definition imply that the behavior in question is "sick" or pathological, the product of a disordered mind. Actually, the overwhelming majority of people who engage in deviant behavior are remarkably normal in most ways. In fact, deviance doesn't even have to be unusual or statistically rare—nor is rare behavior necessarily deviant. It is statistically unusual to take three baths a day, but no one who does so will be condemned or punished as a result. Likewise, nearly all of us tell lies from time to time, so lying is very common. But if you are caught at it, you will be criticized. In short, to know what is deviant, you must find out what kinds of behavior elicit disapproval in others.

Sociologists call those people who observe and evaluate behavior and condone, encourage, or punish the perpetrators of deviance an **audience.** An audience is simply an actual (or potential) collection of people who do or might witness an act, or who hear about it from others. Which others, however? Whose reactions decide what is and is not deviance? After all, if we looked hard enough, we could find *some* people who would condemn almost anything we might think of: dancing, chewing gum, drinking wine at meals, smiling. You name it; someone is against it. Are these activities deviant? No. Deviance is a matter of degree. What is and is not deviant is decided in part by numbers—how many people condemn an act—and in part by the intensity of the hostility, the outrage, or the punishment an act touches off. Acts that excite disapproval in only a few scattered individuals are not deviant acts; likewise, acts the generate only mild disaproval, even in many people, may not be deviant either. Obviously, if someone reacts to something you do by saying, "I'm not too sure if what you're doing is such a hot idea," that reaction is less disapproving than a slap in the face would be. The more people who disapprove of an act, and the more extreme their disapproval, the more deviant is the act.

Deviance and Relativity

Americans accept and take for granted some forms of behavior—such as wearing bathing suits on a beach—that would amount to deviance elsewhere; and activities that are acceptable elsewhere—like hearing voices or seeing visions—are strange or even mad here. Different societies punish very different activities; this is the principle of "sociological relativity" (see Chapter 3).

In some societies, the use of any kind of psychoactive (mind-altering) drug, even alcohol, is regarded as deviant, and anyone who violates this rule will be condemned. In other parts of the world, the use of

Deviance Behavior that offends some people in a society and that moves them to disapproval, condemnation, or punishment of the actor.

Actor Someone who engages in behavior.

Audience Individuals with whom an individual, or a group of individuals, interact, and who witness and react to their behavior.

such drugs as marijuana, cocaine, peyote, and opium is regarded as quite acceptable. Cultural relativity is basic to the study of deviant behavior (Edgerton, 1976).

Customs and norms vary not only from place to place but also from time to time. In Spain during the Inquisition, and in seventeenth-century Puritan New England, religious heretics were often hunted down, persecuted, and even killed. Nowadays, religion is pretty much a personal matter, even in Spain, to say nothing of New England. We must recognize the historical relativity inherent in perceptions of deviant behavior.

Some acts—like incest and murder—are condemned by most societies, so we cannot adopt a completely relativistic approach. Nonetheless, the variability in what is regarded as deviant behavior should impress us more forcefully than the uniformity. Of course, the idea of cultural relativity does not imply that certain activities are not really harmful. Nor does it say that everything and anything is morally acceptable simply because it may be acceptable somewhere. Whether or not a certain action is "really" wrong or right is a question altogether different from whether or not it is regarded as wrong or right. Infanticide—killing babies at birth—may well be truly evil and undesirable, even though it has been widely practiced in different places at different times. Our views concerning infanticide have not prevented it from being tolerated and encouraged elsewhere. It is the punishment or the acceptance of acts that makes them deviant or conventional. Whether they are intrinsically and inherently evil—how we personally feel about their moral status—is really beside the point. The study of deviance from a relativistic position does not address itself to the ultimate good or evil of behavior—only to how it is viewed in certain situations, in certain places, at certain times.

We cannot, therefore, decide whether or not a specific kind of behavior is deviant until we look at people's actual, past, or potential reactions to it. "Deviance is in the eyes of the beholder" (Simmons, 1969, pp. 3–11).

THEORIES OF DEVIANCE

Demonic possession Being possessed by spirits and forced to do evil things; a popular explanation for deviance in the Middle Ages.

Explanations of deviance have engaged the minds of experts and ordinary observers for centuries. In medieval Europe, the dominant explanation was **demonic possession**—the idea that spirits enter human souls and make them do evil things (Pfohl, 1985, pp. 17–42). Over the years, religion lost its hold on the public's mind, and the philosophers of the Enlightenment (the eighteenth century) proposed a new explanation. According to them, the human mind at birth is without knowledge of good or evil and is armed only with a preference for pleasure over pain. Experiences teach us what is pleasurable and what is painful. If we want to change behavior, the Enlightenment philosophers thought, we must first control experience. For instance, society's punishment for wrongdoing should cause just enough pain to ensure that people refrain from behavior that may be pleasurable to them but that violates social norms.

By the nineteenth century, it was recognized that human beings are not mere pleasure-pain machines—that we engage in behavior, deviant and otherwise, for a wide variety of reasons aside from seeking pleasure and avoiding pain. Each scientific discipline—at first, biology; later, psychology; then, sociology—developed its own explanations for deviant behavior.

Biological Theories of Deviance

A Nineteenth-Century Theory. One of the earliest biological theories of deviant behavior was worked out by an Italian physician named Cesare Lombroso (1835–1909). Attempting to extend Darwin's theory of evolution, Lombroso argued that criminals and other wrongdoers were actually ape-like, or "atavistic," throwbacks, genetic accidents representing a more primitive life form in the human evolutionary chain. They were biologically defective, "born criminals," who had been accidentally deposited in the wrong era of human history.

There are innumerable flaws in this silly theory, not the least of them the fact that most apes are less violent than humans. Lombroso simply equated violent and criminal behavior with "primitive" behavior—a totally incorrect idea, as it turns out. Moreover, Lombroso picked and chose his cases, selecting criminals he regarded as "ape-like"—with low foreheads, protruding ears and lips, receding chins, and so on. He did not compare the distribution of these traits in the criminal population with their distribution in the population at large. As a result, Lombroso's claims were totally worthless from a scientific point of view. Such a systematic statistical comparison, made by Charles Goring (1913), an English physician, showed that criminal and noncriminal populations do not differ with respect to physical or biological makeup.

Twentieth-Century Theories. Another biological theory, which explained criminal behavior by body type, or **somatotype,** enjoyed a brief vogue in the 1940s and 1950s (Sheldon, 1940; Sheldon et al., 1949). According to the body-type theory, **endomorphs** (short, plump people) and **ectomorphs** (thin, frail, ones) are much less likely to become juvenile delinquents than **mesomorphs,** muscular, athletic people. This theory rests on a foundation of common sense, at least for the few criminal and deviant acts that really do require muscles. A "96-pound weakling," for instance, is not likely to assault someone who is muscular and twice that size—not without a gun, anyway. However, body-type explanations are not regarded as useful by researchers in the field today, because the overwhelming majority of criminal, delinquent, and deviant acts can be committed by persons of any and all body types.

Somatotype Body type or physical characteristics; one theory of why some people commit crime and deviant behavior.

Endomorph A plump individual.

Ectomorph A thin, frail individual.

Mesomorph A muscular, athletic individual.

Genetic abnormality Pathological chromosomes; one theory of why some people commit crimes.

Genetic Abnormality. Recently, biological factors have again been invoked to explain the causes of deviance and crime (Wilson and Herrnstein, 1985). This new thoery forcuses on **genetic abnormalities.** Most males have what is called the XY chromosomal pattern: forty-six microscopic strands, called chromosomes, that determine their inherited makeup. Some men have what is known as an XYY pattern—an "extra Y" chromosome. Such men tend to be significantly taller than average and to have lower-than-average IQs. Some criminologists argue that "extra Y" males tend to commit a disproportionate number of crimes and that their genetic abnormality is the cause. One problem with this theory is that the XYY chromosomal pattern is very rare; it appears in only one out of every 1,500 to 3,000 men. And is does not appear in women at all.

Objections. All biological theories of deviance and crime suffer from the same two basic flaws. First, biological characteristics cannot and do not directly cause any form of behavior, deviant or otherwise. What crucially influences behavior is not physical characteristics but their impact on others. To return to our body-type example, for instance, a small thin boy is much less likely to be recruited into a fighting gang than a muscular, athletic boy. Physical and social factors are closely intertwined. People react to our physical characteristics, and these reactions, not the physical characteristics themselves, shape our behavior.

The second problem with biological theories of deviance is that rules, norms, and laws are always defined by society. What is regarded as law-abiding, conventional behavior in one culture is deviant in another. Our chromosomes and our muscles know nothing of society's rules and laws. How can a biological characteristic know that it is wrong in one society or social context to kill people, but right in another?

Psychological Theories of Deviance

Within psychiatry and psychology, many different theories attempt to explain the causes of deviant behavior. For the most part, they all have one thing in common: the premise that the key factor is the personality of the offender. Deviance, in this view, is the product of disordered, neurotic, or abnormal minds. Personality theories generally stress early-childhood experiences. Early, painful traumas produce a certain type of abnormal personality that, in turn, expresses itself in antisocial acts, or deviant behavior. Psychological theories assume that this process takes place independently of the culture, subculture, or society in which the personality is raised (Hendin, 1975; Socarides, 1975).

Most psychological explanations treat deviant behavior as a kind of adaptive mechanism, an attempt to deal with certain personality problems. Much of the process is not understood by the actor, whose unconscious mind is largely in control. People in their "right minds" do not freely choose to engage in deviant behavior, this perspective argues; deviation is not, and cannot ever be, intrinsically satisfying. Human beings are driven to deviant behavior by some sort of psychopathology. It is thus not the behavior itself that counts—only what the behavior represents to the actor. The expert understands this behavior but the actor does not.

Psychoanalysts, whose ideas derive from the work of Sigmund Freud (1856–1939), argue that what they call the "Oedipus Complex"—a young boy's unresolved desire to compete with his father for the sexual attentions of his mother—is the unconscious foundation for most deviant behavior. In this view homosexuality, for instance, is produced by the boy's desire for sex with his mother—and her encouraging, seductive behavior toward him—coupled with a strong feeling of guilt about incest that makes all women off-limits sexually and forces the individual to adapt by substituting men as sexual objects (Bieber et al., 1962; Socarides, 1978).

Objections. One problem with many psychological theories of deviance is that they have mostly been worked out from studies of people who have sought psychiatric help or had it forced on them by getting into trouble. In almost every conceivable respect, these people are quite different from those who engage in the same deviant and criminal behavior quietly, people whose activities remain hidden from psychiatric or public scrutiny. We certainly would not build a theory about why some people become truck drivers based solely on the experiences of those drivers who seek out psychiatric help or who have been arrested. Even personality tests administered by psychologists are never given to random, unbiased, representative samples of the population as a whole. So the first problem with personality theories of deviance is their reliance on small, unrepresentative, often clinical samples—those based entirely on patients. Clearly, generalizations drawn from such samples cannot inspire confidence.

Second, psychiatric and other personality diagnoses are notoriously vague, subjective, unreliable, and strongly influenced by the social and personal characteristics of the clinician (Mechanic, 1980, pp. 154–164). Psychiatrists and psychologists cannot even agree among themselves about how to define and measure such crucial concepts and conditions as "neurosis," "maladjustment," "mental illness," and "psychopathology." One study defined psychological abnormality so broadly that its authors claimed that 80 percent of the people in midtown Manhattan suffered from some sort of "mental disorder" (Srole et al., 1962). Psychological theories assume that mental abnormality is roughly equivalent to physical illness. This is called the "medical model" or the "disease analogy." In fact, mental abnormality is a hazy concept; physical disease is less hazy. The analogy may therefore be invalid. One psychiatrist has even gone so far as to say that the whole concept of mental illness is a myth (Szasz, 1961).

The third problem with psychological theories of deviance is that they tend to be individualistic: They attempt to explain behavior as a product of isolated individuals' acting on impulses from within. Yet, as you know from the chapters on interaction and groups, you cannot fully predict how someone will act just by knowing his or her individual characteristics. Deviant behavior, like behavior in general, is typically a "collective effort," because most people behave one way alone and another way in the presence of others. Social context is the most important factor influencing what people do. Social context makes some behavior deviant, other behavior conventional. Any theory ignoring it or minimizing the influence of social contexts will be incomplete or invalid.

Sociological Theories of Deviance

Sociological theories about deviant behavior do more than just explain why specific, isolated, scattered individuals engage in unconventional acts. They tackle the broader issue, too: the social conditions that create patterns of deviant behavior. Most sociologists are more concerned with rates of deviance than with the reasons why this or that person engages in it. Why is crime more frequent in cities than in small towns? What are the chances that juvenile delinquents who are placed in correctional facilities will become professional career criminals, as compared with delinquents who commit the same crimes but are not caught? Which forms of deviance are whites and Blacks, respectively, more likely to commit, and why? These are the sorts of questions that sociologists ask.

In addition, sociological theories of deviance examine not only the behavior and the actors who engage in it but also the audience reaction to both. How does an act come to be regarded as deviant? Why does a society punish some forms of behavior and not others? Who makes the rules? Who gets punished for violating them and who gets off scot-free? Biological and psychological theories of deviance take social rules, laws, and norms for granted. They assume that people who violate them must be different from people who do not. Sociologists consider the creation and enforcement of the rules, laws, and norms a part of the problem to be investigated.

Anomie A social condition of normlessness, where traditional values have lost their hold on people.

Anomie.   In his classic, *Suicide*, Emile Durkheim (1951; originally published in 1897) argued that people kill themselves as a result of social conditions, not individual conditions. He called one of these social conditions **anomie:** a state of normlessness, where restraints have been lifted from the members of a society and traditional values and rules have lost their hold on the people. Under these conditions, Durkheim tried to show, the suicide rate is high.

Decades later, an American sociologist named Robert K. Merton expanded this idea. Merton contended that not only suicide but all forms of deviant behavior result from anomie. Merton suggested (1968, pp. 185–214) that one specific source of anomie—the discrepancy between the cultural goal of material success and the means that society provides to achieve that goal—produces "deviant behavior on a large scale." In our society, every member is encouraged to achieve a high standard of living. We cannot grow up in this society, Merton argued, without being influenced by this goal; indeed, we all wish to achieve it. But not all of us can. No society can possibly provide the means by which all its members achieve material success on a grand scale. Certainly, ours does not. Many Americans find the high road to fame and fortune blocked by the millions of people who are already struggling along it.

What do people do about these frustrations? What "adaptations" do we make to them? Merton wanted to know. The first "mode of adaptation" is simply faith: We must have faith in the American dream of success. We then go about achieving this success (if we can) in the legal, legitimate, culturally approved manner: We go to school, get a degree, find a job, work hard, and try to climb up the ladder of success. Merton called this route "conformity."

But suppose the ladder is blocked? Many people press forward anyway. Others abandon the legitimate, culturally approved route and seek to achieve material success through illegal, illegitimate, or deviant means. They seek wealth and power through such means as pimping and prostitution, organized crime, burglary, robbery, or white-collar crime. "Innovation" is what Merton called this mode of adaptation, and he devoted as much attention to it as he did to all the other modes combined. Innovation is a way of dealing with the need for success in a society that does not allow everyone to achieve that need legally and conventionally. One solution to this kind of pressure is to select an illegal, unconventional means to the same end.

"Ritualism" is another mode of adaptation. It involves abandoning the goal of success but keeping faith with the legitimate means of achieving it. Ritualists are rule followers who have forgotten the purpose of the rules. An example would be the petty bureaucrat who follows all rules down to the tiniest detail, even when the rules undermine the goals of the organization (See Chapter 7).

"Retreatism," another mode of adaptation, involves abandoning both culturally approved goals and the legitimate means of attaining them. Retreatists do not seek to become materially successful—either through legitimate *or* illegitimate means—usually because they have tried and failed at both. Examples of retreatists are psychotics, skid-row alcoholics, and drug addicts. These are society's "two-time losers" because they failed to make it in the conventional world *and* in the underworld.

"Rebellion" represents a mode of adaptation that is quite different from the others. It denies culturally approved goals and the legitimate means of achieving them, but it substitutes different goals and means. The rebel proposes a revolutionary model of what society could be like—perhaps, say, a socialist utopia. Examples of rebels include the 1960s political radicals who attempted to generate a revolution.

LIMITATIONS.   When Merton's theory of anomie was put forward, in the 1930s, the dominant perspective (within and outside sociology) viewed deviance as a kind of pathology: a defect, a sickness, or a behavior produced by unusual traits or conditions. Merton, on the contrary, argued that the routine workings of conventional values and institutions create definite pressures that push us all toward nonconformity. In a sense, Merton attempted to "normalize" deviance.

The second contribution of Merton's **anomie theory** was its emphasis on society-wide, systemic factors that encourage deviant behavior, not individual factors. He wanted to know what led members of whole societies, or members of large groups and categories within them, to exhibit high rates of deviance, not what leads specific individuals to go astray. Although his was certainly not the very first theory to adopt this perspective—Durkheim had raised precisely the same issue—Merton's theory represented a significant achievement. The article that first presented it remains even now the most often quoted work in the entire literature of sociology.

Contrary to Merton's claims (1968, pp. 188, 200), however, his theory did not explain the full range of deviant behavior. It may well account for such forms of deviance as prostitution, professional crime, and embezzlement. But many deviant activities probably do not result from blocked aspirations. Do all or even most alcoholics drink to excess because they have not become materially successful? Why should we think so, when there are so many overachievers who cannot control their drinking? Are smoking marijuana and snorting cocaine on weekends "retreatist" forms of behavior? And what of homosexuality: How does it fit into the scheme?

Anomie theory An explanation that locates the cause of deviance in the discrepancy between the cultural goal of material success and the means society provides to achieve that goal.

Many, and probably most, forms of deviance simply are not illuminated or explained by anomie at all. But as a limited explanation of some forms of deviance, anomie still has enormous value.

Culture Transmission.   No large, complex society ever teaches or enforces one single set of standards. Some subcultures (see Chapter 3) and groups teach unconventional values straightforwardly, as a matter of course. Culture-transmission theorists, such as Edwin Sutherland, argue that deviant, criminal, and delinquent behavior are learned through close interaction with intimates, much as conventional, law-abiding behavior is learned. Deviance, they say, is what happens when people are drawn into circles of acquaintances whose values and norms conflict with prevailing standards. The more intimate and frequent anyone's contacts with those who hold deviant values are, the greater is the chance of their actually embracing and acting out those values. Because the transmission of a deviant subculture involves interacting with its members and, at the same time, reducing interaction with the members of conventional society, this idea is called the "theory of differential association" (Sutherland and Cressey, 1978, pp. 80–83). This theory asserts that to become deviants, we must associate with people who embrace deviant values and beliefs.

According to one application of this theory, differential association begins at birth, when we learn the culture of our parents. Walter Miller, an anthropologist, holds that most delinquency is committed by boys at the bottom of the ladder of social class. Lower-class values, according to the **culture-transmission theory,** actually encourage these boys to break the law. The constant search for excitement, thrills, danger, risk, and "action," leads many lower-class boys into violence. Another value of this subculture—the ability to outwit, dupe, or "con" others—tends to devalue ordinary jobs and to encourage certain illegal activities. The desire of working-class boys to demonstrate their independence of authority and restraint (including parental restraint) leads them into constant run-ins with the police. In short, Miller claimed that children growing up in a lower-class subculture, are more likely to engage in illegal, delinquent and deviant acts than are children growing up in a middle-class environment. The middle class "lays down the law"; the working class must follow or suffer the consequences (Miller, 1958).

LIMITATIONS.   Like all other theories of deviance, culture transmission has its flaws and limitations. To begin with, not all deviant behavior is learned—at least, not straightforwardly. The theory works well for deviant activities—like juvenile delinquency, organized crime, drug use, and homosexuality—that have won acceptance among certain groups. But what about child molestation? A tiny minority of child molesters finds this activity acceptable and encourages others to participate in it (McCaghy, 1967). And what about embezzlers? Surely they emerge more or less on their own, almost never as a result of socialization in an embezzling subculture (Cressey, 1953). Many forms of deviance and crime are solitary in nature. They arise in large part as a result of some kind of independent invention, not through learning.

The culture-transmission theory also does not explain why certain individuals commit deviant acts and others do not. Miller's theory would suggest that all lower-class boys would become delinquent, but only a small minority actually does so. Miller's theory also fails to explain why men and women become homosexual—only how they do so. No doubt, becoming gay involves a learning process: associating with men

Culture-transmission theory A perspective that explains deviant behavior in terms of learning unconventional values in a straightforward fashion.

or women who are already gay. But why do some people associate extensively with homosexuals while others do not? Culture transmission pinpoints a crucial process in deviance—but not a cause. Learning is a means of becoming deviant—though not a *necessary* means—but it does not explain why some choose to do something and others do not. Learning can, likewise, explain how you master sociology, but not why you decided to take it in the first place. Learning must be supplemented with other theories.

Conflict Theory. All the theories of deviance we discussed so far try to explain why certain people violate society's norms and laws. **Conflict theory** turns the question around. It asks, Why are certain actions regarded as deviant? Why are certain laws passed and enforced? Why are some lawbreakers caught and punished, others not? In answering these questions, conflict theory tries to show how making and enforcing rules, norms, and, especially, laws helps to maintain social control.

Most theories treat social control as society's effort to protect its structure and values. They assume that most people share the same set of values and accept a common social order. Conflict theorists disagree. They want to know whose values and whose version of the social order social control protects. Values, norms, rules, and laws are not held in common by all members of any society, nor do they protect all members of society. Quite the contrary, the dominant values, norms, and laws exploit many people. Defining certain acts and people as deviant or criminal helps dominant groups and classes enforce their own particular views of right and wrong—that is, their own special interests. They define what they themselves think and do as "good" and "legal," and what less powerful people think and do as "bad," "deviant," and "criminal." Conflict theorists ask which groups have the power to legitimate their beliefs, behavior, and interests, and to stigmatize and criminalize those of other groups. Their answer: the most powerful groups in society.

LIMITATIONS. As with all other theories of deviant behavior, conflict theory provides only a part of the picture. Some forms of behavior are widely condemned, sometimes for reasons that reflect the interests and the views of many classes, not just the ruling class. Certain norms and laws do protect the members of the society at large—those that prohibit robbery, murder, and rape, for instance. In addition, conflict theory does not ask why certain individuals or categories engage in deviant or illegal behavior—only why that behavior is deivant or illegal in the first place. On the other hand, certain laws, like the tax laws or the lenient laws lightly punishing corporate crimes, do protect the interests of the powerful. As a limited explanation, conflict theory has great value, but it is still only one piece in a very large puzzle.

Labeling Theory. Sociologists use the word **stigma** to denote the public scorn that deviant behavior and deviant actors attract (Goffman, 1963). Behavior that elicits ridicule, avoidance, or snubs is called "stigmatizing behavior." People who are thought by others to engage routinely in deviant behavior are said to be "stigmatized." The process of stigmatizing individuals or behavior is called "labeling" because it makes the label of "deviant" stick.

Labeling theory (also called **interactionist theory**) is a perspective that examines the impact of being caught and stigmatized as deviant. Labeling theory, which focuses on reactions to deviance, deals mainly

Conflict theory A sociological perspective arguing that exploitation and coercion dominate social relations among groups in society.

Stigma The public scorn or condemnation that deviant behavior attracts to the perpetrator.

Labeling theory A perspective within sociology that focuses on the impact of being caught and stigmatized as a deviant. (Also called **interactionist theory**.)

208

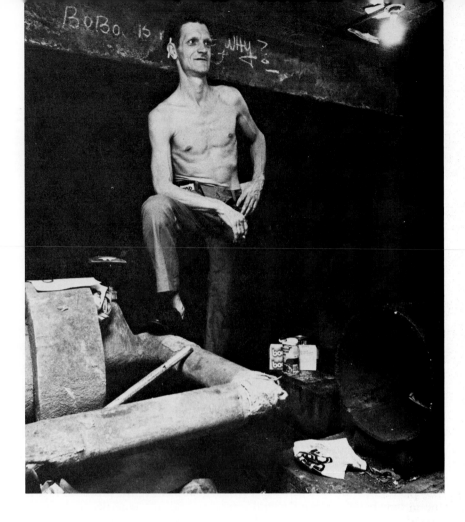

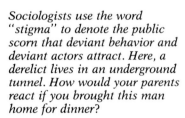

Primary deviation The simple commission of a deviant act. (See **Secondary deviation**.)

Secondary deviation The attempt by deviants to deal with the problems created by labeling.

with the consequences of being "singled out, identified, and defined as deviants" (Traub and Little, 1985, p. 277). Its forerunners were Frank Tannenbaum (1938) and Edwin Lemert (1951). Tannenbaum emphasized that nearly all boys in slum areas engage in mischievous, even delinquent acts. Those who are not caught or punished for their misdeeds grow up to become law-abiding citizens. Those who are have taken a "decisive step in the education of a criminal" (Tannenbaum, 1938, p. 51). Punishment and the entire labeling process, argued Tannenbaum, produce more deviance, crime, and delinquency—not less.

Lemert pursued this insight. He distinguished between primary and secondary deviation, or deviance. **Primary deviation** is simply the enactment of deviant behavior itself—any form of it. Lemert argued that primary deviation is caused by a wide range of factors (Lemert, 1951, pp. 75–76; 1972, pp. 62–63). In fact, Lemert argued, the original cause or causes of a particular form of deviance are not especially important. What counts is others' social reaction to the behavior. **Secondary deviation** is the attempt by deviants to deal with the problems created by labeling. The secondary deviant "is a person whose life and identity are organized around the facts of deviance" (Lemert, 1972, p. 63).

According to several of is most prominent proponents (Becker, 1973, pp. 177–208; Kitsuse, 1972, 1980), labeling theory is not as much an explanation of why certain individuals engage in deviant behavior as it is a perspective whose main insight tells us that the labeling process is crucial. Labeling theory shifts the attention of sociologists away from "Why do they do it?" to how and why judgments of deviance come to be made. Why are certain acts condemned at one time and in one place, but tolerated at another time and in another place? Why does one person do something and get away "scot-free," while another does the same thing in the same society and is severely punished for it? What happens when someone is caught violating a rule and is stigmatized for it: What consequences does this stigma have for that individual's subsequent behavior (Clinard and Meier, 1985, pp. 78–80; McCaghy, 1985, pp. 79, 82, 84)? In a nutshell, these are some of the major issues with which labeling theorists have been concerned.

Labeling theory emphasizes the following concepts in the drama of deviance and stigma: relativity, audiences, contingencies, reflexivity, and the "stickiness" of labels.

RELATIVITY. The most important characteristic of an act, according to labeling theorists, is how a society views it and how people react to it and to someone who enacts it. **Relativity** is variation in judgments by different cultures, subcultures, or time periods of whether a given act is good or bad. Behavior is not deviant in itself; it only becomes deviant when it is seen and reacted to in a given society or at a given time. Is adultery deviant? Not in some societies, like the Lepcha of Sikkim, a tiny state in northern India. The Lepcha tolerate and even encourage adultery. In other societies, like Saudi Arabia, however, adultery is most decidedly deviant; couples caught engaging in it will be severely punished. What is crucial here is not the nature of the act itself, which is basically the same in both places, but the actual or potential reactions by others to the perpetrators.

Relativity Variation in judgments by different cultures, subcultures, or historical time periods about whether a given act is good or bad.

AUDIENCES. The key process in deviant behavior is the labeling of behavior as "deviant" and the labeling of individuals as "deviants." This labeling process is effected by *audiences* (see page 130). We have seen that an audience is simply an individual, or any number of individuals, who observe and evaluate an act or the person who engages in it. An audience could consist of your friends, the police, your teachers, a psychiatrist, bystanders—even yourself, because you can be an observer and an evaluator of your own behavior (Becker, 1963, p. 31). The role of the audience in influencing the behavior of deviants is a major research issue for labeling theorists. So important is this process of labeling that, for certain purposes, it may not matter whether or not an individual who is accused of a given act of deviance actually committed it: According to labeling theory, a falsely accused deviant is still a deviant (Becker, 1963, p. 20) and often resembles people who really do commit the acts that they are accused of committing. Women and men burned at the stake for witchcraft in the sixteenth and seventeenth centuries, for instance, were deviants in the eyes of the authorities or the community (Currie, 1968).

CONTINGENCIES. Not everyone who violates a rule or a law will be criticized or punished by those who witness the deed. Labeling theorists argue that rule breakers are not punished or condemned just because they have violated society's rules. Actions that are deviant to most people in a society may be tolerated by individuals or groups within it. Moreover, ideas about what should be tolerated and what should be punished are not held in common by all members of any large, complex society. Even when people disapprove of behavior, they do not always condemn or punish those who engage in it (Becker, 1963, p. 12; Kitsuse, 1962). Labelists emphasize the role of **contingencies** in the labeling process. A contingency is a seemingly incidental or accidental feature of an event

Contingency A seemingly irrelevant or incidental feature of an act that actually influences the labeling process—that is, whether it or its actor is condemned or not.

or a phenomenon. In the world of deviance, a contingency would be anything that logically shouldn't influence the labeling process, but actually does. For instance, for committing the same crime, a poor person is more likely to get arrested than an affluent one. Poor individuals who have mental breakdowns are sent to state hospitals, and are administered drugs or electroshock treatment; wealthy individuals who have mental breakdowns are said to be suffering from "nervous exhaustion," are sent to private sanitoriums, and are given personalized psychotherapy. According to one observer sympathetic to the labeling perspective, we could say, "that mental patients distinctly suffer not from mental illness, but from contingencies" (Goffman, 1961, p. 135). As a general rule, the greater the prestige and power of the deviator, the greater his or her likelihood of avoiding or resisting being stigmatized as a deviant. The less prestige and power the deviator has, the higher the likelihood of his or her being successfully stigmatized or negatively labeled. In short, the application of the label "deviant" is strongly influenced by factors that lie outside the deviant behavior itself.

Reflexivity The condition or process of seeing ourselves through the eyes of others—at least, as we think others see us.

REFLEXIVITY.   **Reflexivity** simply means looking back at ourselves in large part through the eyes of others. Labeling theory is based on a seemingly simple but fundamental observation: "We view ourselves through the eyes of others, and when others see us in a certain way, at least for long enough or sufficiently powerfully, their views are sure to have some effect" (Glassner, 1982, p. 71). Being stigmatized by others is certainly not the only factor that influences what people do, but it is an important one. In addition, not everyone who enacts behavior that would be punished if it were discovered is caught. At the same time, nearly all people who violate society's major norms know that they would be punished, condemned, and stigmatized upon discovery. Thus, they move around in a world in which they are aware that their identities and their behavior are potentially punishable. In other words, both **direct** and **indirect labeling** operate in the world of deviant behavior (Goode, 1984, pp. 63, 176). People who violate norms have to deal with the probable as well as the actual reactions of the conventional, rule-abiding majority (Goffman, 1963a, pp. 41 ff). All violators of major norms must at least ask themselves, "How would others react to me and my behavior?" If the answer is, "They will react with hostility," then the rule breaker must try to avoid detection or be prepared for condemnation, perhaps punishment.

Direct labeling Being caught and condemned as a deviant for engaging in deviant behavior.

Indirect labeling Being aware that one's behavior and identity are strongly condemned, or widely regarded as deviant, without actually being caught or condemned for engaging in it.

THE "STICKINESS" OF LABELS.   Labeling theorists believe that stigmatizing someone as a socially and morally undesirable character, whether directly or indirectly, has important consequences for that person's further rule breaking. Under certain circumstances, being labeled may intensify one's commitment to a deviant identity and to further deviant behavior—though labeling does not always have this effect. "Obviously, everyone caught in one deviant act and labeled a deviant does not move inevitably toward greater deviance" (Becker, 1963, p. 36). Still, it is difficult to shake off the label of "deviant." Ex-convicts, for instance, have difficulty finding employment after being released from prison; ex-mental patients are carefully scrutinized for odd or bizarre behavior. Such **stickiness of** social **labels** must have an impact on the labeled person's further behavior, although the nature of that impact must be studied empirically.

Stickiness of labels Because deviant labels are difficult to shed, they often "stick" to us for a long time.

One psychologist (Rosenhan, 1973) tested the persistence of deviant labels by arranging for eight totally "normal" and sane people to be admitted to mental institutions around the country. These people claimed that they heard voices saying "empty," "hollow," and "thud." Once they were admitted, the eight behaved quite normally. They stayed in these hospitals for periods ranging from seven days to fifty-two days, with an average of nineteen days, so there appears to be a certain "stickiness" to the label "insane." As the author of the study put it: "Once a person is designated abnormal, all of his other behaviors and characteristics are colored by that label" (Rosenhan, 1973). Of course, the fact that these pseudopatients were eventually released indicates that a deviant label, although sticky, may not be permanent.

LIMITATIONS.   The labeling, or interactionist, perspective shifted the focus of attention away from the causes of deviant behavior and focused it on *who* gets labeled, *why*, for *what* sorts of behavior, and with *what* effects. Widely regarded as a major contribution to the field, the labeling perspective has nonetheles encountered a great deal of criticism from many sources.

For starters, the perspective has been criticized as a nontheory, because it does not explain the causes of such acts as rape, murder, homosexuality, robbery, and so on. It is concerned only with reactions to these acts. Labeling theory, the critics say, is inadequate in the most basic dimension of any theory: explanation. However, labeling theorists disarm this criticism by agreeing that their approach is not a theory, because it does not deal with the question of causality, and by arguing that it was never intended to explain primary deviation (Kitsuse, 1972, p. 236; Becker, 1973, p. 179). Labeling theory, they say, is just a way of looking at the world that helps the observer understand key processes and variables. Like all other perspectives, it is incomplete and requires aid from other perspectives.

CRIME

Although most deviant behavior is also criminal, some of it is perfectly legal. You are quite free never to bathe, or to insult everyone you meet. No doubt, you would be labeled an eccentric, a fool, or a "weirdo," but you would not be arrested. Deviance and crime overlap, but not completely.

Hostile interpersonal— as opposed to legal—reactions to deviant behavior form the arsenal of "informal" social control. In a small, more-or-less homogeneous society—a village or small tribe, where everyone knows and cares about everyone else—informal social controls usually keep members in line. Small societies and tribal villages generally do not have or need more complex forms of social control. As a society grows in size, diversity, and complexity, it comes to include strangers—people who do not share the same memories and values. Strangers can often ignore one another's feelings and attitudes. Informal social controls no longer work. We do not steal from our friends and relatives, because we fear their disapproval. It is much easier to ignore a stranger's disapproval. Growing contact among strangers creates an altogether different mechanism: "formal" social controls. Society now spells out, explicitly and in detail, which actions are illegal, and it designates and empowers specific authorities—the police and the courts—to enforce the law. Informal social controls work by making us fear the opinions of others. Formal controls work by making us fear punishment.

However, violating certain laws results in no punishment at all—no arrest, no prosecution, no prison sentence. Nonmarital sex is against the law in most places, and so too is gambling with friends for small sums of money. But hardly anyone is arrested for these offenses. Indeed, many laws cannot possibly be enforced. For instance, the state of Idaho (for reasons best known to itself) "forbids a citizen to give another citizen a box of candy that weighs more than 50 pounds. In Kentucky every citizen is required by law to take a bath once a year. It is illegal in Alaska to look from the window of an airplane at a moose" (Viorst, 1981).

It is therefore useful to keep in mind the distinction between illegal but insignificant acts, such as these, and behavior that is highly likely to result in arrest, like murder and armed robbery. To understand what is and is not a crime, we must look not only at the law but also at the law in action—at patterns of law enforcement. To sociologists, a crime is an illegal action that is likely to bring forth punishment if the offender is caught.

Types of Crimes

Index crimes Crimes used by the FBI to measure or indicate the nation's overall crime rate: murder, rape, robbery, aggravated assault, burglary, motor vehicle theft, and larceny-theft.

When we think of crime, we tend to think of "street crime." The Federal Bureau of Investigation (FBI) tabulates the incidence of such crimes in its annual "Uniform Crime Report," *Crime in the United States*. The report focuses almost exclusively on seven so-called **index crimes**: murder, rape, robbery, aggravated assault, burglary, motor vehicle theft, and a catch-all category called "larceny-theft. (Arson was added in 1979, but few criminologists investigate arson.) These crimes serve as an overall measure, or indicator, of crimes in general (see Table 8–1).

The FBI's Uniform Crime Reports do give us a glimpse of crime in the United States, but only a partial glimpse. They probably conceal almost as much as they reveal. These reports are based on official police figures, and many victims of crime refuse to get in touch with the police. Conducting "victimization surveys" helps avoid this problem. When national surveys ask random samples (see Chapter 2) of Americans whether they have been victims of crimes during the previous year and, if so, which ones, it becomes clear that official police statistics enormously underreport the incidence of crime. In one such victimization survey, only 28 percent of all victims of crimes reported them to the police, so crime may be as many as four times as common as official statistics (reported in Table 8–1) show (Skogan, 1977).

Clearly, some crimes are much more underreported than others. Motor vehicle theft is the most frequently reported crime because victims want to collect on their insurance. Most assaults are not reported, because, typically, they involve friends or acquaintances who get drunk, argue, and fight; the victim cannot always be distinguished from the aggressor. Petty crimes, like "larceny-theft," are strongly underreported because, in most cases, the items taken have little value. Rape is regarded as shameful for the victim, and most of its victims do not report it, out of a very realistic fear that they will be humiliated by the police and even by their own friends. Nonetheless, the proportion of rape victims who report their ordeal to the police is rising. Murder, finally, is almost always reported or, at any rate, almost always comes to the attention of the police. All official crime statistics must be read with the very important qualification that most of these crimes are seriously underreported.

■ TABLE 8–1 Crime in the United States, 1985

	Offenses Reported to the Police	
CRIME	NUMBER OF OFFENSES	RATE PER 100,000 INHABITANTS
Murder	18,976	7.9
Rape	87,340	36.6
Robbery	497,874	208.5
Aggravated Assault	723,246	302.9
Burglary	3,073,348	1,287.3
Motor Vehicle Theft	1,102,862	462.0
Larceny-Theft	6,926,380	2,901.2

Definitions

Murder and Nonnegligent Manslaughter: "the willful killing of one human being by another."

Forcible Rape: "the carnal knowledge of a female forcibly and against her will." This definition includes "assaults or attempts to commit rape by force or threat of force," but does not include statutory rape, without force.

Robbery: "taking or attempting to take anything of value from the care, custody, or control of a person by force or threat of force or violence and/or putting the victim in fear."

Aggravated assault: "an unlawful attack by one person upon another for the purpose of inflicting severe bodily injury."

Burglary: "the unlawful entry of a structure to commit a felony or theft."

Motor Vehicle Theft: "the theft or attempted theft of a motor vehicle."

Larceny-Theft: "the unlawful taking, carrying, leading, or riding away of property from the possession of another. It includes crimes such as shoplifting, pocket-picking, purse-snatching, thefts from motor vehicles, thefts of motor parts, bicycle thefts, etc., in which no use of force, violence, or fraud occurs." This category does not include embezzlement, confidence games, forgery, and passing worthless checks.

Source: United States Department of Justice, FBI Uniform Crime Reports, Crime in the United States, 1985, Washington, D.C.: U.S. Government Printing Office, 1986, pp. 7–39.

In large urban environments, there is a great deal of contact between strangers. Hence, people can ignore their feelings, and even commit crimes against one another. The fear of being victimized by a crime is high in large cities.

Richard Hutchings/Photo Researchers

The seven crimes in the Uniform Crime Reports—the so-called street crimes—fall into two basic categories. Crimes of violence—which criminologists call "crimes against the person"—include murder, aggravated assault, rape, and robbery. "Crimes against property" include burglary, vehicle theft, and larceny-theft. In general, crimes against the person involve face-to-face confrontations, as well as violence, force, or the threat of force. Crimes against property involve no confrontations, no violence, and no force or threats of force against individuals. They are almost ten times as frequent as crimes against the person (see Table 8–1). Most people who commit crimes do not wish to confront their victims or hurt them physically—in part because they do not want to get hurt themselves.

The level of fear of crime is extremely high in many communities; in some, as a precaution against kidnapping, children are fingerprinted.

Bettye Lane/Photo Researchers

Several distinctly different types of crimes, buried deep in the Uniform Crime Reports, are not included in the FBI's seven index crimes: prostitution, gambling, and marijuana possession, among others. These are called public-order crimes or victimless crimes (Schur, 1965). Some crimes do not appear in the FBI's annual reports at all, most importantly white-collar crimes.

Crimes against the Person. MURDER. Compared with many other countries of the industrial world, the United States is a violent country. It has, for example, the highest murder rate of all industrialized nations: just under eight criminal homicides a year for each 100,000 people—over four times as high as Australia (1.9) and Israel (1.8), five times as high as Hong Kong (1.6), Italy (1.6), and Austria (1.5), over seven times as high as West Germany (1.2), Spain (1.1), France (1.0), and Japan (1.0), and some 16 to 20 times as high as New Zealand (0.5) and England and Wales (0.4) (Barlow, 1987, p. 133). Many experts trace the homicide rate to handguns, because the number of guns in an area or a country correlates almost perfectly with its murder rate. Almost 65 percent of the murders in the United States are committed with firearms. Most homicides start with an argument between two people. Usually, the killer is the person with the better weapon or greater skill at handling it. According to official statistics, only 17 percent of all murders in the United States occurred during other crimes, like robbery and rape (FBI, 1986, p. 11). Murder is almost always spontaneous, rarely planned.

ASSAULT. Assault is the crime that most resembles murder. The essential difference is that in assault, the victim does not die, usually because the offender uses a knife or fists instead of a gun. The "wheres," "hows," and "whys" of assault are almost identical to those of homicide. As one criminologist put it, assault "is really a first cousin of murder" (Reckless, 1973, p. 186).

RAPE. The FBI's Uniform Crime Reports for 1986 tabulated more than 87,000 rapes, but the actual number was at least two to three times higher—perhaps higher still. Rapists used to be regarded as deranged men who jumped out of bushes or dark alleys and grabbed complete strangers. Recent studies show that rapists are about as likely to choose victims they know as to choose complete strangers (Amir, 1971). Most rapists are depressingly average. Some observers feel that rape simply exaggerates certain basic American cultural ideas, notably male supremacy. According to this view, it expresses masculine contempt for women and a desire to impose one's will on a victim whose resistance or desires have no importance (Griffin, 1971; Brownmiller, 1975; Scully and Marolla, 1985).

ROBBERY. Robbery is a bit different from murder, assault, and rape, for the victim and the criminal very rarely know each other personally. Power, masculinity, and the desire to humiliate are only marginally relevant to robbery, which is characteristically a crime between strangers, most often in large cities. (According to the FBI, the robbery rate is over 60 times as high in cities over a million people—965 robberies per 100,000 in the population—as it is in rural areas—fifteen per 100,000). Cash is a highly impersonal commodity, and the robbers are in essence "businesspeople" who seek to acquire it as quickly and safely as possible.

Crimes against Property. Often, cash or goods are stolen without any confrontation with the victims, violence, or threat of violence. Property crimes account for some 90 percent of all the crimes in the FBI's annual report. Burglary, auto theft, and larceny-theft are the most important property crimes classified by the FBI. Larceny-theft is a miscellaneous category that includes such activities as picking pockets, shoplifting, and burglary.

Because property crimes are reported much less often than are violent crimes against the person, police statistics represent only the tip of the iceberg. Unlike robbery, property crime is not overwhelmingly urban. Burglary, for instance, is only a bit more than twice as frequent in big cities as in rural areas (not more than sixty times as frequent, as with robbery). What's more, suburban burglary is growing faster than urban burglary.

Avoiding confrontation with the victim helps thieves in more ways than one: They are better able to avoid not only being detected but also defining themselves as "real" criminals. The absent victim is:

> an impersonal abstraction, and the wrong that is done is diminished in the eyes of the wrongdoer by the lack of any direct encounter. . . . If the possessions of another are obtained by stealth . . . the meaning of the criminal behavior is more easily repressed or ignored. The sense of "real" harm is weakened and the internal mechanisms of guilt or self-disapproval are brought into play with a greatly reduced force (Sykes, 1978, pp. 93, 94).

Crimes without Victims. **Victimless crimes**—for instance, gambling (32,000 arrests in 1985), public drunkenness (964,800 arrests), prostitution (113,800 arrests), and drug possesion and sale (811,400 arrests)— are not included in the FBI's index crimes. As the name implies, the offenders themselves are the only direct victims in these crimes.

The absence of a victim in these "public order" crimes means that, in them, there is no "complainant": no one to file a charge against the

Victimless crime An illegal action that is voluntarily engaged in by the participants, the consequences of which, with respect to harm, are debatable.

Robbery is a crime that typically takes place between strangers. As a result, there are 10 times the number of robberies in large cities, where anonymity is greatest, than there are in rural areas.

Wide World Photos

offender, testify, or give evidence. The police must rely on undercover work, or informants, or sheer luck to gather evidence and make arrests. The number of arrests they do make is only a tiny fraction of the full extent of victimless crimes. According to the National Institute of Drug Abuse, over 18 million Americans used marijuana once or more during the previous month in 1985, and yet, only about 400,000 of them were arrested during that year.

Before 1973, women who sought out abortions in the United States, and doctors who performed abortions, were criminals. (Antiabortionists consider an aborted fetus to be a victim; proabortionists do not.) Today, abortion is legal; tomorrow, it might be redefined as a crime. Many people feel that victimless crimes should be decriminalized completely (Schur, 1965). They argue that activities that are basically voluntary— activities that people participate in because they have chosen to do so and that harm no one but themselves—cannot be controlled. In this view, the law, the police, and the courts should concentrate their efforts on crimes that have victims. Arresting prostitutes, drug users, homosexuals, and public drunks, they say, is an arrogant abuse of public power and a waste of taxpayers' hard-earned money.

White-Collar Crimes.   During the nineteenth century, businesses could operate their factories in any way they chose, however dangerous. They could pollute the water and the atmosphere; make blatantly false advertising claims; sell ineffective and even harmful food or drugs, including cocaine and morphine; and form monopolies to choke off competition. In the last third of the nineteenth century—first in the states and then at the federal level—laws were passed to control these and other business practices. Violations of these laws were called **corporate** or **white-collar crime.** Offenders can be arrested, fined, and sent to prison for violating them.

Corporate crime Illegal actions enacted by representatives of large companies on behalf of the interests of those companies.

White-collar crime Illegal actions committed by affluent individuals of high socioeconomic status in the course of their occupational activities; typically refers to corporate crime.

In the 1940s, criminologist Edwin Sutherland systematically studied white-collar crime by examining the actions of some seventy major corporations in the United States. These seventy had accumulated almost 900 convictions for unfair labor practices, restraint of trade, patent infringement, illegal financial manipulations, and so on. Sutherland concluded that white-collar crime is "real" crime, just as street crime is. He suggested, as well, that white-collar crime is profitable for business, that it is common but rarely detected, and that it is rarely punished with rigor (Sutherland, 1949).

The public still does not think of white-collar criminals as criminals. The police are not equipped to enforce the law against private businesses, and, for the most part, do not attempt to do so. Criminologists rarely study illegal business practices. And corporate executives—no matter how many laws they violate—see themselves as "hard-headed businesspeople," not, as the law defines them, as criminals. Yet the economic impact of corporate illegality is vastly greater than that of street crimes. We pay for corporate crime a few cents or a few dollars at a time, however, so the total cost is never clear to us. Yet it is very high, even to each individual—and it represents in all billions of dollars a year. But the victims are scattered; responsibility is complex and difficult to trace; and the offenders are "respectable" citizens.

Who Commits Crimes?

The FBI's Uniform Crime Reports do more than tabulate information on crimes that come to the attention of the police. They also tabulate the characteristics of suspects arrested for various crimes. (Of course, not everyone who is arrested has committed the crime for which he or she was arrested, but the vast majority are.) The FBI's data show that 82 percent of these suspects are men; nearly 27 percent are Black, and over seven out of ten are white. As a group, arrested suspects are much younger than the population at large (although very young individuals—13 or younger—are less likely to commit crimes than the population as a whole): while 14 percent of all arrestees are between the ages of 14 and 17, only six percent of the United States population is this age; while 19 percent of arrestees are 18 to 21, seven percent of the whole population is; and while thirteen percent of those arrested are 22 to 24, in the population as a whole, only five percent are. This is an over-representation of more than two times their number in the population for the age range extending from adolescence to young adulthood.

Most criminologists consider these three factors—sex, race, and age—the most important variables for predicting who will and who will not commit crimes. Males are roughly four times more likely to commit crimes than women are. Blacks are roughly twice as likely to commit crimes of all kinds that whites are—more than two and a half times more likely to commit index crimes. And young adults, especially those in their late teens to early 20s, are three to five times more likely to commit a wide range of criminal activities than the rest of the population.

How accurately do the FBI's figures on arrests reflect the true rate of criminal activity? The answer would have to be imperfectly, quite imperfectly.

We already know that many crimes are not reported to the police—for the index crimes, about seven out of ten, or 72 percent. Of those index crimes that are reported, the majority—four out of five—do not result in arrest. Of course, the exact figure varies from crime to crime. Some 72 percent of all murders do result in arrest, and 54 percent of all reported rapes, but only 25 percent of all robberies, and only 14 percent of all burglaries (FBI, 1986, p. 155).

Because the people who get arrested are a small proportion of the total number of criminals, these unlucky few are almost certainly different from the miscreants who get away. In crime, as in any other field of human endeavor, there are successes and there are failures, and it is the failures who populate the FBI's social profiles of arrestees. How different are arrested offenders from those who get away?

Sex. No criminologist doubts that men commit more crimes, person-for-person, than women do. To be sure, women are committing more nonviolent crimes than they once did (Adler, 1975). But the fact is that, except for prostitution, men are still committing more of all types of crime than women are. In fact, "sex status is of greater statistical significance in differentiating criminals from noncriminals than any other trait" (Sutherland and Cressey, 1978, p. 130).

Race. If we turn to race and crime, the picture is much more complicated. One problem—the subject of a heated controversy—is that police officers may (or may not) be more eager to apprehend and arrest Black criminals than white ones. The profile of arrested offenders is therefore suspect. On one side of the argument stand those who claim that the law and the police are fair, nondiscriminatory, and even-handed, so that arrestees do represent an accurate statistical portrait of offenders as a whole, including those who are not caught or arrested. On the other side are criminologists who say that the police patrol more heavily in Black and poor neighborhoods and are more likely to arrest Black suspects than white ones. So, according to this view, police statistics on crime reflect the facts of official discrimination, not the facts of crime (Nettler, 1978, pp. 65–70).

One ingenious way of resolving this controversy, at least in part, is to take a victimization survey, the same technique used to determine the true extent of crimes. A way of getting around the problem of discrimination in arrests is to ask victims of certain crimes about the characteristics of the offenders. Obviously, this technique works only for those crimes—robbery, rape, and assault—in which the victims see the offenders. Victims of these three crimes are asked about the offenders' race. By comparing the racial distribution of the victimization surveys with the racial distribution of the FBI's arrest data, we can test the extent to which the latter reflect police discrimination (Hindelang, 1978).

Two messages emerge from such surveys. First, Blacks are more likely than whites to be caught and arrested for committing two of the three offenses. Blacks figure in 48 percent of the arrests for committing rape, but only 39 percent of the victim-designated rape offenses; they appear in 41 percent of all arrests for assault, but only 30 percent of all assaults as identified by victims. This pattern of bias does not hold for the crime of robbery. The second message is that bias does not appear to account totally for the different arrest rates of whites and Blacks. Something else is at work (McNeely and Pope, 1981). The conclusion seems unavoidable: In a significant number of cases, for a number of crimes, Blacks are more likely to be arrested in part because of the color of their skin.

Age. No criminologist has any doubt that the crimes most feared by the public are most likely to be committed by young men in their late

Persons Arrested by Sex, Race, and Age, 1984, 1985

Sources: Statistical Abstract of the United States, 1986, *Washington, D.C.: U.S. Printing Office, 1986, p. 26; and Uniform Crime Reports*, Crime in the United States, *Washington, D.C.: U.S. Justice Department, 1986, pp. 174–175, 176, 178, 182.*

teens and early 20s. It is true that young criminals are more likely to be caught than older, more experienced, professional criminals. Even so, criminal behavior peaks in late adolescence and young adulthood (Sutherland and Cressey, 1978, pp. 124–130). Many experts trace this pattern to the segregation of young people (in schools) from the rest of the population. Not only does this weaken the links of the young to older adults, say these experts, but it also results in there being no clear-cut rules for the adolescents to follow. Moreover, adolescents, whose unemployment rate is very high, have a great deal of free time— time for mischief, among other things (Glaser, 1978, pp. 157–197). One expert attributes the relationship of age (and sex) with crime to the fact that many crimes require strength and energy, assets most likely to be found in young men in their late teens and early twenties (Gove, 1985).

The Crime in Question.   Even if the characteristics of arrestees do reflect those of undetected criminals, most of us still measure the overall crime rate by looking only at certain crimes. The social profile of criminals must depend upon which crimes were used to typify criminal behavior. For instance, Blacks and the poor are more likely to commit certain crimes but less likely to commit others. A profile based solely on those who commit white-collar crimes would indicate that Blacks and poor people are among the most law-abiding segments of our population. Of course, what such a profile would really show is that few Blacks and poor people are in a position to commit white-collar crimes.

The crimes of the street and the crimes of the business world are thus committed by two quite different groups of people, with markedly different social and economic characteristics. Criminologists typically study not crime in general, but a particular style of illegal behavior—a distinctly working- or lower-class style of criminality.

> Everyone commits crime. Many, many people, whether they are poor, rich, or middling, are involved in a way of life that is criminal. . . . Criminality is not simply something that people have or don't have; crime is not something some people do and others do not. . . . [The] label "criminal" is a matter of who can pin the label on whom. . . . [Criminal] acts are widely distributed throughout the social classes. . . . [The] rich, the ruling, the poor, and the working classes *all* engage in criminal activities on a regular basis. . . . What difference there is would be a difference in the type of criminal act, not in the prevalence of criminality (Chambliss, 1973a, pp. 21, 22).

From Arrest to Sentencing

Arrest is only one of many important steps in what some experts call the "correctional funnel" (Wickman and Whitten, 1980, pp. 458–459). At each step of the way, suspects are released and allowed to return to society. Only a very small proportion of arrestees ends up in jail or prison. By law, police officers must take arrested suspects into custody, escort them to local police stations, and there charge them with crimes. Actually, most arrested suspects are released, without official prosecution, before appearing in court. Many of these are released unofficially, at the discretion of the police. For instance, the overwhelming majority of people arrested on a charge of public intoxication—over 964,000 for the charge of "drunkenness," and 671,000 for "disorderly conduct" in 1985—are held overnight and released the next day, when they are sober, without ever being charged with a crime (Sutherland and Cressey, 1978, p. 426). Charges against another sizable proportion of suspects are

WHAT DO YOU THINK?

Is a High Crime Rate Always Bad?

Although crime rates have declined somewhat in the 1980s, they are massively higher than they were a generation ago. And the crime rate that prevails in the United States is strikingly higher than it is in all other industrialized nations of the world. The question is why? Many explanations have been proposed: poverty, the failure of our criminal-justice system, and so on. Although these factors certainly have something to do with crime, one crucial explanation has nearly always been overlooked by observers writing on the subject: our culture values freedom and the rights of the individual over the needs of the society as a whole. "Of all the large societies of the world," asserts sociologist Stephen Cole, "the United States is perhaps the one that places the greatest emphasis on individual rights and the least on collective needs" (Cole, 1983). This value simultaneously tolerates and even indirectly encourages the commission of crime on a massive scale; it also stimulates creativity, diversity, and individual liberties. In other words, something that we value has both good and bad consequences at the same time.

This stress on individualism appears in a number of forms, according to Cole. Social control operates both externally, in the form of reward and, especially, punishment—for instance, by the police, the courts, and prisons—and internally, in the form of the internalization of values as a result of socialization from infancy. Externally, the American public and our fifty state judicial systems are reluctant to apply the ultimate punishment to perpetrators of even the most heinous crimes. Capital punishment is very rare in the United States—only a few dozen murderers have been executed in this country since 1967, as opposed to thousands in such nations as China and the Soviet Union. (It should also be pointed out that Great Britain has no death penalty at all, and, yet, its rate of lethal violence is only one-fifth of ours.) In addition, our rules of evidence in the courtroom are so strict that individuals known to have committed serious crimes are allowed to walk free because of technicalities and loopholes. At the same time, our emphasis on civil liberties (which are nonetheless sometimes violated) attempts

---

Plea bargaining "Negotiated justice," whereby a defendant gives up the right to a trial and, in exchange, is convicted on a lesser charge, which draws a lighter sentence.

dropped or dismissed for insufficient evidence, either by the police themselves or by the prosecutor. One study of California's criminal justice system showed that although almost a quarter of a million felony arrests were recorded in 1973, only a bit more than 62,000 led to convictions (Gibbons, 1982, Chapter 19). In 1979, over a half million felonies were reported to the police in New York City. More than 100,000 people were arrested on suspicion of committing felonies, but only 16,000 were officially charged with felonies. Roughly 1 percent of all felony arrests actually leads to a term in prison (Shipp and Fried, 1981). Most often, arrested offenders are released before court proceedings even start.

If the evidence is sufficient to convict, the court will reach a decision to prosecute, and a defendant will get a chance to enter a plea. In about 90 percent of all cases, the defendants "cop a plea," more formally called **plea bargaining** or "negotiated justice." When this happens, the defendant gives up the right to a trial and in exchange gets a lesser charge and a lighter sentence (but also a conviction). Elaborate and dramatic to ensure that innocent parties are very rarely arrested. The less concerned the police and the courts are with the legal rights of the individual, the more real criminals will be convicted and imprisoned, but, at the same time, the more the innocent will be, too. It is better to let 1,000 guilty go free, we believe, than to convict a single innocent party. Thus, a stress on civil liberties is a mixed blessing—one that most Americans are willing to accept. Unlike citizens in many nations of the world, our citizens walk around with a feeling of freedom, knowing that they are very unlikely to be arrested or convicted on the basis of flimsy evidence.

The internal mechanism of social control, internalization, is also weaker here than it is in most other places. Americans tend to have relatively little respect for authority. We are used to criticiz-ing "everything from our national leaders to our schools to our local laws." Criminals "are frequently portrayed as heroes in American popular culture"—"from Butch Cassidy to the Godfather." As a result of this lack of respect for authority, Cole asserts, "many people in the United States do not internalize a strong belief that it is wrong to violate the law."

It is easy to condemn the lack of respect that Americans have for authority and the law. . . . But again there is another side to the coin. The same attitude toward authority, the same loose commitment that we have to social rules also allows for great innovation and creativity. The stronger the norms or social rules are, the more likely people will be to learn them as children, and then follow them later as adults. But societies that do not tolerate nonconformity will generally have both low crime rates and low levels of creativity. . . . I am not trying to say that crime is good. I am trying to point out that the same type of culture that leads to a high crime rate also leads to many good things such as great personal liberty and much creativity. . . . If we move toward the type of society that places a stronger emphasis on meeting collective needs and maintaining social order, there is danger that we may be losing some of what is great about America: our individual freedom and a society that encourages diversity and creativity (Cole, 1983, p. 56).

Do you agree? What do you think?

---

trials, such as the ones we see on television and in the movies, are quite unusual. Trials are expensive and time-consuming, and the court often assumes guilt—contrary to law, which grants the defendant a presumption of innocence—and wishes to convict as efficiently as possible. Thus, defendants accept automatic guilt and conviction for a reduced charge and penalty. For instance, a charge of "possession of a dangerous drug with the intent to sell" might be reduced to "simple possession," or attempted murder may be reduced to assault. In cases in which defendants face more than one charge, a negotiated plea may require the prosecutor to drop some of them in exchange for conviction on the others.

Bias in the Criminal-Justice System.   The criminal-justice system puts poor people at a disadvantage in a number of ways. Many of them cannot raise enough money to post bail. In some communities, the proportion of suspects who cannot do so from their own funds is as high as 90 percent (Sutherland and Cressey, 1978, p. 429). This means that poor

The nation's jails and prisons are overcrowded. Most inmates of jails are suspects who cannot afford bail. Prisons house those who have been convicted of "street" crimes. White-collar criminals are very rarely incarcerated.

Nelson/Picture Group

defendants must either go to bail bondsmen and borrow money at very high rates of interest or serve jail sentences without having been convicted of any crime. At a given time, a clear majority of all jail inmates are simply awaiting trial—punishment for poverty, not for crime. One observer referred to jails as the "poorhouses of the twentieth century" (Goldfarb, 1975, p. 27). The longer defendants must wait in jail, the more willing they become to accept plea bargaining, regardless of whether they are guilty or innocent. Moreover, the sentence for many offenses is a fine. Defendants who cannot pay it—and many cannot—go to jail (Goldfarb and Singer, 1973, p. 127). The difference between going to jail and not going to jail is a matter of cold cash.

Poor people are more likely to be convicted than others are. In legal jargon, "indigents" are defendants too poor to pay for their own lawyers. Such defendants now have the right to be represented by court-appointed lawyers. One study found that indigents are about 10 percent more likely to be found guilty and, in addition, much less likely to receive probation or a suspended sentence (Nagel, 1966, p. 6).

Prison

Rikers Island is located in New York's East River, a few hundred yards from a busy airport. It is the largest penal colony in the United States, housing some 7,000 men, women, and adolescents.

> It is a crowded, noisy, and potentially explosive place. Inmates, let out of their cells . . . at least fourteen hours a day, are jammed into the open cell-blocks, dormitory corridors, and yards they share with edgy corrections officers, who are used to having their prisoners behind bars. . . . The uneasy, day-to-day truce between the inmates and the officers on Rikers Island exists only because of an unspoken agreement by which the authorities simply don't enforce many of the prison's rules and regulations (Pileggi, 1981, p. 24).

About two-thirds of these inmates are detained at Rikers Island because they could not raise money for bail. For days—and sometimes months—they wait behind bars to appear in court.

The Functions of Imprisonment.   What are the acknowledged functions of imprisonment? Are they achieved? And what about unacknowledged functions? Most criminolgists say that the punishment of criminals has four main goals (Sykes, 1978, pp. 480–495): retribution, deterrence, incarceration, and rehabilitation.

RETRIBUTION.   We commonly feel that wrongdoers should be made to suffer, especially if there is a victim. **Retribution** represents vengeance: an attempt to balance the harm done to victims or to the moral order by the sufferings inflicted on the offender. This rationale is ancient, and dates at least as far back as the injunction, "An eye for an eye, a tooth for a tooth."

Retribution One goal or function of punishment: revenge.

DETERRENCE.   The second function of punishment is **deterrence,** which has two distinct forms: specific and general. "Specific" deterrence aims to ensure that offenders do not repeat their crimes. A prison sentence, for instance, is supposed to be unpleasant enough to make those who suffer through it dread the prospect of another sentence. "General" deterrence, in contrast, acts to discourage potential wrongdoers, those citizens who might contemplate breaking the law but are restrained by the punishment.

Deterrence One goal or function of punishment: discouraging people from committing crimes.

INCARCERATION.   Third, punishment in the form of **incarceration** or sequestration locks up criminals and protects society from them. Some people are thought to be so dangerous to society that they must be isolated.

Incarceration Imprisonment, isolation from the rest of society, incapacitation, or sequestration.

REHABILITATION.   Lastly, there is the rationale of **rehabilitation.** Rational and humane programs of treatment and training—psychological counseling, education, and vocational instruction, for instance—sometimes give prisoners new attitudes and skills and make it possible for them to function in the "straight" world. As a result, they abandon the life of crime.

Rehabilitation One goal or function of punishment: conducting programs that turn the miscreant away from a life of crime.

Does Prison Work?   Some of these goals are more easily measured than others.

RETRIBUTION.   Vengeance requires that offenders suffer for their crimes and makes punishment an end in itself. We do not literally exact "an eye for an eye," but many observers feel that imprisonment is worthwhile simply because wrongdoers deserve to be punished, period. By definition, punishing offenders does fulfill the aim of retribution. Some observers feel that it would do so more effectively if more offenders were sent to jails or prisons, and the sentences were longer. Still, every time a criminal is punished, the motive of retribution is fulfilled.

DETERRENCE.   General deterrence is much more difficult to ensure and test than specific deterrence. No doubt, many people who consider committing crimes decide not to do so from fear of punishment. But we cannot know just how many. To resolve the issue, we would have to compare two societies similar in every way but one: the existence of formal punishment for offenders in one and the absence of such punishment in the other. No such "natural laboratory" exists.

Measuring specific deterrence has its own problems. The 1976 edition of the FBI's Uniform Crime Reports had statistics that showed that almost two-thirds (64 percent) of the people who were arrested and released in 1972 had been rearrested four years later. Of those who had served their full prison sentences and were then released in 1972, 74 percent had been rearrested within four years. Of those who had served partial sentences and were placed on parole in 1972, 71 percent were "repeaters." Of those who were convicted of crimes but were placed on probation without any prison sentence, only 57 percent had been rearrested during this time period. So far, it seems that imprisonment, far from deterring crime, actually encourages it: Those who served their full prison sentences had the highest rate of rearrest, whereas those who served no sentence had the lowest. However, this tendency is somewhat reversed by the "repeat" record of those persons who had been arrested but who were acquitted in court or had their cases dismissed in 1972: 67 percent were rearrested for new offenses within four years.

Of course, it is possible that those offenders who were not rearrested were simply more clever in avoiding detection. Even if they were not, we cannot be sure that the subsequent arrest record of 1972's "class" of criminals was really each offender's punishment experience or the lack of one. For instance, those judges who placed offenders on probation might have had enough insight to choose those with the lowest likelihood of committing crimes in the future. (That, of course, is the basic premise of parole.) So the crucial factor may be that offenders on probation were not hardcore criminals to begin with—not that they failed to serve time. What *is* clear is that a prison sentence is no guarantee of deterrence in the future. The typical released ex-prisoner does return to crime and is rearrested within four years of release. Viewed in this light, prison sentences fail to achieve special or specific deterrence.

INCARCERATION.   On the face of it, we might suppose that prisons, by their very nature, always manage to isolate offenders. After all, in prison, inmates are removed from the sight of respectable members of society. They are locked up and out of harm's way—but only in a very narrow sense. Prisoners can do no damage to the nonprison population; but they can do a great deal of damage to one another. You are much more likely to be murdered in jail than anywhere else, and if you are, your murder is much less likely to lead to formal charges of homicide than would a killing outside a prison. Fights between guards and prisoners often end in the prisoners' deaths—guards are killed much less often in these scuffles—and guards are almost always let off with a ruling of "justifiable homicide." And homosexual rape is epidemic in prisons. One study estimated that during a two-year period, nearly 2,000 of the 60,000 inmates who passed through the Philadelphia prison system had been raped by other prisoners (Davis, 1968). Rather than prevent inmates from committing crime, prisons localize them—within prison walls. "Isolation" is achieved only in a very narrow sense. Moreover, prisons are in effect a finishing school in which local talent gets professional instruction in the arts and sciences of crime.

REHABILITATION.   To judge by the amount of resources devoted to rehabilitating criminals, this function seems to be very much in the background of the American prison system. We spend only about 4 or 5 percent of the budgets of our correctional facilities on rehabilitation: academic and vocational education; and counseling by psychologists, psychiatrists, and social workers. The ratio of staff to inmates is one to more than 4,000 for psychologists, one to more than 2,000 for psychiatrists, and one to more than 1,000 for academic and vocational teachers (Wickman and Whitten, 1980, p. 535). For the most part, guards and prison administrators deny that inmates can be rehabilitated. In any case, they cannot be rehabilitated at the present, pitifully inadequate, levels of spending and effort.

Prisons: An Overview. Prisons are doing their job poorly. But if correctional facilities don't seem to work, what would? Almost certainly, if there were no system of formal punishment, many more crimes would be committed than are committed now. In other words, though specific deterrence has failed to work on convicted offenders, general deterrence probably does work on some potential offenders.

Many problems of our prison system, and of its efforts to deter crime, lie outside the system itself. It is quite unlikely that any particular offender will be punished at all. Researchers have estimated that a mugger's chances of being arrested are about 12 percent per mugging. The chances that a mugger will be imprisoned after the arrest are about 10 percent, so that the likelihood of being sent to jail is a bit more than 1 percent for each offense (Shinnar and Shinnar, 1975). Swiftness and certainty of arrest and punishment deter crime much more effectively than cruel and unusual, but rare, punishment. In short, we really cannot ask our prisons to solve the crime problem. And, to date, no one has proposed a workable alternative to our present correctional system. The present mess will be with us for some time to come.

SUMMARY

1. Societies could not exist without some basic minimum level of social control.

2. Most rules and norms, however, are symbolic: They act not to protect the members of a society from the physical danger that

some actions present, but to protect a certain overall vision of how people ought to behave.

3. Sociologists define deviance as behavior that some people in a society find offensive and that excites, if discovered, disapproval, punishment, condemnation, or hostility toward the individual who engages in that behavior.

4. What is regarded as deviance varies considerably throughout the world; acts that are accepted and tolerated here are punished elsewhere, and vice versa.

5. Over the centuries, people have sought to explain why certain individuals engage in deviant behavior. The earliest such explanation was demonic possession.

6. In the second half of the nineteenth century, biological defects were used to explain wrongdoing, especially crime. Defects in the personalities of wrongdoers, likewise, were the common thread in a number of psychological theories of deviance.

7. Sociological theories are concerned with the general conditions that make for patterns of behavior and rates of deviance. These theories are not concerned with why any particular individual engages in deviance.

8. Anomie theory, a major sociological explanation for deviance, suggests that our culture stresses the goal of material success but gives many people few opportunities for achieving it. This gap generates a high rate of deviance.

9. Another sociological theory of deviance is the culture-transmission perspective, which argues that deviance, crime, and delinquency are learned in a straightforward fashion from one's intimates, just as conventional, law-abiding behavior is learned.

10. Conflict theory seeks to explain the making and the enforcing of rules and laws, not their breaking. It locates the explanation in the upper reaches of the power structure.

11. Labeling theory is concerned with what happens when behavior is defined as deviant and when an individual is stigmatized as a deviant. This process, labeling theorists argue, has important consequences for further deviance.

12. The larger and more socially complex a society becomes, the less informal social control works to keep people in line, and the more formal social control (laws, the police, courts, and prisons) becomes necessary.

13. The major types of crimes that take place in an industrialized society, such as the United States, are crimes against the person, crimes against property, victimless crimes, and white-collar crimes.

14. Determining who commits crimes is a difficult job for criminologists, because of nonreporting, differential detection, and biases in patterns of arrest. Still, most criminologists agree that males, adolescents, and young adults are significantly more likely to commit most crimes than females and older adults. Discrimination against Blacks by law-enforcement authorities exaggerates their crime rate.

15. If white-collar crimes were taken into consideration, the more affluent, middle-class members of society would have a signifi-

cantly higher crime rate than they do—possibly as high as that of the poorer members of society.

16. Most suspects who are arrested are released before being convicted of a crime.

17. About nine out of ten of all convictions are obtained as a result of "plea bargaining," whereby a suspect receives certain conviction in exchange for a less serious charge and a lighter penalty.

18. Poor people are at a disadvantage in the criminal-justice system in a number of ways: They are less likely to be able to post bail and must therefore await court appearances in jail; they are more eager to plea bargain; they are less likely to be able to pay fines and often have to serve jail sentences instead; and they are more likely to be convicted in court, and less likely to receive probation or suspended sentences.

19. The main goals of prison—retribution, deterrence, incarceration, and rehabilitation—are not adequately achieved. Unfortunately, no criminologist has suggested a workable alternative.

SUGGESTED READINGS

Nachman Ben-Yehuda, *Deviance and Moral Boundaries*. Chicago: University of Chicago Press, 1985.
A fascinating analysis of the ways in which deviance both stimulates change and, at times, promotes stability by redefining society's "boundaries." Examines a number of forms of factors—witchcraft, deviant sciences (such as the study of UFOs), deviance in science (mainly "fudging" the results of experiments and plagiarizing), science fiction, and occult phenomena—not generally studied by sociologists of deviance. This book attempts to expand the scope of the field.

James W. Coleman, *The Criminal Elite: The Sociology of White Collar Crime*. New York: St. Martin's Press, 1985.
An excellent overview of corporate and government crime, including their causes, laws, and enforcement.

Edward E. Jones et al., *Social Stigma: The Psychology of Marked Relationships*. New York: Freeman, 1984.
Examines relations between people who bear stigmas ("deviants") and those who do not ("normals"). Adopts a broad conception of deviance, which includes physical stigmas: obesity, handicaps and disabilities, disfigurements, mutilations, and so on. Looks at the phenomenon from the point of view of both the stigmatizers and the stigmatized.

Charles H. McCaghy, *Deviant Behavior: Crime, Conflict, and Interests Groups* (2nd ed.). New York: Macmillan, 1985.
A basic textbook on the subject. Includes a fairly broad coverage of different types of deviance and adopts a "soft" conflict theory approach.

Gwynn Nettler, *Killing One Another*. Cincinnati, Ohio: Anderson, 1982.
Explores the many factors associated with criminal homicide: terrorism, psychopathy, lust, self-defense, cultural influences, and killing for wealth and power. Interesting, though occasionally idiosyncratic.

John Peer Nugent, *White Night*. New York: Rawson, Wade, 1979.
A terrifying description of the rise and fall of Jim Jones, engineer of the infamous Jonestown mass suicide. At least two things make the People's Temple phenomenon—and cults generally—sociologically fascinating. One is that, through group pressure, individuals can be induced to engage in behavior and hold beliefs that they would have previously thought impossible. And two is that, by using a variety of neutralizing devices, it is possible to engage in a wide range of behavior that most members of society would regard as deviant, even deranged, and not to incur serious sanctions for it.

Edwin M. Schur, *Labeling Women Deviant: Gender, Stigma, and Social Control*. New York: Random House, 1984.
A provocative essay arguing that women tend to be devalued in sexist society and are thus more likely to be both victimized and stigmatized as deviants. Well worth reading.

David R. Simon and D. Stanley Eitzen, *Elite Deviance*. Boston: Allyn & Bacon, 1982.
A discussion of corporate and political crime and other harmful and dangerous behavior inflicted by the powerful on the American public, consumers, and workers. Adopts a conflict approach.

James Q. Wilson, *Thinking about Crime* (rev. ed.). New York: Vintage, 1985.
Essays on the causes of and solutions to crime by an influential conservative political scientist.

chapter 9

SOCIAL STRATIFICATION

I n New York City, a white Rolls Royce Silver Cloud glides down Fifth Avenue toward its intersection with 57th Street. The car stops at the curb, in front of an elegant building that bears the name "Tiffany and Co." above the front door. The driver, a uniformed chauffeur, gets out of the car and opens the door. An expensively and tastefully dressed man and woman in their 60s step out onto the sidewalk and enter the building. The chauffeur waits for them. Inside, they purchase a $50,000 sapphire and diamond necklace and a $25,000 solid gold watch.

In Peru, a sandaled, simply dressed peasant is ushered into a large room where a landowner sits at a heavy wooden desk, flanked on either side by burly employees. The peasant walks slowly toward the desk and stops. Holding his hat in hand, he looks down at the floor, speaks softly, and addresses the landowner with great deference. The man behind the desk responds in a familiar, almost condescending way and in the end sends him away, his request unfulfilled.

In South Africa, a Black man is interrogated by the police for the offense of walking through an exclusively white neighborhood.

In England, reporters are chatting idly with one another, or with several tournament entrants who have just finished their matches, in a large locker room in a tennis club. Suddenly, a player enters the room. The reporters stop what they are doing and rush to her side, shoving microphones in her face and asking her questions. The other players keep their eyes on her; they are clearly awed by her presence. She is last year's tournament winner, competing for another crown; they are unseeded players, lucky to be in the competition at all. When she tires of answering the reporters' questions, the champion excuses herself and leaves by a side door, accompanied by the tournament's officials.

In a large, open room in a building located in a midwestern American city, several dozen women, mostly in their 20s, sit at desks and type letters. Emerging from time to time from a smallish, cluttered office is an office manager, a middle-aged woman, who assigns work to the typists and criticizes them for their mistakes and their slow pace. In a suite of middle-sized offices sit a half-dozen men and women in their 30s dressed in suits. They talk on

229

the phone, keep appointments, and hand assignments to a secretary, located at a desk in a nearby vestibule, whose services they share. Down the hall from these offices is another office. Its antechamber is itself an office, occupied by a woman in her 40s. She is an executive secretary to the man in the large office, who is in his 60s. His office, the largest one on the floor, contains a mahogany desk, several leather-covered chairs, a sizable couch, and a number of large green tropical plants. Adjoining the office is a personal washroom. When this man walks through the office, the employees are quiet and attentive. He is the president of the company.

WHAT IS STRATIFICATION?

There are very few universals in human societies: major activities, customs, or institutions that exist everywhere and at all times. Social differentiation is one such universal. In all societies, members distinguish between one another on the basis of three fundamental characteristics: (1) gender, or sex; (2) age; and (3) kinship, or family status. However, not all differences among people, even if they are recognized and regarded as important, are used as the basis for inequality. We make many distinctions among people and categories of people that do not automatically imply inequality. It is not necessarily better or worse to belong to one family than another, for example, or to be a man instead of a woman.

In this chapter, we explore the kinds of social differentiation that do create inequalities. Some people have more than others do—more money, more power, more prestige or respect, even more in the way of basic human rights. These kinds of differences define the subject matter of **stratification.**

Differentiation that results in the unequal distribution of significant social rewards is called social stratification. Stratification is a way of ranking people. What some people do, are, or have is considered to be significantly better than what others do, are, or have. Stratification means that some people have, and others do not have, things that are valued.

The word "stratification" conjures up geological imagery, with layers of earth, rock, and soil piled up on top of one another (Berger and Berger, 1972, p. 120); in fact, sociologists did borrow the term from geologists. In a sense, societies too are "layered," or stratified, so far as their members possess (or do not possess) certain rewards, or valued things. In short, the distribution of rewards and values—who gets what—is unequal pretty much everywhere in the world. Whatever people may want, "some people get more of it than others" (Gerth and Mills, 1953, p. 306). The extent of inequality varies a great deal in different societies, but some kind of stratification is just about universal. Think of the many social rewards that people might have, anything that people might want. Some people drive Rolls Royces; others can't afford bicycles. Very few people possess awesome power—such that a mere suggestion from their lips becomes a command to thousands, hundreds of thousands, or millions. Other people can't seem to get anyone to do anything they want. Some people are the objects of mass adoration. Others are so disgraced

Stratification A system or means of ranking people in a hierarchy according to whether or not they possess things that are valued, such as wealth, prestige, and power; distribution of social rewards.

and dishonored that no self-respecting person wants even to be near them.

Of the many social rewards available to the members of a society, three stand out most prominently: **income, power,** and **prestige** (Weber, 1946, pp. 180–195). Virtually everywhere, it is better to be rich than to be poor, to be powerful than to be powerless, and to receive more respect, prestige, or social honor from others than to receive less of it. Sociologists debate which of these three social rewards is the most important, but they all agree that, taken together, these social rewards are distributed unequally, and that these differences in distribution lie at the core of social stratification.

Stratification is a crucial social characteristic. It does more than just locate individuals in a society with respect to power, income, and prestige. These three dimensions of stratification are closely connected to every person's access to many other aspects of life, such as adequate housing, medical care, and nutrition; long life; protection from legal injustices, crime, and violence; and higher education. Stratification is a basic feature of social life that influences almost everything about every one of us. Its study is central to sociology.

Income The money or other gain received by an individual for labor or services or from property.

Power The ability to get one's way, despite the resistance of others.

Prestige Positive evaluation or social honor bestowed by others; often used in evaluating an occupation.

TYPES OF STRATIFICATION SYSTEMS

Inequality, which today assumes different forms throughout the world, has also assumed different forms throughout history. The earliest, simplest, and least unequal of all forms of inequality is embodied in the "classless" society—the individual stratification system of hunting and gathering societies. Here, there are no true classes, because there are no positions that generate specific social rewards. Positions or rewards cannot be passed from parents to children. The "classless" or individual system of stratification is rare, however; it also has not attracted much interest among sociologists, who have concentrated almost exclusively on structural stratification systems. Three basic kinds of such systems exist—caste systems, estate systems, and class systems—which are delineated by the degree of access they provide to society's rewards and values. Closed stratification systems are based on "ascription," which automatically and inflexibly requires all individuals to inherit their ancestors' social positions. They cannot change their positions through personal achievements. In open stratification systems people can move up or down the class hierarchy, according to their accomplishments or lack of accomplishments. Although no stratification system is ever totally open or closed, all such systems can be classified according to the *extent* to which they are open or closed.

Caste Systems

Castes stand at the closed end of the spectrum: Here, social status is inherited, or **ascribed.** When the stratification hierarchy is organized around castes, it is nearly impossible, in a single lifetime, to move up substantially in prestige, and it is extremely difficult to move up in terms of wealth or power. Each person's position in a **caste system** is determined overwhelmingly by the position of his or her parents. People

Ascribed status A position to which one is assigned through no effort of one's own.

Caste system A system of stratification in which social position is nearly entirely ascribed, or inherited.

Race relations in South Africa is an example of a caste system. Blacks are not allowed to live in or enter certain exclusive white areas, and segregation is strictly maintained.

United Nations

born into high positions do not have to achieve anything to keep them, nor can any personal achievement raise anyone's caste position.

India is a good example of a caste system. A number of analysts (Srinivas, 1962; Singh, 1977) have emphasized the complexity of India's caste system. India has about 3,000 subcastes, some of which have risen or fallen collectively, and some fuzziness and lack of agreement exists about the relative position of some subcastes in the system. Nonetheless, mobility is low in caste systems, and ascribed status is emphasized over **achieved status.**

Achieved status A position that is acquired or attained through one's own efforts.

Contemporary South Africa also exhibits most major features of a caste system: Whites earn four to five times what Blacks earn; discrimination is written into law; for the most part, what are regarded as "uncivilized" (or unskilled) jobs are reserved for Blacks, whereas "civilized" (skilled) jobs are reserved for whites; Blacks are not allowed to live or even enter certain exclusive white areas without authorization; Blacks are deprived of many legal and political rights granted to whites; and a wide range of social contact between the races is against the law. Many white South Africans believe that every white is automatically better and more deserving of privilege than every Black—a sure sign of a caste system.

Estate Systems

Estate system A partly closed system of stratification based on the ownership of land and inherited titles; ascription, or birth, is the main criterion of rank, although some movement up or down is possible.

In some ways, the **estate system** resembles the caste system, because estates are partly closed. In an estate system, the main criterion of rank is birth; rank itself is based on one's family's ownership of land: The larger the estate and the longer it has been in the family's hands, the higher the rank. Theoretically, it is possible to move up or down in an estate system, though only within limits. Estate systems usually have rich and powerful nobilities that control most of society's rewards. Occasionally, a commoner can achieve great social rewards. For instance, in medieval Europe, some sons of commoners became knights, fought for their kings, and were rewarded with titles of nobility. By the end of the Middle Ages daughters of wealthy commoners frequently married less wealthy nobles. The sons of commoners, however, married the daughters of nobles much less often. In England (though not in Continental Europe) only the eldest son of a noble family could inherit the title and estate. Younger sons had to leave their parental homes to become soldiers, adventurers, priests, or scholars. Sometimes, serfs who worked on the land migrated to the growing cities and became successful artisans or even wealthy merchants. Some social mobility, or movement up or down the social ladder, was thus possible, but it was actually quite restricted.

Class Systems

Just as land is the basis of all estate systems, **capital** is the unit of wealth in all **class systems** within a capitalist economy. Capital is any resource or asset that can be turned to profit: money, a factory, a great deal of property, even a highly marketable education, such as a law or medical degree. Clearly, the sources of capital today are much more varied and more readily acquired than was simple land ownership in medieval times. Thus, a class system is far more open than closed. The defining characteristic of a class system is its high degree of social mobility. People are able to change their statuses through personal accomplishments. Achievement, not ascription, is the chief determinant of position in the class system. Nearly everyone must achieve his or her rank in the stratification hierarchy; few people are assigned to one as a birthright.

Children born into affluent, privileged families do, of course, have distinct advantages over the children of the poor and the unprivileged— a head start at the very least. But a head start toward a social position is not the same thing as the position itself. Most children cannot coast on their parents' money and achievements; they must work and achieve themselves to maintain their positions in society. Well-educated, well-to-do (but not enormously wealthy) parents with high-prestige occupations cannot directly pass their privileges to their children or give them a lifetime's income. Privileged as they are, these children must achieve social positions and incomes for themselves. At the same time, as we discuss later in this chapter, achievement is not based solely on native ability. The children of successful parents do have a head start in the race for success. Successful parents pass on certain values and skills to their children that make it likely that these children will succeed. Thus, although the class system is theoretically "open" with respect to mobility, in practice, it is better described as only "partly open." In addition, opportunity is not extended equally to everyone, even in a fairly open class system. Social-class background, race, and ethnicity exert an influence, even today, in one's achievement. These ascribed characteristics (see Chapter 4) are considerably less important than they are in caste and estate systems—but they are influential nonetheless.

In addition, the more industrialized a society becomes, the more it resembles a class system, and the less it resembles a caste or an estate system. The contemporary United States has a class system of stratification, even though it has some caste-like features—for instance, the differences between the way we treat Blacks and whites. Yet, overall, birth now counts less than achievement does for most people.

Capital Any resource or asset that can be used to make a profit, such as money, a factory, or property.

Class system A stratification system in which social position is determined primarily by one's achievement in economic pursuits, especially income and occupation.

WHY STRATIFICATION?

Why has inequality developed in every society that has ever existed? Why are some societies stratified so much more sharply than others? Why do significant inequalities persist even in societies that call themselves "classless"?

Several theories have been developed to explain the reasons behind social stratification. The two best-known are functionalism and conflict theory.

Functionalist Theory

In Chapter 1, we discussed functionalism as a general theory. Now we must explain its specific application to stratification.

The functionalists argue that not all jobs are equally important (Davis and Moore, 1945). Some contribute far more than others to the "functioning" of society. Likewise, some jobs require much more skill or intelligence than others. Not all people are equally capable of handling the demands of different jobs. The functionalist theory of stratification holds that the most important jobs are usually the most demanding.

Consequently, it is quite crucial to match up the most capable people with the most "functionally important" jobs. To do so, the most intelligent and qualified people must be motivated to want the most important jobs. By attaching the greatest rewards to crucial jobs, society attracts the best people to fill and perform them. In short, "social inequality," as the functionalists see it, is "an unconsciously evolved device by which societies insure that the most important positions are conscientiously filled by the most qualified persons" (Davis and Moore, 1945, p. 243). Stratification, the functionalists argue, is good for society. This idea does not, of course, explain why there are such great differences between the haves and the have-nots—only why the differences exist in the first place.

Functionalists point out that their explanation of stratification does not necessarily justify it. But a more nearly perfect justification cannot be imagined. Those who occupy society's privileged positions want to feel that they deserve to be at the top, that they contribute more than others to society's well-being. They also want to feel that those who occupy the bottom rungs of the stratification ladder belong there because they are stupid or untalented or lazy.

Criticisms of Functionalist Theory.   Functionalist theory has been attacked on many different grounds (Tumin, 1953; Anderson and Gibson, 1978, pp. 106–111). It assumes, for instance, that existing mechanisms for recruiting people into "functionally important" occupations are more or less based on ability. If the talented people are to be matched up with the most functionally important jobs, there must be some way of identifying and nurturing that talent. In opposition to the functionalists, some people argue that, far from stimulating the discovery and development of new talent, all stratification systems tend to discourage it: Even if one generation of able individuals did manage to secure high-paying, highly prestigious jobs, these people would wish to make sure that their children, regardless of ability, had jobs and social rewards very much like their own. And most of them would succeed in doing so. Besides, successful parents give their children greater self-confidence, and this eventually becomes a "self-fulfilling prophecy." Among society's disadvantaged, fatalism is common: Why should they make an effort if it produces no result?

What, besides, is the "functional importance" of different jobs? Try to imagine what would happen if all the workers in any occupation went out on strike. Certainly, more people would die if doctors and nurses refused to do their jobs than if manufacturers of expensive jewelry did. The great importance of sanitation workers can be judged when they strike, and garbage piles up on the streets. In fact, the connection between a job's functional importance and social rewards is quite weak, possibly imaginary.

The functionalists also claim that certain skills are scarce and must therefore be rewarded more generously than other skills. The critics of functionalism say that talent, as distinguished from developed skill, is widespread, and that stratification in effect prevents most people from developing their talents. Stratification, they insist, is a means of stifling ability—not of encouraging it.

Finally, the critics of functionalism point out that functionalism treats society as a single body capable of united action. Terms like "in the interests of society," or "social value," or "for the good of society" reflect the view that a certain belief or institution has more or less the same impact on everyone. This view of society promotes the mistaken idea that society is a cohesive entity that can act on its own. The truth is that "society" does not act; individuals within a society act. "Society," taken as a whole, does not apportion the good things of life among its members. Nor do people in certain occupations receive rewards because they help society as a whole. People in these occupations are rewarded because they are helpful or profitable to the corporations or organizations that need them. If a tax accountant working for a huge corporation earns a salary of $100,000, while a lumberjack makes only $20,000, does the accountant make five times the lumberjack's contribution to society (Anderson and Gibson, 1978, p. 108)? More likely, the accountant saves the corporation a lot of money in taxes: good for the company but not, necessarily, for society. Moreover, the economic processes play a role here: Not only does a company profit more by hiring an accountant, but also, accountants are harder to come by than lumberjacks.

According to the critics, different segments, groups, and **classes** in any complex society have *conflicting* interests. Stratification cannot contribute to the "functioning" of a whole society and everyone in it. The results of stratification must be good for some parts of the population—those who receive great social rewards—and bad for others—those who are deprived of these social rewards. Stratification, say the critics, serves special interests, not the general interests of society. This, in fact, is the central thesis of the conflict theory of stratification.

Class A layer or stratum of people with the same socioeconomic status.

Conflict Theory

Conflict theory proceeds from the premise that stratification may be "functional" for the elite but not for most members of any society. Not all conflict theorists dislike every aspect or outcome of stratification, but they all do agree that, in general, it harms most people. By this explanation, stratification is a means of exploitation, a source of disharmony, and, according to some conflict theorists, a path toward revolution.

Bourgeoisie In Marxism, the factory owners, the capitalist class.

Proletariat According to Marxist theory, the working class in a capitalist economy; those who must sell their labor to live.

Class consciousness The shared, mutual awareness of members of a social class of their own class interests.

Many sociologists argue that stratification stifles the expression of ability and talent. Fatalism is common among society's disadvantaged; poor parents typically pass on this fatalistic attitude to their children.

Edward Lettau/Photo Researchers

Marxists prefer to speak of "social class," not of stratification. Karl Marx, the founder of conflict theory, defined social class as an individual's relationship to the "means of production": land, tools, money, and labor. To Marx, there were two major classes in industrial society: the factory owners, or capitalists—who made up the class he called the **bourgeoisie**—and the factory workers, or **proletariat.** The bourgeoisie owned the means of production—factories, land, banks, anything that could produce wealth (or *capital*) on a large scale. Members of the proletariat only owned their capacity to work, "labor power," which they sold to stay alive.

These two classes were much more separate from and hostile to each other than employers and workers had been in preindustrial times. The industrial mode of production required a huge investment. This produced a very unequal and, according to Marx, exploitative relationship. The wealth the workers produced was expropriated for the capitalists' profit. No matter how much money the workers' effort might earn for the factory owner, the workers received only subsistence wages, barely enough to keep them and their families alive.

Marx believed that the economic conditions in which workers lived would eventually bring about an awareness of these conditions. The more exploited workers are, he thought, the more they come to realize that they would be better off by organizing to overthrow the capitalist system and institute a socialist economy. Marx called this heightened awareness, which comes about as a result of exploitation, **class consciousness**—awareness of membership in a social class and of its interests. Because Marx thought that capitalist exploitation must breed working-class consciousness, he thought that capitalism would be inherently unstable. As the workers became increasingly aware of their common suffering and common interests, they would rise up in revolution.

Marxists believe that social class position is the primary fact of existence in a capitalist society, because it determines just about everything else of importance. The three social rewards mentioned in the beginning of this chapter—wealth and income, power, and prestige—could, in Marx's scheme, be reduced to only one: ownership of the means of production or the lack of it. Marxists feel that prestige and political power reflect social class. An extremely wealthy person will receive a great deal of prestige as well, because wealth determines prestige. The same holds for power. It is silly, Marxists feel, to examine three independent dimensions. Wealth is really the only one that matters.

Today's "mainstream" sociologists criticize Marxism most harshly for its concentration on economics. How does the Marxist perspective apply to ordinary men and women? How can we understand human behavior solely by knowing any person's relationship to the means of production? A tiny number of capitalists own those means, and everyone else owns practically none whatsoever—no income-producing land, no factories, no great wealth. This means that most contemporary occupations—janitor, television repairer, lumberjack, clerk, mailcarrier, artist, and truck driver—are actually in the same social class, the proletariat, in that these workers do not own the means of production. According to Marx's scheme, small entrepreneurs—the self-employed, small shopkeepers and the owners of small factories—would eventually be forced out of business and "hurled down into the ranks of the proletariat." So what we are heading toward, as Marx saw it, was an increasingly two-class system, with only capitalists and workers. Many sociologists feel that this approach is extremely limited, and suggest that three dimensions, not one, be used to measure social class.

The Weberian Approach

What is now the "mainstream" approach to stratification in the United States originated with Max Weber (see Chapters 1 and 7), who emphasized not one but three dimensions, which he called "class, status, and party" (Weber, 1946, pp. 180–195). These three refer to what we would today call income, prestige, and power. Weber reasoned that an individual's standing in society has three separate (though related) dimensions. Unlike Marx, Weber believed that it was possible to find many people who ranked high on one of these dimensions but low along the others. In India, for instance, many merchants and traders were extremely wealthy but did not command as much respect, or honor, as Brahmans, who made up the highest caste, though some of them were quite poor. Likewise, in the contemporary United States, a first-year medical intern and a sanitation worker may earn the same income, but the first is in general respected much more than the second. A union official may have far more power, but far less money, than a successful rock musician. In Weber's scheme, each dimension is at least partly independent of the others. Weber's approach is not a theory in the sense that Marx's was; Marx, after all, put forth explanations and predictions. In contrast, Weber describes more than he explains. Nonetheless, Weber's approach to stratification has been extremely influential among contemporary researchers.

Wealth and Income. Classes, for Weber, were not all-or-nothing entities, as they were for Marx. Each dimension of stratification could be regarded as a continuum. We can all, for instance, be ranged on a continuum of income, starting with those who have no income at all up to the richest individual in society. There is no particular point at which the continuum divides into two fixed groups. Although Marx and Weber both used "class" primarily as an economic concept, they meant quite different things by it. Marx defined it as how anyone fits into the structure of the capitalist system of production and exchange—as an owner or as a worker. Weber, in contrast, described class as more or less identical with the ability to purchase what he called "life chances," which is determined, above all, by income. In other words, the members of a class have the economic ability to provide themselves with a certain level of material comfort and to maintain their economic position. People within each class share a similar level of ability to possess or acquire the goods, living conditions, "personal life experiences," land, factories, cattle, money, or "objects that can be exchanged for money," a house, cars—anything, in short, that can be purchased or has economic value.

Prestige. Weber argued that classes need not become true communities or groups with common interests. People do not necessarily come together and interact with one another on the basis of their shared economic position. Why do they interact? Weber argued that common lifestyles often forge a sense of community. For instance, the sons and daughters of families who share the same status are much more likely to intermarry with one another than are the children of families who share a common economic level. Weber believed that status and its acquisition are more of prime movers than are economic interests. Individuals who are accorded the same level of prestige also tend to share the same lifestyle. They live in equally fashionable (or unfashionable) neighborhoods, dress in the same styles, belong or don't belong to the same social clubs, and so on. Lifestyle is a quite different concept from life

Income makes it possible to purchase what Max Weber called "life chances." Wealthy members of society have the ability to provide themselves with a high level of material comfort.

Southern Living/Photo Researchers

chances: Two people could purchase equally expensive items, with the same economic value, yet one may symbolize a high-prestige lifestyle, and the other, a much lower one. A $15,000 vacation to St. Moritz, Cannes, and Florence expresses a high-status lifestyle; the same amount of money spent on a gambling jaunt to Atlantic City and Las Vegas expresses a much less prestigious one. Style of life is not, strictly speaking, an economic concept, but a status concept.

Prestige, or status, groups also lead to friendships and personal relations, particularly marriages within their own circles. Individuals who are accorded the same levels of respect or honor tend to restrict their significant social intercourse to one another. Equally esteemed (or dis-esteemed) families invite one another over for dinner or parties, and they tend to avoid the company of those with markedly different levels of esteem. More specifically, high-prestige circles keep out those of lower prestige to protect their own social privilege; they tend to be snobbish, cliquish, and clannish.

For Weber, status groups—groups whose members share a common lifestyle—not classes, become true communities. It is typically status groups, not classes, that compete with and struggle against one another. Weber agreed with Marx that conflict was normal but thought that conflict over social respect was more important than conflict over economic issues. For the most part, contemporary sociologists have agreed with Weber.

Power.   Weber did not discuss power in the same detail as he did income and prestige. He defined power as the ability to get one's way, in spite of the resistance of others (Weber, 1946, p. 180). Some individuals possess a great deal of power but very little prestige; others, the reverse. Power is unquestionably a crucial aspect of stratification. Yet power is far more difficult to study than income and prestige, in part because it cannot be so easily measured. Consequently, sociologists rarely examine power as a dimension of the stratification system. Instead, they tend to deal with power as a somewhat independent phenomenon.

SOCIOECONOMIC STATUS

Most sociologists today adopt the Weberian (or multidimensional) approach to stratification. Even when they use the term "social class" to describe someone's position in society, they intend the term to evoke several dimensions, not just one. A class is a group or category of people who share roughly the same ranking in the stratification hierarchy. Its members have about the same social rewards: income and wealth; prestige or respect; and power. A slightly more technical term for social class is **socioeconomic status** or, for short, **SES.** Each dimension of stratification (except for power) can be measured fairly precisely; each individual can be given a score on an overall scale that ranks him or her in all of these dimensions.

Socioeconomic status A position along a continuum of income, prestige, power, or education, or a combination of them.

SES Abbreviation for "socioeconomic status."

Income

Income is an easily quantified concept. Sociologists usually ask how much an individual—the head of a household—or an entire family earned during the previous year. Of course, there are some minor problems with assessing income. Obviously, $25,000 does not stretch as far in a family of five as in a household of only a single person. The same income in Alaska (which is a very expensive place to live) doesn't buy as much as in a rural area of Mississippi. Still, income is very easy to measure. It is universally desired, and it commands respect pretty much everywhere. It is also "linear": It can be calculated by an exact number of dollars earned per year.

Individuals can be arranged into income "strata" or levels. If the median family income in a given study is $25,000, then all respondents above that level can be classified as belonging to the upper-income stratum, while those below it can be categorized in the lower one. The number of income strata that exist in a given study or society is a bit arbitrary; it can be two, three, four, or many more, depending on the purpose of the classification scheme.

Occupational Prestige

Since 1925, studies have been conducted every few years to examine one aspect of prestige—*occupational* prestige—as an indicator of SES. All of the early studies were conducted in the United States, but recently, they have been done in some fifty-seven countries. Respondents are asked to rate the prestige of various occupations. Certain occupations, like physician and scientist, rank high in prestige, whereas others, like janitor and street sweeper, command very little (see Table 9–1).

By itself, this finding is not very surprising. At least two very striking facts do emerge from these studies, however. One is that the general public's ranking of the occupational prestige has been remarkably stable since the 1920s. Second, the ranking of occupations is fairly uniform from one country to another.

There is a pattern to the occupations that receive certain levels of prestige. Draw a line (on Table 9–1) between office clerk (with a prestige

■ TABLE 9–1 Occupational Prestige Score, Average for 57 Countries

Occupation	Prestige Score	Occupation	Prestige Score	Occupation	Prestige Score
Physician	77.9	Building Contractor	53.5	Mason	34.1
University Professor	77.6	Actor	51.5	Plumber	33.9
Trial Lawyer	70.6	Bookkeeper	49.0	Sales Clerk	33.6
Head of a Large Firm	70.4	Traveling Salesman	46.9	Mail Carrier	32.8
Civil Engineer	70.3	Farmer	46.8	Truck Driver	32.6
Banker	67.0	Electrician	44.5	Bus Driver	32.4
Airline Pilot	66.5	Insurance Agent	44.5	Miner	31.5
High School Teacher	64.2	Office Clerk	43.3	Barber	30.4
Pharmacist	64.1	Garage Mechanic	42.9	Shoemaker, Repairer	28.1
Armed Forces Officer	63.2	Shopkeeper	42.4	Waiter	23.2
Clergyman	58.7	Printer	42.3	Farm Hand	22.9
Artist	57.2	Typist, Stenographer	41.6	Street Vendor, Peddler	21.9
Primary Teacher	57.0	Policeman	39.8	Janitor	21.0
Journalist	54.9	Tailor	39.5	Servant	17.2
Accountant	54.6	Foreman	39.3	Street Sweeper	13.4
Minor Civil Servant	53.6	Soldier	38.7		
Nurse	53.6	Carpenter	37.2		

Source: Donald J. Treiman, Occupational Prestige in Comparative Perspective. *New York: Academic Press, 1977, pp. 155–156.*

score of 43.3) and garage mechanic (42.9). Except for farmers, all the occupations above the dividing line are nonmanual and involve working with the mind or with people, records, and files. All the jobs below that line (except for shopkeeper, typist, policeman, and sales clerk) involve mainly physical work. Sociologists call nonmanual jobs "white collar" occupations, and jobs that involve physical labor, manual, or "blue-collar," occupations. As a general rule, white-collar occupations rank higher in prestige—as well as in income and in the levels of education required for them—than blue-collar occupations do. Note, however, that this ranking system is somewhat fuzzy and inexact in the middle of the hierarchy.

Further divisions can be made within each of these strata. Some white-collar jobs involve a great deal of skill, training, or education, such as engineers, lawyers, or airline pilots must have. Sociologists call them "professional" occupations. In addition, certain occupations entail the supervision of subordinates or the ownership of a business—the business stratum. Together, the jobs in this professional and business stratum make up the "upper-white-collar" group of occupations. White-collar jobs that require no such training, skill, or education—or that do not involve management or ownership—are called "lower-white-collar" occupations; these are mostly clerical or sales jobs. Taken together, they form the SES level just below the business and professional stratum.

Similarly, some manual or blue-collar jobs require a fair amount of skill, training, or experience, or some sort of apprenticeship. These are "skilled" manual occupations—for instance, mechanics, carpenters, electricians, and plumbers. But some blue-collar jobs require little training or skill. Almost anyone could be a dishwasher or a street sweeper. Skilled occupations have more prestige than unskilled ones.

To make broad socioeconomic distinctions among occupations, we can divide the white-collar from the blue-collar jobs, creating two broad socioeconomic strata. Another way is to create four broad SES strata; the highest is the business and professional stratum, which is followed (in descending order) by the clerical/sales stratum, the skilled manual stratum, and the unskilled manual stratum.

Education

Another dimension of stratification often used to measure SES is education. Although it does not fit neatly into the "income-prestige-power" triad, it does have a number of advantages as an indicator of socioeconomic status. First, it correlates well with the other dimensions; as a general rule, the greater your education, the greater your income and occupational prestige. Second, education, like income, is easily quantifiable. Years of schooling can be ranged in a continuum, a linear dimension, with ladder-like cutoff points.

Wealth

Wealth Significant economic assets.

Even though most adults earn an income of a certain magnitude, very few of us have any significant **wealth**—that is, capital—like stocks, property, or factories that can themselves generate income. The typical American family owns little more than a mortgage on a house and a car or two. Although wealth can be used as a dimension of stratification, it should be kept in mind that most individuals who rank high in income, occupational prestige, and power have very little in the way of wealth. At the same time, approximately half of the wealth of this country is in the hands of 5 percent of the population.

SOCIAL CLASSES IN AMERICA

Marxists generally use the term "social class" to refer specifically to access to wealth, or the means of production. Most sociologists do not follow this practice. In contemporary "mainstream" sociological usage, social classes are equivalent to levels of socioeconomic status. Someone who holds a job with little prestige—or no job at all—earns very little money, and is uneducated belongs to the "lower" class. Someone who has a prestigious job, earns a high income, has great inherited wealth, and is well educated belongs to the "upper" class. Social classes, in this view, are made up of individuals who rank at roughly the same levels in the dimensions of socioeconomic status.

Although these dimensions of stratification are to some degree independent of one another, they are strongly related, or correlated. For the most part, individuals who work at jobs that rank high in occupational prestige are also highly educated and well-to-do. At the opposite end of the spectrum, individuals who have low-prestige jobs also tend to be poorly educated and earn low salaries. Because of this clustering of status characteristics, sociologists often refer to five socioeconomic strata or classes in American society: the lower class, the working class, the lower-middle class, the upper-middle class, and the upper class (Rossides, 1976). Each class displays a number of distinct sociological characteristics.

Far from being hard and fast, however, the number of classes designated is somewhat arbitrary. In addition, social classes are not totally distinct from one another, with sharp breaks or boundaries between them, like blocks piled up, one on top of another. Boundaries between them are gradual, and sometimes even fuzzy.

The Lower Class

The lower class is the stratum at the bottom of the stratification order. It is poor, underprivileged (Matras, 1975, pp. 60–179; 1984, pp. 129–130), deprived of access to social rewards and resources. This stratum is made up of people who are chronically unemployed and underemployed or on welfare—people who usually lack an education or marketable skills. Racial discrimination thrusts many members of minority groups into the lower class, although most of the people in it are white. Physical disabilities, too, make it impossible for a great many people to earn a living.

Poor people are economically insecure, powerless, and deprived. Many of them develop a suspicious, even cynical attitude toward conventional social institutions or activities—such as voting and joining voluntary clubs and organizations—and toward efforts to achieve social action and reform. Many lower-class people are fatalistic about the possibility of social change. They attribute their stations in life to "luck" and "fate." Although these beliefs and attitudes do not in themselves make people poor, some observers feel that they help perpetuate poverty. In many ways, the poor are "outsiders" in their own society. The agencies with which they deal, such as schools and welfare offices, are administered by members of other classes, who are largely unsympathetic to, uninterested in, or even hostile toward lower-class values. The mass media, such as television, display a social world with which they have no direct contact. And they rarely travel, socially and physically, outside their own world (Knupfer, 1947; Cohen and Hodges, 1963).

The Working Class

Members of the working class have blue-collar or manual jobs. They are construction workers, truck drivers, mechanics, steel workers, electricians, bartenders, and the like. What distinguishes this stratum from the lower class is, first, longer periods of employment—and therefore more stable incomes—and, second, employment in skilled or semiskilled occupations, not unskilled ones. Although unemployment hits all levels of the American economy, including those of skilled and semiskilled workers, it is most common at the bottom of the class structure and increasingly less common at each level upward. Members of the working class tend to regard welfare as a stigma. They consider themselves to be respectable and hard working and they look down upon members of the "lower" class, whom they often consider to be shiftless, disreputable, and too ready to exploit public assistance.

Most people in the working class have at least high school educations. Many have some experience of college (especially community college), though few are college graduates. Unionization has helped the working class, but an unstable economy and frequent periods of high unemployment make it difficult for most of its members to accumulate substantial savings. Purchasing a house for people in this stratum is extremely difficult, although a certain percentage may inherit houses from their parents. (Homeowning rises with social class.)

A sizable portion of the members of the working class take relatively little satisfaction in their jobs, because much of their work is routine and frustrating. As a result, many seek their main satisfaction in recreational activities. Many members of this stratum would like to accumulate enough money to leave their jobs and start their own businesses, though few make it. Many pin their aspirations on their children, hoping that they at least will rise in the ladder of success, American-style.

The Lower-Middle Class

In the United States the lower-middle class is made up of families whose chief breadwinners work at nonmanual, lower-white-collar jobs. These people are owners of small stores, managers of small-to-medium-sized organizations and businesses, police officers, nurses, sales personnel, elementary school teachers, dental technicians, and so on. Only a few of these jobs require college educations, although almost all demand some training beyond high school. Members of the lower-middle class are more commonly college graduates than are members of the working class. On the average, the jobs in this lower-middle-class stratum are less subject to unemployment and pay higher salaries than working-class jobs. Job satisfaction is higher than it is in the working class, and most members of the community regard these occupations as higher in standing and prestige. Homeowning is the norm in this category, although both members of a young, newly married couple will have to work for a number of years to accumulate enough savings to buy a house. The members of this social class encourage their children to attend college and hope that they will eventually work at more prestigious, higher-paying jobs.

Members of the working class have blue-collar, or manual, jobs. They tend to be employed longer and are paid higher salaries than members of the lower class. They work at a skilled or semi-skilled occupation.

Cary Wolinsky/Stock, Boston

The Upper-Middle Class

The upper-middle class is made up of the professional and business stratum. The heads of households of families at this level work at upper-white-collar jobs; they are physicians, dentists, successful lawyers, judges, upper-level managers at medium-to-large corporations, well-established accountants. The vast majority of the members of this stratum are college graduates, and a very high proportion also have advanced degrees—a requirement for many of the occupations at this level. These parents expect their children to maintain the economic and occupational level of their parents. Upper-middle-class people have sufficiently high salaries to give them economic stability, sizable savings, and modest wealth. The overwhelming majority of the families in this class are homeowners; they generally live in the fashionable neighborhoods in their communities.

The Upper Class

There are actually two upper classes in the United States. One is made up of families with "old money," which we discussed earlier, in the section on ancestry. This is called the "upper-upper" class. Members of the upper-upper class are distinctive in that they are not only successful professionals, proprietors, and business managers, but they also have wealthy parents and grandparents. The DuPonts, Rockefellers, Vanderbilts, Roosevelts, Cabots, Lowells, and Lodges are representatives of upper-upper class families. Preservation of family fortunes is crucial to the members of the upper-upper class, who are very powerful and who are disproportionately represented not only in the upper management of huge corporations but also in top political positions, such as the federal cabinet (Domhoff, 1983). Members of this stratum typically send their children to elite private schools and colleges, partly so they can strengthen social relationships with "their own kind" and partly so they can meet future marital partners. Marriage within the upper-upper class is both encouraged and expected.

The *lower-upper* class is made up of people with wealth, but not inherited wealth stretching back over several generations. Its members are the "newly rich," the "self-made" millionaires. They are not yet listed in the *Social Register*, although their children or their grandchildren may be. Lower-upper class people may be accepted by the upper-upper class in certain social functions but not in really close social relations. The taste of the lower-upper class may be ostentatious: "If you've got it, flaunt it." In contrast, upper-uppers pride themselves on what they view as their quiet elegance. However trivial these differences between upper-uppers and lower-uppers might seem to most people, they are crucial to members of these classes.

The upper-middle class is made up of the professional and successful business stratum. The members of this class work at upper-white-collar jobs, are usually college graduates, and earn considerably more than the national average.

Dick Luria/Science Source/Photo Researchers

CORRELATES OF SOCIOECONOMIC STATUS

Art Kowalski, a Chicago steelworker, bowls in a local league every Wednesday night. When he is out, his wife, Mildred, visits her parents, who live across the street from her. Mr. Kowalski spends his two-week

Correlates of socioeconomic status Aspects of people's lives that are related to their social-class positions.

vacation with childhood friends at a fishing lodge in Michigan's Upper Peninsula. Mrs. Kowalski stays at home and takes care of their children.

Graham Adams, a Boston attorney, belongs to a tennis club and plays every Wednesday night with his wife, Robyn, and another couple, John and Denise Clark. Mrs. Adams is an assistant professor of history at a college in the suburbs; the Clarks manage their own accounting firm. The Adamses and Clarks took a week-long jaunt to the Italian Riviera on their last vacation.

Sociologists have studied the many **correlates of socioeconomic status:** aspects of people's lives that are related to their social-class positions. It is no secret that people employed at working-class jobs enjoy forms of recreation quite different from those professionals or business executives enjoy. Just about all aspects of our lives—from the newspapers we read to the ways we make love, from the food we eat to our political ideologies and behavior—are either correlated or causally connected with our socioeconomic statuses. For instance, most studies conducted on the relationship between socioeconomic status and voting verify the generalization that the higher the SES, the greater the likelihood of voting Republican in a given election; the lower the SES, the greater the chances of voting Democratic (Erikson, Luttbeg, and Tedin, 1980, pp. 165–180).

Thousands of differences in the attitudes and behavior of the social classes in America and elsewhere have been discovered by many studies researching socioeconomic status. What are some of the differences between the social classes in America? What, in short, are the correlates of socioeconomic status?

Authoritarianism and Permissiveness

More than a generation ago, a study revealed that lower-SES people were significantly less likely to tolerate "nonconformity"—that is, to grant the rights of communists, socialists, atheists, and other political, ideological, or religious minorities to speak in public or hold jobs (Stouffer, 1955). The higher the SES, this study found, the greater the acceptance of nonconformity in behavior and ideas. This difference remains today. It is one of the more striking contrasts between individuals who occupy high and low socioeconomic strata in the United States. Low-SES beliefs tend to stress conformity, "an unwillingness to permit other people to deviate from paths of established belief." Such conformity implies "not only an intolerance of deviant political belief, but also intolerance of any beliefs thought to be threatening to the social order—religious beliefs, ethnic and racial identifications, even beliefs about proper dress and deportment" (Kohn, 1969, p. 201). This phenomenon is sometimes called "working-class" **authoritarianism** (Lipset, 1963, pp. 87–126).[*]

Authoritarianism A rigid, hierarchical view of social life and human relations, usually accompanied by intolerance for a diversity of views and the belief that rules should be strictly obeyed.

"Permissive," or nonauthoritarian, people accept diversity in behavior and belief, dissent in ideology. They reject the notion that everyone must conform to a single standard or set of standards. Authoritarian individuals believe that rules should be strictly obeyed, and that people who are different, "deviant," strange, should be made to conform—or punished. The evidence shows that as the level of education increases, permissiveness also increases; the lower the level of education, and there-

---

[*] This working-class authoritarianism idea has been criticized (for a summary, see Beeghley, 1978, pp. 162–167), but not, in the author's opinion, very convincingly. Data that have been presented are just too difficult to explain away.

fore the lower the SES, the higher the level of authoritarianism. In child-rearing, the higher the SES, the greater the chances that parents stress self-direction, curiosity, and autonomy. The lower the SES, parents are more prone to stress obedience to external authority (Kohn, 1969).

Economic Liberalism and Conservatism

To judge from the strong relationship between SES and permissiveness, it might seem that people at the top of the stratification ladder would be more liberal on all issues. Not so. Low-SES individuals tend to be "conservative" on noneconomic issues, but they are "liberal" on economic issues; high-SES individuals are more conservative on economic issues. The lower a person's SES, the more likely he or she is to think that the government should help people through social-welfare programs. Asked if "the government should do more to improve the conditions of the poor people," only 28 percent of all respondents earning $20,000 and more agreed, whereas 57 percent of those who made less than $5,000 did so. When asked if there should be a "government insurance plan which would cover all medical and hospital expenses," agreement increased from 35 percent for the top income group to 66 percent for the lowest. Agreement with the question of whether the government should "see to it that everyone who wants to work has a job and a good standard of living" increased from 21 percent among the most prosperous of these respondents to 51 percent among the least prosperous (Erikson et al., 1980, pp. 154–155).

Economic liberalism—a belief in government-supported medical insurance, strong welfare programs, greater taxation of the rich, and so on—is supported much more strongly by the poor, by the workers in low-prestige jobs, and by the least well educated. This differential support for specific aspects of the "liberal-conservative" ideological dimension shows that beliefs are extremely complex and cannot be reduced to a pat formula.

Civic Participation

Better-educated individuals working at higher-prestige, higher-paying jobs are more active in the political process. They are more likely to vote, to join voluntary associations (like the Parent Teachers Association, clubs, hobby groups, fraternal associations), to be involved in community or neighborhood organizations, to read newspapers, even to attend religious services.

Lower-SES individuals, in contrast, tend to be less active in all aspects and phases of civic participation, including participation in voluntary associations and organizations. In one study, the percentage of all respondents who belonged to two or more voluntary associations increased steadily, from 7 percent for respondents with grade school educations to 31 percent for all those who had college educations—a more than four-fold increase; respondents belonging to no voluntary associations at all increased from 51 percent for the college educated to 76 percent for the grade school educated (*The Gallup Report*, nos. 201–202). The same pattern prevails internationally. In a study of respondents living in six different countries, the higher the socioeconomic status, the greater the participation in voluntary associations in each country. (Curtis, 1971).

Voting in elections is one clear-cut way that participation in civic life varies by socioeconomic status. In the 1984 presidential election,

One dimension of stratification is the possession of honor, respect, and esteem. Some people, like Pope John Paul II, are the objects of mass adoration. Others are so dishonored and disgraced that no one wants to be near them.

Blair Seitz/Photo Researchers

■ **TABLE 9–2 Percent Who Registered and Voted in the 1984 Election by Education (Years of School Completed)**

Education	Percent Registered	Percent Voted	Total Number (in Millions)
0 to 8 Years	53	43	20.6
1 to 3 Years of High School	55	44	22.1
High School Graduate	67	59	67.8
1 to 3 Years of College	76	68	30.9
College Graduate	84	79	28.6

Source: U.S. Department of Commerce, U.S. Bureau of the Census, Current Population Reports, Series P-20, No. 397. Advance Report, Voting and Registration in the Election of November, 1984. Washington, D.C.: U.S. Government Printing Office, 1985.

as is shown in Table 9–2, nearly four-fifths of all college graduates voted (79 percent), but less than half of those with no high school education (43 percent) did so. However social class and socioeconomic status are measured, as they rise, voting also rises; as they drop, voting, likewise, drops. These differentials in voting point to one of the many ways that upper-strata individuals exert more influence on all aspects of society than lower-strata individuals do.

Civic participation, from voting to joining and participating in voluntary associations, is a measure of optimism—a feeling that what you do matters, that your efforts contribute to meaningful change. People at the bottom of the class structure have been defeated so often that they frequently feel pessimistic and believe that nothing they can do will alter society or their own lives. This results in something of a "vicious circle" whereby deprivation produces a feeling of pessimism and a lack of participation in activities that might change things (Cohen and Hodges, 1963, p. 323). Individuals who participate in the civic realm have more political power and influence, because politicians pay more attention to citizens who vote, give money to their campaigns, write letters to them, and so on.

Achievement Orientation

Classes tend to perpetuate themselves. This is not to say that movement up or down the class ladder does not occur; indeed, this happens quite a bit, as we see shortly. What it does mean is that there are mechanisms that retard a society's rate of mobility; there is a certain degree of inertia in the class system. One of the sources of this inertia is the fact that the members of each class pass on to their children certain values, which equip or fail to equip them for occupational success. High-SES parents tend to have high financial, educational, and occupational aspirations for their children. Low-SES parents are more likely to have scaled down aspirations for theirs. What's more, higher-SES parents are more likely to have a clear idea of what their children must do to ensure that they will be materially successful.

The children of the privileged are trained to expect privilege. They have higher occupational aspirations and higher educational achievements. They are more likely to complete their educations, and less likely to drop out at any given level. The privileged are trained to master the "social graces" considered appropriate to their parents' class, and they are encouraged, and given opportunities, to mingle with their social peers (Matras, 1975, pp. 153–157).

In contrast, the children of the economically "underprivileged" lower strata are more likely to believe that the educational system is irrelevant or a nuisance, and that monetary and occupational success is based on luck rather than individual effort or achievement. In fact, for the most part, education *is* irrelevant to the lives of the most underprivileged. In their neighborhoods, the relationship between hard work and success is tenuous at best (Matras, 1975, p. 169). Parents teach values and beliefs to their children that equip them to fit into the class structure at a certain level. High-SES parents teach their children how to reach their level; likewise, lower-status parents do the same for their children. Although other factors are involved, socialization tends to retard mobility and perpetuate class privilege.

INCOME AND INCOME DISTRIBUTION

Of the principal indicators of socioeconomic status, only one directly measures a resource that, by itself, obtains life's basic necessities: income. Other dimensions are not necessarily less important than income: What makes income so crucial is that it determines access to what sociologists call "life chances": material goods, medical care, food, shelter, clothing, transportation—in short, anything that can be purchased.

Some societies allocate material goods, income included, quite equally. As we've already seen, an economy with little or no material surplus—such as a hunting and gathering society—has very little inequality of goods. Other societies are extremely unequal. An economy that is much more productive, with a vastly greater material surplus—like the great agrarian empires of ancient Egypt, Rome, and China—is full of very large inequalities between rich and poor. Industrial societies distribute their incomes more equally than agrarian societies do. Even societies at the same economic level display quite different degrees of inequality.

How Is Income Inequality Measured?

We need some kind of measuring rod, something that will help us to compare the degree of inequality in different societies.

The diagonal line in the accompanying figure, "Income Distribution—Equality and Inequality," shows us a type of income distribution that does not exist anywhere in the world. An almost straight diagonal line indicates that the poorest fifth of the population earns a shade less than a fifth of the national income of that country; likewise, the wealthiest fifth of the population earns a shade more than a fifth of the national income. In short, everyone has about the same income. It is useful to see a graph like this one, not because such an income distribution actually exists anywhere, but because it can serve as a basis of comparison with income countries that do exist. The further a nation's income distribution departs from the diagonal line, the greater income inequality there is.

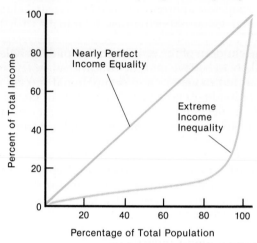

Income Distribution—Equality and Inequality

The other line in the figure—"Extreme Income Inequality"—represents almost exactly the opposite type of income distribution: Here, the poorest four-fifths of the population earns less than one-fifth of the national income, while the richest fifth earns more than four-fifths of it. Although no society has nearly perfect income equality, as illustrated in the first figure, societies do exist with extreme income inequality, as depicted in the second one. The income distributions of countries with comparatively high degrees of income equality will look more like the first figure; the income distributions of countries with high degrees of income inequality will look more like the second.

Income Distribution the World Over

Look at income-distribution figures for the United States from 1947 to 1984 (see Table 9–3). Three clear-cut facts emerge very strongly. First, income distribution in the United States is most decidedly unequal: The bottom fifth of the population (in income) earned only 4.7 percent of the total money earned in 1984, and the top fifth earned nearly ten times as much—42.9 percent. Second, the income distribution in the United States is not at either extreme—total inequality or total equality—but somewhere in the middle. Third, over time, things have not

■ **TABLE 9–3 Percentage Share of Total Family Income**

	Lowest Fifth	Second Fifth	Middle Fifth	Fourth Fifth	Highest Fifth
1984	4.7	11.0	17.0	24.4	42.9
1977	5.2	11.6	17.5	24.2	41.5
1967	5.5	12.4	17.9	23.9	40.4
1957	5.1	12.7	18.1	23.8	40.4
1947	5.0	11.9	17.0	23.1	43.0

Sources: U.S. Department of Commerce, U.S. Bureau of the Census, Current Population Reports, Series P-60. Money Income of Families and Persons in the United States: 1981. *Washington, D.C.: U.S. Government Printing Office, 1983, Table 17; and* Statistical Abstract of the United States, 1986, *p. 452.*

changed at all. The figures for the United States in 1947 are almost identical to those for 1984, allowing for a little random fluctuation from year to year.

Now examine income inequality around the world (see Table 9–4). Of course, these figures are not precisely comparable, but they do give a rough idea of how equally income is distributed around the world. The first thing we notice is that income is more equally distributed in communist countries than in capitalist and in industrializing countries. In Czechoslovakia and East Germany, two representative communist countries, the bottom fifth earns roughly 10 percent of the total earnings, while the top fifth earns about 30 percent. This means that the poorest people in communist countries receive more of those countries' total resources than do the poorest Americans. Of course, the resources of the United States are much greater than those of any communist country. Still, income here is more unequally distributed than it is in Eastern Europe.

It should come as no surprise that South Africa, a country with an official racial separatist policy (apartheid), distributes its income more unequally than the United States does. The poorest fifth there receives less than half the proportion of the total income that the same group receives here, while the highest fifth receives over 15 percent more. Incomes in countries whose economies are still agricultural, that are not yet fully industrialized, are more unequally distributed than they are in more fully industrialized societies. Still, in all industrial societies, great inequality remains.

In this respect, the United States does not fare exceptionally well against industrialized noncommunist nations. Our income seems to be a bit more equally distributed than that of France, but the poorest fifth of the population in the United States commands a smaller slice of the economic pie (4.7 percent) than that of Japan (8.8 percent), Canada (6.7 percent), Great Britain (6.6 percent), West Germany (5.7 percent), and Sweden (5.2 percent). However, the proportion of the total income earned by the wealthiest fifth is about the same in all of these countries except Japan. This indicates that the economic means by which income "filters down" to the poorest segments of the population do not work as well in the United States as they do in other industrialized nations. Our poorest fifth is more underprivileged than the poorest fifths in comparable countries around the world. (Remember, this is a comparative statement, not an absolute one. Our poorest fifth earns a lower *proportion* of the total income earned—although it may earn more in absolute number of dollars than the poorest fifth in some countries.) So we must examine how income in the United States is related to what Weber called **life chances.** What does income buy to make life more materially comfortable?

Life Chances

The connection between socioeconomic status and certain attitudes—opposing abortion, for instance, or believing that homosexuals should have equal rights—and most forms of behavior—like drinking alcohol or voting for a certain political party—is complex and often indirect. The connection between income and life chances is far simpler and much more direct.

Health Care and Longevity. Money buys good health in America—or better health, in any case. The poor live shorter, unhealthier lives than

■ **TABLE 9–4 Percentage Share of Total Income Received by Lowest and Highest Fifth of Population in Various Countries***

	Lowest Fifth	Highest Fifth
Canada	6.7	40.0
Czechoslovakia	11.1	31.5
Ecuador	1.8	72.0
France	3.1	51.5
Germany, East	10.4	30.7
Germany, West	5.7	45.6
Great Britain	6.6	40.3
Japan	8.8	37.6
Peru	2.8	62.6
Sierra Leone	1.1	72.8
South Africa	1.8	62.0
Sweden	5.2	44.1
Tanzania	2.3	63.3
Turkey	2.9	60.6
United States	4.7	42.9

* These figures are not precisely comparable; income figures are computed somewhat differently in different countries. Nonetheless, the observer must make use of what information is available, take note of its limitations, and generalize from it with caution.

Source: Shail Jain, Size Distribution of Income: A Compilation of Data. *Washington, D.C.: The World Bank, 1975.*

Life chances Anything that can be purchased: material goods, medical care, food, shelter, clothing, transportation.

Infant mortality The number of deaths of babies, before they reach the age of 1, per 1,000 births in a given year.

the affluent. There is a direct relationship between income, on the one hand, and ill health and premature death, or what the medical profession calls "morbidity," on the other hand.

There are many ways to document this relationship. Perhaps the most valid is to compare the rates of **infant mortality** among the different economic levels. Infant mortality means the number of deaths of babies, before they reach the age of 1, per 1,000 births in a given year. The death rate for infants under the age of 1 is extremely high, and is exceeded only by the rate for individuals over 65 years old. In modern industrial societies, about three-quarters of all infants who die in the first year do so during the first four weeks, the "neonatal" period.

One researcher asked: "Is poverty hazardous to an infant's health?" (Gortmaker, 1979, p. 281). One study divided parents into two groups: those whose income was below the "extreme poverty level" and those whose income was above this level (which was determined by family size, the consumer price index, and income). It is clear that living in poverty is strongly related to infant mortality: Significantly more infants born to parents living in extreme poverty died during the neonatal period (22.8 per 1,000) than infants born to parents not living in poverty (14.4). This difference was even more extreme for children in the postneonatal period: 10.3 per 1,000 births for the poor as opposed to 4.5 for other groups (Gortmaker, 1979, p. 284). This relationship was maintained even when the education of the mother and father, the age of the mother, the mother's previous pregnancies, if any, and so on, were taken into account. In other words, there is a causal connection between poverty and infant mortality. Individuals who become motorcycle dare devils or smoke three packs of cigarettes a day jeopardize their lives by willful acts. Infants born into extreme poverty are innocent victims of social inequality.

The same picture—higher rates of premature death for infants born into poorer families—holds for adults, too. At age 45, a white man with at least some college education stands to live 2.2 years longer than his counterpart with only four years of elementary school education. Among white women, this differential is even greater: 7.7 years. (For some reason, in this study, these figures were not computed for Blacks.) One of the statistics used by sociologists who study human population, called the "mortality ratio," is computed by figuring out the odds (or statistical chances) that a member of a given category will die during a certain year. If this figure is set at 1 (an arbitrary number) for the overall average of a whole population, then by looking at the mortality ratios for various specific categories, we can immediately see whether they are higher or lower.

In one study (Kitagawa and Hauser, 1973, p. 18), the mortality ratios for white males and females, aged 25 to 64, living in high-income households were .84 and .86 respectively, well below the average 1 for the whole population. For their counterparts in the lowest income households, the mortality ratios were 1.51 for men and 1.20 for women, significantly higher. (Again, data for Blacks were not tabulated in this study.) This means that poor men are about 70 percent more likely to die in a given year than affluent men; and poor women, about 35 percent more likely than affluent women. Obviously, the bottom of the heap in our stratification system is dangerous to life and limb!

A country's infant mortality rate is a "direct measure" of its "physical quality of life." It is, in fact, "sensitive to even small improvements in national health care" (Kurian, 1979, p. 284). As nations go, our rates of premature mortality are not exceptionally good. The citizens of roughly twelve to fifteen nations live longer, healthier lives than we do. Twenty countries in the world, most of them European nations with some form of socialized medicine (Taylor and Hudson, 1972, p. 253; Kurian, 1979, p. 284), have lower rates of infant mortality. The United States is fifteenth in the world in male life expectancy—that is, in fourteen other countries, men live longer—and fifth in female life expectancy. We rank thirteenth in the maternal mortality rate (the measure of how many women die in childbirth). Again nearly all of the countries with lower maternal mortality rates—like Sweden, Norway, Denmark, and the Netherlands—have national health plans. The United States ranks twelfth in the number of physicians per million of population (Kurian, 1979, pp. 259, 281–286).

Housing

Another aspect of life chances that still varies directly with income is housing. As income increases, the quality of housing improves along with it. This improvement is far more than simply being able to live at a fashionable address or own a home with a swimming pool. To begin with, home ownership is strongly related to income: The affluent are more than twice as likely to own their own homes as the poor are. Although 65 percent of the American people live in houses they own, 43 percent of the lowest—and 90 percent of the highest—income categories do (U.S. Department of Commerce, 1979, p. 1). This difference, although large and most decidedly significant, does not adequately convey the real differences in the quality of the housing lived in by rich and poor. Poor families are more likely to live in dwellings that lack adequate plumbing facilities; have too few bedrooms; are infested with mice or rats; and have structural deficiencies, cracks in ceilings and walls, and holes in floors.

Quality of housing extends beyond the walls of a building. Families do not merely own or rent houses or apartments; in a sense, they own or rent whole neighborhoods. The rich live in more comfortable, congenial surroundings than the poor. They have superior recreational facilities, access to better hospitals and health clinics, more efficient transportation facilities, and more effective police protection. The poor are more likely to live in areas with unsatisfactory shopping facilities, boarded up or abandoned structures nearby, and streets littered with trash (U.S. Department of Commerce, 1979, pp. 41–45).

Education

We've already seen that affluent and well-educated parents are more likely to socialize their children into values compatible with future success. Parents are also able to directly purchase more education and a superior education for their children. Access to education is one of the most basic of all life chances, every bit as crucial as health and housing, because it influences or determines future socioeconomic position. Children from poorer families are significantly less likely to attend college than children from well-to-do families, even making adjustments for parents' education. Indeed, children with low measured intelligence who come from high-income families are just as likely to go to college as highly intelligent children who come from low-income families (Sewell and Shah, 1967; Cross, 1971; Krauss, 1976).

POVERTY

Who are the poor? Measuring poverty is a complex and tricky matter. Clearly, a seasonal migrant laborer with ten children and an income of $4,000 a year is poor by any conceivable definition. Not all poor families are poor in such obvious ways. The United States Census has set up a complicated system for determining degrees of poverty. It is based (among other things) on income and the number of members in a family. The maximum income that a single unrelated individual must earn to qualify as poor is about $5,500; for two people, a shade below $7,000; for three, about $8,500; for four, about $11,000; for seven or more family members, just about $16,600. What proportion of our people lives in poverty? It depends on where you draw the line. By the definition of the United States Census, 15.2 percent of the population of the United States lived below the poverty line in 1983, a total of 35.3 million people. The number of poor dropped between the election of John F. Kennedy as president in 1960 (39.5 million) and the last days of Jimmy Carter's administration in 1980 (25.3 million)—marked by twelve years of Democratic, and eight years of Republican, rule. However, with the election of conservative Ronald Reagan, who cut back or eliminated many poverty programs initiated during the Democrats' tenure, the number of poor people began to rise again. In the first three years of Reagan's administration, the number of Americans living in poverty rose by 6 million (Kilborn, 1984).

Who Are the Poor?

Which segments of the American population are living in poverty? Which categories or groups are more likely to remain below the poverty line than others? (See Table 9–5.) Although roughly two-thirds of the poor are white (22.9 million out of a total of 33.1 million), Blacks are about three times *more likely* to be poor than are whites: 31.3 versus 11.4 percent

TABLE 9–5 Persons Living in Poverty, 1985

All Persons	Percent Each Category 14	Number (in Millions) 33.1
White	11.4	22.9
Black	31.3	8.9
Female householder, no husband present	33.5	16.4
Female head with related children	53.6	6.7
Unrelated individual, age 65 and over	25.6	2.3
Male	20.5	.4
Female	27.0	1.9
Hispanic origin	29.0	5.2

Source: Statistical Abstract of the United States, 1987, *pp. 442–444.*

for whites. In fact, a great deal of the poverty in the United States can be located among our racial and ethnic minorities (see Chapter 10).

Much of America's poverty can be found, too, among households headed by women—over a third of which (33.5 percent) live in poverty. If a woman living without a husband has one or more children under the age of 18 living with her, their chances of being poor are greater than even: 53.6 percent. Of all population categories, female-headed households produce the greatest number of poor people. If a family is both Black and female-headed, it faces doubly formidable difficulties, as we see in Chapter 10.

In addition to racial minorities and women, a third concentration of poverty is regional. Some areas of the country simply present fewer economic opportunities than do others. As a result, their residents are considerably more impoverished. For instance, in 1983, the per capita income of the poorest states, such as Mississippi ($6,801) and Arkansas ($7,388), was only slightly more than half that of the most affluent ones, such as Alaska ($12,900) and Connecticut ($11,897). The Appalachian Mountain range, which extends from southern Pennsylvania to northern Alabama, is a major regional zone of poverty. For instance, more than one-third of the people living in the Appalachian region of Kentucky live in poverty.

The fourth concentration of poverty in the United States is among the aged, particularly those who live alone. The aged are an unusual group economically, because they contain a higher-than-average proportion of very wealthy individuals as well as a higher-than-average proportion of very poor ones. Thus, their overall income is very close to that of the population at large. At the same time, the aged are more likely to live in poverty than the rest of the population. More than a quarter of all "unrelated individuals" aged 65 and older are poor, a total of slightly more than 2 million men and women. Because women outlive men, and because so few older women work regularly at gainful employment, four times as many elderly women are poor as elderly men (see Table 9–5).

The fifth poverty segment in the United States consists of the disabled. Over 13 million Americans are classified as disabled. Only one in five of these workers (19.8 percent) is employed full-time; the rest are permanently work-disabled, unemployed, or only part-time workers (*Statistical Abstract of the United States, 1985*, p. 396). A fifth of the disabled live below the poverty line. Disability benefits, even for those who receive them, almost automatically put their recipients either below or very near the poverty line, if that is their sole means of support. The family of a miner stricken with black-lung disease receives $488 a month in benefits if the claimant has no dependents; a minor's widow receives $348 per month (*Statistical Abstract of the United States, 1987*, p. 359).

The last group of poor comprises the unemployed. The official unemployment figure during 1987 was 6 percent, a significant but not sharp drop from the early 1980s, when the rate was roughly one worker in ten. About a third of these workers lived in households that received no income aside from unemployment. Many of the unemployed do not receive even that, because the average length of time that a worker remains unemployed is much longer than it used to be, and the benefits run out. Many of these workers cannot find jobs at all. Some observers believe that the 1980s may be a time of high "structural" unemployment—unemployment caused by a permanent excess of untrained workers, not economic fluctuations.

The figures on the number of out-of-work employees who receive unemployment benefits do not, of course, include those whose benefits run out and those who have given up looking for work ("discouraged" workers). Nor, however, do they include those who work in the "underground" economy: those workers and businesses that do not report their incomes. Not all unemployed workers necessarily live in poverty. Some have spouses who work, and some work at jobs "off the books," either full- or part-time. Still, for a highly industrialized nation, our economy has a relatively high rate of unemployment. The Japanese, the Swedes, and the Swiss, for instance, have rates of only 2 percent—one third of ours.

Another side of the "underground" economy comprises illegal aliens. No one knows exactly how many of them now live in the United States, but the figure certainly totals at least several million. Because the nations they left—such as Mexico, Haiti, and Colombia—are considerably poorer than the United States, these workers are willing to work at extremely low wages. In the western part of this country, these workers are mostly agricultural laborers; in New York City, most work in clothing "sweatshops." They can be exploited and underpaid because they have few alternatives and little legal protection. This sector of poverty is largely "invisible," but it exists.

Why Poverty?

Why does poverty endure amid wealth? Who benefits from poverty? Marxists hold that the poor and the unemployed are a kind of "reserve army of the unemployed," which keeps employed workers docile by reminding them of their fate should they become too militant and demanding. Capitalists, Marx held, pay workers just enough to keep them alive and productive. In the Marxist view, poverty is "functional" for capitalism, because exploitation creates profit (Gans, 1973). Actually, in Marx's day, many factory workers did earn "subsistence" wages—just enough to keep them alive and little more. Marx did not foresee that labor unions would successfully raise the wages of average factory workers well above the poverty line. In fact, many organized workers in highly industrialized nations earn significantly more than the average income.

Most Americans have a distinctly individualistic explanation for poverty: They believe that poor people are responsible for their poverty. Upper-income people are especially prone to believe this idea. When one study asked whether "personal attributes account for poverty," 62 percent of the wealthiest whites in the sample agreed, whereas only 17 percent of the poorest Blacks, and 30 percent of the poorest whites, did so (Rytina, Form, and Pease, 1970, p. 713). This mentality is called "blaming the victim" (Ryan, 1976). Do the rich deserve their riches, or the poor, their poverty?

Turn back to Table 9–5. Nearly 7 million out of 33.1 million poor Americans are divorced or single women with children. One poverty-stricken person in fifteen (2.3 million out of a total of 33.1 million) is elderly and has no supporting family. Over 2 million are disabled and physically prevented from working. Millions of Americans live in economically depressed areas with unemployment rates of 20 percent, 30 percent, or even 40 percent. And millions of Blacks, Hispanics, and Native Americans still suffer from pervasive discrimination.

Close scrutiny of the poorest segments of society does not support the view that lack of ambition and unwillingness to work account for poverty. Clearly, something else is at work. What? Simply this: The American economy, in its present form, cannot provide full employment to all able-bodied workers and a sufficient livelihood to those who, through no fault of their own, are not able to work for livings. In an effort to reduce poverty, liberals typically seek more effective welfare and government benefit and employment programs. Conservatives argue that stimulating the economy through private enterprise is the answer. Yet poverty is still with us, and income inequities remain substantially the same over the generations, despite a variety of governmental policies and programs. Income has not successfully "trickled down" to the poor in the United States to the extent that the politicians have claimed it would. In absolute terms, the poor are a bit better off than they were thirty or forty years ago, because the total economy is more productive than it was then. But the bottom fifth of the economic pile still earns less than 5 percent of the total pie, as was true a generation or two ago. As a result, we should be asking some questions: Why is poverty so persistent, so difficult to eradicate? Why are there so many poor people in our rich country? What makes poverty such a basic part of the American economy?

Despite Marx's failure to foresee the enormous expansion of the middle class and the factory worker's higher standard of living in advanced capitalist economies, he did have a valuable and still valid insight about poverty. Poverty was, and continues to be, advantageous for the rich. It is not that the wealthiest and most powerful members of society consciously plan and conspire against the poorest and least powerful ones. But when a phenomenon so pervasive and detrimental endures for so long, we are forced to ask, Who profits? Poverty, in other words, must serve some important functions, not for society as a whole, but for the most affluent and influential members of society. They act in such a way to ensure that the poor remain poor. It would be disadvantageous to the wealthy for the poor to become financially secure and comfortable.

Government benefits, such as food stamps, attempt to reduce poverty. Income has not successfully "trickled down" to the poor in the United States. Sociologists attempt to answer the question of why poverty is so persistent and difficult to eradicate.

Tom McHugh/Photo Researchers

SOCIAL MOBILITY

Social mobility Movement up or down the class structure.

Social mobility refers to any kind of movement that is sociologically relevant. Movement can be up, down, or sideways. And it can be of almost any type: geographical, generational, occupational. Sociologists who study stratification are interested mainly in movement in socioeconomic status. More specifically, they are interested in two dimensions of socioeconomic mobility: whether it is upward or downward and whether it is within one's own lifetime (**intragenerational mobility**) or from one's parent's to one's own lifetime (**intergenerational mobility**). If someone starts out as a truck driver and ends up owning a large trucking firm, that is an example of upward intragenerational mobility. If someone whose mother washes floors him- or herself becomes a successful trial lawyer, that exemplifies upward intergenerational mobility. Of course, both intra- and intergenerational mobility can be downward as well as upward. Someone who starts out as a junior executive and ends up a dishwasher would represent downward intragenerational mobility. Someone whose parents are both employed in executive or professional occupations but who becomes a taxicab driver has experienced downward intergenerational mobility.

Intragenerational mobility The amount of movement from one socioeconomic status level, or social class, to another within an individual's lifetime.

Intergenerational mobility The amount of movement from one socioeconomic status level, or social class, to another, from one generation to the next.

Different societies encourage and permit different amounts of social mobility. A true class system is based on a relatively high degree of mobility—at least in theory. In a class system, nearly everyone (with a few outstanding exceptions) should attain, or achieve, his or her rank in the stratification system. Hardly anyone is automatically assigned to any class as a birthright. Children born into affluent, privileged fami-

Since the middle 1970s, downward mobility has accelerated somewhat in the United States, and it is possible that the size of the lower class will increase over time. Homelessness is clearly a growing phenomenon in America's cities.

P. Sudhakaran/United Nations Photo

lies do, of course, have a head start in achieving high positions themselves. But inheriting a head start is not the same thing as inheriting a specific position. Most children cannot rest or coast on their parents' achievements; they must *do* something themselves.

At the same time, social classes do "reproduce" themselves from one generation to the next in various ways. In agrarian societies, eldest sons inherit their fathers' estates, thereby ensuring generational continuity. And in industrial societies, likewise, parents with capital—wealth, land, or a business—"can simply give or will the business to their children or provide them with investment capital to start their own businesses" (Robinson, 1984, p. 183). Children with parents who have substantial assets and resources thus start with an enormous advantage in the race for economic success. Most find themselves in the enviable position of managing their inheritances rather than having to earn them on their own, which is considerably more difficult to accomplish. Thus, even though they do have to "do" something to maintain their positions, clearly, what they have to do is of a different order than what someone who did not begin with their advantages would have to do to reach the same position.

In addition, classes reproduce themselves through a process of *differential socialization.* The children of managers and professionals are taught self-reliance and inner-directed motivation, a decided asset in a materialistic, achievement-oriented society. On the other hand, the children of manual laborers are more likely to be taught the value of obedience and conformity, and to be prodded by a motivational system that is dependent on external rather than internal influences—values that tend not to be rewarded by success in capitalist society (Bowles, 1978, pp. 325–326). As a general rule, the higher the parents' social-class position, the greater the likelihood that "they are to value self-direction, self-reliance, independence and curiosity for their children; the lower their class position, the more likely they are to value conformity to external authority" (Robinson, 1984, p. 193). This generalization holds for a great variety of nations (Kohn, 1981) and cultures (Ellis, Lee, and Peterson, 1978) around the world. The evidence further shows that success is strongly influenced by whether or not one adopts these class-linked values. As a general rule, the more self-reliant and self-directed an individual, the greater his or her chances for achievement in an industrial society (Kohn and Schooler, 1982; Edwards, 1984). And it is precisely these values that high-achievement parents pass on to their children. As a result, once again, children who are raised in an upper-socioeconomic status family have a sizable head start over those who do not.

Social Mobility in Industrial Society

How much social mobility occurs in the United States? And how does our rate compare with that of other highly industrialized nations? Clearly, mobility has two more or less separable components: **micro-level** factors (Why do some people move up or down, while others do not?) and **macro-level** factors (What structural factors make for a high or low rate of mobility?). Let's concentrate for a moment on intergenerational mobility, defining it as the movement, either up or down, across the line that separates manual from white-collar work. Many studies indicate that the rate of mobility is quite high in all industrialized societies. About one-third of all sons have jobs at significantly different socioeconomic strata from those of their fathers. (Most of the studies on this

Micro-level A perspective that focuses on the movement and location of individuals within a given social structure, such as the rate of social mobility of men vs. women in the United States.

Macro-level A perspective that focuses on the characteristics of entire social structures or types of social structures, such as the rate of social mobility in agrarian vs. industrial societies.

WHAT DO YOU THINK?

Downward Mobility

A specter is haunting young adults today—the specter of downward mobility. Many people in the "baby boom" generation, now in their 20s and 30s, will probably be economically worse off than their parents were. Many of the material things they grew up with and took for granted now seem out of reach, perhaps forever. Many such people fear they have missed "the last boat to the middle class."

Many of their parents were upwardly mobile. They grew up during the Great Depression and World War II, a period of scarcity and deprivation. But they entered the job market at a time of economic expansion and upward mobility. In time, many could afford houses and comfortable, often affluent lifestyles. "People who came of age in the forties and fifties enjoyed the good fortune of having their expectations shaped during the worst of times and their achievements realized during the best of times—an unbeat-

able match." Their children, today's young adults, had precisely the opposite experience: They grew up during economically comfortable times, and entered the job market during a recession. "Growing up in the fifties, the assumption for most people was that they would equal or do better than their parents. Upward mobility was an immutable fact of American life" (Schumer, 1982, p. 22). In fact, many people who grew up in those times "may never achieve the relative economic success of the generations immediately preceding it or following it. The pinch means that many of the amenities that today's middle class grew up with and came to accept almost as a birthright now seem beyond reach" (Schumer, 1982, pp. 22, 20).

Even though the current generation may earn more than its parents did at the same age, that income does not purchase as

many goods and services. To begin with, there is inflation. An income of $101,000 in 1982 is equivalent to $28,000 in 1952. Because money is worth so much less today, an apparently much higher income has much less purchasing power. And because the percentage of income that gets taxed rises as incomes rise, the current generation gets to keep less of its income, so its seemingly higher incomes are even less substantial. A married couple whose combined income was $66,000 in 1981 paid about 40 percent of that in taxes; in 1962, the taxes on an equivalent income, $22,000 in 1962 dollars, came to only 27 percent. An earned income of $50,000 put a person in the top (50 percent) tax bracket in both 1972 and 1982, even though that sum was worth only $21,561 in 1972 dollars (Schumer, 1982, p. 22). Economists call this phenomenon "bracket creep."

A second grim economic fact

kind of mobility concentrate on men—an unfortunate bias; thus, we refer here to "fathers" and "sons." Now that half of all adult women work full-time, the mobility of women is also crucial.) Social mobility occurs in Europe and Japan at about the same rate as it does in the United States. All highly industrialized societies seem to have about the same rate of intergenerational mobility (Lipset and Bendix, 1959, pp. 17–28; Blau and Duncan, 1967, pp. 432–433).

But the movement across the blue-collar–white-collar line may not represent an altogether valid measure of intergenerational mobility—especially these days, when this distinction becomes fuzzier all the time. Many highly skilled manual jobs are rising in prestige and pay, while many lower white-collar jobs are becoming "proletarianized."

Mobility studies show that father-to-son mobility steps are typically quite small. Rarely does a son get a job much higher or lower than his father's in occupational prestige or pay (Blau and Duncan, 1967, p. 28).

facing those now in their 20s and 30s is the cost of housing, a cost that has outstripped even the overall rate of inflation. Interest rates on mortgages are three to four times the levels of the 1940s and 1950s, so it is "impossible for most in the baby-boom generation to afford the houses they grew up in" (Schumer, 1982, p. 21). In 1955, the editors of *Fortune* predicted: "Certainly the day is close at hand when almost anyone with a job can afford to own a house" (Schumer, 1982, p. 23). Today, "almost anyone" should read, "very few."

To add to the woes of today's young-adult generation, there is the problem of too many people in the same age cohort (see Chapter 18), and this causes more competition for jobs, lower pay, and slower movement up the career ladder. More babies were born between 1946 and 1957 than in the previous thirty years. As the members of this "baby-boom" generation move through their careers, they find that in "almost every occupation, the competition is up

and the rate of promotion down." A Ph.D., an MBA, a law or medical degree mean so much less today because there are so many more of them. "Why does it seem that everywhere you look everyone is trying to do what you're trying to do?" complained one financial analyst, age 30 (cited in Schumer, 1982, p. 24).

And then there is the subjective dimension—the realm of expectation and perception. Even if they are affluent, by today's income standards, the generation of young adults living in the 1980s *feel* deprived "because of pervasive factors rooted in their psychology, their upbringing, and their culture." They grew up facing an economic horizon of seemingly limitless possibilities. Today's economic realities have made things that once seemed possible or even inevitable downright inconceivable. There is perceived downward as well as real downward mobility. The inability of today's young-adult generation to achieve the level of social mobility its parents achieved is frus-

trating. Many members of this generation feel deprived.

Growing up in middle-class homes taught the members of this baby-boom generation to grow accustomed to the finer things in life—art, books, good clothing, and travel. The tastes into which they had been socialized do not match their current budgets. Adjustments and compromises have to be made. "Like the privileged but strapped classes before them, the children of the affluent fifties cling to their notions of quality and taste. . . . [They] are apt to deal creatively with limitations of space. Their apartments become pocket museums, filled with prints, books, and *objets d'art*." Explains one New York resident who feels deprived even though he and his wife earn $35,000 each: "You know, you don't have to give in to it. . . . We can still have it all—just in a different way" (cited in Schumer, 1982, p. 26).

Source: Schumer, 1982, pp. 20–26.

Intergenerational movement up and down the blue-collar–white-collar line usually means a transition from skilled labor to clerical or sales work, or the reverse. Movements from the bottom to the top of the occupational structure, or the reverse—from street sweeper to physician, for instance—are very rare.

Even so, it might be instructive to examine the *relative* frequency of large father-to-son mobility moves. The data show that social mobility from manual or working-class jobs into elite occupational levels—the professions—is rare in all countries but most common in the United States (Miller, 1960; Blau and Duncan, 1967, p. 434; Lopreato and Hazelrigg, 1972, Lipset, 1982). (These studies almost never examine the downward mobility of sons with elite fathers into manual labor.) Nearly 10 percent of the sons of manual laborers attain "elite" or professional status in the United States, but this is true of only 1 percent in Denmark, 1.5 percent in West Germany, 2 percent in Great Britain, between 1.5

and 3.5 percent in France, and 3.5 percent in Sweden. The sons of manual laborers most commonly work at their fathers' occupational level.

In all industrialized societies throughout this century, upward mobility has been more common than downward mobility, for two main reasons. First, in industrial economies generally, and in the United States specifically, the top of the occupational structure has grown and the bottom has shrunk. Thanks to automation and increased mechanization, manual jobs form a decreasing proportion of the total. Technical expertise and professional training are required for more and more jobs. Professional and technical workers—the top occupational stratum—increased from 4 percent of all job holders in 1900 to 15.7 percent in 1985. Farmers (most of them working small subsistence farms) dropped from 20 percent to 1.2 percent; and farm laborers, from 18 percent to less than 1 percent (*Statistical Abstract of the United States*, *1987*, pp. 385–386). Just between 1970 and 1982, some 500,000 farm jobs were lost, and experts predict that by 1995, another 300,000 will disappear (*Statistical Abstract of the United States*, *1985*, p. 405). As a result of expansion at the top and contraction at the bottom, more people move up than down. (The process could work the other way around, as well— for instance, when skilled workers' jobs are eliminated, demand for low-paying service work, like taking orders in hamburger stands, increases.) This phenomenon is known as **structural mobility**. It facilitates individual mobility, but it should not be confused with it. The nature and the shape of the stratification system influence the extent to which people move up or down within it (Tyree, Semyonov, and Hodge, 1979).

The second reason why upward mobility has been more common than downward mobility is that the birth rate is lower at the top of the SES levels. Highly educated married couples with high-paying, high-prestige jobs barely have enough children to reproduce their own numbers. Consequently, this leaves openings at the top of the occupational structure for upwardly mobile sons and daughters of lower-status parents. The lower birth rate of groups at the top of the stratification ladder continually generates occupational, economic, and educational opportunities for the less privileged groups.

What Generates Mobility?

What social factors make for upward (and downward) mobility? What are the characteristics of mobile individuals? What facilitates a move into a new stratum? Clearly, the more education you have, the more likely you are to enjoy occupational and financial success (Hauser and Daymont, 1977; Parelius and Parelius, 1978, pp. 284–286). Like any other generalization, this one has its exceptions. But the lifetime mean income for men with bachelor's degrees is just under $1.2 million; for men with only high school diplomas, it is $861,000—a difference of more than $300,000. Women (whose careers are usually interrupted by childrearing) who get bachelor's degrees can expect to earn $523,000 over a lifetime; those with only high school diplomas, $381,000. The lifetime earnings of men who dropped out of high school average $601,000; of women, $211,000 (*The New York Times*, March 14, 1983, p. A12).

What complicates this picture is that the well-educated are not all equally likely to succeed. At any level of education, the socioeconomic status of parents, especially their income, is correlated with the occupational achievements of their children. Well-to-do, well-educated parents help for a number of reasons. They can afford to steer children to private colleges and universities rather than public ones, and to academically superior colleges and universities (Haveman and West, 1952, pp. 166–

Structural mobility Movement up or down the class ladder that is caused by the opening up or the shrinking of positions in a given economic system or structure.

185; Feldman and Newcomb, 1969, pp. 106–150). Research shows that the undergraduate institutions from which we get our degrees can make a great deal of difference in our future earning power. In one study, graduates of Harvard, Yale, and Princeton earned almost 30 percent more than did graduates of other Ivy League schools (like Columbia, Cornell, and Dartmouth); almost 50 percent more than graduates of all technical and engineering schools, and those of twenty small, prestigious Eastern colleges (like Amherst, Williams, and Tufts); a bit more than 50 percent more than graduates of the "big ten" schools (Illinois, Indiana, Michigan, and so on); and almost 75 percent more than those who got their B.A.s from any other colleges or universities (Haveman and West, 1952, pp. 178–179). Ivy League schools are expensive—and so too are the majority of private colleges. Those students whose parents can afford them enjoy an important competitive edge.

The same study found a strong relationship between parental financial support during college and income after graduation. Common sense seems to argue that students who worked their way through school would be more ambitious and, therefore, more successful later in life. Exactly the reverse turns out to be true: Students whose way was paid entirely by their parents went on to earn significantly more money in their careers than those who paid their own way through school, and the more students earned in college, the less they earned as college graduates (Haveman and West, 1952, pp. 166–177). Of course, those students who worked their way through school had less affluent parents than the students whose parents paid the bills. A higher proportion of the latter entered the higher-paying professions (like medicine, dentistry, law), which require the kind of demanding, extensive postgraduate training for which parental economic support is a distinct asset. (It is very difficult—almost impossible—to work at a part-time job and go through four years of medical school.) Affluent parents can afford to support their children during the four, five, or six years necessary to become trained as a highly paid professional. Through these and other mechanisms, we can see exactly how parents of high socioeconomic status are able to use their privileges to help their children—even though these privileges are rarely inherited directly. A head start is usually sufficient.

The Matter of Luck. Predictable factors do not account entirely for success and mobility, or the lack of them. There will always be a measure of unexplained variation: luck, being in the right place at the right time, working in "growth" industries or prosperous companies, having supervisors who recognize and reward ability, and living and working in prosperous areas of the country—just for starters. The American economy is sometimes chaotic and difficult to predict. Typically, we cannot know much about the economic future in advance, and thus part of our economic fates is a matter of chance. In the 1960s, for instance, teachers were in short supply at all levels, so millions of students embarked on programs of advanced educational training. By the time they had graduated, an oversupply existed, and there were no jobs waiting for them. The demand for engineers has fluctuated from year to year, and the success of an engineering major depends, in part, on what year he or she enters the job market. The income of workers in the building trades depends on factors beyond their control—like the interest rate on home mortgages, the cost of building supplies, inflation, and so on. Any major life event—getting divorced, for example—can have a great impact on our levels of income. A man's marrying a woman who pursues a career can mean the difference between mere survival and prosperity. Sociologists who study social mobility will never be able to predict movement up and down the stratification hierarchy with complete accuracy (see Jencks, et al., 1979).

SUMMARY

1. In all societies, members distinguish among one another by age, sex, and kinship status.

2. Stratification entails a distinct kind of differentiation: the unequal distribution of significant social rewards.

3. In most societies, stratification is structural in nature: People who occupy certain positions receive a certain quantity of social rewards.

4. Of the many social rewards that are granted to holders of certain positions, the three most important are income, power, and prestige.

5. The three basic types of stratification systems are caste, estate, and class systems. They are defined by how open or closed they are: Open systems are based mainly on achievement, whereas closed systems are based mainly on ascription, or inheritance.

6. Stratification has evolved over time from hunting and gathering societies—with the least amount of differentiation between members at the top and bottom of the stratification ladder—to agrarian, with the most; industrialized societies are less stratified than agrarian ones.

7. Functionalist theory of stratification holds that inequality is good for society, as well as necessary and inevitable. Most contemporary observers dispute this argument.

8. Conflict theory, contrary to functionalism, holds that stratification is exploitative, oppressive, and based on coercion.

9. Most contemporary sociologists base their view of stratification on the approach of Max Weber, who considered the dimensions of stratification—income, prestige, and power—to be somewhat independent of one another. Weber also stressed the role of life chances (what money can buy) and lifestyle (which is related to group differences in status).

10. Sociologists measure position in the stratification hierarchy by means of three main indicators: occupational prestige, education, and income. Individuals who rank at about the same level on these three dimensions are said to belong to the same socioeconomic stratum.

11. Most contemporary sociologists use the term "social class" more or less interchangeably with socioeconomic stratum (SES). Individuals who belong to the same social class have roughly the same occupational prestige, income, and education. Sociologists call the principal social classes in America the "lower" class, the working class, the lower-middle class, the upper-middle class, and the upper class.

12. Socioeconomic status, or social class, is a continuum with a number of attitudinal and behavioral correlates. They include authori-

tarianism versus permissiveness, economic liberalism versus conservativism, beliefs regarding sexual equality and appropriate sex roles for women and men, hedonism versus puritanism, different ideals regarding what constitutes happiness and satisfaction, family size, participation in civic life, religious beliefs and activities, and achievement orientation.

13. Income is distributed more equally in industrial societies than in agrarian societies, and more equally in communist than in capitalist societies.

14. Income inequality has not changed much in the United States in the past generation or two.

15. In the United States, access to basic life chances—such as adequate health care, housing, and education for one's children—is strongly related to income.

16. Poverty is strikingly greater in some segments of the population than in others, particularly in racial minorities; in households headed by a woman; in certain geographical areas; and among the aged, the unemployed, and the disabled. Most sociologists agree that poverty is the result of the inability of the economic system to provide enough jobs or livelihoods to these sectors of the population, rather than the result of a lack of ambition or ability on the part of the poor.

17. Marxists argue that poverty is profitable for the most powerful and affluent in society, and that this is why it is perpetuated.

18. Social mobility refers to movement up and down the stratification hierarchy. Although industrial economies generate the greatest amount of mobility, even there, parents strongly influence the eventual class positions of their children.

SUGGESTED READINGS

G. William Domhoff, *Who Rules America Now? A View for the '80s.* Englewood Cliffs, New Jersey: Prentice-Hall/Spectrum, 1983.
A revision of a book originally published in 1967. Domhoff's thesis is that a tiny upper-class elite dominates American government and business. Although critics argue that Domhoff exaggerates in many details, his basic thesis is undeniable. An important book.

Michael Harrington, *The New American Poverty.* Holt, Rinehart & Winston, 1984.
A critique of neoconservative policies to deal with poverty, and an analysis of the sources of America's economic troubles by "an unabashed socialist."

Judah Matras, *Social Inequality, Stratification and Mobility* (2nd ed.). Englewood Cliffs, New Jersey: Prentice-Hall, 1984.
A detailed, rigorous textbook on the subject.

Frances Fox Piven and Richard A. Cloward, *The New Class War: Reagan's Attack on the Welfare State and Its Consequences.* New York: Pantheon, 1982.
A critique of the Reagan administration's cut of billions of dollars from the federal budget's poverty programs. The authors argue that big business supports these cuts because they stimulate a plentiful supply of cheap labor; at the same time, the authors argue, these cuts are harmful to the poor.

Terry J. Rosenberg, *Poverty in New York City: 1980–85.* New York: Department of Research, Policy and Program Development, Community Service Society of New York, 1987.
A detailed empirical study of the characteristics of the poor in one American city. A sobering statistic: the number of poor in New York City has increased between the late 1970s to the middle 1980s from 1.4 million to 1.7 million, from 20 to 23.5 percent of the city's population.

William Ryan, *Equality.* New York: Pantheon, 1981.
A forceful argument documenting that equality does not exist in America. Inequality can only be perpetuated by existing conservative policies, and it can be reduced by adopting a number of innovations: affirmative action, the Equal Rights Amendment, a national health care program. Ryan puts forth the case for a Fair Shares society—that is, one based on collectivism—and debunks what we have now, a Fair Play society—one based on individualism.

Melvin M. Tumin, *Social Stratification: The Forms and Functions of Inequality* (2nd ed.). Englewood Cliffs, New Jersey: Prentice-Hall, 1985.
A brief, readable introduction to the field of stratification.

chapter 10

RACIAL AND ETHNIC GROUPS

Lucas, a 14-year-old South African Black, discusses his anger at police repression of basic human rights in his homeland. His goal is to join an armed resistance movement against South Africa's racist policy of apartheid. When he is 18, he explains, he will join a guerrilla cadre. "Then, instead of stones, I will have a bazooka." Pointing to an armored police vehicle, he says, "I just want to get the bazooka and kill" (Cowell, 1985, p. 30).

In 1983, Uwe Reinhardt, a Princeton professor, attended a meeting of the university's graduate school admissions committee. Looking over the list of applicants, the committee came to the name of a clearly qualified Asian-American student. One committee member said, "We have enough of them." Another member of the committee turned to Professor Reinhardt and said, "You have to admit, there are a lot." Although Asian-Americans attend Ivy League universities in far greater proportions than their representation in the general population, a lower proportion of Asian-American applicants are accepted than applicants overall. "My hunch is if you look at the top 20 percent of the Asian-Americans being rejected at Ivy League schools," Professor Reinhardt said, "they are better qualified academically than the bottom part of the class that is accepted." Admissions officers do admit that most Asian-Americans' academic credentials are strong, but acceptance is not based on tests and grades alone. Other qualities, such as leadership, musical, theatrical, and athletic talent, are also important, they explain— qualities that Asian-Americans are less likely to possess. Most Asian-Americans suffer from one-sided strength in the sciences. Many Asian-Americans wonder if perhaps this isn't simply a genteel form of discrimination (Winerip, 1985).

In 1960, Clarence Dickson was the first Black to graduate from the Miami police academy. He ranked third in a class of sixteen. Proudly, he stood for the class photograph with his fellow graduates. Several days later, when Dickson was out on patrol, an "official" all-white picture was taken without him. Apparently, in 1960, top officials of the Miami police department didn't want the world to know that their force included a Black officer. In 1985, poetic justice was served when Dickson became the first Black to be installed as Miami's chief of police. This time, he could not be excluded from the department's official portrait (Serrill, et al., 1985).

Race According to the dictionary, a group of persons related by common ancestry or heredity; according to sociologists, a category of persons believed, by themselves or others, to share a common ancestry.

One of the reasons why **race** is a crucial topic to sociologists is that it is strongly related to stratification and inequality. Such important things as income, political self-determination, treatment at the hands of law enforcement, and access to higher education and to certain jobs are all influenced by one's racial status.

By itself—as a strictly physical characteristic—race is no more sociologically relevant than height or body weight. Sociologists are interested in the use we make of these characteristics, not the characteristics themselves. How do members of different races relate to one another? What is the nature of their social relations—how, in other words, do they interact with one another? Perhaps the most central question concerns inequality. In just about every society on Earth, race and status are in some way connected. Everywhere, the good things of life—income, power, prestige—are unequally distributed along racial lines. Not all societies are equally racist and discriminatory, but racism and discrimination seem to be very widespread, perhaps even universal. Every large, diverse nation on Earth has a racial and ethnic problem.

Race and stratification are connected in at least two key ways; first, through an unequal distribution of a society's resources and rewards and, second, through the different degrees of respect and honor accorded by various societies to the members of different races.

WHAT IS A RACE?

Most people use the term "race" in a sloppy, imprecise way. There is, in fact, a dual character to those categories referred to as races. One aspect is physical and biological; the second is social and cultural. Physically, human categories do differ from one another in a number of ways, although these differences are more likely to be statistical than absolute. The physical characteristics that have been used to classify individuals as members of specific racial groups include skin color, eye color, thickness of lips, shape of nose, hair form, shape of head, height, and eyelids. Using these criteria, a tripartite typology of race results: Caucasian, Mongoloid, and Negroid. Caucasians are commonly referred to as whites, and their ancestry stems from Europe, North Africa, and the Middle East. The ancestry of the Mongoloid category can be traced to Asia. Negroids or Blacks originated in Africa.* Clearly, there are physical differences among the members of these broad categories—for instance, in skin color. But these categories are not air-tight—that is, it is not possible to divide the peoples of the world into distinct races, with no (or even a small number of) in-between or ambiguous cases. There are at least four problems with using race as a scientific concept based on biological differences among people.

One problem is that there are large groups of people who do not clearly belong in any one of these three categories. For instance, Australian aborigines have dark skin, which should place them among Blacks, but they also have wavy hair, a Caucasian feature. Many East Asian Indians, likewise, have very dark skin and wavy hair, along with a thin or "European" nose. American Indians are commonly classified as Mon-

---

* Actually, if the paleontologists are correct, the ancestry of all of us stemmed ultimately from Africa, hundreds of thousands of years ago. As my colleague Bruce Hare says, "Africa is the mother of us all."

goloid, but they tend to be much taller and have more aquiline noses than most East Asians. Thus, the classification of the world's races into three categories is inadequate because it leaves many millions of people outside of the classification scheme altogether.

A second problem with using race as a scientific, biologically based classification scheme is that there is tremendous overlap among the categories—that is, there is great variation from category to category. Once again, the differences are statistical, and not absolute. For instance, Europeans tend to be taller than Asians, on the average, but many Asians are taller than the average European. Thus, height cannot be used as a definitive or absolute criterion to determine race, because the overlap is so great. Whites are more likely to have longer trunks and shorter legs, whereas Blacks are more likely to have shorter trunks and longer legs—but again, with many whites and many Blacks, the reverse is true. The huge overlap among the races shows how imprecise these categories are.

The third problem with using race as a biological grouping is that there is a tremendous variation within each racial category. For instance, the Pygmy and the Watusi, two groups in Africa, are both classified as Negroid, but the first has the shortest stature and the second, the tallest, among any groups on Earth. Some North Africans and Middle Easterners look European: They have light skin and straight or wavy hair, and sometimes, hazel, green, or even blue eyes. Others have more Negroid features: dark skin, tightly curled hair, flat noses, and full lips. The within-category variation is so enormous that it is difficult to think of its representatives as belonging to the same race.

A fourth problem is that racial mixing has been taking place for millions of years, further confusing the issue. There are no "pure" races. An extremely large number of the members of every race have some ancestors who stemmed from another category. For instance, North Africans (or "Moors") lived in parts of southern Europe for hundreds of generations, and made a significant contribution to the physical characteristics of the local population. In the United States, much of the population designated as white has some Indian ancestry; likewise, much of the population designated as Indian has some white ancestry. The same holds for racial mixing in the South; one anthropologist claims that white Americans have, on the average, 5 percent Black or African ancestry and that Black Americans have, on the average, 25 percent white or European ancestry. (See the accompanying box, "Who Is Black? Who Is White?") Wherever and whenever members of different races have interacted, there has been sexual contact and racial mixing. Racial purity, therefore, is a myth.

For these and other reasons, it is inaccurate to refer to races as scientifically valid categories. Although physical differences among people are based in part on ancestry, dividing the human population into categories based on these physical differences produces a scheme that can only be described as loose, sloppy, and very fuzzy around the edges.

Dictionaries typically define a race as "a group of persons related by common descent, blood, or heredity." This definition is a bit misleading. Picture two circles. One encompasses a group of human beings defined solely by physical characteristics—"common descent" and "heredity." The second circle encompasses a group of human beings who have been defined as a race by the members of a given society, including themselves. The first circle would be determined by physical, genetic, and biological characteristics—which, as we have discussed, are very imperfectly distinguishable among categories. The second circle—the one that interests sociologists—would be a creation of popular beliefs (and misconceptions) about what makes a race and who belongs to which race. We would find the two circles—the "biological" one and the "popular" (or "cultural") one—overlapping very imperfectly. Many people who popular opinion unites in a common racial category do not have a common ancestry. Popular opinion also puts into different categories some people who actually do have a common descent. In other words, the popular conception of race is a social creation. A race exists sociologically because it is thought of as a race—not because it has a solid basis in physical or biological reality. There is, nonetheless, some *degree* of common ancestry in each racial and ethnic group, but it may be a great deal, or very little. The important thing about races is that people think that their members share a common ancestry. In this way, a genetic fiction becomes a social reality.

Consider the distinction between "Blacks" and "whites" in this country. Most Americans, Black and white alike, regard *anyone* with *any* recognizable African ancestry as "Black," whether it be 1 percent or 100 percent. But the line between Blacks and whites might conceivably have been drawn at any point along the Black-white spectrum. Why, for instance, isn't everyone with *any* degree of white ancestry "white"—including those with 99 percent Black ancestry and 1 percent white? Why isn't the line drawn at the 50 percent point, or at 25 percent, or at 1 percent? The reason has nothing to do with ancestry itself but with the way we conceptualize it.

Race, then, rests on what might be regarded as shifting sand—cultural conventions—and not solid, bedrock biological reality. What most of us think of as a race is, thus, partly fictional. At the same time, we must not fall into believing the opposite fallacy: the idea that "race" is totally unreal, a mere illusion that must be swept away by science. What is socially real is real, even if it is also mythical. The common descent of a racial group may be biologically real or biologically fictitious, but when it is believed to be real, the belief has powerful, very real sociological consequences. This phenomenon has been called the "Thomas theorem" because an early sociologist, W. I. Thomas, said, "If men define situations as real, they are real in their consequences." (Like everything else, this is true only up to a point.)

Are races, then, "subjective" or "objective" categories? They are subjective in the sense that although they are widely believed "to be the natural divisions" of humankind, they rest on "arbitrary" distinctions, like skin color. In one sense, however, they are *not* subjective, because we cannot belong to whatever race we choose. Racial "categories are objective in that they are well-established beliefs held in common by a great many people, and they are objective in that they exist independently of the desires of any particular individual. The classification of people in any community is a matter of consensus, and as far as any given individual is concerned, it is a part of the external world to which" we must adjust (Shibutani and Kwan, 1965; pp. 46–47).

ETHNIC GROUPS

An **ethnic group** is a collectivity of people who share a common culture or subculture that is passed down from one generation to the next. Included in this culture are language, religion, and, usually, nationality.

Ethnic group A collectivity of people who share a common subculture that is passed down from generation to generation and who are usually regarded, and regard themselves, as sharing a common ancestry, as well.

Members of ethnic groups perceive their generational continuity. Some sort of common ancestry is usually but not necessarily implied by ethnic-group membership. For instance, Puerto Ricans living in the United States are not, strictly speaking, a "race," but an ethnic group. They are racially diverse in their makeup: Some are almost totally white; some, almost totally Black; most, a complex blend of the two, with an admixture of Native American ancestry, as well. Despite their lack of common ancestry, they do share a common cultural heritage.

Jews, too, are not a race. Judaism is a religion, but many Jews are completely secular yet still regard themselves as completely Jewish. The racial diversity of Jews can be seen in the faces of Israel's people. Some, whose ancestors lived for thousands of years in the Middle East, have light brown skin and look like Arabs. Others, whose parents immigrated from Germany, Poland, and the Ukraine, are light-skinned, and often blond and blue-eyed. Most American Jews came from Europe, and their genetic makeups may be as much European as Middle Eastern. When Jews settled in a new area, and remained in it for more than a few generations, they intermarried with the host population and began to take on its physical appearance. (For instance, the Jews of China, who emigrated to that country at some point afer 200 A.D., are completely Chinese in appearance. The Jews of Ethiopia (or Falasha), most of whom now live in Israel, are very dark-skinned; they are thus indistinguishable from other Africans from that region. The Jews, then, like the Puerto Ricans, are not a race. Yet they are more than a religious communion. They must be regarded, more properly, as an ethnic group.

In the United States, ethnic groups largely overlap with national background. The members of most ethnic groups immigrated here from specific countries, and that common national background is the basis of the shared identity. The immigrants from each country shared a culture that was to some degree different from the culture of other Americans.

No ethnic group is totally homogeneous. There are usually significant differences among groups within the same ethnic group. Bavarians, who come from southern Germany, have a reputation for being warmer, earthier, and more fun-loving than the Prussians, from northern Germany,

America is a land of many races and ethnic groups, a country made up of immigrants and the descendants of immigrants from many nations. Here, 10,000 immigrants become U.S. citizens in the largest swearing-in ceremony in history.

Guy Gillette/Photo Researchers

Who Is Black? Who Is White?

The very words "white" and "Black" suggest absolutely clear differences between the two. But are they so clear?

In 1982, a Louisiana woman who is the descendant of an eighteenth-century Black slave asked a New Orleans court to officially declare her white. Her birth certificate records that she is Black. State law (invalidated in 1983) labeled anyone with more than one thirty-second part "Negro blood" as Black. According to the state, the woman, Susie Guillory Phipps, a light-skinned woman with Caucasian features, has three thirty-seconds part Black ancestry.

Ms. Phipps said that she was totally unaware of her Black ancestry until five years ago, when she applied for a copy of her birth certificate to obtain a passport. "I am white," Ms. Phipps declared to the court. "I was raised as a white child. I went to white schools. I married white twice." The state's attorney said that her birth certificate was filled out by Ms. Phipps's parents, who listed their children's race as Black because that was what their own birth certificates read. Several of Ms. Phipps's relatives testified for the state, saying that they regarded themselves as Black and raised their children that way.

Testifying for Ms. Phipps was a professor of anthropology, Munro Edmonson, who summoned research demonstrating that the average white American has 5 percent "traceable Negro genes," and the average Black American has 25 percent "traceable white genes." Ms. Phipps said that none of her relatives would testify on her behalf because they were fearful that the state would change the birth certificates of their blond, blue-eyed children from white to Black.

If the designation that more than one thirty-second Black or African ancestry—that is, more than one great-great grandparent—should not determine who is Black, what should? Here are four other possible definitions of race:

- A Louisiana Health Department lawyer who represented the state in the Phipps case argued that the proper way to define whether someone is Black or not is if that individual has "any traceable amount" of Black ancestry. This was, in fact, the legal definition of race that ruled Louisiana law until 1970, when the "one thirty-second" rule was passed by the legislature. Because this law was repealed in 1983, it is possible that, once again, Louisiana will revert to the "any traceable amount" rule. By this definition, Ms. Phipps would have to be regarded as Black.

who are said to be more sober, serious, severe, and hard-working. Still, the two groups resemble each other more than either resembles other, different ethnic groups. Ethnicity forms the basis for an identity; despite variation among members, it creates a common *bond*, which is reinforced by traditions, values, customs, norms, and beliefs. Moreover, members of *other* ethnic groups assign us to appropriate ethnic groups, even if our own senses of ethnic identity are weak. Indeed, such ethnic "labeling" by others can create identities that may not even exist to begin with.

PREJUDICE AND RACISM

Prejudice A preconceived, unfavorable opinion of a social category based on racial, ethnic, religious, or other characteristics.

Prejudice is a preconceived, unfavorable opinion of members of racial, ethnic, religious, or national groups—or indeed of the members of *any* social category: Southerners, the rich, homosexuals, men, women, the young, the old, artists, farmers, conservatives, communists, or even soci-

- *The New York Times*, editorializing on the Phipps case, proposed that: "If society must make a distinction, at least let it split the difference evenly: a person is white if 51 percent white, black if 51 percent black" (September 26, 1982). According to this definition, Ms. Phipps is clearly white, because only three of her great-great grandparents were Black.

- The United States Census permits each respondent to designate his or her own racial status. Accordingly, whoever thinks, "I am white," is white, and whoever thinks, "I am Black," likewise, is Black. By this definition, Ms. Phipps is white, because she regards herself as white.

- Lastly, there is the community definition: Someone's race is defined by how that person is regarded in the general community. The facts that Ms. Phipps was "raised as a white child," that she attended predominantly white schools, and that she "married white" twice indicate that she was widely regarded as white rather than Black.

Thus, by two of the five commonly used definitions of race—the "one thirty-second" law and the "any traceable amount" law—Ms. Phipps is Black. By three of them—criteria based on more than half of one's ancestry, self-designation, and community definition—Ms. Phipps is white. Which is she: Black or white? Clearly, race is not a clear-cut phenomenon, as this case shows. To which race someone "belongs" is a bit arbitrary—a matter of definition, not hard fact.

Perhaps a more basic question than how Black and white should be designated is the question, why bother with racial designations at all? Historical research shows that the designation of race on official documents in the New Orleans area served the purpose of maintaining "control over land ownership." Its purpose was "to keep the landowner from having to share his land with his illegitimate children who were family members" (Marcus, 1983).

Why should it make any difference what race someone is? What purposes do racial designations serve nowadays?

Sources: "Black and White," *The New York Times*, editorial, September 26, 1982, p. E18; "A Woman Seeks Change in Racial Designation," *The New York Times*, November 23, 1984, p. A28; and Marcus, 1983.

---

ologists. Most commonly, however, the term is used in the context of race and ethnic relations and refers specifically to negative attitudes toward members of racial and ethnic groups.

The idea that certain races are inherently inferior or superior—**racism**—was advanced in the late eighteenth century. It was made scientifically respectable—for a short time—by an improper extension of Darwin's theory of natural selection: "the survival of the fittest." These nineteenth-century racists claimed (contrary to Darwin himself) that certain races are less advanced on the evolutionary scale, more "apelike," and less highly evolved, whereas certain other races are "superior," more intelligent, more highly evolved, more "advanced" in the biological sense. Contemporary evidence totally refutes these notions.

Racism A negative, hostile attitude toward members of a minority group. (See **Prejudice**.)

Stereotypes

Racism and prejudice almost always involve stereotypical thinking about minority groups. A **stereotype** is a rigid image of the nature and characteristics of a group and its members, one that is held more or less without regard to the facts. Not all stereotypes involve race or ethnic groups; there are, in fact, stereotypes about every conceivable kind of

Stereotype A simple, rigid, and often negative image held about the members of a group without regard for the facts.

social category, including fishermen, lovers, and engineers. Nor are all stereotypes negative in character. But stereotypes influence the thinking of majority-group members concerning minorities, especially when there is intergroup hostility. Some stereotypes are totally fabricated. For instance, in Nazi Germany, it was believed that Jews had an unusually strong sex drive directed, in particular, at blond, Nordic types. Many stereotypes contain a grain of truth but are grossly exaggerated. For instance, many Americans believe that Jews are financially successful. This is true, but this is not the whole truth. Although Jews have per capita incomes higher than almost any other American ethnic group, the per capita incomes of several other groups are just as high; in addition, a sizable number of Jews are quite poor.

Stereotypes tend to ignore the "whys" that explain the "whats." Prejudiced whites believe that a great many Blacks on welfare live well without working. It is true that Blacks are more likely than whites to live on welfare. But most welfare recipients are white. What's more, the overwhelming majority of Blacks are not on welfare, and many of those who are on it are victims of racial discrimination. Stereotypes are also highly selective, biased, and impervious to fact. If actions, individuals, or characteristics do not fit the negative image, they are reinterpreted in a negative light. For instance, prejudiced whites who believe that Blacks are particularly musical and athletic may also think that they are "primitive," uncivilized, and physical. What on the surface might appear to be a desirable characteristic is recast as a bad one.

Of course, not all white people hold negative stereotypes of Blacks, and vice versa. It is even possible that the majority of each race holds an unstereotyped view of the other racial group. Still, when stereotypes are held, they have a fascinating inner dynamic. The very positive characteristics that the members of one race see in their own category are reinterpreted as negative by the members of the other race. Thus, whereas whites see themselves as intelligent, industrious, ambitious, and individualistic, the dominant stereotype of whites held by Blacks is that they are deceitful, sly, treacherous, and selfish. Likewise, whereas Blacks tend to see themselves as religious, sportsmanlike, athletic, musical, and pleasure-loving, the most common white stereotype of Blacks is that they are superstitious, happy-go-lucky, loud, ignorant, and lazy (Stephan and Rosenfeld, 1982, pp. 99–101). Clearly, in the stereotyping process, we are in the realm of fantasy rather than reality.

The Causes of Prejudice

What causes people to develop hostile attitudes toward minority groups? Which segments of the population are especially prone to racism? No neat formula can explain all, or even most, prejudice. At least four theories have been developed to explain it, though: theories that stress economic and political conflict, personality factors, authoritarianism, and traditionalism. The first tries to explain why the majority holds negative attitudes about minorities in general but does not examine why members of majority groups differ in this respect. The latter three theories attempt to understand and explain why some individuals are more prejudiced than others.

Economic and Political Conflict. When two readily identifiable racial or ethnic groups inhabit the same geographical area, they will very probably compete for scarce resources. When different groups greatly desire something—land, money, status, or power—their members usually believe that this something is in short supply and that each group's resources must be won at the expense of the other groups. The stage is set for racism, prejudice—or worse. When economic or political conflict in sharply divided along racial or ethnic lines, prejudice will flourish. The race or ethnic group that triumphs wants to feel that it deserves its good fortune. Likewise, it will view the misfortunes of minority groups as a sign of their inferiority. Racism becomes an ideological rationalization for the economic and political *status quo.*

In the United States, racism was a means of justifying slavery. The only way to maintain a clear conscience while living in—and profiting from—a slave society was to believe that Black slaves were not fully human: hence, the idea that Blacks are inferior specimens of humanity and deserve their condition of servitude. Once established, such a belief has a force of its own. Likewise, when white settlers moved into territories occupied by Native Americans, they became aware that the rival claims of the two groups could only be settled by force. It was easier for whites to feel comfortable about stealing the land and killing its inhabitants if those inhabitants could be regarded as mere "savages," vastly inferior in almost every conceivable respect to whites. Racism automatically equates "different" with "inferior." This process is known as "neutralization," and it is especially common when one group or individual oppresses or exploits another.

The conflict theory explanation of prejudice and racism obviously is not complete because members of every majority group differ among themselves in their attitudes toward minorities—and their differences often cannot be accounted for by economic interests. In any case, once the original economic factor has been removed—once slavery is abolished, North America is settled by whites, and Native Americans have been driven from their ancestral lands—why do racist attitudes persist? Perhaps new economic and political factors keep alive hostility toward minority groups. Why, however, do patterns of racial and ethnic preju-

Prejudice is stronger among some groups and individuals than others. Here, members of the Ku Klux Klan march in a rally to recruit new members as a Black photographer records the event.
UPI

dice change over time? What accounts for the reduction in intergroup hostility in the United States during the past ten or twenty years? We need more than economic conflict theory to explain racism.

Personality.   Prejudice serves a psychological function for majority-group members who, for some reason, feel inadequate. People who feel inferior attribute inferiority to racial or ethnic scapegoats. Some people derive perverse psychological satisfaction from hating members of an out-group. They reason to themselves, "As low as I may sink, there's someone—a whole race of people—who are lower." This sort of nonsense lessens the pain of their own personal inadequacies, like a sort of moral anesthetic. Racists may project onto the peoples they hate the inadequacies they recognize in themselves.

Authoritarianism A rigid, hierarchical view of social life and human relations, usually accompanied by intolerance for a diversity of views and the belief that rules should be strictly obeyed.

Authoritarianism.   Negative, hostile attitudes toward minority groups may also be an outgrowth of **authoritarianism:** a rigid, hierarchial view about human relations, a tendency to view reality in simple, black-or-white terms, ignoring its many shades of gray (see Chapter 9). "Authoritarian personalities" are preoccupied by rules and regulations, with who gives orders and who takes them, with the different levels of power and status enjoyed by different individuals and groups. Authoritarians see life as a competition between winners and losers, a dog-eat-dog struggle (Adorno et al., 1950). Authoritarian personalities are likely to ask, in every situation, "Who's in charge here?" They are uncomfortable in egalitarian situations and strive to establish dominance.

Key elements in authoritarianism are suspicion, fear, and rejection of anything that is different. White authoritarians are hostile toward Blacks; gentile authoritarians, toward Jews and other non-Christians. Majority attitudes about racial and ethnic minorities tend to resemble the majority's attitudes toward deviant minorities. One researcher found that people who wished to place great social distance between themselves and deviants were the same people who wished to place great social distance between themselves and Chicanos, Blacks, Chinese-Americans, and Jews. Those respondents who felt little or no hostility toward deviants tended to feel little or no hostility toward racial minorities. "The tendency to accept or discriminate against those who differ seems to be a basic part of a person's way of looking at the world" (Simmons, 1969, p. 13).

The original study of the authoritarian personality (Adorno et al., 1950) assumed that both authoritarianism and racism were psychologically abnormal belief systems. Sociologists, however, use the dimension of authoritarianism as a *cultural* variable, and are quick to point out that both authoritarianism and prejudice toward minority groups may be entirely "normal," in the sense that they are learned from society at large. Like it or not, a strain of racism and authoritarianism is built into our culture.

Traditionalism A wish to preserve tradition and resist change.

Traditionalism.   In fact, this leads us to the final approach to racism: **traditionalism,** a wish to preserve tradition and resist change. In the course of social and cultural change, certain attitudes become outmoded, old-fashioned, anachronistic, inappropriate. Other attitudes and beliefs replace them. Racism is one of these formerly respectable attitudes that have steadily lost respectability.

Racism is clearly on the decline in America, though it has not yet disappeared, and the economic and political condition of Blacks may not have changed a great deal. In 1933, 84 percent of white college students believed that Blacks were "superstitious"; in 1967, 13 percent did. In 1933, 75 percent of the students believed that Blacks were "lazy"; by 1967, only 26 percent did (Karlins, Coffman, and Walters, 1969, pp. 4–5).

One indicator demonstrating the decline in racist feelings among white Americans is their attitudes toward racial intermarriage. In 1958, Americans were asked if they "approved" or "disapproved" of interracial marriage. Ninety-two percent of whites living outside the South disapproved, as did 99 percent of whites living in the South; only 5 and 1 percent approved, respectively (Gallup, 1972, pp. 1572–1573). In 1983, the same question was asked, and disapproval had dropped to 56 percent of all whites in the nation as a whole; approval, meanwhile, rose to 38 percent. (Among "nonwhites," only 20 percent disapproved and 71 percent approved.) Although white opposition to interracial marriage is still strong, it has declined sharply over the years (Gallup, 1984, p. 96). Perhaps the sharpest decline in racist attitudes came about in the South. When a sample of Southern white parents was asked, in 1963, "Would you, yourself, have any objection to sending your children to a school where a few of the children are black?," 61 percent said that they would object (Gallup, 1972, p. 1824). By 1981, this figure had declined to only 5 percent (Gallup, 1982, p. 24).

The decline in prejudice and racism in the United States underscores the role of traditionalism as a cause of intergroup hostility: The more traditional people may be, the more likely they are to be racist. For instance, older people are more likely than young ones to hold the racist attitudes dominant in the past. Racial and ethnic prejudices are not psychologically "abnormal"; they merely conform to an outmoded standard, because some people cling to standards that the majority is abandoning.

DISCRIMINATION

"Prejudice" and "discrimination" overlap but are nonetheless distinct. Prejudice is an attitude toward a racial or ethnic minority. **Discrimination** is a kind of behavior. The distinction is crucial. Prejudice is a predisposition to act, but much of the time, many of us are constrained from acting out prejudices toward minority-group members by other factors.

Discrimination Treating racial, ethnic, and other minorities unfairly and unjustly, judging them according to irrelevant criteria.

An Imperfect Fit

The distinction between prejudice and discrimination was clearly made in a classic experiment conducted in the 1930s by sociologist Richard LaPierre (1934). LaPierre recorded the treatment of a Chinese couple who asked for service at hotels, motels, and restaurants. Of the more than 250 establishments approached, they were refused service only once. Discrimination—actual *behavior*—was almost totally absent. After a lapse of six months, an inquiry was sent to the same establishments, asking, "Would you accept members of the Chinese race as guests in your establishment?" Only one "yes" response was received. Clearly, then, there is a certain lack of agreement between what we say and what we do (Deutscher, 1973, p. 14)—in this case, for the better. People who feel prejudice and express it verbally may or may not manifest their feelings in discriminatory behavior. Likewise, those who deny feeling any prejudice may engage in strongly discriminatory behavior.

Sometimes, a prejudiced person may refrain from racial or ethnic discrimination from fear of its economic, political, or legal consequences. Likewise, a person totally free from prejudice may be forced to engage in discriminatory practices because the setting makes it unprofitable to do otherwise. The "unprejudiced discriminator" has no feelings of animosity toward any racial or ethnic group or minority yet discriminates because the social, personal, or economic cost of insisting on equality would be too great. In most areas, for instance, real estate agents will not show their Black clients houses in white neighborhoods. This practice, called "steering," is illegal but common. Not all real estate agents who act in this way are prejudiced against Blacks; many of them do so because they believe that their jobs depend on it.

Consider the equally common case of the "prejudiced nondiscriminator." Like "fair-weather liberals," prejudiced nondiscriminators alter their behavior to fit the demands of the immediate situation. They are timid bigots who harbor negative and hostile feelings toward minority-group members but feel constrained from discriminating against them when doing so would threaten other important values. The "timid bigot" is a conformist. If nondiscrimination is called for in a particular situation, he or she will not discriminate. A racist restaurant owner will serve Blacks because refusal to do so is illegal. An anti-Semite might do business with Jews because it might be inconvenient not to. It is possible, of course, to find people who try to reconcile their attitudes and behavior toward minority groups. Active bigots express their prejudice in discriminatory actions, regardless of the cost. Like unprejudiced nondiscriminators, active bigots are consistent; their attitudes and behavior match. For the active bigot, prejudice and discrimination are ends in themselves (Merton, 1949; Rose, 1974, pp. 102–106).

Types of Racial and Ethnic Discrimination

There are three basic types of racial and ethnic discrimination: direct legal discrimination, direct nonlegal discrimination, and institutional racism.

Direct legal discrimination
Discrimination that is supported by law. This form of discrimination no longer exists in the United States.

Direct Legal Discrimination. Today, **direct legal discrimination** against racial and ethnic groups is fairly rare. But it prevails in South Africa, where Blacks cannot vote, own property in most of the country, hold most better-paying jobs, or attend prestigious universities. In Germany, during the 1930s, Jews were not allowed in public on certain days; their property was confiscated; and they were barred from government and professional jobs. In the 1940s, the German government attempted to murder all Jews living in Germany and in other countries, as well.

Direct legal discrimination does not exist in the United States today. A form of it existed until very recently, however. Only in 1967, for instance, were state laws forbidding interracial marriages declared unconstitutional. World War II was fought by racially segregated combat units. And after the United States Government declared war on Japan, it herded all Japanese residents of the West Coast into detention camps. These people had committed no crime; they were being punished for being Japanese.

Direct nonlegal discrimination
Discrimination that is not embodied in law, but that results from actions by individuals.

Direct Nonlegal Discrimination. A second basic form of discrimination is **direct nonlegal discrimination,** which does not involve the direct

As recently as World War II (1941–1945), the United States armed forces fought in racially segregated units. Most Black soldiers were under the command of white officers. Here, a troop convoy makes its way to Liberia.

U.S. Army Photograph

intervention of the state. Discrimination is not embodied in law but results from actions taken by individuals. The government does not officially support such actions but either ignores or deals impotently with them. Direct nonlegal discrimination against minorities manifests itself in nearly all realms of social and economic life. Blacks are barred from a sizable number of white neighborhoods by discriminatory real estate practices. Blacks are almost excluded from a number of higher-paying jobs and, in general, are promoted less rapidly than whites. Even justice is not blind: Blacks tend to receive stiffer prison sentences for the same crimes than whites do.

Our very language reflects derogatory attitudes toward minority groups and, correspondingly, flatters the majority. Consider such phrases as, "that's white of you" and "free, white, and 21." Ethnic jokes, too, reflect and reinforce negative stereotypes and remind minorities that the majority perceives them in negative terms. Of course, many people who tell these jokes may not realize that others find them enormously offensive.

Discrimination in abundance fills our mass media, too. Even today, for instance, Black models are vastly underrepresented in advertising. News about the Black community is almost always "invisible." All things being equal, the murder of a white person receives much more media attention than the murder of a Black one (Hentoff, 1981). The Hispanic community is even more "invisible" in advertising and the mass media.

Some people claim that ethnic slurs, though derogatory, do not have enough impact to be discriminatory: The white readers of a white-owned newspaper are chiefly interested in news about their own community and are by no means actively hostile to the Black community. This argument, a common one, reflects the common belief—by whites, at any rate—that Blacks are not subject to real discrimination. A Gallup poll found that more than two-thirds of the whites (71 percent) in this country appear to think that Blacks are treated "the same as whites." Only 44 percent of all Blacks agreed (Gallup, 1979, p. 219). In a survey

In spite of gains in many areas, discrimination against Blacks in the United States is still the rule. While direct discrimination in this country is not written into law, the government either ignores many discriminatory actions or deals with them ineffectually.

Danny Lyon/Magnum

of New York City's residents, only one-quarter of all whites questioned believed that the city paid "too little" attention to Blacks (23 percent), whereas seven of ten of the Black respondents (71 percent) agreed (Roberts, 1985). Over twice as many whites as Blacks thought that the city's courts "are fair to all races" (26 versus 10 percent). And half as many whites as Blacks thought that the police "are often brutal to Blacks" (36 versus 70 percent). Clearly, a high proportion of whites are not fully aware of the racial problems that Blacks face, even if they are not outright racists.

Discrimination is rarely a pure and simple matter of racial hostility. Other motives (economic ones, for instance) also play a role. Even when it occurs, pure discrimination is not easy to document. This difficulty gave rise to the powerful and valuable concept of institutional racism (Carmichael and Hamilton, 1967).

Institutional Racism.   Most whites do not accept the reality of discrimination because they look only at the discrimination that individuals deliberately inflict on one another. This kind of discrimination, though by no means dead, is indeed less common than it was in the past. Even so, discrimination itself is just as real, just as vicious as ever. Something more basic than individual intentions is at work. What is this something? It is what sociologists call **institutional racism** or **indirect discrimination** (Kitano, 1985, pp. 3, 54).

Sociologists believe that society is far more than the sum of its individual parts. Discrimination, for instance, is not just a matter of individuals' discriminating against other individuals. The more pervasive (and thus important) forms of discrimination result from the workings of institutions, not just of isolated individuals acting on their own. An institution is a set of stable social arrangements that cluster around a particular purpose. Individuals usually act not on their own but within institutions, and the arrangements they impose. Those arrangements may produce results that negate the desires or intentions of the individuals who must act within them. An exclusive focus on individual prejudice,

Institutional racism A pattern of treating minority groups that results in continuing existing racial inequality, even without formal discrimination.

Indirect discrimination See **Institutional racism.**

racism, and discrimination is thus bound to mislead. Human beings may engage, both individually and collectively, in actions that are not meant to be either prejudiced or discriminatory but that still contribute to existing racial inequities. Because our economic, political, and educational institutions are organized in a certain fashion, even formally non-discriminatory actions often perpetuate inequality. To discover the source of racial and ethnic injustice in any nation, we must go beyond the intentions of individuals, down to the very foundations of a society. Even if the majority of individuals become markedly less prejudiced—which has actually happened in the United States over the past few decades—racial inequality remains. Even if acts of individual discrimination decline sharply—or even disappear altogether—racial inequality will remain if we do not recognize and deal with institutional racism.

In the words of the two authors who coined the phrase, institutional racism "keeps Black people locked in dilapidated slum tenements, subject to the daily prey of exploitative slumlords, merchants, loan sharks, and discriminatory real estate agents" (Carmichael and Hamilton, 1967, p. 4). Suppose two would-be businesspeople want to establish and operate a local retail store; one is white and the other Black:

> A financial institution considering a loan application examines the credit history of the applicant, the collateral to be held against the loan, the prospects for business success, and other related criteria. The black man is more likely than the white man to have a poor credit record. . . . Black people usually have no property or investments that could be used as collateral. And finally, the black businessman who wishes to locate in his own community, where the income level is at or near the poverty line, will have poorer prospects for success than the white merchant. . . . The black businessman is also plagued by insurance costs which are as much as three times higher than those that whites must pay. Insurance companies are hesitant to cover ghetto property due to the danger of possible damage in civil disturbances; only very high premiums will draw them . . . into the black community. . . . *The present standards, when applied without regard to race, will lead to more white ownership of enterprises and less black participation in the economy* (Knowles, Prewitt et al., 1969, pp. 16–17).

Consider a specific case of institutional racism: Blacks and whites competing for the same jobs. Even when Blacks and whites are evaluated by the same criteria, those criteria frequently result from white cultural standards, not from the basic work-demands of a job. Police departments, for example, usually require applicants to take written examinations, and Black applicants tend to fare less well on these exams than whites do. Yet written exams typically have little or nothing to do with a candidate's qualifications as a police officer. Take another case: Two high school graduates with equally good grades are accepted by an expensive college. One of the students comes from an affluent white family, the other from a poor Black one. Neither is awarded financial assistance. In the formal sense, no discrimination has taken place, because both students have been treated in the same way. But the poor student will find it much more difficult to raise enough money to attend the school. Given social reality, what seems to be equality of opportunity turns out to be very unequal. Social realities of this sort are the cornerstone of institutional racism.

Discrimination in housing works in two ways. Sometimes, real estate agents refuse to show Blacks houses in certain neighborhoods. This is called "steering." Although technically illegal in America, steering, an example of *direct* discrimination, is widely practiced. But another technique does not require blatant or direct discrimination. By prohibiting builders from putting up multiple-dwelling housing units (like apartment houses) and permitting only single-family units on large lots, communities can price Black people out of the market. These communities may not literally exclude Blacks, yet they keep them out.

Think of some parallels. Imagine a rule that stipulates that all candidates for a given job be 5 feet 8 inches or taller. Most women, automatically, would not qualify. Although the rule applies equally to all, it is not equal in its consequences. Imagine (as was true at one time in the United States) a requirement of owning property to be able to vote. Again, it was a formally nondiscriminatory rule, in the sense that it was applied universally. But, as it worked out, it disenfranchised the poor, the Black, and, at that time, all women. The lesson is a simple one: Rules that apply equally to all are not equal in their consequences. In the words of the French writer Anatole France: "The law, in its majestic equality, forbids the rich as well as the poor to sleep under bridges, to beg in the streets, and to steal bread."

The concept of institutional racism rests on the fact that equal rules applied to unequal situations produce unequal outcomes. Because the present and historical situation of American Blacks is different from that of American whites, true racial equality cannot emerge from equality of opportunity, even when it actually does prevail. In recent years, therefore, Blacks have shifted from demanding equality of opportunity to demanding equality of result. In other words, the proof of racial equality in the United States will be actual economic, political, and educational equality between the Black and white communities. But for the time being, the survival of such inequities demonstrates the power of institutional racism in America.

BLACK AMERICANS

In an industrial economy like ours, income is probably the most critical determinant of social stratification. Since the end of World War II, the median Black-family income has fluctuated somewhere between 55 and just over 60 percent of the median white-family income (see Table 10–1). The small gains made by Black families in the 1960s and early 1970s were wiped out during the late 1970s and 1980s. Today, Black families earn about 59 cents for every dollar white families earn; the 1970 to

■ **TABLE 10–1 Median Family Income in Current and Constant (1985) Dollars, 1967 to 1985**

	Current Dollars		Constant (1985) Dollars		Black-White Ratio
	WHITE	BLACK	WHITE	BLACK	
1967	7,449	4,325	24,001	13,935	.58
1970	9,097	5,537	25,203	15,340	.61
1980	18,684	10,764	24,392	14,053	.58
1985	24,908	14,819	24,908	14,819	.59

Source: Statistical Abstract of the United States, 1987, p. 431.

1983 period represented a slight set-back for Black families (as it did for whites, as well). As we see shortly, another important aspect of Black-white stratification is their respective rates of employment and unemployment. The Black unemployment rate has consistently remained about twice as high as that for whites. In 1987, when about 6 percent of whites were officially unemployed, about 15 percent of Blacks were. (Experts regard the actual rate roughly twice these figures.) Moreover, the unemployment rate for Black teenagers is close to 50 percent. But, at every level, at every age, in every kind of area, the rate for Blacks remains about twice as high as the rate for whites, a striking difference.

The Black Economic Position: Has It Improved in the United States?

The question of whether the economic position of Blacks has improved, deteriorated, or stagnated during the past generation or so has engaged scholars and political leaders throughout the 1970s and 1980s. To answer the question, it is necessary to be very precise about what we mean. Economic position can be measured by several different indicators; rate of unemployment, percent in the labor market employed, educational attainment, median worker income, family income, percent of the population living in poverty, and occupational distribution are several such indicators. There are at least two different ways to measure changes in the economic position of Blacks over time: computing relative and absolute change (Farley, 1984, pp. 13–15). Computing *relative* change entails comparing the economic position of Blacks versus that of whites over time. If the gap between Blacks and whites in such key indicators as income, unemployment, or percent above or below the poverty line becomes smaller, then the economic situation is improving for Blacks. If this gap is widening, then the situation is getting worse for Blacks, relatively speaking. Computing *absolute* change refers to determining the economic position of Blacks today as compared with yesterday—regardless of what it is for whites. If there is improvement on a number of key indicators, then, in an absolute sense, the economic position of Blacks is improving; if not, then it is not getting better.

On one side of this controversy stand the "optimists." Most optimists are political conservatives, although this is not an absolute rule. Optimists believe that since the end of World War II (1945), and especially since the early 1960s, the economic position of Blacks has improved dramatically. William Julius Wilson (1980) states that by the 1970s, workers were no longer being hired or promoted on the basis of race, but ability. Blacks, he states, have made "unprecedented" economic progress since the 1960s. Two observers (Wattenberg and Scammon, 1973) agree, arguing that since 1960, as Blacks have become more educated, they have increasingly entered blue-collar jobs, and they have begun to earn incomes very close to those of whites. For the first time in history, they believe, a majority of Blacks are middle class. Another observer (Freeman, 1976) claims that the evidence clearly shows that by the mid-1970s, college-educated Black men entering the labor force earned as much as white men. There has been, he states, "a dramatic collapse in traditional discriminatory patterns in the market for highly qualified Black Americans" (Freeman, 1976, p. 33). Summing up a glowing picture of improvement in the United States, conservative George Gilder states:

> The last thirty years in America . . . have seen a relentless and thoroughly successful advance against the old prejudices to the point that it is now virtu-

ally impossible to find in a position of power a serious racist. Gaps in income between truly comparable Blacks and whites have nearly closed. Problems remain, but it would seem genuinely difficult to sustain the idea that America is still oppressive and discriminatory (Gilder, 1982, p. 155).

The pessimistic view, in contrast, holds that racial progress is a "myth" (Pinkney, 1985). The pessimistic position is more likely to be believed by liberals, and especially radicals, who hold that the Black-white economic gap remains substantial. (Some conservatives, such as Thomas Sowell, 1981a, 1981b, believe that the situation is not improving, but that this is the fault of such liberal policies as too much government intervention in business and too much welfare for the poor). For instance, Hill (1981) presents statistics that show that economic recession and inflation has had a significantly greater negative impact on Blacks than on whites in recent years. During economic downswings, Hill states, unemployment rises more sharply for Black workers than for whites. Reich (1981) argues that recent improvements in the economic position of Blacks relative to that of whites are in fact illusory. What has improved, he argues, is the structural and demographic position of Blacks: They are moving to the North and into the industrial sector, and away from the South and the low-paying agricultural sector. When these changes are accounted for, the income difference between Blacks and whites remains as substantial today as it was in the past.

In some respects, whether we conclude that the economic position of Blacks is improving or not depends to some extent on which part of the elephant we are examining. In specific areas clear gains have been made; in others, the picture is considerably bleaker. Recall that, in Chapter 2, we explained that which indicator we select to portray a concept is crucial. The fact is, we can verify the pessimistic or the optimistic view by selecting the appropriate indicator of economic improvement. Clearly, then, to present an accurate view, we must select a fairly wide range of relevant and decisive indicators. Farley (1984) shows that along certain key indicators, there have been striking gains in the economic position of Blacks, both relatively and absolutely. At the same time, other indicators show precisely the opposite picture—no improvement, or an actual deterioration in the economic position of Blacks. Two indicators that show improvement are the earnings of employed workers and occupational distribution. Indicators that are mixed, show no improvement, or show a deterioration, are: (1) the rate of unemployment, including (2) the rate of "nonparticipation" in the labor market; (3) median family income; and especially (4) the number and proportion of families living in poverty. One indicator that shows long-term improvement but stagnation during the 1980s is educational attainment. Let's examine each of these indicators in turn.

The educational attainment of Blacks displays a very strange pattern. Both absolutely and relative to whites, the education of Blacks improved significantly and strikingly in the four decades between 1940 and 1980. In 1940, well over a third of the Black population (42 percent) had less than a fifth grade education; only 7 percent had four years of high school or more; and only 1 percent were college graduates. By 1980, only 3 percent had only a fifth grade education, over 70 percent had four years of high school or more, and 16 percent had full college educations. In 1940, the median number of years of education of American Blacks was 8.6 years, a grade school education; in 1980, this had reached 12.5 years, at least some college education. However, during the 1980s, the strong upward surge in the educational attainment of American Blacks was halted, and a stagnation or even decline set in. (This trend is also true of whites, by the way, although their trend is less dramatic.) Perhaps

Whites Own Ten Times the Wealth of Blacks

Although the family income of Blacks in the United States is roughly 60 percent of that of whites, the gap in wealth or financial assets is much greater. A study released by the Census Bureau in 1986 revealed that, on the average, white Americans own ten times the assets of Blacks. Wealth or assets were measured by savings, stocks, housing, and automobiles—minus debts. Three out of every ten Blacks are part of a household that possesses no significant assets at all; for whites, the comparable figure is only 8 percent. The median net worth of white households in 1984 was $39,135, but it was only $3,397 for Black households. Over a quarter of white households (26.2 percent) had a net worth of over $100,000; for Blacks, this figure was only one in twenty-five (3.9 percent).

The size of the disparity surprised even the economists who conducted the study. They were, indeed, at a loss to explain why the Black-white difference is so huge. Some factors they pointed to include a long history of discrimination and low income among Blacks, segregation and a lower quality of schooling, and a high proportion of female-headed households (see Chapter 13). The disparity in assets between whites and Blacks was significantly smaller among families with both parents present, especially if both worked.

Gordon Green, assistant director of the Census Bureau's population division, who supervised the study, said that the ownership of assets is as crucial a measure of prosperity as family income. Racial disparities in wealth, previously ignored by the Census Bureau, will now be examined every two years or so.

Source: Kilborn, 1986, pp. 1, 46; see also Statistical Abstract of the United States, 1987, p. 449.

the conservative policies of the Reagan administration (1981 to 1989) has been at work here, because government aid to education has been drastically cut back. In the age group in which education trends become most apparent (ages 25 to 29), 22.1 percent of all Americans had achieved four or more years of college in 1980, but by 1984, this had actually declined slightly to 21.9 percent. The median number of years of schooling for Americans aged 25 to 29 was 12.9 in 1980, but, by 1984, this had slipped a bit to 12.8. For Blacks, too, stagnation and decline was the rule in the educational realm. In 1984, 12.9 percent of all Blacks aged 25 to 29 had attained four or more years of college, but in only one year, by 1984, this had slipped to 11.6 percent. The median number of years of education achieved by American Blacks aged 25 to 29 in 1980 was 12.6: in 1984, it was still 12.6 (*Statistical Abstract of the United States, 1986*, p. 133). Clearly, the strong educational gains posted by Blacks in the four decades between 1940 and 1980 were eroding in the conservative 1980s. Thus, over the long run, Black educational gains have been encouraging, but during the course of the 1980s, depressing.

In the key indicator of earnings of employed workers, there has been a clear movement toward closing the Black-white gap over time. In 1959, Black men earned only 61 percent as much per hour as white men; twenty years later, this figure was 74 percent. In 1959, Black women earned 61 percent as much per hour as white women did; a generation later, the racial gap all but disappeared: the comparable figure for 1979 was 98 percent (Farley, 1984, pp. 194–198). Adjustments have to be made for the number of hours each worker is employed during the year and the education and skills of the workers, Black and white. According to one estimate, when all the relevant factors are taken into account, among young (25 to 34) men with the same education, hours of work per year, and geographical residence, employed Blacks earned roughly 90 percent of what whites earned in the early 1980s. Among women, the races earned almost precisely the same figure (Farley, 1984, p. 197).

The occupational distribution of Blacks relative to whites improved significantly between the early 1960s and the early 1980s. In 1960, Blacks made up 10 percent of all workers, but they held only 3 percent of the professional and managerial jobs. In 1980, this figure had doubled to 6 percent (Farley, 1984, p. 195). Clearly, then, the occupational distribution of whites and Blacks is converging somewhat. In spite of substantial improvement, however, "a very large gap still distinguishes the occupational distribution of Blacks from that of whites. . . . Blacks are still overrepresented at the lowest rungs of the occupational distribution. . . . The occupational distribution of Blacks will catch up with that of whites only if there are several more decades of change similar to the 1960s and 1970s" (Farley, 1984, p. 50). For most well-paid, prestigious occupational categories, the percentage of Blacks has increased—although in most, very marginally—in the past generation (with the curious exception of dentists and physicians), while the proportion of Blacks in occupational categories at the bottom of the income and prestige ladder (such as janitors, private household workers, and agricultural workers) has declined.

These three economic measures—educational attainment, income of employed workers, and occupational distribution—demonstrate clear gains for Blacks, both absolutely and in comparison with whites over the past generation or so. At the same time, for two indicators—employment and unemployment rates and family income, including the proportion of families below the poverty line—the news is not so good. Here, Blacks have lost substantial ground. For some aspects of these two measures, the deterioration has been relative only; for other aspects, it has been both absolute and relative.

The unemployment rate among Blacks is not a cause for celebration. Month by month, year by year since the end of World War II, roughly twice as many Blacks as whites have been officially unemployed. In 1950, the unemployment rate of Blacks was 10 percent; for whites, it was 5 percent. In 1985, 15 percent of all Blacks in the labor market were officially unemployed; for whites this figure was 7 percent. Even though unemployment fluctuates substantially from year to year, and even from month to month, the unemployment figures for Blacks and whites over time almost seem to be running along a parallel track, one consistently about twice as high as the other. In short, using unemployment as an indicator, the absolute economic position of Blacks has declined significantly in the past generation and a half; relatively speaking, however, it has remained stable.

We've already seen at least one economic indicator on which Blacks have fared strikingly less well today as compared with the past—that is, one area in which their economic position has deteriorated in recent years: participation in the labor force, or the "employment rate," the flip side of the unemployment rate. Participation in the labor force is a more accurate economic measure than unemployment, because the latter does not include individuals who are simply not in the labor force at all—who have never worked, who have given up looking for work, and so on—and are never tabulated in the nation's unemployment statistics. In 1965, 74 percent of all adult Black men were gainfully employed; by June, 1983, the figure had dropped over fifteen points to 57 percent. The drop among white men was much smaller—only 5 percent. Adult Black women's employment remained stable during this period, at 44 percent, while white women's employment rose by 12 percent, from 36 to 48 percent (Cummings, 1983). Thus, in terms of percent working and getting paid at a job, the position of Blacks has deteriorated both in an absolute and a relative sense.

We've already said that employed Black workers have advanced significantly in recent years. However, in spite of these advances, the incomes of Black families relative to those of whites have remained stagnant for forty years. In absolute terms, Black family income rose significantly between 1945 and 1973, but declined slightly between 1973 and 1985. White families experienced precisely the same trend: a sharp rise in income, then a slight drop. Thus, although for the total period, Black family incomes doubled, they also doubled for whites. As we can see from the Black-white ratio (consistently between .55 and .60 between 1945 and 1985), in relative terms, the Black-white family income gap has remained fairly constant over the past generation or so.

Why are the incomes of Black workers almost uniformly on the rise even though family incomes show no improvement at all? Isn't this a contradiction? The answer to the apparent puzzle lies in the consistently higher Black unemployment rate, the declining Black participation in the labor force, and recent changes in the Black family. Most experts agree that these three trends are strongly influenced by discrimination. Thus, it should be clear that the issue of changes in the economic position of Blacks over time does not present a simple, clear-cut picture. Anyone carefully examining the evidence is forced to admit that, in some ways, the economic position of Blacks in America is improving; in some ways, it hasn't changed much; and, in some ways, it is deteriorating. For employed Black workers, especially for young, well-educated Black couples in which both husband and wife work, economic gains over the past decade or two have been striking. Indeed, for this segment of the Black population, the economic position is likely to be very nearly identical to that of whites. On the other hand, this is a small, atypical segment of the Black population. For the unskilled and the uneducated, for the family headed by a woman without a husband, for the out of work, the picture is every bit as bleak as it has been in the past. When viewed accurately and in detail, the economic picture for Blacks does not provide support for either the "optimistic" or the "pessimistic" view. As with so many other things in life, the true picture is a curious blend of the two.

HISPANIC-AMERICANS

Hispanics do not form a single racial category; they include members of all races. The term includes anyone of Spanish cultural heritage. Many Cubans are Black, many are white—of purely Spanish descent. Chicanos, or Mexican-Americans, are mainly of a mixed Spanish and American Indian ancestry (Mestizos), but some are pure Indian, and some are pure Spanish. Puerto Ricans range from Black to white, usually with some American Indian ancestry as well, but most are Mestizos. Many Filipinos have Spanish surnames and substantial Spanish ancestry, but they are usually classified as Asians. A fairly large number of Americans trace their ancestry directly back to Spain. Many of them live in areas, like New Mexico, that once belonged to the Spanish Empire, and then to Mexico, and were acquired by the United States in the midnineteenth

WHAT DO YOU THINK?

Affirmative Action: Is It Fair? Does It Work?

The 1980 election of conservative Republican Ronald Reagan as president of the United States marked the end of an era with respect to the government's role in fostering the economic progress of American minorities. Between 1964 and Reagan's election, federal officials agreed that the government had a responsibility to actively help minorities catch up to whites economically. Although liberal and Black critics often charged that the government wasn't doing enough along these lines, it was nearly universally recognized that this goal guided policy, however successfully—or unsuccessfully—in Washington. Officials attempted to implement this goal in at least three ways. First, money was spent on education and job training in such a way that minorities were awarded a substantial slice of the benefits. Second, the federal government supported a hiring policy in both the public and the private sectors that gave something of an edge to minority applicants. And third, the government increased welfare and other benefits to families unable to work (Jencks, 1983, p. 33).

Giving an advantage to minority candidates over those from a majority group is called **affirmative action.** Suppose two college seniors apply to medical school—one white, the other Black. The record of the white candidate is slightly better—higher grades, higher scores on standardized tests, slightly more enthusiastic recommendations from professors. At the same time, the Black candidate clearly has the ability to complete medical school and become a competent physician. A medical school that accepts the Black applicant over the white one in order to increase the proportion of Black physicians is practicing affirmative action. Now suppose that a police department in a city whose population is 50 percent minority, but that has less than one out of ten minority officers on the force, decides to redress this imbalance. It hires one minority candidate for every white hired, and promotes one minority officer for every white promoted. The goal of this policy is racial and ethnic balance. This police department, too, is practicing affirmative action. (Though the same principle could work equally as well for women, here we focus on racial minorities.)

The American public is ambivalent about the issue of affirmative action. In a poll taken by the Anti-Defamation League of B'nai B'rith, a Jewish civil rights organization, nearly three-quarters of all Americans (73 percent) "reject racial quotas in affirmative action programs and think that all hiring and promotion should be based solely on merit." Even a majority of the poll's nonwhite respondents (52 percent) "said that companies should hire the most qualified applicants regardless of race or ethnic background and should not be required by law to hire a fixed percentage of members of minorities." At the same time, the word "quota" has a negative-sounding ring to most Americans. When asked by a Harris poll if they favored "affirmative action provided there were no quotas," nearly seven out of ten respondents (69 percent) said yes. In the Anti-Defamation League's poll, about half (49 percent) of the minority respondents said that it is fair "to give preferential treatment to minority job seekers"; however, only 20 percent of the white respondents agreed (Gruson, 1983). Clearly, the American public's support for affirmative action depends in large part on how the question is asked and who is being asked.

Since 1980, affirmative action has fallen into disfavor in Washington. Critics of the practice call it a "quota system," a policy of "reverse discrimination" or "racism in reverse." They argue that it is unfair to white applicants and candidates, that it leads to giving preference to unqualified candidates, and that it is counterproductive: It actually hurts minorities because it stifles initiative and the desire to achieve. To encourage minority achievement, conservatives believe, the emphasis should be on equality of opportunity rather than on arbitrary guarantees of equality. If equality of opportunity exists, then it's up to minority candidates to make maximum use of that opportunity. "The promise of equality has never meant the guarantee of success; only that responsible individuals take their fate in their own hands" (Lynch, 1984).

Supporters of affirmative action disagree. To begin with, they assert, none of its supporters believes that unqualified candidates should be hired. When faced with a choice between a qualified white candidate and an unqualified minority candidate, the choice is clear-cut: Always hire the qualified candidate. Affirmative action should never become a policy by which the clearly incompetent are hired. All it says is that the edge should be given to the minority candidate when both are qualified, even though the white one may look slightly better on paper.

The point about "reverse discrimination" or "racism in a different guise," supporters of affirmative action argue, is totally invalid, as well. In the past, racism and discrimination have been used as tactics by more powerful, privileged groups to make sure that powerless, disadvantaged groups did not get ahead. Today, affirmative action attempts precisely the reverse: to accelerate the progress of groups that have been held back in the past. It seems bizarre, its supporters insist, to call two policies racist or discriminatory that have precisely contrary goals—one to deprive minorities of economic equality and the other to grant economic equality to minorities.

Critics charge that it is not fair to hold whites responsible for the position of minorities, because they did not do anything to hold minorities back, nor did they profit from it. Supporters say that this is not altogether true. Whites have always profited from discrimination against minorities. In the past, minorities have been relegated to the bottom of the class structure, often doing jobs that whites did not want, earning salaries that were possible only in a racist society. Because of discrimination against minorities in the past, whites received preferential treatment; many achieved positions they could not have achieved otherwise. Although the goal of affirmative action is not to punish whites, closing the economic gap may entail specific whites' being denied positions they would have otherwise received. But because the position of whites prior to affirmative action is a result of discrimination to begin with, it is not unfair to attempt to redress the balance in the opposite direction.

And as for the charge that affirmative action discourages minority ambition and achievement, its proponents argue that there is absolutely no evidence to support it. This is a rational-sounding argument that actually helps to maintain the privilege of the already privileged and to retard the achievement of disadvantaged groups. Someone who begins a race at a disadvantage cannot make maximum use of an opportunity. It is not enough that two students are accepted at the same college and are encouraged to succeed. If one does not have the kind of background that is conducive to academic success, it is almost inevitable that he or she will not do as well as one who does. And if doing well—or poorly—is systematically related to certain sociological factors, like socioeconomic background and race, then the injunction for all to do well is an empty slogan. There must be some sort of mechanism that helps to make sure that equality of opportunity is translated into equality of result. In hiring and in acceptance to professional schools, affirmative action is one of those mechanisms.

In sum, in the words of one supporter:

Those who have latched onto the color-blind slogan appear to be victims of a simplistic error in reasoning. They have been unable to distinguish between the long-term objective of the civil rights movement to ultimately create a society where race or other such irrelevant attributes do not determine one's fate and the policies required to bring about such a society. There is no logical inconsistency between the desire to create a society where color is irrelevant to success and the use of color-conscious strategies to bring such a society about. Indeed, under the present circumstances, given the racism of our society and the extremely unequal distribution of power and resources, there is no alternative to race-conscious policies (Swinton, 1985).

In some respects, this debate is an empty one, because affirmative action is no longer the policy of the federal government. For the moment, the opponents of the preferential treatment of minorities have won the debate.

Source: Days, 1983; Gruson, 1983; Reynolds, 1983; Feagin, 1984, pp. 365–371; Goodman, 1984; Huron, 1984; Lynch, 1984; Swinton, 1985.

Affirmative action The practice of favoring minority-group members in hiring, promotion, and other economic, political, educational, or housing decisions.

■ **TABLE 10–2 America's Racial and Ethnic Origins, 1970–1980**

	1970	1980	Percent Increase
White	178,098,000	188,340,790	5.8
Black	22,580,289	26,488,218	17.3
American Indian, Eskimo, Aleut	792,730	1,418,195	71.8
Asians and Pacific Islanders	1,538,721	3,500,636	127.6
Spanish	9,072,602	14,608,673	61.0

Source: Merrill Sheils, Diane Weathers, Lucy Howard, and Ron Given, "A Portrait of America." Newsweek *(January 17, 1983), p. 22.*

century. Hispanics are not a race, but an ethnic group. To be even more precise, they are several separate ethnic groups: Puerto Ricans, Cubans, Mexican-Americans, and South and Central Americans.

Obtaining precise information on historical changes in the Hispanic population over time is almost impossible, because until the 1980 United States Census, Hispanics were classified as white. In 1980, the Census finally included a separate category for Hispanics, and there is no doubt of their currently large numbers. After Blacks, Hispanic-Americans are our largest minority, with some 14.6 million people, 6.4 percent of the United States population. And that is almost certainly an undercount, for there are at least a million illegal aliens from Mexico and South and Central America, mainly in the Southwest, Florida, and the New York City area. Next to Asian-Americans and Native Americans, Hispanics are the nation's fastest-growing minority: Some population experts expect them to overtake Blacks by 1985 (Lindsey, 1979); others, by the year 2000 (Fitzpatrick and Parker, 1981). Roughly 60 percent of American Hispanics are Chicanos (Mexican-Americans); 15 percent, Puerto Ricans; 7 percent, Cubans; 7 percent, South or Central Americans. The rest belong to some other category—mixed ancestry or heritages, Spanish (direct from Spain), or Filipinos (most of whom regard themselves as Asian-Americans rather than Hispanics).

More than two-thirds of all Puerto Ricans in the United States live in New York City, which has the largest concentration of Hispanics in America—some 1.4 million. More than 800,000 Mexican-Americans live in Los Angeles, the third largest "Mexican" city in the world. In San Antonio, some half a million Hispanics, mostly Chicanos, form a majority of the city's population. Roughly as many—both Chicanos and Puerto Ricans—live in Chicago. In some cities, like Miami, Florida, and Union City, New Jersey, Cubans are a majority of the population.

In many ways, Americans of Spanish ancestry suffer most of the problems of both direct and indirect discrimination that Blacks experience in the United States. Consequently, their educational and occupational attainments lag behind the national average. In 1984, Hispanics had achieved an average of an eleventh grade education—a median of 11.3 years of schooling. Though this was up significantly from a ninth grade education in 1970 (an average of 9.6 years of schooling), it prevents Hispanics from moving up the occupational ladder. In 1984, the median income for families of Spanish origin was $18,833—68 percent of the average white family income but 22 percent more than the average Black family income. In 1984, 28.4 percent of the Spanish-origin population in the United States lived below the poverty line, a total of 4.8 million people. For Blacks, the comparable figure was 33.8 percent (9.5 million individuals), and, for whites, it was 11.5 percent (23 million). In terms of income, then, Hispanics are located somewhere between Blacks and whites in America, although they are somewhat closer to Blacks than to whites. (*Statistical Abstract of the United States, 1986*). Clearly, then, they are a racial and ethnic minority in every sense of the word.

Puerto Ricans

Puerto Rico is a small island in the Caribbean, about 100 miles off the coast of Florida, with a population of slightly less than 3 million inhabitants. It is a self-governing commonwealth of the United States, neither a state nor a colony. Elections have repeatedly indicated that Puerto Rican voters desire neither statehood nor independence, but prefer to maintain the current arrangement. Puerto Ricans are American citizens and can freely migrate to the mainland, which they do, because the island is densely populated and has a high unemployment rate. After a few years, the majority return to Puerto Rico. Although Puerto Ricans move northward chiefly for economic reasons, prosperity seems to elude them, because many do not speak English, and many come from the rural parts of the island and are not prepared for the urban, industrial economy of the mainland.

Puerto Rican immigration to the United States mainland did not really begin until the end of World War II. This was a new and different kind of immigration. Puerto Ricans migrate readily back and forth from the island to the mainland; they are far less likely to stay put than the European immigrants of the late nineteenth century. Consequently, Puerto Ricans have deeper roots in their native land than earlier immigrants did, and a weaker American identity. Puerto Ricans are also more likely than earlier immigrants to continue speaking their native language, Spanish, and to feel more ambivalent about English. All these factors retard Puerto Rican assimilation and, consequently, their economic success in the United States.

In addition, Puerto Ricans (like Blacks) have been handicapped by prejudice and discrimination. In fact, they face additional institutional barriers, stemming from cultural and linguistic differences. For instance, politicians are rarely willing to invest in the kinds of programs—like bilingual education—that could promote economic, political, and educational parity with non-Hispanic whites.

Mexican-Americans

Although Mexican-Americans are victimized by discrimination and institutional racism, it is nonetheless difficult to substantiate their social and economic position with accuracy because a large (but unknown) number are illegal or "undocumented" aliens. The most recent estimate for the number of illegal aliens in the United States is between 2 and 4 million (Pear, 1985b), perhaps half of whom are Mexicans. They "have no papers to prove their identity, at least none that are legitimate. They have no birth certificates, no resident alien cards, no passports, no Social Security numbers. They usually have no fixed address and no bank account. Many have no driver's license, no credit card, no charge account and no medical records, not even names that are their own" (King, 1984). As a result, they rarely appear in official statistics on income,

Puerto Rico is an American commonwealth; its residents are automatically U.S. citizens. Puerto Ricans travel freely from their island to the United States mainland. For the most part, they maintain a dual loyalty and identity.

Terry Rosenberg

Mexican-Americans make up a diverse and relatively dispersed ethnic group. Here, a Chicano family relaxes on their front steps.

Hella Hammid/Rapho/Photo Researchers

Along with Eskimos, American Indians are the nation's only "Native Americans." There is a great deal of cultural and linguistic diversity among the many American Indian tribes, of which the Navajo is the most populous. Here, a young Crow receives a high school diploma.

Jim Carter/Photo Researchers

education, and occupational distribution. Naturally, the income of these workers is far below the average, both for the population generally and for Mexican-Americans specifically. Because they are in a vulnerable economic and legal position, they can be exploited easily; they also tend to work at the most menial jobs in the economy, especially migratory farm labor.

Mexican-Americans are considerably more diverse than Puerto Ricans are. They are far more dispersed, although a majority live in Texas, California, New Mexico, and Arizona. They live in urban areas and in rural areas, as well. Although most Mexican-Americans are recent immigrants, many such families have been living in the United States for 200 or more years. As a result (unlike the Puerto Ricans), some Mexican-Americans are assimilated into the norms of American culture. Two experts who say that Mexican-American occupational gains have been "sluggish" over the past generation (Pachon and Moore, 1981) argue that there is a kind of "dual labor market" of Mexican-American workers. One segment works at regular blue-collar, semiskilled, and lower white-collar jobs, but a sizable second segment—migrant, part-time, and menial laborers—works at poverty-level jobs outside the economy's mainstream, for wages far below the minimum wage.

Like Puerto Ricans and Blacks, Mexican-Americans do not participate in the American political process proportionally as much as whites, on the average. Despite the elections in recent years of Mexican-American mayors in San Antonio, Texas, and Denver, Colorado, and a Mexican-American governor and senator in New Mexico, they are vastly underrepresented in the corridors of power. Would-be Mexican-American politicians must contend with the fact that in the very area where potential Mexican-American voting strength is greatest—the Southwest—they face the greatest degree of white hostility. Many Southwestern whites fear that successful Chicano politicians threaten their economic and political advantages. In addition, Black voters may suspect that political gains made by Mexican-Americans would come at their expense. This fear inhibits Black-Hispanic political alliances, especially in the Southwest, where they would be most effective.

NATIVE AMERICANS

Along with Eskimos, American Indians are this country's only Native Americans. Many whites see Indians as a homogeneous racial and ethnic group. In fact, however, there is as much cultural and linguistic diversity among different North American Indian tribes as among the societies of Europe. Indians are not a single tribe, speaking a single language, but dozens of distinct and markedly different tribes, speaking distinct and different languages. Moreover, some Indians are much more assimilated than others. Some speak only their tribal tongues, follow ancient customs, and associate only with fellow tribal members. Others, who have lost their traditional ways generations ago, speak only English, and are completely integrated into the American mainstream.

The westward movement of European settlers across North America inevitably encroached upon Indian lands and created conflict and violence between whites and Native Americans. For the most part, whites viewed Native Americans as subhumans, unworthy of the land they inhabited. They were massacred outright, killed off by disease and malnutrition, and forcibly removed from their ancestral land, their economic foundation thus torn from their lives. Some tribes fought back, but white numbers and weapons were overwhelmingly superior. Originally, the Native American tribes were considered foreign nations—Indians became United States citizens, with voting rights, only in 1924—and the federal government negotiated some 400 treaties with them. The federal government violated every one of these treaties. "The treaties, part of United States law, were often masterpieces of fraud; consent was often gained by deception or threat" (Feagin, 1984, p. 182). By 1890, when some 300 mostly unarmed Native American men, women, and children were massacred at the battle of Wounded Knee, in South Dakota, the continent's original population had been militarily defeated, almost totally "pacified" (to use a term from the Vietnam era).

When Europeans first arrived at the shores of the North American continent in the fifteenth century, the population of Native Americans in what is now the United States was between 1 and 2 million. By 1850, only a quarter of a million remained. Today, their numbers have risen to 1.4 million, though one observer (Deloria, 1981) argues that this includes a sizable number of "wanta-bes," who have only a small portion of Native American ancestry. Yet possibly an equal or even greater number of Native Americans was missed by the 1980 Census, for a variety of reasons, including the total assimilation of some and the inaccessibility of others.

On the average, Native Americans are at or near the bottom of the stratification heap in America. The proportion of Native American men who complete college is only one-fourth that of whites—and for women, it is one-eighth. The unemployment of reservation Indians is about four out of ten workers; the majority, 55 percent, live below the poverty line. Native Americans living off the reservation have an average income about 75 percent of that of whites; about one-quarter live in poverty, and one out of ten is unemployed (Simpson and Yinger, 1985, pp. 198, 200). Thus, the economic position of nonreservation Indians is considerably better than it is for Blacks, but reservation Indians are considerably worse off than Blacks. Politically, Native Americans are even more disadvantaged than Blacks and Chicanos are, because their numbers are smaller, their voting rates are even lower, and their political representation in the form of elected officials is practically nonexistent. In recent years, protests and demonstrations have focused attention on the plight of Native Americans, but this has had little impact on actual conditions. In fact, in general, no evidence suggests that the economic or political status of Native Americans will improve in the foreseeable future.

ASIAN-AMERICANS

The number of Asian-Americans living in the United States has increased explosively in recent years. In 1970, there were 1.5 million Americans of Asian ancestry; a decade later, 3.5 million. This 128 percent increase,

Asian-Americans are the nation's fastest-growing racial and ethnic group. Their numbers have more than doubled in the past decade. Here, young Vietnamese immigrants train for a job in California.

Lawrence Migdale/Photo Researchers

the largest recorded for any other major racial or ethnic group, has come about mainly as a result of immigration. At the start of the 1970s, 373,000 immigrants were admitted to the United States each year, a third from Europe and a quarter (roughly 94,000 individuals) from Asia. Ten years later, immigration from Europe had been cut in half, but that from Asia had doubled (189,000 immigrants). California has more than a third of all Americans of Asian and Pacific ancestry, but nearly every state in the union now has a sizable Asian-American minority (Chaze et al., 1983; Hacker, 1983, pp. 41–43; Sheils et al., 1983).

In at least two respects, Asian-Americans make up a very atypical racial minority: income and education. Asians have the highest median family income of any racial group in the country. In 1980, according to the Bureau of the Census, Asians averaged $22,075; whites, $20,439; and the nation as a whole, $19,908 (Lindsey, 1982, p. 25). According to a slightly different tabulation, Chinese-American families earned an average of 12 percent more than American families as a whole, and Japanese-American families, 32 percent more (Jencks, 1983, p. 34). In addition, 75 percent of Asian-Americans have at least a high school education, whereas 69 percent of whites, 51 percent of Blacks, and 43 percent of Hispanics do (Lindsey, 1982, p. 25). Although some Asian-American families, especially recent immigrants, are poor, their average income figures are remarkably high. Thus, in the sense of material deprivation, Asians do not display all of the typical characteristics of a racial minority. Nonetheless, their history in this country is marked by blatant, systematic discrimination and racism.

Chinese-Americans

Chinese immigration to the United States began as a trickle in the 1840s and increased rapidly after the California Gold Rush of 1849. In the three decades following 1850, more than 300,000 Chinese arrived on American shores. Most were laborers on the railroads, miners, or (in Hawaii) agricultural workers. The work was very difficult, conditions were harsh, and exploitation and low pay were universal. The overwhelming majority of these early Chinese immigrants were unmarried men or men whose wives had remained at home; many had to wait decades before they could send for wives in China or arrange marriages with Chinese brides. Only in Hawaii did intermarriage with other groups take place to any significant degree.

During the 1870s and 1880s, an economic recession forced many American workers out of their jobs. Chinese laborers were willing to work long hours at low pay, so some employers preferred them to white workers, who were beginning to organize labor unions. Many white workers felt that the Chinese were taking their jobs away, and this belief generated hard feelings. During the 1880s, anti-Chinese prejudice erupted in many Western communities, culminating in riots and even lynchings. In 1882, the Chinese Exclusion Act ended virtually all Chinese immigration to the United States. The Act was repealed in 1943, and replaced by one that permitted an annual quota of only 105 Chinese immigrants. Not until 1965 were strict quotas based on national origin abolished.

Chinese inhabitants of this country are more likely to live in segregated neighborhoods than any other racial or ethnic group, in part because of the white majority's hostility to them and in part because they wish to keep their national heritage intact. They tend to resist assimilation and typically maintain their traditions, language, and ties to China.

Chinese communities used to be stable and secure; illegal activity was tightly controlled or regulated by members of the communities themselves, and outside authorities were rarely resorted to, except in cases of murder. With the recent wave of Chinese immigration, this isolation is beginning to crack. Traditional leaders now face competition from newer, younger immigrants, who hunger for success in America. Moreover, some younger leaders of this country's Chinatowns are now forging economic and political links with other racial and ethnic groups and communities. We cannot yet know where this trend will lead.

Japanese-Americans

Like the Chinese, the Japanese were brought to the United States to work as laborers, mainly in agriculture, in the 1800s. They too suffered from prejudice and discrimination at the hands of the white majority. For a time, Japanese-born immigrants were barred from American citizenship, even if their children were born in the United States. For years, California and other Western states prohibited Japanese immigrants from owning land. In 1942, 120,000 Japanese-Americans and Japanese nationals living on the West Coast were forced to live in camps for the duration of World War II. The internment of ethnic Japanese was recommended by General John DeWitt, Commanding General of the Western Defense Command. DeWitt's report stated:

> In the war in which we are now engaged racial affinities are not severed by migration. The Japanese race is an enemy race and while many second- and third-generation Japanese born on United States soil, possessed of United States citizenship, have become "Americanized," the racial strains are undiluted. . . . The very fact that no sabotage has taken place to date is a disturbing and confirming indication that such action will be taken (from a summary of the report of the Commission on Wartime Relocation and Internment of Civilians, which appeared in *The New York Times*, February 25, 1983, p. A12).

President Roosevelt relied on this report in signing Executive Order 9066, which authorized United States military officials to exclude any and all persons deemed disloyal from designated areas. Shortly thereafter, all individuals of Japanese descent were prohibited from living, working, or traveling on the West Coast of the United States. "Not a single documented act of espionage, sabotage, or fifth column activity was committed by an American citizen of Japanese ancestry or by a resident Japanese alien on the West Coast" (Miller, 1983, p. A12). At the war's end, many Japanese-Americans returned to vandalized and pilfered homes; some lost their property forever. Not until 1983 did a congressional commission declare that the internment was a "grave injustice," motivated by "racial prejudice, war hysteria, and failure of political leadership" (Miller, 1983, p. 1).

Today, though seven out of ten Japanese-Americans live in California and Hawaii, they are highly assimilated into the American mainstream. They have the highest per capita income and educational achievements of any racial or ethnic group in America; some nine out of ten of them have college educations. By comparison with other Americans of Asian ancestry, Japanese-Americans are much less likely to live in exclusive ethnic enclaves and much more likely to live in racially integrated neighborhoods (Ima, 1976; Kitano, 1976; Wilson and Hosokawa, 1980). The recent economic triumphs of Japanese firms, and an upsurge in racial and ethnic pride by members of all groups, have revived interest in Japanese culture by younger Japanese-Americans.

SUMMARY

1. Racial characteristics are both physical and social phenomena; sociologists are interested in the ways members of different races relate to one another.

2. In all societies, there is a strong relationship between race and socioeconomic status. Income, power, and prestige are unequally distributed along racial lines.

3. Race as a cultural and social category overlaps very imperfectly with the concept of race as a physical category. Some physical distinctions are ignored and some are emphasized in the way that people categorize one another racially.

4. Although race is a biological fiction, because it is believed to be biologically valid and real, it has very real and very powerful sociological consequences.

5. An ethnic group is a collectivity of people who share a common culture or subculture, passed down from one generation to the next; members usually assume that they share a common ancestry, although this assumption is frequently false.

6. Intergroup relations are often marked by a great deal of conflict, often over competition for power or scarce resources.

7. In most areas, one racial or ethnic group dominates another; the dominant group is called a "majority" group, and the dominated one is called a "minority" group, regardless of their numbers.

8. Majorities have dealt with, treated, or related to minorities in a number of ways, such as assimilation, pluralism, population transfer, continued subjugation, and extermination.

9. Prejudice is a preconceived unfavorable opinion against members of racial, ethnic, religious, or national groups.

10. Racism and prejudice almost always entail stereotypical thinking—viewing group members in narrow, rigid, biased terms without regard to the facts.

11. Several explanations have been offered for racial prejudice, including economic and political conflict, personality factors, authoritarianism, and traditionalism.

12. Prejudice and discrimination are related phenomena; they overlap heavily, but are not identical. Prejudice is an attitude toward a racial or ethnic minority. Discrimination is a kind of behavior. It is possible to find unprejudiced discriminators as well as prejudiced nondiscriminators.

13. Three types of racial and ethnic discrimination may be located, isolated, and studied: direct legal discrimination, direct nonlegal discrimination, and institutional racism.

14. Institutional racism, or indirect discrimination, contributes to existing racial inequality. Because our economic, political, and educational institutions are organized in a certain way, even formally nondiscriminatory actions often perpetuate inequality.

15. Improvement in the economic position of Blacks in the United States in recent years has been uneven. By some indicators, the

improvement has been significant; by others, nonexistent. Indeed, in some ways, the economic position of Blacks is deteriorating, both relative to that of whites and in an absolute sense.

16. Black family income remains about 55 percent of that of whites. Blacks remain unemployed at a rate about twice as high as that of whites. The percent of Black families living in poverty has not improved much in recent years, and, in fact, seems to be increasing slightly. The proportion of adult Black men who are employed has dropped from nearly three-quarters in the 1960s to just over half in the 1980s.

17. On the other hand, the education gap between Blacks and whites is closing. *Employed* Black workers are earning more relative to whites, and Black women and white women with jobs earn almost identical salaries. Over time, Blacks are also improving their representation in high-paying, prestigious occupations, and decreasing their representation in occupations at the bottom of the stratification ladder.

18. Thus, in general, whether the economic position of Blacks is improving or not depends on which indicators of economic improvement we use.

19. Hispanic-Americans form a large and growing ethnic group; like Black-Americans, they have suffered significant discrimination in the United States.

20. Native Americans have experienced a long history of severe discrimination and deprivation; for centuries, extermination was the policy of many white settlers. Today, Indians remain the most economically disadvantaged of all racial minorities.

21. Mainly as a result of immigration, Asian-Americans have become the fastest-growing of all racial or ethnic groups in the United States; their numbers here have more than doubled in the past decade. Economically and educationally, Asian-Americans fare better than the white majority.

SUGGESTED READINGS

Reynolds Farley, *Blacks and Whites: Narrowing the Gap?* Cambridge, Massachusetts: Harvard University Press, 1984.
Addresses the question of the Black-white economic gap and whether it has changed over the past generation or so. A dispassionate, strictly empirical analysis. An absolute must-read on this issue.

Joe R. Feagin, *Racial and Ethnic Relations* (2nd ed.). Englewood Cliffs, New Jersey: Prentice-Hall, 1984.
A "conflict-oriented" analysis of racial and ethnic relations in the United States.

Harry H. L. Kitano, *Japanese Americans* (2nd ed.). Englewood Cliffs, New Jersey: Prentice-Hall, 1976.
The history and current position of Japanese-Americans, seen through the eyes of a fellow group member.

Harry H. L. Kitano, *Race Relations* (3rd ed.). Englewood Cliffs, New Jersey: Prentice-Hall, 1985.
A textbook describing and analyzing race relations with an emphasis on the United States.

Stanford M. Lyman, *Chinese Americans*. Englewood Cliffs, New Jersey: Prentice-Hall, 1974.
A sociological and historical description of the position of Americans of Chinese ancestry.

Joan Moore and Harry Pachon, *Hispanics in the United States*. Englewood Cliffs, New Jersey: Prentice-Hall, 1985.
A description and analysis of the sociological characteristics, politics, social institutions, culture, and language of the Hispanic peoples—mainly Mexican-Americans, Puerto Ricans, and Cubans. A valuable book.

George Eaton Simpson and J. Milton Yinger, *Racial and Cultural Minorities: An Analysis of Prejudice and Discrimination* (5th ed.). New York: Plenum Press, 1985.
Something of a "bible" among textbooks on racial and ethnic relations, this book has remained in print for over three decades. Insist on the latest edition.

William J. Wilson, *The Declining Significance of Race* (2nd ed.). Chicago: University of Chicago Press, 1980.
The author argues that social class, not race, is the most formidable barrier for Blacks. This is a highly controversial book.

chapter 11

WOMEN AND MEN

All societies, now and in the past, have regulated the behavior of women and men. All have rules and regulations about what men can and should do, and what women can and should do—and also about what men and women cannot and should not do together. What men and women do, alone and with each other, is governed by norms and sanctions. But although all societies have such rules, the rules themselves vary a good deal. This is the most important fact about them.

The second-most-important fact about these rules is that, everywhere, most people regard them as inevitable, inborn, biologically determined, based on the intrinsic nature of men and women. Most of us assume that men are "naturally" dominant and that it is "normal" for them to rule over the family, and society in general. We assume as well that women have a "genetic" predisposition to be nurturing rather than challenging, emotional rather than rational and calculating, passive rather than active, submissive rather than dominant, etc., etc., etc.

In this view, the separate natures of men and women cannot be changed. To deny this separateness or, worse, to attempt to transcend it by taking on the traits of the other sex is to violate biological destiny. Dominant women and emotional men would thus violate the very foundations of the cosmos.

The sociological perspective rejects these traditional, "common-sense" ideas. Sociologists argue that our ideas about men and women are largely products of culture, not of biological destiny.

WHAT IS SEX?

The term **sex** refers to organic differences between males and females. It also refers to erotic activity, but let us set that aside for the moment. Organic, or biological, differences between men and women are genetic, anatomical, or hormonal. When, after sexual intercourse, the female ovum and the male sperm unite to produce

Sex The condition of being a biological male or female.

Chromosomes Material in cells that determines hereditary characteristics.

Primary sex characteristics Physical characteristics of the body that pertain specifically to reproduction, such as the genitals.

Secondary sex characteristics Physical characteristics that develop during adolescence as a result of the action of hormones, such as facial hair on males and breasts on females.

Hormones Chemicals secreted into the bloodstream by specific organs called glands; they stimulate or inhibit certain biochemical processes.

Gender The culturally determined traits associated with, and roles played by, males and females.

a fertilized egg, which eventually develops into a human being, each contributes twenty-three **chromosomes:** material in cells that determines hereditary characteristics. One of these matched pairs of chromosomes determines the embryo's sex. Some human traits are indeed carried genetically—hemophilia, color blindness, baldness in men, for instance. Note that these are physical characteristics. No scientist has yet been able to connect a specific gene with the behavior, the emotions, or the personalities of men and women. Anatomical differences between men and women are easy to observe, of course. These anatomical differences are of two kinds: **primary sex characteristics**—the genitals—and **secondary sex characteristics**—facial hair and breasts, which develop through the action of **hormones,** chemicals secreted into the bloodstream by organs called glands.

Gender

Gender overlaps with, but is separate from, sex in the biological sense. **Gender** is a sociological concept that refers to the roles each sex is assigned by society and plays within it. Gender comprises all those social and cultural distinctions that distinguish women from men.

Everywhere, most biological men and biological women play out the gender-specific roles assigned by society. Thus, the concepts of sex and gender are clearly interrelated, but not identical. The exceptions—biological males who adopt female roles and biological females who adopt male ones—often tell us more about the reality of sex roles than do people who conform to social expectations.

Is Biology Destiny?

Sociologists recognize that men and women differ biologically, of course. But by comparing gender roles in different societies around the world, we see that, in most cases, culture can override biological factors. It is true that men and only men can impregnate women and that women and only women can menstruate, become pregnant, bear children, and lactate. *No other sexual differences are dictated by biology.* Other sex-linked forms of behavior may be influenced by biology, but that is a different matter entirely. After puberty, for instance, men become 10 to 15 percent larger than women—and thus stronger and faster, at least potentially. Men therefore have a certain physical edge where size, strength, and speed are important. (Of course, some women are bigger, stronger, and faster than many men are.) As a result of this edge, no amount of practice can make the very best women tennis players beat the very best men tennis players. So the extreme likelihood that Martina Navratilova will never beat John McEnroe may very well have biological origins. But Martina Navratilova can trounce more than 99 percent of the world's male tennis players, because she has worked longer and harder at it.

Consider the course of men's and women's athletics over the years. Until recently, women were not encouraged to compete in sports, a fact their athletic performance reflected. Today, women's athletics is more often encouraged and rewarded. Women are participating in greater numbers and with greater enthusiasm and expertise, and their performance is improving much more rapidly than men's, though men are still ahead. Fifty years ago, the very best male athletes were running and swimming more slowly, and jumping and throwing shorter distances, than the best female athletes today. In the 1928 Olympics, for example, the gold medal time in the 100-meter free-style swimming event was 58.60 seconds for men. In 1976, the best women's time for the same event was 55.65 seconds (Davidowitz, 1980). The best women marathon runners can complete the race (all twenty-six miles, 385 yards of it) in about two hours and twenty-one minutes. That time would have beaten *all* runners, men or women, in any marathon before 1970.

Of course, some sports demand sheer size and upper-body strength; in these, women generally perform less well. Women will never challenge men in boxing and football. But for most sports, training, socialization, encouragement, experience, and rewards are more important than biology. If this fact is true for sports, an activity in which physical performance is admittedly important, it must surely be even more true for those traits and activities that do not hang so largely on physical characteristics.

Sociologists insist that biology is always "mediated" through culture. Every society makes a somewhat different use of these biological characteristics, which are not very numerous anyway. In every society, for instance, some people are stronger than others, partly as a result of biological traits. In some societies, the physically strongest men have the most power and influence. But not in most. In general, the most powerful people in most societies tend to be middle-aged or elderly men, who are less physically strong than much younger men. Obviously, social power does not result solely and simply from physical power.

Recent achievement by female athletes have proven false Freud's claim that women are passive and uncompetitive because of their sex. Here, Mary Deker competes in a long-distance event in Los Angeles.
UPI/Bettmann Newsphotos

GENDER ROLES

Gender is probably the core of human existence. Gender awareness among children comes earlier than awareness of any other status—race, social class, religion, and so on. Almost every aspect of human life ties in to gender, because the experience of being human is filtered through sexual status. No one, in our society, can be human and only human; each of us must be a male human or female human. Sex is largely an ascribed (or inborn) status; gender is achieved. Still, every society masks its artificial character, palming it off as "natural." Boys are supposed to be aggressive and play with guns, rockets, and baseball bats. Little girls are expected to be soft and cuddly and to play with dolls and dishpans. Even well-informed mothers and fathers believe that boys instinctively like rockets and guns and that little girls instinctively like dolls. Yet when Margaret Mead, the anthropologist, brought dolls to New Guinea, it was the boys who were most interested in playing with them, singing to them, rocking them to sleep, and behaving in a manner that we would call "maternal." Gender socialization begins early in life, and the actions we regard as innate really begin during the days following birth.

Margaret Mead

Decades ago, anthropologist Margaret Mead tested the proposition that women and men had innate, biologically determined characteristics and personalities. Mead studied three New Guinea tribes—the Arapesh, the Mundugumor, and the Tchambuli—that lived within a few miles of one another. She reported her findings in her classic, *Sex and Temperament* *in Three Primitive Societies* (1963; originally published in 1935).[*] In two of the three tribes, women and men displayed basically the same temperament, or personality. Among the Arapesh, both women and men behaved in ways that we would call "feminine": They tended to be gentle, unaggressive, nurturant, unambitious, lacking in sexual passion, and "maternal." Among the nearby Mundugumor, both women and men were "ruthless, aggressive, positively sexed . . . with the maternal, cherishing aspects of personality at a minimum. Both men and women approximated to a personality type that we in our culture would find only in an undisciplined and very violent male" (Mead, 1963, p. 259). If standard, inborn, sex-linked personality traits exist, the members of these tribes seem never to have heard of them.

Among members of the third tribe, the Tchambuli, men and women differed strikingly, but (according to Mead) it was Tchambuli women who were dominant, aggressive, and ambitious. The men were emotionally dependent on the women, and the women dominated the tribe. They controlled the currency and made the mosquito nets the Tchambuli traded with other tribes. The women gave some of the currency to the men and allowed them to "shop" for personal pleasure. Shopping among Tchambuli men involved much indecision and fickleness. And what did they buy? Holiday attire, perfume, costumes, feathers, flowers, necklaces, girdles—ornaments to make themselves more attractive to women.

The women viewed the men with kindly condescension and tolerance, a kind of amused appreciation. Men had a chiefly decorative, ornamental, and ceremonial function; they especially cultivated their artistic and esthetic gifts: flute playing, dancing, carving, and painting. Their beauty was thought to be their most valuable attribute. Women, in fact, evaluated men according to their grace, attractiveness, and clothing. Men were thought to age faster than women, because they were judged primarily by their looks, which were thought to decline in middle age. Older women commonly courted and married younger men, who traded their looks for the power, prestige, and money of older women. Women were evaluated as good or bad providers. Men played the emotionally subservient role and depended on the security given to them by the women. Women, not men, chose their sexual and marital partners. Here, in short, is a social world almost exactly the reverse of our own, except in one respect: Women had the chief role in raising children.

Mead's research among these three tribes exposed the arbitrary and culture-bound nature of gender roles. Many, if not all, of the personality characteristics we call "masculine" and "feminine" are linked to each sex "as lightly as clothing." Human nature, Mead concluded, "is almost unbelievably malleable" (1963, p. 260). The same infant could be socialized to become a full participant in any one of these three societies, or our own, or any other.

After her study of sex roles in three New Guinea tribes, Margaret Mead concluded that gender is largely (but not entirely) a product of culture. Here, a Cunan Indian woman checks her appearance.

Doranne Jacobson/United Nations Photo

[*] Margaret Mead's research on the experience of adolescence in Samoa, *Coming of Age in Samoa* (1928), has come under strong criticism recently by an Australian anthropologist, Derek Freeman, in his book, *Margaret Mead and Samoa: The Making and Unmaking of an Anthropological Myth* (1983). Freeman's study does not deal with Mead's writings on New Guinea. The book, however, does attack Mead's writings on Samoa on both a specific, concrete level (that is, it claims that she misrepresented the details of Samoan culture) and on a more general level: It attacks Mead's environmentalist point of view. Anthropologists feel that many of Freeman's specific criticisms are valid, but argue that he has overextended his argument at the more general level. The book is not, in fact, an adequate or valid refutation of Mead's environmentalist position. Freeman's book has generated a counterresponse (Holmes, 1986), which argues that Freeman's description of Samoan culture is flawed, and Mead's is the more accurate.

Economic Activity

When we examine the evidence of many societies, we see that only a very few economic activities are assigned exclusively to men—hunting large marine animals, like sharks and whales, for example. Cooking is a predominantly, though not exclusively, female activity. Men typically have most or all of the power. Men almost always do all the fighting in warfare. These very few near-universals are vastly outweighed by the huge variations among societies. Most economic activities are not overwhelmingly assigned either to men or to women. Yet most societies justify their own sexual division of labor by claiming that it rests on the intrinsic traits of men and women. In some societies, men carry the heavy loads—because men are stronger than women, or so it is claimed. In other societies, women carry the heavy loads—and here it is said that women have stronger backs than men do, or are used to difficult work, or don't complain much. The huge cross-cultural variation in the sexual division of labor shows that no such division can be "natural."

Let's consider one example that shows how different societies divide powers and responsibilities between the sexes: the percentage of women in the labor market. In many Eastern European countries, a majority of the women hold jobs outside the home. But in most Middle Eastern countries, only a small percentage do. Clearly, the extent to which women participate in the work force is determined by economic, cultural, and, in some countries, religious factors. Yet in those countries where most women do not work, most people assume that a "woman's place" is by nature in the home. The plain fact is that cross-national comparisons show that women do not have an unvarying "place" or "nature." Woman's place in society is an open question—a social, cultural, economic, and political issue that must be decided by human beings, not by nature, fate, or destiny.

WOMEN IN AMERICAN SOCIETY

Many men and many women now say that the sexes should be equal in all things. That equality is embodied in many laws and many government policies, but not, or not quite, in reality. Americans pay a good deal of lip-service to sexual equality, but most of us are "nonconscious sexists" (Bem and Bem, 1970). Black and white alike, most men feel that their wives should do most of the housework—even if the husband and the wife both work full-time (Ferretti, 1980). Moreover, hardly any American men accept equal responsibility for raising their children— that is "woman's work." Domestic equality does have some ideological support, though. Only 43 percent of respondents to one survey agreed that marriage was "more satisfying" when "the husband provides for the family and the wife takes care of the house and children." And 48 percent approved when "the husband and wife both have jobs, both do housework, and both take care of the children" (Meislin, 1977). What couples do in real life is quite another story, however.

By regarding women primarily as housekeepers and childrearers, we ignore the reality of women's lives as they actually are lived. Today's divorce rate is about four marriages in every ten (see Chapter 13). Millions of women get divorced, and when they do, they find themselves thrust, unprepared, into the job market.

Even when families remain intact, nonworking women face a related, though not identical, problem. For women in the United States, the median age of marriage is 23, and from 90 to 95 percent of all American women eventually marry. A majority of American women bear their last child by the time they have reached their late 20s or early 30s. By their middle to late 30s, childrearing is a part-time activity for typical married women, because by then their youngest children are in school. The average American woman's life lasts an additional thirty-five to forty years. Thus, for the first twenty-three years of their lives, women are socialized to accept childraising as their chief function, yet they spend less than twenty years as full-time mothers. Unless a woman is able to move beyond motherhood, some sort of depression is almost inevitable during the second half of her life.

Finally, more and more women do not marry at all or marry later than they used to. These women must face the realities of the job market from the moment they leave home or school, realities that must eventually be faced by most women.

Women in the Workplace: A Cause for Optimism?

Has the position of women in the workplace improved in recent years? Our answer to this question depends on whether we are optimists or pessimists. Some things have improved dramatically, whereas others have remained the same. Perhaps the most dramatic change has been in the rate of employment for women. A strikingly higher percentage of women work for incomes today than did in the past. In 1890, only 18 percent of all adult women were in the labor force. This figure rose very slowly until 1940—when it was one-quarter—then rose dramatically during World War II (1941–1945)—when it was over a third—dropped in the postwar years, and then began to rise again in the late 1940s (Fox and Hesse-Biber, 1984, Chapter 2; Serrin, 1984). In 1950, 34 percent of all adult American women worked; in 1960, 38 percent; in 1970, 43 percent; in 1980, 51 percent; and in 1983, 53 percent. The Bureau of the Census estimates that in 1995, six out of every ten adult women in the United States will work for a living (*Statistical Abstract of the United States*, 1985, p. 392).

Perhaps even more remarkable is that today, unlike in the past, the changes that are taking place are only slightly affected by women's marital and family statuses. In 1960, 30.5 percent of all married women were in the labor force; in 1984, this figure was 52.8 percent. Even more striking is that, in 1960, only 18.6 percent of all married women with children under the age of 6 worked; in 1984, this figure was 51.8 percent (*Statistical Abstract of the United States*, 1985, p. 399). In 1940, only a bit more than a third of the female labor force was married (36 percent). But, by 1984, nearly six female workers in ten (or 59 percent) were married (*Statistical Abstract of the United States*, 1985, p. 398). Focusing only on the most heavily employed segment of the population, more than two-thirds of all women aged 25 to 54 are in the labor force (Serrin, 1984, p. 32). As of 1983, women made up 43.7 percent of the work force. The Bureau of Labor Statistics estimates that women will hold seven out of every ten jobs created in the 1980s and 1990s (Serrin, 1984). Clearly, then, by any reasonable standard, the rate of employment among women has increased dramatically during this century, and especially

**Percent of Married Women
in the Labor Force
1960 versus 1984**

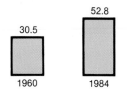

**Percent of Married Women
with Children under the Age of 6
1960 versus 1984**

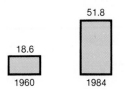

over the past generation or so. This increase is likely to continue in the years to come. (Table 11–1 details the rise in the female employment rate in the United States from 1890 to the 1980s.)

In the realm of wages, the picture is not quite so rosy. Even today, there is a sizable "gender gap" in women's earnings versus men's. Between 1955 and 1970, the average income of women working full-time, year-round, compared with that of men actually dropped somewhat, from 64 percent to 59 percent. However, between 1970 and the 1980s, this figure inched up a bit such that women earned 64 cents for every dollar earned by men (see Table 11–2). Part of the reason for the income disparity between men and women is that women are more likely to be concentrated in a few low-paying occupations, as we see. But even at the same occupational levels, women earn roughly 60 percent as much as men (Rosenbaum, 1980b). Consider some examples: Although women hold 90 percent of the nation's bookkeeping jobs, they earn an average of $98 less than men holding the same jobs. Male administrators of elementary and secondary schools earn an average of $520 a week; women with comparable jobs earn $363. Although women hold about two-thirds of the jobs as health technicians in hospitals and clinics, they earn an average weekly wage of $273 versus $324 for men with comparable jobs (*The New York Times*, March 7, 1982, p. 25). The gender gap in pay is still very much a fact of life for the working woman.

There are a number of reasons for the gender pay gap. One is that certain professions have been open to women only for a short time; as a result, the peak earning years for the women who entered them recently are a few years in the future. In addition, a very high proportion of the women who have entered the job market recently are married women with children, who wish to work part-time, part of the year, or who are willing to compromise by taking jobs to fit their childrearing schedules—something men rarely have to do. In fact, on the average, working wives earn only $430 for every $1,000 their husbands earn (Hacker, 1984, p. 127). The wage discrepancy is narrowed when we compare men and women at roughly the same stage in their lives. Single women earn an average of $867 for every $1,000 earned by single men (Hacker, 1984, p. 126). In a number of occupations that were once nearly all-male, the wage gap, although significant, is modest. Women lawyers average $701 for every $1,000 earned by men. Among college teachers, the figure is $803; among physicians and dentists, $809; and among journalists, $850 (Hacker, 1984, p. 127). In 1983, according to the Bureau of Labor Statistics, women in the youngest age category, under 25, earned 90 percent as much as men. The Rand Corporation, a research organization, predicted that in the year 2000, women's wages overall will be 74 percent of those for men (Serrin, 1984). Thus, when we compare sex differences in income, we discover a somewhat mixed message. On the one hand, much progress has been made. On the other, it will be many years before the incomes of women approach parity with those of men.

Most studies suggest that when women and men do the same job and have the same experience or seniority, pay rates tend to be similar. Most of the dollar differences stem from the fact that women tend to be more recent entrants and have fewer years on the job. Whether women embarking upon a career will attain pay equality with men rests on at least two factors. First, will most of them continue full time on their jobs after they have children? A break in their employment, or a decision to work part time, will slow raises and promotions—as it would for a man. Second, will male-dominated companies elevate women to higher-paid jobs at the same rate they elevate men? In some fields, this has clearly not happened. Many women, for example,

TABLE 11–1 Employment Rate for Adult Women, 1890–1983, and Projections for 1990–1995

1890	18.2
1950	33.9
1960	37.7
1970	43.3
1980	51.5
1983	52.9
1990[*]	58.3
1995[*]	60.3

[*] Projections

Sources: Mary Frank Fox and Sharlene Hesse-Biber, Women at Work. *Palo Alto, California: Mayfield, 1984, Chapter 2; William Serrin, "Experts Say Job Bias against Women Persists."* The New York Times, (*November 25, 1984), pp. 1, 32; Statistical Abstract of the United States, 1985, p. 392.*

TABLE 11–2 Median Annual Earnings for Year-Round, Full-time Workers, Women versus Men, 1960–1983[*]

	Men	Women	Income Ratio
1960	$ 5,417	$ 3,293	.61
1970	$ 8,966	$ 5,323	.59
1980	$18,612	$11,197	.60
1983	$21,881	$13,915	.64

[*] Figures are not adjusted for inflation.

Source: William Serrin, "Experts Say Job Bias against Women Persists." The New York Times (*November 25, 1984), p. 32.*

have committed their lives to teaching careers, yet relatively few become principals or superintendents of school systems (Hacker, 1984, p. 127).

In the sphere of occupational distribution, the disparity between men and women is great, although narrowing very slowly. In some occupations, the increase in the proportion of women workers is startling, but mainly because the numbers were so small to begin with. From 1962 to 1982, the proportion of all engineers who were women rose from 1 percent to 6 percent. Among physicians, the proportion increased from 6 to 15 percent, and among medical students, to 25 percent. Similar increases took place in a number of other occupations during the same period: among mail carriers, from 3 to 17 percent; among insurance agents, from 10 to 26 percent; among bartenders, from 11 to 50 percent; among bus drivers, from 12 to 47 percent; and among college teachers, from 19 to 25 percent. Women now make up a majority of insurance adjusters, bill collectors, psychologists, and assemblers. At the same time, according to Janet L. Norwood, United States Commissioner of Labor Statistics, although "employed women are clearly moving into higher paying jobs," the "actual number engaged in these occupations remains relatively small." For example, the number of women lawyers increased more than five-fold between the early 1970s and the early 1980s, "but there are still less than 100,000 in the legal profession, and they make up only about 15 percent of the total" (Serrin, 1984, p. 32). Only 2.5 percent of the skilled, high-paying highway construction jobs are filled by women. And only eight out of every 1,000 employed women hold high-level executive, administrative, or managerial jobs, according to Catalyst, a research group. Women occupy 455, or only 3 percent, of the 16,000 seats on the boards of directors of the country's thousand largest corporations listed by *Fortune* magazine (Serrin, 1984, p. 32).

The fact is, even today, there remains a great deal of occupational sex segregation (Fox and Hesse-Biber, 1984; Roos, 1985). Women and men, overwhelmingly, hold different jobs. Women tend to be concentrated in a smaller number of occupational categories than men. In 1983, 99 percent of all secretaries, 96 percent of typists, 97 percent of receptionists, 90 percent of telephone operators, 91 percent of bank tellers, 84 percent of cashiers, 96 percent of registered nurses, and 97 percent of child-care workers were women. Moreover, half of all men work in sixty-five of the 250 occupations listed by the Bureau of the Census, half of all women work in only twenty-one of them. In fact, one-quarter of all female employees work in just five occupations: secretary/stenographer, household worker (servant, domestic, or "cleaning lady"), bookkeeper, school teacher, and waitress (Blau, 1979, pp. 278–279). Whereas men are clearly much more widely distributed throughout the occupational structure, women tend to be confined to and concentrated in a relatively small number of occupations—a tendency that is as strong today as it was in 1900.

In fact, women are so segregated into specific and limited occupations that there are in effect two labor markets, one male and one female. Women are concentrated in the very few jobs that most of them can actually get. Women bring "special qualities" to the work force: They are relatively inexpensive to hire, relatively easy to fire, and relatively well educated. And there are lots of them. "Industrial society needs a pool of cheap but educated labor, and this need has kept women in low-paying, well-schooled jobs." Women are hired when they are needed, in times of economic boom; during recessions, "they are, like blacks, last hired and first fired" (Tavris and Wade, 1984, pp. 269, 272–273).

A sex-segregated marketplace supports . . . salary differences by making use of the fact that most women's primary allegiance is to their families. "Women's" jobs do not require long-term commitment or extensive sacrifice of time, so a woman can take a job, quit, and return as family responsibilities change. Because service and clerical jobs exist all over the country, women whose husbands are transferred can travel with them and pick up work in the new city. Employers, for their part, do not have to provide much training for female employees or invest time and resources in them. Geographically, married women are a captive labor force. Where they work is determined by where they live, which in turn is determined by where their husbands work. Further, most wives have to consider other attributes of a job than income and interest: They want their hours to correspond to the children's school hours, for example, or they decide to work nights while their husbands are home with the kids (Tavris and Wade, 1984, p. 272).

The Sexual Funnel

Each job has what might be called a **sexual funnel.** In jobs where both men and women work in large numbers, women tend to be less successful; they become scarcer with every step upward in every profession. Most social workers are women, but most social-work supervisors are men. Most librarians are women, but most directors of large libraries are men. Most school teachers are women, but most principals and district supervisors are men.

Consider the academic profession—teaching at the college and university level. As we can see from Table 11–3, women suffer from the double disadvantage of having lower salaries than men at each rank and lower likelihood of holding higher-ranked or tenured positions. Depending on rank, in 1985, women earned between $2,000 and $5,000 less than men at each rank, and they were roughly 25 percent less likely to hold tenured positions. (Tenure is a lifetime position, and is usually granted at the Associate Professor level.) In addition, women were over twice as likely to be on nontenured "tracks"—that is, to hold jobs that will never be granted tenure. Clearly, the sexual "funnel" applies to jobs in higher education: Women are increasingly scarce the higher up on the academic ladder we look. And women are less well paid in the academic world. The median academic salary in 1985 for women with Ph.D.s in the humanities was $30,900; for men, the salary was $36,100. In the sciences, the comparable salaries were $35,600 for women and $46,100 for men.

Similar salary gaps may be found on most campuses around the country, at some of the finest—and some of the humblest—institutions. The University of Wisconsin at Madison pays male full professors an average of $5,000 more than their female counterparts. At Harvard, in 1985, only 5 percent of all tenured faculty were women, as compared with 20 percent nationwide. Thirteen of Harvard's departments have no tenured women at all (Rohter, 1987).

Observers agree that, for the most part, a majority of the "horror stories" of blatant, overt sexual discrimination no longer take place. Yet, in spite of the gains of the past decade or two, women's progress up the academic ladder is significantly slower than that of men's, and their pay at each rank and each level of qualification is strikingly below that of men's. Though the academic profession has "come a long way" in reaching gender equality, it still has a long way to go.

In many ways, the status of women parallels the minority status of Blacks (Hacker, 1951; Bird, 1970). **Sexism** is no less strong than racism—perhaps, as feminists argue, it is even more deeply rooted and more widely accepted. Like racism, too, sexism has institutional roots, because

Sexual funnel A situation that exists whereby the higher the stratificational position, the smaller the proportion of women there are.

Sexism The ideology or behavior that supports gender inequality.

Women face many barriers to occupational and economic achievement. Despite these obstacles, an increasing number of women reach the executive level in their chosen careers.

Alex Von Koschembahr/Photo Researcher

■ **TABLE 11–3 Academic Gender Inequality in Income and Tenure**

Average Salary for Faculty at Institutions with Doctoral Programs
1985–1986

Academic Rank	*Salary*	
	MEN	WOMEN
Professor	$47,660	$42,470
Associate	34,480	32,320
Assistant	29,330	26,650
Instructor	22,130	20,050
Lecturer	26,140	22,650

Tenure Status for Ph.D.s Employed at Academic Institutions, 1985[*]

Humanities		
	MEN	WOMEN
Total	47,000	17,900
Tenured	75%	51%
Untenured, on track	11	20
Nontenure track	10	24
Average salary	$36,100	$30,900

Science and Engineering		
Total	171,402	32,287
Tenured	63	38
Untenured, on track	16	23
Nontenure track	14	31
Average salary	$46,100	$35,600

[*]Percentages do not add up to 100 because totals include postdoctoral appointees, for whom tenure does not apply.

Source: American Association of University Professors; National Research Council; Larry Rohter, "Women Gain Degrees, But Not Tenure," The New York Times (January 4, 1987), p. E9.

indirect discrimination against women creates economic and political gaps that are just as wide as those created by direct discrimination. Institutional sexism assumes many guises in our society.

Although, as we have discussed, a higher education is no guarantee of a higher income, still, on the average, <u>education is correlated with income</u>. The educational sphere is one area in which we might assume that success is related directly to ability and effort. However, pressures operate on women in colleges and universities in a way that few men have to face. Women tend to drop out of higher education at a disproportionally higher rate at each step along the way. <u>Something of a sexual funneling</u> thus takes place in the achievement of academic degrees. At the lowest levels of higher education, women's attainment is as great as or greater than men's. At the higher levels, women are significantly underrepresented. In 1982, 10.9 million students were enrolled in colleges in the United States; just under 50 percent were male and just over 50 percent, female. Slightly more than 1 million bachelor's degrees were awarded that year, about 49 percent to women and 51 percent to men. At the master's level, women earned about 51 percent of all degrees. But at the more advanced levels, the picture changes. Women earned only 28 percent of the 32,000 Ph.D.s awarded in the United States in 1982. In the same year, women earned 25 percent of all M.D.s, 15 percent of dental degrees, 33 percent of law degrees, and 11 percent of all engineering degrees (*Statistical Abstract of the United States, 1985*, pp. 157, 159). Even though this represents a huge advance over degrees granted in the past, it is still far below women's potential. (Table 11–4 documents degrees granted by sex in 1960 and 1982.)

Women's exit from the higher reaches of the educational system in greater numbers than men's is typically not a result of academic or emotional difficulties. There are several reasons for sexual funneling in the educational sphere. The first is marriage and childbearing. Whereas men rarely leave school for such marital reasons as the need to support a family, women very often drop out to support their husbands through school or to raise children. Our society's expectation that women have a primary obligation to their husbands and children, rather than to their own educations and careers, is a major institutional barrier to women's occupational achievement. A second reason is that girls and women are not encouraged in school to the same educational heights as men are, and they come to believe that they are incapable of maximum educational achievement. A study by Karen Erikson Paige found that whereas the primary influence on men's choice of an occupation is the income it earns, for college women, the strongest influence is its sex composition (Tavris and Wade, 1984, p. 270). Women come to scale down their educational and occupational sights, accept lower levels of academic achievement as well as enter fields that are traditionally female-dominated.

Sexual funneling also operates in the choice of field of study in high school and college. "Women (correctly) perceive that they will have difficulty being employed in math and science fields, which are male-dominated, so they don't take math and science courses. High-school girls think they'll have a better chance of getting work if they learn clerical skills, so they don't learn technical skills—even though carpenters are better paid than secretaries" (Tavris and Wade, 1984, pp. 269–270). This begins as a steering process practiced by teachers and counselors: Girls are told that they are better suited to certain fields and not at all to others. Eventually, they come to believe that they are incapable of studying certain areas, and so they are closed off to them forever. And the direction that this steering process takes tends to follow income lines: Women tend to be encouraged to pursue fields with lower-paying careers

■ **TABLE 11–4 Degree Earned by Sex, 1960 and 1982**

	1960 Total			1982 Total		
	PERCENT		NUMBER (IN	PERCENT		NUMBER (IN
	MALE	FEMALE	THOUSANDS)	MALE	FEMALE	THOUSANDS)
Bachelor's	65	35	395	51	49	1,205
Master's	68	32	75	49	51	295
Doctorate (Ph.D.)	90	10	9.8	72	28	32.7
Medicine (M.D.)	94	5.5	7.0	75	25	15.8
Dental (D.D.S. or D.M.D.)	99	0.8	3.2	85	15	5.3
Law (J.D. or L.L.B.)	97	2.5	9.2	67	33	36.0
Engineering	99	0.4	45.6	89	11	100.6

Source: Statistical Abstract of the United States, 1985, *pp. 157, 159.*

and discouraged from pursuing fields with higher-paying careers. Only a minority of bachelor's degrees in 1982 were awarded to women who majored in such high-paying fields as economics (33 percent), engineering (11 percent), business (40 percent), and natural sciences (26 percent). On the other hand, a majority of those majoring in such lower-paying fields as foreign languages (76 percent), education (76 percent), and fine arts (63 percent) were women (*Statistical Abstract of the United States, 1985*, p. 158). And so, in a very real sense—in terms of future earnings—sexual funneling operates in choice of field of study, as well.

Women, Men, and Socioeconomic Status.   Today, as of old, women are judged primarily as reflections of their fathers, husbands, sons, and sons-in-law. A woman is rarely viewed by others as a wholly independent human being. Single women are commonly thought to go to work solely to meet suitable husbands. Men can move up the ladder of social class through their own accomplishments, but for many women, marriage remains the only major path of social mobility. A man pulls himself up the social ladder; a woman moves up by marrying a man who is moving up or has already done so. Women are twice as likely to marry "up" the stratification hierarchy as are men.

The Mentor Connection.   A second major institutional factor holding back women's achievements, especially at the professional and managerial levels, has been called the "mentor connection," the "protégé system," or the " 'old boy' network" (Epstein, 1970; Sheehy, 1976; Dullea, 1981a; Tavris and Wade, 1984, p. 262). In many fields, advancement hangs wholly or in part on the assistance and advice of older, wiser, more powerful, and better-connected colleagues or supervisors. These connections are usually informal: They are distinct from the specific work demands of an occupation. Successful men typically select promising, younger men as their protégés, and men on the rise usually look for male mentors. These informal networks tend to be relatively closed to women. It is therefore difficult for women to "break into" the upper ranks in many fields because successful men do not feel comfortable cultivating women as protégés.

The few exceptions to this rule demonstrate just how pervasive and powerful it is. Germaine Greer (1980) found that, without exception, the very few great women painters in history had mentors to guide their artistic careers—usually relatives, like fathers or older brothers. Margaret Hennig (Hennig and Jardim, 1977) selected twenty-five high-level women executives and conducted an intensive study of each stage of their careers. She found that, early on, all these women had accepted the assistance of specific male bosses. Many of the best-known and most accomplished women in history followed this protégé-mentor pattern—anthropologists Margaret Mead and Franz Boas, writers Simone de Beauvoir and Jean-Paul Sartre, filmmakers Lina Wertmüller and Federico Fellini, authors Mary McCarthy and Edmund Wilson, for instance.

Diminished Expectations.   A major barrier to occupational, educational, and financial success for women is their own diminished expectation of success, an expectation that is often quite realistic. Until quite recently, men were thought to be by nature more ambitious than women. Not so. A woman's conscious drive for success stems from her perception of her actual chances for it. In one study of male and female employees (Crowley, Levitin, and Quinn, 1973), 64 percent of the men but only 48

It is difficult to attribute male supremacy to capitalism, since many preindustrial societies severely restrict the rights and activities of women. In many Islamic societies, women are carefully watched and controlled.

Ronny Jaques/Photo Researchers

percent of the women said they wanted promotions. Two-thirds of these women employees did not expect to be promoted. "We would guess that to avoid frustration, women, like men in the same situation, scale down their ambitions" (Crowley et al., 1973). Another study seems to verify this conclusion (Kanter, 1976b). In one corporation (like most others), secretaries and clerks were mostly women with little chance of advancement. These women were not ambitious. But the few women who worked in high-ranking sales jobs had career aspirations identical to those of their male counterparts. "Ambition, self-esteem, and career commitment were all flourishing among women in sales jobs, who were well paid and on the way to top management" (Kanter, 1976b).

Tokenism.   Another institutional mechanism that slows down the economic progress of women is **tokenism** (Tavris and Wade, 1984, pp. 262–267). The presence of a few women (or Blacks) in high-level positions serves to persuade white males that the system is fair and nondiscriminatory. Most people do not think systematically about the world around them. When they see a few exceptions, they think they see a rule. They think, for instance, that the few dozen women and Black members of the House of Representatives show that women and Blacks are represented, and fairly, in the United States Congress. But a few cases cannot make a rule or disprove one—at most, they merely indicate that no rule is absolute. The success of a few token Blacks or women may actually hinder equality by making us think that discrimination no longer exists.

Tokenism With regard to the sexes (and races), granting a few women (or Blacks) high-level positions to indicate that the system operates fairly and without respect to sexual (or racial) status.

The Mass Media

Look at relevant statistics describing what men and women do in their daily lives. Listen to what people—lots of different kinds of people—say to one another. Talk to them about what they think. Look at television commercials, magazine advertising. Inspect photographs, letters, films, jokes—any cultural products of our society at all. Find out who says what, who does what. Catch some people at a time when they are making an important decision, embarking on a new path in their lives—say, a significant career move. Find out who makes what decisions, on what basis, in whose interests. Everything you scrutinize will say basically the same thing: In this society, a woman has importance mainly as a wife and mother. Men are important mainly because of what they do in the marketplace.

Although the mass media project an image that is half fantasy and only half reality, they both reflect and influence real-life social behavior. Unlike real-life behavior—which is submerged, fleeting, and difficult to study—the mass media's imaginary vision of life can easily be pinned down and studied systematically. Sex roles in the mass media have, in fact, been studied extensively (Busby, 1975; Goffman, 1979), and the studies show that women appear chiefly in secondary, dependent roles. They catch husbands, get married, do housework, change diapers, prepare meals, serve men coffee, etc., etc., etc. Men tend to be shown in far more independent roles. They achieve; they are active and strong—or become so if they purchase the right product—they seek adventure; they work for a living; and they are served, sought after, and loved by women. When the mass media show women who work for a living, they work at jobs subservient to men, as secretaries or airline attendants, or they deal with children (as schoolteachers, for example), or they work in the "helping professions" as nurses or social workers. Women almost never give orders to men in television commercials: They almost always take orders, except in household matters, an exception that reinforces the truism that women's "place" is in the home.

Consider the findings of one study of television advertisements (Dominick and Rauch, 1972). Of all the females in these TV ads, 38 percent were shown inside the home, compared with 14 percent of the men. Men were much more likely to be shown outdoors or in business settings than women were, and twice as many women as men were shown with children. For men, forty-three different occupations were recorded; for women, only eighteen. And of the nearly 1,000 voice-overs, only 6 percent used female voices.

Another study, of more than 1,000 television commercials, found that nearly half of these commercials were severely restricted. A third of the women were shown doing household tasks; a third, as "domestic adjuncts to men"; and about a sixth (17 percent), as sexual objects for men. Less than one-half of 1 percent (0.3 percent) of these portrayals "showed women as autonomous people, leading independent lives of their own" (Hennessee and Nicholson, 1972, p. 12). "Watching commercials," the authors of this study write, "is like being blasted by some casually malevolent propaganda machine dedicated to the humiliation of women" (Hennessee and Nicholson, 1972, p. 13).

The mass media are controlled by a fairly small number of people, who tend to be relatively conservative in outlook and wish to market products that reflect mainstream values. Bombarded by products that reflect the *status quo*, the public is in effect "conditioned" to accept it. Such products have an especially profound effect on children. With this in mind, Linda Busby (1975) examined children's television programs on the commercial networks, hoping to determine the roles men and women played. She found the following: When compared with the females, the males were more ambitious; less affectionate; less sensitive; more competitive; more adventuresome; more realistic; more knowledgeable; more violent; more independent; more active; braver; stronger; more aggressive; less emotional; more sturdy; more dominant; more logical; bolder; more individualistic; more outgoing; more often leaders; more patient; and more bossy. When compared with the males, the females, consequently, were less ambitious; more affectionate; more sensitive; less competitive; less adventuresome; less realistic; less knowledgeable; less violent; less independent; less active; less brave; weaker; more submissive; more emotional; more fragile; less dominant; less logical; more timid; less individualistic; more often homebodies; more often followers; less patient; and less bossy.

In a detailed study of how men and women are depicted in magazine advertisements, sociologist Erving Goffman discovered some of the following:

> (1) overwhelmingly a woman is taller than a man only when the man is her social inferior; (2) a woman's hands are seen just barely touching, holding or caressing—never grasping, manipulating, or shaping; (3) when a photograph of men and women illustrates an instruction of some sort the man is always instructing the woman—even if the men and women are actually children (that is, a male child will be instructing a female child!); (4) when an advertisement requires someone to sit or lie on a bed or a floor that someone is almost always a child or a woman, hardly ever a man; (5) when the head or eye of a man is averted it is only in relation to a social, political, or intellectual superior, but when the head or eye of a woman is averted it is always in relation to *whatever* man is pictured with her; (6) women are repeatedly shown mentally drifting from the scene while in close physical touch with a

Sex on a Stamp

In 1981, the British Post Office released two stamps bearing an official portrait of Prince Charles, eldest son of Queen Elizabeth II, and his bride, Princess Diana, standing together. In the portrait, the Prince towers over his wife; the top of her head barely reaches his chin. Those who have seen the royal couple were puzzled by the stamp because Charles and Diana are almost the same height: The Prince is 5′11″ tall, the Princess 5′10″.

In the photograph that served as the basis of the stamp, the Prince was standing on a box—hence, his seeming height advantage. Why? An official statement issued from Buckingham Palace claimed that British stamps always bear a silhouette of the monarch in the upper right-hand corner. In this case, the silhouette had to be located right above Princess Diana's head, which meant that a blank space had to be created there—hence, the height discrepancy (Tower, 1981).

Some sociologists argue that relative size is a way of expressing or reinforcing differences in power and prestige. Men are typically taller than women, though some women are taller than some men. But they are hardly ever depicted as taller, except when men are shown to be subordinate in some crucial respect (Goffman, 1979, p. 28). Thus, a woman who is shown to be as tall as a man would not be regarded by observers as inferior in status and might actually be regarded as dominant. Had Prince Charles and Princess Diana been shown to be about the same

Cambridge Essex Stamp Company, Inc.

height—as they are in real life—this equality would imply that the Princess is not inferior in status.

Which argument makes the most sense to you: the demands of the design of the British stamp or the need to depict Prince Charles as superior in rank to Princess Diana?

---

male, their faces lost and dreamy, "as though his aliveness to the surroundings and his readiness to cope were enough for both of them"; (7) concomitantly, women, much more than men, are pictured at the kind of psychological loss or remove from a social situation that leaves one unoriented for action (e.g., something terrible has happened and a woman is shown with her hands over her mouth and her eyes helpless with horror) (Gornick, 1979, p. viii).

Women, then, are depicted in the media as helpless, unserious, weak, and protected by men—in fact, much like children (Goffman, 1979). Although controversy still prevails over the extent to which the media influence our attitudes and behavior, it is clear that they reflect a social relationship in which women are the inferior party.

Consider, too, the roles played by women and little girls in children's preschool and school picture books. Usually, these books are given to children, not chosen by them, at a time when they are working out their own sexual identities. One study (Weitzman et al., 1972) found that girls and women are above all sharply underrepresented in the titles, central characters, roles, pictures, and plot lines of these books, which had about eleven times as many male as female characters. Females, the researchers concluded, "are simply invisible . . . often play insignificant roles, remaining both inconspicuous and nameless." Any child who reads children's books would be "bound to receive the impression that girls are not very important because no one has bothered to write books about them" (Weitzman et al., 1972, pp. 1128, 1129). Those girls and women who did get into these books are overwhelmingly *passive*. And this passivity has serious consequences. "Stories [the researchers write] have always been a means for perpetrating the fundamental cultural values and myths. Stories have also been a stimulus for fantasy, imagination, and achievement. Books could develop this latter quality to encourage the imagination and creativity of children" (Weitzman et al., 1972, pp. 1147–1148).

Still, times are changing. Pressure from the women's movement and from women editors has forced publishing companies to include more women in their children's books, to present these women in a wide range of activities—not just stereotypical ones—and to avoid sexist language. Consider, for instance, a passage from a children's book published in 1960, and the same passage as published in 1978. The 1960 version read as follows: "Most of the work of looking after passengers is done by women called stewardesses. The job of a stewardess is to make people comfortable. She helps people who are old or sick, and women with babies. Many stewardesses are very pretty. But it takes more than a pretty face to make a good stewardess." The same passage published in 1978 read as follows: "Most of the work of looking after passengers is done by women and men called flight attendants. The job of flight attendants is to make people comfortable. They help people who are old or sick, and help parents with children. Many flight attendants are very good looking. But it takes more than good looks to make a good flight attendant" (Collins, 1978).

It costs a lot of money to write, edit, produce, and purchase nonsexist textbooks, so many school districts are hanging on to their old ones, sexism notwithstanding. Besides, it may take a generation to complete valid studies of the newer books' impact on sex roles (Collins, 1978).

THE FUTURE OF SEX ROLES

"You've come a long way, baby," proclaims a commercial advertising a brand of cigarettes aimed at women smokers. The advertisement is silly, but it is perfectly true that when cigarettes were first sold commercially, men objected to the women who smoked them. Comparisons between the position of women today and in the past are important because they can tell something about the future of sex roles.

Such comparisons do not, however, point in a single direction. At least one observer (Harris, 1975) believes that male supremacy is "on the way out," that it was useful for a brief period in human history, but no longer serves any evolutionary purpose. Others believe that male supremacy is necessary, and that efforts to introduce sexual equality will lead to "sexual suicide" (Gilder, 1975).

Even if we cannot tell *how* sexual relations will change in the future, we can see with our own eyes that they have changed and are changing. At one time, American women could not vote, or work in most occupa-

A small number of women are entering professions that were once exclusively male. In many astronaut crews, women are full and equal partners with men.
NASA

tions. Male supremacy was certainly more complete in the nineteenth century than it is today. Visitors from abroad commonly remark—often critically—on the freedom and independence of American women. To these visitors, it seems that American women have almost been granted equality with men. But a glass that is half full is also half empty—it depends on your perspective. Few feminists doubt that American women have won rights that they did not have in the past and that women in most other countries do not have today. But these same feminists believe that social change has been too slow in the United States, and too "cosmetic," or too superficial.

Conscious efforts have been made, with the government's support, to eradicate certain aspects of sexual inequality in a few countries— Sweden, the Soviet Union, and the People's Republic of China, among them. None has attempted to eliminate all aspects of sexual inequality, and none has been a complete success. Perhaps a look at the Swedish example will show us possibilities for our own future.

No Western government has attempted to eliminate sexism more vigorously than Sweden has. In 1968, the government officially proclaimed that men and women should have the same rights and "the same responsibility for the upbringing of children and the upkeep of the home," and that "achieving this equality would require a radical change in deep-rooted traditions and attitudes." The government even insisted that "active steps must be taken by the community to encourage a change in the roles played by both" men and women (quoted in Camerini, 1976, pp. 277–278).

Such steps were taken, yet in the 1970s, only 57 percent of adult Swedish women worked, as compared with 86 percent of Swedish men. Part of the problem was the government's failure to provide enough day-care centers; despite an official ideology that makes childrearing a joint responsibility of husbands and wives, most Swedes still see it as women's work. Although the government provides a paternity leave program allowing fathers to take seven months off from work—at 95 percent of full salary—to raise their children, in 1976 only 7 percent of all eligible

WHAT DO YOU THINK?

Gender Inequality in Education and the Economy: Is Full Equality Just around the Corner?

When the 1980s are compared with the 1970s with respect to a wide range of measures of equality and inequality, it is extremely difficult to deny that more gender equality exists in the area of economic life now than in the past. This is true in nearly all the nations of the industrialized world. The Organization for Economic Cooperation and Development (O.E.C.D.) compared men and

Percentages of Female Students in Colleges and Universities

	1970	1982/1983
Australia	33	46
Austria	29	41
Finland	48	48
Japan	28	35
Netherlands	28	42
Sweden	42	46
Switzerland	23	33
United States	41	51
West Germany	27	42

Average Hourly Earnings in Nonagricultural Activities of Full-Time Female Workers as a Percentage of Those of Men

	1970	1981
Australia	65	86
Austria	68	72
Britain	60	70
Finland	70	77
France	79	80
Netherlands	73	77
Sweden	80	90
Switzerland	63	68
West Germany	69	73

Percentage of Men and Women of Working Age Who Are Employed

	Men		Women	
	1975	1983	1975	1983
Britain	92	88	55	58
France	84	79	50	52
Japan	90	89	52	57
Netherlands	83	80	31	39
Sweden	89	86	68	77
United States	85	85	53	62
West Germany	87	80	50	50

fathers actually took the paternity leave (Tavris and Wade, 1984, pp. 345–346). In high school, girls continue to select subjects according to traditional patterns—mostly the humanities, social studies, nursing, and clerical and other "service-oriented" fields, overwhelmingly taught by women. Male students mostly take courses in math, the natural sciences, women on three such indicators: the percentage of students enrolled in universities and other institutions of higher learning, the average hourly pay of workers, and the percent of each sex who are employed. For each of these indicators in nearly all industrialized countries, there was greater gender equality over time.

In nine of the countries examined by the O.E.C.D. in 1970, women comprised a third of all students enrolled in universities; by the early 1980s, this figure had climbed to 43 percent. (And in the United States specifically, this figure was a majority.) The average hourly earnings of women workers in nine countries was just under 70 percent of that of male workers in 1970; by the early 1980s, this had grown to 77 percent for these nine countries. In the period between the 1970s and the 1980s in seven countries of the industrialized world, male employment slipped by an average of three percentage points, from 87 percent of adult men to 84 percent. During this same period, women's employment actually rose some 5 percentage points, from 51 percent to 56 percent of adult women. Clearly, these indicators point to considerable progress in closing the gender gap in education, wages, and employment in just one decade or so. Can full equality be just around the corner?

Many experts argue that this is not a reasonable expectation for the forseeable future; for the remainder of the century, at the very least, some measure of gender inequality will continue to plague the women of the industrial world. In fact, it is entirely possible that full gender equality is an unattainable goal. In the words of one observer: "Throughout the industrial world, women are catching up with men in education and earning power. But if some current trends continue, they may never achieve equality" (Lewis, 1986).

Here are some indications that point to this conclusion:

Although women have achieved parity or near-parity in university enrollment in the United States, Canada, and the Scandinavian countries, their numbers are lagging in several other countries, such as Japan, Britain, and Switzerland.

Women still tend to be underrepresented in each nation's most prestigious institutions of higher learning, such as France's "grands écoles," and are much more likely to attend schools that do not lead to high-paying, rewarding careers.

Whereas men dominate the sciences, engineering, business, and the law in university studies, women tend to concentrate in literature, languages, and education—majors that are less likely to lead, again, to high-paying, rewarding careers.

Legislation providing for equal pay for equal work has been enacted in twenty-four of the countries belonging to the Organization for Economic Cooperation and Development. Yet significant income disparities between men and women persist.

Though women's employment has been rising in the face of a decline in manufacturing world-wide, most of the positions that women fill are service jobs that require few skills and pay comparatively poorly.

In any job category, women tend to be paid less than men for the same work. Women tend to be kept longer in less lucrative positions and to receive fewer promotions and less overtime pay.

The Organization for Economic Cooperation and Development concludes its report on gender inequality with the following gloomy words: "Serious inequalities between girls and boys and between men and women persist. . . . A serious gap remains between official objectives [proclaiming gender equality] and actual practice" (Lewis, 1986).

Is gender equality in the industrial world's future? Or will inequality between men and women in education, income, and employment be a permanent fixture of our society? What do you think?

Source: Lewis, 1986, p. 20E.

technology, and engineering—all mainly taught by men. "It is obvious that girls are not being sufficiently stimulated to pursue studies leading to more skilled or nontraditional careers" (Camerini, 1976, p. 281).

In the best-paid government administrative posts, only 2 percent of the officials are women; but in the lowest-paid positions, 76 percent are. In 1976, only two out of eighteen cabinet ministers, 20 percent of the members of the national legislature, and 15 percent of the members of local-government bodies were women (Camerini, 1976, pp. 282, 283). A detailed study of the division of household tasks in Uppsala, a city in Sweden; in three Soviet cities; and in Helsinki, the capital of Finland, found almost no differences at all (Haavio-Mannila, 1975). In all three nations, most women did the traditionally female tasks. The women always prepared breakfast for 76 percent of the Swedish couples, prepared dinner for 86 percent, did the daily cleaning for 80 percent, and fed small children for 70 percent. The figures were almost identical for Finland and the Soviet Union. "Househusbandry may be an approved way of life in Sweden, but it is far from a popular practice" (Tavris and Wade, 1984, p. 346).

Similar conclusions may be drawn from two experiments in sexual equality: the Soviet Union and China. In the former, women tend to be overrepresented in the lowest paid, most menial occupations; the high-status, more highly paid jobs are almost totally monopolized by men. Very few women hold positions of power in the government or the Communist party. Of 360 members of the Central Committee of the Communist party, only fourteen are women (Mandel, 1975). Although three-quarters of all Soviet physicians are women, physicians there are not as well trained and are paid less than their American counterparts.

In China, some 90 percent of all women work outside the home, and there is a fairly extensive network of nurseries and day-care centers attached to the factories, hospitals, housing projects, and businesses where the parents work (Tavris and Wade, 1984, p. 343). Still there is almost no sexual activity before marriage; rural families, even today, generally prefer to have sons; significant pay differentials still exist between men and women who do the same work; many jobs (for example,

Most men are still not ready to share equally in the performance of household chores, even if their wives are employed outside the home. There is a growing number of exceptions to this rule, and, one day, most households may be completely egalitarian.

Ken Karp

Many feminists argue that social change has been too slow in coming and too "cosmetic" once achieved. Other observers think the move toward sexual equality has been dramatic and unprecedented, and that full equality is inevitable. Which view do you share?

Bettye Lane/Photo Researchers

primary school teachers, day-care attendants, and nurses) are filled almost exclusively by women; and women are still a tiny minority in top political circles. Even so, mainland China's approaches toward sexual equality have been impressive because they have been made so quickly: In 1949, at the time of the communist revolution, China was among the most male-dominated societies in the world.

These cross-cultural examples teach us valuable lessons. First, government sponsorship of sexual equality has an impact but cannot change the personal relations of men and women—not very quickly, at any rate—or dramatically change the sexual distribution of powers and rewards. Second, these three cases show that fundamental social change must take time to effect—perhaps several generations—and can only be effected unevenly.

Sex roles are not isolated from the other social and cultural institutions. Eliminating sexual inequality will require comparable changes in other spheres of life, particularly the economic one. There are small but definite causes for optimism. Couple by couple, household by household, office by office, company by company, profession by profession, women are winning equality with men. Full sexual equality will not be achieved in this century, but milestones in that direction will be detectable each day, month, and year. The signs are unmistakable; progress, though slow, is inevitable. Sex roles have changed more in this century than in the previous 10,000 years. The glass is half full, not half empty.

SUMMARY

1. All societies, past and present, have regulated the behavior of women and men.

2. These sex-linked rules are justified as based on the intrinsic nature of the sexes; to deny that they are natural and inevitable is to deny one's biological "destiny."

3. *Sex* refers to the organic characteristics of males and females—mainly genetic, anatomical, and hormonal.

4. *Gender* is a sociological concept that refers to the roles the sexes are expected to play in society.

5. The dominant sociological view of sex and gender maintains that many of the differences between men and women are cultural in origin; "nurture" can usually overcome the few significant "natural" differences that exist between the sexes.

6. Gender is socially constructed: We learn what society expects of men and women, and we act accordingly.

7. Recent theories that attempt to overemphasize the role of biology in male-female behavior are often misleading.

8. Margaret Mead's study of sex and temperament in several New Guinea tribes demonstrates the malleability of sex roles.

9. Sex-role assignment is evidenced in the economic activity of men and women the world over: Although a few of these activities are assigned exclusively to one sex or the other, most are distributed fairly evenly.

10. Likewise, the proportion of women in the labor force varies from one society to another. In some parts of the world, most adult women work, whereas in others, only a tiny proportion do so.

11. There is an income gap between men and women working in industrial societies; women tend to be paid less, even for the same job. This gap occurs at every educational level.

12. The jobs women do most are strongly sex-segregated: Women work at a smaller number of different jobs than men do.

13. Each job has its own "sexual funnel": In every profession, the higher the occupational position, the lower the proportion of women.

14. There are several explanations for this "sexual funnel": direct and indirect discrimination, a stronger expectation that women

will assume full domestic and childrearing responsibilities, the lack of a "mentor connection," diminished expectations, and tokenism.

15. One of the most remarkable changes in the workplace in recent years is the huge increase in the number of women working for a living, including women with young children.

16. The "gender gap" in income between men and women may be narrowing, but at an extremely slow rate.

17. In addition, the occupational distribution of men and women working in certain jobs is changing, although slowly. Change has been dramatic in certain occupations, but nonexistent in others.

18. Women are depicted in the mass media, for the most part, in traditional, sexist terms.

19. Economic and occupational discrimination against women serve a number of functions for the capitalist economy.

20. Several nations have pledged to eliminate sexism, but inequalities still remain in these countries.

21. Full sexual equality is probably inevitable, although attaining it will be a long, slow process.

SUGGESTED READINGS

James A. Doyle, *Sex and Gender: The Human Experience.* Dubuque, Iowa: William C. Brown, 1985.
    A textbook covering a wide range of aspects of gender and sexuality. The first part examines the subject from a variety of perspectives: the biological, psychological, sociological, and anthropological. The second part examines gender and sex in a number of areas of life: power, language, education, work, religion, politics, the family, and mental health.

Ethel Klein, *Gender Politics: From Consciousness to Mass Politics.* Cambridge, Massachusetts: Harvard University Press, 1984.
    Raises the question of why the feminist movement emerged and grew in the 1960s and 1970s and not earlier. Argues that major factors influenced the deterioration of the traditional image that women are only wives and mothers: the entry of women into the labor market, decreased fertility, a longer female life span, and a higher proportion of women who remain single. A necessary precondition for the emergence of the women's movement was the acceptance of the cause of sexual equality by the general public, a condition, the author argues, that was met in the early 1970s.

Jean Lipman-Blumen, *Gender Roles and Power.* Englewood Cliffs, New Jersey: Prentice-Hall, 1984.
    This book argues that relations between women and men make up a blueprint after which all power relationships are patterned.

Not everyone will agree with the author's thesis, but it is well argued and worth reading.

Ruth Schwartz Cowan, *More Work for Mother: The Ironies of Household Technology from the Open Hearth to the Microwave.* New York: Basic Books, 1983.
    Argues that, far from saving time and permitting women to do other things, so-called labor-saving devices have actually added to the domestic chores of women by raising the standards of adequate housework.

Hilda Scott, *Working Your Way to the Bottom: The Feminization of Poverty.* Boston: Pandora Press/Routledge and Kegan Paul, 1984.
    Almost half of all families living in poverty are headed by women. Out-of-wedlock births are increasing strikingly. The divorce rate is inching perilously close to one marriage in two. This book explores these and other trends of the recent economic plight of women.

Carol Tavris and Carole Wade, *The Longest War: Sex Differences in Perspective* (2nd ed.) New York: Harcourt, Brace, Jovanovich, 1984.
    A first-rate, highly informative, detailed evaluation of sex roles and sex differences. Probably the place to start in any examination of the subject.

chapter 12

AGING

A lthough we age from the moment of conception to the moment of death we do not normally talk about aging children. For most of us the term "aging" carries some connotation of decline or deterioration in health and vitality. Most people think of aging as something that happens to us somewhere after middle age, although we are not very precise in specifying when this begins. Given the fact that the median age of college students is 22 and that only a few college students are beyond the age of 35, why should they be at all concerned with aging? Because, however young they may be now, they all hope to live to old age. Moreover, if they do live to old age this period will be just as important a part of their total lives as childhood, adolescence, or adulthood. Successful adjustment to old age will be just as important a part of their life histories and personal well-beings as adjustment to adolescence.

Today, most Americans who survive the first and most dangerous years of their lives will live to reach old age. This was not always so. In 1900 the average life expectancy at birth for women in the United States was 51 years; for men, 48 years. By 1984 life expectancy for women had increased to 78.3 years; for men, to 71.1. While life expectancy had generally increased by twenty-five years, the sex difference in life expectancy had increased from 3 to 7.2 in favor of female longevity.

Both the number and percentage of the total United States population living to 65 and beyond have increased dramatically since 1900. In 1900, 3 million Americans were over age 65, and they comprised approximately 4 percent (one in twenty-five) of the total population. In 1970, 20 million Americans were over age 65, and they comprised approximately 10 percent (one in ten) of the total population. In 1980, 25,544,000 Americans were over 65, and they comprised approximately 11 percent (one in nine) of the total population. Demographers estimate that, by the year 2000, 36 million Americans will be over age 65, and they will comprise approximately 13 percent of the total population, and that, by the year 2030, 64 million Americans will be over 65, and they will comprise approximately 19 percent of our total population (U.S. Bureau of the Census, Social Security Administration).

At age 65, Americans are confronted with a series of developmental and adjustment problems. Most older persons experience strong inducements from employers to retire at age 65 or before. Retirement brings a loss of status, privilege, and power that were associated with one's position in the occupational hierarchy. A major reorganization of life must take place because the 9 to 5 workday is now meaningless. Those whose identities and personalities were shaped by the demands of their occupational roles will be forced to change their definitions of self. There can be a considerable degree of social isolation if new activities are not found to replace work-related activities. Finally, individuals must often search for new identities, meaning, and value for their lives (Cox, 1984, pp. 11–12).

The reorganization of life that takes place at the time of retirement can be viewed in light of both gerontology and geriatrics. Gerontology studies the social, economic, political, and related social aspects of aging; geriatrics is a branch of medicine that deals with the problems and diseases of old age.

In sorting out the problems of old age, gerontologists often have difficulty with the mind-body dualism observed by the early philosophers. Events in one's social life, such as the loss of a lifelong marital partner, can lead to loss of the will to live and the onset of a series of physical and medical problems. Conversely, certain physical disabilities, such as diabetes, prostate trouble, or arthritis, may diminish one's capability to assume the role of husband or wife and so alter one's social world. The physical and social adjustment of older Americans are often interrelated and difficult to separate.

Growing old is physiologically inevitable, and it is commonly experienced as a progressive decline in organic functioning and as a gradual decline in sensory and cognitive capacities. These losses, however, vary considerably from individual to individual, and there is no predictable pattern by which all individuals will experience these losses.

AGING AS A SOCIAL PROBLEM

Even though aging is an irreversible biological process, the ways people grow old are influenced by social and cultural factors. Three main social factors affect the aged in the United States (Atchley, 1978). The first is our confusing system for defining who is old and who is not. The "official" age for an "old" person in America is 65, the Social Security system's age of eligibility for retirement benefits. Otherwise, the age of 65 has no special meaning. Different people age at different rates, so chronological age is not a consistently accurate measure of aging. It is possible to be a "young" 65 and an "old" 55. Yet most Americans think of age 65 as the time when physical and mental signs of old age begin to take their toll. People of that age are thus thought to be "old," regardless of how much (or little) they have really aged.

Second, in our country, the economic system is based on the assumption that everyone can and should get an adequate income from work. This implies that everyone is physically able to work, to live in a household independent from others, to get to work, and so forth. Many old people, however, can do none of these things. Others are removed from the labor force by mandatory retirement and are thus required to live on pensions and savings. The result? Income for Americans aged 65 and over is half that of Americans aged 55 to 61 (U.S. Department of Health and Human Services, 1981). Many older Americans live below the poverty line because they depend on Social Security and on pensions that do not keep up with inflation. Older people living on fixed or slowly rising incomes during a period of inflation cannot always buy enough food, shelter, clothing, and heat. For some 80 percent of all retired Americans, Social Security benefits are the only source of income (Atchley, 1978).

The third social factor that affects aging is that poverty itself speeds up with the aging process. Premature aging is most common among the poor, perhaps as a result of the stresses of lower-class living (Atchley, 1978). Many older persons become dependent on other people or on welfare agencies, and this dependency can promote psychological difficulties. Even with Medicare—public health insurance—millions of our old people cannot get adequate health care because they still lack money or mobility, and because Medicare does not cover preventive care, eyeglasses, and dental care. "American society still has a great distance to go in meeting the health-care needs of its old people" (Atchley, 1978, p. 11). The aged in America, particularly if they are poor, have great difficulty coping with the problems that accompany the aging process.

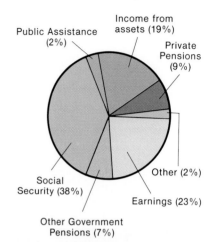

Percent of Aggregate Money Income of Older Persons by Source

Income from assets (19%)
Public Assistance (2%)
Private Pensions (9%)
Social Security (38%)
Other (2%)
Earnings (23%)
Other Government Pensions (7%)

Source: Chartbook on Aging in America. *Compiled by Carol Allan and Herman Brotman. Published by the White House Conference on Aging in America, March 1982, p. 61.*

AGEISM

One social problem that confronts the aged and only the aged is **ageism:** prejudice and discrimination against older people because they are old. Ageism embodies a negative stereotype that depicts the aged as ill, tired, sexless, mentally slow, forgetful, grouchy, withdrawn, unproductive, isolated, defensive, and self-pitying (McTavish, 1971, p. 97). Many older people are none of these things, yet the negative stereotype of old age is widespread and resistant to change (Larson, 1978; Ward, 1979; Atchley, 1980). Only rarely in modern times does age produce respect; most societies view it as absurd, revolting, or tragic (Ward, 1979). This stereotype not only assigns the elderly to an inferior social status, but it may also have created an irrational fear of aging (Neugarten, 1971).

Even though this stereotype may be inaccurate, it is a reality in the minds of the people who accept it. General attitudes and opinions and, sometimes, even behavior are based upon it. One study of humor, by Erdman Palmore (1971), clarifies some common social attitudes toward aging. (Humor can be an important indicator of attitudes, because it usually reflects social stereotypes.) Palmore analyzed 264 jokes about old people. More than half were clearly negative. The most disparaging jokes were those dealing with physical abilities, personal appearance, concealment of age, mental abilities, and "old maids." Jokes about old men, especially jokes in which male "old-timers" still performed sexually, tended to be much more positive than jokes about old women. Most jokes about concealment of age made fun of women's attempts to appear younger.

Two age groups appear to have the most negative attitudes toward old age: young adults and middle-aged adults. Children have little negative feelings about the old: They usually think that old people are "good" and "wise," and that they lead "happy" and "exciting" lives (Thomas

Ageism The prejudice and discrimination that aged persons face because their role in society is not valued.

and Yamamoto, 1975). This research suggests that most people adopt the negative stereotypes of aging as they themselves begin to feel threatened by age. As people grow older, they feel less attractive and, perhaps, less important.

Our attitudes toward old age, and toward the other stages in the life cycle, are not entirely consistent. In 1975, the Harris poll asked two groups of Americans, one aged 18 to 64, the other 65 and older, which had been the "best" and "worst" years of their lives. Those aged 18 to 64 ranked the 20s as the best age, followed by the 30s. Persons 65 and over rated the 30s as the best age, with the 20s and 40s tied for second place (see Table 12–1). People aged 18 to 64 regarded the 70s as the worst age—closely followed by the teens. The group of individuals 65 and over also considered the 70s to be the worst age—followed by the 60s. The respondents in the Harris survey believed that each stage of life has both negative and positive features. Teenagers have little responsibility and pressure, as compared with older people, and are thus more free to enjoy life. Yet they are often unstable and rebellious. The respondents viewed the 40s and 50s as a time of financial security, wisdom, and experience but also as a time when health might begin to decline. The 60s and 70s brought with them diminished responsibility and renewed opportunities to enjoy life, provided people of that age were not ill, poor, lonely, or immobile. Older people were thought to be "friendly," "warm," and "wise from experience." For many older people, the age of retirement and freedom from responsibility may indeed be pleasant. Yet overall, the social image of aging is not a positive one.

Sources of Ageism

Why? What are the sources of these negative attitudes? There seem to be two (Ward, 1979). First, all societies have values, some of which negatively shape our perceptions of the aging process. Second, these stereo-

▉ TABLE 12–1 Attitudes in a National Sample about the "Best" and "Worst" Years of a Person's Life (Percentage of Population)

	"Best" Years		"Worst" Years	
	18–64	65+	18–64	65+
Teens	16	7	20	10
20s	33	17	5	7
30s	24	22	3	5
40s	13	17	3	3
50s	3	8	6	4
60s	1	6	12	14
70s	0	2	21	21
Other	1	2	6	7
Wouldn't choose any age	7	15	17	22
Not sure	2	4	7	7

Source: Louis Harris and Associates, Inc. The Myth and Reality of Aging in America. *A study prepared for The National Council on the Aging, Inc.,* Washington, D.C., 1975.

325

typic views are often false and frequently result in the elderly's being seen as inferior by others in society. Finally, we fear old age and the problems we associate with it (Ward, 1979).

Aging and Social Values. The stereotype of old age reflects what we as a society value and what we fear to lose (Ward, 1979). One of the things we value is productivity, or active work. We fear to lose the role of productive and active contributors to society. Modern societies, like ours, remove the aged from the mainstream of social activity, through planned retirement, usually when older people are no longer responsible for childrearing, financial support, and the other tasks central to family life. The good news is that they get the freedom to pursue their own interests and enjoyments, without work and family responsibilities. Nevertheless, retirement is a status that is not particularly important in achievement-oriented societies. In essence, the elderly go to the sidelines, while younger people assume the active social roles that are rewarded by our social system.

Americans are expected to be active, achievement-oriented, and productive. Older people generally do not meet these expectations. Ours is a youth-oriented society, as most consumer goods and advertising attest. Therefore, to be old is to enter a stage of life that is socially devalued because the aged no longer fully participate in normal adult roles.

This youth-oriented society emerged in the recent past. To show how it did so, in *Growing Old in America* (1977), David Fischer examined the impact of modernization on the elderly. In colonial days, less than 2 percent of our population was 65 and older. Mortality rates (see Chapter 18) were high and old age relatively rare, so colonial Americans regarded the aged as special. Elders were placed in charge of the churches and held the important positions in the meeting houses. The old were esteemed not just out of affection or deference to age but even along religious lines. Retirement because of age was unheard of, so the elderly leaders of the church and community usually continued in office until they died.

Not all of the elderly were regarded with veneration, however. The elderly upper classes were held in high esteem. The aged poor, in contrast, were scorned. Nonetheless, the general lot of the aged in colonial times was one of authority and respect—and it was reinforced, among the affluent, by the fact that land was usually owned by the oldest male, which thus forced his younger relatives to treat him with respect, if not fear.

The cult of old age was weakened in the eighteenth and nineteenth centuries, and eventually replaced by a cult of youth. Wealth replaced age and inherited social position as the chief qualification for leadership; fashions became oriented toward youth; and derogatory terms were coined, like "gaffer," "codger," "fuddy-duddy," and "geezer," which poked fun at older people. With the establishment of mass education for the young, and retirement programs, residential separation, and diminished income for the aged, older people were pushed into a lower status. The country turned to youthful heroes: Daniel Boone, Andrew Jackson, the defenders of the Alamo, George Armstrong Custer, Teddy Roosevelt, and the like.

Stereotypes of the Elderly. The ageism that exists in our society today results in a number of stereotypes about age that simply are not true. Perhaps one of the most common stereotypic views of the 65 plus group in America is that all old people are alike. This simply is not the case.

Some older people find it difficult to cope with the aging process. They feel alienated, lonely, and deprived of a meaningful existence. Poverty compounds these feelings and has been shown to hasten the aging process.

Charles Gatewood

Some Facts and Figures on the Elderly

As we see in more detail in Chapter 18, the population of the United States is getting older. In 1820, the median age of all Americans was 16.7—half the population was older and half was younger. In those days, the infant mortality rate was extremely high, many women died in childbirth, and very few people lived to a ripe old age. By 1920, the median age of all Americans had risen to 25.3, and by 1981, to 30.3. An increasingly greater proportion of the population is surviving to old age. Population experts predict that by the year 2000, the median age will be 36 years, 38.4 by 2010.

Today, just over one American in nine (11.4 percent) is 65 or older. The state with the oldest residents is Florida; its median age is 34.7, and 17.3 percent of its population is 65 or older. The youngest state? Alaska, with a median age of 26.0, and only 3 percent 65 or older. Women, as we all know, live longer than men: 9.3 percent of the male population of the United States is 65 or older, but 12.6 percent of the female population is. Women are about twice as likely to reach the age of 80 as men are. Whereas almost four out of five men aged 65 or over (79 percent) are married, only half as many women (39 percent) are.

Only one elderly man in six (17.8 percent) is employed, and only one elderly woman in thirteen (7.7 percent). Roughly one out of every seven men aged 65 or older (14 percent) and four out of every ten women of that age (41 percent) live alone. The median income of such "unrelated individuals," as the government calls them, was $5,746 for men and $4,957 for women, in 1981.

The government classifies a quarter of these men (24 percent) and a third of these women (32 percent) as impoverished. Overall, slightly fewer than one person aged 65 and over in six (15.7 percent) lives in a household below the poverty line—38 percent for the Black elderly and 31 percent for the Hispanic elderly.

Source: Statistical Abstract of the United States, 1982–1983, pp. 26, 28–29, 30, 31, 442.

There is considerable variation in the world of the aged. One elderly person may be living in a one-room apartment in downtown Detroit, attempting to survive on a meager Social Security check. Another elderly person may have a condominium in Miami, Florida, where he or she spends the winters and a cabin in Canada, where he or she spends the summers. To think of these two individuals and their lifestyles as being anything alike is simply an error (Cox, 1984, pp. 16–17).

Another common stereotype of the elderly is that they are isolated. A small proportion of the elderly are isolated; they spend almost their entire time within the confines of a house or apartment. The majority of the elderly, however, are married, independent, and mobile. They visit friends and family throughout the community, are active in social clubs, entertain, and travel. The view of the elderly as sick, feeble, and homebound is simply not an accurate picture of the majority of elderly people in the United States today.

A third common stereotype of older people is that retirement is a period of crisis and adjustment that is forced on them by their employers. In actuality most of the elderly look forward to retirement and, if given the choice, will retire early. James Schultz found that of every 1,000 retirees, only seventy were forced to retire. The remaining 930 apparently chose their retirements voluntarily (Schultz, 1980). Herbert Parnes reports that, in his study of retirees, seven out of ten had retired before age 65 (Parnes, 1981, p. 27).

Another common misconception of the elderly is that retirement undermines the physical health of the person and often leads to death.

Many, upon observing an acquaintance, friend, or relative die shortly after retirement, presume that retirement shortens life. What is misunderstood is that at any age some people will die, whether working or not. Longitudinal studies indicate that most retirees show a slight improvement in their overall health following retirement and that there is no difference in the mortality rate for this group and those remaining in the labor force. Retirement simply does not precipitate death (Parnes, 1981, pp. 93–131).

Fear of Aging and the Aging Process. The third source of our negative perceptions of old age is our fear of age and of the evils we associate with it: low income, poor health, loneliness, senility, and death. To be old, most of us feel, is to be retreating from life, little by little. Some people thus struggle to maintain their youthful looks and attitudes as long as they can, in order to avoid recognizing the plain fact that they are indeed old.

The onset of old age comes at different times for different people. We do not know the exact cause of the aging process. The two leading theories state that aging may largely be due to deterioration in the space between the cells of one tissue and those of another, or to some form of preset genetic program. Even if the onset of aging has a single cause or related set of causes, the course of the aging process involves biological, genetic, social, and psychological factors. Once begun, the single most obvious sign of aging is the appearance of the skin, which tends to dry out and wrinkle. Sight and hearing are sometimes impaired. Muscles start to shrink and become weaker; joints stiffen and swell; the heart, lungs, kidneys, and bladder operate at lower levels of effectiveness. The body's output of hormones begins to diminish, too, and the body becomes increasingly susceptible to stress, infection, and, especially, to such degenerative diseases as cancer, heart disease, and diabetes. The aging process makes death inevitable for all kinds of life.

Most of us become aware of the aging process during middle age (40 to 55) (Cox, 1984). At this point, many people have less energy than they had in the past, and they begin to pursue intellectual activities instead of physical ones. Their work careers usually reach a plateau, and most of their children will have left home. Death now becomes a reality, not just something that happens to other people.

Later maturity (55 to 75 years) is troubled by a marked reduction in energy, vision, and hearing. Chronic health disorders become common. Income is reduced by retirement, and the deaths of friends and relatives curtail social interaction. Most women are widows by the time they are in their mid-60s. The period of later maturity can nonetheless be pleasant for those who plan for it, keep their vigor and spirits, and are prepared to make use of their new-found free time. Older people who begin second careers may even continue to be highly productive members of society.

Old age (75 and over) is more likely than all other stages of life to be a time of loneliness, boredom, and diminished intellect and self-esteem. Older people take longer to respond to stimuli and to recall recent events, probably because the aged are *more easily distractible* than younger people. Memory of past events, in fact, is usually quite good. Considerable memory loss can be a sign of organic brain damage, but even though this is more common *in older people*, it does not occur in all of them. Alzheimer's disease, which is becoming widely studied by the medical community, is one of the diseases associated with organic brain damage. There are no known cures for Alzheimer's disease today. Another particular problem for the elderly is physical frailty and the possibility of being so disabled that physical mobility must be restricted or denied.

Physical and mental infirmities—the reality of being tired, ill, dependent, and closer to death—can and do produce severe depression among the elderly. Old age is thus a time of life that many people fear, yet it happens to all those who live sufficiently long. And many of those people manage to keep enough vigor and mental awareness to enjoy themselves. Old age can be a pleasant time of life, but often it is not.

ADJUSTMENT TO OLD AGE

So far, we have found that although aging and the devalued social role associated with it are widely feared, it has some positive aspects, too. What's more, old age affects different people quite differently.

Age alone does not make men and women happy, intelligent, and healthy, or unhappy, senile, and sick (Neugarten, 1971). Bernice Neugarten and her colleagues carried out a longitudinal study, which followed the adaptational patterns of about 2,000 persons aged 70 to 79 over a period of fifteen years. Three principal areas of life were examined: personality, life satisfaction, and activity. The researchers concluded that the aged can be divided among four major personality types: (1) integrated; (2) defended; (3) passive-dependent; and (4) disintegrated.

The researchers found that a majority of the aged in their sample managed to maintain "integrated" personalities. These older people took great satisfaction in life; had good cognitive (intellectual) abilities, self-confidence, and maturity; and were open to new experiences. One subtype among people with integrated personalities consisted of those the researchers called "reorganizers," who engaged in a wide variety of activities, such as business and community affairs. The second subtype, the "focused," comprised people who remained active, but only in a few select roles. The third subtype, the "disengaged," took satisfaction in their lives but were not highly active. Despite their apparently high self-esteem, they had voluntarily withdrawn from role commitments and were content with the "rocking-chair" approach to old age.

The researchers called the second major personality type the "defended." These were hard-driving, ambitious, achievement-oriented people who were very defensive about aging. The defended personality group comprised two major subtypes. First, the "holding on" group continued to work hard and to maintain relatively high levels of activity, in hopes of getting satisfaction from life. Next were those defended personalities described as "constricted"—people who used diet and exercise to try to defend themselves against aging. They minimized any kind of social activity or interaction in which they might be seen as old or inferior. They hoped against hope to maintain youthful physical appearance.

The third major personality type among the aged consisted of those the researchers described as "passive-dependent." There were two subtypes common to this group. "Succorance-seeking" individuals had a strong need to be dependent and to have other people respond to them. Somewhat active, they seemed to adjust to aging in a positive manner as long as they had other people to depend on. The other subtype—a relatively rare one—comprised the "apathetic." These people were pas-

WHAT DO YOU THINK?

Golden Sunset

The American divorce rate is now at an all-time high. Yet a century ago, when divorce rates were vastly lower than they are today, few couples lived long enough to celebrate their fortieth or fiftieth wedding anniversaries. Today, many do. What characterizes the marriages that survive?

Gerontologists—researchers who study the elderly—find that such marriages tend to fit one or two basic types: the "golden-sunset" couples, whose members are extremely happy with each other, and "survivors," whose marriages have lasted from sheer endurance rather than a sense of satisfaction. Golden-sunset couples say that their marriages have improved with each passing year. Survivors say, "Well, we made it" (Sweeney, 1982).

Today's elderly grew up at a time when divorce was not an option. Judy Todd, a psychologist at California State University at Dominguez Hills, who studied older couples, explains: "When we asked why they didn't divorce, they looked at us really puzzled. . . . They had never thought of it" (cited in Sweeney, 1982). In the future, there will be fewer survivors and more golden-sunset couples, because the survivor types will divorce rather than endure unsatisfying marriages.

What makes for "golden-sunset" marriages? One factor, according to Professor Todd, is that couples with less rigid sex roles are happier. When the men do many things traditionally done by women, and vice versa, the cou-ples "had more enthusiasm for each other, more growth and change" (Sweeney, 1982). The golden-sunset couples did not worry about "who's boss."

Many couples with children have so little time to themselves that communication between husband and wife declines. By the time the children are old enough to leave home, husband and wife have become "intimate strangers." Spouses must often get reacquainted. "They may go through some real anxiety, depression, conflict, and sweat, but as they do they reach a new stage of marriage that's far better than anything they had before," one gerontologist explains. "Not very many—twenty-five percent—can manage to do that. Some split up. Most just avoid the whole thing" (Sweeney, 1982). Certain couples find that they stuck together mainly because husband and wife wanted the approval of others and adhered to stereotyped role expectations. They stuck together because they believed they were expected to. But the "golden-sunset" couples, who had vital marriages, "were tolerant of differences in others and were concerned with their own values and each other's needs" (Sweeney, 1982). The other factors that make for "golden-sunset" marriages? Researchers point to strong commitment to the spouse as a person, good communication, shared decisions, and mutual support and respect.

Consider a specific case: Ruth and Hal Axe "are deeply, demonstrably in love. They hold hands, ride their tandem bicycle from their Los Angeles home to the beach and sing each other's praises like a blissfully happy, newly wed couple." Hal, 80, a retired high school math teacher, and Ruth, 78, a retired reading teacher, have been married for fifty-four years. Both are physically active. Ruth wrote a biography that is about to be published in its second edition. She swims twenty laps a day in their backyard pool. They share such hobbies as bicycling, classical music, and sailing. A few years ago, they rode their tandem bicycle twice from San Francisco to Los Angeles, a distance of more than 400 miles. Ruth Axe explains the secret of their success: "We're terribly interested in the other's viewpoint, even if it differs. I feel that much of the basis of our happiness is that we have learned to listen to each other." Arguments can frequently degenerate into a question of, "Am I going to win or is she?" Hal comments. "If you can avoid that . . . it makes it a lot easier. Marriage is more apt to be happy if each builds up the other," he adds. "See how Ruth builds me up. That's wonderful, and I like to build Ruth up. It makes me so happy when Ruth is happy. That's part of the things that help make our marriage so beautiful." Ruth Axe summed it up by commenting: "We're a mutual-admiration society" (Sweeney, 1982).

Source: John Sweeney, "Long Marriages—Good and Bad" (Part II), *Newsday*, August 23, 1982.

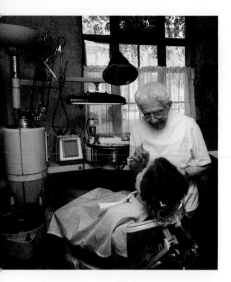

Researchers find that a large proportion of the aged take great satisfaction in their lives, maintain their intellectual ability, retain their self-confidence, and are active and vigorous. Here, an 86-year-old dentist practices his craft.

Blair Seitz/Photo Researchers

One theory of aging holds that we age in ways that are consistent with the attitudes and personalities we develop as young people. Old age, then, is just the predestined end of youth and adds little to our overall make-up.

Bjorn Bolstad/Photo Researchers

sive, had little interaction with others, engaged in few activities, and seemed to have little interest in life.

The fourth major personality type among the aged was the "disintegrated." Very few people belong in this category, which comprises all those who demonstrated gross psychological disorganization and could live outside institutions only because of family help or because other people in their social networks tolerated them.

Neugarten's typology of aging may not be complete, by the way; Neugarten admitted that there may be other personality types, other patterns of aging, among the aged. Nor do all specific individuals fall neatly into one category or another. This typology, like all others, separates out patterns that, in real life, are usually combined. Its value is its ability to make us see differences among people who may be superficially similar.

Neugarten came to two main conclusions. First, she pointed out that older people deal with aging in a great variety of ways. Variation, not similarity, seems to be the rule among the aged and, according to Neugarten, may become even more pronounced in the future. The reason: Past studies of aging have often included people who were poor, foreign-born, and poorly educated. As those Americans who have enjoyed the relative affluence and high educational standards of the midtwentieth century grow old, they will demand greater freedom to choose their own lifestyles.

Neugarten's second major conclusion was that men and women age in ways that carry forward the attitudes and personalities they developed as young people. When we look into it, she found, we usually find that whiny, defensive, silly, and unhappy old people were once whiny, defensive, silly, and unhappy young people, too. Likewise, if we have self-confidence, judgment, and good humor today, we will probably have them when we are old. There is little or nothing about the process of aging itself that imparts any particular emotional color to old age. Old age is just the predestined end of youth and does little more than develop any virtues and vices we may have picked up en route.

Personality is not the only variable that helps us understand how different older people adjust to aging. Three especially significant variables are health, sex, and socioeconomic status. Several studies suggest that health is the most important single determinant of an elderly person's self-assessment (Ward, 1979). Pessimism about health seems to generate anxiety and poor adjustment to aging; optimism about health, an absence of these problems. As for sex, denial of aging appears to be more typical of women than of men. Research shows, for instance, that women generally perceive the onset of old age later than men (Drevenstedt, 1976), a tendency perhaps related to American sex-role stereotypes, which equate female beauty and sexuality, on the one hand, and youth, on the other. With very few exceptions, older women are not perceived as "beautiful," although older men often qualify as "distinguished." Older men marry younger women much more often than younger men marry older women.

The third important variable is socioeconomic status. The assumption that old age is a great leveler because it affects rich and poor alike is not necessarily true (Hochschild, 1973). To coin a phrase, "'Tis better to be old and rich than old and poor." The upper social classes tend to live longer than the lower classes do, and the shorter a person's life expectancy, the poorer that person's health and morale. Lower-class people may begin to "feel" old at earlier ages than people who are better off.

Aging in Japan: A Contrast

We have seen that, in the United States, modernization diminished the social status of the aged. Japan, too, is a modern country, yet in Japan, the elderly still enjoy a high degree of respect. Richard Cohn (1982) investigated this situation in order to test Donald Cowgill's (1974) theory that modernization is a disaster for the elderly—that the more modernized a society, the lower the status of the elderly. Cowgill's theory does fit the general pattern of development in most modern nations, including ours; Cohn found that it does not fit Japan. Japan has a slightly higher proportion of older workers than other countries do, and the elderly are more likely to be employed there, too. But these conditions do not, in Cohn's view, exempt Japan from the rule that modernization hurts the status of the aged. What has? Japan has an institutional system of permanent employment. Employees of large companies usually remain with the same employer until retirement, which in most Japanese firms comes at the age of 55 (see Chapter 17). Cohn insists that permanent employment gives older workers an established position in Japanese businesses, and this keeps their status high.

Another important factor that works to the same end is Japan's ancient tradition of Shinto, a religion strongly influenced by Confucianism and ancestor worship. Confucianism defined the elderly as wiser and thus superior to the young; ancestor worship, which attributes certain dark powers to the dead, also had the effect of raising the status of the aged. Since 1963, Japan has even had a national holiday, Respect for the Elders Day, that commemorates the elderly. Japanese children are taught to be respectful to the old; seats on buses and trains are reserved for the elderly. The elderly in Japan are also much more likely to live with their children than the elderly in other countries—about 75 percent of all elderly Japanese live with their relatives, compared with only 18 percent of aged Americans (Palmore, 1975)—and they are much more likely to fulfill important functions in the family, such as child care and housework, so that many Japanese women with preschool children can work outside their homes (Morgan and Hirosima, 1983). Clearly, the aged Japanese have greater social status than the aged in Western nations. Modernization does not explain everything.

Stereotypes of the elderly in the United States are usually negative. In our youth-oriented society, the elderly are often demeaned or neglected. In contrast, the elderly in Asian countries tend to be treated with dignity and respect, even by the very young.

A. I. Parnes/Photo Researchers

SOCIOLOGICAL THEORIES OF AGING

How do people grow old? What experiences do the aging share? Do the aging experiences of the elderly differ along key dimensions, factors, or variables? Social scientists have developed several theories to explain the social role of the aged and the processes that generate the role. Four of the most influential are disengagement theory, activity theory, continuity theory, and age-stratification theory. Each has its own special strengths and weaknesses.

Disengagement Theory

Disengagement theory, which stems from the functionalist perspective (see Chapter 1), is the most influential—yet also the most controversial—theory in social gerontology, the study of aging. Disengagement theory

Disengagement theory The theory that people disengage from society because their social roles require it once they reach a certain age. Disengagement is thought to be beneficial for society because it allows younger people to assume the vacant roles, and older people to withdraw to enjoy the benefits of retirement.

embraces three basic propositions (Cumming and Henry, 1961): (1) The process by which aging individuals withdraw from society is quite normal; (2) it is also inevitable; and, finally, (3) it is necessary for "successful" aging.

All individuals must eventually die. Society's institutions must survive independently of these individuals. This survival maintains social stability and cohesion; it is "functional." Society must therefore have an orderly way of transferring power from the older to the younger members of society. It must phase out those individuals whose sudden withdrawal would be disruptive. The process of phasing older people out from society's mainstream thus becomes institutionalized. Stable norms indicate which individuals should be disengaged and when, and which forms of behavior are appropriate thereafter. Norms, for instance, decree that individuals should retire from work at a certain age; a retirement ceremony often celebrates the occasion. Disengagement, however, is usually not a single event; it is a gradual process that, over time, separates people from their regular social roles and activities.

The withdrawal of society from the individual is only half of the disengagement theory. The other half is the idea that individuals themselves choose to withdraw from certain social roles as they become older. The more roles from which they withdraw, the less they are bound by society's norms. As retired people, they can fill a social role that allows them to become increasingly self-centered. According to disengagement theory, the more fully they assume that role, the more likely they are to be "successful" in retirement.

Disengagement theory is controversial. For example, it does not seem to occur in certain social institutions—political institutions, for instance. The relatively older ages of United States senators and, particularly,

Disengagement theory argues that societies must have a means of phasing out older people from the mainstream. Gradually, the elderly must relinquish power and authority, and take on more marginal roles.

United Nations Photo

United States Supreme Court justices (the average age is 64) seems to cast doubt on the idea that disengagement is a "functional necessity."

Disengagement theory may not adequately account for individual disengagement, either. People who have accepted and fulfilled society's norms for younger people may have difficulty coping with retirement, however "functional" it may be for society as a whole. Far from actively desiring retirement, they may resist it and all other forms of disengagement.

Disengagement theory is important nevertheless because it describes the social processes that sometimes occur when older people, as a result of age, withdraw from their usual roles. The theory is particularly applicable to situations in which retirement is mandatory. It also helps explain those cases of societal disengagement in which the individuals affected accept their new roles. The strength of disengagement theory is that it demonstrates that, in some sense, the interests of society require older people to accept new roles. The result is often the disengagement of those older people. By setting a specific age, usually 65, as the time of retirement, disengagement becomes institutionalized, orderly, and inevitable—just as aging itself is inevitable. For many people, some degree of personal disengagement also appears to be inherent in the aging process.

Activity Theory

Activity theory is essentially an action theory of successful aging (Havighurst, 1963). It makes three basic assertions: (1) most normal aging people maintain fairly constant levels of activity; (2) their engagement with or disengagement from society is influenced by past lifestyles and socioeconomic considerations, not by the inflexible needs of society, as disengagement theory suggests; and (3) older people must maintain or develop substantial levels of social, physical, and mental activity to age "successfully." In Havighurst's view, the norms for old age are identical to those of middle age, whose successes and failures strongly influence the course of the aging experience. Activity theory asserts that those who age successfully behave, as far as possible, like people in middle age.

Some research supports activity theory. A study at Duke University, carried out over a ten-year period, found that older men did not become less active or less satisfied with life, whereas older women did, but to only a small (but statistically significant) extent (Palmore, 1969). Temporarily lowered levels of activity during illnesses were usually followed by increased levels of activity. There was little or no overall change.

These data came from relatively healthy people. Disengagement may thus be more typical of the less healthy. The point, however, stands: Disengagement is not an inevitable result of aging. Throughout the ten-year period of the study, the participants kept up consistently high levels of activity, and those who were more active had higher morale and life satisfaction—happiness, in a word. The study concluded that engagement, not disengagement, was typical of normal aging and that people who have been active in youth and middle age will be active thereafter. Disengagement, when it occurred, usually did so only just before death.

Activity theory suggests that some people—perhaps a majority—do not disengage from society when they become old. If they retire from their occupational roles, they make up for it by engaging in some other type of satisfying activity. So far, so good. But activity theory suffers from two basic flaws. First, it assumes that older people judge themselves

Activity theory The theory that people who kept active are those who age the most successfully.

Activity theory holds that if we are to age successfully, substantial social, physical, and mental activity must be maintained. Here, senior citizens challenge one another to a game of chess.
United Nations Photo

by middle-age standards, and it does not explain what happens if they do not follow these standards. Second, it does not explain what happens to those older people who are prevented from maintaining a middle-age standard of living for physical, mental, or socioeconomic reasons. Like disengagement theory, activity theory explains the behavior of some, but not all, people.

Continuity Theory

Another major theoretical approach to the social experience of aging is based on the idea that the various stages of the life cycle are marked by great continuity (Neugarten, 1964). This so-called **continuity theory** maintains that as men and women pass through the life cycle, they develop relatively stable values, attitudes, norms, and habits, which become an integral part of their personalities. As people grow old, they attempt to maintain these personality traits, and this attempt dominates their reactions to the aging process.

Continuity theory The theory that people have a basic core personality and that their behavior thus continues more or less unchanged as they age.

Continuity theorists do recognize that such personality traits are often modified by experience, because human beings change by adapting to new situations. Some people who look forward to retirement, for example, are not really prepared for it and therefore do not enjoy it. Experience teaches them to change their attitudes—or, if they are wise, to adapt to retirement by learning how to enjoy it.

Continuity theory has the virtue of explaining certain aspects of aging much more fully than disengagement or activity theory can. But it can also be very hard to implement in research (see Chapter 2), because it requires extensive and valid knowledge about individual life histories and attitudes.

Age-Stratification Theory

If you have ever studied Spanish history, you may have run across the term, "The Generation of '98." It refers to a group of Spanish writers who came to maturity at the time of Spain's defeat in the Spanish-

American War, a humiliation that ended centuries of imperial glory. Those Americans who came to maturity in the 1950s are sometimes called "The Silent Generation" because their relative political apathy seemed odd to the members of the "Depression Generation," men and women who came to maturity in the 1930s.

These tags remind us that groups of people born at more or less the same time progress through life together and share common experiences, loves, and hates. At the same time in their lives, they have all been children, teenagers, young adults starting careers and families, middle-aged persons, and old. Such a group constitutes an **age cohort,** which moves through the same life course and shares a common history of past events, like the Great Depression, World War II, the Korean War, and the Vietnam War. Researchers interested in **age-stratification theory** study members of the same age cohorts and also the differences among age cohorts. Take a look at your own family the next time you go to a wedding. Compare the songs played for your grandparents with those the band plays for the bride and groom. Look at the way your parents and other members of their generation dress, and compare it with your own clothing and that of your friends. If you probed more deeply, you would probably uncover differences in political attitudes, sexual behavior, and just about everything else. These differences are the stuff of age-stratification theory.

Age-stratification theory allows us to analyze the social characteristics within and among different age groups, and it illuminates the effect of age behavior and attitudes. To date, it has not been used extensively. More research is needed to test its value.

Age cohort A group of people of the same age who move through the life course together.

Age-stratification theory The theory that allows us to analyze the people who belong to age cohorts that have different characteristics. These differences explain why people of different generations hold attitudes particular to that cohort and dissimilar to other cohorts.

DEATH AND SOCIETY

Death, like aging, generates attitudes and social norms. Phillipe Aries, a French social historian, argues (1974) that in the Middle Ages, Europeans did not worry quite as much about death as we do now. Medieval people did not want to die, or at least they were in no hurry to do so, but when death was near, they seem to have approached it as a familiar aspect of life. Death—the common destiny of our species—was then accepted as a part of the natural order.

Except when death was sudden or unexpected, it usually involved a familiar ritual. First, the dying person was supposed to die in bed. A ceremony was organized by the dying person, who was expected to follow a prescribed sequence of behavior. The dying person was supposed to express sorrow about the end of life and to recollect beloved persons, events, and things. He or she was expected to pardon the (usually numerous) companions gathered around the deathbed for anything they may have done, and then to make a final prayer requesting forgiveness of his or her own sins. After a priest administered the last rites, the gathering waited for death. Dying was a public and familiar act, and the dying person's room was entered freely by relatives, friends, and neighbors. Aries, for example, claims that from A.D. 1100 to 1800, no portrayal of a deathbed scene was without children. Usually, there was no great show of emotion at the deathbed, because behavior was guided by a formal death ritual.

In modern society, we no longer experience death in this ceremonial manner. Nor do we take death for granted. Modern men and women die in fear, anxiety, and isolation. From the Middle Ages on, our attitudes toward death have been changing because (as Aries notes) Western society has gradually come to fear death. One source of this change, Aries claims, was Christianity. Although some early Christian martyrs died without fear—indeed, in joyous anticipation of heaven—Christianity by and large made Westerners fear death by making them fear the Judgment Day, the day when the soul of a newly dead man or woman was committed to hell or to purgatory (and, eventually, to heaven). The security imparted by the collective ceremony of death was in part undermined by the dying person's belief that he or she would soon stand in judgment before the Lord.

Medieval Christianity, thought Aries, was not wholly responsible for the growing fear of death, however. From about 1750 to 1850, the artistic and philosophical movement called Romanticism contributed to this fear by extolling nature and the expression of strong emotions. Death was now regarded as a painful undoing of nature's beauty and joy. Acute fear of death became a social norm because death separated the dying from beloved persons or objects. Later in the nineteenth century, dying people were encouraged by social norms to regret their failure to accomplish all their goals.

"Acceptable" death The modern practice of dying quietly, even though intense anxiety is associated with the event for all concerned. "Acceptable" death reduces social disruption.

By the twentieth century, the collective minds of the West had come to fear death quite thoroughly. Efforts had to be made to control that fear by making death as unobtrusive as possible. The new goal was an **"acceptable" death:** a death that would not be unpleasant for the survivors, an idea whose origin was the medieval belief that each person's death was closely related to that person's life. At the moment of death, it was then thought, the dying person's life flashed before his or her eyes, in a final illumination that provided each life with its conclusion and ultimate meaning. Death was the moment when you truly came to know yourself, or so medieval people thought. To "die well" was thus very important.

The twentieth century took this idea and reinterpreted it, not for the benefit of the dying person but for that of the survivors. Instead of a death marked by powerful—and perhaps disturbing—insights, the men and women of the twentieth century wanted to think of death as calm and orderly, as "acceptable." Death became "forbidden," and modern society sought to hide it. This was the more easily accomplished because, today, fewer than one-third of the deaths in American society take place at home, at work, or in public places.

Most people now die in hospitals. This put an end to the traditional death ritual, because death in hospitals is controlled not by the dying but by their physicians. Death occurs under the jurisdiction of people who are strangers to the dying person, and in a physical location that is quite cut off from the rest of society. Death has been removed from the sphere of the ordinary because it occurs mostly among older people—about two-thirds of all deaths in industrial societies result from biological decay and the ills of old age—something that was not true in previous centuries, when relatively more people died quite young. Older people are more removed from the mainstream of social life, so their deaths are usually less disruptive, and therefore less noticed, than the deaths of younger people.

Modern anxiety has forced society to develop norms and values that push aging and dying out of sight and out of mind. Social life can then continue, while the rest of us try to forget about these experiences.

SUMMARY

1. A major problem confronting old people is ageism, their devaluation by the young, which is reflected in negative social stereotypes of the elderly. These stereotypes are largely inaccurate.

2. Recent research suggests that most older people are relatively happy and satisfied with their lives. Life satisfaction in old age seems to be affected by the variables of health, sex, and socioeconomic status.

3. The most influential theory in the field of social gerontology, or the study of aging, is disengagement theory, which views retirement and other aspects of the disengagement of older people from society as good, both for society and for older people themselves.

4. Disengagement theory has been challenged by activity theory, the idea that activity (engagement) keeps older people happy.

5. Two relatively recent theories—continuity theory and age-stratification theory—offer important perspectives. Further refinement of these theories is needed before their validity can be fully assessed.

6. The aged are not now a genuine minority group in American society, and, as a result, they do not have as much political and social power as their numbers would seem to warrant. Because their numbers are continuing to rise, both absolutely and in proportion to our total population, the aged may eventually represent a much greater social force in our society than they do now.

7. Finally, social attitudes toward death have changed greatly since the Middle Ages. Death is now a cause for anxiety, and societies have tried to reduce that anxiety by putting death out of sight, in hospitals, and out of mind.

SUGGESTED READINGS

Robert C. Atchley, *The Social Forces in Later Life* (3rd ed.). Belmont, California: Wadsworth, 1980.
  An introductory survey of social gerontology intended to provide the reader with an overall view of the field.

Harold Cox, *Later Life: The Realities of Aging* (2nd ed.). Englewood Cliffs, New Jersey: Prentice-Hall, 1988.

Arlie Russell Hochschild, *The Unexpected Community*. Englewood Cliffs, New Jersey: Prentice-Hall, 1973.
  A study of the social relationships among a group of aging women in an apartment house for the elderly in San Francisco. The group developed into a "sisterhood."

Herbert S. Parnes, *A Longitudinal Study of Men, Work, and Retirement*. Cambridge, Massachusetts: MIT Press, 1981.

James Schultz, *The Economics of Aging*. Belmont, California: Wadsworth, 1980.

Jan D. Sinnott, Charles S. Harris, Marilyn R. Block, Stephen Collesano, and Solomon G. Jacobson, *Applied Research in Aging*. Boston: Little, Brown, 1983.
  A guide to methods and resources for students interested in studying elderly persons.

U.S. Population Aged 65 & Older, 1900–2030. Source: United States Bureau of the Census, Social Security Administration.

Russell A. Ward, *The Aging Experience: An Introduction to Social Gerontology*. New York: Lippincott, 1979.
  Another comprehensive review of the literature in social gerontology.

chapter 13
MARRIAGE AND THE FAMILY

In 1983, Royston Potter, an ex-Mormon, was dismissed from a police department in a suburb of Salt Lake City. The reason: He is a polygamist, married to three women at the same time. Mr. Potter says that he took three wives "as a matter of religious conviction. . . ." "It's not so much that you decide that you want one," he explains, referring to another wife. "It's necessary as far as a theology goes." Now a janitor, Mr. Potter is suing to be reinstated in his old job. He maintains three separate residences, and he visits each one "on a rotation-type thing, normally one night at each place." His wives are Denise, 30 years old; Joann, 30, and Mary, 23. Estimates have it that about 20,000 Utah residents are living in polygamous households. Mr. Potter was excommunicated from the Church of Jesus Christ of Latter Day Saints for his polygamous behavior. Mormon spokespersons rejected Mr. Potter's claim to religious righteousness, holding that practices that were acceptable in nineteenth-century Mormonism do not necessarily guide contemporary theology (*The New York Times*, September 12, 1983, p. A16).

Menlo Park, California, is a small, affluent suburb south of San Francisco—the perfect place, its residents claim, to raise children. The three houses occupied by Peter and Karen Ward, Jan and John Lahr, and Sandy Ward, all located within eight blocks of one another, in many ways reflect the upheaval experienced by many American families in the 1980s. Four years ago, Peter was married to Sandy, and Karen was married to John. When Peter and Sandy's relationship disintegrated, Sandy moved out and Peter retained custody of the children. Then John and Karen separated. Karen and Peter then married; she moved, with her children, into Peter's house. And Jan and John then married, moving into his house. Then Sandy bought a house nearby, forming what they now call "the Bermuda Triangle." Five adults share four children, "all of them . . . linked in a new social network, a new American extended family." Home base for the four children, who range in age from 7 to 11, is with Karen and Peter Ward. Every other weekend and one evening a week, the children pair off and spend time with their "noncustodial" parents, John and Jan Lahr, and Sandy Ward, who lives alone. The adults drop off the children at each others' homes. "I think we're very much like the old extended family," Sandy says.

"Some of us get along better than the others, just like in any other family." Although not all of the adults agree, for the most part, the children count their assets. "Hey, did you know I have two mommys and two daddys and two houses and a brother and two sisters and six dogs and a cat and. . . ?" says 7-year-old Nils Lahr (Norman, 1980, pp. 28, 44, 54).

One night, just before the outbreak of World War II, Richard Carmichael brought his seven sons together in the living room of his Springfield, South Carolina, farmhouse. He held a long, thick stick in his hand, and he asked each of his sons to place a hand on the stick. "Now break it," the father commanded. Each of the sons exerted his strength to break the stick, struggling and twisting, but the stick wouldn't break. Then Richard Carmichael took the stick out of their hands and snapped it over his knee. The stick, the father explained, represented the unity of the family. "You are brothers," he said. "You hold together, like this stick. The only one who can break you apart is me." The brothers subsequently contributed $10 each to the family business. Today, they operate a multimillion dollar business operation in Queens, New York. The business includes a service station, a diner, a liquor store, a bus company, and a commercial building. It is very much a family enterprise in that each brother runs a different phase of the operation. When one brother, David, showed up late for work too often and missed too many assignments, he was temporarily banished from the business; he will be invited back only when the other brothers decide he is ready to assume his share of the responsibility.

There are nine Carmichael children, who learn the business by helping out at work, and eleven grandchildren. Several of the brothers have been offered jobs outside the family business; they have always turned such offers down. "If you can do it for someone else, you can do it for kin," one brother explains. Even though the Carmichael brothers have left the farm and lead modern lives in a hectic city, they still own land in the country in which they grew up. "They still return for . . . reunions, and they still cling to those dinner-table lessons about life that were handed down, like property, from grandfather to father to son" (Gross, 1984, p. 29).

Sometimes, it can be misleading to call a diverse institution, like the family, by a single name. For some Americans, the "family" means a father, a mother, and a sibling or two, living together in a stable household. For others, the father is absent much of the time, and the mother is the head of the household. Still other Americans grow up in families that consist of parents, siblings, grandparents, cousins, and aunts and uncles. What some of us have experienced as the family differs quite a lot from what others have experienced.

Anthropologists and sociologists call a family unit made up only of parents and their children a **nuclear,** or **conjugal, family.** Families made up of additional members are called **extended families.** The size of American families varies a good deal, and so does the number of generations that live within them. If we look beyond the borders of the United States, we find that families differ in many other ways, too. In fact, the variation is almost infinite.

Many of us are dimly aware that in some societies, one man may have a number of wives at the same time—an arrangement called **polygyny.** We may also have heard that in a few societies, one woman is permitted to have several husbands at once—an arrangement called **polyandry.** (The more general term, which includes both polygyny and polyandry, is **polygamy;** marriages that involve more than two partners.)

Nuclear family See **Conjugal family.**

Conjugal family A family unit that is made up only of parents and their children; also called nuclear family.

Extended family A family unit made up of more than parents and their children.

Polygyny A marital arrangement whereby one man may be married to more than one woman.

Polyandry A marital arrangement whereby one woman is permitted to marry more than one man.

Polygamy Marriages that involve one individual married to more than one partner.

The traditional extended family consisted not only of parents and their children but also of such relatives as grandparents, aunts, uncles, and also of servants—all living under a common roof. The high divorce rate of recent years has created a "new" extended family, made up of parents who have been married more than once and their children by former husbands and wives.

Michael Philip Manheim/Photo Researchers

And that is only the beginning. Many are the ways in which men and women come together to create the family.

Despite this global variability, the conjugal family, one husband living with one wife and their biological offspring, is the most common family form. Even in societies that permit other forms—in Islamic nations, for instance, a man may have up to four wives—the conjugal pattern is the most frequent one (W. J. Goode, 1964, pp. 46–49; 1982, p. 5). Moreover, the world-wide trend, over time, is clearly toward the conjugal pattern (W. J. Goode, 1963). The sensitive student of the sociology of the family must be aware both of the family's variation and its commonalities.

WHAT IS A FAMILY?

Do we really have to define the family? Surely, "everyone knows." Alas, things aren't quite so simple! The classic definition, offered by anthropologist George Peter Murdock decades ago, described a family as a "social group characterized by common residence, economic cooperation, and reproduction" (Murdock, 1949, p. 1). This definition encompasses polygamous and monogamous unions, as well as conjugal and extended ones. It is a satisfactory description of the overwhelming majority of all those unions that sociologists and anthropologists would call families. However, we do not have to search far and wide for exotic exceptions to discover that not all families share the same residences, that not all cooperate economically, and that not all are involved in the biological reproduction of offspring. Consider the following description of life among the Ashanti, a West African tribal people:

> As night falls young boys and girls can be seen hurrying in all directions carrying large pots of cooked food. One can often see food being carried out

The family is an institution that assigns responsibility for raising and maintaining children to a specific set of parents. No other institution does so well with equal effectiveness, so the family is a true cultural universal: It exists everywhere, in all societies.

Richard Hutchings/Photo Researchers

Family The social institution that assigns responsibility for the physical survival, upbringing, and socialization of children.

of a house and a few minutes later an almost equal amount of food being carried into it. The food is being taken by the children from the houses in which their mothers reside to those in which their fathers live. Thus one learns that husband and wife often belong to different domestic groups, the children perhaps sleeping in their mothers' houses and eating with their fathers (Fortes, 1963, pp. 63–64).

An even more curious case could be found among the Nayar, a people living on the southwest coast of India, before the twentieth century. Nayar women contracted strictly ceremonial marriages before reaching puberty. Their husbands neither consummated the marriages nor lived with them. Immediately after the wedding, the husband disappeared from his wife's life—usually forever. After puberty, the woman had sexual liaisons. However, her ceremonial husband—with whom she had never had intercourse—was the socially acknowledged father of her children. Neither her husband nor any of her lovers owed her or her children economic support, because she lived on an estate that passed through the female line (Gough, 1964).

Although these unusual marital arrangements have by now fallen into disuse, they once prevailed among many peoples around the globe. They leave us, once again, with the unanswered question, What is a family?

Childrearing

The birds and the bees are born knowing what they must do to produce and raise their young. But human beings need rules and regulations to ensure that their children receive care and protection. The **family** is an institution that assigns responsibility for the physical survival, upbringing, and socialization of children. Only by teaching systematic, socially sanctioned norms can a society ensure its own continuity from generation to generation. The family serves this crucial function. In this sense, the family is a cultural universal: It exists everywhere.

Clearly, the concepts of marriage and the family overlap a good deal. Not all married couples will produce a family complete with children, and not all families include married parents. Nonetheless, most married couples throughout the world produce children, and most children are the product of formal marriage agreements. Typically, marriage represents a culturally approved contract geared specifically to the prospect that the partners in the marriage will produce offspring. No society separates these two social institutions, marriage and the family.

In contemporary nation-states, with their formal codes of law, marriages may be either "legitimate" or "common law." Legal marriage is marriage as most of us know it: the proposal, the ceremony, the signing of a formal marriage contract. Common-law marriages just "happen." The partners start living together without, necessarily, intending to get married. After a certain number of years (which varies from place to place) the woman and her children acquire specific legal rights over the name and property of the man, who becomes a husband whether he likes it or not.

Most of the terms of marital agreements involve the relationship between the marital partners and their offspring, not between the marital partners themselves. The specific terms of those agreements vary a great deal from society to society. But all of them attempt to give actual or potential children some sort of a place in the social world. The family is our first and primary link with the rest of society. In some societies, a person has no social existence outside membership in a specific family.

Perspectives on the Family

Every human society has some type of family structure. What does the family offer that is absent in other institutions? The family's role in society has been analyzed quite differently by two major sociological theories. Functionalism argues that the family makes a positive contribution to society as a whole; in contrast, the conflict perspective holds that the family helps preserve existing inequalities and contributes to the exploitation of the powerless.

Functionalism.   Over thousands of years, we have devised social arrangements that make our existence viable. Without these arrangements, our survival would be chancy. Just as we cannot live without food, water, and air, so too we cannot live without cooperation among the members of society. Social institutions are the theater in which the rules of cooperation are acted out. Functionalists view the family as the foundation of any society. It contributes to the social order and makes collective life possible. Some of its functions can be performed by other institutions, but the family appears to perform them most effectively. The very universality and persistence of the family bear witness to its contribution to society.

REPRODUCTION.   Societies constantly need to replace their members from one generation to the next; otherwise they would die out. Men and women can procreate without marrying and without forming a family unit of any kind. In all societies, however, informal arrangements that do so lack full social approval (Malinowski, 1930; W. J. Goode, 1960a, 1977, pp. 374–375).

PHYSICAL MAINTENANCE.   Adults have to be motivated not only to bring forth children but also to care for them and nurture them to adulthood. The family provides what is usually a reliable, stable means of ensuring children's physical survival, because it lays that responsibility on specific parents. No other social arrangement or institution performs the functions of reproduction and physical maintenance quite as well as the family.

SOCIAL PLACEMENT.   Early in life, children are placed in society by their parents' social "locations." Societies have a conservative tendency to maintain themselves, and the inheritance by children of their parents' social positions is one mechanism for ensuring social stability. Achievement-oriented societies, in which adults, through their own efforts, acquire social locations different from those of their parents, require special mechanisms to retain their stability.

SOCIALIZATION.   The process of socialization begins in the family. Children are totally dependent on their parents for nurturance and love and are therefore especially sensitive to parental influences. Families serve the function of passing on a society's culture—its values, norms, beliefs, attitudes, and language. Of course, there are other such agents—peer groups, schools, the mass media—but the family is the earliest, the most fundamental, and, for many aspects of life, the most influential.

EMOTIONAL SUPPORT.   Another essential function of the family is to provide its members with emotional support. It is "a haven in a heartless world"—a place where members can recover from the difficulties and uncertainties of society. Love is unconditional in the family, granted rather than earned—support that makes it possible for us to continue functioning in our other social roles, where people expect us to "perform." The family provides an emotional foundation to human life.

SOCIAL CONTROL.   Last, the family begins the job of teaching us to distinguish right from wrong. Every society needs at least a minimal amount of social control—mechanisms to ensure that members obey the rules. Without effective social controls, a society would collapse into chaos. Everywhere, families serve to keep children in line; thus, everywhere, children get their first taste of rules and regulations from their parents. In this way, the family helps preserve the social order.

Conflict Theory.   Conflict theorists do not assume that any social institution benefits society as a whole. They ask which groups or segments of society profit from the workings of the family—and which lose out. If the family does contribute to the social order, say the conflict theorists, it preserves existing inequities. Therefore, the family helps maintain the privileges of the privileged classes and the subordination of those below them. It locks in the existing class structure.

In addition, say the conflict theorists, the family preserves male supremacy. Men have more power than women because social arrangements and institutions—especially the family—maintain sexism and sexual inequality. Following Marx's collaborator, Friedrich Engels (1970), conflict theorists argue that before the emergence of agriculture, men and women had more or less equal power and status. Women gathered fruit and vegetables and tended small animals; men hunted large animals; both contributed equally to survival. No double standard existed: Men and women were allowed the same sexual privileges, and there was no need for one sex to dominate the other. With the coming of agriculture, men began to take on more essential economic tasks, and women became increasingly dependent on men for survival. "Women's work" did not give them a position of power. Men monopolized the

The functionalists argue that to survive, society must devise institutions and rules that make life tolerable for its members. The family is one such arrangement. It ensures that children will be born, raised, and taught. And it gives comfort to its members in a world that is often cold and heartless. Conflict theorists add that by doing so it helps to preserve social unjustices.

Earl Roberge/Photo Researchers

means of production—the land, work animals, and the plow—and, as a result, they dominated women. Women came to be considered the property of men. Industrialization further entrenched these tendencies, because men worked in factories, while women remained at home as housewives, taking care of their husbands and bringing up another generation of workers (Szymanski and Goertzel, 1979, pp. 285–287, 300).

Some conflict theorists—mostly Marxists—argue that sexual inequality cannot be eliminated until capitalism is overthrown and replaced by socialism. Others—mainly feminists—hold that a vigorous women's movement can eliminate male supremacy, without overturning the present economic system. All conflict theorists agree that alternate family arrangements are needed to liberate us from oppressive tradition (Breines, 1981, p. 4).

LOVE AND MARRIAGE

The Rules of the Game

Every society has rules that govern who may, and may not, marry whom. These rules are of two basic types: exogamy and endogamy. Exogamous rules dictate that each member of a society marry outside his or her social category or group, and endogamous rules require each member to marry within his or her category or group.

Exogamy. The most obvious rule of **exogamy** requires us to marry people of the opposite sex. The **incest taboo,** which forces people to marry outside their own family units, is another exogamous rule, a nearly universal one. (The only recorded exceptions are the royal families of ancient Egypt, Hawaii, and the Incas.) However, the boundaries of the family unit vary from society to society. Some forbid marriages with about half of all the members of a tribe or a village; others exclude only the nuclear family, first cousins on one side, blood aunts and uncles, and grandparents. Even in the United States, the definition of incest varies: Some states allow first cousins to marry; others do not.

It is commonly thought that the incest taboo originated as a means of preventing the disastrous genetic effects of inbreeding. This explanation is faulty, because many societies of the world do not have a clear idea of the facts of biological paternity, let alone of genetics. More likely, the rule developed as a way of clearly demarcating role relationships within the family. If father and son were to compete for the sexual and romantic attentions of the father's daughter, the unity of society's most basic institution would be undermined. If the family was strained by erotic competition, it would become a sexual battlefield, not a force for stability and social order. Moreover, the father's authority would be undermined by his role as his daughter's suitor and his son's rival. The mixing of the two roles—one as a superior, the other as an equal—would hopelessly confuse relationships among the members of the family, because there must be some degree of predictability in relationships.

Endogamy. The rules of **endogamy** are more numerous and far more complicated than the rules of exogamy. Societies everywhere insist that

Exogamy Marrying outside one's own group or category.

Incest taboo A rule prohibiting family members from marrying or having sex with one another.

Endogamy Marrying within one's own group or category.

Homogamy The tendency for people with similar characteristics to marry one another.

members marry within certain boundaries. Social rules attempt to prevent marriages—and even, typically, sexual contact—between individuals of different age categories, ethnic groups, races, religions, social castes, and social class. **Homogamy** is the technical term for the old maxim, "Like marries like,"—that is, the tendency for people with similar characteristics to marry one another. Social rules create pools of eligible marital partners—young men and women who obey society's marital norms by making endogamous marriages. Over time, parental control of their children's selection of mates seems to have broken down, and, as a result, the traditional rules of endogamy seem to have lost force. But these rules still exist and still partly govern our choices.

Most Americans think that they are free to date and marry more or less whomever they please. After all, isn't love "blind"? Yes and no. It is true that, in America and in western Europe, as well, love is almost universally considered to be a requirement for marriage. It is also true that Western society was, until recently, the only culture that regarded romantic love as a legitimate basis for marriage (W. J. Goode, 1959, 1973, pp. 245–260); other societies assumed that love would develop after marriage; and still other societies consider love to be beside the point. Love is unstable, disruptive, sometimes maddening. Often, it is a threat to order and stability, the foundations of family life and of society itself. Most societies have therefore preferred to base marriage on such considerations as social respectability, social alliances, property, or the support of marriageable daughters. Romantic love has existed throughout the world, but for most societies, it was not a sound reason for two people to marry.

Everywhere, however, prearranged marriages are giving way to greater freedom of choice, and romantic love is gradually taking over as a legitimate justification for marriage—or as a requirement for it. But even in the United States, love is not blind. We tend to fall in love with and marry people who are similar to ourselves in predictable ways. Despite the old proverb, "opposites attract," the facts suggest that most marriages take place between people who are no more than a few years apart in age, belong to the same races and religions, have about the

The rules of endogamy require the members of a society (or of any group within it) to marry within the group, however defined—by age, race, religion, social class, or anything else. In the United States, such rules are applied most strictly to race.

James Fotte/Photo Researchers

Katrina Thomas/Photo Researchers

same amount of education, are roughly equal in physical attractiveness, and belong to the same social class.

Like Marries Like

With parental control and even influence constantly diminishing, why should these decidedly unromantic considerations continue to guide our choice of mates? Isn't it a contradiction to say that romantic love is the main justification for marriage and also that unromantic forces tend to determine whom we marry?

No. You need not be scheming, materialistic, or prejudiced to marry largely within your own social group or category. Nor need you be a slave to social pressures. Cupid's wings usually flutter only around certain kinds of people, and for several very specific reasons.

First, we must separate those characteristics that are universally recognized as "hierarchical" from those that make people different, but not necessarily better or worse. Hierarchical characteristics include wealth and attractiveness, because nearly everyone agrees that it is better to be rich than poor and better to be physically attractive than ugly. Nonhierarchical characteristics include religion and, to a large extent, ethnic-group membership. For instance, in the United States Protestants, Catholics, and Jews typically do not assert that one denomination is better than others, but parents of each faith often do argue that their children would get along better with spouses of their own religions.

Dating and Courtship as Exchange. Courtship and marriage may be looked upon as a kind of *market, exchange,* or *bargaining system* for characteristics that most of us want (Waller, 1937, 1970, pp. 169–180; W. J. Goode, 1977, pp. 376–379; 1982, p. 52). Every potential partner has a certain "price" on the marriage market; in other words, potential partners (and their parents) will regard others as relatively desirable or undesirable insofar as they have certain traits or characteristics. Young men and women are ranked according to certain qualifications and they feel—as their parents do—that they should marry individuals of at least equal standing in this ranking system. People who are ranked more or less as equals—who command the same "price" in the dating and marriage market—end up being matched with each other. An unusually handsome young man from a poor family may marry a less attractive young woman from an affluent family. In this case, the two parties have "exchanged" their valued qualities and characteristics. Without doing so consciously, each has added up his or her total "value," arrived at a "price," and sought out a partner who can "pay" it. (W. J. Goode, 1964, p. 36).

Of course, some people violate this ranking system. Sometimes, love is truly "blind." Remember, too, that everyone's personal value and ranking system is to some extent unique. A certain woman may value a man's sense of humor more than any other quality; a certain man may above all wish to find a wife who shares his interest in *Spiderman* comics. And the value systems of men and women are not identical. Men stress the physical attractiveness of a potential partner more than women do; women are more likely to be concerned with intelligence, considerateness, and sociability (Berscheid, Dion, Walster, and Walster, 1971, pp. 179–180)—and also a man's career prospects.

PHYSICAL ATTRACTIVENESS. In our society and time—especially among adolescents and young adults—physical attractiveness seems to be the quality most desired in wives and husbands. Everyone may wish to date the most attractive man or woman around, but in reality we tend to date only those whom we regard as roughly equal to ourselves in attractiveness. Because men stress looks more than women do, they are more likely to miscalculate their attractiveness to women than the other way around.

One study (Silverman, 1971) sent teams of observers—two men and two women—into bars, social events, theater lobbies, and other places where dating couples appeared in public. The research teams each independently rated the dating partners for attractiveness on a five-point scale. In 60 percent of the couples, the partners were separated by a half a point or less, and in 85 percent of the couples, by one point or less. No couple was separated by more than 2.5 points. The researchers also recorded whether or not the couples engaged in various kinds of intimacies—holding hands, walking arm-in-arm, and so on. Sixty percent of all the couples that were matched in physical attractiveness engaged in some form of physical intimacy, but only 46 percent of the moderately similar couples, and 22 percent of the couples that were not well matched in physical attractiveness, did so.

Looks can be regarded as a kind of "master trait," because it assumes central importance in the minds of a majority of the people in our society, especially during courtship. We believe that attractive people have many desirable personality characteristics and are more likely to secure good jobs, experience happier marriages, be better parents, be happier, and lead more fulfilling lives (Dion, Berschied, and Walster, 1972). Do these stereotypes have a grain of truth? No matter. The important thing is that they are widely believed and therefore have great impact on mate selection in the United States. Courtship is a kind of "flesh market." Physical appearance has more influence on the choice of an eventual marriage partner than does any other single factor.

SOCIAL STRATIFICATION.   A second factor, not quite as clearly hierarchical as looks, but hierarchical nonetheless, is stratification—the income, power, and prestige of a potential spouse's family and the career prospects of the potential husband. In high school, dating tends to take place between members of the same social class. In one study, 61 percent of the partners in all dates belonged to the same social class, and 35 percent belonged to the class next to that of their date (Winch, 1962).

Here, as with looks, the matching and exchange process can be detected even in this early stage of courtship. When boys dated across class lines, in two out of three cases they dated a girl from a lower class position; but when girls dated across class lines, they "dated up" in two out of three cases. Boys and girls who "dated up" had some special quality: The girls were unusually attractive; the boys were outstanding athletes (Hollingshead, 1949, pp. 230–232). These girls and boys "were able to gain the advantage of dating with a person in a higher class position by offering in exchange another valued trait" (W. J. Goode, 1964, p. 33).

Among college students who attend a school away from home, social-class background tends to be less powerful, and more subtle and indirect, than it is for young people who do not go to college at all and for those who go but continue to live with their parents. Away from home, the dating behavior of young men and women cannot be closely scrutinized by parents, friends, and the community at large. When a young man tells his date that his father—who may live 2,500 miles away—is a carpenter, a physician, or a ditchdigger, this fact does not have as much impact on her as it would if she lived in her date's community and had to deal with the reality of his social position on a daily basis.

Nonhierarchical Characteristics.   Physical attractiveness and, to a less extent, social class are hierarchical factors in courtship and mate selection. Certain other characteristics are not necessarily regarded as good or bad, but as "just different"—that is, they are not regarded as good or bad by everyone in a given society. Greek-Americans may or may not believe themselves to be "better" than other people, but many of them still want to marry other Greek-Americans, as do Catholics, Protestants, and Jews. To begin with, most people find it easier to meet potential spouses with similar backgrounds and to get along with them—to find areas of common interest. Most people also feel a certain social pressure, especially from their parents, to date within certain boundaries. The more social characteristics two people have in common, the more likely it is that they will actually meet each other socially, enjoy each other's company when they do get together, and receive approval from others during the dating or courtship process. If we must rely on common sayings "birds of a feather flock together" describes the courtship process much more accurately than "opposites attract."

PROPINQUITY.   Consider the factor that sociologists call "propinquity"— in plain English, "nearness." Studies show that something like half of all marriages between city dwellers unite partners who lived a mile from each other. Of course, neighborhoods tend to be fairly uniform with regard to social class, income, race, and several other factors, so there are many reasons for this correlation. People of higher socioeconomic standing tend to seek their marital partners further afield than do people lower down on the stratification ladder. In one study of unskilled laborers, future spouses had lived an average distance of five blocks apart (Koller, 1962, p. 476; Eshleman, 1985, pp. 285–288). Of course, propinquity plays a major role in the courtship and marriage of college-educated partners, too. But the propinquity of their families matters less than that of their classmates: Students who attend the same colleges are highly likely to date each other and, eventually, to marry. It is impossible to court someone you've never met, and most people do not stray very far afield to mingle socially.

COMPATIBILITY.   Many studies show we tend to enjoy the company of people who are compatible with us, and the more compatible they are, the more we enjoy their company. The things that most of us consider crucial—religion, politics, notions of how men and women should treat each other (equality versus male dominance, for instance), attitudes toward sex, the expression of physical affection and intimacy, childrearing practices, attitudes toward ambition and material success, and so on— vary among different social groups. Social class, for instance, is probably more important as an influence on compatibility than as a means of determining anyone's "value" in the dating market because social class is strongly correlated with beliefs and behavior in many areas of life (see Chapter 9).

The Process of Endogamy

The *process* of endogamy—the tendency to marry within one's own social group or category—is much more complex and subtle than the *rules* of endogamy. Because each of us belongs to many different groups, we must all "marry in" and "marry out," too, particularly in a society like ours, where love sometimes triumphs over class and religion.

But the strongest rule of endogamy is still observed almost universally. That rule concerns *race*. Friends, parents, other relatives, and neighbors—even complete strangers—enforce this rule vigilantly. Both Blacks and whites face a great deal of social pressure not to marry into the other race. But whites are much more hostile to interracial marriage than Blacks are. When a random sample of Americans was asked, "Do you approve or disapprove of marriage between whites and nonwhites?" twice as many Blacks (66 percent) as whites (32 percent) approved. Whites were almost three times as likely to say they disapproved—58 percent as against 21 percent (Gallup, 1979, p. 218). Until 1967, interracial marriages were actually illegal in some states. With or without such laws, the rule of racial endogamy clearly has an impact, albeit a diminishing one, on marriage patterns in the United States. In 1960, there were a total of 148,000 interracial marriages in the United States; by 1970, 310,000; and by 1984, 762,000 (*Statistical Abstract of the United States, 1986*, p. 36). Although the increase has been dramatic in absolute terms, interracial marriages still constitute only slightly more than 1 percent of all marriages.

The most potent taboo seems to surround Black-white marriages, which make up less than one out of four of all interracial marriages (175,000 out of 762,000). Somewhat more common than Black-white interracial marriages were white-Japanese and white-American Indian marriages, although Blacks are much more numerous in our society than either Japanese-Americans or American Indians. The explanation, probably, is that whites are much more hostile to Black-white marriages than to any other kind of racial exogamy. For this and for other reasons, Black-white marriages are about one and a half times more likely to

Men and women who share common social characteristics are more likely to meet, more likely to enjoy each other, more likely to date, more likely to date seriously, and more likely to get married than are men and women who lack social bonds.

Southern Living/Photo Researchers
Will McIntyre/Photo Researchers

end in divorce than white-white and Black-Black marriages (Reiss, 1980, p. 336). At first glance, it might seem that the extremely high incidence of interethnic marriage invalidates the principle of homogamy. (See the accompanying box, "Interethnic and Interracial Marriage in the United States.") Although ethnic barriers have broken down to an unprecedented degree in the United States today, they still operate—more weakly than in the past, to be sure. Individuals marrying today are still more likely to marry people who have the same ethnic backgrounds as they do, on a statistical basis, than they are to marry people of any other ethnic background. For instance, Americans of full or partial Italian ancestry make up roughly 5 percent of the United States population (or 11.6 million individuals). If the principle of homogamy did not operate, we would expect interethnic marriages to represent no more than 5 percent of all marriages involving Italian-Americans. In truth, the figure is between 40 and 50 percent—considerably higher than it was in the past, but much lower than it would be if marriages took place randomly with regard to ethnicity.

Sex Ratio and Group Size.   The rules of endogamy—even racial endogamy—lose a great deal of force when few eligible partners of the "right" ethnic, racial, religious, or social class are available. Men and women may then have to choose between marrying out or not marrying at all. In the nineteenth century, something like nine out of ten Chinese immigrants to Hawaii were men, because the time and expense of bringing a bride from China were usually too great. Many Chinese men therefore married Hawaiian women, custom notwithstanding.

The sex ratio is not the only factor increasing the chances of racial and ethnic out-marriages. Another is group size. Some groups are simply too small in number to support endogamy. For instance, in communities in which Jews form a tiny minority, their rate of marriage with non-Jews is much higher than in communities with large numbers of Jews.

Letting Love Happen.   Romantic love is a powerful, even central, force in mate selection. But many factors channel and limit its role. Love is not a bolt of lightning out of the blue. To be sure, love has an irrational, accidental quality. Still, we can only fall in love with someone we meet, and we tend to meet and date—and, even more, date "seriously"—people who are similar to ourselves in key ways. Usually, we "let love happen" only within specific social limits, within a "pool of eligibles." Who is in that pool? Who is excluded? The answers derive partly from cultural and partly from personal notions of the sort of person who would be an appropriate "match."

THE MARRIAGE RELATIONSHIP

The United States has one of the highest rates of marriage in the world—close to 95 percent. In Sweden, Ireland, and several Caribbean nations, such as Jamaica, 20 to 30 percent of the population never marries. (However, in some countries, "common-law" marriages, though common, are not included in the official statistics.)

WHAT DO YOU THINK?

Interethnic and Interracial Marriage in the United States

Joseph Giordano lives with his wife and nine children in a suburb of New York City. They are ethnically intermarried. Mr. Giordano's ancestry is Italian; his wife, Mary Ann's, is Irish, Scottish, and Dutch, "with the Irish predominating," she says. Mrs. Giordano grew up in a totally Irish neighborhood. "I remember everyone was horrified when one of the houses across the street was sold to an Italian family. Those differences were important back then, but Joe and I haven't experienced anything like that kind of negative response." None of their neighbors seems to care what their ethnicity is nor that their national origins are different. The Hurds, married for twenty-three years, have not always had the same kind of acceptance. Hugh Hurd is Black; his wife, Merlyn, is white. They live in New York's Greenwich Village. "I don't notice it anymore," Mrs. Hurd says, "but I used to be able to see the look of curiosity or shock as we walked along the street. . . . Once, we looked a long time for an apartment, and I was the one who rented it. But when the landlord first saw us together, I almost had to give him smelling salts." Mr. Hurd feels that, in his present environment, his marriage is no longer much of an issue; they both feel that there has been "a tremendous amount of change" on the issue. Still, he feels discriminated against in subtler ways, like catching a cab. Mr. Hurd rejects the term "interracial" to describe his marriage: "It's an arbitrary distinction, used simply to maintain differences." Mrs. Hurd adds, "I think we are all one race" (G. Collins, 1985). Do most Americans agree with this assessment?

In 1980, for the first time, the United States Census asked questions about national origin of the nonforeign-stock American population. (The Census is still not permitted to ask questions about religion, however, so intermarriage between religious groups could not be studied from the 1980 Census.) Previous censuses had asked questions about the country in which someone was born, and the country in which his or her parents were born, but none had asked about the ancestry for third-or-more generation Americans. This new information sheds light on interracial and interethnic marriage in the United States. Doing a secondary analysis of the Census data, sociologist Richard Alba paints a truly remarkable portrait of the relationship between marriage, race, and ethnicity in the United States.

No major surprises emerged on interracial marriage from a study of the 1980 Census. As we might have expected, racial barriers to marriage are still formidable; interracial marriages, although increasing in number, are very rare. About 99 percent of non-Hispanic whites marry non-Hispanic whites. Among Blacks, 97 percent of men and 99 percent of women marry other Blacks. For both categories, however, younger individuals are strikingly more likely to out-marry than older ones. For the generation born 1920 or before, the rate of out-marriage is about one-half of 1 percent. For the generation born after 1950, however, the rate is 2 percent for whites, 6 percent for Black men, and 2 percent for Black women. Crossing racial lines to choose a marital partner is much more common for three other racial categories: Just under 30 percent of Hispanics marry non-Hispanics, just under 30 percent of Asians marry non-Asians, and just over half of American Indians marry non-American Indians. Thus, Indians, Asians, and Hispanics readily marry outside their racial categories, whereas Blacks and whites are extremely unlikely to out-marry. Many factors contribute to this pattern, including group size. Among these factors, the strength of cultural taboos cannot be discounted.

The real news to emerge from the 1980 Census, however, was about marriage across ethnic lines. Ethnic barriers, so rarely breached in the past, have crumbled with respect to marriage. Interethnic marriages are now more common than marriages to individuals who share entirely the same ancestry. Particularly noteworthy was the extraordinarily high rate of interethnic marriage among whites that prevailed in the United States. (A similar analysis of ethnic groups among Asians, Indians, Hispanics, and Blacks was not conducted.) In

1980, marriage across ethnic lines among whites was not only common—it was the norm. Only one out of four American-born whites of non-Hispanic heritage (or 27 percent) was married to someone with an ethnic background identical to his or her own. Nearly half (46 percent) are married to spouses with no ancestry at all in common. And 27 percent are married to individuals whose ancestry overlaps partially. This tendency to out-marry ethnically among native-born Americans of European ancestry is strikingly more likely the younger the individual is, and strikingly more likely among some ethnic groups than others. For instance, among individuals entirely of Italian ancestry, about 60 percent born in 1920 or before married others also entirely of Italian ancestry; for those born after 1950, this figure was only 20 percent. Among individuals entirely of Polish ancestry, the comparable figures were 50 percent and 10 percent. On the other hand, ethnic groups that are larger and whose residences in the United States stretch back many generations—for instance, the English, Irish, and Germans—have had a mixed ancestry for some time; for them, change is likely to be more gradual, and, hence, the differences between older and younger generations is small and sometimes nonexistent.

One result of the extraordinarily high rates of interethnic marriage among Americans of European ancestry is that there are a large number of individuals in the United States with mixed national heritage. Just under half (47 percent) of all non-Hispanic whites in the United States have a mixed ancestry, as do 31 percent of those born in 1920 or before, and 60 percent of those born after 1960. Among individuals with all or some ancestry stemming from certain countries, especially ethnic groups who have been in the United States for many generations, the proportion who are mixed makes up a clear majority—the English (53 percent mixed), Germans (65 percent), Irish (75 percent), French (77 percent), and the Scots (90 percent). As a consequence of the large number of individuals of mixed ancestry, the interethnic marriage rate in the future is likely to grow even more, because these individuals have a weak hold on any ethnic identity, and thus overwhelmingly marry people with different ethnic backgrounds.

The implications of these findings for our understanding of marriage and ethnic identity are almost revolutionary. Sociologists have always considered marriage and intermarriage as an indicator of acceptance and equality between families and groups. Max Weber, a late nineteenth- and early twentieth-century German sociologist, saw the restriction on caste and class intermarriage as a measure of the power and prestige of the highest caste or class and the social distance it placed between itself and lower castes and classes (Weber, 1946, pp. 311, 405–408; Bendix, 1960, p. 160). Equality is implied where intermarriage is accepted and freely practiced. The "social distance" scale devised by Emory Bogardus in 1928 considered the acceptance of members of another ethnic group "to close kinship by marriage" as the ultimate test of acceptance, tolerance, intimacy, and lack of social distance between ethnic groups.

What do the data from the 1980 Census tell us about interethnic group tolerance and acceptance? Do we live in a society in which race is still significant but ethnicity is not? Some social scientists would answer this question in the negative; they see a different message in the 1980 data. New York Senator Daniel Patrick Moynihan, author of the so-called "Moynihan Report" on the Black family and coauthor, with Nathan Glazer, of *Beyond the Melting Pot*, a book about ethnicity in New York City, is quoted as saying: "There may be a lot of intermarriage, but there is also a strong persistence of ethnic identity and memory. . . . I'd bet that now each year there are two times as many ethnic parades in New York than . . . a quarter of a century ago." William C. McCready, program director at the University of Chicago's National Opinion Research Center said: "It is not established that marriage is the ultimate test of ethnicity. If anything, marriage seems to be less of an ultimate commitment than it was 40 years ago. People go in and out of them. . . . Linkage between ethnicity and marriage choice may be breaking down, but linkages are still strong to ethnicity in areas like childrearing, styles of political participation, patterns of substance abuse and ways that people react to things like illnesses" (G. Collins, 1985).

Sources: Alba, 1985a; G. Collins, 1985.

■ TABLE 13–1
Median Age at First
Marriage, 1890–1985

	Male	Female
1890	26.1	22.0
1900	25.9	21.9
1910	25.1	21.6
1920	24.6	21.2
1930	24.3	21.3
1940	24.3	21.4
1950	22.8	20.3
1960	22.8	20.3
1970	23.2	20.8
1980	24.6	22.1
1985	25.5	23.3

Source: Statistical Abstract of the United States, *various editions*.

Choosing and being chosen by a partner in marriage is only the beginning. Only in fairy tales do handsome princes marry princesses and live happily every after. Each married couple works out or stumbles on its own special relationship, which, like everything else in the social world, is patterned, not random. Couples get along, each in its own way, largely because of specific sociological forces. Our job is to understand those forces.

Postponing Marriage

One of the more interesting trends of the past generation is the rise in the median age of couples at first marriage. From 1890 to 1950, the average age at first marriage in the United States actually dropped. Then, after 1960, it began to rise (see Table 13–1). Couples are postponing marriage longer than they did 20 or 30 years ago, and they will probably continue to do so for the foreseeable future.

Why? To begin with, many more women attend college today than did so a generation ago. In 1960, there were only 1.2 million women at American colleges; in 1985, 6.6 million. College attendance is a major reason for later marriages. Second, far more women work today than did so in the past, and the movement of women into the labor market also delays the age of marriage. Third, the women's movement may have helped delay marriage (Glick, 1975, p. 17; Gagnon and Greenblat, 1978, p. 221); by challenging the idea that a woman's role is to marry and become a mother as soon as possible.

Fourth, many more couples today are living together without being officially married than did so in the past. For many such couples, "living together" simply postpones the wedding date. For others, it is an experiment—a kind of informal, unofficial, "trial marriage," which can be ended without the trouble and complication of a divorce. As recently as the late 1960s, students were being expelled from college for cohabiting or "living together"; indeed, many were expelled from school on

More and more women and men are getting married, and therefore having children, later in life. Many present-day women have their first children in their 30s.

Edward Lettau/Alpha

being discovered in the room of a member of the opposite sex. Today, most campuses have coed dormitories, and some even have coed bathrooms.

The Bureau of the Census estimated that, in 1986, over 2.2 million unmarried couples were living together in the United States, well over a doubling from 1977, and an increase of four times since 1970 (Glich and Norton, 1977; *Newsday*, December 17, 1986, p. 14). Although unmarried live-in couples make up only 4 percent of all couple households (far below Sweden's 12 percent), living together is far more than a passing fad. In an October, 1977, CBS/*New York Times* poll, 82 percent of the men and 69 percent of the women aged 18 to 29 said that living together was "OK" or "doesn't matter." Among respondents aged 30 to 44, 59 percent and 52 percent, respectively, did not object to living together, but among 45 to 64 year olds, only 37 percent and 22 percent (Quindlen, 1977), didn't. Clearly, for a sizable and rapidly growing minority, cohabitation is a thinkable and practical alternative to marriage. Most of these cohabiting men and women will eventually marry—odds are, to each other—but they are not rushing to the altar.

Despite all the doomsayers and the visionaries, conventional heterosexual marriage will, for generations, remain the lot of the overwhelming majority of American couples. Alternative arrangements—cohabitation, communes, homosexuality, celibacy, and institutional living—will appeal only to a relative few.

Ambivalence about Marriage

Western culture is strongly ambivalent about marriage. Almost everyone eventually marries. We regard marriage as the foundation stone of our society, the stitching that holds the social fabric together. A person who has never been married is considered something of a deviant. Not without a trace of irony, we speak of "wedded bliss" and "holy matrimony." Even divorced men and women are quite likely to remarry within a few years.

But there is a darker, more negative side to our feelings about marriage. Cartoons like "The Lockhorns," "Andy Capp," and "Grin and Bear It," and such TV characters as Archie and Edith Bunker, represent hostility between husband and wife as not only routine but also humorous. Derisive jokes about marriage, most told by and to men, abound in Western culture. "Every woman should marry—and no man," said the nineteenth-century British politician and novelist, Benjamin Disraeli. A popular saying goes, "Bigamy is having one wife too many. Monogamy is the same." Arthur Schopenhauer, a philosopher, wrote, "To marry is to halve your rights and double your duties."

Men commonly see marriage as a trap, a burden, a limitation. Folklore represents them trying to avoid it until they are "caught" by scheming, manipulative women and burdened with responsibilities, screaming children, and nagging, scolding wives. They yearn to be "out with the boys" or out "chasing women" (Bernard, 1983). Marriage, however, is also thought to have a civilizing effect on men: disciplining them, taming their passions, keeping them out of trouble. Married men, in fact, lead longer, happier, healthier lives than unmarried men do (Durkheim, 1951; Gilder, 1974; Bernard, 1983). Writes one sociologist, "It might not be farfetched to conclude that the verbal assaults on marriage indulged in by men are a kind of compensatory reaction to their dependence on it" (Bernard, 1983).

The Impact of Marriage

It is ironic that men, who appear to shun marriage, seem to be improved by it, whereas women, who used to regard it as their life's work, seem in a number of ways to deteriorate because of it (Tavris and Wade, 1984, pp. 274–276). A number of studies have investigated the relationship between marital status and mental illness. Consistently, they show that married women and single men are worse off psychologically than single women and married men. Regardless of how we define mental illness or distress, women are psychologically less healthy than men, and wives, less healthy than husbands (Gove, 1972; Campbell, 1975). We are forced to conclude that marriage benefits men but not women. Why?

Many observers feel that a high proportion of married women suffer from what is called "the housewife syndrome" (Tavris and Wade, 1984, pp. 276–280). Their identities are tied up with a role that is secondary, inferior, and relational. They derive their senses of worth from serving others, not from their own achievements. In a survey (Shaver and Freedman, 1976) conducted among the educated and fairly affluent readers of *Psychology Today*, housewives reported significantly more anxiety than employed wives did (46 versus 28 percent), more loneliness (44 versus 26 percent), and more feelings of worthlessness (41 versus 24 percent). Even married women working as clerks and typists were happier with themselves and their lives than were comparable women without jobs (Ferree, 1976). Social contact with the outside world provided mental stimulation that was lacking in the lives of full-time housewives. And the working woman's paycheck enabled her to contribute to the financial well-being of the family and thus to have more power and respect within it—as full-time homemakers could not.

Another study compared a sample of full-time housewives with a sample of married professional women. The researchers wanted to find out how full-time housework related to self-esteem, feelings of uncertainty, the expression of creativity, and the feeling of attractiveness to men (Birnbaum, 1975). They found that the housewives had much lower senses of self-esteem, more often felt uncertain about their identities and desires, were ten times as likely to miss challenges and opportunities, and tended to feel "not very" attractive to men. In fact, the married professionals were much more likely to feel themselves happily married than the full-time housewives were (Birnbaum, 1975).

Working wives also have some unique problems, however. In effect, a married and employed woman has *two* jobs: the regular 9 to 5 and the job of taking care of her family. Men generally do not share equally in the housework (R. Collins, 1985a, pp. 175–177). One study found that "Working wives still bear almost all the responsibility for housework." Although working wives do less housework than wives who are full-time homemakers, "they still do the vast bulk of what needs to be done. Husbands of women who work help out more than husbands of homemakers, but their contribution is not impressive. Even if a husband is unemployed, he does much less housework than a wife who puts in a forty-hour week" (Blumstein and Schwartz, 1983, pp. 144–145).

Sex Segregation

Some cultures keep the sexes apart, especially in public. In strongly Islamic countries, for instance, men and women do not socialize together in public—no talking, laughing, sipping coffee, dancing, or just plain "hanging out." Only men congregate together in public; they even dance together, a sign of male domination, not homosexuality. Women who appear in public are regarded as immoral or "loose." In such cultures, men and women do almost nothing together, at least in public.

In the rural areas of the Mediterranean, in Muslim areas around the world, and in much of South America, a man and a woman "must never be left alone together, or the worst will happen" (Cornelison, 1977, p. 20). The sexual passion of men is thought to be almost uncontrollable, and a man's honor requires him to guard his daughters' virginity and his wife's fidelity. To most Westerners, this pattern seems grim and restrictive. Most of us do not automatically impute a sexual meaning to contact between the sexes. Before adolescence, young boys and girls inhabit separate worlds. They associate primarily with members of their own sex, to whom they look for approval. This pattern is called **homo-social.**

Homosocial Sex-segregated.

Beginning in early adolescence, young men and women generally begin to associate **heterosocially**—that is, with members of the opposite sex. What members of the opposite sex think begins to be important, and young men and women tailor their behavior accordingly (Gagnon, 1977, pp. 168–170; Gagon and Greenblat, 1978, pp. 136–137). For many young men and women, however, this transition from homosociality to heterosociality is not complete. They remain attached chiefly to companions of their own sex, care little about the opinions of the opposite sex, and socialize with members of it mainly to "get what they want," not because they value the company of men or women (as the case may be). As a general rule, the more equality any social group concedes to women, the more heterosocial its marriage relationships will tend to be, and vice versa.

Heterosocial Sex-integrated; a quality that characterizes marriages that are egalitarian, companionate, and sexually integrated.

Communicating

For the newly married, marriage inevitably entails an at least partial entry into the world of the opposite sex. Even the most homosocial of marriage partners, people who think of men and women as totally different creatures, must have some contact with their husbands or wives. For just this reason, young men and women may find the early years of marriage troubling and puzzling. They repeatedly fail to see or understand the cues given off by their spouses, whose concerns and interests they find either incomprehensible or "trivial and boring" (Komarovsky, 1967, p. 55). Some partners have to seek help to "translate" messages from their husbands or wives. One young husband, a 23-year-old man with a grade school education, admitted to a researcher that "when I was first married, half the time I didn't know what she was driving at, what it was all about. . . . Sometimes I'd think I'd got her all figured out and then I don't make her out at all. The women in her bunch understood her pretty well though. . . . They seemed to understand her better than I did sometimes. They'd tell their husbands about her and the fellows would tell me." This man's wife added: "Men are different. They don't feel the same as us—that's one reason men are friends with men, and women have women friends." A 25-year-old woman with a tenth grade education added, "The fellows got their interests and the girls got theirs, they each go their separate ways" (Komarovsky, 1967, pp. 33, 150, 151).

Homosociality is more firmly entrenched among less well-educated couples who do blue-collar work, and their children, than among professional people. It is especially strong when the wife is a full-time house-keeper not employed outside the home. The norms of middle-class, white-collar, college-educated married couples require a more "companionate" relationship between husband and wife—more sharing, "more exploration of feelings, and more exchange of them" (Rubin, 1976, p. 119). In other words, middle-class norms call for the husband to empathize with the wife, and vice versa. Middle-class couples tend to do more things together, as a couple, and it is less common for the man to run off with his buddies and the woman to stay home taking care of the children or chatting with her women friends.

Some observers feel that, over time, couples of all classes are adopting the heterosocial and companionate pattern. "Suddenly, new dreams are stirring. *Intimacy, companionship, sharing*—these are now words working-class women speak to their men, words that turn both their worlds upside down" (Rubin, 1976, p. 120). Change is almost always painful. Transforming patterns inherited from the remote past will not be easy or comfortable. Couples, especially the men, who grew up with homosocial models will find the shift bewildering and threatening. But many couples will have no choice but to adapt. A whole new set of expectations demand fulfillment. Working-class couples will have to do what they have always done: survive and, if they are lucky, learn (Rubin, 1976, pp. 120, 133).

CHILDREN

In 1800, when our economy was overwhelmingly agricultural, an average American family had about seven children. By 1900, when industrialization was in full swing, an average family had a bit more than 3.5 children (Degler, 1980). And by the late 1970s, the average family had only two children (Nordheimer, 1977). Before industrialization, the infant mortality rate (deaths of children less than a year old) was so high that a family would have had to produce eight or nine children to be sure that two would survive to adulthood and replace their parents (Gagnon and Greenblat, 1978, p. 316). A large number of children was also an economic asset, because the children could start working at an early age and thus contribute to the family's support. Children were also expected to support their parents in their old age.

Today's Small Family

The nature and composition of the American family has changed drastically over the past 200 years, but one thing remains constant: Today, as always, most married couples want to have children. In the early 1980s, less than 6 percent of all American wives aged 18 to 34 expected to have no children (Reiss, 1980, p. 359). The proportion of American couples that do not want children has risen a bit, but population experts expect it to stay well below 10 percent for the rest of the decade (Blake, 1979). An overwhelming majority of all married couples, and about half of all divorced couples, will have at least one child. Still, the number of children that couples have and wish to have is going down quite strikingly. Today, more married women—49 percent—want to have no more than two children (Reiss, 1980, p. 359).

The *total fertility rate* for any year is the total number of children that any 1,000 women in a country would bear if each had the average number of children born to mothers in that country. For instance, if the total fertility rate for a certain year was 3,000, that would mean that a cross section of 1,000 women would, over their lifetimes, bear 3,000 children—three for each woman. Given current death (or mortality) rates and assuming no migration, in or out, a total fertility rate of 2,110 represents zero population growth, or simple replacement of the population. In 1981, the total fertility rate of the United States was 1,815, or less than two children per woman, below replacement level. (The United States population continues to grow because of immigration.) Today's fertility rate is almost exactly half the rate of the 1950s, during the postwar baby-boom era; the total fertility rate from 1950 to 1954 was 3,337, and from 1955 to 1959, it was 3,690.* From the late 1950s on, the fertility rate has dropped steadily (*Statistical Abstract of the United States*, 1985, p. 57). Experts predict a baby "boomlet" or a baby-boom "echo" during the 1980s, because the baby-boom children have grown up and are having children of their own (Family Service America, 1984, pp. 22, 24). This "boomlet" will be extremely modest, however, and will represent only a slight rise in the birth rate. Baby boomers are marrying later and having fewer children than their parents did, and so their fertility rate will be very low, even though they are now in their childbearing years. In sum, then, although the overwhelming majority of American women today still expect to bear and raise at least one child, the number of children they expect to have and do have has fallen drastically.

This decline represents a revolutionary change. It demonstrates that couples have a large measure of control over childbearing. The availability of more effective birth-control techniques accounts for some of the decline. But the decision to *use* contraception results from economic, cultural, and individual changes, including the rise in the average level of education and the increase in the proportion of wives who work.

The Individualistic Family

The small size of the typical contemporary American family demonstrates its individualistic character. Such decisions as how many children to have and when to have them are made by each couple, usually in the light of very practical considerations. A couple's parents, for example, may wish to be grandparents and make their wishes clear. But those wishes, usually, are only one factor among many.

Child care, too, has an individualistic character in the United States. In nearly all other cultures, childraising is the responsiblity of an extended family, a group of close relatives, or an entire village. Many cultures have a "microcommunity" (Whiting, 1977) of two or three dozen mothers and other parents who watch over, take care of, control, protect, and "parent" children. Children are surrounded not only by two biological parents but by "parental surrogates."

The American system of child care is totally different. Typically, the mother and father—and they alone—care for their children. Parents are more or less isolated in their parenthood, because they get little help from others. This "all-your-eggs-in-one-basket" system in child care

---

* This figure represents the number of children that would be born to all women, both married and unmarried; obviously, the fertility rate of married women, or the average number of children born to all married couples, would be a bit higher than this.

(Skolnick, 1987) strains the parent-child relationship—a situation that the extended family of surrogate parents manages to avoid. American parents do not have a network of relatives to back up their decisions, so their authority tends to be weak and indecisive. Weak parental authority makes children rebellious, resentful, and independent, especially as they grow older and cultivate peer ties outside the family unit.

Parenthood is perhaps the most difficult of all adult roles—especially for mothers, because the father typically contributes far less to parenting (Rossi, 1968). Other major roles—like those involving marriage and work—provide a much longer transitional period, which prepares us for those roles by socializing us into them. Parenthood, in contrast, starts abruptly. From the very first, the "new mother starts out immediately on twenty-four-hour-a-day duty with full responsibilities" (Skolnick, 1987, p. 313). If she finds that the role doesn't suit her, it is too bad: Parenthood is forever. You can get divorced, or quit a job—even change your sex—but you cannot stop being a parent.

Working Mothers

The contemporary American family contains both traditional and modern elements. On the one hand, mothers are still doing most of the child care, and when fathers pitch in, they say they are "helping out the wife," not doing work that is properly theirs. On the other hand, an increasing number and proportion of women are working at jobs outside the home, a trend that is not likely to reverse. According to the United States Census, a shade more than 40 percent of women with preschool children work; this proportion slowly rises as children grow older and more self-sufficient. More and more working wives are in the "double bind," facing urgent demands both from family and job. The double binds puts great stress on the mother and, as a result, on her marriage and on her whole family, too.

Three possible ways of relieving the burden are now emerging: first, child-care services; second, a more active role in child care by the father; and third, more flexible working conditions for working mothers. Between the late 1960s and the late 1970s, the percentage of all children aged 3 and 4 enrolled in nursery schools went up from 15 percent to 30 percent (Reiss, 1980, p. 458). This trend will almost certainly continue.

As for the man's role inside the family, it has not changed as rapidly as the woman's role outside the home (Skolnick, 1987). Still, it is beginning to change. One indication of this is that more and more divorced fathers are seeking and getting custody of their children. A generation ago, almost none did. Social change is likely to be slow and fitful. Fathers will continue to resist child-care responsiblities. But the pressures upon them to become equal parents will surely mount. The more important a woman's career becomes, and the more her income approaches her husband's, the more husbands will be forced to accept child-care responsibilities (Rappaport and Rappaport, 1976; Bird, 1979; Hall and Hall, 1979). It is just a question of time.

The conditions of employment will probably be the last to change. More flexible work hours ("flextime") suiting women's home schedules would make childrearing easier. So would job sharing (the practice of allowing two or more workers to fill one full-time job), child-care leave with guarantees of reemployment, and day-care facilities on the job. So far, these changes have been adopted by relatively few businesses. They are resisted not only because they challenge present-day social norms but also because employers regard them as troublesome and expensive.

More mothers work outside the home today than ever did so in the past. Many women must raise children and, at the same time, hold full-time jobs. One way of relieving the burden might be to set up day-care facilities in factories and offices. So far, there are few such facilities.

Porterfield-Chickering/Photo Researchers

DIVORCE AND REMARRIAGE

Some 40 percent of all American marriages now end in divorce (Glick and Norton, 1977). In the late 1970s and early 1980s, somewhat more than a million divorces were granted each year, and slightly more than 2 million marriages. However, the divorce rate is not 50 percent, because many of these divorces involved couples that married in the past.

Divorce is much more common today than it used to be, but that does not necessarily mean that today's marriages are unhappier than those of the past. A hundred years ago, "it was taken for granted that even substantial difficulties were not . . . adequate grounds for breaking up. Perhaps in most Western societies it has been assumed until fairly recently that spouses who did not love one another and who fought in private should nevertheless be civil in public and maintain the marriage simply for the sake of their children and their respectable standing in the community" (W. J. Goode, 1982). Today, even temporary marital problems may lead to divorce because it has become much more acceptable. In a film called *Lovers and Other Strangers*, a young wife leaves her husband because "his hair doesn't smell like raisins anymore." No doubt she had other reasons too, but couples clearly break up for vastly less substantial reasons than used to be thought necessary for divorce. Over the past generation (twenty-five or so years), the divorce rate has almost tripled. The best expression of that rate is the number of divorces each year per 1,000 married women. From the end of the Civil War (1865) to the beginning of World War I (1914), that rate rose from only one per 1,000 married women to eight per 1,000. From 1920 to the early 1960s, the divorce rate remained more or less stable. But from the 1960s to the present, the rate has again increased dramatically, from nine per 1,000 married women to twenty-two per 1,000.

In western Europe and North America, the divorce rate has gone up in tandem with the pace of industrialization. However, the connection between the two is not universal. The Arab world, Africa south of the Sahara Desert, and Japan before industrialization all had a good deal of divorce (W. J. Goode, 1963, pp. 155–162, 195–199, 358–365). A society's divorce rate has many causes, which may be unique to each society. Perhaps we should concentrate on divorce in Western society, especially the United States, and only during the past generation.

Age at Marriage and Divorce

One of the most important influences upon the likelihood that a couple will eventually divorce is each partner's age at marriage. Couples who marry before the age of 18 are two to three times more likely to be divorced than couples who marry in their 20s. A very high proportion of teenage marriages are arranged because the wife-to-be is pregnant— not an ideal way to start a life together. Even teenage marriages that are not brought on by pregnancy tend to be very unstable. They are typically inspired by purely physical attraction between the partners, who wish to legitimate their sexual activity. But the body decays over time, and, meanwhile, most people change and mature. Such couples frequently grow emotionally and intellectually distant. When they reach adulthood, they find that they have little in common.

Divorce and Socioeconomic Status

The divorce rate of the lowest socioeconomic stratum is higher than that of groups further up the social ladder. Divorce, in fact, tends to be most common at the bottom of the class structure and least common at the top, notwithstanding the well-publicized divorces of a few celebrities. (One slight wrinkle in this pattern: Women in secure, high-paying professions tend to have a higher divorce rate because they know that they can support themselves.) Clearly, economic difficulties take their toll on a marriage.

Divorce and Religion

Because the United States Census is prohibited by law from asking respondents their religion, religion's role in divorce is less clear than that of many other factors. By itself, religious identity does not seem to be a major cause, because at the same socioeconomic levels, Catholics, Protestants, and Jews have about the same rates of divorce. Two religious factors do, however, seem to play a role. The first is the degree of religious identity, devoutness, and traditionalism, because very devout couples are much less likely to get divorced than less devout couples, and couples who identify with no religion at all have the highest rate of divorce. Second, interfaith marriages also tend to be more unstable than those between people with the same religious backgrounds, probably because interfaith couples tend to be unorthodox, untraditional, and unconventional.

Incompatibility and Divorce

In fact, the general rule is that the more important social factors a wife and husband may have in common, the less likely they are to be divorced, and vice versa. This rule, like any generalization, has its exceptions, but it predicts the likelihood of divorce about as well as anything else. It applies not only to interfaith marriages but also to interracial couples and to couples with markedly different social statuses, levels

The younger the couple at marriage, the greater the likelihood of divorce. Having children usually compounds a young couple's problems.

Susan Kuklin/Photo Researchers

of education, ages, and so on. Because, as we have seen, "birds of a feather flock together," the very forces that usually influence the choice of a mate also determine the success or failure of most marriages. Compatibility in marriage is partly, even largely, determined by sociological similarity.

Divorce and Remarriage

Common sense would suggest that most people whose marriages have ended in divorce would not wish to remarry. Why be a two-time loser? Common sense is dead wrong: Divorced people are eager to remarry, and the overwhelming majority of them do so within five years of getting divorced. Divorced people are far more likely to get married (again) than are people of the same age who have never been married. Three-quarters of all divorced men in their early 30s eventually remarry, and two-thirds of the women. Widows and widowers have much lower remarriage rates than divorced people, too. (Young widows and widowers are almost as likely to get remarried as young divorceds, but older widowed people are much less likely to do so than older divorced people.) In part, widowers and, especially, widows are less likely to get married because there is a shortage of eligible men, especially at the older ages. But if this shortage were the only reason, then all the widowers would get remarried, and they do not.

Divorced people do not dissolve their marriages because they reject the institution of marriage. Most of them love being married; they have merely rejected their marriage partners. Widows and widowers do not choose that status; fate inflicts it on them. Many remain emotionally loyal to their dead spouses; prospective spouses may fail to "measure up."

THE FUTURE OF MARRIAGE AND THE FAMILY

Conservatives fear that contemporary trends, especially toward sexual equality, will inevitably destroy the family and society as we know it (Decter, 1974, pp. 107ff; Gilder, 1975, pp. 252–265, 278). Radical critics of the family argue that it is sexist by its very nature and that full sexual equality must destroy it (Firestone, 1970, p. 233; Millett, 1970, p. 127; Greer, 1971, p. 232). Alternatives to the family include test-tube babies, communes, unmarried motherhood, childlessness, celibacy, and the creation of an independent, all-female "lesbian nation."

From the perspective of the 1980s, however, it appears that these fears and hopes are not realistic. For the foreseeable future, most men and women will seek and find more-or-less monogamous relationships with people of the opposite sex. A high proportion of these relationships will culminate in conventional marriage. A high proportion of them will produce children. The experience of divorce will not deter most of the men and women who pass through it from remarrying. The increasing numbers of divorced parents who marry each other will result in a new and broader definition of family relations. Greater sexual equality will redefine and restructure the family, not destroy it. The constantly increasing number of working wives and mothers will produce new sex roles, and new definitions of right and wrong—new and different, but not unrecognizable. Some form of marriage and the family will survive.

SUMMARY

1. Many family forms exist the world over; having grown up in one form does not necessarily give a person full knowledge of all forms.

2. The family is one social institution; it fits in or "hangs together" with others. The family usually reinforces other aspects of society, and vice versa.

3. The family is an institution that assigns responsibility for the physical survival, upbringing, and socialization of the child. In this sense, the family is universal in all societies.

4. Functionalism argues that the family is both universal and historically persistent because of its positive contribution to society as a whole.

5. Conflict theory holds that the family preserves existing inequality and contributes to the exploitation of the powerless.

6. All societies have rules governing who may and may not marry whom.

7. Rules of exogamy govern marriage outside our own group or category; marrying outside our sexes or genders and outside our family units are the two most common exogamous rules.

8. Endogamous rules dictate that members of a society marry within a certain category.

9. Categories of people that can be arranged in a hierarchy— whereby they can be ranked according to certain universally valued characteristics—can be described as a kind of market, exchange, or bargaining system.

10. Mate selection on the basis of nonhierarchical characteristics— whereby people are considered to be "just different" and not necessarily better or worse—involves propinquity (nearness), compatibility, and social acceptance.

11. Two other factors that influence mate selection are sex ratio and group size.

12. Couples in the United States are waiting longer to marry than in years past.

13. Western culture is strongly ambivalent about marriage; we have a "love-hate" relationship with the institution.

14. As measured by several criteria, the impact of marriage on men seems to be largely positive; its impact on women seems to be more negative.

15. In some marriages, called homosocial, men and women assume markedly different roles and do not socialize together. Other marriages, called heterosocial, involve spouses who do not rigidly separate their roles and their social lives.

16. Today's family is significantly smaller than families of the past.

17. The individualistic character of the contemporary family causes a special tension and difficulty in family life.

18. Some 40 percent of all American marriages now end in divorce.

19. Age at marriage, socioeconomic status, religion, and the couple's compatibility; all contribute to the success or failure of the marriage.

20. It is highly likely that divorced individuals will remarry.

21. Although society and individuals are changing, the family—in one form or another—will continue to flourish.

SUGGESTED READINGS

Philip Blumstein and Pepper Schwartz, *American Couples: Money, Work, Sex*. New York: William Morrow, 1983.
A massive study based on interviews with 300 couples—120 heterosexual (seventy-two married and forty-eight cohabiting), ninety lesbian, and ninety gay male couples—living in the Seattle, San Francisco, and New York vicinities, and some 12,000 questionnaires returned by the couples. As the subtitle says, the main topics covered are money, work, and sex.

Leonard Cargan and Matthew Melko, *Singles: Myths and Realities*. Beverly Hills: Sage, 1982.
A study of the social life of singles. Makes a number of interesting comparisons with married men and women.

Andrew J. Cherlin, *Marriage, Divorce, Re-marriage*. Cambridge, Massachusetts: Harvard University Press, 1981.
An interesting sociological and statistical study on remarriage—its trends, causes, and consequences.

Randall Collins, *Sociology of Marriage and the Family: Gender, Love and Property*. Chicago: Nelson-Hall, 1985.
A textbook on the family by a conflict-oriented theorist.

William J. Goode, *The Family* (2nd ed.). Englewood Cliffs, New Jersey: Prentice-Hall, 1982.
A brief but rigorous textbook on the family. Makes excellent use of cross-cultural materials.

Judith Lewis Herman, with Lisa Hirschman, *Father-Daughter Incest*. Cambridge, Massachusetts: Harvard University Press, 1981.
A feminist analysis and study of incest. Extremely persuasive and compelling. For now, this is the definitive statement on the subject.

Diana E. H. Russen, *Rape in Marriage*. New York: Collier Books, 1982.
A shocking study of women who have been sexually assaulted by their husbands. The author argues that marital rape is "the crime in the closet." The first of its kind and a revelation.

Charles Vert Willie, *A New Look at Black Families*. Bayside, New York: General Hall, 1981.
A Black sociologist's defense of the Black family.

chapter 14

RELIGION

In rural North Carolina a modest wood-frame church rocks with joyous gospel songs pouring from proud, enthusiastic Black voices.

In the streets of New York, half a dozen young men and women in saffron robes and sneakers clang finger cymbals and chant "Hare Krishna." Hundreds of pedestrians swarm past them, oblivious to their devotions.

On a Sunday morning in Los Angeles, a family wakes up, dresses, gets into the station wagon, and travels to a nearby drive-in theater to hear a sermon delivered by a polished and well-dressed preacher. He asks this automotive flock to contribute money to help him deliver his message on TV.

In Iran, a monarch is overthrown by angry mobs loyal to an exiled Muslim leader, who soon returns and rules the country with an iron fist, executing thousands of alleged infidels and sinners.

In Rome, millions gather at St. Peter's Square to pray for the recovery of Pope John Paul II, injured by the bullets of a would-be assassin, a fanatical Muslim.

In the hills near a Mexican village, a circle of worshipers sits around a night-time campfire and ingests psychedelic mushrooms. The men and women have visions until the rise of the morning sun.

All these events occurred fairly recently. Yet in the nineteenth century, many intellectuals believed that religion would eventually be replaced by science. Religion, they believed, was irrational, only one step removed from magic and superstition. Science would answer all the questions that plagued humankind—and in a more effective and valid way than religion possibly could. Science was based on fact, religion on fantasy, or so these thinkers held. To Karl Marx, for instance, religion was the "opiate of the masses." It existed chiefly to pacify the poor, by turning their attention away from their wretchedness in this world and toward a happier (but unreal) one. When the workers penetrate the mystery of religion, Marx held, it would be discarded; under socialism, it would become totally irrelevant and obsolete. Even more recently, in 1965, two sociologists predicted a "post-christian era" for the United States (Glock and Stark, 1965).

Skeptics were wrong. Religion is alive and well almost everywhere today—even in communist countries like Poland.

367

Religion does take somewhat different forms from century to century and decade to decade, from society to society and city to city. And the number of the faithful may vary a good deal. Still, we find some type of religion flourishing almost everywhere and at all times. Like the family, religion is a universal cultural institution.

WHAT IS RELIGION?

Religion A system of beliefs and practices relative to sacred things that unite adherents into a kind of moral community.

What then is a **religion?** Sociologists define it as a system of beliefs and practices relative to sacred things that unite their adherents into a kind of moral community (Durkheim, 1915, p. 47). The "sacred" is infinitely above and beyond everyday reality. It generates reverence, awe, and a sense of mystery. In short, the sacred is felt to be holy. The opposite of the sacred is the "profane"—whatever is ordinary, everyday, secular. The two worlds of the sacred and the profane are kept separate. Worshipers, for instance, are not supposed to gossip during the celebration of a Catholic mass. All societies distinguish things that are sacred from those that are profane.

The "moral community" of like-minded believers is also central to religion. Although some individuals hold totally unique and private sets of beliefs, and follow unique and private sets of rituals and practices (Luckmann, 1967), these people do not generate social structures centered around their own private religions. Though this type of private or "invisible" religious expression is interesting, it is not as sociologically important as organized religions are. Nearly all religions have followings, memberships with common identities, practices, and world views that bind people together and set them apart from other groups.

Sociology does not assess the literal "truth" or "falsity" of religions any more than it attempts to determine whether a certain type of family is "valid" or "invalid." Not, of course, that the sociological approach to religion is completely "objective." Each sociologist's religious beliefs certainly influence the way he or she views a certain religion. Sociologists can also discuss issues that are relevant to good and evil. For instance, they can assess whether or not religion or a particular religion meets common human needs, like satisfying a spiritual hunger or creating social cohesion. Sociologists' main concern, however, is to determine the impact of religion on society or segments of it. Sociologists might

Sociologists define religion as a system of beliefs and practices concerning sacred things—things above the everyday reality of the world. A religion unites its believers into a moral community.
Sandra Baker/Photo Researchers

say, for instance, that one religion legitimates social inequality, that another promotes social change, and that a third helps its followers achieve material success. Judgments on these questions, though controversial, are neither endorsements nor condemnations of any religion. Sociologists deal with religion's role in society. The subject matter of the sociology of religion is the influence of religion on secular society and the influence of secular society on religion.

WHY RELIGION? TWO VIEWS

Sociologists have analyzed religion from a variety of perspectives. Two of the most influential are the functionalist and the conflict theories (see Chapter 1). As it does with other areas of social life, functionalism insists that institutions found in societies the world over must be beneficial, or "functional" to society. Religion must make a contribution, the functionalists reason, because human societies have always had some form of it. Conflict theorists adopt the opposite point of view. Religion, they claim, is one of the many ways that powerful elites exploit the masses. It benefits that elite, not society as a whole.

The Functionalist Theory of Religion

All societies raise and answer questions of ultimate meaning concerning the role of human beings in the universe and about life after death. Even among the archeological remains of some stone-age societies, we find indications of a spiritual quest. Why is religion a universal human institution? This was among the first questions raised by sociologists.

Emile Durkheim (see Chapter 1), who was one of the strongest influences on American sociology, believed that religion arose when human beings recognized that the society as a whole exists prior to, and will outlive, every individual within it. Religion, he argued, is the worship of society itself. In the act of worship, through religious rituals, society's members renew their bonds with one another and with society (Durkheim, 1915). Later, the functionalists added (along similar lines) that religion contributes to the stability, the cohesion, and the survival of all societies by binding a society's members together and making them loyal to it.

Religion serves to explain and justify our place in the world. It legitimates a certain version of empirical reality and of right and wrong, true and false. Religion tells its believers that the practices of a specific society are not a mere accident of history but cosmic in origin: eternal, inevitable, God-given. Religion offers a version of reality that "makes sense" out of a vast, confusing, and basically senseless universe. The basic function of religion is "universe-maintenance." Religion provides meaning in a world that might otherwise seem meaningless (Berger, 1967, pp. 22–28, 29–44).

The Conflict Perspective

An alert sociologist must examine religion's negative functions as well as its positive ones. Functionalism assumes that religion has pretty much the same influence on all segments, groups, and classes in a society. In contrast, Karl Marx argued that religion exists because it helps the ruling elite keep the masses docile, controllable, and exploitable. It does so in two ways: directly, by preaching that existing social arrangements are not only fair but sacred, and indirectly, by focusing the believer's attention on a world beyond. Marx, in short, found that religion serves to legitimate the social, economic, and political order. In this respect, his analysis was similar to that of the functionalists. But Marx took a step beyond this point and argued that religion helps the ruling class and not society as a whole. He also held that religion is not necessary; it is universal only because exploitation is universal. The end of exploitation would therefore be the death knell of religion. Or so said Marx.

A Synthesis

Marxism notwithstanding, human beings do have a persistent need to "make sense" out of the world and to understand what lies beyond the everyday events of individual lives. Certain questions seem so troubling and pressing that only religious explanations seem to suffice. Science, for instance, cannot satisfactorily explain why a lover or a child dies. Nor can we be emotionally or spiritually satisfied with the idea that death has no meaningful explanation, that it "just happens." The universe is full of "whys"—questions that can only be answered in the territory of the sacred. Human beings need to believe that their way of life is "good" and even "sacred." And though many religions serve the *status quo*, others have challenged it—witness Black churches in this country, for example.

THE BUILDING BLOCKS OF RELIGION

Many Westerners believe that their religions are special and unique—like no other religions in the world. Yet all religious bodies do share certain common elements—building blocks that make each religion a religion.

Beliefs

Monotheism Belief in the existence of only one God.

Polytheism Belief in the existence of a number of gods.

As Durkheim's definition indicates, the thing that makes the religious approach to reality distinctive is its acceptance of the sacred—forces that operate outside ordinary worldly forces, "a reality that does not belong to this world but nevertheless affects it" (Wilson, 1978, p. 34). Some religions (like Christianity, Judaism, and Islam) are strictly **monotheistic:** They accept only one God. Others, such as Hinduism, are **polytheistic** and accept many gods. Yet all accept some sacred force, not explainable by routine, earthly forces.

All religions have a body of beliefs that form a more or less unified system. Generally, these beliefs attempt to answer questions of ultimate meaning—the meaning of life and our place within it. Stories, myths, and events support each religion's overall interpretation of ultimate meaning. For instance, the Biblical account of Abraham's willingness to sacrifice his son Isaac demonstrates the virtue of absolute devotion to God. Hinduism's acceptance of castes supports the belief in reincarnation and in divine retribution (karma) for actions in past lives. Among

Muslims, the belief in almsgiving demonstrates the unity of Islam. Religious beliefs tend to be a part of a "package deal": There is a degree of internal consistency in the beliefs of the world's religions.

Not all the members of any religious body accept every item of belief and doctrine. Invariably, some people will hold certain beliefs but not others. Within Christianity, some denominations are quite firm about the literal truth of every statement in the Bible, whereas others believe that Biblical accounts are myths designed to teach basic truths. Some Muslims believe that all non-Muslims are "infidels" in need of conversion, whereas others accept diversity of religious belief.

Rituals and Practices

Rituals are generally specific, prescribed acts that take place within concrete, sacred contexts, such as private prayer or public church services. Practices are somewhat broader and might include the way you lead your day-to-day life. Sometimes, however, ritual and practice are not easy to distinguish. Both refer to the outward behavioral expression of a religion, the way that adherents act out their devotion. Participation in ritual not only symbolizes faith but also reaffirms and sustains it. When Christians take the communion wine and wafer, symbolizing Christ's blood and body, they renew their ties with Christianity as a whole. When Muslims face Mecca to pray, they renew their ties with Islam.

As with beliefs, so too with rituals: Not all adherents of a religion follow the same ones. Among some Christians, church going is a sometime affair. Not all Muslims pray five times a day. Indeed, the way that believers translate their faith into earthly practices often seems to contradict the teachings of their religion. Christianity, for instance, supports a belief in the brotherhood and sisterhood of humanity, yet some Christians are openly racist. Such hypocrisy is not unique to Christianity: It is not always possible to predict just how a religion's teachings will influence day-to-day practices and behavior.

Religions do nonetheless have an impact on the lives of believers. Eighteenth-century ascetic Protestantism influenced the rise of industrialism in Europe (see Chapter 20). Today, many fundamentalist Protestants in this country support a wide range of conservative political policies. An Islamic movement toppled the regime of the Shah of Iran in 1979. Clearly, religions demand that their followers go out into the world and practice their faith through actions. Clearly, too, the behavior of believers in different religions can often be very different indeed.

Community

Organized religions exist as a community of believers. Although many individuals, especially in an urbanized, industrialized society, hold to their own unique, private, or "invisible" religions (Luckmann, 1967), sociologists have not focused much of their attention on them. This is because such private religions do not have much impact on a society unless they win converts. Religion is not just the product of a private quest to answer troubling questions of meaning. To participate in religion is to participate in peoplehood—in what Durkheim called a "moral community." It is the affirmation of belonging to a group of like-minded souls. We need not go so far as to say, with Durkheim, that the worship of the sacred is the worship of society itself. Still, religious participation intensifies religious feeling. Religious forces are moral forces: They emanate from, and are renewed by, a collectivity. In many societies of the

Religious rituals, like this one in Iran, give individual believers a practical way of affirming their membership in the moral community of believers.

J. Isaac/United Nations Photo

world, there is not a single religious community, but several, sometimes at odds with one another. Religion generates conflict as well as cohesion. Nonetheless, Durkheim was correct in arguing that religion cannot exist apart from the group that sustains it.

Organization

In tribal societies, religion is simply one aspect of the tribe's total way of life. Religious and tribal practices are almost indistinguishable from each other; all members of the tribe are adherents of its religion, and vice versa. In larger and more complex societies, several things distinguish religions from tribal practices. First, the role of religious functionary (or priest) is a full-time job, with designated individuals leading the ceremonies and "representing" the tribe, village, or community before the gods. A religious organization emerges and positions and functions are filled by particular individuals. Second, a hierarchy develops within this organization. The position of priest acquires power and esteem, and people compete for it. Third, reformers generate new and unorthodox interpretations of religious truth, seek converts, and set up independent religious organizations. When this occurs, society and religion are no longer one and the same; individuals cannot be believers simply by belonging to the tribe.

FORMS OF RELIGIOUS ORGANIZATION

Charisma

In societies that grow from small and tribal to large and complex, religion ceases to be solely a source of cohesion and consensus. It becomes a potential source of competition and conflict. The challenge to religious tradition comes from men and women who are seized with an absolute certainty that their own private revelations are divinely inspired. This pattern of personal revelation characterized the Old Testament prophets, Jesus, Muhammad, Joseph Smith (founder of the Mormons), Mary Baker Eddy (founder of Christian Science), Elijah Muhammad (founder of the Black Muslims), Gautama Buddha, and George Baker ("Father Divine"). Prophets claim to have direct contact with the divine, announce a break with established religion, and proclaim that this break is not only legitimate but necessary.

Most prophets attract little or no following and create no viable organization to sustain their inspirations. Some societies are not ready for certain prophets or doctrines, and some prophets do not have enough of the quality sociologists call **charisma** (Weber, 1963, p. 46ff, and passim; 1968, pp. 1111–1157). Charisma is a characteristic possessed by a few rare individuals, who may inhabit almost any walk of life. Charles Manson, a convicted mass murderer, had this quality—unfortunately—as did John F. Kennedy, Martin Luther King, and Alexander the Great. Presidents Richard Nixon, Lyndon Johnson, and Gerald Ford never had it.

Charisma is a Greek word that means "gifts of the spirit." Charismatic leaders are endowed by their followers with "supernatural, superhuman, or at least specifically exceptional powers or qualities that are regarded

Charisma An exceptional power or quality attributed to certain leaders.

as of divine origin" (Weber, 1947, pp. 358–359). Charismatic leaders are "natural" leaders: They do not have to hold office to inspire and exercise power over followers. "The bearer of charisma enjoys loyalty and authority by virtue of a mission believed to be embodied in him" (Weber, 1968, p. 1117).

Charisma is highly unstable, and this hinders the establishment of a new religious order. A charismatic prophet may win many converts, but what happens when the prophet dies? How do the prophet's disciples transform this original charisma into a structure, an organization that will endure? And what happens to the prophet's message once it is "exposed to the conditions of everyday life," conditions that usually frustrate the message in its pure form? The leader and the followers wish to "maintain the purity of the spirit," but they also want the movement to survive. So "the charismatic message inevitably becomes dogma, doctrine, theory, . . . law or petrified tradition" (Weber, 1968, pp. 1121, 1122).

Compromises are required to create a religious organization that can hold the faithful and win new converts, to raise revenue, to manage relations with the "powers that be," and to pass on the prophet's mantle of religious authority. Prophets lead by dint of personal magnetism. Subsequent leaders derive authority from the offices they occupy. In other words, authority becomes "routinized" (adapted to the demands of the real world) and "bureaucratized" (institutional rather than personal). When religions do not deal with these practical problems or create true organizations, they die out.

Once established, religious organizations take a number of different forms. Although the beliefs and doctrines preached by various religions differ quite strikingly, there are also interesting parallels in religious organizations. Sociologists have identified four basic forms of religious organization. They are the cult, the sect, the church or ecclesia, and the denomination. The sociological usage of these words does not conform precisely to the popular one, but sociological usage offers special insights into religious organization.

Cults

The term **cult** is used very loosely by the general public and by the media to mean any unusual, "kooky" religious body with a strong hold on its followers. The most widely accepted meaning of the term cult in sociology is "the beginning phase of an entirely new religion," one that provides "a radical break from existing religious traditions" (Roberts, 1984, p. 242). Cults "do not have a prior tie with another established religious body in question. The cult may represent an alien (external) religion, or it may have originated in the host society" as a result of radical innovation, not splitting off from a parent religious body. Either way, the cult is something new and radically different with respect to other existing religious bodies. "Cults, then, represent a deviant religious tradition in a society" (Stark and Bainbridge, 1985, pp. 25, 26).

There are three different types of cults: audience cults, client cults, and cult movements (Stark and Bainbridge, 1985, pp. 26–30). **Audience cults** are loosely structured, diffuse entities which lack formal religious organizations. They have no true membership; followers float in and out of affiliation—indeed, even what determines "affiliation" is unclear. A strong leadership—or, in fact, any leadership at all—is lacking. People who are extremely involved with astrology would constitute an audience cult. So would those interested in flying saucers and UFOs. Audience

Cult A religious body that is novel in a society, strikingly different from the religious mainstream, and that does not arise from existing religious bodies.

Audience cult A loosely structured, diffuse religious entity which has no formal organization and whose adherents rarely meet.

cults may gather occasionally at conventions or other meetings, but adherence to, participation in, and consumption of cult doctrine takes place mainly through radio, television, magazines, newspapers, and books.

Client cult A cult based on giving and receiving specific services, such as therapy, success, and peace of mind.

Client cults are somewhat more organized than audience cults. Here, adherents are seeking a specific service—like therapy, success, enlightenment, spiritual guidance, or divine salvation. Their commitment to the cult, although stronger than that of the followers of an audience cult, is partial rather than all-embracing. Scientology, est, Dianetics, rolfing, and bodies that are generated around certain Eastern gurus are examples of client cults.

Cult movement A full-fledged religious organization that attempts to satisfy its members' religious needs in their entirety.

Cult movements arise when leaders are able to convince clients, followers, or adherents to attend services regularly and to abandon loyalties to other religious organizations. "Cult movements are full-fledged religious organizations that attempt to satisfy all the religious needs of converts. Dual membership with another faith is out. Attempts to cause social change, by converting others, become central to the group agenda" (Stark and Bainbridge, 1985, p. 29). The degree of commitment cult movements are able to extract from their members varies. Some are weak organizationally, little more than study groups. Some are much like more conventional churches and denominations in the degree of commitment and loyalty their members display. A few cult movements are able to generate intense, extreme commitment—a total way of life. "They require members to dispense with their secular lives and devote themselves entirely to cult activities. . . . Their lives are circumscribed wholly by the demands of the cult. Usually they live in. If they hold jobs, it will be only where and when they are directed to do so, in enterprises the cult owns and operates" (Stark and Bainbridge, 1985, p. 29). The Unification Church ("Moonies"), Reverend Jim Jones's People's Temple, before their mass suicide, the "Hare Krishna" movement, Synanon, the Divine Light Mission of Guru Maharaj Ti, and Rajneesh are examples of cult movements.

Cult movements come into extreme tension with the society in which they are located, unlike audience and client cults. The greater the loyalty and commitment a cult is able to mobilize from its members, the greater the tension with conventional society (Stark and Bainbridge, 1985, pp. 35–36). When members cut off their ties with relatives and friends and organize their lives around the cult and its demands, and when the behavior that is demanded of members clashes sharply with commonly accepted norms, opposition and hostility from others is likely to be aroused. Not uncommonly, legal authorities are called in to settle disputes, handle complaints, or make arrests; to rescue children held against their will, investigate charges of "brainwashing," deal with sexual abuse, violence, or other crimes, and so on. For instance, Synanon's members were accused of assaulting outsiders, physically abusing (including beating) members, and attempting to murder a lawyer with a rattlesnake (Ofshe, 1980, p. 121). Strong cult movements also tend to have strong, charismatic leaders whose will is either unopposed or who carries the day against feeble membership opposition. For instance, Charles Dederich, the leader of Synanon, successfully demanded that all members give up their right to have children—that men undergo vasectomies and women have abortions—and that all existing couples terminate their present relationships and be paired up with other partners (Ofshe, 1980, pp. 122–123). Reverend Jones of the People's Temple was able to make his followers give up all their money, their property, and their freedom; to confess to acts they did not commit—like homosexual behavior and sexually molesting their children—to subject themselves to beatings and verbal humiliation; and, ultimately, to give up their lives in a mass suicide (Mills, 1979).

Sects

There are parallels between the cult movement and the **sect.** Both entail a fairly radical break with at least some aspects of conventional society and established religion. Both stress a degree of separateness by members from the secular world and a certain exclusiveness in relations with fellow members. And both encourage conversion of members, and conversion by members of new members. Sects also experience a degree of tension with the society at large. However, sects and cults do diverge. Whereas a cult arises anew or externally, a sect is an offshoot of a parent religious body, usually a church. In theological terms, sects are *schismatic* groups; their existence "began as an internal faction of another religious body" (Stark and Bainbridge, 1985, p. 24). However, they claim not to be new, but to be old—that is, they "left the parent body not to form a new faith but to reestablish the old one, from which the parent body had 'drifted'. . . . Sects claim to be the authentic, purged, refurbished version of the faith from which they split" (Stark and Bainbridge, 1985, p. 25).

Sects tend to be fairly dogmatic—that is, they tend to see the world in black-and-white, all-or-nothing terms, to be unwavering and unquestioning in their beliefs, and to feel superior to and self-righteous toward all nonbelievers. They also tend to be fundamentalistic in their theology: The original revelations and scriptures represent the only authentic, true expression of the faith. For instance, members of Christian sects believe that every word in the Bible is literally true now and for all time. Adherents of sects see themselves as "faithful remnants" of God's people, a fellowship of the elect, a kind of priesthood or community of "true believers," who alone listen to God's word. Sects are characterized by a high level of lay membership participation, and they usually underplay the clergy. Sects are hostile or indifferent to secular society, which is considered evil and corrupting. Sect members also underplay the material dimension of life and emphasize otherworldly issues: heaven and hell, salvation, moral purity, and deliverance. A common belief among sects is that, when God is revealed, only the righteous—that is, they alone—will achieve salvation (Yinger, 1970, pp. 251ff; Wilson, 1982, pp. 91–92; Johnstone, 1983, pp. 77–79; Roberts, 1984, pp. 224ff). Examples of sects are most contemporary "born-again" Christian bodies, Jehovah's Witnesses, Seventh-Day Adventists, and most Protestant denominations during their very inception (such as Methodism, Lutheranism, Presbyterianism, and the Baptist bodies).

As with nearly all sociological variables, "sectness" is a matter of degree; some sects are more sect-like than others are. In addition, some religious bodies rely less on conversion for their membership than on natural reproduction, and, yet, they have most of the other features of sects, such as originating in a split or schism from a parent body and withdrawing from or being indifferent or hostile to secular society. These are called **established sects.** Examples include the Amish, the Mennonites, the Hutterites, and the Mormons (Wilson, 1982, p. 102; O'Dea and Aviad, 1983, p. 83).

Over time, as successful sects attract a more stable and successful membership, they become increasingly wealthy, respectable, and conservative. Such a sect has now become a denomination. That, in brief, is

Sect A schismatic religious body—one that split off from a parent church—that possesses a strong sense of its own righteousness and of the error of other religious bodies and that remains somewhat aloof from secular society, which it views as corrupt.

Established sect A sect that rejects the secular world and the general society, but whose membership relies less on conversion than on natural reproduction.

the history of Methodism from the eighteenth century to the twentieth (Niebuhr, 1929) and of the Mormons from the nineteenth century to the present (O'Dea, 1957). The dispossessed form the sect, and new prophets, as with new revelations, arise to serve them.

The last decade or two have witnessed an explosion of sects in the United States. But although sect members generally are not as affluent or as well educated as the majority of Americans, sects no longer appeal exclusively to the dispossessed. Today, something else is afoot in the world of religion.

The Church

Church An established religious body that has a rigid hierarchy, an extensive bureaucracy, and a powerful influence over secular society, especially the government, and that claims universalism in a society—that is, it claims all the members of a society as members of the church. As a general rule, the church is conservative: It compromises with and supports existing social values and social structures, especially the stratification and political systems.

Ecclesia See **Church.**

The **church** (sometimes also called the **ecclesia**) claims to be *universal*—to include as its members all or nearly all individuals living in a given society. Those who do not belong (for instance, Jews in medieval Europe) automatically have an inferior legal, political, and religious status. Churches, in other words, exercise a religious *monopoly*. As the established religion, churches usually claim to have a hold on theological truth. They also tend to dominate the secular state; many churches are also state religions. They are large, powerful, hierarchical, and extensively bureaucratized. Churches employ a full-time professional clergy who have been trained in formally approved and sponsored institutes that impart official credentials and ordination. For the most part, members tend to be born into the church; it gains new members as a result of natural reproduction and the socialization of children. The church has a favorable relationship with secular society; unlike the sect, it has made compromises to maintain its position. It supports the *status quo*, including its values, its structures, and the existing stratification system. Churches place a great deal of emphasis on the intervention of the clergy between the laity and God; the sect, in contrast, emphasizes the individual's direct relationship with God. In a church, it is important that the clergy properly interpret the word of God to the membership (Yinger, 1970, p. 257; Johnstone, 1983, pp. 79–80; Roberts, 1984, pp. 228, 232–239). Excellent examples of churches are the Eastern Orthodox Church during the nineteenth century and before in Russia, Greece, and Bulgaria; the Roman Catholic Church in medieval Europe; and Lutheranism in the Scandinavian countries during the seventeenth, eighteenth, and nineteenth centuries. Note that "churchness," like sectness, is a matter of degree; certain examples (like the Catholic Church in Spain during the Inquisition) approximate an "ideal type" more closely, whereas other examples (such as Lutheranism in Sweden today) have some features of the church, but are missing most others. At the same time, the church, the sect, and the cult, are clearly distinct types of religious bodies.

The Denomination

Denomination A religious organization that accepts the validity of other religions, is fairly secularized, and generates a fairly mild religious commitment.

Secularization A process of becoming influenced by nonreligious forces and losing a more intense and "purer" religious orientation.

When the church loses its monopolistic hold on a society, and when a number of religious bodies achieve equal legal and political status, denominationalism is the result. A **denomination** is one religious body among several; denominations stress religious pluralism, tolerance, and cooperation. Members of denominations are not dogmatic. They regard affiliation with one or another religious body as a matter of religious choice or an accident of birth, and they do not attribute spiritual superiority to themselves or inferiority to others. Denominations have become prey to **secularization**—that is, they have been permeated with and by the values and practices of the workaday world. The religious faith of most members is not terribly strong, and religion is usually a marginal commitment and activity.

> In the modern state, the churches . . . tend to become denominationalized, as they lose their claim to special status, and as orthodox religious commitment weakens. Voluntarism becomes the norm in religion . . . and established churches, which long ago lost their power to coerce, have increasingly lost even the force of conventional influence over the masses of the population, just as they have been forced to abandon the position of mutual reinforcement that they once enjoyed with the agencies of the secular state. To all this, we add the force of secularization, which has meant a loss of power for conventional religion (Wilson, 1982, p. 93).

In the United States, denominationalism is characteristic of nearly all of the larger Protestant bodies, Reform and Conservative Judaism, and much of the Catholic church. America is a land of religious diversity, and denominationalism tends to be strongly held and widely practiced in the religious mainstream here. Of course, as with the other religious types, denominationalism is a matter of degree. Some American denominations (like Southern Baptists and Missouri Lutherans) display sect-like features, whereas others, like Congregationalists, Northern Baptists, and United Methodists, more closely approximate the "ideal type" of a denomination.

MAINLINE AMERICAN RELIGIONS

In the United States, contemporary mainline religions both compete with and anchor a series of nonreligious identities and interests. Compared with religious bodies that call for a more intense religious commitment (like sects), in the mainline bodies, religious doctrine is less crucial; the secular meaning behind the religious identity assumes great importance. Although members of various mainline denominations do hold somewhat different beliefs, these beliefs tend to be strongly shaped by secular statuses, such as the individuals' social classes and educations, and the region of the country in which the individuals live. About 95 percent of all Americans say that they believe in a personal God, but most of them also think, "You shouldn't go overboard about it." As we see a bit later in this chapter, religions have undergone a certain kind of secularization—that is, they have been influenced by nonreligious, material forces. This is not to say that Americans have turned their back on religion and have abandoned its worship and beliefs. In fact, in many ways, religion in America is stronger than it has ever been in this century. What this means is that the very nature of religious observance has undergone a transformation that most earlier worshipers would describe as a turning away from their conceptions of a true religion—indeed, as its very corruption.

At the same time, late twentieth-century religious expression does have its own distinct character. Some say that nationality and the political sphere have acquired a sacred aura—the so-called "civil religion" thesis. Many observers argue that religion serves a number of secular functions for its adherents, especially ethnic affiliation, social status, and organization participation. And finally, some observers hold that the contemporary religious mainstream is stronger than it has ever been, that religious belief and participation are higher than at any time in this century. Let's examine each of these assertions in turn.

Ethnic Affiliation

The memberships of most local churches in the United States are ethnically homogeneous. In some denominations, membership itself affirms and reinforces ethnic identity. Relatively few Reform Jews are religious in the strict sense of the word; most attend services only a few times each year. But belonging (and contributing) to a local synagogue, marrying within the faith, having a religious wedding ceremony, sending their children to Hebrew school and having them Bar Mitzvahed or Bat Mitzvahed—all are ways of keeping their ethnic identity alive, of reminding themselves that they are a people distinct from all others.

Each Eastern Orthodox church—the Bulgarian, Armenian, Greek, Russian, and so on—consists of a single ethnic group, and serves the same function for its members. The church services and religious beliefs are a vehicle around which to organize an identity of peoplehood—whether Bulgarian, Armenian, Greek, or Russian. The church sponsors activities that involve wearing national costumes, cooking and eating ethnic food, and singing songs and dancing to music from "the old country," all of which serve to remind the participants that "I am Greek," or "I am Armenian."

Are Catholics Different from Protestants?

Despite their name ("catholic" means universal), a very high proportion of Catholic churches are ethnically uniform. Certain local churches are almost entirely Irish, Italian, Hispanic, Vietnamese, or Polish in composition, and a Catholic is likely to join—or avoid—one on that basis, according to his or her own ethnic background. Thus, as with Judaism and the Eastern Orthodox churches, Catholicism continues to exist, in part, because it serves as a symbol of ethnicity.

Based on a misunderstanding of Max Weber's theory of the Protestant ethic and the spirit of capitalism, an earlier generation of researchers believed that Catholics held religious views and followed religious practices that were distinctly different from those of the Protestant majority (Lenski, 1963). Contemporary evidence refutes this view. Almost seven out of ten Catholics (69 percent) said that "divorced Catholics should be permitted to remarry in the Catholic Church." Almost three-quarters (73 percent) said that Catholics should be allowed to use artificial birth control (Gallup and Poling, 1980, Table F). Almost the same proportion of Catholics as Protestants said that abortion should be "legal, under any circumstances" (18 percent of Protestants, 20 percent of Catholics) or "legal, under certain circumstances" (58 percent of Protestants, 53 percent of Catholics), indicating no difference of opinion on this crucial aspect of Catholic dogma (Gallup, 1978, p. 32). Slightly *more* Protestants than Catholics said that extramarital sex was "always wrong" (71 versus 64 percent) (Gallup, 1978, p. 207). Catholics once tended to be strikingly more active churchgoers than Protestants were; in the 1950s, more than seven out of ten Catholics (72 percent) attended church weekly. By 1984, however, this figure had declined to about half (51 percent). Meanwhile, the figure for Protestants was significantly lower (39 percent), indicating something of a convergence for the two religions (Gallup, 1985, p. 271). Clearly, Catholicism is no longer as great a religious force in the lives of its adherents in the United States as it was a generation ago. The church has become more secularized. It was these trends that moved

Pope John Paul II, aware of the forces of secularization acting on America's Catholics, to issue a number of declarations, directed specifically at American Catholics, reaffirming the church's traditional stand on abortion, birth control, nonmarital sex, and divorce. It is unlikely that these statements will have much of an impact, because such beliefs and practices are the result of powerful social forces, and are not a simple act of forcing one's faith in an approved direction.

Social Status

Another nonreligious function served by mainline American denominations is the affirmation of social status. For example, those Jews who belong to Temple Emanu-El, in New York City, are well-to-do and highly assimilated; the members of the small *schuls* (synagogues) on New York's Lower East Side are mostly poor, unassimilated, and old. Religion can be looked on as a kind of consumer item, like a car or a house. Belonging to the "right" denomination is a symbol of place in the stratification hierarchy. People who rise in the class system often change their religious membership, just as they might change their neighborhoods. In the seventeenth and eighteenth centuries, as Pennsylvania's Friends (Quakers) became wealthy, they gradually became Episcopalians, because the Episcopal church had more social distinction than the Society of Friends (Baltzell, 1958). This same "matching" process takes place today: The Baptist lawyer from Georgia who moves to Los Angeles and becomes rich may well decide he would be more comfortable as a Methodist; the Orthodox Jewish physician who moves to the suburbs may decide to join a Conservative temple; the daughter of a Midwestern German Lutheran family who receives a Ph.D. and gets a job teaching at a university may become a Unitarian. These cases are so common that they fall into a clear-cut pattern.

A Nation of Joiners

This country's denominations serve additional functions, too—besides affirming ethnic and class identity. We are, for example, a nation of joiners, and in many ways belonging to a church or a synagogue is rather like belonging to the PTA or a local birdwatchers' club. In fact, there is a high correlation between participation in religious groups and participation in secular groups (E. Goode, 1966, 1980).

The one function that seems to have declined in importance over the last generation or so is the specifically religious and spiritual function. As society at large becomes less and less spiritual, the "mainstream" or mainline religions must try to hold to their increasingly skeptical and materialistic flocks. Meanwhile, the members who are concerned with spiritual matters are increasingly looking outside the mainstream for spiritual comfort and guidance. As we can see from Table 14–1, the membership of the mainstream denominations, which are ecumenical and liberal in their orientation, is declining, either in absolute numbers or relative to the general population. Between 1960 and 1983, the Episcopal church lost nearly half a million members. During this same period, the United Methodist church, another mainstream denomination, lost over a million members. As a general rule, the more fundamentalist, the more sect-like, and the more conservative the denomination, the more it has grown during the past generation or so. The Mormons more than doubled their numbers between 1960 and the 1980s, while the Southern Baptists added roughly 4 or 5 million members to their rolls. Sects, such as the Assemblies of God, the Church of God of Cleveland,

■ **TABLE 14–1 Church Membership, Selected Denominations, 1960–1980s**

	1960	*1984/1985*	*Percent Change*
Mainline Denominations			
Episcopal	3,269,000	2,794,000	−15%
Lutheran*	5,269,000	5,250,000	−1%
United Methodist	10,641,000	9,292,000	−13%
Presbyterian**	4,249,000	3,203,000	−25%
Conservative Denominations			
Southern Baptists	9,731,000	14,342,000	+47%
Mormons***	1,642,000	3,794,000	+131%
Missouri Lutherans	2,391,000	2,628,000	+10%
Sects			
Assemblies of God	508,000	2,036,453	+301%
Church of God (Cleveland, Tennessee)	170,000	506,000	+198%
Church of the Nazarene	307,000	516,000	+68%
Jehovah's Witnesses	250,000	698,000	+179%
Salvation Army	254,000	421,000	+66%
Seventh-Day Adventists	317,000	684,000	+116%

Figures rounded off to the nearest thousand.
* Lutheran combines the membership of the American Lutheran Church and the Lutheran Church in America.
** Presbyterian combines the Presbyterian Church in the United States, the Presbyterian Church in the United States of America, and the Cumberland Presbyterian Church.
*** Mormons combines the Church of Jesus Christ of Latter Day Saints and the Reorganized Church of Jesus Christ of Latter Day Saints.
Source: Constant H. Jacquet, Jr. (ed.), Yearbook of American and Canadian Churches, 1986. Nashville, Tennessee: Abingdon, 1986, pp. 231–241.

Tennessee, and the Jehovah's Witnesses have doubled and tripled their membership—or more—over the past generation. (See Table 14–1.)

By and large, though, the membership of the mainstream denominations is declining steadily. (A June 19, 1985, article published in *The New York Times* proclaimed "Church Rolls Up; Long Decline Ends." However, the tabulation it cited combined mainline with conservative denominations, along with sects as well, making a meaningful evaluation of membership trends all but impossible.) There is clearly a growing loss of interest in the secularized, ecumenical, mainstream Protestant denominations. The Catholic church, also subject to forces of secularization, is also declining in membership. (Until recently, Catholicism managed to grow yearly, but mainly because of immigration from Catholic countries.) Between 1983 and 1984, the number of Catholics in the United States decreased by roughly 100,000 (Goldman, 1985). Clearly, the established, liberal denominations in America are in deep trouble. We examine why shortly.

Has There Been a Religious Secularization in America?

Certainly a great deal of secularization has taken place in American society over the course of its history. Churches have considerably less power than they had in past centuries. Individuals may defy bans and traditions once strongly sanctioned by religious bodies without penalty or serious repercussion; such issues as abortion, divorce, premarital sex, the Sunday "blue laws," out-of-wedlock birth, heresy, and blasphemy illustrate this generalization: The churches no longer punish violators or individuals who have engaged in these practices to the degree that they once did. It is difficult to deny that religion is less intrusive in the lives of ordinary members of society than it was at one time. We might be tempted to argue from this that religion has become irrelevant in the lives of contemporary men and women. At the same time, we would be wise to resist this temptation. Has American culture become entirely secularized in recent years? Has the specifically religious aspect of our mainstream religions been relegated to the sidelines? Though, admittedly, the sacred and godly dimension has remained strong for fundamentalism, is this also true of the religious mainstream?

Researchers are not entirely in agreement on the answers to these questions. Is it possible to make a meaningful comparison of the degree of religious expression now versus that of the past? As with so many areas of life, we find ourselves resorting to *indicators* of religiousness. How would we measure the degree to which religion is important in our lives? Has American society become less religious over the years—or more? And how would we determine this? According to a 1983 Gallup Poll, summarized in *The New York Times* (March 11, 1984, p. 22E), weekly church attendance in the United States grew from 1950 (39 percent) to 1955 to 1958 (49 percent), and then declined steadily after that (to 40 percent). In 1957, when respondents were asked, "Do you believe that religion can answer all or most of today's problems?" 81 percent said yes. This percent declined steadily until the 1980s, when the figure was slightly more than half (54 percent). Clearly, as measured by some indicators, the influence of religion has declined in the past generation or so.

This conclusion is not universally accepted, however. Between 1977 and 1981, a team of researchers (Caplow, Bahr, and Chadwick, 1981; Caplow, Bahr, Chadwick et al., 1983) compared the religious beliefs and practices of the residents of a small Midwestern city, given the pseudonym of "Middletown" (which was, in fact, Muncie, Indiana) with those of 1924, when the same city was studied by sociologists Robert Lynd and Helen Merrill Lynd and reported in their classic book *Middletown* (1929). Surprisingly, on a number of measures or indicators, religious observance is actually higher today than it was over a half a century ago. Only a quarter of all Middletown's married couples attended church regularly in 1924, whereas recently, half did so. Half of the 1924 respondents reported no church attendance at all, whereas recently, only one-sixth did. In 1924, there was one church for every 870 residents, whereas currently, there is one for every 538. Tithing—giving one-tenth of one's income to the church—was practiced by only one out of the 100 families on whom the Lynds had such information; currently, a third of the active church members tithe. Overall, the authors say, these data demonstrate a "strong persistence of religion in America. . . . As Middletown people have become more egalitarian, more hedonistic, more affluent, and more educated, they have become more zealous in religion than their grandparents were" (Caplow et al., 1981, p. 37).

On the other hand, as the authors also point out, the very nature of religious commitment and expression has changed in contemporary society. For one thing, religious dogmatism has declined. Although faith in God, Jesus, and the Bible remains high today, the view that one's own beliefs are the only valid religious beliefs has plummeted during this century. When the Lynds asked Middletown's entire high school population in 1924 if they agreed with the statement, "Christianity is the one true religion, and all people should be converted to it," 94 percent agreed.

The same question presented to a comparable contemporary sample elicited only 38 percent agreement. Thus, although adherence to religion remains strong—indeed, seems stronger than in past decades—the very content of that religion has changed:

> The onerous parts of religious observance—long sermons, afternoon services, compulsory fasts—have been mostly abandoned. Sin is still regularly denounced from the pulpits, but sinners are treated with consideration. Divorced persons are admitted to communion; suicides are buried in consecrated ground; wayward youths are counseled, not excommunicated. In every measurable way, Middletown's religion has become less puritanical in the past two generations, that is, less conscience striken about faults, less censorious about shortcomings, less emphatic about rewards and punishments, and less preoccupied with sex. . . . Divorce, suicide, bankruptcy, and unmarried pregnancies are treated as disasters, not as crimes, by Middletown's ministers and churchgoers, and the victims are much more likely to be consoled than to be ostracized. . . . The new tolerance is the most striking change in Middletown's religion in the past half-century; indeed, it represents a signal departure from Christian practice throughout history. Not only do Protestants speak well of each other and benignly of Catholics, they abstain from condemnation of the heathen and favor teaching about Buddhism in the public schools. There is no longer any preaching against the pope at revival meetings. There are no more diatribes against the Jews in Easter sermons. The rise of Islamic fundamentalism in the late 1970s and the anti-American vituperation of Moslem mobs during the Iranian hostage crisis did not provoke any discernible anti-Moslem reaction in Middletown's churches. . . . Religion of any kind is no longer perceived as a legitimate object of aggression. The wrath of the godly is now reserved for such secular targets as bureaucrats, abortionists, and pornographers (Caplow et al., 1983, pp. 283, 287).

Thus, though American religions are alive and well, religious expression and belief have become less intense, less dogmatic, less exclusive, and more tolerant—in short, somewhat watered-down.

FUNDAMENTALISM IN AMERICA

If mainstream religious groups have become secularized to the extent that belonging to them is no different from belonging to the PTA, what does religion offer that's special? Some say that the mainstream churches are in trouble because a secular society has no need for religion. Others say that they are in trouble because they have become *too* secularized, too removed from the spiritual needs of the people (Kelley, 1977, pp. 20–21, 36ff). Perhaps both points are correct—but each point is correct for different sets of people. While the liberal, mainstream denominations are declining in membership, the sects—the "strong" religions, the ones that declare themselves to have a monopoly on truth, the fundamentalist Christian churches—are growing at an explosive rate. They are growing despite the expectations of almost all experts on the sociology of religion. The decline of the mainstream religious groups and the amazing expansion of fundamentalist sects have gone together, hand in hand.

Sectarianism

Sects reject denominationalism, the idea that all religions are of equal validity and worth. Sects view society as corrupt and seek to change it or withdraw from it. Their members tend to be dogmatic. In addition,

Protestant sectarians are fundamentalists: They believe that the Bible issued directly from God and is wholly without error. Fundamentalists believe that the Lord created the heavens and the Earth in six days and six nights and that Jesus was born of a virgin. The more literally Christians interpret the Bible, the more likely they are to believe that their own church is absolutely right about theological questions and that other churches are wrong.

As with every sociological variable, sectarianism is a matter of degree; some religious groups have more of it than others. Of all large American religious groups, the United Church of Christ (the Congregational church) is the least sectarian, the most **ecumenical** (cooperative with other religions), the most tolerant of other religious bodies, the least inclined to fundamentalism, and the most secular. In a study conducted in the 1960s, only 40 percent of all Congregationalists in the sample said, "Jesus is the Divine Son of God, and I have no doubts about it" (Stark and Glock, 1968, p. 33). Only 41 percent said that they had no doubt concerning the existence of God! In many ways, Congregationalism represents an almost "pure type" of denomination, American-style.

Consider the Southern Baptist Convention. Unlike the liberal, mainline religious groups, the Southern Baptists—distinct from those of the North—have enjoyed spectacular growth in recent years. In 1960, they had 9.7 million members; in 1980, 13.6 million—a 36 percent increase, nearly twice that of our population as a whole (Jacquet, 1986, pp. 231–241). In the same 1960 study, 99 percent of the Southern Baptists said that they did not doubt the existence of God; 99 percent said that they did not doubt the divinity of Jesus; 94 percent expected Jesus to return to Earth; 92 percent said that they believed, literally, in Biblical miracles; 97 percent believed in a life after death; 97 percent said that acceptance of Jesus as Savior was "absolutely necessary" for personal salvation; and 61 percent said that belief in the Bible as "God's truth" was "absolutely necessary" for it (Stark and Glock, 1968, pp. 28, 33, 34, 36, 37, 43). Twenty-five percent said that the Jewish religion was "definitely," and 28 percent "possibly," a "barrier" to salvation. In August, 1981, the president of the Southern Baptist Convention said (on national TV), "God Almighty does not hear the prayer of the Jew, for how in the world can God hear the prayer of a man who says that Jesus Christ is not the true Messiah?" In most ways, the beliefs of Southern Baptists more closely resembled those of sectarians than those of the other large groups.

Denominationalism, as sectarians see it, reflects the erosion of religious faith, not just tolerance and open-mindedness. For the most part, they are right. Within the framework of a strong fundamentalist faith, the rejection of the idea that all religions are equally valid is logically inevitable. After all, scientists believe that the principles of evolution are literally true, and therefore that the Biblical account of creation is literally false. Fundamentalists avow religious truth in much the same spirit.

The Fundamentalist Revival

Fundamentalism has flourished precisely because it created a strong religious commitment in the midst of a highly secular society. The mainline denominations have largely ignored the chief function of religion: making sense of human existence, building a sacred world, creating a world of meaning for believers. Fundamentalist churches offer their members salvation, eternal life, perhaps the strongest of all inducements to membership. Secular organizations are not competing in this market,

Ecumenical Practicing cooperation among a number of religious bodies.

Fundamentalist churches are growing explosively in the United States—because they provide activities and a sense of common purpose for their members.
Milton Potts/Photo Researchers

Fundamentalism In Christianity, belief in the literal and infallible truth of the Bible; more generally, adhering to an orthodox doctrine and practice.

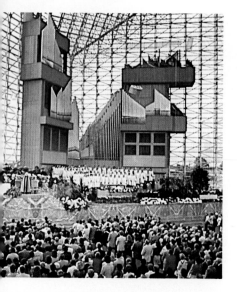

Contemporary urban society fosters the emergence and growth of religious organizations whose services are similar to the mass media, with a huge audience, a largely one-way communication, and impersonality combined with pseudo-intimacy.

Zimberhoff—Gamma/Liaison

so the fundamentalists, unlike the mainstream denominations, can offer something that the secular world cannot. Denominations offer, not salvation, but symbols of status and ethnicity, and they must therefore compete with secular organizations for members (Kelley, 1977, pp. 91–93). Denominations do not have the inducements, the organizational methods, or the commitment that sects do, and this is the chief reason for their rapid decline and the sects' rapid growth.

Fundamentalist churches offer definite, simple, black-and-white answers in a bewildering world. At a time when community and family ties are weakening, these churches offer a surrogate community and a substitute family. They seek to restore faith in the political process, patriotism, and government (Bellah, 1970). Their members are warm, emotional, and communal in spirit, whereas the denominations tend to be impersonal and formal. They offer solace amid the political, social, moral, and emotional anguish of our day. And, today's fundamentalists (unlike the sectarians of the past, who tended to be the poorest and least well-educated members of society) approximate a cross-section of our society—not just the materially dispossessed but the spiritually dispossessed.

Precisely to the extent that the mainstream of American culture becomes more secular and irreligious, fundamentalism flourishes on the sidelines. Our society seems to have polarized between those who are moving away from religion altogether and those whose religious commitment is becoming deeper and stronger. We seem to be developing "two societies" in religion. The religious mainstream—which, remember, still includes the majority of our population—appears to be breaking up; "the center cannot hold."

THE "NEW RELIGIONS"

On July 1, 1982, 2,075 couples, all followers of the Reverend Sun Myung Moon, were married in a mass ceremony in Madison Square Garden. The bridegrooms were dressed in identical blue suits; the brides wore identical lace and satin gowns made by the sect's members. The couples were matched by Reverend Moon, and many had met only a few weeks before. A number of them had no common language and had to speak through interpreters (Montgomery, 1982).

Reverend Moon's sect, the Unification Church, underemphasizes the romantic and personal side of marriage. Marriage, to them, is just a means of attaining spiritual perfection. Celibacy is the ideal. "We admit that what we are doing is not normal in the eyes of many," one sect member stated. "It is our dedication to God, not to self, that enables us to do it." Georgia Sherman, a Liberian, who married Richard Lewis, a Welshman, said, "Because we hold Reverend Moon in such esteem, there is trust" (Austin, 1982, p. B4).

Why would more than 4,000 people marry spouses they hardly knew? The Unification Church is one of a number of bodies collectively described as the "new religions." They comprise the unconventional, non-Jewish, non-Christian, and fringe Christian faiths that cropped up here in the 1960s and 1970s (Needleman, 1970; Marty, 1976, pp. 126–157). Some of these new religions are not really new, but they did not exist

WHAT DO YOU THINK?

Are Conservative Protestants Anti-Semitic?

Studies conducted by sociologists in past decades have suggested that there is a connection between Christianity and anti-Semitism. More specifically, the stronger their religious faith and the more orthodox, conservative, and fundamentalist their religious beliefs, the greater the likelihood that Protestants will be prejudiced against Jews (Glock and Stark, 1965). Apprehensive because of the possible implications that this finding might have for Jews, considering the recent rise in religious conservativism, the Anti-Defamation League of B'nai B'rith, a Jewish civil rights organization, commissioned a nationwide poll on the relationship between religious conservativism among white Protestants and anti-Semitism. Episcopalians, Presbyterians, Unitarians, and Congregationalists (that is, members of liberal Protestant denominations), as well as Catholics and Blacks were not included in the study.

Respondents were selected according to several criteria of religious conservativism, attending church frequently and saying that religion played an important role in their lives principal among them. Just over three-quarters (77 percent) described themselves as born-again Christians. Baptists were most heavily represented in the sample (36 percent), followed by Methodists (12 percent), Lutherans (10 percent), and mem-

bers of the Church of Christ (7 percent); the rest were members of other Protestant denominations.

Did the conservative Christians in this study have a negative view of Jews? Is there a connection between conservative Christianity and anti-Semitism? The B'nai B'rith's study's findings do not answer this question conclusively, but the answer that emerges is a qualified no. The vast majority of the conservative Christians who were interviewed did not have a negative image of Jews and could not be regarded as anti-Semitic.

In 1981, the then president of the Southern Baptist Convention was quoted as saying, "God does not hear the prayer of a Jew." When asked for their opinion on this statement, 86 percent of the sample disagreed. Even among Baptists, only 12 percent agreed. The statement, "Christians are justified in holding negative attitudes towards Jews since the Jews killed Christ," elicited 90 percent disagreement among the study's respondents.

When asked directly about their overall opinion of Jews, roughly half (49 percent) said that they had either a "very favorable" or a "somewhat favorable" opinion. Forty percent said that their opinion was "about average," and only a tiny minority (4 percent) admitted that their opinion was unfavorable.

The study asked several ques-

tions that pertain to secular stereotypes that are sometimes used to characterize Jews. Over half (51 percent) agreed with the statement, "Jews are tight with money." However, among those who agreed, the majority (60 percent) saw this trait in a positive, not a negative, light. Thirty-nine percent agreed that "Jews want to remain different from other people and yet they are touchy if people notice these differences." However, of those who did agree, three in ten (30 percent) saw this as a positive trait. Over a quarter (27 percent) agreed with the statement, "because Jews are not bound by Christian ethics, they do things to get ahead that Christians generally do not do."

Fifty-seven percent of the respondents interviewed did not agree with any of these anti-Semitic stereotypical characterizations. However, one-fifth (22 percent) agreed with one out of seven of them, and another fifth (21 percent) agreed with two or more. The director of the Anti-Defamation League saw this finding as "troubling."

Did the study by the Anti-Defamation League confirm the view that there is a connection between conservative Christianity and anti-Semitism? Or refute it? What do you think?

Source: Chavez, 1987, p. A22.

When more than 2,000 couples who belong to Reverend Sun Myung Moon's Unification Church got married in a collective ceremony on July 1, 1982, all the grooms wore identical suits and all the brides wore identical gowns. Such sects promote a sense of belonging among members, but at the cost of their individuality.

Ken Karp

in America before. Others emerged only recently. The new religions are "cults." Among them are many varieties of Hinduism, such as the Divine Light Mission and the "Hare Krishna" movement; various occult groups, like the Process; followers of witchcraft and Satanism, Scientology, Synanon, Tibetan Buddhism, and Subud.

The number and variety of these proliferating cults is vast, so it is difficult to generalize about all of them. There do seem to be several common denominators. The new religions are similar to fundamentalist Christian sects: They are "strong" religions; they tend to be authoritarian, to demand an intense and total (rather than a weak and marginal) commitment; they stress discipline and conformity among their members; they proclaim that they and they alone have a monopoly on truth; they condemn secular society as corrupt; and they actively seek committed converts.

Second, most of the new religions were founded, and continue to be sustained, by strong charismatic leaders. Some—the Unification Church, for instance—have created organizations that will probably survive the leaders' deaths. Others depend solely on the leaders' charisma to maintain the commitment of the faithful. While a leader lives, his word—very few of such religious leaders are women—is sacred and unchallengeable. Followers attribute to these leaders infinite wisdom and a sacred nature, and they are originally attracted to these sects primarily by a leaders' charisma. In fact, such a leader may well live a life of luxury made possible by the contributions of his followers. (When a reporter asked a relative of the then 16-year-old Guru Maharaj Ji, leader of the Divine Light Mission, about his Rolls Royce, the response was, "Do you expect him to ride on a donkey?"; Cohen, 1975, p. 82.) The followers, by contrast, often live in poverty and self-denial. Jim Jones, the leader of the People's Temple, seems to have had sex with any follower he chose, male or female, yet ordinary members could have sex only with Jones's prior approval. Synanon, which began as a community for treating drug addicts, but became a religion in 1975, forced all its male members to undergo vasectomies—sterilization—in 1977. The sole exception was Charles Dederich, Synanon's powerfully charismatic leader. The more charisma a leader may have, the more the faithful tend to see him as "above the rules." By contrast, the ministers of fundamentalist Christian sects are expected to practice what they preach.

A third feature of the new religions is their highly communal nature. Social and emotional bonds tend to be very close. Members socialize mainly with one another and let outside friendships lapse. The leader encourages this exclusiveness and limits contact with nonmembers to missionary work and fund raising. The members of some of these new religions live exclusively with one another in communal settlements, thereby minimizing contact with the outside world and maximizing the leadership's control over the flock. Members value these strong ties, which is one of their main reasons for joining. Many of these members hungered for intimate contact and caring, which they found lacking in the secular world. By joining, they found an instant substitute family, a close-knit group of peers who cared about them—as long as they conformed to the cult's belief and practices.

Conflict with Secular Society. These three factors—organizational strength, the leader's charisma, and the social isolation of the membership—combine with the unorthodox views of the new religions to place them in sharp conflict with secular society. The leader may insist that any challenge to his power attacks the sacred values—or the divine itself.

He may decide that any and all means may be used to repel such threats. These means bring many new religions into conflict with the rest of the world.

In 1973, Pat Halley, a journalist on an "underground" newspaper in Detroit, hit Guru Maharaj Ji in the face with a shaving-cream pie. A week later, two men went to the journalist's apartment and nearly bludgeoned him to death with a blackjack. Most of the guru's followers feel that the attack was justified. One told a television interviewer that if he caught someone who had thrown a pie at the guru, he would "cut his throat on the spot." "On the spot!" he repeated (Cohen, 1975, p. 90).

Probably the most well-publicized criticisms of the new religions involve charges that certain leaders have held members against their will and "brainwashed" them. Often, parents of devotees attempt to win them back, sometimes forcibly, and to "deprogram" them (that is, remove the influence of the cult from their minds). Ted Patrick, a former Protestant minister, has a full-time business retrieving cult members and "deprogramming" them. He has often been sued by these cults and arrested by the police on kidnapping charges.

Social Composition. One of the most crucial, interesting, and revealing features of these new religions is their social composition. Fundamentalist Christian churches and sects draw their memberships from a fairly wide cross-section of the population. But the "upper-middle class"— highly educated professional and business people—and also the very poor are probably somewhat underrepresented in the fundamentalist churches. Fundamentalism attracts whole families—the young, the old, parents with children, people of all ages. The new religions, in sharp contrast, recruit mainly among the middle and upper classes and overwhelmingly among adolescents, young adults, and whites (Wuthnow, 1976). Young people tend to be less skeptical, more trusting, more open to new ideas, less formed intellectually, and more susceptible to unorthodox, unconventional, untraditional beliefs. They are also very vulnerable to group and peer influences, so the importance the new religions attach to the sharing of beliefs by a community of peers acts as a powerful recruiting device and as a way of sustaining loyalty and commitment.

Why do these groups recruit largely among the middle and upper-middle classes? Perhaps because many young people in them are alienated from our society and its traditions, including religion. They seek a meaning to life—something more than what many of them may regard as a bland, tame, and sterile life of material comfort. Their parents have taught them to question authority and to be tolerant of nonconformists—lessons that are much less commonly learned by young people from lower socioeconomic strata—so they are much more receptive to new messages of all sorts.

The Future of the New Religions. These new religions will not just "go away." A few, like the Unification Church and Synanon, have built large and very profitable financial enterprises—in fact, some people charge that these groups are not really religions but businesses using religion as a "front" to get tax-free status. Whether or not these or other charges are true, new religions do answer the deep-seated spiritual needs of many Americans. No doubt, the mass media exaggerate their importance—for their exotic beliefs and flamboyant leaders make interesting news—but their combined membership certainly approaches that of some Protestant denominations. Because they control so much of their

Some cults are highly successful and have followers all over the world. Here, Hare Krishna worshippers pray and chant through a park in Caracas, Venequela.

Douglas R. Shane/Photo Researchers

members' lives, their impact on American society may grow in the coming years, for good or for evil. As sociologists, we cannot judge the new religions, but we can and must try to understand them.

THE BLACK CHURCHES IN AMERICA

Black religious institutions in the United States are every bit as diverse as those that are predominantly white. There are Black Christians of every variety, Black Muslims, Black Jews, and Black members of the new religious sects. Contrary to popular belief, the importance of religion among American Blacks is more than a reaction to prejudice, discrimination, racism, and poverty. But these consequences of the minority status of American Blacks have certainly played a role in the unfolding of their religious patterns and institutions.

The Black Churches Yesterday and Today

Before the Civil War, white slaveowners attempted to erase all traces of African culture from Black slaves, but they were not completely successful. Many African influences survived, including, in religion, enthusiastic congregational participation and the prominence of music and song in services. The slaveowners saw in religion, especially in the afterlife, a way of reconciling their slaves to the hardships of slavery. If the slaveowners themselves believed that Black slavery was authorized by the Bible, they need not feel guilty about it, and if the slaves believed that slavery was so authorized, they would be less likely to rebel. In fact, though, several slave revolts had their roots in religious inspiration.

Before the Civil War, almost all Christian churches in the South described slavery as "God's will." Many Northern churches opposed it, but they were, and remain to this day, overwhelmingly segregated: With some measure of truth it is said that the most segregated hour in America is 11 A.M. on Sunday morning, because American churches are for the most part 100 percent white or 100 percent Black.

Religious segregation should be considered at both the national and the local level. A number of denominations have very few Black members so that local segregation is not necessary. Because of the ethnic link, there are few Black Lutherans, Jews, and members of Eastern Orthodox churches. Except in the state of Louisiana, the Catholic church was not strong in the slaveowning areas of the South. Relatively few Episcopalians and Presbyterians are Black, because the members of these denominations tend to be quite well-to-do. And the Mormons, whose theology views Blacks as inherently inferior, therefore attract very few Blacks.

What about the denominations like the Baptists and the Methodists, which would be expected to attract Black members? These denominations did not allow Blacks into local churches and forced them to set up their own. Just after the Civil War, Blacks founded separate denominations, usually within a Baptist or Methodist theological framework. Even now, the majority of all Black Christians are concentrated in six separate and almost totally Black denominations; only a tiny minority of Black American Protestants belong to denominations that have a substantial number of whites. (There are slightly over 1 million Black Catholics, making the Catholic population just under 3 percent Black.)

Paradoxically, this system of institutional segregation has nurtured Black leaders since the Civil War. Because these denominations are all Black, Blacks lead them and, in some cases, have risen to national prominence. Had Black ministers attempted to rise in integrated but white-dominated church hierarchies, the path would have been blocked by discrimination. Even where Blacks make up a sizable proportion of a church's membership, as they do in the Jehovah's Witnesses, Black leaders are almost totally lacking. Consequently, racial segregation permitted talented Black religious leaders to rise and shine.

The Role of the Black Churches

Religion plays a much greater role in the lives of Black Americans than in the lives of whites. Black ministers command far more respect and influence in their communities than the white clergy does in theirs. (But among a minority of Blacks who are hostile to religion, they attract more criticism. See Hamilton, 1972, for both sides.) Politicians, both Black and white, must court the Black clergy to win the Black vote. Blacks are much more likely than whites to attend church and accept traditional religious tenets. When asked, "Did you, yourself, happen to attend church in the last seven days?" 31 percent of the white Protestant men who responded—and 38 percent of Black men—said that they had. For the women, the figures were 40 percent and 49 percent, respectively. Interestingly, Blacks (and whites) tend to be more religious in the South than in the North.

Black churches encourage spontaneous congregational participation. Shouts of "Amen!" and "Praise the Lord!" and "Sweet heavenly Jesus!"

fill the air. The participation of the worshipers reflects the intensity of their religious feeling.

Politics and Religion

Ever since Karl Marx described religion as the "opiate of the masses," its political role has been debated. One study found that political militancy among Blacks varied inversely with religiosity—the more religious a Black person was, in other words, the less militant on the issue of civil rights, and vice versa. But a majority of the most militant Blacks in this study were classified as "very" or "somewhat" religious (G. Marx, 1967). Church members who believe that "everything is in God's hands" and who emphasize the afterlife tend to be politically inactive. But church members who believe that "God helps those who help themselves" and who emphasize the here and now tend to be militant on civil rights. This militant but Christian outlook, whose greatest symbol was the Reverend Martin Luther King (1928–1968), fueled the civil rights movement of the 1950s and 1960s and is still the inspiration for such contemporary organizations as the Southern Christian Leadership Conference and for Black-activist religious leaders like the Reverend Jesse Jackson.

In short, for some believers, the Christian religion does tend to inhibit militancy. For many Black Christians, however, religion is an inspiration for political change and reform, not a political "opiate." As two sociologists of racial and cultural minorities put it, "There are some among the oppressed who use religion as a shield against the misfortunes of life; but others are armed with righteous anger" (Simpson and Yinger, 1972, p. 518; 1985, p. 325). Some churches—Black and white—admittedly do adopt otherworldly attitudes in the face of worldly evil. Many fundamentalist sects avoid politics altogether because they see it as unreformable or unimportant. For other believers and religious bodies, belief contributes to militancy, not passivity.

Religion tends to be more powerful in Black families and communities than is true among whites. Moreover, the Black church has more often been a force for progressive social change than white religious organizations.

The Black Muslims

One Black religious body that received much media attention in the turbulent 1960s was known popularly as the "Black Muslims" and officially as The Nation of Islam. Before 1975, it adhered to a sharply anti-white theology. Whites were dubbed "blue-eyed devils," and all contact with them was rejected as corrupting and degrading to Black men and women. The sect taught that Black Americans should form a separate nation within what is now the United States. Eventually, it claimed, a "Battle of Armageddon" would destroy all white nations on Earth. From then on, the world would be ruled by the principles of Islam.

In their daily lives, Black Muslims stress thrift; hard work; abstinence from drugs, alcohol, and cigarettes; and marital fidelity. The eating of pork is forbidden. Men, they believe, should be head of the family; women should return to their traditional place "alongside" their husbands. As for Christianity, they reject completely what they call the "white man's religion." Like the white race, for them it has no future. Muslims have set up many successful businesses and farms, and the sect has succeeded in reforming many Blacks away from lives of crime, drug addiction, and alcoholism (Lincoln, 1973).

In 1975, the leader and founder of the Nation of Islam, Elijah Muhammad, died. His son, Wallace, assumed command of the organization. The younger Muhammad transformed the Muslims almost overnight. He changed their name to the World Community of Al-Islam in the West (W.C.I.W.); dropped its racist, antiwhite doctrine; and announced that whites were welcome to join. (A much smaller organization, still called the Nation of Islam, split off from the original body and retains its all-Black policy. Its leader, Louis Farrakhan, became notorious during the 1984 presidential campaign by issuing anti-Semitic statements and calling Judaism a "dirty religion.") Adherents were encouraged to participate in political activity, such as voting, which had previously been forbidden. Wallace Muhammad even supported Jimmy Carter for president in 1976 and attended his inaugural ceremony. Wallace lived more modestly than his father had done, too, and paid off the organization's staggering debts. The Black Muslims had joined the American religious mainstream and began to attract a more middle-class following. The organization's subsidiaries sought and got business from the United States government, including a $22 million Defense Department contract to supply food to the Army. The Black Muslims had ceased to be a sect; they had become a denomination (Gans and Lowe, 1980; Muhammad, 1980).

SUMMARY

1. During the nineteenth century, and even until fairly recently, many intellectuals, including social scientists, believed that religion—based on ignorance and superstition—would eventually disappear. Clearly, they were wrong: Today, religion is alive and well practically everywhere.

2. Sociologists define religion as a system of beliefs and practices

relative to sacred things that unite their adherents into a kind of moral community.

3. Sociology is not concerned with the theological or the empirical "truth" or "falsity" of religion; it is interested in studying the influence of religion on secular society and the influence of secular society on religion.

4. Functionalism argues that religion makes a positive contribution to society as a whole.

5. Conflict theory views religion as a means that the powerful have of exploiting and oppressing the masses.

6. All religions share at least one defining element, a concern for the sacred or the supernatural, and three basic elements or building blocks: beliefs, rituals and practice, and a community.

7. Many religions begin with the inspiration of charismatic leaders.

8. A basic problem for religions is stabilizing the enthusiasm generated by charismatic leaders into organizations that permit the religions to endure and help solve life's problems.

9. There are four basic types of religious organizations: the cult, the sect, the church, and the denomination.

10. Cults represent an entirely novel religion in a specific society. Contemporary thinking in the sociology of religion delineates three different types of cults: "audience" cults, "client" cults, and "cult movements." Audience cults are loosely structured, diffuse entities which lack formal religious organization and whose adherents rarely meet. Client cults are made up of members who seek specific services—like therapy, peace of mind, success, or salvation. Cult movements are full-fledged religious organizations that attempt to satisfy their members' religious needs in their entirety.

11. A sect is typically an offshoot of a parent religion; it possesses a strong commitment to the truth of its beliefs and the falsity of other religions. Sects generally consider secular society to be corrupt and remain somewhat aloof from it.

12. The church is an established religion—large, powerful, with a rigid hierarchy, an extensive bureaucracy, and a strong influence over secular society, especially the government.

13. A denomination is a religious body that tolerates diversity and accepts the validity of other religions; denominations flourish in a multireligious society, such as the United States.

14. Sects typically appeal to the dispossessed, the occupants of the bottom of the class structure. However, as their members become more affluent and respectable, sects gradually become transformed into denominations.

15. "Mainline" American denominations offer a lukewarm religious commitment; much of their appeal lies in functions indirectly related to religious feeling—such as ethnic affiliation, an affirmation of social status, and organizational participation.

16. Many observers argue that societies tend to generate "religions" based on patriotism, nationalism, the sacredness of their political institutions, and a sense of specialness in the eyes of the divine entity. For the United States, this is called "American civil religion."

17. Has American religious expression become secularized over the past generation or two? Many experts believe that religious observance has increased, but the content of religious belief and practice has become less intense, less dogmatic, and less puritanical.

18. In recent years, fundamentalist religious organizations have grown rapidly, while the "mainline" denominations have stagnated.

19. Religious orthodoxy, or fundamentalism, is related to sectarianism: Generally, the more fundamentalist a religious body is, the more it rejects the validity of the truth of other religions.

20. Fundamentalism offers a strong religious commitment, which is one of the reasons why it has been experiencing a revival in recent years.

21. A number of "new religions" have emerged recently—unconventional, non-Jewish, non-Christian (or "fringe" Christian) faiths—that offer an even more intense religious commitment than the traditional sects.

22. Religion tends to be more important in the lives of American Blacks than whites; most Black Christians belong to segregated, nearly all-Black churches.

SUGGESTED READINGS

Willa Appel, *Cults in America: Programmed for Paradise*. New York: Holt, Rinehart & Winston, 1983.
Who joins cults? What happens when someone does? What are the steps of indoctrination? What happens to someone who leaves a cult? This book explores the many sides of the "cult" phenomenon.

Theodore Caplow, Howard M. Bahr, and Bruce Chadwick, *All Faithful People: Change and Continuity in Middletown's Religion*. Minneapolis: University of Minnesota Press, 1983.
A study of the religious beliefs and practices of the residents of a small American city, "Middletown" (Muncie, Indiana). A major feature of the study is its comparison with studies conducted in 1924 and 1935 by Robert S. Lynd and Helen Merrell Lynd, *Middletown* and *Middletown in Transition* (1929, 1937). The authors document the fact that there has been a strong continuity of religious faith and practice in the contemporary generation.

Calvin Goldscheider and Alan S. Zuckerman, *The Transformation of the Jews*. Chicago: University of Chicago Press, 1984.
An historical and sociological analysis of the social, political, and economic institutions of the Jewish people.

C. Eric Lincoln, *The Black Church since Frazier*. New York: Schocken Books, 1974.

A description of the Black style of religious expression in the United States.

Thomas F. O'Dea and Janet O'Dea Aviad, *The Sociology of Religion* (2nd ed.). Englewood Cliffs, New Jersey: Prentice-Hall, 1983.
An excellent, brief overview of the subject of the sociology of religion.

Keith A. Roberts, *Religion in Sociological Perspective*. Homewood, Illinois: Dorsey Press, 1984.
A detailed basic textbook on the sociology of religion.

Gordon Shepherd and Gary Shepherd, *A Kingdom Transformed: Themes in the Development of Mormonism*. Salt Lake City: University of Utah Press, 1984.
A sociological analysis of how Mormonism accommodated itself to a number of internal and external forces during its first century and a half.

Rodney Stark and William Sims Bainbridge, *The Future of Religion: Secularization, Revival and Cult Formation*. Berkeley: University of California Press, 1985.
The results of a series of studies on religion—sects, cults, and religious movements. A good place to get a sense of what sociologists do when they conduct research on religion.

chapter 15
EDUCATION

The *Manifesto of the Communist Party*, written in 1848 by Karl Marx and his collaborator, Friedrich Engels, puts forward a platform of ten reforms that might be made in the immediate aftermath of a socialist revolution. They include the abolition of all private income-producing property and state ownership of all banks and all means of transportation and communication. The tenth plank is "free education for all children in public schools" and an "abolition of children's factory labor." In this respect, at least, the scribblings of two revolutionaries have become a reality in the Western world. Today, we take the universal, even compulsory, schooling of young people from 6 to 16 for granted. It is surprising to learn that in Western society generally, and in the United States specifically, state-supported education is a fairly recent development. In Marx's time (1818–1883), the children of manual laborers began to work in factories, mines, and farms at the age of 6 or 7, for twelve to fifteen hours a day. Most of them never saw the inside of a classroom, and remained illiterate to their dying day. They never received what we today call "an education."

Almost without exception, Americans approve of the educational changes that have taken place since Marx and Engles's time. We all, it seems, endorse our universal, compulsory public educational system. And yet, in recent years the educational system has come under strong criticism from observers who feel that it has failed to fulfill its task. In the early 1980s, the federal Department of Education sponsored a study that was conducted by the National Commission on Excellence in Education; it cost three-quarters of a million dollars to complete. The report released by the Commission in 1983 expressed its concerns eloquently in its title: *A Nation at Risk*. The report stated: "The educational foundations of our society are presently being eroded by a rising tide of mediocrity that threatens our very future as a nation and as a people. . . . If an unfriendly foreign power had attempted to impose on America the mediocre educational performance that exists today, we might well have viewed it as an act of war. As it stands, we have allowed this to happen to ourselves" (Fiske, 1983a, p. 1; National Commission on Excellence in Education, 1983, p. 1).

A few months after the publication of this report, the Carnegie Foundation for the Advancement of Teaching issued its own report evaluating the American educational system (Boyer, 1983; Fiske, 1983b). The Carnegie Foundation admitted that schools cannot cure all of society's ills. Moreover, it stated, the educational system is a symptom of society's problems, and not the disease itself. "A report card on public education is a report card on the nation," it stated. "Schools can rise no higher than the communities that surround them." At the same time, the Carnegie Foundation's report also found serious problems with the American educational system. It stated:

> There remains . . . a large, even alarming gap between school achievement and the task to be accomplished. A deep erosion of confidence in our schools, coupled with disturbing evidence that at least some of the skepticism is justified, has made revitalizing the American high school an urgent matter. . . . Without good schools none of our problems can be solved. People who cannot communicate are powerless. People who know nothing of their past are culturally impoverished. People who cannot see beyond the confines of their own lives are ill-equipped to face the future. It is in the public school that this nation has chosen to pursue enlightened ends for all its people. And this is where the battle for the future of America will be won or lost (Boyer, 1983; Fiske, 1983b, p. A13).

Is this nation failing to achieve its educational goals? And what exactly is our educational system like?

A BRIEF HISTORY OF EDUCATION

Education The institution devoted to the transmission of knowledge, beliefs, and values by individuals occupying formal instructional positions ("teachers") to individuals occupying learning positions ("students").

Education is an institutional form of teaching and learning. It is not so different from the process of socialization (see Chapter 6)—the larger or more general meaning of the word. But in large, complex, urban, and industrialized societies, education has another meaning, too—a narrower and more specific one. In small, homogeneous, tribal societies, children are mostly educated by being included "in adult activities so that they may observe, imitate, and learn through doing. In these ways children acquire the language, values, world view, and skills of their culture. Under circumstances such as these, all adults are teachers, and there are few, if any, special places or times when learning is formally supposed to occur" (Parelius and Parelius, 1978, p. 23). Only a few specific skills, such as magic or woodcarving, are consciously, deliberately taught to children by designated specialists.

At the tribal and preagrarian level, therefore, education and socialization are pretty much the same thing. When society accumulates an economic surplus above and beyond the level of subsistence, its increased resources can be used to support specialists who do not participate directly in the production of food. Some of these specialists are made responsible for education. This chapter is about education in this narrower, more modern sense: The structure and process through which people (called "teachers") who hold formal positions transmit knowledge to people ("students") who hold "reciprocal positions."

The earliest educators, probably magicians and priests, imparted specific skills to their students. As societies grew larger and the division of labor expanded, rulers needed to have bureaucracies with more and more skills—to govern the people, build roads and cities, collect taxes, make war, put down rebellions, and so on. These skills had to be taught to succeeding generations of administrators, officers, and engineers. By the time that the great agrarian empires of early China, Egypt, and Mesopotamia were established, some 5,000 or so years ago, education had been established as a secular occupational specialty.

Education and Industrialization

At this stage, however, education served almost exclusively to transmit skills useful to autocratic rulers. The mass of the population did not benefit directly from education: Only an elite of birth or talent received any kind of formal training. Not until the late nineteenth century, in fact, could a majority of people in western Europe and North America even read or write. For most of human history, formal education has been monopolized by a privileged few. In the nineteenth century, however, the establishment of an advanced industrial economy added greatly to the number of skills needed to run industry. Universal public education and, as a consequence, near-universal literacy largely resulted from the need for a technologically sophisticated labor force. Of course, the process of creating such a labor force extended well into the twentieth century. If we compare, on the one hand, the amount that different countries spend to educate their citizens and the literacy rate of each country and, on the other, their level of industrialization, we find an almost perfect correlation between the two. Highly industrialized countries, like the United States, the Soviet Union, and Japan, have literacy rates well above 95 percent. Countries with practically no industry at all have literacy rates on the order of 5 percent to 15 percent. Partly industrialized countries, like Turkey (65 percent literacy), Egypt (54 percent), and Brazil (75 percent), are also in-between with respect to literacy. The more industrialized a nation may be, the lower its illiteracy rate; the less industrialized it may be, the higher its illiteracy rate. Although not perfect, this correlation is very close. And like many relationships, it is a two-way street, for an illiterate nation can only industrialize slowly, if at all.

THE ROLE OF EDUCATION

What is the purpose of education? What functions does it serve? It might seem that these questions can be answered in a fairly simple, straightforward fashion. As in most other areas of sociology, however, functionalism rivals conflict theory. The functionalist approach to education emphasizes its positive contributions to the society as a whole. The conflict approach, in contrast, stresses the way in which our school system perpetuates inequality.

The Functionalist Perspective

On the most general level, the **functionalist perspective of education** claims that education fosters the smooth maintenance of society and maximizes its chances of survival. Education contributes to the social order. In small, preagricultural tribal societies, just about everyone pitches in and contributes to a child's education; in industrial societies,

Functionalist perspective of education The view that the educational system acts to contribute to the stability, cohesion, and consensus prevailing in a society.

specialists do the job. In either case, education promotes integration, stability, and consensus, just as they, in turn, promote education (Parsons, 1959; Goslin, 1965, pp. 1–18).

Cultural Transmission. Functionalists argue that all societies survive by perpetuating themselves—by passing on their cultures to each succeeding generation. Schools are among the most crucial of these inculcation mechanisms. Through them, society imparts its norms, values, beliefs, and customs to the young. Socialization takes place in all sectors and institutions of society, but it is made most explicit in the course of formal education. In school, children participate in ceremonies, songs, pledges, and drama, all of which reinforce the messages being taught to them. These rituals are as much an emotional as an educational experience. For instance, most young Americans do not know the meaning of many key words in the Pledge of Allegiance, but the ceremony still generates a positive feeling about our country and our government. One of the functions of education is a conservative one, especially at the elementary and grade school levels: The children learn "to love and revere the established and traditional institutions of society. These include the family, religion, the government, and the general economic system." In short, schooling serves the function of "cultural reproduction" (Parelius and Parelius, 1978, p. 23). American schools socialize us to accept hard work, rugged individualism, private property, God, the traditional family, democracy, equality, and law and order; they also teach an active, practical orientation to life (Parelius and Parelius, 1978, p. 24).

Social Control. A culture must not only be taught but enforced. The young must be induced to behave in what society designates as the appropriate manner. Social control comprises all those mechanisms that a society uses to keep its members "in line." Schools reward children who practice culturally approved principles, and they punish those who do not—in short, conformity is encouraged and deviance, discouraged.

Such school rituals as the flag salute and the Pledge of Allegiance generate positive feelings about our country and government.

Susan McCartney/Photo Researchers

Students receive gold stars not only for academic performance but for obedience, as well. Without learning to follow a huge array of rules and regulations, no student can ever hope to emerge successfully from any educational institution. Of course, it is not enough merely to keep students in line by applying positive and negative sanctions. Schools try to get students to internalize a culture's value system, so they will be "self-policing and supportive of the social order" (Parelius and Parelius, 1978, p. 24). Social control operates more indirectly than this, too, because schools act as custodial institutions for the young, keeping children and adolescents off the streets for a considerable length of time.

Training in Intellectual Skills. It might seem unnecessary to point out that education teaches students to think and grow intellectually. Illiterates are at a hopeless disadvantage in a technological society, so schools begin with the three r's—"reading, 'riting, and 'rithmetic." Beyond this first step, however, they impart reasoning power and knowledge: the power to solve problems that have yet to be encountered. Schools are a bulwark against ignorance and the powerlessness it inevitably entails. Schools are more than just a mechanism of personal development, however; as the functionalists emphasize, a well-educated and informed citizen body contributes to stability and to social order.

Selecting for Ability. Functionalists argue that the most capable members of society must be selected to perform the most functionally important occupational roles, and they must be motivated to want to perform them (Davis and Moore, 1945). In short, as the functionalists see it, the best people end up in the right jobs. One major function of education is thus to identify a society's most capable young people and guide them into those occupations in which they can make the greatest personal contributions, contributions that will, in the functionalist view, benefit society the most. Schools channel students into appropriate careers by marking out the brightest and hardest-working students for the most rewarding jobs, and sending the others to positions in which they can make their more modest contributions to society. The functionalists consider academic ability and performance to be predictors of real-life ability and performance, and therefore to be valid screening mechanisms for the various occupational fields.

Assimilation. Large, complex nations face problems not shared by small, preagricultural, tribal societies: For instance, the former must often absorb and resocialize immigrants from other countries and cultures. Assimilation is more difficult for older migrants than for younger ones, in part because children are less fixed in their ways than adults, in part because children are still in school. In the past, schools in the United States attempted to eradicate the influence of foreign cultures on our children and to Americanize them. Today, many school systems recognize the value of encouraging children to keep in touch with foreign cultural traits and customs. At the same time, American schools try to assimilate foreign-born students into the mainstream of our society. Teaching the English language is probably the most crucial aspect of this effort.

Large, complex societies must also deal with subcultures that do not share many values of the dominant culture. The educational system must attempt to integrate into the mainstream children from various racial, ethnic, religious, regional, and social-class subcultures. Although schools do not seek cultural homogeneity, they—more than any institu-

In a varied society like ours, school must integrate children from many social, national, religious, and racial backgrounds into the cultural mainstream.

Irene Bayer/Monkmeyer Press

tion—are responsible for society's effort to resocialize such students in accordance with a common core of shared values.

The Conflict Perspective

Conflict theorists—following their general line of argument—insist that the educational system does not have a uniformly positive impact. On the contrary, they claim, it works to the advantage of the powerful and the affluent and helps keep the poor in their place. Conflict theorists regard education as an arena of struggle among various social and economic groups, not as a source of consensus and stability. Conflict theory insists that all existing societies, especially the capitalist ones, are divided between dominant and subordinate groups, or classes. The dominant group controls the educational system and uses it to impose self-seeking views on the rest of society, by making sure that it promotes values and skills advantageous to the elite. Far from being fair and and equitable, the educational system perpetuates and justifies exploitation. The function of schooling, especially in a capitalist society, "is to produce the kind of people the system needs, to train people for the jobs the corporations require and to instill in them the proper attitudes and values necessary for the proper fulfillment of one's social role" (Szymanski and Goertzel, 1979, p. 188).

This **conflict perspective of education** may seem to resemble the functionalist position, because both theories view education as an assembly line that supplies society and the economy with cooperative citizens and workers. There are, however, also crucial differences between the two views. Conflict theorists consider the educational system to be unfair (because they think it only serves the interests of the ruling elite), coercive (because it imposes the values of one group on all the others), and riddled with conflict (because it is a struggle for dominance that sometimes breaks out into actual violence).

Far from sorting out, encouraging, and rewarding the most able and intelligent students, say the conflict theorists, education stacks the deck in favor of the sons and daughters of the elite. The best education—that is, education that commands the greatest esteem and financial rewards—is nothing more than an article of commerce, a thing that is bought and sold for money. Intelligence and academic performances have relatively little to do with it, they say. Thus, the educational system passes on the existing system of stratification to future generations by

Conflict perspective of education The view that education is an arena for a power struggle among different social and economic groups in a society, the result of which is the imposition of the most powerful group's ideology on everyone else.

awarding the most valuable educational credentials to the children of the elite. In most cases, too, say the conflict theorists, the educational requirements or credentials for high-paying, prestigious occupations are not related to a job's actual performance demands. For the most part, educational requirements are a means of weeding out candidates with the wrong social and economic backgrounds and of awarding elite jobs to the elite. Demanding that candidates for executive positions hold MBAs from Harvard, Stanford, Columbia, and the like is a not-so-subtle way of ensuring that these jobs go to children whose parents could afford such a high-priced education. Even middle-level jobs are caught up in this unjust **credentialism,** because secretaries, receptionists, nurses, and police officers are increasingly required to have bachelor's degrees. How much do these degrees help on the job? According to conflict theorists, little or not at all. Relevant skills and training are generally picked up on the job. Credentialism turns out to be another way of perpetuating inequities in a capitalist society (Berg, 1970; Collins, 1971, 1979).

Conflict theorists do not maintain that the ability to get a "good" degree is totally unrelated to performance or ability, only that schools favor children from families in the higher socioeconomic brackets. They argue, too, that high-socioeconomic parents teach their children values that tend to be rewarded in school—politeness to teachers, punctuality, neatness, cooperativeness, and so on. Those articulate and highly talented members of the working class who do manage to excel in school are, in effect, bribed by the system, which has an interest in rewarding them with high grades, scholarships, and success. Thereby the system "coopts" them—neutralizing any desire they might have to challenge it. The process of **cooptation**—absorbing able sons and daughters of the working class into the elite—is another way that education, say the conflict theorists, justifies injustice and inequality.

A Synthesis

A synthesis of the functionalist and conflict theories is possible; both are flawed, and both are valuable. Education, for the most part, imparts knowledge, beliefs, and values whose overall impact is a conservative one. But the conservatism of education is not unique to capitalist societies; in fact, schools in the Soviet Union and in other communist countries are even more bound to the *status quo* than our schools are. In those countries, conformity and discipline are much more rigid and thoroughgoing, and deviance is less tolerated and more often punished (Bronfenbrenner, 1970, pp. 23–69). The fact is—and here the functionalists are correct—no society could survive if it did not teach its younger members the skills and values that permit it to survive. In this sense, education is inherently conservative. This should not be considered a condemnation of the educational system of capitalist societies specifically—which is the way conflict theorists see it—but an expression of how things are more or less everywhere.

Another strike against the conflict theory is the impossibility of reducing an educational system to "nothing more" than a means of defending the *status quo.* In many times and places, both in capitalist and socialist societies, the primary focus of rebellion has typically been educational institutions—and, more specifically, colleges and universities. For instance, a high proportion of the rebels who in 1979 overthrew the Shah's regime in Iran were university students. In South America, universities are periodically closed down by governments fearful of suspected radical and revolutionary activity on campus. Even in the United States, during the Vietnam War, the focus of opposition to the government was the

Credentialism Setting up arbitrary, formal educational requirements for elite, high-paying jobs that bear little connection to the actual job requirements. Its unstated purpose is two-fold: first, to exclude children from less privileged families from these jobs and to give a competitive advantage to those with upper-middle-class backgrounds; and second, to socialize future occupants of these high-paying positions into conservative, *status quo* accepting values and norms.

Cooptation The process of absorbing able sons and daughters of the working classes into the ranks of the affluent so that they won't threaten the *status quo*; this helps solidify the rule of the elite.

universities—especially the elite ones, such as Berkeley, Columbia, and Harvard. Besides, though many Marxists say that university social science departments are "mostly geared to providing legitimation to the corporate system" (Szymanski and Goertzel, 1979, p. 191), the social sciences are in fact the most left wing of all disciplines (Ladd and Lipset, 1975, pp. 74–75). The popular image of the "pinko" college professor does have some basis in truth. In fact, "academics are more likely than any other occupational group . . . to identify their views as left or liberal, to support a wide variety of egalitarian social and economic policies, and to back small leftist parties" (Lipset, 1982, p. 144). These facts get in the way of the conflict theorists' charge that education, especially higher education, is an "appendage" to the capitalist system, legitimating it as "the best of all possible worlds."

Another objection to conflict theory is the fact that even though the educational system favors the children of the elite, many children of the classes below it rise in the class hierarchy through educational attainment (Blau and Duncan, 1967; Duncan, Featherman, and Duncan, 1972). Conflict theorists underplay the role of intelligence in educational attainment (see Heyns's, 1978, comments on Bowles and Gintis, 1976). One careful observer (Heyns, 1978) concluded that ability (defined as IQ) probably accounted for half of the total variation in the amount of schooling that different people receive and is therefore a major influence on success and income (Sewell, Hauser, and Featherman, 1976). Both intelligence and social class operate powerfully—and more or less equally—class more than intelligence for women, and vice versa for men (Sewell and Shah, 1967). (With greater numbers of women attending college and entering the job market, this difference between them will probably diminish.) This part of the argument is a draw.

Credentialism.   The conflict theorists may have more of a point in the "credentialist" part of their argument. If it were true that education, particularly higher education, selected out of the best and brightest students and trained them for skilled jobs, we would expect to find some relationship between grades in college and occupational success. In fact, no such relationship exists; "grade point average in college does not predict either occupational status or future earnings with any degree of consistency" (Hurn, 1978, p. 38). Even among physicians, who must pass through a long and rigorous program of training, medical school grades are weak predictors of job performance later on.

Clearly, the educational system does serve primarily to manufacture and distribute credentials much more than to provide knowledge and skills.

> Instead of saying that educational institutions teach the skills that are necessary for the performance of complex occupations, it can be argued that educational credentials are used to ration access to high status occupations. Employers who are faced with many potential applicants for few jobs can use educational credentials as a convenient screening device that appears to be quite impersonal and fair. . . . Those who have high levels of education do, of course, generally obtain higher status jobs than those with less education. But this does not seem to be because of the cognitive skills that educated people learned in school. It is the possession of the educational credentials, rather than the acquisition of the cognitive skills that those credentials denote, that seem to predict future status (Hurn, 1978, pp. 39–40).

Educational Consensus?   The functionalist argument can also be faulted for exaggerating the extent to which all Americans agree on a set of core values and beliefs that can be instilled through education.

At least in grade school and high school, the views of racial, ethnic, and political minorities are largely unrepresented in the educational process. Blacks, women, working-class people, and the young are less influential than are whites, men, the higher socioeconomic strata, and older people in determining the content of society's cultural institutions—including education.

Even today, students in the United States are exposed to an interpretation of reality that favors the dominant social classes over all others. To pick one subject—history—it is clear that historians (and history courses) have largely ignored women (until the 1960s, at least) and racial minorities. Blacks, American Indians, Asians, and other minorities are less nearly invisible in American history courses than they used to be, but we still have a lot of catching up to do before their contributions to our society get full recognition. "World history" concentrates on the history of the white world—Europe and North America—and practically ignores the history of Africa, Asia, and South America. And history is for the most part confined to the doings of the mighty—kings, emperors, and presidents. The common people scarcely seem to deserve mention. History is by no means worse, in these respects, than the other academic disciplines. Clearly, the role and the views of dominant groups occupy a more central place in education than do those of less powerful groups—because the dominant groups record their own doings.

THE AMERICAN EDUCATIONAL SYSTEM

Our system of education is almost unique. Canada and Europe have universal, free, compulsory education, as we have. But our students tend to remain in school much longer than their students do. The turning point in our educational system was, roughly, the years from 1870 to 1910. In 1870, the entire United States had only 500 public schools and only 80,000 high school students. Only 2 percent of all 17 year olds received high school diplomas. By 1910, 10,000 public high schools had been set up, more than a million students were enrolled at the high school level, and 9 percent of all 17 year olds received high school diplomas (Trow, 1973; Parelius and Parelius, 1978, pp. 59–60).

In the early years of this century, a substantial proportion of school-age children did not attend school, and, in fact, they never did so in their entire lives. In 1910, only half of all 6 year olds in the United States saw the inside of a classroom; by the age of 7, still only three-quarters did. Even by the peak ages of attendance, 11 and 12, only nine American children in ten were in school just after the turn of the century. And by the age of 16, only half of American children were in school. Clearly, the average amount of schooling received by the country's children only one lifetime ago was brief. As we can see from Table 15-1, the contrast between the percent of individuals enrolled in school in 1910 and 1980, especially at the younger and the older ages, is striking. As compared with earlier in this century, Americans today enter school at a younger age and stay in it until a much older age. More than four times as many 4 year olds, nearly twice as many 6 year olds, and three times as many 18, 19, and 20 year olds are attending school in the 1980s as did in 1910 (Bogue, 1985, p. 383).

■ **TABLE 15–1 Percent Enrolled in School at Selected Ages by Sex, 1910 and 1980**

	Males		Females	
Age	1910	1980	1910	1980
5	17	76	17	76
6	52	98	52	97
7	75	99	75	99
9	86	99	86	99
11	91	99	92	99
12	89	99	92	99
14	81	99	82	99
16	49	93	52	92
17	34	84	37	84
18	22	62	23	62
19	15	42	14	44
20	9	34	8	35

Source: Donald J. Bogue, *The Population of the United States: Historical Trends and Future Predictions*. New York: Free Press, 1985, p. 383.

This photograph of a public school in Valdez, Alaska, was taken at about the time when our educational system was making a "great leap forward." In 1870, the United States had only 500 public schools. By 1910, we had 10,000 public high schools alone.

National Archives

■ **TABLE 15–2 Median Years of School Completed, by Age and Race, 1940 to 1983**

Age 25 Years and Over:

	ALL PERSONS	BLACKS
1940	8.6	5.7
1950	9.3	6.8
1960	10.6	8.0
1970	12.2	9.9
1985	12.6	12.3

Age 25–29 Years

	ALL PERSONS	BLACKS
1940	10.3	7.0
1950	12.0	8.6
1960	12.3	9.9
1970	12.6	12.2
1985	12.9	12.7

Source: Statistical Abstract of the United States, 1987, p. 121.

The first distinctive feature of our current educational system is therefore its scope, because almost all Americans are educated in some type of school. And the second is its length, because we educate a greater proportion of students to a higher level of education than does any other nation. Today, seven out of ten Americans aged 15 to 19 are enrolled in some kind of educational institution. At this age, only Japan's rate is higher. (Note that Japan doubled its rate in less than one generation, from 1960 to 1975—an astonishing accomplishment.) By the ages of 20 to 24, more than one American in five (22 percent) is still in school—the highest rate in the world for this age group. (Note again that Japan tripled its rate from 1960 to 1975, from 5 to 15 percent; we did not even double our own, which went up from 12 to 22 percent.) Even at the relatively advanced ages of 25 to 34, about one American out of every twelve is enrolled in school. The United States is committed to higher education for the mass of the population. Only Japan has a comparable commitment in this respect. Japan, however, has already outstripped us in some ways, especially in science and engineering. In 1977, it graduated more than 19,000 electrical engineers at all levels (bachelor's, master's, and doctorate), while the United States—with twice Japan's population—graduated only 14,000. "And that gap is believed to have been widening" (Stockton, 1981, p. 52). For a recent summary of the Japanese educational system, see Ezra Vogel, *Japan as Number One* (1979, pp. 158–183).

Besides having a lot of students in colleges and universities, the United States has a high level of educational attainment (see Table 15-2). Starting in 1970, the average American had at least some college education—a median of 12.2 years of education, so half of the population had less and half had more. In 1985, the average level of education for Americans in their late 20s was almost one year in college. The more recent the generation, the greater its educational attainment; indeed, for the youngest adult generation, even the educational gap between whites and Blacks is extremely small.

These changes came about because Americans—the general public and also local, state, and federal officials—were willing to spend rapidly rising sums of money on education. Taking inflation into account, the national average annual expenditure for elementary and secondary schools came to less than $400 per pupil in 1930 (as expressed in 1977 dollars; it was far lower in 1930 dollars). Educational spending rose each decade thereafter until the late 1970s, when it reached $1,782 per pupil (*Social Indicators III*, 1980, p. 291).

More recent developments yield a somewhat darker picture. From 1946 until the early to middle 1950s, there was a population "bulge"—the so-called postwar baby boom (see Chapter 13). After that, the birth rate declined. It follows that, gradually, over time, fewer and fewer children will be of school age. As a result of this decline in the birth rate, the number of students enrolled at all levels of education is gradually declining. The peak for elementary school students—over 37 million—was reached in 1970. In the early 1980s, there were almost 6 million fewer elementary school students. As for enrollment, it reached its peak—15.8 million—when the elementary school students of 1970 became teenagers, in 1977. Since then high school enrollment has dropped sharply, by almost 2.5 million students. Now we come to college enrollment. In 1978, for the first time in any year-to-year period (except during wars), it dropped—from 11.5 to 11.1 million. The number of college students has risen since then, to 12.5 million in 1985, in part because older students, mainly women, have been returning to school to begin or complete degrees they hadn't been able to get years before.

Thousands of schools, in communities throughout our country, have been closed, and hundreds of thousands of teachers have been thrown out of work. Colleges and universities have experienced cutbacks, layoffs, attrition, retrenchment, and, in some cases, closings. In the 1970s, double-digit inflation, combined with rapidly spiralling operating costs, forced cutbacks in teaching facilities and services to students. And the Reagan administration reduced federal expenditures on education at all levels, especially higher education, quite sharply—adding to the problems of educational budget makers. Our educational system is in deep trouble, and it will remain so for some years to come.

Primary Schools

It is very hard to generalize about the educational institutions below the college level: There is so much variety. Religious schools are not like secular schools, and private schools are not like public schools. Schools in large cities are difficult to compare with schools in small communities. Schools with well-to-do students are very different from schools with poor students. Inner-city schools differ markedly from suburban schools. Integrated schools have certain characteristics that are not shared by all-white or all-Black schools.

Probably the most important influence on our elementary schools is the social-class composition of the students. Each school in a community large enough to enroll students in several schools, located in different neighborhoods, will probably be somewhat homogeneous with regard to class because most communities are segregated by class. The more affluent families live in certain neighborhoods; poor families live in others. Typically, urban public elementary schools get their pupils from a fifteen to twenty-five square-block area, from a square mile or so. "Consequently, the elementary schools reflect the socioeconomic differences of the neighborhoods in which they are located" (Havighurst and Levine, 1979, p. 47).

A study of the elementary schools of Chicago identified four basic types of schools (Havighurst, 1964):

1. "High-status schools," usually located in high-income areas or near the "edges" of the city or in the suburbs.
2. "Conventional" schools, usually located in neighborhoods in which lower white-collar (or lower-middle-class) families predominated.
3. "Common-man schools," in areas where a majority of the families were employed blue-collar (or manual) laborers.
4. "Slum" schools, in low-income areas with high population turn-over and high crime rates.

Chicago's teachers could readily distinguish among these four types of schools and could easily classify them by taking into account nine characteristics (Doll, 1969): (1) the teaching role; (2) attitudes toward nonacademic duties expected of teachers; (3) degree to which teaching emphasized academics; (4) student hostility; (5) parents' attitude toward school; (6) students' and parents' respect for teachers; (7) students' exposure to cultural experiences in their everyday lives; (8) students' values; and (9) school climate.

Problems. Because teachers and administrators feel called on to socialize students into "mainstream" American values, students from poorer households do not quite fit into our schools. For the most part, our schools are not tailored to the wants, needs, expectations, or feelings of these students, who therefore tend to perform less well than students who come from middle- and upper-status families.

Some educators attribute this lower performance to lack of motivation or intelligence. In reality, it is caused by the discontinuity, the lack of fit, between the institution (our schools) and its personnel (the students). Imagine taking a group of children from a white, affluent

American primary education is characterized by strong segregation by socioeconomic status from one school to another, an inappropriate "fit" with the interests and abilities of children from lower and working class families, and low performance compared with other industrialized nations of the world.

Jim Carter/Photo Researchers

neighborhood and placing them on the streets in a poor and tough one. How many would survive or "make it" in such a setting? Not very many, chances are.

Two sociologists of education (Havighurst and Levine, 1979, pp. 196–201) have systematically studied the difficulties faced by poorer students, and the sources of these difficulties. They have identified eight basic problems:

1. *Inappropriate curriculum and instruction.* School lessons and materials often lack relevance to the culture and the lives of working-class children and are often ill suited to their special interests and talents.

2. *Lack of parental and peer reinforcement for educational norms and experiences.* Working- and lower-class families mostly regard schools as institutions to be tolerated or rebelled against, not valued and used. To the low-status pupil, the school is an *alien* institution, run by outsiders with meaningless, meddlesome values. Neither family nor peer group sees teachers and administrators as "significant others." More often than not, family and peer groups do not back up the demands of educators.

3. *Teacher perceptions of student inadequacy.* On the first day, teachers of low-status students typically walk into classrooms believing that they have slow learners on their hands, and they act on that belief.

4. *Lack of previous success in school.* Expectations of failure tend to become self-fulfilling prophecies. Teachers almost automatically regard lower-status students as slow learners. The students thus acquire self-concepts that reinforce their teachers' images and become slow learners.

5. *Difficult teaching conditions and lack of adequately prepared teachers in low-status schools.* Many observers believe that most teachers have not been adequately prepared for the problems of low-income students, in part because this preparation almost never includes teacher-training programs (Havighurst and Levine, 1979, p. 197).

6. *Lumping together low-status students within schools and classrooms.* Low achievers tend to be set apart in special classes and in separate classroom groups that are supposed to benefit from special instruction. Unfortunately, this segregation often reinforces their feelings of inferiority and academic incompetence. They may conclude that they have been put in a class of "dummies," isolated from the better students. Many educators now feel that heterogeneous (mixed) ability groups are better for teaching (Havighurst and Levine, 1979, p. 198).

7. *Ineffective delivery of services in classrooms with many low-status students.* Far less teaching goes on in the lower- and working-class schools because far more time must be spent dealing with day-to-day problems and moment-to-moment disruptions.

8. *Low standards of performance.* Low-achieving students tend to be advanced to the next grade without adequately meeting the requirements of the previous one. Low-status students are not expected to achieve much, and they are led to believe that low performance is acceptable to their teachers. In a sense, they are victimized by systematically low expectations, which give them very mistaken notions about the level of work required for success in school (Massey, Vaughn, and Dornbusch, 1975, p. 9).

The Minority Factor.   These problems are compounded by racial factors—especially for Black students—and by the language problems faced by children who speak Spanish at home. These two minorities suffer most from the gap between their own everyday lives and the dominant white, middle-class values that inspire our schools.

Certain schools, those in which parents have actively attempted to have input and in which a large proportion of teachers belong to minority groups, have tailored their curricula to the needs of minority students. These efforts have had mixed results. On the one hand, among the youngest adult generation, Black educational attainment is now very nearly equal to that of whites. On the other, many problems arise from the fact that local schools are not insulated from the rest of the society but belong to the institutions that surround them. At each succeeding step in the educational ladder, from elementary school to graduate school, American society as a whole is dominated by white middle-class values and standards. Schools that try to make their programs suit poor and minority students run the risk of failing to prepare them for success in the outside world. These schools must try to balance conflicting needs to reach and educate their students to become members of the greater society.

An International Comparison.   It seems fair to say that the first characteristic that would strike almost any observer of our primary schools is the extent to which they vary according to the social backgrounds of their students. Probably the second feature an observer notices is that students here are granted much more freedom than they are in other countries. Other industrialized nations of the world do have free, compulsory, and universal systems of primary school education, but the nature, character, and content of education vary enormously from one industrial society to another.

To European, Japanese, and Chinese teachers and administrators, typical American classrooms seem chaotic: Discipline is loose if not wholly absent. To American teachers and administrators, French, Russian, and Japanese students seem very well behaved, well disciplined, obedient, and hard working. The teachers receive much more respect and have more authority than teachers do here, and students are much more likely to listen to and obey them. There are many reasons for this difference, but much of it results from the fact that these countries have a stronger sense of nation and community than the United States does. Especially in communist countries, schools systematically train students to accept the aims of the state. Soviet and Chinese schools are more densely interwoven with and integrated into the students' lives than ours are.

An American visitor to a number of Soviet schools at all levels was above all impressed by their students' "good behavior." In their external actions, he explains, "they are well mannered, attentive, and industrious. In informal conversations, they reveal a strong motivation to learn, a readiness to serve their society, and . . . an idealistic attitude toward life. . . . The discipline of the collective is accepted and regarded as justified, even when severe as judged by Western standards." It is apparent, this educational expert writes, that "instances of aggressiveness, violation of rules, or other antisocial behavior are genuinely rare" (Bronfenbrenner, 1970, p. 77).

What is so remarkable about the Soviet and the Chinese educational systems is the way that the influence of peers supports rather than undermines educational objectives and methods. When a group of American 12 year olds were asked whether they would be more or less likely to engage in misconduct, like cheating on exams, if their classmates knew about it, they turned out to be more inclined to engage in misconduct, not less so. By contrast, in the Soviet Union, classmates are about as likely to control misbehavior as parents and teachers are. The Soviet primary school peer group not only tends to reinforce adult-approved behavior but also to induce its members to police one another (Bronfenbrenner, 1970, p. 80).

This strong discipline, emanating both from teachers and from the students themselves, is a mixed blessing, of course. Such schools are breeding grounds of conformity. They try to stifle creativity, imagination, and spontaneity. One observer of Soviet primary schools discussed her misgivings about the Soviet educational system with a Russian friend, who responded: "You keep talking about the individual. . . . Individual rights, individual work, the individual mind. But what you call individualism, we call egotism. And we consider our system of education successful if it eradicates this egotism." Reflected the author: "I have always regarded the development of the individual as the only legitimate goal of education. . . . The only valid measure of a school may be how much fight is left in its students at the end of their academic careers. Soviet schools are extraordinarily good at squeezing the fight out of the individuals they process. That is why I would hesitate to borrow too much from them" (Jacoby, 1974, pp. 241–242).

The High School

High school is an almost universal fact in the lives of American adolescents: Just over 93 percent of our 14 to 17 year olds are enrolled in a high school (Bogue, 1985, p. 385), and about three-quarters of them get high school diplomas (Molotsky, 1984). Contemporary American adolescents are something more than children but considerably less than adults; adolescence is a new thing under the sun. Until quite recently, people of this age were defined as adults. They worked at demanding, full-time jobs; got married; and raised children. Previous centuries, and today's nonindustrial societies, have not even had a social category of "adolescence." In tribal societies, young people were prepared for adulthood and, at a specific age—often 12, 13, or 14—underwent ceremonies that anthropologists call "rites of passage" to initiate them into it. The transition from childhood to adulthood was sudden, often taking no more than a few months of training. An in-between period of adolescence, combining some of the privileges and restrictions of childhood with adulthood, simply did not exist. The Jewish Bar Mitzvah ceremony—in which 13-year-old boys announce, "Today I am a man!"—is a remnant of the rite of passage, though it no longer initiates the boy into real (societal as opposed to biological or ritual) adulthood.

In contemporary industrial society, the transition from childhood to adolescence to adulthood takes from five to fifteen years. Biological maturation clearly plays a role in the onset of adolescence, though improved health conditions and better diet cause biological puberty to start earlier today than it did in the past. When girls begin to menstruate and develop breasts, and boys begin to develop facial hair and deeper voices, and the sexual urge begins to gush forth in both sexes, they no longer think of themselves as children. Yet the most important changes of adolescence are not the physical ones but a transformation in consciousness and behavior.

Perhaps the most significant of these changes is the growing importance of peer groups. In childhood, parents have at least as much influence on children as peer groups do. But in adolescence, other adolescents

Japanese students are far more disciplined and better-behaved than their American counterparts. Note that these students are wearing uniforms.

Robin Mayer/Time, April 13, 1987

become the major reference group, the major agent of socialization, and the focus of interaction and intimacy. A generation ago, *The Adolescent Society* (Coleman, 1961) argued that a strong high school peer subculture had developed separately from mainstream adult culture, and was even at odds with it. In industrial society, the family had lost much of its hold, and the schools were too impersonal and removed from the concerns of adolescence to fill the void. Enter the peer group, which provided the very kind of support young people needed.

High schools are the chief stage of the adolescent peer group because they throw hundreds or thousands of young people into close contact, segregating them from people of other ages—something that was quite uncommon in preindustrial societies. High school students are forced "inward," into their own age group, and made to carry on almost their whole social lives with people of their own age. The adolescent peer group "comes to constitute a small society, one that has most of its important interaction within itself, and maintains only a few threads of connection with the outside adult society (Coleman, 1961, p. 3).

In Coleman's study, adolescents placed success in athletics at the top of their value hierarchy for boys. Sports heroes were considered the most popular boys and the ones most likely to be picked as friends, to be regarded by girls as the most desirable dates, and to belong to the school's "elite." Athletes who were good students ranked higher than those who were not, and good students who were not athletes tended to rank higher than poor students who were not athletes. But good athletes ranked ahead of good students—far ahead. Getting good grades was relatively unimportant for boys; for girls, it was even less important and actually detracted from their popularity with boys. The important things for girls were being physically attractive, being a cheerleader, coming from the "right" family, and wearing the "right" clothes.

Of course, not all high schools are identical, nor does the youth subculture constitute an all encompassing way of life radically opposed to adult society in every particular. In fact, there is a generational continuity from parents to children: Teenagers are much more like their own parents than like other teenagers' parents. But, in most respects, they are also more like their peers than like their parents. Adolescence marks the point in one's life when parental influence begins to diminish and peer influence begins to increase.

Student Alienation.   What about the academic side of high school? It would not be rash to say that most students do not enjoy school. They do enjoy being with their friends; they enjoy hanging out; most like dating the opposite sex (though many find dating awkward and even painful); some enjoy sports and love the competition and the glory that comes with it; and most consider high school to be a necessary evil. But most of them do not enjoy high school as a learning experience. Because teachers are the adults who have the greatest amount of contact with students, they bear the brunt of the students' hostility or indifference.

One survey of thousands of students and teachers from fifteen high schools throughout New York State found that exactly two-thirds of the students surveyed did not enjoy school. They felt that their teachers did not help them, did not understand them, did not teach them very much, and did not care about their academic futures. The teachers, alas, were totally unaware of these attitudes. More than half of the teachers evaluated the overall academic process as "positive," whereas only a bit over a quarter of the students agreed. More than half of the teachers rated school morale as "positive"; almost two-thirds of the students rated it as "negative." When both teachers and students were asked about how much teachers help students, teachers appeared to think very much more highly of their ability to help students than the students themselves did. The one issue on which they agreed was that students did not understand the special problems of teachers (Fleischmann, 1973, p. 49).

Another study rigged up a clever experiment to determine how involved, mentally and emotionally, students were with their classes. Members of a sample of seventy-eight high-school students were equipped with paging devices that for a week emitted electronic signals at random. When they heard the signals, these students recorded where they were, whom they were with, what they were doing, how they felt about being where they were, and how high or low their levels of concentration might be. The researchers found that the students' levels of boredom were highest, and their levels of concentration lowest, in the classroom. On average, it appeared that the students in this study were paying attention less than half the time they were in classrooms (Csikszentmihalyi, Larsen, and Prescott, 1977).

Academic Performance.   This alienation from the academic side of high school is reflected in students' academic performance. Although teachers award significantly more As and Bs today than they did a decade ago—the so-called grade inflation—standardized tests seem to show that students are learning less and less. The Scholastic Aptitude Test (SAT) is supposed to evaluate the students' knowledge and preparation for college. These multiple-choice tests, taken by more than a million high school seniors each year, are among the most significant of all admissions criteria used by colleges. The scores range from a possible low of 200 to a possible high of 800. When the test was originally designed, a score of 500 was set as the national average. Although there are flaws in the SAT—as in every test that has ever been devised—it is regarded as a valid measure of a high school senior's knowledge, academic achievement, and ability.

A report released by the Educational Testing Service, which designs the test, shows that test scores on the SATs declined between the late 1960s (in 1967, the average score for the verbal section of the test was 466, and for math it was 492) and the early 1980s (in 1981, the verbal was 424, and the math, 466). Between the early and the middle 1980s, SAT scores rose slightly—in 1985, they were 431 verbal, 475 math (Fiske, 1984a; *Statistical Abstract of the United States, 1987*, p. 135). Nonetheless, almost no expert doubts that high schools are in deep academic trouble.

Why? Educators have many explanations for the recent decline in the overall academic performance of American high school students. Some of these explanations try to account for the problems of teachers; others, for the problems of students. Both sets of explanations show how social, cultural, an economic changes in our society as a whole affect teachers and students alike.

High on the list of things that make teachers less effective is their growing alienation. High school teachers often consider their work to be "just another job," not a special calling that demands unusual dedication. In one city after another, budget crises and teacher strikes have often halted the educational system for weeks or even months, and when the students return, their teachers cannot make up the lost time. Even those systems that have never been shut down have been bled slowly to death by financial cutbacks in school budgets. These cutbacks reduce the resources available to teachers and often produce layoffs of teachers themselves—layoffs that also result from the shrinkage in the adolescent population of this country. Many teachers must work with the knowledge

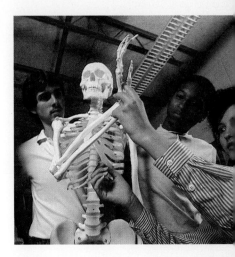

Many educators detect a decline in educational quality and the motivation of students during the past generation. There are signs that this trend may be reversing itself, however.

Will & Deni McIntyre/Photo Researchers

that sooner or later they will probably "get the axe." By 1976, the supply of newly qualified teachers exceeded the demand by some 80,000 (Boocock, 1980, p. 137). In the mid-1980s, the situation reversed itself, and once again, teachers are in demand—at salaries half of what they could earn in another line of work. These economic realities lower morale and promote alienation and demoralization among teachers, so it is much harder for most of them to become fully committed to teaching.

Some of the problems that teachers face have been at least partly self-imposed. As the teaching profession has become more unionized, it has also become more bureaucratic—partly as a result of pressures imposed (through unions) by the teachers themselves and partly as a result of pressures imposed upon them, through school boards and administrators. Each side, for its own reasons, wishes to base advancement and salary increases on easily quantifiable criteria: usually, years of service and coursework beyond the undergraduate degree. Quantifiable criteria prevent favoritism, protect teachers from the hostility of administrators, give administrators the illusion of scientific management, and free administrators from the need to justify their decisions.

Teacher's unions, on their side, have made it practically impossible to fire a teacher for nonbudgetary reasons—for instance, for incompetence. Administrations and school boards have instituted curricula that encourage conformity, homogeneity, and rigidity and that punish experimentation (Boocock, 1980, pp. 136–137). Meanwhile, the supposed beneficiary of our educational system—the student—receives a less and less rewarding educational experience.

Why do students seem to be less able to learn? Both teachers and the lay public have opinions on this subject. Six factors are often mentioned:

1. *Television.* Watching TV is a passive activity that demands little or no intellectual involvement and diminishes the attention span of the average viewer. Typical teenagers spend more time before TV sets than in classrooms. Television undermines the ability to understand and take an interest in the written word, the basic medium of the classroom.

2. *Excessively permissive childrearing.* Dr. Spock taught the mothers of the post-World War II era to respect their children's individuality. He and similar postwar oracles of the baby boom are believed by some to have encouraged a decline in self-discipline, an inability to delay gratification and to plan and work for the long run, an increase in self-centeredness, and a general insensitivity to the needs of others.

3. *A decline in the legitimacy of authority figures.* The young increasingly distrust teachers, parents, politicians, psychiatrists, the clergy, experts, and authorities of any kind. They no longer feel that they owe anyone cooperation or belief simply by virtue of his or her position. Teenagers often suppose that they know as much as teachers do.

4. *The breakup of the traditional family.* Parental authority is diminishing; family ties are weakening; and the divorce rate is rising. Parents do not support educational aims or methods as they once did, nor do they have the same power over their children.

5. *The deterioration of the civic community.* Schools are an expression of civic pride. Our people no longer have as much of a stake in their communities as they once did. Families move often, ignore

The Coleman Report

In 1964, President Lyndon B. Johnson and Congress commissioned a massive, nation-wide survey of our educational system. Its initial purpose was to document racial inequalities in our schools and to propose solutions to that problem. Headed by sociologist James Coleman, the study gathered data from 4,000 schools, 60,000 teachers, and some 600,000 students (Coleman et al., 1966). The study—popularly known as "The Coleman Report"—found just the opposite of what it was expected to find: Although minority and white students typically *do* attend separate, segregated schools, and minority students *do* perform less well on a variety of standardized tests, the Coleman Report claimed that Black and white schools were pretty much alike in many measures of educational quality. Expenditures per pupil were approximately equal, and so too were teachers, laboratory facilities, school buildings, and so on. The white schools did not seem to be better in most significant respects.

Coleman went on to make an even more startling claim—that the quality of a school had little or no effect on the educational achievement of its students. What really counted, the study argued, were the social characteristics of the student body and of the families from which it was drawn. Blacks do less well in school, Coleman reported, not because less money is spent on their education, but because they attend schools in which most students are lower-class and academically unmotivated Blacks, and because their parents give them little academic motivation or guidance.

These findings "sent shock waves through government, schools, and academia" (Parelius and Parelius, 1978, p. 309). Immediately, the report was awash in controversy. It seemed to indicate that higher spending on minority schools would be a waste, because they were already equal to white schools and because better schools had apparently failed to produce better-educated students. The report also seemed to be blaming Black students for their own academic difficulties—what some sociologists call "blaming the victim," not the system. One sociologist charged that the report's research was "compromised," because it had been shaped by the government and policymakers. In fact, the findings were ignored by the Johnson administration but "marketed" by President Nixon to justify cuts in the federal education budget (Rash, 1980). The Coleman Report's findings have been empirically supported (Mosteller and Moynihan, 1972) and refuted (Rutter, Maughan, Mortimore, and Ouston, 1979; Williams et al., 1981a, b, c). To this day, *Equality of Educational Opportunity* remains one of the most controversial sociological studies ever published.

community and school affairs, and resent schools for consuming their "hard-earned tax dollars." The decline of local schools is just one example of the general unravelling of the community fabric, a weakening of the bonds that hold society together.

6. *The rise of disorder, deviance, and crime in the schools.* High schools today must cope with much violence and crime. Vandalism, assaults on teachers, fights between students, the use of alcohol and marijuana during school hours—all these occupy a large place on the school scene. All make teaching and learning more and more difficult.

These problems are part of our society—not just of our educational system—and only our society as a whole can possibly deal with them. Educational problems are the consequence, not the cause; only large-scale social change can reverse long-term social trends. The "back to basics" movement (Parelius and Parelius, 1978, pp. 376–378; Ravitch, 1978) may or may not be desirable in itself, but its assumption that the system's problems are mainly internal seems to be unrealistic. Reading, writing, and arithmetic may be necessary, but they are not enough.

Higher Education

In a given year, the United States now has some 12 million students enrolled in about 3,000 institutions of higher learning. More than a million additional students are working toward advanced professional or academic degrees. The Bureau of Labor Statistics tallied more than half a million college or university teachers. These are vast numbers. They conceal an enormous diversity in institutional, educational, and occupational situations and experiences. Indeed, the United States probably has the most diverse collection of institutions of higher learning in the world. Some are tiny and enroll only a few hundred students; others accommodate hundreds of thousands of students at all levels. Some are religious; most are secular. Some are private, and, in them, tuition alone may cost $18,000 a year. Others are funded by state, county, or local governments. Some rank among the most distinguished universities in the world. Others are glorified high schools—and bad ones at that!

Of the many ways of looking at the profession of higher education, one involves seeing it as a kind of hierarchy. Some colleges and universities have more prestige than others; and some may do a better job of teaching their students. Individual academics are usually ranked within the systems of their own colleges or universities—from the professor level on down.

The Great Divide. At all levels of the academic world the most significant hierarchical line divides tenured ("senior") faculty, who can only be dismissed in unusual circumstances, from nontenured ("junior") faculty, who are hired for a specific number of months or years. Superimposed on this fundamental distinction is the hierarchy of ranks. Instructors are usually teachers who have not yet completed their Ph.D. degrees but will be considered for promotion to assistant professor when they do. About three to seven years after an assistant professor receives the Ph.D., he or she is considered for tenure—if, that is, the assistant professorship is on the tenure-track "line." Assistant professors on the tenure-track line are usually appointed for two or three years, with options for renewal; assistant professors who are not on the tenure track are usually let go at the end of a year. Tenure decisions operate on an "up or out" basis: Those who are denied tenure usually must leave the college or university within a year or two. Being denied tenure is equivalent to being fired, though the actual departure may take several years.

Adjunct professors stand outside this system of tenure. They are part-time faculty who teach, and are paid for, one course at a time. Adjunct faculty may be graduate students trying to earn livings while they complete their degrees; or they may be full-time faculty members at other schools who need the extra pay. Finally, they may belong to a new class—the "academic proletariat" of people who have completed their Ph.D. degrees but have not been able to find full-time academic jobs. Adjunct teaching is very hard work at very low pay. People who teach four or five courses at different colleges or universities on an adjunct basis work twice as hard as ordinary assistant professors for half the pay. Unhappily, this is not just a theoretical example; it now happens quite often.

Promotion to an associate professorship usually carries tenure. The tenure decision is usually made when the candidate is 30 to 35 years old—so the consequences of that decision may be felt for thirty or forty years. The granting (or denial) of tenure is probably the most crucial

WHAT DO YOU THINK?

Does Education Have an Impact on Scientific Beliefs?

Does acquiring an education make a difference in what we believe to be true? Do poorly educated people hold different beliefs about how the material world works than well-educated people do? Although untangling cause and effect here is a tricky and complicated matter, researchers have found large, significant, and even striking differences between the lower and upper levels of the education continuum. Well-educated people are much more likely to reject pseudoscientific beliefs and more likely to agree with current opinion among scientists with respect to what is true. Yet, interestingly, the better-educated are more likely to be skeptical of and have less blind faith in "leaders and experts" as purveyors of the truth. In one study (Miller, 1986), only a minority of respondents who left high school without graduating (43 percent) believe that astrology is "not at all scientific," whereas a sizable majority of those with graduate degrees (75 percent) believe this. When asked whether or not they agree with the statement, "Human beings as we know them today developed from earlier species of animals," only

a minority of high school dropouts (38 percent) agreed, whereas a majority of respondents with graduate degrees (71 percent) did. High school dropouts are much more likely to believe that "Some numbers are especially lucky for some people" (60 percent) than are holders of graduate degrees (25 percent).

The author of this study argues that the poorly educated tend to be "scientifically illiterate." What does our scientific world, he asks, look like to this segment of the population?

First, "the language of our society includes a lot of words and terms without meaning to this group."

Second, "this group has difficulty distinguishing between science and pseudo-science."

Third, "for people living in a scientific culture who do not understand it, the world will tend to look hostile and dangerous." For instance, they are more likely to believe that "scientific researchers have a power that makes them dangerous" (71 percent agree versus 36 percent of holders of graduate degrees).

At the same time, the author

says, "there is a broad recognition among less well educated citizens that they must depend on leaders and experts to explain the world around them." They are strikingly more likely to agree with the statement, "In this complicated world of ours, the only way we can know what is going on is to rely on leaders and experts who can be trusted" (81 percent versus 36 percent of the best-educated citizens). The author argues that the results of this study "point toward a pre-collegiate education system that provides an inadequate conceptual framework for the later inclusion of new information. By failing to address directly issues like astrology and luck, the schools have left gaps in knowledge." Agents (like the media) who fill those gaps "have not been careful or responsible in differentiating between entertainment, science fiction, and science." It is time, the author feels, to address this flaw in the educational system.

Source: Miller, 1986.

point in the career of an academic. Today, budgetary problems have made it much harder for large universities to award tenure than it was a decade ago. Many professors who are denied tenure cannot find academic jobs anywhere and must leave academic life. Besides the frustration and bitterness this creates among faculty members who are denied tenure, it also generates much anxiety among the junior faculty awaiting tenure evaluations in the coming years.

The Future of Higher Education.   The academic profession has gone through cycles of hard years and good years. The 1950s and 1960s were a time when the number of students, student aid, academic resources, and research funds grew and grew, and teaching loads diminished. By the late 1970s and the 1980s, student populations, financial assistance to students, and resources in general tended to shrink or hold stable while costs and tuition spiraled: The trend had been reversed. Some fields have produced so many Ph.D.s that a majority of them cannot find academic jobs—history and English literature, for instance. In certain other fields, like economics and engineering—which have applications outside the university—the job market is still in excellent shape. Sociology is somewhere in between: Most brand-new Ph.D.s who are willing to search far and wide and are not too choosy about where they work can find academic jobs. How the academic profession will respond to these and other economic and demographic changes is not yet clear. What is clear is that it will face severe challenges in coming years, challenges that will test its ability to survive in anything like its present form. Hard economic times may not make higher education worse, but they will inevitably make it a different place in which to work and study.

EDUCATION AND INCOME

Does being educated pay off? Why struggle through high school and college when one can drop out of school and begin earning money right away? After all, many individuals with advanced degrees earn very little money and many without high school diplomas earn a great deal. Is it worth it financially to stay in school? For both Blacks and whites, a distinct income advantage does come to those who receive higher educations. As a general rule, the more education that one receives, the higher one's income is likely to be. "Rich rewards are paid by the American economy to those who attain an advanced education" (Bogue, 1985, p. 571). A senior in high school wondering whether it is worthwhile to attend college should note that the family income of someone with only a high school diploma is $12,000 lower than that of someone with a college degree—about $3,000 for every year of college for the rest of one's life, or $45 for each working day of the worker's life (Bogue, 1985, p. 572). For both whites and Blacks, there is roughly a tripling in family income from the bottom to the top of the educational ladder. Clearly, then, though some well-educated workers are poor, and some wealthy individuals have received very little education, "they only provide exceptions to what is a very marked and a very consistent relationship" (Bogue, 1985, p. 572).

This same comparison is highlighted even further when we compare the lifetime earnings of workers at each level of educational attainment. As we can see in Table 15-3, workers with less than high school educations earn roughly half of what workers with one or more years of postgraduate educations earn. This tendency is so striking that it is difficult to understand the behavior of students who are capable of remaining in school and who choose, nonetheless, to drop out. "The male who fails to complete high school suffers a lifetime loss of more than a quarter

■ **TABLE 15–3 Lifetime Earnings by Educational Attainment**

	Lifetime Earnings	
	MEN	WOMEN
Educational Attainment		
Less than high school	$ 601,000	$211,000
High school graduate	$ 861,000	$381,000
1 to 3 years of college	$ 957,000	$460,000
4 years of college	$1,190,000	$523,000
5+ years of college	$1,301,000	$699,000

Source: Donald J. Bogue, *The Population of the United States: Historical Trends and Future Predictions*. New York: Free Press, 1985, p. 573.

of a million dollars. By going on to complete college after high school graduation, he adds more than $300,000 to his lifetime earnings. . . . Although the rewards to women are smaller in size, they are proportionately similar" (Bogue, 1985, p. 575).

The relationship between education and income exists; of that there is no doubt. There is some doubt, however, as to exactly what causes this strong relationship. Why do workers with more education earn so much more money than workers with very little education? The answers that functionalists and conflict theorists offer to explain this question are very different.

Functionalists, whose views on education we encountered earlier in this chapter, argue that the process of being educated entails receiving "functionally important" knowledge—knowledge that contributes to the functioning of the society as a whole. Once this knowledge has been transmitted, the educated individual is then capable of taking on a job that contributes to society's functioning. And because of the contributions that such jobs make, their occupants are rewarded with high salaries (Davis and Moore, 1945).

This theory is rejected by conflict sociologists. Although it most emphatically agrees that better-educated individuals are paid more, conflict theory argues that the relationship exists not because of the contributions that better-educated individuals occupying positions that demand more education make to the society as a whole. Indeed, conflict theory argues that the educational requirements for certain high-paying jobs bear very little relationship to the real work demands of those jobs. Most jobs can be performed competently by individuals with much less education than they formally require (Berg, 1970). Conflict theory argues that the link between education and income, far from demonstrating that academic achievement has its just and appropriate reward, actually shows that education maintains the existing stratification system and retards social mobility. Education serves the function of *credentialism,* a concept we encountered earlier. Demanding educational credentials sets up requirements for jobs that are unrelated to actual job performance; its purpose is to make sure that only individuals who can afford to spend several years in school, not earning an income, and whose families can afford to support them during this period, can receive high-paying, high-prestige jobs.

Moreover, conflict theorists argue, education does serve a socializing function that has nothing to do with transmitting technical knowledge necessary to perform on the job. Rather, education ensures that future professionals and executives are taught the norms and values appropriate to elite occupations. Because the elite dominate the educational system, the values that are transmitted in higher education tend to be conservative and to support the *status quo* (Collins, 1979). Although the educational system does not weed out all aspiring individuals with lower- and working-class backgrounds, it does give a distinct competitive advantage to the children of the elite and the upper-middle class, as we saw in the chapter on stratification (Chapter 9).

In short, conflict theory explains the link between education and income by arguing that the educational system is a mechanism whereby the privileged pass on their economic advantages from one generation to the next. Through this process, too, the children of less privileged families are, for all practical purposes, excluded from economic achievement. Far from offering the children of the poor an avenue to social mobility, education is a means of keeping them from rising in the class system and of maintaining existing privileges.

SUMMARY

1. In preagricultural societies, education was an unspecialized activity: Everyone pitched in and engaged in it. Education and socialization were identical.

2. With the development of agriculture, education came to be a specialized activity; it became the job of specific individuals to teach the young a designated body of knowledge.

3. Education and industrialization are closely connected: The more industrialized a society is, the lower is its rate of illiteracy.

4. Education has been analyzed from at least two contrasting perspectives: functionalism and conflict theory.

5. Functionalists emphasize the positive contributions that education makes to the society as a whole; its functions include cultural transmission, social control, training in intellectual skills, selecting for ability, and assimilation.

6. The conflict perspective stresses the ways that schools perpetuate existing inequalities and justify exploitation.

7. Many contemporary observers believe that a synthesis of the two views is necessary; although both are flawed as total perspectives, they both have much to offer.

8. The system of education in the United States is practically unique; only in Japan is as high a proportion of the population educated for as long a period of time.

9. In the late 1970s and early 1980s, for the first time in history, American school systems nation-wide began to experience a decline in the number of students enrolled.

10. Another recent trend is the decline in the occupational value of a higher education.

11. Perhaps the most crucial characteristic influencing the nature

of a secondary school is the social-class composition of the neighborhood in which it is located.

12. In working-class schools, teachers face a number of distinct problems in their educational tasks.

13. Minority students experience a gap between their own everyday
lives and the white, middle-class values that govern the schools;
this often generates educational difficulties.

14. Compared with schools in other nations, American schools seem
chaotic and American students, undisciplined; in contrast, Russian, European, Japanese, and Chinese students tend to be well-
behaved and hard working.

15. In industrial societies, the adolescent peer group has a unique
influence on adolescents.

16. Many adolescents do not regard the high school as a locus of
interesting learning experiences.

17. According to a number of criteria, high school student performance has been declining in recent decades.

18. Experts point to a number of factors contributing to this decline,
including television, excessively permissive childrearing, a decline in the legitimacy of authority figures, the breakup of the
traditional family, a deterioration of the civic community, and
the rise in crime and drug and alcohol use in the schools.

19. Higher education houses a complex ranking system, in which
the granting of tenure is the most important criterion.

20. There is a very strong and consistent relationship between education and income: The more education one has, the more one is
likely to earn.

SUGGESTED READINGS

Jeanne H. Ballantine, *The Sociology of Education: A Systematic Analysis*.
Englewood Cliffs, New Jersey: Prentice-Hall, 1983.
A well-written, informative basic textbook on the subject. Each
chapter concludes with a section entitled "Putting Sociology to
Work."

Samuel Bowles and Herbert Gintis, *Schooling in Capitalist America:
Educational Reform and the Contradictions of Economic Life*. New
York: Basic Books, 1976.
A much-discussed Marxist-oriented analysis of the functions of education for capitalist America. According to the authors, education
reflects and sustains the existing class structure and the capitalist
system. Education has never provided equality of opportunity here,
they argue, because it is rooted in the inherently unequal conditions
of a capitalist economy.

Peter W. Cookson, Jr., and Caroline Hodges Persell, *Preparing for Power:
America's Elite Boarding Schools*. New York: Basic Books, 1985.
How do elites pass on their values and positions to the generation
that follows them? The maintenance of privilege in a large, diverse,
formally democratic capitalist society like the United States is a
complex process, but no one doubts that education plays a major
role. This book demonstrates how boarding schools "help transmit
power and privilege" and how wealthy families "use the schools
to maintain their social class." The book is a result of personal
observations by the authors; interviews with hundreds of headmas-
ters, alumni, and students in fifty-five American, ten English, two
Cuban, and one Israeli boarding schools; some 2,500 anonymous

questionnaires filled out by first-year students and seniors; interviews with 382 teachers; and archival data—directories, cata-
logues, alumni surveys, speeches, and alumni contributions. Assembling all these data, the authors conclude that elite prep schools
socialize their students into shared beliefs and lifestyles consistent
with upper-class life and prepare them for positions of power.

Daniel V. Levine and Robert J. Havighurst, *Society and Education* (6th
ed.). Boston: Allyn & Bacon, 1984.
An excellent textbook on the sociology of education.

National Commission on Excellence in Education, *A Nation at Risk*.
Washington, D.C.: U.S. Government Printing Office, 1983.
A report whose conclusions hold that American education is suffering from a "rising tide of mediocrity." Some of the changes the
Commission sets forth include tightening educational requirements raising college admission standards, extending the school
day and the school year, requiring more homework, and raising
teachers' salaries. Although this report has received a great deal
of attention, its impact is less clear.

Lois Weis, *Between Two Worlds: Black Students in an Urban Community
College*. Boston: Routledge & Kegan Paul, 1985.
An ethnographic study of the subculture of Black students attending an American community college. The author argues that educational institutions unwittingly collude in maintaining existing racial and class antagonisms.

chapter 16
POLITICS

I n New York State, the incumbent senator is defeated in an election, and his rival is voted into office. In Minneapolis, a municipal antipornography bill is vetoed by the mayor, a woman. In Nevada, a reclusive billionaire instructs an aide to donate $50,000 to a presidential hopeful's election campaign. In West Virginia, a coal mine—less rigorously inspected than in the past because of a relaxation in federal safety regulations—collapses, killing several miners. In Philadelphia, a Black mayor is elected for the first time in the city's history. In Hamilton County, Tennessee, private industry is contracted to administer, for profit, the county's jails and to provide custodial and security services. In Houston, a human rights amendment that aims to include homosexuals under its legal protection is defeated by the voters by a margin of four to one. In Washington, D.C., after eight years in office, a conservative administration manages to cut federal spending on pollution control and clean-up in half—from $4.5 billion to $2.2 billion. In North Dakota, a group of farmers holds an angry meeting to determine what to do about rising expenses, falling profits, and farm foreclosures and bankruptcies.

All of these actions or consequences are political by their very nature. **Politics** may be defined as *"who gets what, when, and how"* (Lasswell, 1936). The central dimension in politics is **power**—the ability to get one's way despite the resistance of others (Weber, 1946, p. 180). The game of politics is the game of exercising power. Someone's wielding power means that his or her actions have consequences. By relaxing pollution and safety regulations on industry, for example, the Reagan administration made certain business ventures more attractive for investors, but also endangered the lives of workers and the public (Tolchin and Tolchin, 1983a, 1983b). By making campaign contributions, donors made the election of chosen candidates favorable to their interests more likely (Clymer, 1984, 1985; Oakes, 1984). By shifting public services from government to the private sector, legislators divert jobs from one sector to another—and, many claim, provide the public with less costly and more efficient and effective services (Tolchin, 1985). With the election of minority candidates, power is shifted from white to minority hands; this produces shifts in jobs, patronage, funding, pubic policy, legislative voting patterns, and perhaps even the

Politics The exercise of power. Sometimes defined as the pursuit of power.

Power The ability to get one's way, despite the resistance of others.

public image of minority groups in the eyes of both minorities and the white majority.

Politics is most commonly thought of as the attempt to acquire or hold onto government office. Often, a government official will be accused of "playing politics" by supporting a given piece of legislation. In actuality, all government officials, from the president of the United States to a local dogcatcher, must play politics in nearly every decision they make and every action they take. The line between trying to get or stay in office and conducting government business is fuzzy. Public officials are almost always campaigning for office. Consequently, sociologists do not make a sharp distinction between acquiring office and running the government. Both functions are political by their very nature. Both entail the exercise and the pursuit of institutional power.

POWER AND AUTHORITY

Legitimate power Authority. Power that exists when those subject to it accept the right of others to exercise it.

Authority The exercise of legitimate power.

Illegitimate power Power exercised by individuals against those who reject their right to rule.

The exercise of power is thus the subject matter of politics. In defining power as the ability to get one's way despite the resistance of others, Max Weber made a critical distinction between two kinds of power: legitimate and illegitimate. According to Weber, **legitimate power** means that those subject to it accept the right of others to exercise their power. When American presidents assume office, even those who voted against them agree that they have the right to the keys to the Oval Office. Weber called this legitimate power **authority. Illegitimate power,** according to Weber, is that power exercised by people whose right to rule is rejected by those subject to it. When an unscrupulous business executive influences politicians by giving them huge bribes we see this influence as an illegitimate form of power. A conquering army that forces obedience upon subject peoples may be viewed as illegitimate, but it will be obeyed. Many states and governments have ruled with coercive, illegitimate power for centuries. Nonetheless, when the ruled accept the rulers as legitimate, their power will likely be more stable and longer-lasting. Legitimacy is a resource that politicians use to rule effectively.

Clearly, legitimacy is a matter of degree. Certain efforts to rule will be regarded as illegitimate to nearly everyone in a given political system. The late billionaire Howard Hughes influenced a number of politicians by giving them very large sums of money, usually in cash, and often in secret. Between 1969 and 1970, Hughes attempted to offer then-president Richard Nixon a million dollar bribe to stop atomic testing in Nevada, where he lived—a deal that failed to materialize (Drosnin, 1986, pp. 359–382). Everyone, regardless of his or her feelings toward atomic testing, would regard this effort as illegitimate, an improper attempt to exercise power. (The failure of the attempt indicates just how illegitimate it was regarded, at least by Nixon.) On the other hand, many individuals and organizations do exercise a degree of power by making contributions to politicians. **Political action committees** (or **PACs**) are lobbies or organizations whose purpose is to protect certain special interests. The American Medical Association has a PAC, as do the United Automobile Workers, the National Education Association, Lockheed, Nabisco, the dairy industry, the tobacco industry, and the National Rifle Association.

Political action committee (PAC) An organization that attempts to further its own interests by influencing the political process; a well-organized interest group, a "lobby."

In the 1984 election, winners of Senate seats received an average of $3 million each in campaign contributions. The proportion they receive from PACs has been rising over the years—from 18 percent in 1976 to 29 percent in 1984. Republican Senate victors received an average of 33 percent from PACs and Democrats, 26 percent (Clymer, 1985). One member of the House of Representatives, Dan Rostenkowski, Democrat from Illinois, received $168,000 from PACs in 1983 for his 1982 campaign, although he already had a surplus of a half a million dollars left over— all of which he can put into his personal bank account when he leaves Congress (Oakes, 1984). On balance, winners receive more campaign money overall, and more money specifically from PACs, than losers do. Moreover, contributors are more likely to support politicians who vote their way than those who don't; in addition, politicians are more likely to vote their way in the future, having received substantial contributions from a given source. Is this fair? Is it *legitimate*? Although there will be considerable difference of opinion on these questions, most Americans begrudgingly accept the right of citizens—and lobbies—to contribute financially to the campaigns of politicians, and, in this way, to exercise a degree of influence over them.

Rulers who exercise legitimate power are not necessarily just, fair, democratic, or "good." But their citizens or subjects do feel that they have a right to rule. This feeling may be generated by apathy, ignorance, fraud, hypocrisy, nationalism, ideological commitment, self-interest, stupidity—or by real enthusiasm. These reasons for obedience cover a broad spectrum and make the distinction between legitimate and illegitimate power a continuum, not a wall separating two clear-cut categories.

Types of Authority

Besides offering a useful definition of power, and distinguishing between the legitimate and illegitimate varieties of it, Max Weber also constructed a typology (a model) of legitimate power, or authority. We have already run across two of the three types of authority (in Chapter 14, on religion): charismatic and bureaucratic (or "legal-rational") authority. The third type Weber called traditional authority.

Charismatic Authority. **Charismatic authority** emanates from those leaders who inspire allegiance because of purely personal qualities they are thought to possess, independent of any office. Charisma is not easily measured. It is irrational and elusive—yet powerful. The responses of the people tell us who has it and who does not. President John F. Kennedy had it; President Gerald Ford did not. Until his assassination in 1968, Martin Luther King, leader of the Southern Christian Leadership Conference (SCLC), had great charisma; his successor, Ralph Abernathy, did not. Charismatic authority legitimates the power of certain leaders who command obedience because of their personal qualities, not because of their official positions.

Many charismatic leaders also have bureaucratic positions. But Jesus, perhaps the most characteristic of all charismatic leaders, had none. Some charismatic leaders create formal positions for themselves, as did Fidel Castro of Cuba and Lenin, the first leader of the Soviet Union. Others, in large part through their charisma, win positions that already exist. When the leader's authority is purely charismatic, and he or she occupies no formal position, the problem of succession tends to make movements unstable. Charisma, by definition, is specific to particular individuals. Moreover, it is so rare that no movement can expect that one charismatic leader will follow another. The second generation of

Charismatic authority Authority that emanates from leaders who inspire allegiance because of the special, purely personal qualities they are thought to possess, independent of any office.

Charisma is a special quality of power that some leaders have of inspiring followers. Governor Mario Cuomo of New York attracts followers and voters as much for the force of his presence as by his ideas and programs.

UPI/Bettmann Newsphotos

leaders must retain the followers' loyalty without the extraordinary leader who inspired it in the first place. Some political or religious movements, thus die with their charismatic leaders. Others manage to survive by containing and preserving the leaders' special authority in some sort of formal, bureaucratic structure. The nature of the followers' allegiance is bound to change. It will become weaker, less irrational, less emotional, less spontaneous—but at the same time, more stable.

Bureaucratic authority
Authority that emanates from the public's faith in the rules and regulations governing a particular office.

Bureaucratic Authority. **Bureaucratic authority** emanates, not from a person, but from the public's faith in the legitimacy of the rules and regulations, rights, and obligations governing an office. Each leader occupies an office, a formal position of authority. Both leaders and followers know beforehand the powers attached to the office and what its occupant is supposed to do—and not do—in it. The duties of followers are specified in equal detail. A general, for instance, has authority because privates accept the legitimacy of the office and of the bureaucratic system that created it. One general may be thought a bumbler, another an inspired genius, but both will be obeyed. On the other hand, most bureaucratic structures are limited in scope; the military, in fact, represents an instance of this principle. During peacetime, a civilian can ignore the order of even a general, because the military's authority is not unlimited.

A couple of additional points about bureaucratic authority can be made: First, it is more limited than charismatic authority; the rules define and thus restrict its scope. Professors have the right to flunk students for poor coursework, but they do not have the right to demand that students yield to sexual advances. Charismatic authority is far more diffuse. The duties of a follower are broader, less clearly defined. It depends pretty much how much of a hold a leader has, not on what may be spelled out in rules.

Last, office, by itself, cannot sustain a leader's authority. To be effective, bureaucratic rulers must win the personal respect of those who follow them. An officeholder's ability to exercise the powers of an office are partly contingent upon his or her fitness to exercise them.

Traditional authority Authority based on custom; rulers wield legitimate power because their subjects believe them to possess a sacred right to rule.

Traditional Authority. **Traditional authority** is based on custom. Traditional rulers—kings, queens, monarchs, sultans, dukes, chiefs, emperors, caliphs, shahs, and czars—wield legitimate power because their subjects believe them to have a "divine right" to do so. In certain times and places, traditional rule seems absolute, as it was, for example, in the Chinese, Inca, and Zulu Empires. Yet even at the height of this apparent despotism, traditional rule is always to some degree limited. For one thing, the aristocracy usually has certain legitimate claims to power. For another, the ruling family may be internally divided.

During the last few centuries, as the rule of traditional authority has waned, kings and emperors have more often been deposed not by relatives seeking to replace them but by commoners seeking an end to traditional authority altogether. As long ago as the 1640s, the English Puritans overthrew the royal government and established a republic (overthrown in its turn in 1660). In 1651, King Louis XIV, king "by the grace of God" of France, said, "I am the state!" Yet his great-great-grandson, Louis XVI, was deposed and beheaded in 1792. Over time, traditional authority has declined in importance. In nearly all countries that have kept monarchs, the monarchs no longer rule as heads of government; they have assumed merely ceremonial functions and lack political power, as in Great Britain and Japan. On a more local and regional level—particularly in the less industrialized, rural areas of the world—traditional rulers remain influential. Of course, these areas represent a substantial proportion of the globe, even today.

It sometimes happens that regimes, originally founded on entirely different bases, come to acquire the mantle of traditional authority. When the Soviet army defeated and expelled the Japanese army from North Korea at the end of World War II, it installed Kim Il Sung as the nation's president. After more than forty years in power, Kim's regime clearly rules on the basis of traditional authority. Kim's statue dominates every city and town, his portrait gazes down from most public buildings, and his sayings appear almost everywhere, including on granite slabs next to country roads. In official portraits, he is depicted as a full head taller than everyone else standing around him, as well as the object of their adoring gazes. Over 1,000 books about him are listed in the catalogue of North Korea's major library. His birthday and that of his son are national holidays. To commemorate Kim's seventieth birthday in 1982, an "arch of triumph" was built in the capital—thirty-five feet higher than the original in Paris. Red plastic plaques are mounted over every door of every institution that Kim's son Kim Jong Il has visited; some doors bear as many as twenty-five plaques. It is clear that the younger Kim is being groomed for the presidency of North Korea (Burns, 1985a, 1985b). In short, North Korea bears all the marks of a regime based on traditional authority.

The State

The most basic issue in politics is this: Who has legitimate force in a given territory? Today, what we call the **state** has, by definition, a monopoly on legitimate force in any society. Others may have force, but not legitimate force. If strong disagreements break out in violence or if certain people or areas are in revolt, only the representatives of the state have the authority to suppress the disturbances. Representatives of no other institution can make that claim—not teachers, not the clergy, not business executives, not mothers or fathers. Only representatives of the state. Of course, the local police are the most immediate and visible of these representatives. To put the matter of force another way, the state has a monopoly on legal violence.

One fundamental problem facing all revolutionary regimes is the "routinization" of charisma. The second generation of leaders must retain the followers' loyalty without the leader who inspired the revolution in the first place. China after Mao was forced to shift direction and follow the path that Mao would have rejected.

A. Friend/Time, Jan. 26, 1987

State A political entity characterized by centralized, institutionalized rule and a sense of common identity among the population.

Why Force? If the state is legitimate, why should force be necessary? To begin with, not everyone grants the legitimacy of any particular government—remember, legitimacy, like almost everything else, is a matter of degree. Second, a very small number of people can create a very great deal of disruption. Even if the overwhelming majority regards the government as legitimate, a few hundred people who do not can wreak havoc on a large, modern government by using violence against it.

Of course, many governments are not regarded as legitimate. In 1953, the Shah of Iran was ousted from power by an elected government that the United States government suspected of pro-Soviet tendencies. A bit later, this government was overthrown in a coup organized by the United States, and the Shah was restored. But in 1979, he was again overthrown—this time, for good. The Shah's regime was perceived by many Iranians as illegitimate: The mass of the population rejected it. Force of arms was necessary to put down opposition or criticism to it, until it was overthrown.

Even in legitimate states, citizens may grant the government's right to exercise power in general and in principle but they might still resist certain specific obligations if they did not face the threat of force. We may acknowledge the government's right to collect taxes but resent the taxes levied on our incomes. We may feel that because all other countries maintain armies, ours must, too; if so, we might also accept the government's right to draft able-bodied citizens. But we might still resist the draft if we thought that the army was being put to bad uses, as many Americans did during the war in Vietnam. Many people who felt that way nonetheless let themselves be drafted rather than spend a couple of years staring at the four walls of a cell in a military stockade. In short, the state's use of force or—much more often—the threat of force is needed to extract compliance from the people even when they feel that the government is legitimate. (See W. J. Goode on these and related points: 1972; 1977, pp. 399–406.)

In fact, a large measure of a political regime's legitimacy is passive rather than active. The public accepts rather than rejoices in the government's rule. It calculates that it is easier to comply with the government than to deal with the inconvenience and the pain of resistance.

Some conflicts break out, not between the government and groups or individuals opposed to it, but between different groups or individuals. When such conflicts erupt into violence, the state must step in and enforce its monopoly of legal violence. When a divorce settlement, let's say, has awarded custody of the children to the mother, the state must forcibly uphold the divorce settlement if the father kidnaps them. If it did not, the weak and the peaceful would always be exploited by the stronger and the violent. Without force, no state could survive. All political regimes are and must be sustained by physical force or the threat of it—whether or not they are accepted as legitimate by the people. In short, "force constitutes one of the major foundations of all social structures"—especially of the state (W. J. Goode, 1972, p. 507).

Of course, the amount of physical coercion needed to maintain order varies a good deal from regime to regime. What proportion of a nation's economy must be spent to maintain internal security? How repressive must the military or the police be to maintain civil order? How much support would a rebel force receive from the people? To say that all regimes rest ultimately on force does not mean that all are equally coercive.

Governments are far more effective when they hold the threat of physical coercion very much in the background and appear to be run wholly with the consent of the people. No regime admits to being illegitimate, not even the most repressive and dictatorial. All regimes claim that dissidents against them are few, and they are often believed even when these claims are most decidedly untrue. When a state controls the nation's means of communication, either directly or indirectly, it attempts to create a positive image of its rule, and if the public does not have access to contradicting arguments and facts, it may not be skeptical of this image. For instance, most North Koreans have "fixed dial" radios capable of receiving only broadcasts from the capital. Television sets receive only official stations, which carry patriotic programs extolling the virtues of Kim, his regime, and his son (Burns, 1985a). Most governments use image mongering as their first line of defense, and they use physical force judiciously and only as a last resort, when propaganda has become ineffective.

TOTALITARIANISM

"Totalitarianism" is a term used to define the degree of repression of a regime in power; the more repressive the regime, the more totalitarian it may be said to be. A **totalitarian state** has at least five basic defining features:

Totalitarian state A state that is extremely repressive. Its citizens have neither majority rule nor civil liberties.

1. The decision-making process is highly centralized: A very small number of people have a great deal of power, and the mass of the people have virtually none.

2. Civil liberties are repressed; citizens may be arrested, convicted, and imprisoned on flimsy charges and evidence. Citizens, in short, are "guilty until proven innocent."

3. There is an attempt to mobilize compliance from the entire citizenry. No one may stand outside the system; there are no neutral citizens. "You're either for us or against us," is a common theme of totalitarian regimes.

4. Freedom of the arts and other media of culture is severely repressed; cultural expression not following the party or government line receives no support, or is smashed, or is forced to go underground.

5. Any and all significant efforts at autonomy from the state or the party are repressed; there is an attempt to absorb all institutions into state or party control. No institution, even a chess or a bird-watcher's club, is permitted to be independent of state or party control.

Totalitarianism is, as are most things, a matter of degree. Measuring the degree of repressiveness of the various governments of the world is a difficult task; it is clear-cut only at the extremes. Hardly anyone would charge the Western democracies, such as Sweden and the Netherlands, with totalitarianism. However, at the other end of the spectrum, many of the most repressive totalitarian regimes are military dictatorships, and a number are supported by the United States government; others are communist regimes. Still, not all communist regimes are totalitarian or highly repressive. Most observers agree, for example, that a moderately high level of freedom from repression prevails in Yugoslavia and

Nicaragua. On the other hand, North Korea (as we discussed earlier), Albania, and, to a slightly lesser extent, the ~~Soviet~~ Union are widely regarded in the West as more or less fully totalitarian governments. What is living under a totalitarian government really like? Let's consider some specific cases.

Totalitarian regimes seek to rigidly control the public's access to information, even information that elsewhere is considered not only innocuous but essential to everyday life. For instance, in the Soviet Union, "a common reference tool Westerners take absolutely for granted—the telephone book—is an item of priceless rarity." In Moscow, every fifteen years or so, a new phone book listing private subscribers is published—in editions of only 50,000! Naturally, they sell out within a few hours (Smith, 1984, pp. 471–472). In the absence of a telephone book, individuals can dial for assistance, "but the service is almost always busy"; if someone wants the number of a person with a common name, like Ivanov (of which there are 150,000 in Moscow), he or she "will not be served" (Binyon, 1985, p. 121). A citizen with a phone book is a citizen with a tiny degree of power and autonomy; a citizen without one is a citizen who needs constant assistance and whose requests may be monitored and recorded by the state.

In totalitarian regimes, physical mobility is restricted. In the Soviet Union, travel from one city to another is severely restricted.

> A foreigner living in Moscow cannot just get in his car and drive off. On all roads leading out of every Soviet city there are permanent police check-points. Unless a foreigner has advance clearance, he will be stopped and turned back. A resident journalist cannot buy an internal air-ticket without notifying the Foreign Ministry two working days in advance. Even if he got on a train or bus and was not recognized as a foreigner, he could not stay anywhere, as Soviet hotels accept bookings only if the visa has first been endorsed for the visit (Binyon, 1985, p. 145).

Likewise, physical mobility is sharply restricted for Soviet citizens, as well. For instance, the population of Moscow, regarded as a desirable place to live, has been rigidly set at 8 million. No one who lives elsewhere may simply pick up and move there; the availability of openings depends on the death or out-migration of Muscovites, as well as priority and special permission.

South Africa is another example of a totalitarian regime. Its population is 83 percent Black. Yet Blacks have the legal right to live in only 13 percent of the nation's territory! If the police encounter Blacks in the remaining 87 percent of the country—including all urban areas—those Blacks must have "legitimate" reasons for being there, such as employment by a white family or firm. If not, they are arrested. Until 1986, the physical and geographical mobility of Blacks was monitored by means of something called an "internal passport," which the police had the right to inspect at any time under any circumstances. Without this passport, any Black in South Africa could be arrested. (The Soviet Union still has internal passports.) In 1986, internal passports were abolished in South Africa and replaced by identification cards; now, no one can be arrested for not carrying them. (The chances are, however, that official restrictions on mobility will be replaced by informal ones: police "hassling" of citizens who don't "belong" in certain neighborhoods or areas.)

Restrictions on movement are only the most basic of the assaults on the liberty of South African Blacks, but not, perhaps, the most humiliating. A number of **apartheid** (or segregation) laws regulate almost every aspect of private life: whom South Africans can marry; which restaurants

Apartheid The policy of rigid racial separation that prevails in South Africa.

South Africa's laws of apartied (or racial segregation) require Blacks and whites to use separate facilities. Restrictions on the rights of Blacks are severe and regiment almost every aspect of their lives. The tendency to politicize private life is characteristic of a totalitarian state.

W. Campbell/Sygma

and stores they can patronize; whom they can employ. Furthermore, Blacks in South Africa do not have the right to vote in national elections, to elect their own representatives. Their role is restricted to electing puppet representatives in all-Black townships with no power at all in Pretoria, the nation's capital. In short, much of the Black South African's life, both public and private, is restricted by the totalitarian state.

Total Commitment

As its name implies, in a totalitarian political system, all of social life revolves around the aims of the state. Membership in the party becomes a necessity for career advancement. In communist societies, the party is equated with the state—indeed, with the society as a whole. Everyone in the country must "fit in." No dissent, opposition, criticism, or, in theory, even indifference is allowed. Everyone is expected to serve the state; commitment to the state's interests is supposed to be total. The distinction between the state and society is progressively eroded. Every deviation from the norm is an attack on the state, on "the people." Private matters become weighty political questions. What people do or say in private may become public events—as a result of bugging, telephone taps, the use of secret agents.

A totalitarian regime strives to have a pipeline into every household—with information filtering out and propaganda pouring in. The official ideology is believed to explain everything. The state controls the educational system and dictates the curriculum. It monitors and censors the mass media—newspapers, magazines, book publishing, TV, art, radio, and film. "Alternate" or "underground" media must therefore be circulated through networks of like-minded friends and acquaintances. Independent networks for disseminating information must be concealed from the authorities and, as a result, from the public. In the Soviet Union, dissident authors mimeograph or photocopy their manuscripts, which they then pass from hand to hand; in the Soviet Union, this system is called *samizdat,* or "self-publishing." There, officials have made it illegal to "multiply copies of a manuscript for nefarious or subversive purposes." One must receive official permission from a high-ranking minister, which is very hard to get, to have access to a photocopier. Soviet intellectuals regard a photocopier with sentiments bordering on reverence. The importance of written communication to totalitarian regimes is illustrated by the fact that in Romania, in 1983, ownership of typewriters was limited to official approved persons, with permits.

DEMOCRACY

Democracy A form of government in which a majority rule the electoral system and the citizens enjoy civil liberties.

The term **democracy** comes from the ancient Greeks (it means "rule by the people"). In fact, part of the population of ancient Greece, including Athens, its most democratic city, was made up of slaves, and women—half the population—were regarded as not fully human. These ambiguities about the meaning of democracy persist to the present day. The word has such appeal that communist nations that are far more totalitarian than democratic use the term "democratic" in their names—East Germany, for instance, calls itself the "German Democratic Republic." In addition, the constitutions of many repressive regimes around the world—promising their citizens democratic rights—are practically identical to those of Western democracies.

Although no perfect democracy has ever existed, and the term is often misused, some features are nonetheless common to democratic states. Most contemporary observers agree that their two most basic defining features are equality and liberty (Pennock, 1979, p. 4). Another way of expressing the same idea is to say that the central norms of democracy are majority rule and minority rights (Irish, Prothro, and Richardson, 1981, p. 43).

Equality

The principle that "all men are created equal" does not imply that all men—and women—are literally equal in all respects. Clearly, some people are stronger, more intelligent, musical, academically inclined, mechanically skilled, or artistic than others. "Equal" means that all people, by virtue of their common humanity, have a moral right to participate in the political process, partly because human dignity requires it, partly because only in this way can individuals protect their own interests and safeguard their rights. It was not until the Voting Rights Act of 1965 that Blacks voted in substantial numbers in the South. Partly as a consequence, dozens of Black politicians have been elected in recent years, including to the post of mayor, a trend that we discussed in Chapter 10.

Equality implies majority rule, the political participation of each individual as an individual and thus the triumph of the greatest number of individuals. The electoral process is a logical outcome of the idea of equality, because elections conducted without force or coercion permit the majority to express itself and, in the end, to rule. Political theorists now agree that free and representative elections are a necessary condition for democracy (Pennock, 1979, pp. 6–11).

Marxists, however, deny that free elections are the defining characteristic of democracy. Subtle but powerful forces, they say, make elections ineffective, because all candidates support the existing economic system—and (according to them) economics runs politics, not the other way around. Big business, they say, rules America. To non-Marxist observers, this criticism appears to be self-serving, because formally free elections play an extremely limited role in Marxist regimes. Technically, elections exist in communist states (as they do in South Africa), but they do not operate at the higher reaches of government. The electorate in communist states may generally vote for certain local officials, but not for national positions, such as premier, president, or party secretary;

these positions are typically decided as a result of a vote—often "by acclamation"—of elite governing bodies, such as the Soviet Politboro. What communist governments do not have is elections among genuinely divergent factions belonging to different parties. Only one party exists under communism: the Communist party. Communist states claim to represent "the will of the people," but they never allow the people to express themselves freely. Flawed as the electoral process may be, say democratic political theorists, humanity has never devised a more democratic means of governing. As Winston Churchill, Britain's prime minister during World War II, said: "Democracy is the worst system devised by the wit of man, except for all the others."

Political equality does not imply economic equality. Indeed, by strictly economic measurements, average citizens of communist nations are more equal (though with a lower standard of living) than those of the United States and many other democratic nations (see Chapter 9). American society has not been very successful in distributing wealth equally. In the West, democracy is regarded as a procedure, a mechanism for achieving other goals, such as economic equality. Communist regimes, by contrast, are based on "democratic centralism"—that is, decisions are made by a small elite, supposedly "in the interests" of the majority. If a group of generals overthrows a government and redistributes much of the land to the poor, has the country become more democratic? Economically, yes. But politically, no, because the transfer of power was not accomplished through democratic procedures.

Liberty

A second precondition for democracy is liberty. Democratic theory does not hold that the majority is always right. In fact, in a democratic government, citizens enjoy certain "inalienable" (or "natural") rights—rights that cannot be taken from them, regardless of the will of the majority. (In principle, at any rate; rights must be protected, and the poor often lose their rights because they lack adequate legal services.) Minority rights must also be protected from the majority, should the majority become arbitrary and oppressive. Free speech, though not absolute, is a right granted to every citizen of a democratic state. Democratic majorities do not have the right to curtail free speech if they do not approve of its content. Citizens also have the right to be protected from arbitrary or unwarranted arrest, "cruel and unusual" punishment (such as torture), and unreasonable searches. In a democracy, for instance, the representatives of the state do not have the right to wiretap a citizen's phone without cause or probable cause (strong suspicion that a felony has been committed), to enter and search a citizen's home on a vague suspicion, or to deprive a citizen of free political or religious expression (unless it violates ordinary criminal laws; you cannot, for example, murder a politician and claim as defense your right to exercise free speech).

Though inalienable, **civil liberties** are never absolute. Where does legitimate freedom end? That is a matter for honest argument. Does freedom of speech include the right to falsely shout "Fire!" in a crowded theater? (No, according to a famous saying of Oliver Wendell Holmes Jr. [1841–1935], a justice of the United States Supreme Court.) To make libelous or slanderous statements about someone and tarnish his or her reputation in the community? (Sometimes, yes; usually, no.) To publish classified documents that threaten the national security or reveal military secrets to foreign powers? (No.) To distribute pornographic films showing 12 year olds? (Again, no.)

Civil liberties Rules that exist in democracies, spelling out rights that citizens have regarding free speech, protection against arbitrary or unwarranted arrest, surveillance, and so on.

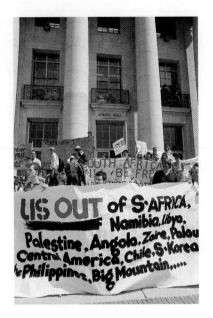

Liberty is one basic condition of democracy, and free speech is one aspect of liberty. Citizens in a democracy enjoy free speech as an inalienable right—it cannot be taken away, even by a majority vote. Such civil liberties protect the right of groups and individuals to protest existing conditions.

Lawrence Migdale/Photo Researchers

Special-interest group An organization or a group that has a fairly specific goal or purpose and that attempts to influence the political process to achieve that goal.

Lobby A certain kind of highly organized interest group, with an office, a staff, and access to legislators and politicians.

Besides, in every democracy that ever existed, civil liberties have been violated in practice. The police in some jurisdictions have even been known to violate a suspect's rights. For instance, the "Watergate" investigations of 1972 to 1974 uncovered a wide variety of constitutional violations either committed directly by high government officials or authorized by them, including burglaries, illegal wiretaps, buggings, opening first-class mail, "dirty tricks" (such as distributing falsely attributed scandalous letters), and requesting tax audits of political opponents. These and other violations of civil liberties occur in all democracies, but, if discovered, they are subject to judicial review. In undemocratic regimes, civil liberties are not guaranteed even in principle. Such governments put their own interests ahead of individual freedom.

THE AMERICAN POLITICAL SYSTEM

Governments make formal rules for the members of societies, and they have the power to enforce those rules. The functions of government include the funding of essential services, the enactment of legislation, the maintenance of military forces, the collection of taxes, and the carrying on of foreign relations. Every action by every government involves making decisions—that is, choices. Why make one choice and not another? Why do Republicans tend to emphasize defense and underplay welfare, while Democrats usually do the reverse? Why did President John F. Kennedy (1961–1963) support the 1961 Bay of Pigs invasion of Cuba? Why did the action fail? Why did Kennedy call for a "quarantine" (in effect, a naval blockade) of Cuba in 1962, when he discovered that the Soviets had placed offensive missiles in Cuba, and why did the Soviets back down and remove them? Why did President Ronald Reagan call for an end to corporate taxes—and why did he withdraw his proposal when it touched off an outcry from Democrats and liberal Republicans?

Political events take place within a specific social, economic, and political context, or structure, and they are understandable only with reference to it. Every political system creates and enforces rules in a way that is both unique (in all its details) and similar to other political systems (in its general outlines). Like all other political systems, ours has certain distinctive features. Two of the most basic are the two-party system and the importance of **special-interest groups,** or **lobbies.**

The Two-Party System

A political party is a group of individuals organized to gain and exercise political power by winning control of government (Irish et al., 1981, p. 132). Totalitarian states usually permit only one party: The Soviet Union, for instance, permits only the Communist party. This one party is presumed to have a monopoly on truth. In these cases, the party does not have to gain power but maintain it—protect it from real or imagined threats. In democratic states, at least two parties must regularly compete for power, although the existence of two or more parties is no guarantee of a democracy; one or more parties could be totally ineffectual, or parties could be identical, "Tweedledum and Tweedledee."

The United States has had literally hundreds of political parties, and it has dozens of them even now. Yet all but a few of them are so small that they have no realistic hope of gaining power, or even of influencing government policy or the outcome of elections—the Democratic Workers party, the Vegetarian party, or the Prohibitionists, to name three. In some areas, smaller parties can influence elections—for instance, the Liberal and Conservative parties in New York. Even at the national level, minority parties can make an impact—as did George Wallace's American Independent party in 1968 and John Anderson's Independent party in 1980. Yet neither Wallace nor Anderson had any realistic hope of becoming president. Their parties acted as pressure groups, not as true parties.

For all practical purposes, then, the United States has a two-party system. Most of the time, minor parties fail to win a single seat in Congress or the governorship of any state. In part, the dominance of the Democrats and Republicans results from our "winner-take-all" system of election. This means that in almost all our elections, on all levels of government, the candidates with the most votes—not necessarily a majority of the vote—win election and take office. Most Western European democracies have systems of election that make it easier for minority parties to elect candidates, either through "proportional representation," which gives parties representation in proportion to their voting strength in the country as a whole, or through a system that forces parties to compromise with one another. In the United States, if a party receives 10 percent of the vote, it receives nothing. In much of Europe and in Israel, if a party receives 10 percent of the vote, it receives 10 percent of the seats in the government. This "winner-take-all" system of election has had a profound impact on our nation's political institutions.

We have not only fewer parties than most other democratic countries but also less ideological parties; if a party with, say, 10 percent of the total vote can elect candidates, then a party can appeal to a relatively small minority of the electorate and still get representation. In contrast, American parties must have broader appeal and, consequently, less clear-cut ideologies. Europeans, for example, find American parties "wishy-washy" on many issues. This ideological vagueness is needed to appeal to the largest possible number of voters. Too strong a stand on too many issues will alienate too many voters.

The ideological differences between the Democratic party and the Republican party are real, but they are neither absolute nor striking. Democrats, for instance, are more likely to favor a national health-insurance plan; Republicans, to oppose it. Republicans are more and Democrats less likely to support large increases in our military budget. Yet many Democrats oppose national health insurance, and some Republicans opposed President Reagan's proposed increases in military spending. On few questions are all Democrats on one side and all Republicans on the other.

Another characteristic of American political parties is their weak hold over the electorate, demonstrated by the very low voter turnouts in recent elections and the fairly high rate of vote switching and ticket splitting (voting for candidates of both parties). Among the twenty-eight nations that have held free elections since 1945, the United States ranks next to last in average voter turnout. In all the elections between 1945 and 1981, only 58 percent of all eligible American voters actually cast their ballots—in the presidential election of 1980, only 54 percent. In some nations, average voter participation is more than 90 percent. Even in Canada, the country that is most similar to the United States, elections draw over 75 percent of the eligible voters. Voting is low here, among other reasons, because American political parties tend to take weak stands on the issues, and the voters therefore respond weakly. In Western

Europe, practically the entire political spectrum is covered by many parties; there is something for everyone. In the United States, the two major parties must settle for a lukewarm response from the voters; not finding the position of either very meaningful, many citizens choose not to vote.

As a result of our relative indifference to our political parties, we tend to switch parties quite often. In 1964, Democrat Lyndon B. Johnson received 61 percent of the presidential vote; in 1972 Democrat George McGovern received only 37 percent of the presidential vote. In the 1980s, President Ronald Reagan was supported by millions of voters who approved of him personally, but supported neither his party nor its policies. These facts show that party loyalty among American voters is not very strong. Even in the same election, vote splitting is quite common. Party affiliation is only one of several factors that influence American voters. We also respond to a candidate's personality and manner on TV, to racial or ethnic pressures, and so on. For instance, in 1983, more than 85 percent of Chicago's white voters, most of whom were traditional Democrats, cast ballots for a Republican mayoral candidate. Why? Because the Democrat was Black. He won anyway, mainly because he got more than 95 percent of a strikingly higher-than-usual Black voter turnout.

None of this means that party affiliation and political ideology are totally unimportant to American voters. The various segments of American society do differ politically, just as the Democrats differ as a rule from Republicans. Compared with the differences among Western Europe's political parties, however, ours are fairly small. The Democratic party embraces a coalition of a number of groups, categories, and statuses. A poll of 1984 voters leaving the polling booth made it clear that although Reagan's vote was substantially greater than Mondale's in nearly every category, support for the Democratic candidate that year remained high among Blacks (90 percent), Hispanics (65 percent), Jews (66 percent), union members (53 percent), the very poor (53 percent), voters who viewed themselves as liberal (70 percent), and the unemployed (68 percent). The vote was nearly evenly split among the least well-educated category (49 versus 50 percent) and government employees (48 versus 50 percent). In contrast, Reagan's support was strongest in the traditional bastions of Republicanism: among white Protestants (73 percent), professionals and business managers (62 percent), high income earners (68 percent who earned over $50,000 voted for Reagan), whites generally (66 percent), the married (63 percent), the religiously conservative (80 percent of all white born-again Christians voted for Reagan), voters who regarded themselves as conservative (81 percent), and older voters (Reagan attracted 63 percent of the vote among those aged 60 and older). One distinctive feature of the 1984 election was that the Republican candidate made inroads into traditional Democratic territory, such as among white ethnics, like voters of Italian descent (57 percent voted or Reagan), voters who live in the South (63 percent of whom voted for Reagan), and younger voters (among those age 18 to 29, Reagan received 58 percent of the vote). Of course, none of these characteristics, or any combination of them, is a guarantee that anyone will vote for the "appropriate" party or candidate. Nonetheless, members of certain social categories do have a fairly stong tendency to affiliate with and vote in certain ways, and the greater number of characteristics one has in a certain direction, the greater the likelihood that one will affiliate and vote in that way.

Interest Groups

A sizable number of Americans feel very strongly about certain issues. They cannot realistically hope to form a separate party, because there are too many issues, and no party can hope to win an election on a single issue, given our winner-take-all system. The next best thing is to form a special-interest group to influence candidates and elected officials. Especially in the past few decades, special-interest groups have emerged in profusion, each with its own special issue: blocking gun control; repealing the United States Supreme Court's 1973 decision legalizing abortion; raising import duties on foreign goods; ratifying the Equal Rights Amendment; preventing its ratification; continuing federal subsidies to tobacco farmers; raising the minimum wage; improving or limiting auto safety; limiting the number of students admitted to American medical schools; taking sex and violence off television; saving the whales; stopping experimentation on live animals; increasing federal funding to the arts; lowering taxes; and literally thousands and thousands of other issues.

Despite this impressive variety, all interest groups are not equal. Big business is the best organized, the most politically active, and the most generously funded of all the major categories of interest groups. Although the business community does not form a unified political force, the business lobby tends to support legislation that favors high profits, low taxes, and reduced government regulation of its activities. In general, for instance, the business lobby opposes further environmental legislation and favors relaxing existing controls.

Organized labor, although no match for the business lobby, also has its own cluster of interest groups, which favor legislation to create jobs in the public and private sectors, to increase job security, to raise wages, and to improve the safety of the workplace. Powerful agricultural groups, professional groups (like the American Medical Association), ideological groups, and even interest groups within the government (like the Pentagon and the Army Corps of Engineers) also try to influence the conduct of government in their respective areas of interest.

Interest groups work in a variety of ways. Financial contributions to candidates are their most direct means of influencing the politi-

The American political system is permeated by special-interest groups. Lobbyists, who represent them, attempt to persuade politicians and bureaucrats to make decisions that will benefit these groups. Large, well-financed lobbies sometimes have more political influence than their membership might warrant.

UPI

cal process. Political campaigns are very expensive—and becoming more so with each election. In 1986, a total of $342 million was spent on the Congressional races—$80 million more than in 1984; $155 million of this went for Senate candidates and $187 million for House candidates. Although money is not the only factor in winning an election, it is extremely important (Tolchin, 1986). And interest groups generate funds more effectively for a candidate than does the general electorate.

Interest groups also mount public protests, organize campaign activities for or against particular candidates, sponsor advertisements, bring and subsidize legal actions, and supply information to politicians and officials. Many special-interest groups have offices and large staffs in Washington, D.C., that carefully cultivate politicians and officials. The collective impact of the lobbyists who influence Congress is so great that they are called the "Third House," in addition to the Senate and the House of Representatives (Morgan, Donovan, and Potholm, 1979, p. 128).

Are interest groups, lobbies, and political action committees good or bad for the democratic process? Some observers believe that the proliferation of different groups, each with its own point of view and program, tends on balance to prevent any single group or interest from dominating the rest. The business lobby, they say, restrains the labor lobby, which in turn restrains business; consumer groups and environmentalist groups check manufacturers; and so on. This argument falls apart in many cases. Lobbies are rarely equal in size or influence; and the largest, most influential lobby usually gets its way. For many issues, only one side is highly organized. Many questions are resolved not by the majority, nor even by the collision of two equally influential interest groups, but by a single well-organized and well-financed lobby that imposes its will by rewarding friendly politicians and punishing unfriendly ones.

Consider, for instance, the role of the National Rifle Association (NRA) in preventing effective gun control—an issue that, poll after poll, year after year, is shown to be overwhelmingly popular. However, the NRA, which has more than a million members, is opposed to any form of gun control, in addition, there is no comparable counterlobby to nullify the NRA's power. Clearly, highly motivated minorities can and do exert an influence far beyond what their numbers would seem to justify.

Part of that influence may be inevitable. Any political process must be dominated by those who are more active than the majority; and governments must always be more responsive to interests that make their demands known by organizing, turning out voters, and influencing (or befuddling) public opinion. Interest groups are an intrinsic feature of American political life, and will continue to be so unless our entire system of government is changed beyond recognition. Reforms may limit some of their more outrageous practices (such as offering bribes to politicians), but these practices are not the real basis of special-interest-group power. A bit of national wisdom goes, "If you can't lick 'em, join 'em." That is what seems to be happening. Previously inactive interests are now organizing and influencing the political process. Ralph Nader's Center for the Study of Responsive Law, for instance, is a consumer lobby. Civil rights organizations, such as the National Association for the Advancement of Colored People (NAACP), is mastering the techniques of traditional lobbyists. Environmental groups, too, are beginning to flex their political muscles. Lobbying will never be a game played between equal adversaries, but it's the only game in town.

The Political Spectrum

Terms like "liberal," "conservative," "moderate," "middle of the road," "radical," and "reactionary" resound through everyday talk. But what, exactly, do they mean? This is not an easy question to answer, because everyone has a slightly different definition of them. Your own political outlook will influence how you define any particular term, and thus all the others. Some Marxists, for instance, see no essential difference between liberals and conservatives; they lump more than 95 percent of the American political system into one more-or-less undifferentiated category. Members of extreme right-wing organizations (like the John Birch Society and the various organizations that call themselves the "Ku Klux Klan") consider the rest of the political spectrum, from conservatism to Marxism, to be a disguised form of communism. Liberals and conservatives do take their differences seriously, of course. They do not take seriously, however, political differences at the fringe. Marxists, for instance, are divided among numerous hostile factions and attack one another on the basis of minute issues of dogma that do not exist for outsiders.

People can be liberal or conservative in different areas of life. Liberalism and conservatism present not one dimension but many. People with blue-collar jobs and only high school educations tend to be more liberal economically than white-collar workers and professionals with college educations, who are more conservative about economic issues (see Chapter 9). On civil liberties issues, blue-collar workers are more conservative, whereas white-collar and professional workers tend to be more liberal. Clearly, the terms used to describe political and ideological positions do not have a universally agreed-upon meaning.

As a result, the American public does not have a clear-cut understanding of what it means to be a liberal or a conservative. As many as 20 percent of the respondents in some polls cannot correctly identify a particular politician's ideology, and an additional 30 percent are "don't knows" (Erikson et al., 1980, p. 57). When asked by a CBS/*New York Times* poll what "the biggest difference between liberal views and conservative views" are, only half of the sample ventured to answer at all. Only 19 percent mentioned government spending or government control. But when respondents were asked to classify their own views, the self-designated labels tended to correspond to the conservative and liberal positions on economic and civil liberties issues, respectively.

In current American politics, conservatives are supposed to believe in economic laissez faire—a hands-off attitude toward government intervention and control. Liberals are supposed to believe in bigger government, more governmental control over the economy, and more governmental assistance to individuals. The truth is that both conservatives and liberals accept certain kinds of governmental control but not others—but they have opposing ideas about what should and should not be controlled. American (though not foreign) conservatives believe that the government should not intervene in economic matters and should let racial and sexual inequality take their "natural" course. They argue that a healthy economy will eventually produce more economic opportunities for Blacks, Hispanics, and women than government intervention will. Conservatives do, however, believe that government should actively intervene against marijuana, abortion, pornography, and "subversive" political activity.

American liberals, on the contrary, want government intervention to uphold living standards and to help eliminate racial and sexual inequalities. But they adopt something of a "hands off" policy in such matters as drug use, sex, and the political activities of "subversive" organizations. Generally, too, they oppose American military intervention abroad. So liberals and conservatives do not really disagree about how much control the government should have over our lives, but over what kind of control, in which areas of life. Let's consider one aspect of the liberal-conservative debate more closely: the economy.

Conservatism.   Conservatives—that is, proponents of **conservativism**—have great faith in the superiority of the "free-enterprise" capitalist economy over all other systems, especially communism. Therefore, conservatives believe that business should be regulated by the government as little as possible. For instance, Ronald Reagan, the fortieth president of the United States (1981 to 1989), in many ways a model conservative, promised to "get the government off our backs." During his administration, many regulations governing pollution and worker safety standards were suspended or ignored; Reagan, like conservatives in general, argued that such regulations stifle and inhibit business and thus cut down on jobs, profits, and prosperity. The interests of business, they believe, should come before all others, for "the business of America is business."

Conservatives, therefore, feel that government assistance to the people—in the form of federal welfare, food stamps, Social Security, medical benefits, educational "head-start" programs, Medicare, Medicaid, employee disability compensation, and school-lunch programs—should be cut back. Also, too much welfare and state assistance, they believe, undercuts the initiative of the people, makes them dependent on the government, and discourages their efforts to find jobs in the private sector. They also feel that federal support of enterprises and institutions that are not profitable—such as the fine arts, social research, higher education, and libraries—should either cease altogether or be drastically reduced. Such cultural and educational activities, they say, should either be put on a profit-making basis, or they should turn for support to the private sector or to state and local governments. The only enterprises and activities that should receive massive government support are those that protect us from external threats—mainly the military and related scientific and technological research.

Some observers make a distinction between "moderate" conservative and "ultraconservative" ideologies. Moderate conservatives favor some foreign aid, accept the idea of moderate government taxation and the use of government spending to help stimulate the economy, and tolerate welfare and other government benefits. Ultraconservatives, on the other hand, "see foreign aid as a giveaway," continue to insist that taxes should be cut to the bare minimum, and continually oppose "any welfare spending, claiming that it destroys moral fiber and saps individual initiative as well as costing them tax money and making it harder to keep wages down" (Domhoff, 1983, p. 91).

Liberalism.   As a general rule, although liberals—that is, proponents of **liberalism**—generally support capitalism at home and abroad no less than conservatives do, their support is more qualified. For instance, conservatives oppose the Marxist Sandinista regime in Nicaragua, fearing a communist "take-over" in Central America; liberals, on the other hand, withhold their support for the *contras*, an army fighting the Sandinistas. Thus, whereas conservatives are strongly anticommunist, liberals could be more accurately described as noncommunist in their orientation. Contrarily, conservatives have more tolerance for right-wing dicta-

Conservativism The political view that the economy should be regulated by the government very little, that welfare and other programs designed to assist the poor should be kept to a minimum, that the military should be strongly supported, and that communism should be contained abroad, even at the cost of supporting extremely undemocratic regimes.

Liberalism The political view that the government should fund programs to assist the poor, that civil liberties should be strictly observed, and that a rapprochement should be reached with communist regimes abroad.

torships in Third World countries, because they are very hostile to communism, whereas liberals tend to be more critical of these regimes. (At the same time, the Marcos regime of the Philippines and the Duvalier regime of Haiti, both repressive dictatorships, fell during the conservative Reagan administration, a fact regarded by some as a human rights coup for Reaganism.) A second plank in the liberal ideological platform is that liberals favor more controls over big business than conservatives do. Liberals usually feel that if the federal government does not attempt to regulate business, especially big business, the economy will move away from a true "free enterprise" system and toward "oligopoly," the control of the market by one or a few gigantic firms. They also fear that without government controls, big business would deceive the consumer, pollute the environment, and exploit and endanger its workers' safety and lives.

Liberals do not think that the "invisible hand" of the free market necessarily distributes economic benefits fairly; wealth, they say, does not automatically "trickle down" from rich to poor. Certain groups lose out if they are not assisted by government, so liberals tend to favor special-assistance programs to the poor, and they do not fear that these programs undercut the work ethic. Most of them also support government aid to the arts and higher education. Last, most liberals believe that conservatives exaggerate the military threat from communism; they do not favor an enormous military buildup. They tend to be critical of the conservative tendency to support American allies, however brutal or undemocratic.

Radicalism. In contrast to both conservatives and liberals, radicals believe that capitalist governments exploit the majority for the benefit of a small ruling elite. **Radicalism** draws heavily from the writings of Karl Marx—though not all radicals consider themselves to be Marxists. Radicals believe that a capitalist economy, by its very nature, creates class, racial, and sexual inequalities, oppression, and exploitation. Government is little more than an "executive committee for the bourgeoisie" (Marx's phrase). Consequently, radicals believe, governments under capitalism require a major overhaul to become more just and more responsive to the needs of the people.

At this point, radicals break into two camps: democratic socialists and revolutionaries. **Democratic socialists** believe that much of the economy should be taken out of the private sector and placed under state control, but that this process can, under certain circumstances, be peaceful, democratic, achieved without a bloody confrontation. The socialist governments of Presidents François Mitterand (France), Felipe Gonzalez (Spain), Mario Soares (Portugal), and Andreus Papandreou (Greece), the labor wing of the Swedish government, and various municipal governments elected, for example, in Bologna, Italy, exemplify this political orientation. On the other hand, **revolutionaries** argue that a democratic and peaceful transition to socialism is not possible. Furthermore, they claim, socialists cannot continue to work with a democratically elected government within the framework of a capitalist economy (unless this is merely one step in a strategy of taking over that government completely). Revolutionaries emphasize the role of armed struggle in the seizure of power, in the literal violent overthrow of bourgeois governments. In addition, democratic socialists accept in principle the idea of an economy with a mix of private and state-controlled industry, whereas revolutionaries believe that the ideal economy should remain entirely in state hands. (It must be said that this is an ideal that no

Radicalism The political ideology that is most closely associated with the ideas of Karl Marx; radicals believe that the capitalist economy is exploitative and oppressive by its very nature, and must be overthrown for socialism.

Democratic socialist Someone who believes that the transition to socialism can take place democratically, through the electoral process, and that socialist governments should be run on a democratic basis, with civil liberties, a toleration of dissenting views, the consent of the governed, and open elections. (See also *socialism* and *democracy*.)

Revolutionary Someone who believes that governments in capitalist states should be overthrown, violently if necessary, and replaced with socialist or communist governments in which the means of production are controlled by the public, not the private, sector.

WHAT DO YOU THINK?

Which Political Label Fits You?

Circle the answer that is closest to your own opinion:

1. Do you think the federal government should spend:
   (a) more money than it has in order to help Blacks and other minorities?
   (b) about the same amount?
   (c) less money than it has in order to help Blacks and other minorities?

2. Which is the most important cause of the social problems faced by Black people?
   (a) racial discrimination
   (b) lack of ambition and other shortcomings

3. To take the place of welfare, would you be in favor of a federally funded guaranteed income which would give every family of four a minimum of $10,000 a year?
   (a) yes
   (b) no

4. In general, do you support the goals of the women's liberation movement?
   (a) yes
   (b) no

5. Do you support the use of busing in order to achieve racial integration of the schools?
   (a) yes
   (b) no

6. Would you be for or against the construction of federally funded, low-income housing projects in your county?
   (a) for
   (b) against

7. The government should introduce a system of socialized medicine, even if this means the income tax would have to be raised.
   (a) agree
   (b) disagree

8. More than ever, it is the duty of the United States to prevent the communists from taking over the world.
   (a) agree
   (b) disagree

9. The federal government should reduce the amount of money spent on national defense.
   (a) agree
   (b) disagree

10. The United States should have fought the war in Vietnam to win, no matter what it took.
    (a) agree
    (b) disagree

11. The United States should reinstitute the draft.

---

communist state has yet attained. Even the Soviet Union tolerates some private enterprise, even though officials are typically embarrassed by its productivity, because it emphasizes the inefficiency of state-run industry.) As these terms are commonly used, revolutionaries are considered more "left wing" and more radical than democratic socialists are.

The far right, See **Reactionary.**

Reactionary Someone whose beliefs are consistent with the extreme right wing of the political spectrum; reactionaries wish to do away with the electoral process, civil rights, and civil liberties.

The Far Right. Radicals are often called "leftists." At the other end of the political spectrum—at **the far right**—lies the domain of the right wing: the **reactionaries**. The reactionaries are considered even more conservative than mainstream conservatives are, although the two philosophies blend into one another in practice. "Ultraconservatives," discussed earlier, share many crucial points of ideology with reactionaries, and to which category someone belongs is largely a matter of degree and emphasis. The crucial defining element of all reactionaries is that they wish to reverse or turn back the hands of time. As the term is

(a) agree
(b) disagree

12. Convicted murderers should be punished by the death penalty.
    (a) agree
    (b) disagree

13. Possession of marijuana should be decriminalized.
    (a) agree
    (b) disagree

14. Because of inflation, the federal government should increase welfare benefits.
    (a) agree
    (b) disagree

15. The federal government should pay for abortions for poor women who want them.
    (a) agree
    (b) disagree

16. Do you think it is all right for a homosexual to be an elementary school teacher?
    (a) yes
    (b) no

17. Do you favor establishing diplomatic relations with Cuba?
    (a) yes
    (b) no

18. Do you think that the federal government should initiate a jobs program to reduce unemployment, even if the program might increase inflation?
    (a) yes
    (b) no

19. Are you in favor of an amendment to the Constitution that would make it illegal to have an abortion?
    (a) yes
    (b) no

20. Do you favor constructing more nuclear reactors in your county to generate electricity?
    (a) yes
    (b) no

How to Score Your Answers

Give yourself one point each time your answers match those in the following list:

1. a	6. a	11. b	16. a
2. a	7. a	12. b	17. a
3. a	8. b	13. a	18. a
4. a	9. a	14. a	19. b
5. a	10. b	15. a	20. b

What Your Score Means

If your score was 13 or higher, your political attitudes most closely resemble those of American liberals. If you scored 9 through 12, your attitudes most closely resemble those of middle-of-the-roaders, or moderates. A score of 8 or less means your political attitudes are most similar to those of conservatives.

Source: Adapted from Bookbinder, 1980, p. 17. © 1980 Newsday, Inc.

commonly used, to be a reactionary is to desire a return to the values and practices of the past, to erase political progress and reforms, and to reinstitute a system that prevailed before they took effect. Extreme examples would be represented by citizens of European nations who believe that a monarchy should be restored, as well as those who believe in fascism, or a repressive, totalitarian, far-right government.

In various European countries today, neo-Fascists and neo-Nazis actually have political parties that run candidates for office—unsuccessfully. These parties and their members are racist, antisocialist, anticommunist, and antimodernist. In Europe and in the United States reactionaries tend to play a somewhat indirect role in politics. Their impact in certain countries of Latin America, the Middle East, and the Far East, however, is more direct. Often, the United States supports reactionary regimes abroad because they tend to be strongly anticommunist. They also tend to be repressive and, if need be, brutal. In this way, our government sacrifices democratic ideas for stability.

THEORIES OF AMERICAN POLITICS

Who rules America? The sociological debate over that question has been dominated by two contrasting approaches or theories: the power-elite model and pluralism. Pluralism overlaps heavily with functionalism. It argues that leaders achieve their positions through ability and that they make decisions on behalf of the majority and its interests. According to the pluralists, these leaders are very responsive to their respective constituencies, and because we have many leaders and many constituencies, power is fragmented into many hands, not concentrated in a few. By the lights of pluralistic theory, democracy is alive and well in contemporary America.

The Power-Elite Theory

A bit more than a generation ago, C. Wright Mills published one of the most controversial books ever written by an American sociologist: *The Power Elite* (1956). Mills died a few years later, at the height of his intellectual powers, but his impact on sociology continues. If anything, the questions and issues raised by the **power-elite theory** are more relevant today than they were when the book was first published. And the controversy over it is still very much alive. Mills's work reflects his commitment to conflict theory, but he was neither an orthodox Marxist nor an economic determinist, so his book has been attacked by the political left as well as by the right (Domhoff and Ballard, 1968). It was, however, translated into Russian and Polish and distributed in communist countries. (Mills used to enjoy telling his friends about the time he met a Russian construction worker, in a remote area of the Soviet Union, who kept a translation of *The Power Elite* in his wheelbarrow and read it during his lunch break.)

The work of Marx had a strong influence on Mills (as did that of Weber), but so too did the work of certain sociologists and political scientists who were really rather reactionary. C. Wright Mills became part Marxist, part American pragmatist, part populist, and part muckraker and reformer.

Power-elite theory The perspective that holds that the most important decisions in American politics are made by a small, highly cohesive group of individuals at the top of major institutions.

One basic tenet of the power-elite theory of C. Wright Mills is that the leaders of political, military, and economic institutions are interchangeable, since they move easily from sphere to sphere.

U.S. Army Photograph

The central theses of *The Power Elite* are awesome in their implications, because, if Mills were alive, he would probably argue that these theses are even more relevant today. Let us consider them, one by one:

1. Some Americans—and almost all of them are men—hold monstrous power over everyone else. In their hands rest the momentous decisions about the freedom or oppression, prosperity or poverty, life or death of everyone else—not just in America but all over the world.

2. This power elite is tiny in number.

3. Its members form a unified, cohesive, centralized group.

4. The power elite is held together by common economic and political interests: Its members want—and get—the same things, things that are both to their individual and collective advantage.

5. The power elite is also held together by a social and cultural unity. Its members acquire common values through social interaction, education at elite boarding schools, intermarriage, working at similar occupations, and membership in country clubs.

6. They exercise their power chiefly by taking control of the very top positions in huge bureaucracies—what Mills called "command posts." In other words, they control and concentrate the "means of administration."

7. Today's dominant bureaucratic institutions deal with the economy, politics, and the military. These three institutions almost completely dominate all other institutions (such as religion and education), which serve the interests of the "big three."

8. Within the economy, the political system, and the military, top administrators have become interchangeable. They are not only socialized to become very much alike but are actually the same people, because they shuttle from command posts in one sphere to command posts in the others.

9. The power elite rules without effective controls. There are no real "checks and balances," no competing elites, few restrictions or restraints. The members of the power elite are basically responsible to no one but themselves.

10. Below the power elite stands the "middle level" of power: labor leaders, members of Congress, local power elites. They do not have enough power to check the national power elite, and, besides, they are the base from which members of the national power elite are recruited.

11. Below this middle level of power is the mass of unorganized people, who lack effective power—the general public. Its members differ in many ways, but all have one thing in common: impotence. That common impotence is not the basis for an effective challenge to the elite.

12. The general public is manipulated through deception, the power elite's control over the mass media, force, fraud—whatever may be needed. The public's consent is sometimes useful to the power elite because that consent disguises the true extent of its power.

13. The powerful do not make decisions "in the interests of the public" or "for the common good," but to further their own private, personal, special interests.

14. The power elite practices "higher immorality." Its members did

not secure their positions of rule as a result of talent, ability, or intelligence, but through the right background, the right connections, and the right degree of ruthlessness and cunning. Their actions are not only in their own interests but, often, against those of the public at large.

15. The power elite's control has increased and is increasing. Its accountability to the public is diminishing.

Pluralism

Pluralism The school of thought that argues that power is dispersed rather than centralized, contingent rather than general, and exercised with the consent of the governed rather than in an unchecked fashion.

Challenging the power-elite theory is a group of sociologists and political scientists who believe that power at the national and local levels is more dispersed, amorphous, and equally distributed than Mills had thought. **Pluralism** assumes that the economic interests of the United States are diverse and conflicting. IBM and U.S. Steel are both big companies, they say, but IBM's interest in foreign sales gives it interests very different from those of any steel company. They see one group or coalition triumphing in one issue; another, triumphing in a differing one. No power elite rules across the board, they say, in all important areas of life; power wielding is "contingent" rather than universal and requires the consent of the governed. Because political and other leaders are accountable for their actions, they promote the interests of society as a whole. In short, pluralism argues that the power structure is diversified, complex, and fragmented, not unified, monolithic, and unchecked, as Mills believed (Riesman, Glazer, and Denney, 1953, pp. 239–259). Lobbies, interest groups, temporary alliances, shifting coalitions, opposing forces, and cross-cutting factions offer a vast and effective system of checks and balances. The unions and big business interests compete with each other in the decision-making process, struggling over wages and working conditions; neither gets the upper hand consistently. Ecologists demand and get legislation setting gas-emission standards and other controls on factories and automobiles, controls that corporations oppose. The resulting legislation is usually a compromise between the two contending positions.

The pluralist position has been dubbed the "multi-influence hypothesis." As one of its chief proponents puts it:

> The relationship between the economic elite and the political authorities has been a constantly varying one of strong influence, cooperation, division of labor, and conflict, with each influencing the other in changing proportion to some extent and each operating independently of the other to a large extent. . . . Further, neither the economic elite nor the political authorities are monolithic units which act with internal consensus and coordinated action. . . . In fact, there are several economic elites which only very rarely act as units within themselves and among themselves, and there are at least two political parties which have significantly differing programs with regard to their actions toward any economic elite, and each of them has only a partial degree of internal cohesion. . . . The National Democratic party . . . generally has a domestic policy that frustrates the special interests of the economic elite. . . . The multi-influence hypothesis sees conflict as often multi-lateral . . . with the sides changing at least partially from issue to issue, and with consensus being achieved only temporarily and on a limited number of issues (Rose, 1967, pp. 2, 3).

Pluralists attach great importance to elections, because voting restrains the power of those who make large-scale decisions. They argue that lobbyists from such voluntary associations as the NAACP, the ACLU, the League of Women Voters, and the American Legion tend to cancel one another out. Some influence politicians in one direction; others, in the opposite direction. Political representatives control the business community; the voters, in turn, control their political representatives. Last, pluralists believe that, by and large, those who fill the most powerful positions in our society—political, economic, or military—have won their powers by virtue of ability, talent, and intelligence—and not because they have the right backgrounds and connections.

A Synthesis

Which approach, the pluralist or the power elitist, offers a better fit with the facts of the American political system? Is it necessary to choose between them? Or do both have something to offer? Today's sociologists believe that a synthesis of the two approaches is fruitful.[*]

No one believes that all people are equally able to impose their political wills. Everyone agrees that some people have more power than others. And no one would argue that ability and intelligence (however measured) are the only qualifications for power, that wealth and social connections cannot buy a good deal of it, that those who wield power represent nothing but the will and interests of the majority, or that the powerful are completely accountable to the public in everything they do. To the extent that we all reject these assertions, we are all "power elitists."

Even so, the power elite is not omnipotent. Political power of any kind has limits. No ruling elite is ever completely united on every issue, nor can any such elite, however powerful, get its way at all times. Compromises have to be made by everyone, the power elite included. Even Mills did not believe that the power elite totally dominates American society. In a comment on the very book in which he spelled out the power-elite thesis, Mills wrote: "The power elite is not a homogeneous circle of a specified number of men whose solidified will continuously prevails against all obstacles" (Mills, 1957, p. 22).

Nonetheless, the differences between pluralism and the power-elite theory are substantial. Which one offers the most adequate view of power in this country? The debate between the pluralists and the power elitists can be summed up in three fundamental questions. First, who rules? Second, in what manner do they rule? And third, in whose interests do they rule?

Who Rules? Much more easily answered than the second and third questions is the first, "Who rules?" Here, the power-elite position wins the argument. The powerful do not represent a cross-section of the nation as a whole in any conceivable respect. If we were to locate the most powerful members of American society, some would be in the economic sector, and some in the political. In the economic sector, the powerful include the presidents, the board chairs, and the key directors of the country's largest corporations. In the political sector, they include the president of the United States, the justices of the United States Supreme Court, United States senators, cabinet members, key members of the House of Representatives, state governors, and the mayors of our largest

Pluralism The school of thought that argues that power is dispersed rather than centralized, contingent rather than general, and exercised with the consent of the governed rather than in an unchecked fashion.

business

state

[*] Marxists and power-elitist-oriented sociologists sometimes claim that pluralism is now considered as something of a fairy tale by most political sociologists, but the continuing vigorous research and publications by pluralists (Dahl, 1982; Lipset, 1982) suggest that this position is alive and well. Furthermore, power-elitist-oriented sociologists' critiques of pluralism (for instance, Domhoff, 1983, pp. 202–210) suggest, again, that an obituary for this position is a bit premature.

cities. Even a glance at those who hold these positions makes it clear that the overwhelming majority are white, male, 45 years old or older, and the children of well-to-do, college-educated parents. Consistently, over the years, about 70 percent of all United States senators and 50 percent of all members of the United States House of Representatives have been lawyers; and so have twenty-five of forty presidents (Domhoff, 1979, p. 159). Anyone who asserts that those Americans who hold the positions of greatest power literally represent the population as a whole—in all its social, economic, and demographic characteristics—is plainly wrong.

Only a very naive pluralist would assert that the powerful form a cross-section of our society as a whole and that all groups and classes have equal access to power. Still, it is surprising just how much certain segments of American society are overrepresented in the ranks of the powerful—and how underrepresented other segments are. A psychologist (turned political sociologist) named G. William Domhoff (1967, 1978, 1983) investigated the dense connection between this country's upper class and its power elite. Our upper class is defined by the possession of "old" money, fortunes that have been in a family's hands for several generations (see Chapter 9). In twelve cities of the United States, a yearly book called the *Social Register* lists "prominent" and "notable" families. (Comparable listings are published in several other cities, as well.) Something like 38,000 families are included in the *Register's* pages, less than 1 percent of our population. Most researchers of stratification agree that a listing in the *Social Register* is a valid, though not perfect, indicator of upper-class status.

Who rules? Some critics of the American policital system argue that the powerful do not represent a cross-section of the population as a whole. This tiny, powerful elite tends to be male, white, middle-aged, affluent, well-educated, and upper-class or middle-class in background. These critics say that the decisions of the powerful reflect this basic fact.

Dennis Brack/Black Star

Domhoff documented his view that the upper class does not merely have a great deal of "old" money but is also a ruling class. The most powerful economic and political positions in our society tend to be dominated by a tiny upper-class elite. About one-third of the members of the boards of directors of the largest corporations are listed in the *Social Register*. Over the past forty years, a clear majority of the chiefs of the most powerful cabinet departments (such as Secretary of State) has belonged to *Social Register* families. At least one newspaper is owned by a *Social Register* listee in every city where it is published, except Pittsburgh. A majority of the very largest donors to the campaigns of our most powerful politicians belongs to the upper class. Half the largest defense contractors come from upper-class families. In other words, the members of our upper class are several thousand times overrepresented among those who hold the most powerful positions in America.

These findings support several of Mills's assertions about the makeup of the power elite. Unless we want to argue that the members of the upper class are thousands of times more capable of exercising power than the rest of us, it would seem that access to powerful positions is not based solely, or even mainly, on talent. Clearly, background and connections play a major role. Likewise, as Mills argued, those who hold upper-level positions in government, business, and the military move back and forth among the three. Of the 100 most important officials of the Reagan administration, one-fourth had a net worth of over $1 million, and almost every one of them entered government service from a top-ranking position in a large corporation (Brownstein and Easton, 1983). Economist John Kenneth Galbraith (1969, p. 20) found nearly 700 retired generals, admirals, colonels, and Navy captains working for the ten biggest defense contractors. United States Senator William Proxmire discovered more than 2,000 retired officers employed at major defense corporations (Galbraith, 1969, p. 21; Proxmire, 1970).

Decision Making. The evidence that the upper class dominates our major institutions seems persuasive, and so does the evidence suggesting that a small group of upper-class movers and shakers moves routinely from business to the government to the military, and vice versa. Not all the elements of the power-elite theory enjoy general recognition, however. Sophisticated pluralists argue that this common background does not show that power is indeed concentrated in the hands of the few or that powerful people consistently make decisions in their own interests. Legislators and government officials need not typify the whole population in their characteristics—only in their decisions. Whose values influence the powerful? The pluralists find that, regardless of their class origins, the values of the powerful reflect those of the general public (Dahl, 1961, pp. 91–92).

The power-elite position does exaggerate the concentration of political power and the cohesiveness of the elites in our major institutions. (Economic concentration is, however, extremely great, as we see in Chapter 17.) In many cases, the power structure of each institution operates independently of other power structures or in shifting coalitions of institutions. The economic elite may be the most powerful, but on some issues its power may be blocked or blunted. Moreover, certain interest groups, as well as the press, have had an influence on decision making, occasionally at the expense of big business.

Business, too, is dependent on and sometimes controlled by large numbers of individually powerless people. Strikes and labor unrest are so costly to industry that executives have good reason to avoid them and usually have to make certain concessions to do so. Consumers ultimately make or break any business, and a successful boycott could destroy a company or even an industry. (We must emphasize that this power is hypothetical and is very rarely mobilized.) Corporate executives are supposed to make sure that things like this do not happen, and that is why public relations is so important to industry. Good business thus requires a relatively satisfied labor force and relatively satisfied customers. Labor and consumers do not "run things," but business is built on their tacit approval. In a crisis, labor can exert a kind of veto power over business by disrupting its routine. As for the general public, big business, for all its power, cannot make anyone buy its products, and the power not to buy, though disorganized, is very great in the long run. Successful executives know this and try to compromise by weighing short-term losses against long-term gains. What may appear on the surface to be an act "for labor" or "in the public interest" may in the end strengthen the self-interest of a corporate enterprise. Clearly, the connections between political and economic institutions are very complex and subtle—so complex and so subtle that this issue is an important theme in the next chapter.

SUMMARY

1. Politics is defined as the institutional exercise of power.

2. Sociologists do not make a sharp distinction between "politics" and "government."

3. The political and the economic institutions are closely intertwined.

4. Max Weber defined power as the ability to get one's way even in the face of resistance by others.

5. Power can be legitimate or illegitimate; legitimate power is called "authority."

6. Authority can be "charismatic," "bureaucratic," or "traditional."

7. States have legitimate force in a given territory. Force is exercised in all nations, although just how much is necessary varies from situation to situation.

8. The modern nation-state is a fairly recent historical development; most contemporary states grew out of empires that were built by larger, stronger societies conquering smaller, weaker ones.

9. States vary in how repressive they are; extremely repressive regimes are totalitarian states.

10. Democratic governments have two basic characteristics: equality and liberty. Although both may be violated in practice, they are institutionalized in democracies.

11. The American political system is in many ways distinctive, even unique.

12. The winner-take-all character of American politics generates relatively low party loyalty, low voter turnout, and a two-party system.

13. Interest groups are a distinctive feature of the American political scene. They have a strong influence on the government, disproportional to the number of members that belongs to them.

14. The American political spectrum is fairly "centrist" compared with that of Western Europe and other nations: We have very few radicals and very few extreme rightists.

15. The pluralist-elitist debate has dominated political sociology for more than a generation. Although the evidence is not conclusive, on the national level, the available data favor a modified version of the power-elite theory.

SUGGESTED READINGS

Michael Binyon, *Life in Russia*. New York: Berkeley Books, 1985; and Hedrick Smith, *The Russians* (rev. ed.). New York: Ballantine Books, 1984.

Avoiding the usual exclusive focus on leaders, these two first-rate books describe what everyday life in the Soviet Union is like for its ordinary citizens. They explode myths both of the political right—for instance, that all Soviet citizens are enslaved and wish to overturn the government—and of some segments of the left, as well—that the Soviet Union is a democratic worker's paradise without crime, pollution, and favoritism. The truth is far more complex—and interesting—than either of these versions. These two books correct the idea that in the Soviet Union, one is a dissident or an ideologue; they show, instead, that most Russians are politically indifferent. Although they want a less repressive regime, most Russians support some version of communism and tend to be fiercely loyal and patriotic.

Robert Dahl, *Dilemmas of Pluralist Democracy: Autonomy vs. Control*. New Haven: Yale University Press, 1982.

A major pluralist political scientist outlines some of the difficulties of significant social, political, and economic change in a democratic society.

G. William Domhoff, *Who Rules America Now? A View for the '80's*. Englewood Cliffs, New Jersey: Prentice-Hall/Spectrum, 1983.

A thorough updating of the author's classic, *Who Rules America?* (1967), this book argues and presents evidence showing that a tiny upper class, consisting of a fraction of 1 percent of the population, disproportionately dominates the most powerful positions in the government and in big business. An entire chapter is devoted to dealing with the criticisms of the earlier edition of this book.

Thomas R. Dye, *Who's Running America? The Conservative Years* (4th ed.). Englewood Cliffs, New Jersey: Prentice-Hall, 1986.

A study of the nation's elite in the major institutional spheres. How "interlocked" are the members of the institutional elite? How do the elite get to the top? How do they make their decisions? This book marshalls data to answer these questions.

Seymour Martin Lipset, *Political Man: The Social Bases of Politics* (expanded ed.). Baltimore: Johns Hopkins University Press, 1982.

An extremely influential collection of articles on a wide range of topics in political sociology. Lipset's sociology is sympathetic to the pluralist approach, and it is often attacked by Marxist and power-elite-oriented sociologists. Read this book and find out why. This edition includes "A Personal Postscript" and updated discussions.

chapter 17

THE ECONOMY

On a cold morning in December, Dale Burr, a 63-year-old Iowa farmer, left his house with a 12-gauge shotgun. When his wife of forty years, Emily, tried to stop him, he shot and killed her. Leaving a note at home, he drove into town, walked through the back doors of the Hills Bank and Trust Company, drew the shotgun from his overalls, and shot the bank's president. He then drove to the farm of a man with whom he had had a dispute over land a few years earlier. Burr shot and killed the farmer, then fired at but missed his fleeing wife and young son. Ten minutes later, a sheriff's deputy pulled Burr onto the shoulder of a road near his house. By the time the officer reached Burr's pickup, Burr had shot himself to death. Burr's farm was heavily mortgaged, and he was in debt to the bank to the tune of some $800,000. Burr, an even-tempered workaholic all his life, suddenly buckled under the enormous financial pressures he faced (Malcom, 1985). Although murder and suicide are clearly extreme reactions to economic problems, depression and stress reactions are common (Brenner, 1984; Farmer, 1986).

During the 1970s, inflation was high, agricultural exports increased dramatically, farm land values were inflated, and bank interest rates and government and lender policies encouraged farm expansion. Many farmers went into debt to modernize and expand their farms. Suddenly, in the 1980s, inflation declined, foreign markets no longer wanted as much American agricultural products, and land values plunged. As a result of economic forces they could not foresee and, even today, do not understand and cannot control, thousands of farmers find themselves in a desperate economic situation. The interest that the nation's 2.37 million farmers owe on loans they have taken out ($21 billion a year) is nearly equal to their entire farm income ($23 billion a year in the past two years). And as farmers are forced off their land, banks who hold the loans on the failing farms also go under, as do surrounding towns, industries and merchants that serve agriculture. "Our little towns are dying," said one rural Midwesterner. "Now we've lost our restaurant. All we have left is a co-op and a beer hall, and it looks like the beer joint may go too" (Robbins, 1985, p. 30).

Economics affects us all. Events that take place on the other side of the globe can influence our incomes—or whether we have jobs at all—the lines of work we decide to enter, the prices of the goods we buy, and even our mental and physical health. No matter how much we may try to control what happens in our lives, every one of us is connected economically with every one else in an immense global ebb and flow of money, goods, and services.

There is an especially intimate connection between the political and the economic institutions, as we saw in the last chapter. Government policy can take money out of our pockets or put more in. Most policies are not simply good or bad for a society as a whole (though some are), but are usually good for some segments of society and bad for others. As a general rule, conservative administrations favor policies that put more money into the pockets of the affluent, whereas liberal administrations follow policies that aim to improve the economic condition of the poor and the working classes. For example, the conservative administration of Ronald Reagan came into office in January, 1981. As promised, Reagan cut back on or dismantled social services that had their principal impact on the poor. The Congressional Budget Office reported that during the period between 1983 and 1985, families earning less than $20,000 lost a total of $20 billion in income from budget and tax cuts. On the other hand, families who earned $80,000 or more gained $35 billion from the same sources. In 1983, households earning less than $10,000 a year lost an average of $270 in income; households earning $80,000 had their income increased by over $7,000 as a result of Reagan's federal policies (Galbraith, 1984, p. 44). Clearly, then, what the government does often influences our economic lives even at the most basic, day-to-day level: our pocketbooks.

Economy The production and distribution of scarce goods and services.

Economics may be defined as the institution that deals with the manufacture and distribution of resources—with money, goods, and services. The **economy** is, above all, a social institution: money, goods, and services do not ebb and flow of their own accord. Economic relations are social relations: People manufacture goods, hire and fire workers, enter and leave the labor market, purchase certain goods but not others, make the decision to spend or save. This should not be interpreted to mean that every one of us is free to do whatever we wish economically. Indeed, our choices are constrained in many cases by events very much beyond our control. Yet, what happens in the economic sphere is a human endeavor, the result of the actions of billions of acting and reacting individuals who produce combined effects that may be contrary to what most would have chosen individually.

In a simple economic system, the resources a society generates and distributes are water, food, and shelter. As a society's technology becomes more complex and productive, its resources become increasingly elaborate. And as a society's resources expand, so do its complexity and diversity; this complexity, in turn, gives rise to new kinds of resources. How a society produces and distributes goods and services, and the nature of the goods and services so produced, help determine many of its most important features.

THE EVOLUTION OF THE ECONOMY

Three great and far-reaching advances in technology have been so powerful that they deserve to be called revolutions. The first was the development of agriculture, the second was the Industrial Revolution, and the third was the emergence of the postindustrial economy. Each advance transformed society beyond recall.

Agriculture

From the dawn of human existence until some 15,000 years ago, the human race subsisted entirely by hunting and gathering food from the wild. Hunting and gathering societies were almost always nomadic, and they did not generate much economic surplus. The material aspects of these early societies tended to be sparse and simple (see Chapter 4). Archaeological remains tell us that human societies began to cultivate food roughly 15,000 years ago, probably in the area we now call the Middle East. It is possible that the discovery arose independently in Southeast Asia, China, India, and Africa, or it is possible that it spread from the Middle East to these locations; there is dispute about this issue. Agriculture did emerge a few thousand years later in North and South America, and Europe almost certainly received the idea from the Middle East. Asians and Africans had refined agriculture to a sophisticated and productive level at a time when Europeans were still hunting huge, dangerous, and now-extinct beasts for food.

Hunting and gathering were not abandoned immediately by societies that developed agriculture. In fact, they coexisted for thousands of years, even in the same society. Early agriculture was arduous and inefficient, and it required a great deal more effort than hunting and gathering. Its principal advantage was that the same quantity of food could be produced on a much smaller area of land. (It is possible that population pressures generated the discovery of agriculture.) Greater efficiency and productivity came only thousands of years after agriculture's discovery, beginning with the invention of the hoe and expanding considerably after the invention of the plow. Food growing commonly took place along with the domestication of animals, especially cattle, which could be used in the process of planting and harvesting. (The dog had been domesticated thousands of years earlier, as an aid in hunting large game animals.) Food growing promoted the emergence of settled communities on a large scale. Because it is so much more efficient and productive to grow food than to search for it, the resources of agricultural societies were vastly greater than those of hunting and gathering societies. There

■ **TABLE 17–1 The Number and Acreage of Farms, 1950–1986** *

	Number (Millions)	Total Land (Million Acres)	Average Acreage per Farm
1950	5.6	1,202	213
1954	4.8	1,206	251
1960	4.0	1,176	297
1965	3.4	1,140	340
1970	2.9	1,102	374
1975	2.5	1,059	420
1980	2.4	1,039	427
1986	2.2	1,007	455

* The definitions of "farms" and "farm acreage" have changed several times since 1950; therefore, the figures in this table are based on slightly different definitions.

Source: Statistical Abstract of the United States, 1987, p. 621.

was much more of everything to go around. The number of people in agricultural societies expanded greatly, too. The economy could now support many more families—hundreds of times as many—than a hunting and gathering economy. All of the material aspects of the agricultural societies blossomed—clothing and devices of all kinds, including, of course, weapons—and so too did their art. Finally, roles and statuses, ranks and positions, jobs and other economically supported activities became very numerous and specialized. In a hunting and gathering society, the chief social divisions were based almost entirely on age, sex, and kinship. In agricultural societies, the social divisions became almost limitlessly complex.

The Merchant Class

Agrarian society An agricultural society in which the primary method of production is the plow.

Merchant Someone who buys and sells goods or commodities for a profit, as an occupation or profession.

Societies based on agriculture (which are called **agrarian societies**) developed urban communities. And with the development of fixed communities and the accumulation of a large economic surplus and, hence, goods far beyond the society's subsistence needs, a new economic opportunity presented itself: buying and selling for a profit. Advanced agrarian societies tended to generate a **merchant** class: an economic category made up of individuals who exchanged money for goods, and then turned around and exchanged those same goods for even more money. They did not acquire these goods to use them, but to sell them to another party for more money than they paid for them. Merchants were not manufacturers; they bought goods from manufacturers and sold them to consumers or to other merchants closer to the consumers. Buying and selling for a profit seems like such a universal activity nowadays that it is difficult to imagine a period of history when it did not exist. But, in fact, a true merchant class did not exist during the hunting and gathering period. Although buying and selling, or, more commonly, the exchange of goods and services, did take place among different tribes and societies tens of thousands of years ago, it was almost exclusively for the use value of the goods exchanged. For instance, a society living near an ocean exchanged salt with the members of a society living in a forest for stone tools. But in this case, the exchange took place between societies and not individuals, and was for the purpose of using the items, and not for a profit.

Merchants did not appear at a specific time in history and so it is difficult to call their emergence a real revolution. Traders and merchants existed in ancient Rome, China, and India, but their numbers were small and their overall economic impact on the ancient world was likewise small. Merchants did not become an important economic class until the thirteenth or fourteenth century, at first in the Italian city-states and later throughout most of Western Europe. Most observers do not regard merchants as true capitalists, and argue that capitalism emerged only with the Industrial Revolution in the eighteenth century—that is, with the emergence of manufacturing, or the transformation of raw materials into usable products, for a profit. Merchants did not manufacture goods; they merely exchanged them for money. At the same time, these early merchants did plant the seed of the Industrial Revolution—*and* capitalism—because of their dedicated pursuit of profit.

Industrialization

Industrialization The transition to an economic system based on the use of inanimate power sources, such as coal or oil, the invention of machines to replace animal or physical human power, and the organization of workers into large productive units.

The second great economic revolution was **industrialization,** which began in the mid-1700s. Primitive manufacturing centers existed much earlier—for instance, foundries to create steel and weapons and craft centers where clothing, jewelry, or stained glass windows were made. Preindustrial economic activity was not, however, characterized by *mass production*, which was the basis of the Industrial Revolution.

Before the Industrial Revolution, manufacturing took place in two main settings: the household and the craft shop. Entire families worked to produce such handicrafts as clothing, rugs, and furniture. This was a very inefficient way of producing goods. These operations were small, and because the whole household pitched in, specialization was not possible. Craft shops were more efficient than households, but they too were relatively small in scope, partly because they were little more than extended families. The guilds to which most workers belonged restricted membership tightly, protected their limited market, discouraged competition and product innovation, and cooperated closely with the government and the nobility.

Mass production, the true factory system, shattered traditional society and laid the groundwork for an altogether new society. Let's examine the new system in detail:

1. *The use of inanimate power sources.* Humans and animals are obviously much weaker and slower than machines powered by steam, coal, oil, or gasoline. Inanimate "prime movers" like the steam engine and the electric generator are far more powerful, efficient, and inexpensive than the muscle power of animals and human beings—by a factor of several thousand times.

2. *The invention of new machines to replace human skills.* In the preindustrial world, everything that did not come fully formed by nature had to be made by hand. The production of all goods was therefore limited by the endurance and speed of individual human workers. From the late eighteenth century onward, machines began to replace human skills in almost every area of manufacturing. Some argue that mechanization debased many goods and the quality of work in general, but it undoubtedly raised the level of production—vastly—and thereby made possible a more equal distribution of property than had prevailed in preindustrial times.

3. *The organization of workers into large productive units—factories.* Instead of households or craft shops with a dozen or two dozen workers, the workplace grew to accommodate hundreds, even thousands, of workers.

4. *The development of highly specialized worker functions and activities.* In preindustrial times, most workers carried through the production of any article from beginning to end. With the coming of heavy industry, workers were assigned to highly specific tasks with very limited scopes, and they repeated the same activity over and over again.

5. *Interchangeable parts.* Before the Industrial Revolution, most products were made to order for specific customers. Each product was thus unique. With the emergence of specialized functions and tasks, most workers in each factory were assigned to produce one specific item over and over again, each identical to and interchangeable with the next. Any part of a given item could be taken out and replaced by another identical part, and the product would work. If, for instance, the trigger on a musket was broken, the manufacturer could replace it with a virtually identical one. Before the Industrial Revolution, the manufacturer would have had to produce a new trigger to fit that particular musket and it alone.

Industrialization did not occur overnight. Even late in the nineteenth century, many factories were still primitive and inefficient. The keys to industrialization were the use of inanimate power sources, such as coal and oil, and the invention of machines to replace human skills. Here, we see an early shotgun factory.

The Bettmann Archive

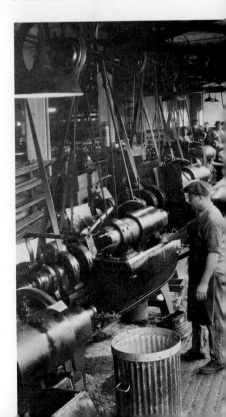

The Impact of Industry. By the mid-1800s, the Industrial Revolution had changed Great Britain irreversibly, much as it was soon to change France and (about half a century later) the rest of Western Europe and North America. Intense competition among manufacturers forced many firms to the wall and, in the end, handed over the markets for many goods and services to a few huge companies. The enormous productivity of the new factories required a mass market in which to sell the manufactured goods. About a century before the start of the Industrial Revolution in Britain, small farms began to be consolidated into fewer, larger ones, while improved agricultural techniques raised productivity. Because fewer farmers and agricultural laborers could now produce more food, many were eventually forced off the land, into rural factories (of which there were many) and cities. The industrial cities grew dramatically.

All these developments created a new class: the proletariat. Farm laborers or even small farmers could loosely be called a "rural proletariat," but they were (and still are) scattered about the countryside, so their common economic conditions did not create a common sense of identity. Factory laborers worked face-to-face with one another and became intimately acquainted with their common poverty and difficult, dangerous working conditions. The type of work that factory laborers performed alienated them from their jobs, because they could not derive satisfaction from being "just another cog in a machine." Workers' movements began to organize unions, strikes, and revolutions. In short, class conflict was born.

Large-scale manufacturing called for large amounts of raw materials. Originally, factories were built close to the areas where these resources were mined and harvested. England and France were early leaders in industrialization because coal (necessary for steam power and for iron-making) was readily available in those countries. Often, however, new technologies, markets, and products demanded new and different natural resources, and new and different sources of them. This, in turn, spurred on (though it did not create) the process of colonization.

Competition spurred efficiency and continual innovation, so old methods and materials were constantly becoming obsolete. Moreover, the people's ability to purchase the new goods and services did not always keep pace with the economy's capacity for producing them.

The Industrial Revolution therefore brought with it faster economic cycles—booms, busts, depressions, financial crises, and so on. The economy became vastly wealthier than it had been in preindustrial times, but vastly more unstable, too.

Industrialization is a matter of degree. It does not happen overnight. At a given moment, one nation may be highly industrialized, another still very agricultural, and a third somewhere between the two. In highly agricultural societies, as much as 80 percent of the work force is employed by agriculture. In highly industrialized societies, the proportion is very low, less than 3 percent in the United States, for example. Even so, American agriculture is so productive that the United States is the world's leading agricultural nation. Many countries that are almost wholly agricultural cannot feed themselves.

As more and more people give up farming, most of the remaining farms become larger and larger, and small farmers find it harder and harder to hang on. In 1950, farms of more than 260 acres made up 15 percent of the total number of American farms; this proportion grew to 30 percent in 1982. In fact, farms of 1,000 acres or more—only 2 percent of all farms in 1950—were 7 percent of all farms in 1982. Such very large farms actually increased in absolute numbers during this period, to 162,000 from 121,000. Well over half of the country's total farm acreage in 1982 (61 percent) was accounted for by 1,000 acres or more (*Statistical Abstract of the United States, 1987*, p. 622). Farming has become rather like big business—"agribusiness."

THE MODERN ECONOMY

Sectors

Economic historians have divided the process of industrialization into three stages: the preindustrial (or agricultural) stage, the industrial stage, and the postindustrial stage. Each one is defined by the proportion of the labor market working in what economists call the primary, secondary, and tertiary economic sectors.

The **primary sector** comprises agriculture and those industries that extract natural resources directly from the land—mining, for instance, and oil drilling, fishing, logging, and so on. The **secondary sector** transforms these natural resources into marketable items. For the most part, the secondary sector is the industrial sector, engaged in manufacturing—turning iron ore into steel, manufacturing cardboard boxes from wood pulp, assembling automobiles, constructing buildings, and the like.

The **tertiary sector** is the "service" sector, which uses manufactured products to perform services—like laundering clothes or repairing cars—or in the course of a job, as a teacher uses chalk and a bus driver uses a bus. In the tertiary sector we find such people as nurses, bankers, college professors, janitors, postal workers, police officers, social workers, and so on.

Agricultural economies have large primary sectors that employ a high proportion of their labor markets. Industrial societies have a lower proportion of workers in the primary sector and a higher proportion in the secondary sector. In one present-day industrial society, the Soviet Union, workers are almost evenly divided among the primary, secondary, and the tertiary sectors. When a nation's economy becomes even more

Primary sector That segment of the economy that extracts natural resources directly from the land—such as mining, fishing, and farming.

Secondary sector That segment of the economy that transforms natural resources into products—such as turning iron ore into steel or wood pulp into cardboard boxes; most of this sector is the industrial sector, or manufacturing.

Tertiary sector The "service" sector of the economy, which uses manufactured products to perform services—a teacher uses chalk, a bus driver uses a bus, and so on.

The primary economic sector comprises agriculture and other industries that extract natural resources directly from the land. Today, only a tiny fraction of the American work force works in the primary sector. Here, farm workers pick beans.

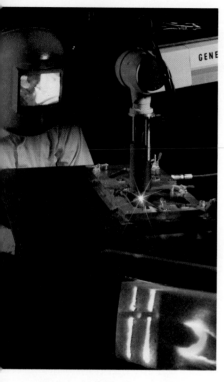

The secondary sector in an economy transforms natural resources into products that can be sold on the market. The secondary sector is made up of workers engaged in manufacturing—such as assembling automobiles. The United States is a postindustrial society, employing only a third of its workers in the secondary sector.

General Electric Research and Development Center

Postindustrial economy An economic system with a highly efficient, productive industry and a majority of its work force in the tertiary or service sector.

■ **TABLE 17–2 Economic Sector of Economically Active Population, 1976, International Comparison**

	Agriculture[*] (Percent)	Manufacturing (Percent)
Australia	6.2	31.4
Bangladesh	77.1	4.6
Bolivia	46.2	9.7
Burma	64.7	7.2
Cameroon	73.8	4.5
Canada	5.9	28.6
Egypt	44.2	12.4
France	10.9	37.3
Great Britain	2.6	40.7
Guatemala	57.2	13.7
Indonesia	64.7	6.5
Iraq	30.1	9.1
Italy	15.4	43.5
Japan	11.9	35.6
Liberia	71.6	1.3
Malawi	84.4	3.6
Philippines	48.7	10.4
Sweden	6.2	34.8
Thailand	73.2	6.7
Tunisia	32.4	14.8
United States	3.9	29.7

[*] Agriculture includes "Agriculture, forestry, hunting, and fishing," almost all of which is actually farming.

Source: Year Book of Labor Statistics, 1980. Geneva, Switzerland: International Labour Office, pp. 32–60; and U.S. Bureau of Labor Statistics, *International Comparisons of Employment,* 1978, p. 25.

efficient and factories employ fewer and fewer workers, the proportions of both farm workers and factory workers drop and the proportion of the labor force employed by the tertiary sector increases. A postindustrial society is one in which a majority of workers is employed in service occupations. In 1900, the United States (like the Soviet Union today) had about the same proportion of workers in each sector. By 1975, over six American workers in ten were in service jobs, and a third were employed in the secondary sector. These employment figures make it clear that the United States has become a **postindustrial economy** (Rossides, 1976, p. 136).

CAPITALISM, SOCIALISM, AND COMMUNISM

■

Goods and services are produced and distributed all over the world, and everywhere they are produced somewhat differently. One of the most crucial of these differences is the ownership of the **means of pro-**

duction. The "means of production" is anything that is capable of producing goods and services. On a small scale, in an agricultural society, a plow would be one among a number of the available means of production. On a larger scale, in an industrial society, a factory, a gold, coal, or copper mine, a sizable tract of farm land, raw materials, and a large sum of money would all represent various means of production. *Capitalism* is the economic system in which the means of production are privately owned and controlled. Firms such as General Motors, General Electric, and General Foods are owned by individuals and families, the stockowners. In contrast **socialism** is the economic system in which the means of production are owned and run by the state, presumably for the good of the general society. According to Marx, when the state takes over the means of production, productive private property is abolished, and, thus, social classes and class conflict are eliminated, as well. Marx regarded socialism as a transitional phase between capitalism and communism. A state "dictatorship of the proletariat" is necessary, because neither a ruling elite, some inequality, nor such values as competition and materialism can be eliminated overnight. Eventually, however, **communism** will emerge out of socialism. Communism is the final, most advanced stage of social evolution, according to Marx. Here, the means of production are owned and run not by the state, but collectively, by everyone. Communism is a classless, stateless, nonexploitative, totally equalitarian utopia. No such society now exists, nor, given what we know about human relations, is such a society likely ever to exist. Still, the idea sounds appealing to many thinkers, writers, and observers.

The terms "socialism" and "communism" are usually used with somewhat different meanings than the ones that Marx intended. Most commonly, non-Marxists, especially popular writers, use the term communism to refer to nations, economies, parties, and ideologies within the Soviet orbit. The American Communist party, for instance, is Moscow-inspired, although by no means does it "take orders" from the Kremlin today. Marx would not have agreed with this definition of communism, because the Soviet Union is very far from his ideal of what communism should be. In fact, most likely, Marx, like many Marxist writers, would have regarded the Soviet regime as a betrayal of communist principles. Likewise, socialism is popularly used to describe nations, economies, parties, and ideologies that favor or have a large measure of state ownership and control of industry. For instance, in the mid-1980s, Greece, Spain, Portugal, and France all elected socialist presidents, who favor, but cannot bring about, state ownership of key industries.

These three concepts—capitalism, socialism, and communism—are ideal types—that is, no economies exist that are quite like them. They represent approximations, rough models, and not precise specifications of reality. In truth, all economies are mixed; pure capitalism, socialism, and communism do not exist anywhere. Moreover, like most distinctions, that between socialism and communism, and those between each of them and capitalism, are a matter of degree. The United States, which is just about the most capitalist of all economies, is in part publicly owned and controlled. Amtrak, a railroad, is government-funded, as is the Tennessee Valley Authority (TVA), a power company. Most of our educational system, even private colleges and universities, is supported by the government. Part of the American system of health care—though far less than in Europe—is paid for by the United States government, chiefly through Medicare and Medicaid. The United States armed forces and police, jail, and prison systems are run and funded by federal, state,

Means of production Anything that is capable of producing goods and services, especially for a profit and on a large scale. Examples are a gold mine, a large tract of farm land, a large sum of money, or a factory.

Socialism State ownership of the means of production. As it is widely used today, the term refers to a "mixed" economy—that is, one partly in state hands and partly in private hands.

Communism According to Marx, the ultimate and highest stage of historical development: a stateless society in which the means of production are owned and run collectively. The term's current, popular, and somewhat erroneous meaning refers to the nations and ideologies aligned with the Soviet Union.

The term "communism" is commonly (but somewhat erroneously) used to describe the state-run economies of the U.S.S.R., Eastern Europe, mainland China, and Cuba. In every socialist or communist economy there is some private enterprise, just as there are some state-run industries in every capitalist economy. Here, Chinese workers make silk thread.

Art Resource/Paula Gerson

The United States has the most capitalist economy in the world. The key feature of capitalism is the pursuit of private profit. Goods and services are placed on the market in hopes of fetching a price higher than their cost of production.

Art Resource/Daniel Brody

or local governments. Likewise, there are certain capitalist features in socialist and communist nations. For instance, in the Soviet Union, citizens are allowed to own small plots of land and grow, and even sell, agricultural produce from those plots. And most of the farms in Poland are in private hands. In fact, in most of the socialist and communist world, government relaxation of restrictions on private commerce has taken place in recent years. In 1985, Havana announced that Cuba was ending the state's ownership of houses and apartments. Beginning that year, the state got out of the business of renting homes and turned over their ownership to residents. With some dwellings, the process would take ten or twenty years, but with many, it was effective immediately (Treaster, 1984). In Bulgaria, the total land area set aside for private use grew throughout the 1980s; it now represents 14 percent of all land under cultivation and yields 28 percent of the country's total agricultural output (Binder, 1985). And in 1982, China began dismantling its farm communes, decollectivizing its system of agriculture, a move announced the previous year (Sexton, 1981). In the cities, shopkeepers began selling goods to the public for a profit (Goldman and Goldman, 1984). Throughout the 1980s, China's leaders encouraged foreign capitalist investment, the play of the market forces of supply and demand, and a limited degree of free enterprise. And yet, each of these economies remains overwhelmingly in state hands, and must be classified as socialist. Clearly, then, no economy is entirely communist, socialist, or capitalist in nature. The proportion of the total economy that is in private or public hands is one important indicator of its status.

The single most distinctive feature of capitalism is the pursuit of private profit. Goods and services are placed on the market in hopes of fetching a price higher than their cost of production. Except for a few essentials, like education, libraries, roads, and so forth, anything that is not profitable for individuals is not undertaken, or must be undertaken solely for the love of the activity itself, like writing poetry. Within the boundaries of legality, capitalist economies make profit its own justification—an end in itself. Junk that makes money is good junk and will be produced as long as the money comes in. The market knows neither good nor evil.

Karl Marx, the founder of socialism and communism, did not produce a comprehensive definition of either. As he himself put it, he declined "to write the cookbooks of the future." He did, nonetheless, make two basic points about the socialist (or communist) future. First, socialism would so increase the amount of goods and services available for distribution that society would be able to "inscribe on its banners, 'From each according to his ability, to each according to his needs' ": Society would no longer have to divide limited resources among the many people competing for them. To put the same thought in another way, there would be no classes, and thus no ruling class. With no ruling class, there would be no need for a state to protect its selfish interests. The state would therefore "wither away." There would be "administration," but not "politics." The second aspect of communism, as Marx saw it, was that it would liberate the whole human being repressed by the division of labor under capitalism. As Marx said:

> In communist society, where nobody has one exclusive sphere of activity, but each can become accomplished in any branch he wishes, society regulates the general production and thus makes it possible for me to do one thing today and another tomorrow, to hunt in the morning, fish in the afternoon, rear cattle in the evening, criticize after dinner, just as I have a mind, without ever becoming hunter, fisherman, shepherd, or critic (Marx and Engels, 1947, p. 22).

No society like this exists anywhere on earth—certainly not in such communist industrial nations as the Soviet Union, where the state has hardly "withered away."

THE MULTINATIONALS

Commerce among nations is at least as old as the Phoenicians, whose trading ships sailed from what is now Lebanon to foreign lands more than 3,000 years ago. Trading routes criss-crossed the globe, as silk, gold, spices, tools, and even clam shells and stone axes were bartered or sold. Although trade was international in scope, production was not. Even in the early stages of the Industrial Revolution, most manufacturing firms were small and confined to a single country. As companies grew, however, they sought raw materials from foreign nations, as well as foreign markets to sell their products. In time, too, many began to manufacture products in foreign lands, with foreign labor, and many opened branch offices in a number of different countries. The phenomenon of the **multinational** (or "transnational") **corporation**—a company that operates in several foreign countries through affiliates that are subject to some degree of central control—was born.

The parent company can exercise its influence over the branches in several ways, including decisions about what to produce, how much of it, at what price, with what technology, for which markets, and under whose management (Committee for Economic Development, 1981, p. 14). To the multinationals, the world is a "company town" (Vaughn, 1978). Most economists agree that for a company to be regarded as a true multinational corporation, it must be large. According to one definition, a true multinational must operate in six or more countries and have foreign sales of more than $1 billion annually.

The multinational corporations play an immense role in the world's economy. The International Chamber of Commerce estimates that Amer-

Multinational corporation A large company that has subsidiary offices, and does substantial business, in a number of different countries.

A multinational corporation operates in several countries, through affiliates subject to central control. According to one definition, to qualify as a multinational a company must operate in at least six countries and have foreign sales of more than $1 billion annually. Most multinationals are American. Here, McDonald's operates on a Tokyo street.

Daniel Sheehan/Black Star

ican multinationals alone generate one-third of the world's gross product (Madsen, 1980, p. 24). According to one estimate, within this decade, only 300 supergiant corporations will produce over half of the world's industrial output (Tyler, 1972). Shell Petroleum, the world's second-largest corporation, operates in 120 countries. Some of the largest multinational corporations have sales larger than the entire gross national products of many countries. The annual sales of Royal Dutch Shell are bigger than the gross national products of Turkey, Venezuela, or Iran; the sales of General Motors surpass the GNP of Switzerland, Pakistan, or South Africa (Solomon, 1978, p. 10). International Business Machines (IBM) has more foreign currency than the governments of Canada or Sweden. International Telephone and Telegraph (ITT), the world's eighth-largest corporation, has annual sales of $20 billion; 200,000 shareholders; and more than 400,000 employees in ninety countries. It owns Wonder Bread, Sheraton Hotels, Hartford Insurance, Avis Rent-a-Car, Burpee Lawn and Garden Products, and Bobbs-Merrill Publishing—among other companies (Madsen, 1980, p. 63).

The multinationals are not only huge, but also truly international. Many earn most of their profits abroad, not in the countries where they maintain their home offices. Exxon earns roughly 75 percent of its profits outside of the United States; Philips, a Dutch firm, earns 90 percent of its profits outside the Netherlands; British Petroleum, 80 percent of its profits outside Britain. Hoffman-LaRoche, a Swiss-based drug firm, does only 3 percent of its business in Switzerland.

Most of us are not aware of the international origins of some of the products we use. Most of us may know that a Sony television is (probably) manufactured in Japan, an Olivetti typewriter in Italy, and a Volvo automobile in Sweden. But how many Americans know that Imperial margarine, Dove soap, Aim and Close-Up toothpastes, and Wisk laundry detergent are trademarks owned by Unilever, a joint Dutch-British firm? Or that Standard Oil is a subsidiary of British Petroleum? That A&P is owned by a German company? That the engine in the Dodge Omni is made by Volkswagen (a German firm) or that Valium is Swiss; Baskin-Robbins, British; and Timex, Norwegian? That Libby's string beans, Pepsodent toothpaste, Brylcreem hair tonic, and Bantam Books are all foreign-controlled? For that matter, how many of us know that Pullman no longer makes railroad cars in the United States but *does* make automobiles in the Soviet Union (Madsen, 1980, p. 26)?

American multinationals, like foreign ones, are deeply involved in overseas markets. Standard Oil of California earns 60 percent of its revenues outside the United States; Texaco, 66 percent. IBM makes a shade more than half of its profits (53 percent) abroad. Colgate-Palmolive earns 58 percent of its profits from foreign investments; Coca-Cola, 46 percent; and General Motors, 22 percent. Foreign operations of American-based firms generate from 30 to 40 percent of total net corporate profits in America (Solomon, 1978, p. 13; Madsen, 1980, pp. 49–99). IBM, the world's seventh-largest corporation, employs almost as many workers abroad (120,000, only 600 of whom are Americans) as in the United States (155,000).

Multinationals are largely, though far from exclusively, American-based. Of the ten largest multinationals, eight have headquarters in the United States—sixty-three of the top 100; twenty-nine are European and eight are Japanese (Vaughn, 1978, p. 16). Roughly 300 of the top 500 multinationals in the world have headquarters in the United States. Yet the multinational corporation "has no national loyalties. It moves over the globe for profit and growth." Multinationals regard having too much concern for American interests as "provincialism," possibly damaging to corporate interests. By ignoring national boundaries and regrouping along global lines, production levels go up and costs go down (Vaughn, 1978, p. 28).

Even so, the multinationals do not necessarily act in the interests of their host countries. In the early 1970s, ITT interfered in the international affairs of Chile, and certain huge corporations, notably Exxon and Lockheed, offered illegal bribes totalling millions of dollars to officials in a half-dozen countries. In short, the multinationals have become quasi-sovereign—more or less independent power centers acting in their own interests, often in ways that hurt their home countries *and* the countries where they do business (Eells, 1976, pp. 239–242).

Multinationals have their supporters, too. They employ many workers in the less developed countries (LDCs), pay local and national taxes, and sometimes stimulate economic growth of local industry and the emergence of a local professional and managerial class (Frank, 1980, p. 144). Despite the many "misunderstandings" between multinationals and the people—especially, the politicians—of the LDCs, many multinationals seem to be "learning to become socially responsible citizens" (Madsen, 1980, p. 235). For their part, the LDCs are working out a "less polarized relationship" with the multinationals, one marked by "greater mutual understanding and accommodation." Perhaps, over time, a pattern of "mutual gain" will emerge (Committee for Economic Development, 1981, pp. 2, 17). So, at any rate, say the multinationals' defenders.

Other economists argue that, on balance, global companies harm the nations in which they do business. These economists say that multinationals compete with local businesses and thus weaken the host country's domestic economy. They claim, too, that the multinationals benefit only the local upper and middle classes, and a small, privileged stratum of the working classes, thereby reinforcing social inequality. Sometimes, the multinationals prop up local dictatorships, and almost everywhere, they spread Western values and undermine local cultures. The critics say, too, that the multinationals tie local economies to the world economy, thereby generating local inflation and discouraging well-rounded, independent local economies.

The emergence of the multinationals may well be the most important economic innovation since industrialization itself, and they will be with us for some time to come. Indeed, by the end of this century, they will produce half the world's industrial goods. For good or ill, they will dominate our economic lives well into the next century—and considerably beyond.

UNEMPLOYMENT

For half a century, General Electric—the eleventh-largest corporation in the United States—had manufactured metal irons in a factory in Ontario, California. Late in February, 1982, GE, almost the only local employer, closed the factory, and in effect closed the town of Ontario. GE was not losing money on the plant, but it was not making enough to satisfy GE's top management. Metal irons are more expensive to manufacture than plastic irons, which have become more popular with Amer-

Unemployment forces many people to leave their communities and criss-cross the country in search of work. The Thom family traveled from Minnesota to Denver seeking a job but couldn't find one. They planned to go to Arizona next. An old bus serves as their home.

The New York Times/Brian Payne

ican consumers. GE claimed that converting the Ontario plant would be too expensive, so the plastic irons would be manufactured in Singapore, Mexico, and Brazil. Workers in those countries get $5 to $7 an hour less than ours do, and they have no troublesome unions.

As for the workers in Ontario, California, seventy-eight were placed in another GE plant. And the Ontario factory, bought by another firm, reopened with 250 workers. Meanwhile, some 500 skilled, former GE workers joined the unemployment lines.

In June, 1987, 7.26 million Americans were officially unemployed, 6.0 percent of the United States work force of 121 million. Nearly 2 million more are termed "discouraged" workers—that is, they have given up looking for a job. Lillian Morris, 32, of Dodge City, Kansas, lost her job when the grocery store where she worked went out of business in 1981. "I had a car—I lost that," she said. "I had my own home—I had to move back in with my mother." She has applied for a number of other jobs, without success (Clymer, 1983b). George Clem, 31, a Jackson, Michigan, worker laid off from a manufacturing job, said, "I've lost everything I ever had—it's all gone. I've lost my job. I've lost my home. I thought I had my future assured, but now I know I have no future" (Nelson, 1983).

Not every jobless person or family endures extreme hardships, but many do. A 1983 poll conducted jointly by *The New York Times* and CBS News showed that in a nation-wide sample of more than 1,500 Americans, 36 percent lived in households where at least one member had been unemployed during the past year. In such households, 63 percent "bought lower quality food" than they had before, 53 percent had had to withdraw money from a savings account to live, and 50 percent had cut back on medical or dental care. A third had borrowed money; a third had missed payments on home mortgages, car loans, or apartments; and 18 percent had accepted food stamps or some welfare (Clymer, 1983b).

The recession of the early 1980s has created a class of "new poor." Many of those who are now unemployed had formerly held steady, high-paying jobs year after year. They "were the backbone of our work force who bought homes, cars. . . . What we're seeing here is . . . people who were breadwinners, purchasers, suddenly finding themselves with little available income" (Stuart, 1982).

Unemployed workers often blame themselves for their problems, and the longer they stay unemployed, the greater the tendency to self-blame—and despair. Economic loss becomes personal loss—a sense of guilt and depression. These emotions often generate such destructive behavior as child abuse, wife beating, murder, and suicide. Harvey Brenner, a public health researcher, found that a 1 percent rise in unemployment, if sustained over a six-year period, is correlated (for men) with a 4.3 percent and (for women) a 2.3 percent increase in first-time admissions to mental hospitals, with a 4.1 percent increase in suicide, with a 5.7 percent increase in the homicide rate, and with a 4 percent increase in admissions to state prisons (Pines, 1982; Brenner, 1984). The high unemployment of the 1980s therefore added about 1,200 additional suicides to the number that would have occurred in a more stable economy (6 percent unemployment, say). A similar rise in the suicide rate took place during the Great Depression of the 1930s.

Underemployment.   Nearly as serious as outright unemployment is the recent upsurge in so-called underemployment. Many college graduates, for instance, are currently working at jobs that do not make use of the

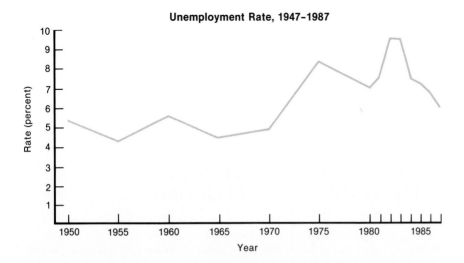

Unemployment Rate, 1947–1987

skills they acquired as undergraduates (see Chapter 15). In a nation-wide survey of 2,500 college graduates, sociologists Jo Carol Phelan and Thomas James Phelan found that one-third reported themselves "under-employed." (This proportion varied from 53 percent for majors in the social sciences to 24 percent for education majors.) College graduates had spent, on average, 2.8 more years in school than their jobs required (Hildebrand, 1983).

Why Unemployment?

From 1965 to 1969, the United States unemployment rate remained steady at about 4 percent. In the 1970s, it rose from 5 to 8 percent, and, in the early 1980s, it reached a post-World War II peak of nearly one worker in ten, or 9.5 percent. In the middle to late 1980s, the unemployment rate eased back a bit to about 6 or 7 percent. For over a half a century, administrations have promised to get the American worker back on the job. Yet the unemployment rate was higher in the 1970s than it had been in the 1960s, and higher in the early 1980s than it had been in the 1970s. Why?

There are many reasons, and not all economists agree on what they are. Some would blame American industry's short-sightedness, for while Japan's executives make plans based on ten- and twenty-year pro-jections, our corporate leaders often look only to next quarter's profits. Other economists argue that the economic slump (and thus unemploy-ment) is the fault of the declining quality of American products, caused, in turn, by the carelessness of American workers. Some economists point to the unreliable availability and cost of key natural resources, such as oil. Demographers emphasize the delayed impact of the post-World War II "baby boom"—the sudden influx of workers who entered the job mar-ket from the late 1960s to the late 1970s.

A few economists even argue that unemployment is actually profitable for certain segments of the American economy, especially those that do not rely on mass consumption of consumer goods. "If everyone could be employed, extraordinarily high wages would have to be paid to toilers in restaurant kitchens, laundries, filling stations, and other humble posi-tions." With a low rate of unemployment, very few young men or women would be willing to enlist in the volunteer army. Unemployment makes

■ TABLE 17–3
Percent of labor force unemployed

1950	5.2
1955	4.3
1960	5.4
1965	4.4
1970	4.8
1975	8.3
1980	7.0
1981	7.5
1982	9.5
1983	9.5
1984	7.4
1985	7.2
1986	6.8
1987 (June)	6.0

Sources: "The Reagan Economy at the Homestretch." *The New York Times* (July 27, 1986); F8; *Statistical Abstract of the United States 1986*, p. 390.

unions more willing to make concessions, and workers, more frightened and cautious. Communities compete for jobs by offering tax and other concessions to private business. Environmental controls may be relaxed. Minorities and women are less likely to demand affirmative-action hiring policies, because there will be little hiring in any case. A sense of futility keeps the country's political mood conservative. Seen from this perspective, "there are far worse phenomena than unemployment. One of them is full employment" (Lekachman, 1977, pp. 36, 38, 40).

DEINDUSTRIALIZATION IN THE POSTINDUSTRIAL ECONOMY

Although there is far from universal agreement on this question, some researchers regard the information explosion as the third technological revolution in human history. Many observers, as we have noted, call a society in which a majority of the workers are employed not in industry but in the tertiary or service sector a postindustrial society (Bell, 1976). Such a society has also been called the "information society" (Naisbitt, 1984); one observer dubbed the revolution that was said to usher it in, and the society based on this revolution, "The Third Wave" (Toffler, 1981). Postindustrial society began in the United States in the 1960s with the development of the computer. In Japan and Western Europe, the information revolution is taking place right now. The postindustrial economy is primarily a service economy. Unlike in the manufacturing sector, in this sector, raw materials are not transformed into a tangible, physical product. Rather, a transaction or some other intangible act is performed: typing a letter, healing a patient, teaching a student, negotiating a will, fixing a car's engine, or arresting a criminal suspect. We must not imagine, however, that jobs in the service sector are automatically higher or lower on the economic scale than jobs in the primary or secondary sectors. Clearly, the service or tertiary sector makes up an extremely mixed bag. It includes clerks and sales personnel, secretaries, physicians, teachers and professors, lawyers, mechanics, police officers, bookkeepers, bus drivers, engineers, social workers, computer programers, telephone operators, garbage collectors, as well as a host of other people whose jobs do not entail the production or manufacture of physical goods.

It is important to keep in mind that manufacturing does not disappear in a postindustrial society. It is simply no longer the sector that employs a majority of the economy's workers. The service sector continues to feed off its industrial base. Many jobs—indeed, probably most jobs—in the tertiary sector are directly dependent on manufacturing. An advertising executive motivates the public to buy a car; sales personnel sell it; a bookkeeper keeps track of its sale; a mechanic repairs it. The car, a product that is manufactured in the secondary sector, is responsible for the jobs of all of these workers in the tertiary sector. Just as agriculture does not disappear when industry matures, likewise, manufacturing is still absolutely essential in the "information society."

What happens when the economy moves from one stage to another? The majority of the work force gives up, or is forced to give up, its traditional lines of work and to move into new ones. At the same time, an industrial society still needs farming: Not all workers employed in the older technology will be forced to abandon their traditional liveli-hoods. The United States, presumably the most highly developed postin-dustrial society on Earth, exports more food, in terms of dollar value, to other countries than any other nation—but only 2.5 percent of our work force is engaged in agriculture for a living. Thus, the proportion of the work force is not a precise reflection of the economic value of a given sector of the economy. As a consequence, these shifts should not be looked upon as absolute. It is a proportional matter: The proportion of the labor force defines a society's stage of economic development. The greater the proportion of a society's work force working in agricul-ture, the more agrarian that society is; the greater the proportion of a society's work force that is employed in manufacturing, the more indus-trial that society is; and the greater the proportion of a society's economy that is employed in the service or tertiary sector, the more possible it is to characterize its economy as postindustrialist.

Each of these technological revolutions has produced casualties. Thousands of years ago, agriculture tied formerly nomadic peoples to fixed locations, hence destroying ancient tribal ways (Eckholm, 1984). We've mentioned the horrifying conditions of the early industrial facto-ries, with their extremely high rates of worker injuries, mutilations, and even deaths. Industrialization has usually meant destroying the landscape and polluting the soil, water, and air. Economic development is never purchased cheaply. Just as millions of farmers and peasants were displaced by industrialization, so, too, will laborers be thrown out of work as a result of plant closings with the shift to a service econ-omy. Economic change will always be a mixed blessing, and the latest technological revolution is no exception.

Is the change worth it? Has the transition from an industrial to a postindustrial economy helped or hurt American society? And what of the years to come—will the economic curve be up or down? There are, as with most things, at least two views on this issue. One side, the optimists, believes that recent economic developments have been more beneficial than harmful and that temporary setbacks are inevitable for some regions of a nation and some segments of the work force, but that, in the long run, the trend line will be upward (Toffler, 1981; Nais-bitt, 1984; Fallows, 1985). The other side, the pessimists, believes that recent economic developments have been harmful and that they will continue to be so if a new direction, based on a more interventionist strategy, is not taken (Bluestone and Harrison, 1982; Alperovitz and Faux, 1984).

In 1980, the President's Commission for a National Agenda for the Eighties issued its report, *Urban America in the Eighties: Perspectives and Prospects*. The Commission, arguing that nothing endures forever, stated that industries, like empires, rise and fall. All dynamic economies will include strong and weak sectors; some will grow and others, shrink. New growth industries will experience expanding business investment; older, stagnant industries will experience **disinvestment**—money will be withdrawn from them and invested elsewhere. Likewise, cities in which declining industry is located will also decline in size, affluence, and vigor. Cities like Cleveland, Chicago, and Detroit cannot survive at their present sizes or in their current forms, the report said. Their decline, like the decline of the industries on which their economies are based, is an inevitability. The solution is not to attempt a revitalization project that is doomed to fail, but to stimulate the migration of their present

Disinvestment The withdrawal of capital from one industry or sector and its investment in another.

residents to other areas of the country where more vital industries are located. Migration selects out the younger, more able, and more ambitious workers, workers who go on to have more successful careers in their adopted homes than those who continue living in economically stagnant areas. The ones who do stay will be older, less capable, and less ambitious. When an area declines and such individuals are thrown out of work, in all likelihood, they will never be as well off or have as good jobs as they did previously. But such, the report maintained, are the personal tragedies of specific people, and they have little to do with the nation as a whole.

This presidential report "amounted to the first shot in the economic battle of this decade" (Fallows, 1985, p. 48). It drew a battle line between the optimists, who saw the change as healthy and the decline of certain industries and regions as inevitable, and the pessimists, who argued that something terribly unhealthy was happening to the American economy, and would continue to do so until drastic measures were taken. Everyone agrees that **deindustrialization** is taking place: A decreasing proportion of the work force is engaged in manufacturing, and capital investment is being withdrawn from certain industries. But again, is this a good thing or a bad thing?

The pessimists point to decaying, abandoned factories, dying communities, stagnant industries, and long unemployment lines. "How can this be good?" they ask. The optimists argue that some areas and industries will experience a decline, while others will grow. The only thing that's different about today's process of deindustrialization, they say, is the cast of winners and losers. What is important, they say, is the overall national picture, and here, the number of jobs continues to grow. Today's economic change is creating more economic opportunities than it has destroyed. Between 1979 and 1986, while roughly 2 million manufacturing jobs disappeared from the United States economy, some 6 million service jobs were added. Between 1984 and 1995, about 16 million jobs will be added to the American economy, according to a Bureau of Labor Statistics estimate, 90 percent of which will be in the service sector.

An argument put forth by the pessimists is that the jobs that are disappearing are high-paying, highly skilled jobs, and the ones that are replacing them are low-paying, low-skill, dead-end jobs. The image they invoke is that of a $20 an hour union steel or auto worker's being laid off and forced to work for $4 an hour flipping hamburgers at McDonald's. The optimists claim that this image is very atypical of the process of deindustrialization. The jobs that are disappearing are not all, or even mostly, good, high-paying union jobs, and the majority of the newly created jobs are not dead-end or low-paying ones, they say. The steel and the auto industries are misleading guides to what's happening in manufacturing. When the recent decline in the steel industry began in 1979, steel workers made up only 1.5 percent of all American workers. Steel and auto workers were, until recently, uncharacteristic, the "aristocracy" of American workers; they earned over one and one-half times what other workers earned. Most displaced workers earn considerably less than this, the optimists point out. For instance, the job category that experienced the sharpest decline in number of workers between the 1970s and the 1980s was private household workers, or domestic servants. Is there any more hopeful sign of progress, asks one observer, than the shrinkage of unskilled, low-paying jobs (Fallows, 1985, p. 61)? At the same time, the job openings for computer programmers, data

Deindustrialization The process and period of transition between a manufacturing and a service economy. During deindustrialization, industrial firms earn a declining share of a nation's total profits and lay off workers; many go out of business altogether.

processors, electrical and electronic engineers, and computer operators are reaching unprecedented numbers. Although some of the newer service jobs are minimum-wage, dead-end jobs, like serving hamburgers, most, the optimists say, are at the upper end of the pay and skill scale.

The pessimists are not persuaded by these arguments. They insist that the process of deindustrialization has done a great deal more harm than good to the American economy. They hold that the economic shifts that have taken place in recent years are not the result of destiny or any "wave of the future," but of decisions made by executives (and secondarily, politicians) to profit big business, regardless of their impact on the rest of the society. What is taking place is not simply a natural transition from one sector of the economy to another, but a conscious decision to close down industrial plants, abandon communities, destroy their economic bases, and dismantle their basic industry (Bluestone and Harrison, 1982). Why should business make such destructive decisions? Even though some of what goes under the name of deindustrialization does represent a shift to the service sector of the economy, much of it entails the relocation of industry to regions with low tax bases, low labor costs, and no unions (and this includes foreign countries), and disinvestment by large conglomerates from certain aspects of their businesses and reallocation of their capital into other phases of their operations.

When the cost of doing business in one area rises higher than it is in another area, firms are likely to relocate. When they abandon one community, they often leave devastation behind. Public facilities, such as schools and municipal services, which had to be installed because the firm located in the area in the first place, are dependent on a population and a tax base. When a firm leaves town, public money has to be cut back on these facilities, and some have to be closed down altogether. Corporations do not have to pay for the disruption they have caused by their departure. When they relocate to another area, they put new demands on their municipal services—schools, the water supply, sewer systems, playgrounds, and so on. They don't have to pay for these changes, either. The total cost of their moves to both the community they leave and the one to which they relocate is extremely high. In fact, if they did have to pay for all the devastation they caused and the services they receive, chances are, they wouldn't relocate.

Ideally, disinvestment "is supposed to free labor and capital from relatively unproductive uses in order to put them to work in more productive ones." Unfortunately, what typically happens, the pessimists say, is that capital disappears from a region or an economic sector, and labor does not find comparable work. For instance, two years after losing their jobs, auto workers earn only 43 percent of their former wages, and even six years later, they earn only five-sixths (Bluestone and Harrison, 1982, p. 10). And the issue is not simply lost wages and lost productivity. Workers and their families suffer serious medical and psychological problems as a result of unemployment and a lowered standard of living (Buss and Radburn, 1983; Brenner, 1984). And whole communities are destroyed in the process.

Meanwhile, the corporation simply looks at the profit-and-loss column. Instead of improving and upgrading old manufacturing facilities, executives often let them run down, "milk" them for large but temporary profits, acquire new businesses elsewhere or in another sector, and then abandon the old plant. Although they improve their profits by following this practice, they destroy lives in doing so—and everyone else has to

WHAT DO YOU THINK?

Are the Rich Getting Richer?

Using data collected by the Federal Reserve Board, the Democrats on Congress's Joint Economic Committee prepared a report demonstrating "a concentration of economic clout" in the United States "that has snowballed to levels not seen since the Great Depression" of the 1930s. The 420,000 "super rich" families in the United States, a mere 0.5 percent of the population, own 35 percent of the total wealth—$3.7 trillion of the nation's $10.6 trillion in assets. A study using 1962 data showed that 0.5 percent of the population controlled a quarter (25.4 percent) of the total national wealth. At the other end of the scale, the poorest 90 percent-

of American households held 35 percent of the total United States wealth in 1962, but only 28 percent in 1983. In other words, over the past generation, the rich have been getting a larger slice of the total economic pie, and the poor have been getting a smaller slice.

The *average* wealth of these 420,000 super rich was $8.85 million. The next-lower economic level, an additional 420,000 families, who were termed "very rich," held 6.7 percent of the total national assets, with an average per family wealth of $1.7 million. And the next layer, the 7.6 million merely "rich" families, owns almost exactly 30 percent of the total United States wealth. Every-

one else, more than 75 million families, divides up a bit more than a quarter of the total economic pie. Their assets, including houses and cars, average just under $40,000 per family. The study concluded that not only is the wealth in this country unequally divided, but its distribution is becoming more unequal over time.

Has the United States ceased to be a "land of opportunity"? Are we becoming a polarized society—where the "haves" are becoming richer and the "have-nots" stay poor? What do you think?

Source: *Newsday*, July 27, 1986, p. 15.

pay for them. All along the line, individual workers and their families, whole communities, and the public sector are picking up the tab to support the profit-and-loss columns of big business.

Much of the process of disinvestment entails firms' leaving the Northeast and Midwest and relocating in the South and Southwest, where taxes and labor costs are lower. Some of the process involves relocating

TABLE 17–4 Distribution of Wealth in the United States, 1983

Economic Level	Number of Families	Percent of U.S. Population	Average Wealth	Total Wealth	Percent of Total U.S. Wealth
Super rich	420,000	0.5	$8.85 million	$3.7 trillion	35.1
Very rich	420,000	0.5	$1.7 million	$0.7 trillion	6.7
Rich	7.6 million	9	$206,000 to $1.4 million	$3.7 trillion	29.9
Everyone else	75.5 million	90	$39,584	$3 trillion	28.2

Source: Democratic Staff of the Joint Economic Committee, United States Congress, *The Concentration of Wealth in the United States: Trends in the Distribution of Wealth among American Families*, July, 1986.

outside the country altogether. For instance, Uniroyal now manufactures tires in Brazil, Turkey, Spain, and Australia. In fact, the overseas operations of a number of American corporations are extremely profitable. For instance, Ford, Coca-Cola, and Citicorp derive more than half of their profits from overseas operations. To a board of directors sitting in New York, whether their profits derive from Korea, Singapore, Brazil, or the United States is of little importance. What counts is the size of their profits. If an accountant tells them they can increase their profit line by 2 percent by moving out of an old plant in Akron, Ohio, into a new one in São Paulo, Brazil, they do it. It is regarded as wise business policy. The destruction of lives and communities does not enter into the equation at all.

Much of this disinvestment from industry entails redirecting capital from manufacturing into nonmanufacturing sectors—in short, diversification. For instance, between the late 1970s and the early 1980s, General Tire diverted a sizable chunk of its profits from the tire business into television, radio, soft drink bottling, and an airline. During the same period, U.S. Steel drew capital away from steel, let its steel plants run down, and reinvested in shopping malls. Mobil Oil acquired Montgomery Ward, a department store. (These firms acquired manufacturing facilities, as well.) In this way, capital is shifted from one sector or company to achieve maximum profit. For the men and women whose lives depend on working for these corporations, the result is economic devastation and personal and psychic disorganization (Bluestone and Harrison, 1982, pp. 25–81).

The proof of the pudding for these two approaches to deindustrialization resides ultimately in what the recent economy has done for the average American income. Here, we find a mixed scorecard. Between the early 1970s and the early 1980s in the United States, the median family income—adjusting for inflation—stagnated, indeed, slipped a bit. However, between 1982 and 1986, median family income increased in real dollars, to $29,458. Between 1985 and 1986, the total number of poor people in the United States declined from 33.1 to 32.4 million, from 13.6 percent of the population in 1983 to 15.2 percent in 1986. So far, the optimists seem to have a slight edge. On the other hand, the income distribution in the United States seems to have suffered a setback. The share of total income received by the most affluent households increased from 43.6 percent in 1970 to 46.1 percent in 1986. The bottom fifth's share decreased from 4.1 percent to 3.8 percent. In short, the rich seem to be getting an increasingly larger slice of the total economic pie, while the poor, though perhaps not quite as badly off economically, seems to receive a smaller slice (Pear, 1987).

Why? Part of the answer is that the postindustrial economy actually does seem to generate far more jobs near the bottom of the pay scale than near the top. The number of highly-paid computer specialists are more than offset by the hamburger flippers. A report released in 1986 by the Joint Economic Committee of Congress revealed that more than half of the new jobs created in the United States between 1979 and 1984 paid less than $7,000 a year, and that two-thirds of them were part-time positions. At the other end of the scale, the number of jobs that paid $28,000 or more actually declined by over 400,000 during this same period ("Low-paying Jobs Held Rising," *The New York Times*, December 11, 1986, p. A31). Thus, for stimulating the economy, it seems that deindustrialization has done something quite different—made it more inequitable.

SUMMARY

1. The economy is the institution that deals with the manufacture, distribution, and consumption of resources—with money, goods, and services.

2. The lives of all of us are influenced by the economy, in ways we may not be aware of and, often, cannot control.

3. There is a close relationship between the economy and other institutions, especially the political and the economic institutions.

4. Directly or indirectly, all humans on Earth are interconnected in an immense global ebb and flow of money, goods, and services.

5. Agriculture emerged roughly 15,000 years ago, and it had a profound impact on all aspects of all societies who adopted it.

6. The emergence of a merchant class—an economic category of individuals engaged in buying and selling for a profit—was a significant economic development.

7. Industrialization began in the mid-1700s and was characterized by mass production and the development of the factory system.

8. Industrialization generated competition among manufacturers, the opening of new markets in which to sell manufactured products, and the search for sources of raw materials.

9. In concert with industrialization, the number of farms and farmers decreased, and the average size of the remaining farms increased.

10. The primary sector of the economy comprises workers who extract natural resources from the land; the secondary sector is made up of workers who manufacture these resources into salable products; and the tertiary sector includes those who are involved in the service occupations.

11. A postindustrial economy is characterized by an already-efficient and productive industry and a growing number and proportion of workers in the tertiary sector.

12. The more industrialized a society is, the more centralized and oligopolistic its economy is.

13. One method of measuring economic concentration is by charting corporate interlocks—executives who sit on the boards of directors of two or more large companies. Corporate interlocks indicate that the American economy is integrated into a single, unbroken network of huge corporations united by multiple interlocks.

14. Capitalism is characterized by private ownership of the means of production and socialism, by state or public ownership of the means of production. In truth, all capitalist and all socialist economies are mixed, and so this distinction is one of degree. Some socialist economies are becoming more profit-oriented.

15. Marx defined communism as a classless, stateless, nonexploitative and totally equalitarian utopia. No such society exists, nor is it likely that one ever will.

16. It is possible that an important economic development—as momentous as the emergence of agriculture and industrialization—is now in the making: the emergence of the multinational corporation, a large company with branches in a number of different countries. Marxists and other radicals denounce the multinational trend, whereas conservatives and moderates see it as beneficial.

17. Roughly 7 percent of the American workforce is unemployed. Unemployment has a devastating impact on the lives of many families so afflicted.

18. With the transition to a postindustrial economy, the United States economy is experiencing the process of deindustrialization, or the withdrawal of capital from basic industry. Whether this is a good or a bad thing for the economy is currently in dispute.

SUGGESTED READINGS

Victor R. Fuchs, *How We Live: An Economic Perspective on Americans from Birth to Death*. Cambridge, Massachusetts: Harvard University Press, 1983.
How our everyday lives are influenced by economic forces. In spite of its strong conservative bias (as you read it, can you see where the author makes unwarranted assumptions?), this book contains a great deal of value. The author adopts a "life cycle" approach: Each chapter deals with a specific stage in the individual's life, from infancy to old age. Contains a great deal of analysis relevant to public policy.

John Kenneth Galbraith, *The Affluent Society* (4th ed.). Boston: Houghton Mifflin, 1984.
A classic essay on the economics of American society, with a chapter commenting on the Reaganomics of the 1980s. Galbraith asks why the Japanese have surged ahead in industrial productivity in recent years. He supplies two answers. First of all, far more of our economy is devoted to wasteful and sterile military expenditures—nearly 8 percent of our gross national product (GNP), versus 1 percent for the Japanese. And second, Japanese executives plan for the long run, whereas ours do not look much beyond the current fiscal quarter and, hence, are short-sighted and fail to see long-term trends at work. Galbraith's analysis is certainly worth pondering.

John Kenneth Galbraith, *The New Industrial State* (4th ed.). Boston: Houghton Mifflin, 1985.
An updating of a classic work. A wise and witty overview of our current economic condition. Informative and fascinating.

Beth Mintz and Michael Schwartz, *The Power Structure of American Business*. Chicago: University of Chicago Press, 1985.
An empirical study of corporate interlocks showing that management in the large banks make the decisions that have the greatest impact on the American economy. The authors argue that the banks determine the economic activities even of the largest industrial firms. A controversial book; not all observers accept its conclusions.

Frances Fox Piven and Richard A. Cloward, *The New Class War: Reagan's Attack on the Welfare State and Its Consequences*. New York: Pantheon, 1982.
An examination of a conservative administration's effort to dismantle government protection of the poor "from the insecurities and hardships of an unrestrained market economy."

Bradley R. Schiller, *The Economics of Poverty and Discrimination* (4th ed.). Englewood Cliffs, New Jersey: Prentice-Hall, 1984.
Who are the poor? What contributes to their poverty? Why does poverty exist at all? This book offers a timely discussion of these and related issues.

Neil J. Smelser, *The Sociology of Economic Life* (2nd ed.). Englewood Cliffs, New Jersey: Prentice-Hall, 1976.
A brief overview of economic sociology, particularly how sociological factors influence economic behavior.

"Adam Smith" (George J. W. Goodman), *Paper Money*. New York: Dell, 1982.
Do you want to know why gasoline prices rose in the 1970s—and then fell in the 1980s? What fuels inflation? What you should do with your money in case of a catastrophe? How the stock market works? What role the Saudi Arabians play in contemporary economic developments? What happens when the anchovies swim away from their traditional waters? This book provides an entertaining, nontechnical look at a very technical subject. Smith calls the creation of OPEC (the Organization of Petroleum Exporting Countries), and its long-term impact, "the greatest transfer of wealth in world history." That's quite a strong statement; aren't you curious to find out what he means by it?

chapter 18

POPULATION AND URBANIZATION

In 1798 a slim volume called *An Essay on the Principle of Population* was published in England. Written by a clergyman named Thomas Robert Malthus, it was to become one of the most important and controversial books ever written. Before Malthus, few observers had given much systematic thought to the relationship between the world's population and its economic resources. Malthus argued that human populations must inevitably increase more rapidly than the supply of food, assuming that they refrain from what Malthus called "sin"—artificial birth control. In the long run, however, starvation and disease will reestablish a balance between food resources and population. Rather than rely on this dismal mechanism, Malthus argued, men and women should practice "moral restraint" by marrying late and controlling their sexual urges.

Malthus tended to confuse moralistic preaching with scientific prediction. But he did put his finger on a crucial and incontestable fact: A country—or the world as a whole—can indeed have too many people for the available resources.

Governments and population experts are still struggling with the relationship between numbers of people, on the one hand, and food resources, on the other. In Africa, for instance, the Sahara Desert is creeping southward, destroying once-productive farm land, and, in 1985, millions of residents of Ethiopia and Sudan starved to death before assistance could reach them. Even though the distribution of food and other resources within a given country is every bit as important as the total amount available for distribution, that amount is often insufficient, whatever the distribution. Malthus was something of a prophet.

THE SUBJECT MATTER OF DEMOGRAPHY

The word "demography" stems from the ancient Greek: "Demos" means people and "graphy" means writing—hence, writing about people **Demography** is the study of human populations in their

Demography The systematic study of the size, composition, and spatial distribution of human populations, as well as changes in all three, and the causes and consequences of such changes.

strictly quantitative aspect. Demographers concern themselves with a population's size, composition, and spatial distribution; with changes in all three; and with the causes and consequences of such changes. No area of sociology is so sharply focused on human beings as numbers. Perhaps you think that you, after all, are not a number or a statistic, but a flesh-and-blood human being. A demographer would reply, "Yes, you are a human being—an individual, with unique characteristics and a personality all your own. But you are also a statistic, or at least, you are *part* of many statistics—and so is everyone else." These two ways of looking at people are different, not contradictory. Even though two 18-year-olds may be different in many ways, they may be counted together by a demographer in the same age category. Even though two couples have very little in common, the fact that they both got divorced the same year is very important to a demographer. It surely does make a great deal of difference if a country has only a few hundred thousand inhabitants, like Iceland, or a billion, like China. Societies in which the average age of dying is 46 are surely different from those in which it is close to 80. A nation in which women bear eight children, on the average, is quite different from one in which they bear only two.

The Birth Rate

Birth rate A measure of how many children the women of a given society or social category bear.

Crude birth rate The number of children born each year per 1,000 people in the total population.

The **birth rate** is a measure of how many children the women of a given society or social category bear. A society's birth rate can be expressed in several different ways. The easiest to understand is the **crude birth rate:** the number of children born each year for each 1,000 people in the total population. For instance, roughly 3.7 million babies were born in the United States in 1984. For a population of 236 million in that year, this yields a crude birth rate of 15.7 per 1,000 in the population. The crude birth rate does not take into account the age or sex ratio of the population, and so it can be misleading under certain circumstances. Still, the crude birth rate is a fairly good measure of a society's fertility. The United States, Switzerland, and Denmark each have quite low crude birth rates—about fifteen per 1,000 in the population. Paraguay, Haiti, Saudi Arabia, and the Philippines each have quite high crude birth rates—more than forty per 1,000. Even without considering the age or the sex composition of these nations, we have a good idea that the fertility of the second group of countries is much higher than that of the first.

The Death Rate

Crude death rate The annual number of deaths per 1,000 people in the total population.

Life expectancy The average number of years individuals living in a given country or social category live, on the average.

The death rate measures the likelihood of dying in a given country or segment of the population. It is usually expressed in the form of the **crude death rate,** the annual number of deaths per 1,000 in the total population. Countries with a crude death rate lower than ten per 1,000 have very low crude death rates, whereas those with rates higher than twenty per 1,000 have very high crude death rates.

A slightly different measure of death is the average **life expectancy** for each country or group in the population—that is, the number of years people live, on the average. The life expectancy of the United States population was 74.6 in 1983—78.8 for white women, 73.5 for Black women, 71.5 for white men, and 64.9 for Black men. A number of countries of the world have an average life expectancy for the general population very near that of 80 years—for instance, Japan (77), Iceland (77), Norway (77), Sweden (78), and Switzerland (79).

The third (and probably most valid) demographic measure of death is the **infant mortality rate**—that is, the number of deaths of children under the age of 1 per 1,000 births in that year. This statistic has fallen dramatically during the course of this century. In 1900, the infant mortality rate of the United States was 100; today, it is eleven. The Soviet Union's infant mortality rate was 273 in 1913; today, it is thirty-six. Even in very recent decades, the drop in this statistic has been impressive. Costa Rica's infant mortality rate was fifty-eight in 1970, and in 1983, it was twenty; Cuba registered a drop from forty-one to twenty. Japan cut its rate in half during this period, from fifteen to seven. Infant mortality rate is very strongly dependent on the health conditions and the hospital facilities that characterize a society or country at a given point in time. This, in turn, is dependent on a nation's economic development, per capita income, and income distribution. Highly industrialized countries, like Japan, Switzerland, France, and the United States, have infant mortality rates roughly at ten or below. Poorer, less economically developed countries, like Ethiopia (142), Nepal (142), Bolivia (107), and Haiti (107), have infant mortality rates over ten times as high as the affluent societies (see Table 18-4 later in the chapter). Countries that became affluent very quickly, such as Saudi Arabia and Libya, and whose income is not very well distributed, have not yet managed to extend adequate medical care to the majority of the population. However, this is likely to change dramatically in the near future.

Infant mortality rate The number of babies who die each year before their first birthday per 1,000 total births.

The Migration Rate

The **migration rate** is the number of people entering or leaving a country for each 1,000 people in its total population. During Ireland's Great Potato Famine, in the 1840s, that country's population dropped to 6.5 million, from 8.1 million, in only ten years (Schrier, 1970, p. 158). That represents a very high rate of emigration, or outmigration. Most of these people came to the United States. From 1820 to 1950, more than 45 million citizens of other nations came here, a very high rate of immigration, or in-migration.

Just as there can be migration from one country to another, or "external" migration, so too there can be migration within the same country, to different geographic areas, or between rural and urban areas; this is called "internal" migration. Today, we see Americans migrating from the Northeast and the Midwest of the United States to the "Sun Belt"—the South, the Southwest, and some of the Pacific states. Our Eastern and Midwestern cities are losing population, and the suburbs and rural areas are gaining it.

Two basic sets of factors are involved in migration: "push" and "pull" factors. "Push" factors are those that push people *out* of an area or a country, those that make it more difficult to live in a given place. A good example would be the nineteenth-century Irish potato famine, mentioned previously. The relatively high unemployment rate that prevails in the Midwest is a major "push" factor in inducing people to move away from that region. "Pull" factors, in contrast, are those that pull people *into* a country or region: They make some areas more desirable places to live. Immigration to the United States remains high, even today, in part because of the country's relatively high per capita income in comparison with the countries from which immigrants generally stem. Within the United States, internal migration to the Sun Belt is clearly stimulated by at least one "pull" factor: its good weather. Most immigration involves "push" and "pull" factors in combination.

Migration rate The number of people entering or leaving a country for each 1,000 people in its total population.

Demography is the study of human populations in their strictly quantitative aspect. Demographers concern themselves with the size, composition, and spatial distribution of a population, with changes in all three, and with the causes and consequences of these changes.

Paolo Koch/Photo Researchers

The Composition of the Population

Demographers are also concerned with the distribution of certain characteristics in a population—in a word, with its composition. There are, of course, many aspects of population composition that demographers study—race, occupation, employment, rural-urban residence, and so on. But age and sex are the most fundamental and important of them. Why? Because they determine a population's future size. Clearly, the older a population is, and the lower its proportion of women, the lower the likelihood that it will grow in the future. If the population has a young average age, and there are at least as many women as men, it has a high likelihood of growing in the future. Demographers have devised a special figure to portray each country's age and sex-specific distribution (see the figures below). It is called the **age-sex pyramid.** In populations with a high proportion of young people, this figure looks like a triangle or a Christmas tree. Such figures characterized almost all preindustrial societies, and some others, including the United States, until a generation or two ago. As a society becomes industrialized, its birth rate drops and the average age of its citizens rises. Its age-and-sex distribution chart becomes flatter and flatter and looks less and less like a pyramid.

As the figures show, the age-sex pyramid of the United States in the nineteenth century had a true triangular shape: heavy in the younger years and sparser in the older years. But today's profile is flatter, more even, because we have many more older people, especially women, in the population. The age-sex pyramid of Mexico, like that of the United States over a century ago, is triangular, because Mexico has many young

Age-sex pyramid A figure demographers use to portray the age and sex distribution of a population; the sexes are divided into each half of the figure, and age groupings are arrayed horizontally from top to bottom.

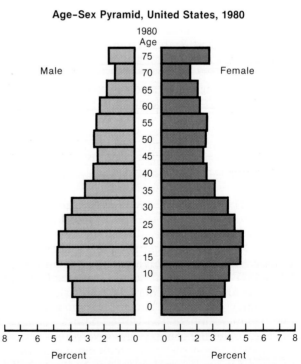

Age–Sex Pyramid, United States, 1980

Source: Paul E. Zopf, Jr., *Population: An Introduction to Social Demography.* Palo Alto, California: Mayfield, 1984, p. 113.

**Age–Sex Pyramid for an Economically Developed Country with a
Low Birth Rate: Sweden, 1985**

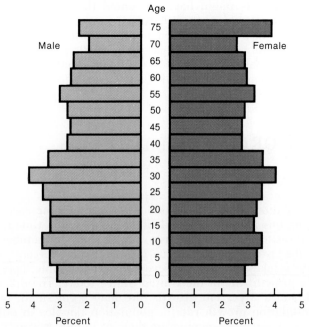

Source: Demographic Yearbook, United Nations.

people and few older ones. Sweden's age distribution is flatter and more evenly distributed than that of the United States today. Certain areas have extremely unusual age-sex compositions.

Clearly, many factors influence the age-sex composition, not industrialization and the birth rate alone. Wars, for instance. Both East and West Germany have very few people, especially men, in the age range from 60 to 69, because of the devastation of World War II. Migration, too, influences the age-sex pyramid: Some regions and even countries have relatively few men in the 20- to 49-year-old range, because they have migrated elsewhere to find employment.

The Age Cohort.   Age distribution points to one of the most important concepts in demography—the idea of the **age cohort:** a generation or a population segment that continues to be roughly the same age over time. The "Depression generation" grew up during the Great Depression of the 1930s and experienced difficult economic times during their formative years. The post-World War II "baby-boom" generation makes up a cohort consisting of people born from 1946 to the late 1950s. Studying cohorts is important because the movement of age categories through life influences many other features of a society. The large size of the baby-boom generation, for example, means that social factors relevant to their particular age group become prominent at each succeeding point in time. Products that appeal to adults in their 30s will be popular in the 1980s, for instance, and those that appeal to men and women in their 40s will sell well in the 1990s. And after the year 2010, the retire-

Age cohort A group of people of the same age who move through the life course together.

ment of the members of this cohort will put a severe strain on retirement-benefit programs, including Social Security. Twenty years ago, a close study of age cohorts might have prevented the oversupply of school teachers that developed in the 1970s; we would have known that too many teachers were being trained for the small number of children that were going to reach school age by the 1970s and 1980s. However, one of the most basic lessons we learn from sociology is that people are not always completely rational when it comes to social planning.

THE WORLD POPULATION

Human populations have a tremendous potential for increase. One way of measuring this increase is to calculate the period of time it takes for the population to double. Obviously, the shorter the number of years this takes, the faster the population is growing. At a 1 percent population growth rate, it takes a population seventy years to double. This is almost exactly the growth rate of the United States today. The difference between a 1 and a 2 percent growth rate may seem small, but at a 2 percent population growth rate, a population doubles in only thirty-five years. At 3 percent, a population doubles in only twenty-two years. At 4 percent, a population doubling takes eighteen years; at 5 percent, thirteen years; and at a growth rate of 6 percent, a population doubles in only eleven years (Weeks, 1986, p. 54).

During nearly the entire first million years of human existence, when we were hunters and gatherers, the population of the Earth grew extremely slowly. By 8000 B.C., the Earth's population had grown to some 8 million. At roughly this point, agriculture became widely adopted (see Chapter 17), and, because of this innovation, the Earth's population began to grow more rapidly. By the time of the birth of Jesus, the population of the Earth had grown to an estimated 300 million. From 8000 B.C. to A.D. 1, therefore, the Earth's population doubled every 1,500 years or so. From the birth of Jesus to the beginning of the Industrial Revolution (roughly 1750), the Earth's population grew to 800 million, a growth rate that represents a doubling about every 1,250 years. From that time on, the pace of population growth on Earth quickened very rapidly. Between 1750 and 1950, the Earth's population increased from 800 million to 2.5 billion—a doubling every 122 years. Between 1950 and 1987, only a thirty-six-year span, the Earth's population doubled again, to 5 billion. The period of time that it has taken to double the number of people on Earth has gotten shorter and shorter. Can anyone doubt that we are in the midst of a "population explosion"? (Weeks, 1986, pp. 52–53).

What is the prognosis for the future? Can our population continue to grow at an ever-faster rate? If present trends were to continue, in a few thousand years, the Earth would become a solid ball of human bodies growing out into space at the speed of light! Clearly, it is impossible for present trends to continue. The Earth's resources simply cannot sustain the population increases that have taken place in the recent past. In fact, population increases are beginning to slow down. Demographers estimate that the doubling from 1987 will take sixty-three years, because in the year 2050, there will be roughly 10 billion people on

■ **TABLE 18–1 World Population, 8000 B.C. to 2050 (Estimates)**

Year	World Population (in Millions)
8000 B.C.	8
4000 B.C.	86
A.D. 1	300
1650	600
1750	800
1810	1,000
1850	1,200
1900	1,680
1930	2,008
1960	3,037
1987	5,000
2000	6,350
2025	8,297
2050	10,000

Sources: Charles B. Nam and Susan Gustavus Philliber, *Population: A Basic Orientation* (2nd ed.). Englewood Cliffs, New Jersey: Prentice-Hall, 1984, pp. 15–21; George Russell et al., "People, People, People." *Time* (August 6, 1984); Paul E. Zopf, Jr., *Population: An Introduction to Social Demography*. Palo Alto, California: Mayfield, 1984, pp. 3–4; Clyde H. Farnsworth, "A Doubling of the World's People to 10 Billion in 2050 Is Predicted." *The New York Times* (July 11, 1985): A1, A4; David Yankey, *Demography: The Study of Human Population*. New York: St. Martin's Press, 1985, pp. 37–42; John R. Weeks, *Population: Introduction to Concepts and Issues*. Belmont, California: Wadsworth, 1986, pp. 52–57.

■ **TABLE 18–2 Geographic Distribution of the World's Population, 1650–2020 (in Millions)**

	World	North America *	Latin America	Africa	Europe *	Asia *	Oceania *
1650	545	1	12	100	103	327	2
1750	728	1	11	95	144	475	2
1850	1,171	26	33	95	274	741	2
1930	2,008	134	110	155	530	1,069	10
1985	4,845	264	406	551	770	2,830	24
2020	7,760	330	752	1,433	871	4,342	32

* North America includes Hawaii; Oceania excludes Hawaii. Europe includes the USSR; Asia excludes the USSR.

Source: John R. Weeks, *Population: Introduction to Concepts and Issues*. Belmont, California: Wadsworth, 1986, p. 69.

the planet Earth. The growth rate of the Earth's population reached a peak in the 1960s, 2.0 percent per year. By the 1980s, this slowed down to 1.7 percent. Still, even at this slower rate, the Earth is adding roughly 83 million people per year to its population. Between 1975 and the year 2000, more than 2 billion new people will be added to the Earth's population—more than the total number of people on Earth in 1930 (Weeks, 1986, pp. 55–58). Thus, even though the population explosion has slowed down greatly in the last two decades, it is a population explosion nonetheless.

Just as important as the total number of people on Earth is the population growth of different areas and nations. As Table 18–2 shows, the growth rate of some continents will continue to be explosive, while that of others will be far more moderate. Between 1985 and 2020, North America's population will grow 25 percent, and Europe's, only 13 percent. However, Latin America's and Africa's populations nearly quadrupled between 1930 and 1985, and between 1985 and the year 2020, Latin America's will increase 85 percent, and Africa's will increase 160 percent. Asia's population more than doubled in the 1930 to 1985 period, and from 1985 to 2020, it will increase over 50 percent. What is the cause of such dramatic increases?

THE DEMOGRAPHIC TRANSITION

■

Prior to the Industrial Revolution of the 1700s, all societies on Earth had very high birth rates and very high death rates. Because birth and death rates were so nearly equal over the long run, populations everywhere tended to increase slowly. The Industrial Revolution promoted medical improvements that drastically cut the death rate, especially the rate of infant mortality. But in the early stages of industrialization, the birth rate continued to be very high. Why the difference? Innovations that reduce the death rate are largely technical and can be carried out by specialists, without regard to cultural attitudes. In any case, most people have reasons to prefer life to death, health to disease. Such medical improvements as better sanitation and smallpox vaccination therefore cut death rates fairly soon after their introduction. Birth rates, however, initially remained high because the decision to have a certain number of children cannot be centralized; it is made by each man and woman. Birth rates thus hang on cultural norms, values, and beliefs, which often promote large families. Even if birth-control methods are available, the people must want to have fewer children. (In agrarian societies, children are an economic asset, because they can work on a farm at an early age.) As societies become more urbanized and industrialized, large families become an economic liability, both to themselves and to society. But this lesson takes several generations to sink in.

For some time, during the early stages of industrialization, the death rate becomes relatively low, while the birth rate continues to be relatively high. During this second phase of the so-called **demographic transition,** industrializing societies experience very rapid population growth—the "population bomb" that exploded in Europe and the United States a century or more ago and is now exploding in Asia, Africa, and Latin America (see Table 18–2). Phase two of the demographic transition hits countries in the early or middle stages of industrialization, or in nonindustrial countries that adopt modern health measures. The birth rate continues to be high, but the death rate continues to fall. The result: still more explosive population growth. In these countries, where birth rates have not yet come into line with death rates, rapidly growing populations outstrip food resources, and many people will starve. As things look now, the situation can only get worse. There is no real hope for improvement during the coming generation.

For mature industrial and postindustrial societies, there is a third phase: a low death rate *and* a low birth rate. The yearly population increase now falls to about 1 percent. Indeed, some industrial nations grow at all only because of in-migration. (The birth rate of the United States is barely below level, but the country continues to grow because of immigration.) The birth rate falls because the married couples of mature industrial and postindustrial societies have fewer children than their ancestors did. Why? In part because of birth control, but mainly because in these societies children are an economic liability, not an

Demographic transition The pattern a society exhibits in population change as a result of industrialization, from having a high birth rate and a high death rate, through having a high birth rate and a falling death rate, to having a low birth rate and a low death rate.

The birth rate of a country is a result of many individuals making choices about their lives. Birth rates depend on cultural norms, values, and beliefs. For a nation to have a low birth rate, many couples must want to have few children. Here, a social worker explains the fundamentals of conception and birth control to a group of Indian wives.
United Nations?ILO

The World's Exploding Population

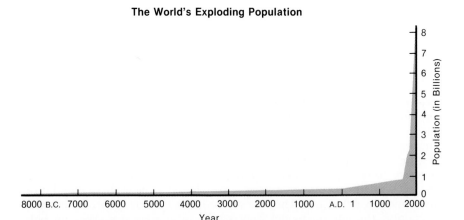

Source: John R. Weeks, *Population*: *Introduction to Concepts and Issues*. Belmont, California: Wadsworth, 1986, p. 53.

asset. The attitudes and values of married couples finally catch up with economic realities. Men no longer require many children as proof of their virility, nor women, as proof of their fertility and devotion to motherhood.

Objections.   This model of the demographic transition may suggest that industrial nations are somehow more virtuous than nonindustrial ones. The truth is that, person-for-person, the industrialized nations use up far more of the Earth's resources—including food—than the less developed ones do. There are no villains in the demographic transition, only victims. And those victims are the starving peoples of the world.

The demographic transition model is basically an accurate description of population dynamics, but it is nonetheless possible that many economically **less developed countries (LDCs)** will never reach phase three, because they will never achieve industrial development. If so, today's less developed societies are not precisely comparable to Western Europe and North America during the past two centuries.

What are the obstacles to industrialization in today's LDCs? One is the fact that their populations grow so rapidly as to wipe out economic gains immediately. Each year, these countries find themselves further and further behind economically—and further and further away from industrial "take off." The birth rate produces a vicious circle: It is so high that population growth remains too high for economic development, and as a result, the birth rate does not fall.

A second problem of industrial development in the LDCs is their status as providers of raw materials and inexpensive labor for multinational industrial corporations. Many companies in the LDCs are controlled and owned by foreigners, citizens of industrial countries. The profits of these companies are exported to the parent countries and do not necessarily enrich the host countries, where the profits were earned.

Another reason many countries of the world will not be able to industrialize in the near future—at least for another generation or so—is their political and military instability. At one time, for instance, Lebanon was a major banking center and the likeliest candidate in the Arab world for rapid economic development. Today, much of Lebanon lies in ruins, lacking government of any kind, while rival foreign armies terrorize

Less developed countries (LDCs) The poorer, less industrialized countries of the world.

The Demographic Transition

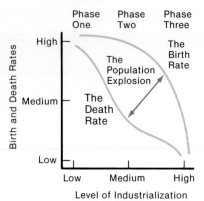

Source: U.S. Department of Commerce, U.S. Bureau of the Census, *Current Population Reports*, *Series P–23*. Washington, D.C.: U.S. Government Printing Office, 1979.

More developed countries (MDCs) The more affluent, more industrialized countries of the world.

one another and the population at large. Today, industrial development in Lebanon is impossible. Unstable political and military conditions in the Middle East, much of Latin America, parts of Africa, and Southeast Asia make industrial development in these "hot spots" almost impossible.

Future Trends. The demographic transition model does, at any rate, provide an excellent description of societies that are already industrialized countries. But it falls down in assuming that all societies will go through all three phases, as Japan, North America, and Europe did. Because the economic, military, and even demographic factors that characterize today's nonindustrial nations are vastly different from those in the West a century or two ago, we should expect their population dynamics to differ, too. The fate of the LDCs cannot be predicted with certainty; the classic model may work—or it may not. We can only predict that things will get worse before they get better. The question is, how much worse?

We do have some recent indications that the world's population growth has slowed down a bit. The 1975 to 1980 world-wide crude birth rate stood at about 28.9 per 1,000 persons. Demographers estimate that the 1985 to 1990 rate will fall to 27.1 per 1,000 persons (Nossiter, 1980). Overall population growth slipped from 1.98 percent per year during the 1965 to 1970 period, to 1.88 during 1975 to 1977 (Reinhold, 1978), and to 1.73 during 1975 to 1980. By the year 2000, some predict an annual growth rate of 1.5 percent (Cowell, 1981).

Smaller families may be coming into fashion even in Asia and Latin America. Contraception is beginning to be used for the first time in some areas of the world, couples are marrying later, and more women are working, which also lowers the birth rate (Ibrahim, 1980). Yet even if the birth rate were to decline drastically—rather than gradually, as seems to be happening—it will take at least several generations before the world's population can be brought into line with its food resources, and the problem will be most acute in the poorest countries. Their citizens will bear the brunt of future population increases and the attendant disasters.

Taken as a whole, the **more developed countries (MDCs)** of the world have a crude birth rate of 15.8, whereas the LDCs have a birth rate nearly twice as high, 31.4. The annual growth rate of the populations of MDCs is under 1 percent—0.62 percent, to be exact. The annual population growth rate of the LDCs is over twice as high—2.04 percent. In 1984, LDCs contained 3.6 billion people, roughly 75 percent of the total world's population, whereas MDCs had about 1.2 billion, or one-quarter. By the year 2000, LDCs will have 4.8 billion people, 79 percent of the total, and MDCs will have less than 1.3 billion, 21 percent. And by the year 2025, LDCs will have 6.8 billion people, 83 percent of the world's total, and the MDCs will have less than 1.4 billion, or 17 percent. Clearly, the differential in birth and population growth rates will shift the world's population more and more in the direction of the less developed third-world nations of the Earth (Bogue, 1985, pp. 14–15).

One last but crucial point about the population explosion: The problem of world hunger is not just a question of population size. In fact, it is largely a question of inequality: the unequal distribution of the world's economic resources, including food. The Earth now grows enough food to nourish its population, and it could grow twice as much food as it now does. The richer nations have not given enough importance to helping the poor ones, or even to saving their people from starvation. And the elites of the LDCs appear to have benefited most from whatever relief efforts have been made, because they, often, have been known to acquire the food supplies from abroad and sell them at a profit.

One solution to the problem of hunger—along with reducing the birth rate drastically—is to bring more land in the LDC under cultivation and to give this land to the poorest peasants, who suffer most from inadequate nutrition. (Less than 60 percent of the world's cultivatable land is now being farmed, according to the United Nations' Food and Agricultural Organization, and only 20 percent is in Africa and Latin America, where the population problem is most severe; (Crittenden, 1981.) More modern and productive farm techniques must be promoted by governments, too, to raise agricultural yields. Right now, however, the problem of hunger seems almost beyond solution. Unfortunately, it is a problem that has many independent causes, not one. All over the world, for some time to come, millions of human beings will be undernourished and millions more will starve.

POPULATION TRENDS

Demographic trends affect us all. Among other things, they mean that some of our current teachers will not find permanent jobs as professors and that you yourself are likely to have much more trouble finding a job than your parents did when they were your age. Demographic trends are also the final result of the activities of millions of individuals, who among them produce large-scale, nation-wide changes. When Bill and Mary Smith complain that their daughter Sally refuses to marry the man she lives with, they may be only dimly aware that hundreds of thousands of Sallys all over the country are doing the same thing. When the apartment building across the street from Mr. and Mrs. Brown, who live in New York City, is destroyed by vandals and then filled by vagrants, alcoholics, and drug addicts, they may not realize that their personal misfortune is mirrored in large cities all over the Northeast and Midwest.

C. Wright Mills (see Chapter 1) distinguished between the "private troubles" of individuals and the "public issues" shared by a whole society, a region, or a social category. Here, individuals have private troubles, but these troubles are also public issues or problems in the big picture. Demography does not look at events taking place in a distant "out there": It studies millions of individual lives, including our own. Often, demographic events happening to us are shared by others who share some of our social statuses. It takes the sociological imagination, as Mills pointed out, to see how what is happening on the individual level is caused by larger social and demographic forces.

Let's take a look at one of the more dramatic demographic changes taking place in this country: the aging of our population (see Chapter 12). In 1970 the median age of all Americans was 28; in 1980 it was 30. Population experts expect it to reach 36 by the year 2000 and 38.4 in 2010. In actual numbers, this country had 15 million more elderly men and women in 1980 than it had a decade earlier. The change has many real-life consequences for everyone in the United States. It puts a strain on government programs, like Social Security and Medicare, designed to assist the elderly. It means that as the school-age population

WHAT DO YOU THINK?

"One Couple, One Child" in China

In 1949, the year of the communist revolution, China's population was 500 million. Early policy toward population control was negative. Chairman Mao declared in 1949: "It is a very good thing that China has a big population. Even if China's population multiplies many times, she is fully capable of finding a solution." And a bit later, he stated: "The absurd theory that increases in food cannot catch up with increases in population, put forth by such Western bourgeois economists as Malthus and company, has not only been refuted by Marxists in theory, but has also been overthrown in practice" in socialist societies. Some China observers believe that this attitude, along with his unwillingness to deal with China's population problem, was the most damaging mistake of Mao's long political career.

In spite of Mao's attitude, China's birth rate and population growth rate did decline in the two decades following the revolution. Still, in 1970, China's growth rate was well over 3 percent per year, and its population, more than 900 million. With nearly a quarter of the Earth's population, it had only 7 percent of the arable land. China had more than four times the number of people the United States did, but only a quarter of the arable land. To the country's population experts, the prospects seemed grim. China's birth rate and population growth threatened to flood the nation with too many mouths to feed. Demographers convinced the politicians that population control was a matter of survival for this land-poor, struggling nation.

In 1979, a radical and controversial policy was adopted: "one couple, one child." In a land where large families were honored, this would not be easy. At first, the policy was loosely enforced. But by 1982, when the population was clearly climbing again, more drastic measures were instituted. Every Chinese belongs to a "unit," a workplace or rural governing body, and every unit has a birth-control committee, headed by officials of the Communist party. The vast majority of all decisions require their approval—who gets housing space, who can grow cash crops, who is allowed to go to college, even who can marry. The birth-control committee makes sure that couples follow state and party policy with respect to birth control. If they refuse, peer pressure is applied. If that doesn't work, reprisals follow. They can be fined and fired from their jobs; their valuables and land can be confiscated.

When a couple has one child, the state strictly requires that an intrauterine device be inserted in the woman. Today, some 70 million IUDs are used in China, half of all those in the world. In addition, if a couple has succeeded in having more than one child, one member must be sterilized. Women who become pregnant after having one child are required to have abortions. In one province, abortion "posses" search the countryside for pregnant women, who are caught, handcuffed, and delivered to a clinic for forced abortions. Abortion is an important means of birth control in China. There were 53 million abortions there between 1979 and 1984, approximately the population of France. In 1983 alone, there were 14.4 million abortions in China. In one not atypical province, one-fifth of the abortions performed in 1984 took place in the

The Chinese government has vigorously enforced a "one couple-one child" policy as a brake on its population growth. This has worked until very recently, when the birth rate began to rise again.

United Nations

■ **TABLE 18–3 Population Projections for the World's Ten Most Populous Nations (in Millions)**

	2000	2025	2050	2100	Total Fertility Rate, 1984 *
China	1,196	1,409	1,450	1,462	2.173
India	995	1,311	1,518	1,639	4.637
Soviet Union	306	339	358	376	2.335
United States	259	286	288	289	1.846
Indonesia	212	284	332	358	4.214
Brazil	181	243	279	299	3.816
Nigeria	169	329	471	593	6.902
Bangladesh	157	266	357	434	6.300
Pakistan	140	229	302	361	5.840
Japan	128	132	129	128	1.710

* "Total fertility rate" is the number of children women have, on average, during their entire lifetimes.

Source: The New York Times (July 29, 1984): E3.)

third trimester, when many fetuses are viable. Doctors have an obligation to make certain that a baby emerging from the womb of a woman with one child does not live.

This drastic policy has worked. Today, China's growth rate is just over 1 percent a year, less than half of what it was in 1970. China's total fertility rate—the average number of children that women have—among the ten largest nations on Earth is higher only than that of the United States and Japan, and lower than that of the Soviet Union. If present trends continue, China's population will level off at roughly 1.4 billion by 2025, whereas most of the other LDCs of the world will continue growing at a rate that will be devastating to their own well-being (see Table 18–3).

Is China's drastic policy of birth control humane? Is it moral? One Chinese health official declared: "It's more humane to kill children before they are born than to bring them into a society of too many people. . . . If you consider the serious difficulties overpopulation creates for people living today, the moral problem of abortion isn't too serious."

There are indications that this seemingly monolithic policy is not quite as strict as it appears on the surface. While couples in the cities are rigidly held to one child, "the rules are much more flexible for the nearly 80 percent of the population in rural areas. A rural couple that gives birth to a girl can usually get permission to try again for a boy. The strict curbs also do not apply to ethnic minorities" (Kristof, 1987, p. A8).

In addition, it became clear in the mid-to-late 1980s that the more-or-less stringent enforcement of China's "one couple, one child" policy began to be relaxed; her birth rate was once again on the rise. In 1985, China's birth rate was 17.8; in 1986, it rose to 20.8.

Family planning controls, "while still vigorous, have been moderated somewhat in the last few years" (Kristof, 1987, p. A8). One reason that is commonly cited is that China has become sensitive to international criticism. The sorts of incidents described above have "aroused indignation in the West and led the United States to cut off support for United Nations population programs, which play a role in China" (Kristoff, 1987, p. A1).

In addition, the general population has become more prosperous in the past two or three years than ever before in China's history. As a consequence, many couples are now able to pay the fines imposed by the government for the "crime" of violating its birth control policies. A Western diplomat overheard a conversation between two friends in a beauty parlor; said one, "I have one child, but I want another. And now I have the money to pay the fine" (Kristof, 1987, p. A8).

The recent trend has demographers and diplomats worried. On the one hand, a rise in China's population may wipe out the nation's recent economic gains and cut into future progress. On the other hand, if Chinese politicians and administrators realize this, it may result in another harsh crackdown.

Clearly, the Chinese are facing a dilemma.

What do you think of China's "one couple, one child policy"? How would you solve this dilemma?

Sources: W. Sexton, 1983, Part II, pp. 4–5; "Tradition Slows China Bid to Curb Births," 1983, Ideas Section, pp. 1, 10; Weiskopf, 1985, Part II, pp. 4, 5, 16; Kristof, 1987, pp. A1, A8.

of the United States goes down (from 58 million in 1970 to 51 million in 1980) facilities designed to serve the young must be closed. It means that the proportion of women in our population is rising, because women live longer than men. (In 1910, there were 106 American men for every 100 American women; by 1950, 98.6 men for every 100 women; and in 1980, 94.4 men for every 100 women.) There are three women for every two men aged 65 and older, and more than two women for every man 85 and older (Herbers, 1981).

As Table 18–4 shows, the over-65-year-old segment of the American population will grow dramatically in the years to come. There were 26 million older Americans counted in the 1980 United States census. By 2050, this older age segment will have increased its number by two and a half times, to 67 million. Their proportion in the total population will have doubled—from 11 to 22 percent. The number of young Americans, in contrast, will decline. In 1980, there were 94 million under-25 Americans, and they made up 41 percent of the population. By 2050, there will be only 90 million of them, and their proportion will decrease to 29 percent. The age segment from 25 to 44 will increase slightly in number, from 63 to 77 million, but in proportion, they will drop slightly, from 28 to 25 percent. The next-to-oldest age segment, 45 to 64, will increase their absolute number from 44 to 74 million, and they will increase their proportion from 20 to 24 percent. Clearly, the American population is aging significantly. Over time, there will be more and more old people and fewer and fewer young ones in the United States.

These numbers and proportions affect people's lives. Elderly widows and divorcees—even single women in their 30s and 40s—have a difficult time finding male companionship. Of course, not all elderly women are looking to get married; elderly men, however, are proportionately more likely to be interested in marriage, because they often want to be taken care of by women. But because the number of elderly men is relatively small, those older women who do wish to marry find the competition for the few available men very stiff. Married elderly women not uncommonly think, "If I were to die tomorrow, there would be twenty women or more on my doorstep, after my husband, the next day." According to the U.S. Bureau of the Census (1976), more than twice as many widowed men as women in their 70s remarried. The explanation is strictly demographic.

Another part of our social lives influenced by the upward age shift is the marketing and advertising of goods and services. From the 1950s through the 1970s, most products were aimed at the "youth market" created by the baby boom. With the gradual aging of our population,

■ **TABLE 18–4 Population of the United States by Age, 1980–2025 (in Millions)**

	All Ages	Age Under 25 Number	Percent	Age 25–44 Number	Percent	Age 45–64 Number	Percent	Age 65 or older Number	Percent
1980	228	94	41	63	28	44	20	26	11
1990	250	90	36	81	33	46	19	32	13
2000	268	92	34	80	30	61	23	35	13
2025	301	92	31	78	26	72	24	59	20
2050	309	90	29	77	25	74	24	67	22

Source: Stanley Kranczer, "United States Population Outlook." *Statistical Bulletin* (January–March, 1984), p. 17.

The number and proportion of specific segments of any population affects the entire society. Here, we see one consequence of the aging of American society: a huge retirement community, Sun City in Arizona.

Georg Gerster/Photo Researchers

more and more products are designed for the over-30 set. In the early 1980s, for instance, Levi Strauss and Company introduced a new style of jeans, cut a bit fuller in the seat and the thighs to allow for middle-age "settling." Skin-care products that claim to promote younger-looking skin—and that are therefore bought by older women—now sell better than they used to. The "Pepsi Generation," to judge from past ads, used to consist chiefly of 15 to 25 year olds. Today, Pepsi's ads include models aged 15 to 75. Johnson's Baby Shampoo, Baby Oil, and Baby Powder are all now used chiefly by adults. Even the candy market is being geared mainly to adult consumers (Span, 1981). Again, the explanations are strictly demographic.

URBANIZATION

The emergence and growth of cities—a process called **urbanization**—is among the most basic and important of all demographic processes. What is a city? Experts define a city as a large settlement with a high population concentration (Fischer, 1984, p. 24). Thus, two defining criteria are absolutely essential to the definition: the size of, or number of people in, a settlement, and how densely settled it is, how closely together the people live. It is difficult to imagine a city without these two criteria. Some commentators include a third criterion, as well: heterogeneity. Cities contain people who may be quite different from one another—in terms of income, ethnicity and race, occupation, age, and so on. According to this criterion, for example, an enormous university campus cannot be regarded as a city because, even though it may contain tens of thousands of people living in close proximity to one another, its residents are too similar to one another in age to qualify. There is just not enough diversity and heterogeneity on a large campus to make a university a true city (Choldin, 1985, pp. 45, 48).

Behind this seemingly simple definition—size, density, heterogeneity—lurks a great deal of diversity. Cities are not all alike; there is enormous variability from one to the other. Some are huge; others, though larger than villages, are relatively small. Some are rich, world centers

Urbanization The emergence of cities and their growth over many centuries.

of commerce and banking. Others are so poor that beggars die in their streets by the thousands each day. Some have broad, paved streets. Others have crooked, cobblestone streets, barely wide enough for donkey-drawn carts to pass through. In some, violence is a routine and expected daily event; in others, violence rarely occurs, and residents feel safe and secure. In spite of all this variability, however, cities do have certain characteristics in common that more rural areas lack. It is on these characteristics that the remainer of this chapter focuses.

The Emergence of Cities

People have lived in more-or-less permanent settlements for only 2 per-cent of our existence, and in real cities (as opposed to small villages) for only half of this relatively brief duration (Fischer, 1984, p. 3). The most important precondition for the emergence of large permanent set-tlements that do not produce their own food was the development of agriculture, and the economic surplus that resulted from it. Hunting and gathering economies can support fewer than one person per square mile. Even primitive farming on fairly fertile soil can support some thirty people per square mile. Agriculture thus permits larger, denser communities. In the Middle East, in Pakistan (the Indus River valley), and in northern China, archaeologists have uncovered cities that are about 6,000 years old. Cities did not emerge in the New World until much later, which shows that agriculture is a necessary, but not a suffi-cient, condition for them. Cities did not emerge in Europe until some 4,000 years ago.

The earliest permanent settlements were not cities but agricultural villages with a cluster of dwellings at the center of fields that radiated out like spokes on a bicycle wheel. These small agricultural communities increased in size and variety and, in time, became cities. Greater size permitted greater differentiation and elaboration in the division of labor. A greater and greater agricultural surplus permitted a larger and larger population base, including an increase in the number of people who did not directly participate in the growing of food. The largest of the most ancient cities held some 20,000 inhabitants. Cities of 20,000 inhabit-ants made a great deal of occupational and social diversity possible. Social classes now emerged, as did the use of metals. Cities became trading centers and stored grain from the surrounding countryside. Most cities were walled, to protect their inhabitants from the barbarians with-out. Still, all of the ancient cities were attacked both by nomadic people and other cities. The last such invasion of nomads—the Mongols—took place only about 800 years ago. Until then, urban life was always fragile.

The tiny cities of antiquity—Rome, the largest of them, had some half a million inhabitants—accounted for only a fraction of the human race. Even by 1800, according to United Nations' estimates, only 2 per-cent of the world's people lived in communities of 20,000 or more people. By 1850, it was 4 percent; by 1900, it had doubled again, to 9 percent. Half a century later, in 1950, 21 percent of the world's peoples lived in cities. If current trends continue, almost four out of ten of the Earth's inhabitants will live in cities of 20,000 or more by the year 2000 (Cousins and Nagpaul, 1979, p. 6). For the past two centuries, the world-wide trend has been very strongly in the direction of greater urbanization, largely as a result of the agricultural and industrial revolutions. Prein-dustrial cities, moreover, were much smaller than cities became after the beginnings of industrialization. In ancient societies, it took some seventy-five farmers to produce enough food to support one city dweller.

With the rise in agricultural productivity that occurred from the 1600s onward, one farmer could feed many city dwellers. Meanwhile, the factory system made it more convenient for industries to concentrate in cities, where labor was plentiful and cheap.

Today, however, most rapidly growing cities are found in the nonindustrialized nations. The largest cities of industrial and postindustrial societies have mostly reached their peak and are growing slowly or not at all. Some are even shrinking. Because most of today's predominantly agricultural societies do not produce food efficiently—they need several farmers to support one city dweller—they cannot feed their large urban populations. Malnutrition and starvation are rife among the new urban migrants, who come to these cities, ironically, in hopes of finding economic opportunity and instead find hunger and unemployment rates that are sometimes higher than 50 percent. A high proportion of these new urban residents live in "squatter's settlements"—wood or tin huts without running water or sanitary facilities. Despite these conditions, such cities continue to grow.

URBAN ECOLOGY

In the field of biology, **ecology** studies the relationship of organisms to one another and to their environment. Sociology has borrowed the ecological model in order to study the relationships among people and institutions living and working in specific physical environments. For instance, settlements are more likely to be built at sea level than at the top of a mountain, in temperate climates than at the North Pole, near water than in the middle of deserts. Over time, settlements are connected by commerce and other forms of communication, and these ties create relationships among them.

Within particular cities, moreover, people tend to be distributed in distinct patterns. No city is populated evenly or randomly. In all cities, some areas are specialized for commerce, for industry, for housing, and so on. Some neighborhoods are poor; others are well-to-do. Some neighborhoods house transient populations; others have been inhabited by the same families for generations. A city's "skid row" is more likely to be located in certain kinds of neighborhoods than in others. Its high-rise apartments are built in one area; its single-family dwellings in another. **Urban ecology** studies such patterns in the spatial relationships among a city's districts.

Urban ecologists are interested in the three basic urban processes they call centralization and dispersal, degree of segregation (or specialization), and invasion and succession.

"Centralization" means the tendency, in many cities, for people and institutions to be packed into a central, or downtown, area: "dispersal" is the tendency, in certain other cities, for people and institutions to be scattered all over the city. Both are a matter of degree. Some cities (like New York) are relatively centralized: A densely populated central area forms the core from which less densely populated areas radiate. Other cities (like Los Angeles) are more dispersed, with no identifiable "downtown" area.

"Segregation" is the tendency of certain people and institutions to congregate in specific areas. Chicago, for instance, is quite a racially

Ecology The study of the physical and geographical interrelationships among groups, neighborhoods, and social categories in a given environment, such as a city.

Urban ecology The study of spatial relationships among people and institutions in cities.

492

segregated city; San Francisco is much more racially integrated. Likewise, New York is a city with specialized institutions located in distinct neighborhoods—the financial district on and about Wall Street, the theater district just north of Times Square, the publishing industry in Midtown, and so on.

"Invasion" and "succession" are concepts that describe changes in a city's physical spacing, and in relationships among people and institutions, often according to identifiable patterns. For instance, the Lower East Side of Manhattan was once peopled mainly by Jewish immigrants; today, it is made up mainly of Blacks and Puerto Ricans. What is now called the SoHo (South of Houston Street) district of Manhattan once had almost nothing but warehouses and small factories; today, it is home to hundreds of artists and dozens of fashionable art galleries. All urban areas and neighborhoods change, sometimes dramatically. Urban ecologists study the dynamic quality of cities.

Urban ecologists have devised three basic models or theories to explain the centralization, segregation, and invasion and succession of cities. The **concentric-zone model** (Park, Burgess, and McKenzie, 1925) argues that cities develop into a series of concentric zones, much like an archery target. The central business district, with its large shops and stores, offices, banks, bus and train stations, and government buildings, is located in the bull's eye. The second circle is called the "zone in transition." Once a neighborhood for well-to-do people, this area comes to attract the poor and homeless, transients, and criminals. Rooming houses, light industry, and "greasy-spoon" diners abound in this area, which is a neighborhood in name only, because it lacks the qualities essential for a true community. The third zone houses stable working-class homes. The fourth zone has more affluent families, most of them homeowners. Beyond the fourth zone lie heavy-manufacturing and outlying business districts and the suburbs. Today, most urban ecologists recognize that this pattern is inaccurate.

The **sector model** (Hoyt, 1939) of urban development argues that a city generates "sectors," or wedge-shaped areas that grow out from its central core, usually along transportation routes, such as highways and railroads. This model rejects the idea that concentric circles completely surround a downtown area. Moreover, it assumes that specialization is not determined solely by an area's distance from a city's central business district. Instead, the sector model suggests that areas can retain a specialized and distinct character in one direction from the central business district. This sector pattern, too, is not universal, but it is more common than the concentric-zone model.

Concentric-zone model In urban ecology, the view (now obsolete) that cities develop into a series of concentric zones, much like an archery target, each with its own specialized function, people, and institutions.

Sector model In urban ecology, the view that cities generate "sectors," or wedge-shaped areas that grow out from their central core, usually along transportation lines.

The third theory of urban development is the **multiple-nuclei model** (Harris and Ullman, 1945), which focuses on many minor centers developing all over a city, not on a single downtown business district. Each center is itself the focus of an area's specialized activity, and such areas are scattered all over a city. One district might specialize in heavy manufacturing, another in light manufacturing, a third in business and commerce, a fourth in entertainment, and so on. This model, like its rivals, works better for some cities than for others.

Contemporary urban ecologists (Berry and Kasarda, 1977; Hawley, 1981; Exline, Peters, and Larkins, 1982), have developed much more sophisticated models, which take into consideration more factors than those early efforts did. Since the end of World War II, our large Eastern and Midwestern cities have declined in population and lost much industry, and commerce. By contrast, the sprawling Sun Belt cities of the South and West have gained both population and business. Moreover, today's cities, all over the country, are being thoroughly decentralized: People and institutions are spreading out beyond city limits. The traditional models of urban development were written before these trends had emerged. Today's urban ecologists realize that a city's economic and social lives are influenced by forces that extend even beyond its suburbs; the "fringes of many of the nation's urban regions have now pushed one hundred miles and more from the traditional city centers." Cities are less and less likely to have central business districts; downtown retailing and manufacturing become less important over time (Berry and Kasarda, 1977, pp. 266–267). Many cities have spread so far that our urban areas are becoming linked to one another in structures vaster and more complex than the early urban ecologists could ever have imagined.

Multiple-nuclei model In urban ecology, the theory that cities develop minor, specialized, geographically scattered centers, rather than a single downtown area.

URBANISM AS A WAY OF LIFE

The early sociologist Max Weber (see Chapter 1) wrote that almost none of the world's greatest religious prophets grew up in a large urban center. They spent their early years in the provinces, the hinterlands, the small towns, and the backwater areas. City dwellers, wrote Weber, become sophisticated and indifferent and lose their capacity for wonder and outrage. Rural people have a more absolute sense of morality, and when they stand face-to-face with corruption and evil, they are more likely to preach a gospel of righteousness. Since Sodom and Gomorrah were destroyed by fire and brimstone, the cities and their people have been regarded as corrupt, decadent, and ungodly. In any case, throughout human history, city dwellers have thought different thoughts and lived different lives from the thoughts and lives of country people. What is it about living in large, dense, diverse communities that influences behavior and belief?

In the first place, the so-called urban lifestyle does not arise automatically. Urban and rural life are different, but not everyone who lives in a city is urbane. Cities create a potential for a certain set of values and lifestyle, but these are not dictated by the cities. In fact, it has been argued that, before industrialization, life in most cities was not radically different from life in the surrounding rural areas. In the preindustrial city, social relationships were based on kinship networks: Who you were depended on your family background. Class lines were very rigid, and there was almost no social mobility. City governments were despotic, and different religious, ethnic, and occupational groups were forced to live in different areas of the city, even separated by walls. Certain groups (like the Jews) did not have full legal or political rights. In many preindustrial cities, such as those of ancient Greece and Rome, slaveholding was common. The preindustrial city was vastly different, sociologically, from contemporary industrial urban centers (Sjoberg, 1960).

Even today, many people living in urban areas are "rural" in outlook and behavior. Despite these "urban villagers" (Gans, 1962), urban people do tend to be different. How—and why?

Community and Society

Gemeinschaft A type of society or social setting characterized by intimacy, informality, closeness, strong emotion, cooperation, and common values and goals.

Gesellschaft A type of society or social setting characterized by formality, emotional reserve, superficial, segmental relations between individuals, and an indifference to community values and goals.

Ferdinand Tönnies (1855–1936), one of the earliest sociologists, pioneered the study of rural-urban differences. He characterized two contrasting types of social structures—in German, called **Gemeinschaft** and **Gesellschaft.** Tönnies was born in a small town in a pastoral area in northern Germany. As he was growing up, he saw the area transformed into a more and more urban setting. The changes he himself witnessed led to his classic *Community and Society* (1957, originally published in 1887). The *Gemeinschaft* (community) type of social structure—note that the word comes from the German root, *gemein*, "in common"—is characteristic of rural areas. People are bound together by a spirit of unity, intimacy, cooperation, and common values and goals. Very often, ties of kinship and family form strong bonds between local residents. Social relations tend to be informal and comfortable, yet also deep and strong. Social control works through interpersonal mechanisms—gossip and face-to-face encouragement, for example. People conform to one another's expectations because they care very much about how others feel about them.

As the size of the community increases, the people living in it have less and less in common. *Gemeinschaft* becomes weaker and weaker, and a new type of social structure emerges: *Gesellschaft* or "society." The *Gesellschaft* is based on people's differences. A large city is the characteristic *Gesellschaft* setting. Most of those we meet are either strangers or people with whom we have only superficial, limited relationships.

Sociologists recognize that urban and rural life tend to be radically different. Cities generate a "Gesellschaft" type of existence, characterized by emotional reserve, impersonality, individualism, and superficial, limited relations among people, while country life is characterized by its opposite, "Gemeinschaft," or intimate, face-to-face togetherness.

Van Bucher/Photo Researchers

Most interaction in cities is impersonal and emotionally reserved. People tend to be highly individualistic and indifferent to community goals and values. Because different beliefs and behavior patterns flourish in cities and because most city people don't care how strangers feel about them, formal mechanisms of social control become necessary—the police, the courts, and jails. Gossip, ridicule, persuasion, and personal encouragement are no longer sufficient. In a *Gesellschaft*, individuals do not belong to a close-knit group and community simply by being born into one. They must find and create social bonds—or go without them altogether—so many city dwellers feel isolated, lonely, and alienated.

The Urban Mentality

Tönnies's work spawned a great deal of sociological research and writing on rural-urban differences. One of the most well-known and influential of these efforts was an essay called "The Metropolis and Mental Life," by Tönnies's fellow German sociologist, Georg Simmel (1858–1918). Simmel (1950, pp. 409–424; originally published in 1902–1903) described the urban mentality as a combination of three basic traits: emotional reserve; an attachment to personal freedom; and a willingness to seek out and reward extreme individuality.

Emotion reserve, or indifference, is a self-protective device, wrote Simmel. The tempo of urban life is so fast, and the images that bombard city dwellers are so diverse, that they must maintain a certain emotional distance from this sensory onslaught. Residents of cities learn to react with their minds, not their hearts. "The reaction to metropolitan phenomena," Simmel argued, "is shifted to that organ which is least sensitive and quite remote from the depth of personality. Intellectuality is thus seen to preserve subjective life against the overwhelming power of metropolitan life" (Simmel, 1950, p. 411).

Individual freedom, the second quality of the urban mentality, stems from the absence in cities of the many "narrow circles" that bind small-town people. This freedom flows directly from the emotional indifference of urban men and women, because the mutual care and concern of rural areas are seen by metropolites as mere "pettiness and prejudice." Freedom has a good and a bad side, however; emotional indifference can create loneliness and despair.

The third trait of metropolitan life, extreme individuality, stems from the need, in cities, to offer something new and different to attract social attention. Buried in a vast community, the would-be celebrity must display some outstanding or unusual quality to be noticed. Metropolitan life encourages "extravagances of mannerism, caprice, and preciousness" (Simmel, 1950, p. 421).

Another influential and now-classic essay strongly influenced by Tönnies's original distinction between urban and rural life was Louis Wirth's "Urbanism as a Way of Life" (1938), probably the most often quoted publication on the subject of urbanization. Wirth emphasized the size, density, and heterogeneity of cities. These characteristics produce a distinctive style of social relationships. Interpersonal interaction in the city tends to be "impersonal, superficial, transitory, and segmental." City dwellers deal in a strictly utilitarian way with most people they meet. What can you do for me? That is the question. In fact, Wirth argued, cities tend to encourage predatory activity: attempts to exploit others. City people are connected to one another by only the most "fragile," "tenuous," and "volatile" of ties. Under these circumstances, "personal disorganization, mental breakdown, suicide, deliquency, crime, corruption, and disorder" become far more prevalent in cities than in rural communities.

Contemporary Views of Urban Life

Contemporary views of urban life are less negative. The early sociologists, like Tönnies, Simmel, and Wirth, were struck by the differences between the swiftly declining rural culture and the exploding metropolis—an explosion they themselves witnessed. From today's vantage point, these early portraits seem exaggerated. No one doubts that urban life is different from rural life. But contemporary sociologists point out that most city dwellers seek out and find oases of personal intimacy and emotional warmth. Relations with others may be largely superficial, but it is still quite possible to have many intimate relationships in a city. Urban life is marked by an ebb and flow between intimacy and impersonality, not by a uniform impersonality.

City people adopt a characteristic style of socializing to combat the city's atomizing influence. One aspect of this style is the growth of voluntary associations. More than rural areas, large cities generate clubs, groups, and organizations that create bonds of intimacy among members. Besides, in many cities, neighborhoods create bonds of closeness no less strong than those in rural areas.

The model that Tönnies, Wirth, and other early sociologists adopted in characterizing the transition from rural to urban life is specific to Western nations. Cities in Asia, Africa, and Latin America retain a more *Gemeinschaft*-type of flavor than those in Europe and North America.

The classic rural-urban model assumes that city life generates a certain kind of mentality, including a sense of rootlessness and alienation. This perspective ignores the possibility that these features of city life are really generated in the countryside. Perhaps, after all, the people who migrate to cities felt rootless and alienated even in the country. Rural life was neither so peaceful nor so close-knit as these early sociologists argued. Their own nostalgia comes through in their writings more than actual conditions in the past do.

What Makes City People Different? Three Views

Hardly any visitor from a smaller, less densely settled area to a city—practically any city that has ever existed—has failed to remark on the differences between urban and rural dwellers. City folk are usually characterized as more sophisticated, more tolerant of deviance and diversity, more prone to engage in unconventional behavior, less traditional, more intellectual, more impersonal, more emotionally reserved, more interpersonally estranged from one another, less open, less helpful and friendly to their neighbors, more aloof, more calculating, more quick-paced, more irritable, more uptight, and less easygoing than their rural counterparts. On these traits, there seems to be a fair degree of consensus. Throughout human history and all around the globe, rural visitors to cities have characterized their urban brethren in these terms.

But what makes for these differences? Why do city folk tend to be different? Three views attempt to explain these widely observed differences.

- Determinist theory argues that population size and density change the way people live and think, and ultimately their personalities, mostly for the worse.

- Compositional theory argues that it isn't cities that change people, but the people who migrate to cities that make cities different.
- Subcultural theory offers a blend of the preceding two theories; it argues that, independently, urbanism and composition make city life different.

Determinist theory—that urban life changes people's outlook and behavior—is associated with the views of Louis Wirth, which we discussed earlier. In order to survive in the city, people have to deal with their environment in a certain way. Indifference and aloofness are survival mechanisms ensuring that urban dwellers not be flooded with demands on their time, attention, and emotions. In addition, urban dwellers' lives are fragmented into bits and pieces. The people they see at work are not the ones they see in the community, who, in turn, are not the ones they see in leisure activities, and so on. Each social circle has only a small, narrow hold. Integration among the many only partly overlapping circles is formal and weak. Social ties are shredded; people are estranged from one another in city life. Consensus and communal harmony do not exist. People respond to such a social arrangement by casting off tradition, rejecting conventionality, and suffering psychic stress.

Compositional theory holds that urban life itself has no effect on personality or orientation. Cities don't change people, this perspective argues. Urban factors such as size, density, and heterogeneity have very little effect on social life. Compositionalists argue that it is the social characteristics of urban dwellers—their ages, races, socioeconomic statuses, occupations, educations, marital and family statuses, sexes, and so on—that give social life in the city its distinctive stamp. For instance, some cities have a lopsided sex ratio, with many more men than women. Generally, such cities have higher rates of crime, especially assaults and other violent behavior. It is the sex ratio that determines this, not the nature of urban life, because men are more likely to commit criminal and violent acts than women, especially if they are isolated from female companionship. Cities with a high proportion of affluent, highly educated residents will support cultural and artistic institutions and give a city an intellectual flavor, whereas cities whose residents are poor and uneducated will be disinclined to do so.

Subcultural theory attempts to blend these two perspectives. It agrees with the compositional school in asserting that a city's social composition influences its social life. And it agrees with the determinist school in arguing that urban characteristics (size, density, heterogeneity) influence social life in the city. But subcultural theory argues that rather than shredding and destroying social groups and ties, as the determinist perspective claims, city life actually strengthens them. Rather than considering urban life to be alienating, anomic, and emotionally cold, subcultural theory considers it to be teeming with intimate social interaction. Cities support the emergence and vitality of distinctive subcultures. How? The key concept in subcultural theory is that of the **critical mass:** the number of people necessary to sustain a given type of social group or organization. For each type of group or social organization, a certain number of people is necessary to form it and keep it going. In small communities, it is unlikely that enough people interested in engaging in a certain activity or forming a certain type of group can be found. The larger the community, the greater the likelihood that enough people can be found. Thus, cities sustain intimate social relations, they do not corrode them:

Determinist theory A perspective urban sociologists use to explain why city life is different from life in less settled areas; it argues that the general characteristics of cities—specifically, size, density, and heterogeneity—determine what social life in urban areas will be.

Compositional theory A perspective urban sociologists use to explain why city life is different from life in less settled areas; it argues that the social characteristics of people in cities generally, and in certain cities specifically, give them their distinctive flavor—and not the qualities that all cities share (size, density, and heterogeneity).

Subcultural theory A perspective urban sociologists use to explain why city life is different from life in less settled areas; it argues that cities sustain groups, institutions, and organizations that are not viable in smaller communities because of the sizes of their populations. See **Critical mass.**

Critical mass The size of community must reach to support a certain type of institution, group, or organization. See **Subcultural theory.**

For example, let us suppose that one in every 1,000 persons is intensively interested in modern dance. In a small town of 5,000 that means there would be, on the average, five such persons, enough to do little else than engage in conversation about dance. But a city of one million would have 1,000—enough to support studios, occasional ballet performances, local meeting places, and a special social milieu. Their activity would probably draw other people beyond the original 1,000 into the subculture. . . . The same general process of critical mass operates for artists, academics, bohemians, corporate executives, criminals, computer programmers—as well as for ethnic and racial minorities (Fischer, 1984, p. 37).

Subcultural theory holds that many of the more unusual interests and inclinations that people have cannot be satisfied in a rural or a small town locale. Moreover, people are more socially isolated, at least with respect to developing social relations based on these interests and inclinations, in small communities than in larger ones. It is only a larger community, which has a critical mass of like-minded individuals, that allows individuals to interact with others on the basis of these somewhat unusual interests and inclinations.

URBANIZATION IN THE UNITED STATES: PAST, PRESENT, AND FUTURE

In 1640, the population of New Amsterdam (whose name was changed in 1664 to New York) was 400; Boston had 1,200 inhabitants. By 1730, New York had grown to some 8,000 inhabitants, Boston to 13,000. In 1820 only twelve cities in the United States had populations of 10,000 or more (Cousins and Nagpaul, 1979, p. 72).

Today, three-quarters of the American people live in communities of 25,000 or more. More than half of all Americans live on only 1 percent of this country's land mass. In less than two centuries, the United States has changed from a country whose people were 90 percent rural to a country of urbanites—three-quarters of our whole population. That transformation came in three stages: (1) preindustrial; (2) urban-industrial; and (3) metropolitan (Gist and Fava, 1974, pp. 56–62).

The preindustrial period stretched from this country's first settlement, in the early 1600s, until just before the Civil War, which began in 1861. The majority of our population was made up of country people, mostly farmers. Our cities were small, and most of the important ones were Eastern seaports. These preindustrial cities were not congested, nor were residential, business, and official districts separated from one another. Cities were small enough for a person to walk comfortably from end to end. Public services—like firefighting, police protection, sewage and garbage disposal, and water supply—were mostly provided privately, by profit-making companies or by volunteers, not by the municipal government.

During the urban-industrial period of the nineteenth century, the number of farmers and other country people declined, the proportion of our population living in cities rose, and our largest cities grew dramatically. Cities of 100,000 and even a million emerged on our shores. Water transport declined in importance during this period, and railroads became the chief means of moving goods and people. As a result, large cities sprang up in the hinterlands. Industrialization took over, and, along with it, the factory system. Specific neighborhoods in the industrial cities took on a specialized character; certain areas within each of them became devoted to manufacturing, residence, retailing, and administration, respectively. Public transportation emerged to carry people to and from these different and sometimes distant areas. Municipal government assumed responsibility for public services, including education, sanitation, water, welfare, and fire and police forces. Cities became far more crowded; large apartment houses were built. It was within this period (more specifically, from 1880 to 1924) that the vast majority of European immigrants arrived on our shores.

There was no clear dividing line between the urban-industrial and metropolitan periods, but the latter was in full swing after World War II, which ended in 1945. The urban-industrial period parallels the shift of the American labor force from the industrial sector to the service sector (see Chapter 17). The Interstate Highways System was built in the 1950s, and trucks and automobiles replaced railroads as the prime means of transporting goods and people. The areas within and around our larger cities became totally "filled in" by the urban sprawl, and the suburbs assumed increasing importance. Middle-income families fled to them, leaving the cities to the poor, to minorities, to the unconventional, and to people rich enough to protect themselves from the city's problems. The suburbs became sociologically, economically, culturally, and economically linked with cities. Areas of the city deteriorated. Build-

The newer cities of the South and West are large and sprawling, with centers that are far less densely populated than are those of Eastern and Midwestern cities. These newer cities depend upon the automobile. The layout of Los Angeles, depicted here, shows this tendency.

Georg Gerster/Photo Researchers

ings, even entire blocks, were abandoned, vandalized, demolished. Whole neighborhoods died. Much industry and many retail stores relocated in the suburbs to avoid crowding, high taxes, rents, and crime rates. Municipal services declined in quality, especially public transportation. The city's tax base declined, and the viability of municipal governments became more and more questionable. Municipal borders between the city and surrounding communities became increasingly meaningless for all practical purposes—except politics, including taxation.

This pattern of urban decline and decay was not duplicated by the cities of the Sun Belt. From 1970 to 1980, every large city east of the Mississippi River, except for Indianapolis and Columbus, Ohio, lost population. By contrast, all of the largest cities in the West except San Francisco and Seattle gained population. By 1981, Los Angeles had overtaken Chicago as the nation's second-largest city, and Houston had passed Philadelphia as the fourth largest. With the oil glut of the mid-1980s, some Sun Belt cities dependent on an oil economy, like Houston, slipped somewhat in population.

The "new" cities of the South and West have been described as "the cities of the future." Instead of the classic pattern—a congested downtown area, with less and less densely concentrated areas radiating out from it—the Sun Belt cities simply sprawl out from a center that is itself a suburb in all but name. "Drives through these cities seem endless," two urban specialists comment, "and that is the point." These cities are best appreciated "through the windshield of an automobile. Newer cities, raised to adulthood in the automobile age, exhibit the spatially dispersed patterns of . . . nothing more than super suburbs" (Goldfield and Brownell, 1979, p. 397). In fact, many of the largest cities of the West—Los Angeles, for instance—are less densely populated than

Demographers and urban geographers and sociologists hold that the entire area from Boston's northern suburbs through Rhode Island, Connecticut, the New York metropolitan area, northern New Jersey, Philadelphia, Delaware, and Baltimore, right down to Washington, is becoming a single unbroken urban area—a megalopolis they call "Bowash."

Ann McQueen/Stock, Boston

many Eastern suburbs. The Western cities that have lost population—San Francisco and Seattle, for example—do not have this "suburban" layout.

In fact, this same process of suburbanization is taking place in the East and the Midwest, but in a somewhat different form. Although the Northern cities are losing population, the areas between these cities—including their suburbs—are becoming so densely populated that boundaries become fuzzier and fuzzier. This suburbanization of America's cities marks the fourth phase in their historical development: the coming of the **megalopolis** (Gist and Fava, 1974, pp. 91–94). The large cities' outer rings, which include shopping malls and large apartment buildings, begin to overlap with those of nearby cities. As a result, there are no real rural areas between them, just densely populated urban areas alternating with somewhat less densely populated urban areas. The suburbs become increasingly urbanized, and the spaces between cities actually become continuous zones.

One such area is called "Bowash" by demographers, urban sociologists, and geographers. It includes the entire zone from Boston's northern suburbs, through Rhode Island, Connecticut, the New York metropolitan area, northern New Jersey, Philadelphia, Delaware, and Baltimore, right down to Washington, D.C. Throughout this zone, no one is ever far from a metropolitan center, even in the few remaining patches of farmland and the more numerous suburbs that still insist on fairly large plots of land around houses. Stretching about 600 miles and encompassing some 57,000 square miles, this area holds about one-fifth of our entire population, more than 45 million people. "Bowash" is a true megalopolis.

Megalopolis A huge "super city" created by the urbanization and suburbanization of previously rural areas between contiguous cities.

SUMMARY

1. Demography is the systematic study of human populations; its subject matter is human beings studied strictly as numbers.

2. There are only three ways a population's size can change: birth, death, and migration.

3. The crude birth rate—the number of children born each year for each 1,000 people in the total population—is a fairly valid measure of a society's fertility. A crude birth rate of fifteen to twenty per 1,000 is low, whereas a rate of forty is high.

4. The crude death rate—the annual number of deaths each year per 1,000 in the population—is a fairly valid measure of the likelihood of dying in a society. A slightly different measure of death is the average life expectancy of each country or population group, or the median age at which people die. A third measure is the infant mortality rate, or the number of babies who die each year before their first birthday per 1,000 total births.

5. The migration rate, or the number of people entering or leaving a country per 1,000 people in its total population, is also studied by demographers.

6. Demographers are concerned with the distribution of certain characteristics in a population—that is, with its social composition. Age and sex are the most important of these characteristics.

7. The age cohort, one of the most important concepts in the field of demography, refers to a segment of the population of roughly the same age; demographers follow age cohorts over time.

8. The amount of time it takes to double the world's population is diminishing over time. Today, the Earth's population is growing rapidly and alarmingly.

9. The population of the poorest and least economically developed countries on Earth is growing fastest. Part of the the reason for the widening of the economic gap between the rich and the poor nations is the rapid population growth in the latter.

10. The demographic transition is a consequence of industrialization and describes a process by which a society changes from having a high birth rate and a high death rate, to having a low birth rate and a low death rate. During the first phase of the process, societies experience an explosive population growth.

11. The demographic transition model is basically an accurate description of population dynamics, but there are problems with it. One such flaw is that a number of less developed nations will not achieve full industrialization in the foreseeable future, due to a number of complex problems.

12. There are some indications that the world-wide population growth has been slowing down somewhat in recent years.

13. The most striking change in the demographic characteristics of the American population is that it is growing older. The median age of all Americans was 28 in 1970, and 30 in 1980; in the year 2000, this will rise to 36, and by 2010, it will be 38.4. This change has many consequences for everyone in the United States.

14. There is evidence in several locations throughout Asia of cities that are 6,000 to 8,000 years old; cities emerged as a consequence of the discovery of agriculture.

15. The world-wide urban population has increased dramatically over the past century and in recent decades. In 1800, only 2 percent of the world's population lived in communities of 20,000 or more; by the year 2000, this will become almost four people out of every ten.

16. Urbanization is occurring more in the world's less economically developed nations than in its industrialized countries.

17. Urban ecology is the study of the spatial relationships among people and institutions in cities.

18. Contemporary urban ecologists have developed sophisticated models of patterns of urban development. Today, urban areas are becoming linked in structures far vaster, more complex, and spatially separated than the early urban ecologists could have imagined.

19. Urban life typically generates a more *Gesellschaft*, or corporate-like orientation, and a less *Gemeinschaft*, or community-like orientation. City life also tends to breed individualism, isolation, loneliness, and alienation.

20. Contemporary views consider urban life to be more complex and less simplistic than the early sociologists painted it.

21. Throughout history, urban residents have been viewed as different from rural dwellers; this is probably an accurate assessment.

Three sociological theories account for this difference: determinist theory, compositional theory, and subcultural theory.

22. The United States has been transformed from an overwhelmingly rural nation during colonial times to a highly urban society, with three-quarters of its population living in communities of 25,000 or more.

23. The population of the United States is shifting from the older cities of the Northeast and Midwest to the "Sun Belt" cities of the South and West. This process slowed down a bit in the mid-to-late 1980s.

24. America's cities are undergoing a surge of suburbanization that is popularizing previously rural areas between cities, creating a series of megalopolises.

SUGGESTED READINGS

Donald J. Bogue, *The Population of the United States: Historical Trends and Future Projections*. New York: Free Press, 1985.
This basic, important, and extremely useful book should not be read from beginning to end. It is a reference guide to the American population today and in the past; it also offers predictions about what the population will look like in the future. Based mainly on United States census data, it covers the size and growth of the United States population, its age, sex, racial and ethnic composition, facts on marital status and divorce, birth and death statistics, migration, education, employment, occupation, income, religious affiliation, and "political demography." Worth browsing through for lots of intriguing facts. I cannot imagine a college or university library without a copy of this volume. If yours doesn't have one, demand that it acquire one.

Harvey M. Choldin, *Cities and Suburbs: An Introduction to Urban Sociology*. New York: McGraw-Hill, 1985.
A useful textbook on urban sociology.

Claude S. Fischer, *The Urban Experience* (2nd ed.). San Diego: Harcourt Brace Jovanovich, 1984.
City life, as seen through the eyes of a sociologist—the physical setting, the social setting, primary and secondary groups, the individual in the city, the city and the suburbs, and the urban future. This is a highly regarded book on the subject.

Jane Jacobs, *Cities and the Wealth of Nations*, New York: Random House, 1984.
Nations, Ms. Jacobs explains, are artificial and arbitrary units, whereas cities are real and natural. Cities create wealth in a number of important ways. Some cities flourish; other fall into a state of decay. Why? This book addresses this crucial issue.

Edward Krupat, *People in Cities*. Cambridge, England: Cambridge University Press, 1985.
Explores the mental images that people have of the cities in which they live. Although the "objective" features of a city—its size, density, per capita income, sex ratio, and so on—are important, so too is the subjective dimension of its reality. For instance, one's objective likelihood of being robbed is twenty times as great in Washington, D.C., as it is in Milwaukee, yet Milwaukee residents feel only slightly safer than Washingtonians. If people feel that certain areas are unsafe, statistics on actual rates of crime are irrelevant: They are not likely to go to those places. Another example: If a place is perceived to be close, people are more likely to go there than if it is perceived to be far. People estimate a route with many twists and turns to be further than one that is straight, even when both are objectively the same distance. Stores near the center of a town are perceived to be closer than ones that are actually closer, but on the outskirts of town. This book summarizes the research on the subjective dimension of urban life.

Charles B. Nam and Susan Gustavus Philliber, *Population: A Basic Orientation* (2nd ed.). Englewood Cliffs, New Jersey: Prentice-Hall, 1984.
A textbook on demography.

Brian M. Schwartz, *A World of Villages*. New York: Crown, 1986.
What was social life like before the growth of cities? The author, a 24-year-old law school graduate at the time, gave up his job as a clerk to a judge and set out on a journey around the world, avoiding cities and seeking out remote villages. A fascinating narrative of adventures in fifty countries. As a contrast, what does this book tell us about city life?

John R. Weeks. *Population: An Introduction to Concepts and Issues*. Belmont, California: Wadsworth, 1986.
An excellent basic textbook on demography.

chapter 19

COLLECTIVE BEHAVIOR AND SOCIAL MOVEMENTS

D id you know that there are thousands of huge, hungry alligators living in the sewers of New York City? They got there because residents brought them back from their Florida vacations and then, when they grew too large, flushed them down their toilets. Did you know that Procter and Gamble, a consumer products manufacturer, contributes 10 percent of its profits to a cult called the Church of Satan and that its logo—the face of the man in the moon in front of a field of thirteen stars—is proof of its link with Satanism? Are you aware that earthworms are ground up into "Big Macs" to increase their protein content? That Colonel Sanders' fried chicken is really fried rat? Have you heard the one about the babysitter who was high on LSD and baked a couple's baby in the oven thinking it was a turkey? Did you hear about the guy who bought an almost new Porsche worth $30,000 for only $50 because the owner ran off with his secretary and told his wife to sell it and send him the money?

All of these stories are, of course, completely false, although they are widely accepted as true. They are **urban legends** (Brunvand, 1980, 1981, 1984, 1986; Dickson and Goulden, 1983; Morgan and Tucker, 1984, 1987), modern stories that are told and believed as true even though they never happened. Urban legends are a type of **collective behavior**—the relatively spontaneous, unstructured, and extrainstitutional behavior of a fairly large group of people. "Extrainstitutional" simply means that behavior of this type deviates from the established, normative, institutionalized patterns of everyday life. Collective behavior operates in situations in which there are no clear-cut definitions from mainstream culture (Turner and Killian, 1986). Urban legends, much like rumor, operate a bit outside the stable, patterned structures of society. They reflect, like all collective behavior, the "maverick" aspects of human behavior.

Collective behavior includes fads, fashions, crazes, panics, some riots, rumor, mass hysteria, mass delusions, and much crowd behavior. Examples include:

- *Streaking*. Between January and May, 1974, apparently world-wide, it was not unusual for one or more individuals, usually young men, to take off their clothes and run completely naked past startled (or amused) spectators at public gatherings, such

Urban legends Contemporary, more or less spontaneously generated stories with certain stereotypical features; they are told and believed as true, even though they are, in fact, quite fanciful.

Collective behavior The relatively spontaneous, unstructured actions of a fairly large number of people responding to a given stimulus.

as football games, graduation ceremonies (it tended to be a college phenomenon), horse races, or, once, an Academy Awards ceremony (Evans and Miller, 1975).

- *The June Bug Epidemic.* In June, 1962, a female worker in a factory in the South complained of a rash, nausea, and dizziness. Over the next four days, sixty-two more workers had the same symptoms and claimed that they had been bitten by bugs. The mill was closed down and health inspectors were summoned; they found only two biting insects in the entire plant, sprayed the place, and left. No more such incidents were subsequently reported. Officials and experts agreed that the complaints were psychogenic in origin and that the outbreak was a case of mass hysteria (Kerckhoff and Back, 1968).

- *UFOs.* During the summer of 1984, the residents of a small upstate community saw strange objects in the sky—a triangle of green, white, and red lights about thirty feet off the ground, spanning roughly the size of a football field. Many residents believe that it was an aircraft from another planet. The police, who tracked the sighting to a nearby local airport, insist that it was five or six small planes, whose pilots were taking part in a deliberately planned hoax, flying in formation (Schmatz, 1984).

- *The Jersey Devil.* In 1735, Mrs. Leeds of Leeds Point, New Jersey, was expecting a baby. Already the mother of twelve children, she prayed to the devil to curse her impending offspring. When the baby was born, it had wings, a tail like a lizard, cloven hooves, and a horse's face. The creature never died, according to the legend. It has been seen stalking the Pine Barrens, an undeveloped area of southern New Jersey, for over 200 years; its most recent sighting was in the 1960s (Rosnow and Kimmel, 1979, p. 91).

Compared with conventional, everyday life, collective behavior is less inhibited and more spontaneous, more changeable and less structured, shorter-lived and less stable (Lang, 1972, pp. 3–4). In reality, collective behavior and conventional behavior tend to blend into one another; behavior fills a spectrum from completely structured at one extreme to almost completely unstructured at the other—and most behavior falls somewhere between the two. Collective behavior is relatively spontaneous and unstructured, but it is not wholly so.

Social movements Organized efforts by a large number of people to change or preserve some major aspects of society.

Social movements are organized efforts by large numbers of people to change or preserve some major aspect of society. Clearly, the civil rights movement is an example of a social movement: the organized effort on the part of Blacks to improve their social and economic positions in American society. Solidarity is a social movement in Poland; its goals include establishing legal labor unions, obtaining the right to strike, and gaining independence from the Communist party. There is a vigorous animal rights movement in the United States, with several million supporters, who regard animals as an oppressed group. Activists demand more humane treatment of animals by humans, and they insist on an end to medical experiments with animals, indecent treatment of farm animals, caging animals in zoos, and hunting animals for sport and their hides. Women's Liberation is another example of a social movement; its goal is to improve the social and economic conditions of women in the United States and around the world.

Social movements share a number of characteristics with collective behavior. Three are of central importance. First of all, both are dynamic:

They reflect or help to generate social change. A highly stable society has neither collective behavior nor social movements; highly fluid, changing societies have both. In short, both represent something of a break with the present. Second, both are extrainstitutional—that is, both violate established norms, the institutions and traditional values of society. Both affront the notion of what ought to be held by the respectable, traditional members of society. Both reflect the "maverick" side of human nature. In line with their extranormative character, both also tend to be minority phenomena; though both are sometimes extremely widespread, they usually attract only a segment of the population of the society in which they take place. And third, both collective behavior and social movements are *collective* phenomena—they are engaged in interaction with others. They are group creations. Although nearly every other form of human behavior can be engaged in alone, collective behavior and social movements are always the product of actions, reactions, and interactions with and in the midst of other people.

Even though, in their violation of norms, collective behavior and social movements are technically examples of deviance (see Chapter 8), they are not typically so regarded by their participants. Collective behavior and social movements occur in contexts that seem to the participants to justify unusual, unconventional responses: They look upon their socially unconventional behavior as appropriate given the circumstances. The very fact that both are "collective" actions means that they arise in group settings and are approved by individuals in the interactional matrix. For the most part, people who engage in collective behavior and social movements are not regarded as deviants, nor is deviance part of their self-image. For example, a civil rights worker of the 1950s would have said, "Maybe much of the community disapproves of what I'm doing, but justice is on my side." A women's liberationist of the 1970s would have said, "We're trying to make American society a more just and more decent place; we're really the wave of the future." A participant in a demonstration that turned into a riot would say, "I just got swept away by the crowd—it seemed like a good idea at the time." Whereas most deviants are aware that they are a stigmatized minority, participants in collective behavior and social movements would say either that everyone else would have done the same as they did under the circumstances, or that they are trying to change society so that, in the future, people will be doing what they ought to be doing.

Even though there are similarities, there are striking differences between collective behavior and social movements, as well. In many ways, their differences outweigh their similarities. In the past, sociological analyses emphasized their similarities and stressed the collective behavior-like features of social movements. In fact, in some analyses, social movements were regarded as a type of collective behavior. Today, the two phenomena are more likely to be regarded by sociologists as distinct, more or less separable in nature. Some of the basic differences that distinguish these two social phenomena include:

- *Duration*. Collective behavior is relatively transitory and short-lived, whereas social movements are relatively enduring.
- *Degree of organization*. Collective behavior is relatively unorganized and unstructured, whereas social movements are relatively structured and organized. A corollary of this difference is that collective behavior is typically leaderless; there is little or no differentiation into leaders and followers. On the other hand, social movements tend to have leaders and active participants.

- *Relationship to the conventional social order.* Both are unconventional. The difference is that, whereas collective behavior stands outside the conventional social order, social movements directly challenge it.

- *Intentionality of participants.* For the most part, participants in collective behavior are unintentional, nonpurposeful, and expressive, and they are more concerned with emotionality than with achieving a specific goal. On the other hand, participants in social movements are intentional, instrumental, and purposeful in seeking to attain specific goals. (They may go about it in an irrational way—that is, the goals they seek may be unattainable, through the means they employ, or even completely unattainable; still, they do set out to achieve those goals in an intentional fashion.)

- *Relationship to social change.* Both are, of course, dynamic phenomena. But whereas collective behavior is an *expression* of social change, social movements seek to *generate* social change.

- *Degree of importance to participants.* Collective behavior entails relatively superficial, trivial aspects of life; social movements entail relatively important aspects of life.

WHY COLLECTIVE BEHAVIOR?

You might think that sociologists would not be able to explain anything as spontaneous and unstructured as collective behavior. By its very nature, collective behavior appears to erupt "for no reason at all." Not so, however: Patterns and regularities mark its causes, because collective behavior emerges and thrives under certain conditions and not others. Sociologists have devised a variety of theories to explain it. The four best known are the value-added theory, contagion theory, convergence theory, and emergent-norm theory (Turner, 1964). Each of these theories approaches the phenomenon from a somewhat different perspective. A fifth theory, the social behavioral/interactionist perspective, or SBI (Miller, 1985, pp. 40–46), is still in the process of development and is not as widely cited as the other four.

The Value-Added Theory

Value-added theory The perspective that isolates six preconditions for collective behavior: structural conduciveness, structural strain, generalized beliefs, precipitating factors, mobilization for action, and operation of social control.

Perhaps the most ambitious theory of collective behavior is called the **value-added theory** (Smelser, 1962). This approach isolates six determining factors, or conditions, that make for collective behavior. If these conditions are missing, collective behavior will not occur; if they are present, it is almost sure to do so. Each individual condition increases the likelihood that collective behavior will take place; the absence of any condition decreases that likelihood. These factors form a sequence; each step generates the conditions that make the next step possible.

Structural Conduciveness.   The major aspects of a social structure must promote or allow collective behavior. For instance, mass looting can take place only in a materialistic society, in which people value the possession of goods. Likewise, there must be retail stores for looting to occur.

Structural Strain.   Smelser argues that collective behavior is problem-solving behavior. Faced with what he called structural strain—stress, deprivation, threats, or uncertainty of some sort—people respond in ways that attempt to alleviate the problem. Prison inmates who experience intolerable conditions and feel that nothing is being done to improve them may erupt in a riot. Rival gangs of Black and white teenage boys may fight in neighborhoods where racial tension is common.

Generalized Beliefs.   Strain alone is not enough to generate collective behavior. Smelser argues that strain must be accompanied by a belief that points the way to a particular solution. Beliefs need not be valid for people to act on them, as long as they are widely held. For instance, in the 1920s and 1930s, hundreds of Blacks were lynched by angry mobs in the South (and some in the North, as well). These actions were fueled by racist beliefs about the inferiority of Blacks and their "proper place" in society. Mass looting in poor neighborhoods is often based on the (usually correct) belief that stores located in them charge higher prices than stores in well-to-do areas, and also on the looters' belief that they have not received their fair share of the nation's material wealth.

Precipitating Factors.   Collective behavior must be set off by triggering events or precipitating factors. A 1983 prison riot in the Ossining Correctional Facility ("Sing Sing") was touched off by a guard who showed up an hour late to let inmates out of their cells for a recreational period (Mack, 1983). In 1977, massive looting in New York City was directly caused by a city-wide power failure on the night of July 13.

Mobilization for Action.   Collective behavior is usually inspired by leaders who take initiative or by the mass media, which can spread attitudes, beliefs, and rumors throughout a community. The 1977 blackout looting began on a large-scale basis only after a small number of street hustlers mobilized passers-by to follow their example.

Operation of Social Control.   Typically, if controls or restraints discouraging collective behavior are absent, it is free to take place. In the case of the 1977 blackout looting, formal social control was almost entirely lacking. For the first three hours of the blackout, the police did not have enough officers on the street to deal effectively with the looting. Said one precinct captain: "By the time we got enough men to do anything that night, it was already too late" (Curvin and Porter, 1979, p. 58). A rumor that the police were not arresting anyone spread through the streets. By the time the police began arresting looters in large numbers, the professionals had already made off with the most valuable merchandise. Most of those arrested were teenagers out for a good time and working-class people scrambling for whatever happened to be lying around. Those who profited most by the looting stood the least chance of being arrested, whereas those who profited least were most likely to be caught (Curvin and Porter, 1979, p. 58).

Contagion Theory

Contagion theory asks, "How do people come to behave collectively, intensely, and oddly?" Its proponents argue that the moods, the attitudes, and the behavior of individuals may be generated, communicated, and intensified by the presence of others (Blumer, 1969a). Suggestibility, enthusiasm, and exuberance are heightened in a collectivity, when individuals are surrounded by people whose attention is focused on the

Contagion theory The theory that argues that the moods, attitudes, and behavior of individuals in a collectivity are generated, communicated, and intensified by the presence of others; hence, contagion causes collective behavior.

Contagion theory argues that suggestibility, enthusiasm, and exuberance are heightened by the presence of others. People in a crowd often do things they would not have done alone. Here, looters, young and old, cart off merchandise through the broken window of a supermarket.

UPI

same event. "Under contagion, people find themselves spontaneously infected with the emotions of others so that they want to behave as others do" (Turner, 1964, p. 390).

Contagion theory helps us understand what promotes collective behavior but cannot itself explain why collective behavior occurs in the first place. A crowd is never whipped into a frenzy for no reason at all, just because its members have assembled in the same place. The power of crowd-suggestion has its limits. Contagion, for instance, does not explain why enthusiasm falls rather than rises when a few members of the crowd go "too far."

Convergence Theory

Convergence theory The theory that argues that people who share certain predispositions come together and act out those predispositions; hence, individual characteristics, not the presence of others, cause collective behavior.

Convergence theory argues that people who share certain tendencies will often come together, or converge, to act out their common predispositions. The crowd adds nothing to the feelings of its individual members, though it may intensify those feelings if they are already present. "The individual in the crowd behaves as he would behave alone, *only more so*" (Allport, 1924, p. 205). Individuals in a crowd "are all set to react to the common object in the same manner, quite apart from any social influence" (Allport, 1924, p. 229). For instance, the lynchings of Blacks during the 1920s and 1930s were overwhelmingly committed by poor, uneducated, frustrated whites, who feared economic displacement (Dollard et al., 1939).

Emergent-Norm Theory

Emergent-norm theory The perspective that holds that many onlookers to collective behavior are initially ambivalent, indifferent, amused, or even quietly unfriendly toward that behavior, thus lending an illusory unanimity of support for it.

Emergent-norm theory asserts that observers attribute too much unanimity, uniformity, and spontaneity to most kinds of unconventional, unstructured behavior. Witnesses to collective behavior are themselves affected by it, and they often exaggerate the number of participants and the oddness of their behavior. "The conspicuous actions of a few individuals are attributed to a whole group, and sentiments appropriate to the behavior and the situation are imputed to all the members" (Turner, 1964, p. 390). For instance, in a riot, many individuals who are on the scene are merely interested or amused bystanders, or are even quietly unfriendly (Lee and Humphrey, 1943). The crowd is full of diverse views, this theory argues; its unanimity is "a collective illusion" (Turner, 1964, p. 390). The overt passivity of many onlookers appears to lend collective support to the actions of a minority. Many onlookers who do not approve of the behavior taking place may be pressured to join in. No doubt, such pressures are real. But so too is the passivity of most members of many crowds.

> At first glance, it often appears that everyone in a crowd is staring at rapt attention at a speaker or that basketball fans are all cheering wildly while looking toward the play that is occurring. But a systematic analysis of photos or film records of such events reveals something quite different. Crowds are seldom completely focused on a single object, and when near unanimous focus occurs it is of short duration. . . . Within crowds various motives for participation exist, diverse feelings are in evidence, and many types of behavior can be observed. For example, those gathered at a protest rally have a variety of motives for being there, in addition to protest. Some may be seeking excitement, sex, or drugs. Police and protest leaders are concerned with maintaining order, while FBI agents are concerned with national security, and those selling protest buttons, with making money. Seldom will all these people express the same feelings or act in unison (Miller, 1985, pp. 25, 46).

All collective behavior is attended by individuals with *degrees* of identification with what's going on. Some are personally and intensely involved and identified; others have a more marginal and lukewarm identification. Contagion theorists err, emergent-norm theorists say, in assuming far too much uniformity in the focus of attention and emotion. And convergence theorists err, they say, in assuming far too much unanimity in the motives and characteristics of individuals assembled at a crowd. In focus of attention, motives, and characteristics of those present, there is far more diversity than previous views posited.

The emergent-norm perspective emphasizes that crowds are not wild, irrational mobs, but are guided by conventional norms (Turner and Killian, 1986). On occasion, however, crowds do face new, unusual, or ambiguous situations for which novel or *emergent* norms arise. For example:

> When people join together to rescue friends and neighbors after a community disaster, an ephemeral or temporary division of labor emerges. The emergent

Convergence theory argues that people who share certain tendencies come together in a crowd and act out their common needs. They behave as they ordinarily would, only more so. For instance, demonstrators favoring Phillipino president Corazon Aquino express their feelings at a vote tally.

James Nachtwey/TIME, February 24, 1986

patterns of authority and lines of communication may be quite different from those extant prior to the disaster. Heavy equipment operators, for example, may find themselves in positions of authority, giving orders to bankers and city officials. Teenagers may become rescue workers and couriers of important information, performing tasks of greater responsibility than usual. To the casual observer, these arrangements may seem chaotic; however, [to the emergent-norm theorist] they are an effective, normatively guided collective response to urgent situations (Miller, 1985, p. 25).

Emergent-norm theorists emphasize the *continuity* between conventional and normative social behavior, on the one hand, and collective behavior on the other.

CROWDS

Crowd A gathering of people physically assembled at the same place at the same time, focused on the same stimulus.

Mass Individuals who are physically dispersed but who share a common attitude or belief and act upon it, sometimes alone, sometimes with others.

A crowd is a gathering of people who are physically present in the same place at the same time. In contrast, masses are physically dispersed but share common attitudes or beliefs, and sometimes act on them. Here, a crowd gathers for the "Live-Aid" concert.
Anthony Suau/Black Star

The many and diverse forms of collective behavior can be reduced to two basic types. In the first, the participants physically assemble in the same place at the same time. Such a gathering of people is called a **crowd.** In the second, the individuals affected by the collective behavior are for the most part physically dispersed, but they share some common attitude or belief and act upon it, sometimes alone, sometimes with others. In this second case, they make up what sociologists call **masses.** Like everything else in social life, the line between a crowd and the masses is not always clear-cut. Sometimes a crowd is so large, scattered, and diffuse that it comprises clusters of smaller crowds, each reacting in the same way to the same stimulus. Still, the distinctive feature of a crowd is the way its members directly encourage one another to action. The physical proximity of its members is what makes a crowd unique.

Crowds have a number of distinctive features, and there are several kinds of crowds. Both their features and their varieties are especially relevant to the study of collective behavior (Lang and Lang, 1961, pp. 111–151; Blumer, 1969a; Turner and Killian, 1986). The first general characteristic of crowds is that the individuals within them feel a sense of anonymity; to be but a "face in the crowd" means to be almost invisible as an individual. Second, members of a crowd are more suggestible than single individuals. It is easy to "get swept along" by what others in the crowd are doing and to do things that individuals would not do by themselves. Crowds thus have great spontaneity: Crowd behavior is more volatile, excitable, and emotional than the behavior of isolated individuals. Last, crowds generate a sense of invulnerability in their individual members. People swept up in a crowd feel a strong and instant sense of being backed up by a force stronger than each specific individual. They feel a sense of strength that they would lack by themselves.

Types of Crowds. There are four basic types of crowds (Blumer, 1969a). "Casual" crowds are loosely structured, made up of individuals who just happen to be in the same place at the same time. They are united solely by physical proximity, not (or not necessarily) by common interests or goals. An example is the crowds that gather daily in and around Times Square in New York, which have no sense of common identity. The members of such a crowd can enter and leave it at any time. A precipitating event—such as an arrest, a fight, or an accident—could generate a common focus of attention and thus give its members some sense of common identity.

"Conventional" crowds come together for specific purposes—to attend a lecture, for example, or to hear a concert or watch a movie. These crowds are "normatively" governed: Their members observe the rules that decree what is and is not appropriate in such settings. Generally, a movie audience does not throw rocks at the screen, and students at a lecture do not hiss the speaker. "Expressive" crowds, too, may have gathered for a specific reason, but they differ from conventional crowds because the main purpose is just the opportunity to belong to the crowd itself. Crowd activity is an end, not just a means. People do not, for instance, attend political rallies chiefly to be enlightened by the speakers; they assemble for the purpose of being in the crowd—to express an emotion, a belief, a sentiment through the crowd and its behavior. Naturally, the line between conventional and expressive crowds is fuzzy. In fact, under certain conditions, a conventional crowd can become an expressive crowd. A loss by the home team or a bad call by an umpire or referee can turn law-abiding fans into an angry, shouting assemblage. Most sporting events, and rock concerts, have elements of both. "Acting" crowds engage in overt behavior, aside from just milling around. Riots, for example, are carried out by acting crowds—as are revolutions, lynchings, violent demonstrations, and mass lootings.

"Conventional" crowds come together for a specific purpose—to attend a lecture, watch a movie, or hear a concert. These crowds tend to be "normatively" governed: Their members observe the rules that decree what is and what is not appropriate at such gatherings. Here, the citizens of a small New Hampshire community come together for a town meeting.

Farrell Grehan/Photo Researchers

MASSES

Not all collective behavior brings its participants into face-to-face contact. Spontaneous, volatile behavior need not be generated in the heat of the moment, in the presence of others. In "mass" collective behavior, the participants are more widely scattered, around the country or a large geographical region, than they are in "crowd" collective behavior, and the action takes place over a longer period of time. Mass collective behavior may last for weeks, months, or even years, though it is more short-lived than the more stable and basic features of a culture or a society.

Mass Delusions

Mass delusion is a type of collective behavior that takes place, not among face-to-face crowds, but among people in many places. There have been many mass delusions throughout history. One of the most disastrous was the persecution of "witches" in Renaissance Europe (Currie, 1968). Another was a forged document called *Protocols of the Elders of Zion*, which turned up in Russia in 1905. It purported to be the proceedings of a conference at which Jews discussed plans to overthrow Christianity and to control the world. The original document was forged by the Russian secret police, to justify anti-Semitic pogroms, but the *Protocols* was widely disseminated—in the United States, in 1920, by Henry Ford's newspaper, *The Dearborn Independent*. The *Protocols* is still being peddled today as an authentic document in some quarters—among an organization of Russian ultratraditionalists, several extreme right-wing groups in the United States, some Japanese extremists, among Nazi immigrants in South America, and in the Middle East (Johnson, 1987).

Mass delusion A mistaken notion, often one that is acted upon, that takes place, not among face-to-face crowds, but among people who are scattered in many places.

A less sinister but more striking case dates from 1938, when actor and director Orson Welles narrated a radio dramatization of H. G. Wells's *The War of the Worlds*, a novel describing a Martian invasion of the Earth, adapted for the present at that time, and set in the United States. The dramatization was extremely realistic. Actual locations of towns and streets in New Jersey and New York were mentioned, and simulated news bulletins, on-the-spot interviews, and life-like background sounds, such as police sirens, radio static, and milling crowds, contributed to the broadcast's credibility. At one point, the on-site reporter, played by an actor whose performance was heavily influenced by the famous eyewitness description of the Hindenberg disaster eighteen months earlier, described creatures that were emerging from a pit where a meteor had landed in a field in Grovers Mill, New Jersey. The narrator was excited, almost incoherent, his voice breaking with extreme emotion. Suddenly, the creatures fired on the crowd in which the reporter was standing. The sounds of the weapons merged with the screaming of the crowd, creating "a chaotic and hair-raising din" (Miller, 1985, p. 105). Then, there was dead silence. After a long period of dead air space, the studio announcer said, "Ladies and gentlemen, due to circumstances beyond our control, we are unable to continue the broadcast from Grovers Mill. Evidently there is some difficulty in our field transmission" (Cantril, 1966, pp. 17–18). An extremely high proportion of the audience of this dramatization believed that they were listening to an actual invasion from Mars. They were frightened out of their wits; many called the police, the National Guard, hospitals, newspapers, and radio stations for information, and friends, neighbors, and relatives for help and assurance. Though the extent of the mass panic has been exaggerated (Miller, 1985, p. 100), there is no doubt that thousands of people were thrown into a state of emotional panic.

A Classic Case. In March and April of 1954, Seattle newspapers carried stories about automobile windshields that had inexplicably been pitted, or "peppered," with small craters. Some drivers found tiny "metallic-looking" particles about the size of a pinhead embedded in the glass of their car windows. In a two-day period in mid-April, damage to some 3,000 cars was reported in the Seattle area. On April 15, the Mayor of Seattle declared that the problem was no longer a local police matter and appealed for assistance to the governor of Washington and the president of the United States. Motorists covered their windshields with floor-mats or newspapers. From April 15 to April 17, 1954, more than 650 column-inches in the local newspapers were devoted to this story. A number of theories tried to explain the damage; the most popular one blamed atomic fallout from H-bomb tests.

A careful scientific study investigaged the windshield pitting and concluded that it had been caused by ordinary road damage—sand and gravel striking the windshields of moving cars. The number of pits increased with the age and mileage of the car. The pits had always been there. After the first newspaper stories, drivers for the first time began to look at their windshields, not just through them.

The epidemic burned itself out as quickly as it had begun. Complaints dropped off sharply; after April 17, there were none at all, and after April 19, not one newspaper story was devoted to windshield pitting (Medalia and Larsen, 1958).

Why Mass Delusions? What generates such mass delusions? Each case is different, of course. In 1938, Europe was on the verge of war; people

WHAT DO YOU THINK?

The Cattle-Mutilation Mystery

Perhaps the most fascinating recent mass delusion was the cattle-mutilation mystery. On September 5, 1967, a horse named Snippy failed to show up for his daily watering at the corral of the King Ranch, near Alamosa, Colorado. The next day, a search party discovered the dead horse, whose flesh, from the shoulders up, had been neatly removed, leaving the skull and shoulder bones entirely exposed. A Denver pathologist was quoted as saying that neither predators nor a knife could have performed the bizarre mutilation. News accounts claimed that Snippy's internal organs, blood, and brain fluid were missing. Not content with one mystery, some observers added another: They blamed UFO activity for the incident. A wave of sensational publicity brought thousands of visitors to the King Ranch for months afterward. Later, the CIA and satanic cults were blamed for the horse's death. Then, from 1967 to the late 1970s, some 10,000 reports came in of horses and cows mutilated with "surgical precision."

In 1979, the First Judicial District Attorney's Office of Santa Fe, New Mexico, submitted to the federal government a grant application that read: "After the death, the animal's rectum and sex organs always are removed in a mutilation case with a precision many investigators believe could be accomplished only with a sophisticated instrument, such as a laser beam. . . . Strong evidence exists that cattle are killed elsewhere, then flown by aircraft to the spot where they are found, and dropped to the ground" (quoted in Rorvik, 1980, p. 121). Headlines in newspapers and magazines read: "Did Poor Horse Poke His Head Inside Radioactive Saucer?," "UFOs Linked to Weird Animal Mutilations," "Is It the Work of a Witches' Cult, Space Aliens, or the CIA?," "Doctor Says Cattle Mutilations May Switch to Human Victims," "Veterinarian Says Flying Objects, Cattle Mutilations May Be Related," "Mutilators Psychotic" (Rorvik, 1980; Stewart, 1980). A study conducted in the mid-1970s of a sample of adults living in South Dakota revealed that just under half (44 percent) believed that the animals had been done in by mysterious agents—cultists, psychotics, UFOs, or the CIA.

Finally, a curious and enterprising sheriff of Washington County, Arkansas, Herb Marshall, rigged up an experiment. Two of his men hid in bushes for thirty hours straight, observing a calf that had died of natural causes. At night, the officers watched through a Starlight Scope, which enables the viewer to see in the dark. They also took numerous photographs. "At the end of those 30 hours," Sheriff Marshall said, "we had us a classic case, a carcass that looked exactly like most of the others that were reported to us. Its tongue was gone, one of its eyes was missing, its anus had been cored out, the whole thing." How had it happened? "First, we observed what any pathologist will tell you happens when an animal dies. The tongue protrudes and lies right out there on the ground; the anus . . . sticks out. . . . Then the predators and scavengers come along and eat the parts that protrude, the soft, easy-to-get-at-parts: the tongue, the genitals, the udder if it's a female. Then as the animal gets colder, the tongue, or what's left of it, retracts back into the mouth so it looks like it was cut off way down deep. The anus retracts, too, and gives the appearance its been operated on, especially after the blowflies have finished with it" (Rorvik, 1980, p. 142). In addition to the blowflies, Sheriff Marshall's men witnessed scavenging forays upon the dead calf's body by a skunk, some buzzards, and a stray dog—"all of which enjoyed a good meal" (Rorvik, 1980, p. 142). The cattle-mutilation mystery turned out to be no mystery at all—just a classic mass delusion.

How would you have responded to the cattle-mutilation mystery—or how did you respond if you knew about it? Are you prone to respond to mass delusions?

Sources: Adapted from D. Rorvik, 1980, p. 121–122, 142–143; J. R. Stewart, 1980.

listening to *The War of the Worlds* broadcast were responding as much to the coming of World War II as to a possible Martian invasion. Anti-Semitism accounted for the acceptance of *The Protocols of the Elders of Zion;* people who hated Jews believed the forgery to be authentic, whereas those who had no such hates did not take it seriously. The persecution of witches was nourished by fear, ignorance, superstition, the emergence of Protestantism, and the breakdown of feudalism (Ben-Yehuda, 1985, pp. 23–73).

Mass delusions show that we often see, not what is really happening, but what we are predisposed to think is happening. People tend to accept whatever confirms their own preconceptions, and to resist facts that do not fit them. Mass delusions are not isolated events; they grow out of the social circumstances of people's lives. No matter how bizarre, they reveal fundamental and common social processes at work.

Fads, Fashions, and Crazes

What do telephone-booth stuffing, goldfish swallowing, flagpole perching, "streaking" (running around in public nude), and smoking banana skins have in common with miniskirts, "punk-style" hair and clothing, the hula hoop, the use of pink and black in men's clothing, and pyramid financial schemes? Just this: Like much of human behavior, these practices were so mercurial—they rose so high and fell so fast—that they belong to the field of collective behavior.

Fads Activities, usually in fairly superficial areas of life, in which a large number of people engage for a short period of time; followers do not become obsessive or fanatical about fads.

Fashions Fluctuating styles in appearance and behavior.

Crazes Short-lived activities, usually in fairly superficial areas of life, in which a large number of people engage for a short period of time. Some of these people are obsessive and fanatical about the activities in question.

Fads are activities, usually in fairly superficial aspects of life, in which a large number of people engage for a short time. **Fashions** refers to fluctuating styles in appearance and behavior. **Crazes** are like fads but become very central in some followers' lives and, especially when accompanied by fanatical behavior, are more intense than fads or fashions (LaPierre, 1938, pp. 488–497, 502–510).

Most fads, fashions, and crazes are discontinued after the initial burst of enthusiasm that propelled them to popularity. The coughing ashtray did not survive a single season; the pet rock was gone within a year. However, some fads, fashions, and crazes are continued for fairly long periods of time by much smaller numbers of people who hang on when others have turned elsewhere. Video games are still played today, but the number of players, and the fanaticism of their play, is a small fraction of what it was at the fad's height of popularity a few years ago. In 1980, 2 million video games and 10 million video cartridges were sold in the United States; in 1982, these figures were 8 and 75 million, respectively. But by 1985, their sales had dropped to 1.5 and 12 million. Their sharp rise and fall indicates their faddish character (Pollack, 1986). Likewise, in 1984 and 1985, Cabbage Patch dolls were so popular that near-riots would break out in stores that received shipments of them; customers would push and shove and snatch dolls out of the hands of other customers. Sales were extraordinary—over $500 million in 1984 and $600 million in 1985. But the fad quickly peaked in the latter year and, by 1986, only $250 million worth of the dolls were sold (Crudele, 1986). Clearly, Cabbage Patch dolls will continue to sell in the future, but their sudden and explosive sales immediately following their introduction, and their precipitous drop in sales only the year after their peak, marks them as an unmistakable example of a fad.

Some fads, fashions, and crazes pass through cycles, and reappear in new forms every few years; one such example is the pyramid game, a "get-rich-quick" financial scam. The hemlines on women's skirts go up and down every few years, and what was "in" one year may have been "in" a decade or two before. But the crucial defining feature of fads, fashions, and crazes is that they are all picked up by large numbers of people for relatively short periods of time—a matter of weeks, months, or a year or two.

Fads and fashions tend to be so transitory and to deal with such trivial aspects of life that they might appear to be unimportant. How can "streaking," goldfish swallowing, or wearing a miniskirt solve any serious problems? Usually, of course, they don't (Lang and Lang, 1961, p. 486; Turner and Killian, 1986). But many of them do serve important social functions that may not be apparent on the surface.

To begin with, fads and fashions serve as mechanisms of identification and differentiation (Lang and Lang, 1961, p. 480). By adopting a fad or a fashion, you identify with one group and hold yourself apart from another. This symbolic affirmation of membership is more important than the fad or fashion that is the means of achieving it.

Many fads are taken up by the young as a relatively harmless way of rebelling against their parents. Other fads serve to announce the unconventionality of those who engage in them. And although fads usually do not have prestige value, fashion often does (Turner and Killian, 1986). Many fashions, in fact, have high status. Some members of the upper socioeconomic strata announce their status and distinguish themselves from people in the middle and lower strata by wearing fashionable clothes. When these styles are imitated on a mass basis, they are abandoned by their original champions and replaced by new styles. Sometimes, however, members of the upper strata take to wearing fashions (like jeans and workshirts) that originated in the lower strata; "reverse snobbery," too, may often have status-identification and differentiation functions, but in the opposite direction.

Crazes, in particular, generally arise when those caught up in them need solutions to their life problems. In today's complex, bewildering world, many therapeutic and quasitherapeutic crazes—the orgone box, Rolfing, "primal scream therapy," to name a few—have sprung up, supposedly, to solve personality problems. Few of these unorthodox practices become established; most fade away almost as soon as they appear. Diet plans based on medical quackery, which promise magically to shed pounds or "cellulite," come and go with regularity, deluding their followers and enriching their inventors. Many crazes are financial in nature. In the 1600s, the Dutch began to invest and speculate in tulip bulbs and plants. The financial transactions became so intense so quickly that tulips were literally worth more than their weight in gold. Families invested their life savings and sold their homes and lands to buy and sell tulips. Inevitably, the bubble burst, leaving thousands of speculators financially ruined and a few lucky ones extremely wealthy.

Rumors

This chapter began with several public **rumors,** specifically, urban legends, that are false although believed by both tellers and listeners. Some rumors are, of course, true (Miller, 1985, pp. 77–79), but most of what is told as true without substantiation is false, and once a rumor is actually substantiated, it is no longer referred to as a rumor. For instance, Rock Hudson was rumored to have contracted AIDS (acquired immune deficiency syndrome) months before this was medically verified and reported to the public. Afterwards, the information ceased to be a rumor

Rumor A story from a questionable or unknown source that is passed from one person to another without verification of its validity. Some rumors turn out to be true; most are false.

and acquired the status of fact. On the other hand, hundreds of celebrities have been rumored to have AIDS who do not. Word-of-mouth communication is highly believable, and the closer we are to someone, the greater the likelihood that we will believe what he or she has to say. It is very easy to exaggerate, simplify, and embellish what someone has told us, to fill in the gaps and supply detail that we did not hear. Dramatic, bizarre stories are a lot more interesting and likely to be told than the mundane truth, and every one of us loves a good story. There are many common-sensical reasons why rumors fly thick and fast.

Sociologists and social psychologists have studied rumors and have verified a number of interesting generalizations about the conditions under which they arise, are transmitted, and are believed. Two key factors are critical: *importance* and *ambiguity*. The more interested people are in a given subject or topic, the greater the number of rumors spread about it. And the less the information, or the greater the ambiguity of the evidence, pertaining to a given topic, the greater the number of rumors spread about it. Rumor is highly likely when people are very interested in a topic and when little or no verified information exists about it. Rumor is highly unlikely when people are not interested in a topic and when a great deal of highly verified information exists about it (Allport and Postman, 1947). According to this model, rumors serve the function of relieving tension and affirming emotion, not acquiring information. Few people have much interest in verifying a given rumor, but a great deal of interest in passing it on.

Shibutani (1966; 1986, pp. 274–275) considers rumor to be a substitute for solid information; it is, in his words, "improvised news." Rumor is likely to occur, Shibutani states, if the demand for news exceeds the supply. This is clearly evident, for example, when formal or institutionalized channels of communication have broken down, such as during a local disaster, when radio and TV stations are unable to operate or provide up-to-date information. During wartime, when there is a partial blackout on strategic information, rumors commonly fly about such restricted areas of vital importance. Gossip about celebrities is common because certain areas of life are both private—information being restricted—and intensely fascinating to much of the public; hence, for the very areas in which demand is great, supply is limited.

Urban legends circulate because public concern about certain issues is great and often overwhelms what information exists about them. Billions of meals are served in fast-food restaurants like McDonald's and Colonel Sanders, but very few of us have any idea of the ingredients in the food. Clearly, the numbers of people who eat in such restaurants have something to do with the rumors that circulate. And fast food is often called "junk" food, which implies that its contents are bad for us. What could be worse than eating worms and rats? Fundamentalist Christians are intensely concerned about the secularization of contemporary society; they denounce homosexuality, abortion, drug use, sexual equality, humanism, liberalism, and the disintegration of the family. So concerned are they about these trends that they fear that they may have their origins in intentional plots or conspiracies. The metaphor "the forces of Satan"—what they see as corruption—takes on a literal meaning in the form of an actual, concrete satanic cult. And a company that sports a logo that seems to smack of occultism becomes the target of these bizarre speculations. Stories about crazy things that babysitters do reflect parents' concerns about leaving their children in the care of people they don't know well enough. Rumors about someone's doing something wrong with a microwave oven reflect our fear of potentially dangerous new technology. Rumors about acquiring very expensive cars for practically nothing reflect our concern with material things and the hope that springs eternal in the breast of nearly every one of us: Maybe, just maybe, today, I could get very lucky!

SOCIAL MOVEMENTS

A group of women demonstrate outside a Times Square movie theater that is showing a pornographic film depicting violence against women. The demonstrators carry placards, distribute leaflets, and chant slogans.

A band of guerilla soldiers enters a nation's capital, drives a dictator into exile, seizes government buildings, and proclaims a new regime.

Members of a civil rights organization discuss the most effective strategy to persuade Black people to vote in an upcoming election.

These very different cases are all examples of social movements, organized, noninstitutionalized efforts by large numbers of people to change or preserve major aspects of society. Fads and fashions are not organized, intentional, or long-lasting, nor do they seek to bring about substantial social change. But social movements are and do all these things. Social movements do not work entirely within the system. When sociologists describe social movements as "noninstitutionalized," they mean that these movements make use of a wide variety of techniques, including boycotts, demonstrations, and even, occasionally, contrived riots to achieve their ends. Not all efforts to bring about social change involve social movements. For example, when the federal government passed the Voting Rights Act of 1965, this was not, in itself, a social movement (even though the civil rights movement did put pressure on the government to pass the Act).

At the same time, we should not conceive of social movements as existing in a world totally separate from mainstream politics. In fact, there is something of a *continuity* between the two. Classical theories in sociology emphasized the similarities between collective behavior and social movements. Both were thought to be "irrational" and spontaneous outbreaks, having little in common with the institutionalized world of politics. Today, however, a cohort of young scholars is challenging that tradition (McAdam, 1982; Morris, 1984; Jenkins, 1985). They offer "a dramatic break with the classic theories," arguing that social movements share more in common with legitimate political institutions than with collective behavior. The newer approach emphasizes "rationality, resources, networks of solidarity, continuities between unruly challengers and institutionalized politics, and the central role of movements in generating social change." The classical collective behavior approach was "built on the faulty assumption of a qualitative break between social movements and institutionalized politics. In this model, social movements were simply a more organized form of collective behavior, which was itself defined in terms of a polar contrast with routinized or institutional action" (Jenkins, 1986, p. 354).

Today in the United States, social movements abound. The Moral Majority seeks, among other things, to make abortion illegal. Women Against Rape protests against pornography. The National Organization for Women (NOW) is dedicated to equality between women and men. The Jewish Defense League (JDL) uses violence against what it regards as anti-Semitism. The diverse groups within the civil rights movement—

Abortion has become a major issue of contention in American Society, with organized movements on each side of the issue mounting protests supporting their positions. The outcome of this struggle is likely to be a consequence of which one is larger and more powerful rather than which one is right.

Bettye Lane/Photo Researchers

such as the National Association for the Advancement of Colored People (NAACP), the Southern Christian Leadership Conference (SCLC), the Urban League, Operation PUSH—seek to protect the interests of blacks and other racial minorities. The FALN seeks to attain Puerto Rican independence through acts of violence and terrorism. The National Association to Aid Fat Americans (NAAFA) fights discrimination against the obese. And literally tens of thousands of other social movements are all struggling for their own objectives. All represent collective, organized efforts by individuals to change aspects of American society, to prevent such changes, or even to undo the changes of the past.

Not all social movements achieve their goals, or even survive; in fact, only a minority do. Many consist of a fairly small core of dedicated leaders and if they abandon the cause, the movements may collapse. Organizations dedicated to causes also have a tendency to splinter into factions over issues of theory, policy, and tactics, or to fall apart when public support or funding dry up, when factionalism takes hold, and when the membership's enthusiasm wanes. Marcus Garvey, for instance, founded the Universal Negro Improvement Association early in the twentieth century. Its goal was to take American Blacks "back to Africa." Garvey was convicted of mail fraud in 1925 and deported to Jamaica, his homeland, in 1927, and his movement died thereafter. The Symbionese Liberation Army, a revolutionary group that gained a great deal of public attention by kidnapping Patty Hearst, was destroyed when the police arrested and killed nearly all its key leaders. The Temperance movement had a temporary success in 1919 with the passage of the Volstead Act, which brought about the nation-wide prohibition of alcohol. However, a high proportion of the American public simply chose not to live a totally sober existence, so Prohibition was abandoned.

Some movements have been successful in achieving their goals. The National Organization for the Reform of Marijuana Laws (NORML) has helped to reduce the penalties for the possession of small quantities of marijuana in almost every state in the country, and it has even achieved outright decriminalization in eleven states. The Women's Suffrage Movement generated the momentum behind the passage of the Nineteenth Amendment to the Constitution (1920), which granted the vote to women in national elections. In the late 1960s and early 1970s, the movement against the Vietnam War helped force President Lyndon Johnson into retirement in 1968 and then created a climate of opinion that made our military withdrawal from Southeast Asia more acceptable. A few movements are even more sweeping and momentous in their impact. Revolutions, for instance, are one type of social movement; those that took place in America (1776), France (1789), China (1949), Russia (1917), and Cuba (1959) resulted in new governments and even new societies.

Types of Social Movements

Many classifications, or typologies, of social movements have been put forward. Each typology arranges them by their various characteristics. One such typology, for instance, is based on the direction and the degree of the changes these movements seek (Cameron, 1966, pp. 22–24). "Reactionary" social movements seek to restore society, or some part of it, to a former condition or state. Racist organizations, for instance, wish to restore white supremacy in all its former vigor, to return to the days when Blacks were even more subservient to whites than they are now. Another movement that looks fondly back to the past is the Moral Majority, whose members seek to return to the time when only marital sex was approved, homosexuality was regarded as a disease, and abortion was illegal and available only to the rich or the desperate.

"Conservative" movements seek to retain the *status quo*, to fight changes that other movements might propose to bring about. The National Rifle Association (NRA), for instance, organizes to prevent the imposition of controls on handgun ownership. Conservative movements "are most likely to spring up when there is a threat of change, and they are frequently organized specifically to combat the activities of some other movement which is making changes" (Cameron, 1966, p. 23).

"Reformist" (or "revisionary") movements wish to make partial or moderate changes in the present state of society. In general, they focus on specific issues or areas: saving whales or baby seals, for instance, or blocking efforts to build nuclear reactors, promoting equal rights for homosexuals, decriminalizing marijuana, and so on.

"Revolutionary" movements seek major, sweeping, large-scale change. Of course, the line between "revisionary" and "revolutionary" movements is not altogether clear. In fact, the same general movement will often contain both reformist and revolutionary movement organizations and tendencies. Some members of the Women's Liberation movement, for example, want society to grant equal rights to women—a major change, to be sure. Other members of this same movement want to make that change even more significant and revolutionary by restructuring the nature of sex roles and sexual relations. Their goals include changing the way men think: making men feel unashamed of the softer, more vulnerable and emotional (or "feminine") side of their personalities; treating women like full human beings and not simply as exploitable objects; taking on such traditional "women's" roles and tasks as housework and childraising; and being less competitive, less elitist, and less "macho." Proponents of these more sweeping changes argue that merely putting more women in traditionally male jobs would not be an improvement for most women. The distinction between revisionary and revolutionary movements actually hangs on how many areas of society a movement seeks to change and how radical that projected change may be. Movements for change can be arranged along a revisionist-revolutionary continuum, some closer to one end, others to the opposite end, and still others in the middle.

"Escapist" or "retreatist" movements do not seek to change society at all but to withdraw from it and its corruption. Marcus Garvey's "back to Africa" agitation was such a movement. So was Jim Jones's People's Temple, whose members withdrew into the jungles of South America, only to commit mass suicide several years later (see Chapter 1). Escapist movements need not withdraw from society physically; they can withdraw by isolating themselves socially and emotionally, limiting contact with outsiders to a minimum. Many religious sects are of this variety. In fact, the line between social movements and some religions is quite fuzzy. These movements are oriented to the individual change of their members rather than social change.

Last, "expressive" movements seek to change the psychic, emotional, internal state of individual members, not external conditions. Their members believe that society and its problems—hunger, poverty, inequality, and injustice, for example—are less important than each individual's attitude toward them. For instance, the movement called est (Erhard Sensitivity Training) began sponsoring the "Hunger Project" in 1977; its supposed aim is to make hunger disappear within two decades, mainly by convincing its members, and sympathetic outsiders, not to feel guilty about the starvation of millions or billions of their fellow human beings. Because guilt is "stupid and counterproductive," eliminating it will eliminate hunger (Babbie, 1980, p. 533).

The Genesis of Social Movements

Although there are many social movements in the United States and in other societies, too, relatively few people in any society join social movements of any kind—an important point. Even if huge numbers of people participate in social movements, they constitute only a small proportion of the total population. Most people are totally inactive, especially in major social movements, like rebellions or revolutions:

> Aristotle believed that the chief cause of internal warfare was inequality, that the lesser [social strata] rebel in order to be equal. But human experience has proved him wrong, most of the time. Sharp inequality has been constant, but rebellion infrequent. Aristotle underestimated the controlling force of the social structure on political life. However hard their lot may be, people usually remain acquiescent, conforming to the accustomed patterns of daily life in their community, and believing those patterns to be both inevitable and just. Men and women till the fields every day, or stoke the furnaces, or tend the looms, obeying the rules and rhythms of earning a livelihood; they mate and bear children hopefully, and mutely watch them die; they abide by the laws of church and community and defer to their rulers, striving to earn a little grace and esteem. In other words, most of the time people conform to the institutional arrangements which enmesh them, which regulate the rewards and penalties of daily life, and which appear to be the only possible reality. Those for whom the rewards are most meager, who are the most oppressed in inequality, are also acquiescent. Sometimes they are the most acquiescent, for they have little defense against the penalties that can be imposed for defiance. Moreover, at most times and in most places . . . the poor are led to believe that their destitution is deserved, and that the riches and the power that others command are also deserved. In more traditional societies sharp inequalities are thought to be divinely ordained, or to be a part of the natural order of things. In more modern societies, such as the United States, riches and power are ascribed to personal qualities of industry and talent; it follows that those who have little or nothing have only what they deserve (Piven and Cloward, 1977, p. 6).

Relative to a society's total population, few people rebel against the existing order or even join movements that protest against their lots in life. Sometimes they accept their lots, however hard, quite cheerfully. Yet in nearly all the world's societies, some people, almost always a minority, do band together to bring about change or to prevent change, or to undo change. In the United States, they add up to millions of people. Social movements, by their very nature, express dissatisfactions—with the way things are or with changes other people want to make. Their participants think that their own values, needs, goals, or beliefs are being stifled or threatened by certain conditions or people, and they want to "set things right." All social movements require three basic conditions to come into being:

1. Some "objective" condition must be capable of creating people's opposition.

2. Groups or individuals must "subjectively" feel that this condition is in fact undesirable and that something can be done to change it.

3. Society must provide some means for making this dissatisfaction collective—that is, organized. This usually means some form of leadership.

Objective Conditions versus Subjective Factors

Each of these three components must be explained. The transformation of an "objectively" undesirable state or condition into "subjective" dissatisfaction is problematic—that is, it does not happen automatically and, when it does, that demands an explanation. The presence of social movements implies that significant numbers of the members of a society are unhappy about the way things are, and that they wish to change them to what they see as a better way. This is both true and obvious—a truism. A truism is not as much wrong as it is insufficient as an explanation. Most people are unhappy about one thing or another in their lives, and wish to change it, but they do not always join or participate in social movements. And large numbers of people who are fairly happy about their lives in general want to change some aspect of it or the society that seems to be making their lives the way they are. Moreover, the objective features of people's lives do not necessarily lead to participation in social movements. Many individuals who are extremely well off are also active participants in social movements, and some of the most miserable human beings on Earth will never join a social movement. Black family income in the United States increased by one and one-half times during the decade of the 1960s, and, yet, participation in change-oriented Black movements skyrocketed during this period. (And, as we know, numerous civil disturbances—riots—also occurred in the 1960s.) To turn things around, between the early 1970s and the early 1980s, Black family incomes did not rise at all in real dollars (neither did white family incomes), and, yet, movement activity remained at a very low ebb at that time. India's untouchable population, tens of millions of people whose standard of living is among the lowest on Earth, has no sustained, vigorous social movement to protest or alter its miserable condition. America's middle class—among the most economically privileged of the Earth's social categories—joined in protest against high taxes (Americans pay a far lower proportion of their incomes in taxes than do citizens of nearly every Western European country), a revolt that lead to "Proposition 19" and other successful tax cutbacks in California and a number of other states, as well. Clearly, then, objective conditions alone do not determine whether members of a given category or group take part in social movements. Something else is also at work. Although objective misery is certainly part of the picture, it is far from the whole picture.

All over the world, human beings fall sick and die, yet they do not, everywhere, believe that anything can be done to remedy the ill. Wars kill soldiers and civilians by the million, but relatively few people in any nation stand up and say, "Hey, let's end this thing peacefully." The environment is being systematically despoiled by industrial development—an objective condition. Yet not all Americans consider ecological degradation to be a problem that should be controlled, or even to be a problem at all. In short, one person's problem is another's fact of life. Both objective and subjective factors help account for the rise and fall of social movements.

However, the main sociological theories attempting to explain social movements concentrate more heavily on one or the other of these factors. The classic Marxist tradition emphasizes objective economic and political conditions, which, they claim, promote class consciousness and, eventually, the process of organizing and leading a revolution. Capitalist society generates protest because it distributes income and wealth inequitably. Some people are privileged, others deprived; some are exploited, others exploit. Protests and, eventually, revolutions occur when the underprivileged become aware of these objective conditions and organize to eliminate them. According to the "objectivist" perspective, subjective class consciousness reflects objective and undesirable social realities. Leaders only act as "midwives," leading the underprivileged to understand the objective state of affairs (Useem, 1975).

Of course, exploitation and oppression exist everywhere, though in varying degrees, yet social movements do not emerge everywhere. Relatively egalitarian societies may spawn many strong social movements, whereas others that are quite oppressive have almost none. Within societies, some exploited groups do not launch social movements against their objective conditions, whereas many privileged groups launch them by the dozen. Moreover, most social movements, at least within the United States, do not protest oppression. Objective conditions certainly are relevant to the emergence of social movements, but we cannot take the subjective factors for granted. If anything, the subjective factors appear to be more important than the objective ones. In other words, we must distinguish between absolute deprivation ("objective" theories) and felt deprivation, or dissatisfaction, because different individuals interpret "the same set of objective circumstances in radically different ways" (Wilson, 1973, p. 77). For a "protest movement to arise out of the traumas of daily life, people have to perceive the deprivation and disorganization they experience as both wrong, and subject to redress. The social arrangements that are ordinarily perceived as just and immutable must come to seem both unjust and mutable" (Piven and Cloward, 1977, p. 12). Moreover, exploitation and oppression are not the only objective conditions that can touch off social movements—many can, including environmental pollution, nuclear energy, abortion, sex and violence on television, high taxes, school prayer: You name it.

Relative Deprivation.   One theory that attempts to fuse the objective and the subjective factors into one explanation of how protest movements, particularly revolutions, emerge is the **theory of relative deprivation.** We find an early expression of it in a pamphlet written, interestingly enough, by Karl Marx and called *Wage-Labor and Capital.* Marx explains:

> A house may be large or small; as long as the surrounding houses are equally small it satisfies all social demands for a dwelling. But let a palace arise beside the little house, and it shrinks from a little house to a hut . . . and however high it may shoot up . . . if the neighboring palace grows to an equal or even greater extent, the occupant of the relatively small house will feel more and more uncomfortable, dissatisfied, and cramped within its four walls. . . . Thus, although the enjoyments of the worker have risen, the social satisfaction that they give has fallen in comparison with the increased enjoyments of the capitalist, which are inaccessible to the worker, in comparison with the state of development of society in general. Our desires and pleasures spring from society; we measure them, therefore, by society [subjectively] and not by the objects which serve for their satisfaction [objectively]. Because they are of a social nature, they are of a relative nature (Marx, 1968, pp. 84–85).

The theory of relative deprivation argues that the degree of objective deprivation that people suffer has no automatic relation to the likelihood they will *feel* deprived—and therefore join a protest movement. People feel deprived not because they are objectively deprived, but because they feel deprived in comparison with others around them or with their own past objective circumstances (Gurr, 1970).

The Theory of Rising Expectations.   One variety of the theory of relative deprivation is called the **theory of rising expectations,** which argues

---

Relative deprivation, theory of
An explanation of how protest movements, particularly revolutions, emerge that attempts to use the objective and subjective factors behind these social movements.

Rising expectations, theory of
A theory maintaining that dissatisfaction often rises as conditions improve, because expectations rise faster than conditions improve—thereby setting the stage for social movements and even revolution.

that improving objective conditions generates subjective expectations of further improvement. As the standard of living rises, we get used to the improvement and take it for granted. The faster things improve, the faster the desire for more improvement rises. If a temporary economic setback lowers the standard of living (or even merely prevents it from rising) after a period of improvement, widespread dissatisfaction sets the stage for protest and revolution. The theory of rising expectations has been used to explain the French Revolution (Davies, 1962, 1969). In Russia, the reign of Czar Alexander II (1855–1881) was marked by the emancipation of the serfs, the introduction of local self-government, and a relaxation of censorship and government control over education. Yet with each new reform, antigovernment protest became more intense, culminating in Alexander's assassination. Almost all historians of Russia agree that Alexander was the most enlightened and humane of the czars, yet his reforms could not satisfy the spiral of rising expectations they created. (See accompanying figure.)

Resource Mobilization.   The theories explaining participation in social movements discussed so far break down into two varieties: (1) those theories that emphasize objective conditions, not the way in which objective conditions are translated into discontent; orthodox Marxism fits this description; and (2) those theories that focus mainly on the way objective conditions are translated into a subjective readiness to participate in social movements; the theory of relative deprivation and the theory of rising expectations fit this category.

A third kind of theory explains participation in protests and social movements as a result of certain kinds of leadership. The "raw material" for a mass movement exists in many times and places. According to this third kind of theory, social movements rise up in some places but not in others because some leaders know how to mobilize and channel the deprivation and dissatisfaction that comes to hand everywhere. What counts, in this view, is the availability of charismatic and skillful organizers and leaders. This type of explanation, the **resource-mobilization theory,** assumes that the true explanatory variable in the process of protest and revolution is not discontent, which exists everywhere, but the way it is mobilized and manipulated by leaders.

The theories of relative deprivation and rising expectations focus on the origins of discontent. Resource-mobilization theory focuses on its mobilization. A good but extreme example illustrating the resource-mobilization theory is the rise and fall of the Italian-American Civil Rights League, an organization founded and directed by Joseph Colombo, the reputed head of one of New York City's most powerful crime syndicates. Colombo's avowed aim was to protest the image of Italian-Americans in the mass media and their alleged persecution by the FBI. Colombo drew some 1,500 contributors to a $125-a-plate dinner in 1970. The League's first "Unity Day" rally drew about 100,000 demonstrators in New York. At Madison Square Garden, Frank Sinatra, along with a large and impressive cast of famous entertainers, raised $500,000 for the League's cause. The League's membership had grown to 45,000 (Hills, 1980, p. 91).

Italian-Americans, like members of every ethnic group in America, have collective grievances. But did these "objective" conditions account for the League's instant and enormous success? Let's consider the fate of the Italian-American Civil Rights League. Between 1970 and 1971, the League fell out of favor with the heads of New York's other crime "families," who believed that Colombo was attracting too much attention to organized crime and that he was using the League as a means

Resource-mobilization theory
The perspective that holds that discontent in a population does not explain social movements, because discontent exists virtually everywhere. The key factor explaining social movements is the ability of leadership to mobilize that discontent.

of milking money from an unsuspecting public. The second annual Unity Day rally was sparsely attended—according to some, because the mobs that are alleged to control certain New York labor unions refused to give their workers the day off to attend the rally. At the rally itself, a would-be assassin's bullet left Colombo permanently paralyzed. The "hit" man, reputedly hired by another crime family, was himself shot to death, and his killer escaped discovery. The Italian-American Civil Rights League soon died in obscurity. The discontent it expressed had been whipped up by a scheming leader, and when he left the scene, the League left with him. Resource-mobilization theorists argue that many, perhaps even most, social movements arise and are sustained in similar fashion. Most, however, do not have the misfortune to incur the disapproval of organized crime, so their leaders can organize and mobilize almost indefinitely.

The theory of resource mobilization does not assume that all social movements are whipped up by manipulative leaders for their own benefit. It makes two valid points. First, because objective deprivation, and thus subjective dissatisfaction, exist to some degree throughout all societies, these two factors do not in themselves explain why social movements arise and flourish. Second, some social movements are, indeed, little more than clever schemes by leaders who exploit the ever-present realities of deprivation and discontent. Many other social movements, however, do genuinely seek to reform major aspects of society.

Consider, for instance, the role played by leaders in mobilizing the Black civil rights movement. That Blacks suffer from collective injustices and deprivations is an objective fact, and it was even more so in the 1930s and 1940s, when the civil rights movement began. Blacks are also dissatisfied with their position in life—in other words, their absolute deprivation has been translated into felt deprivation. The next step, mobilizing this discontent, now demands explanation.

Beginning in the late 1950s, a series of boycotts and sit-ins broke out in our Southern and border states. Blacks demanded to be served in hitherto all-white stores and restaurants and refused to sit only at the back of public buses. What inspired these protests and demonstrations? What created this powerful social movement, which won Blacks access to public facilities and retail stores all over the country, particularly in the South? Deprivation and discontent had existed before this period, but it had not produced an effective mobilization of the Black public.

One observer (Morris, 1984) argues that the boycotts, the sit-ins, and, in effect, the whole civil rights movement did not emerge as a sudden, irrational outburst of collective behavior, but as a rational, almost inevitable outgrowth of preexisting social structures, which gave the movement resources, organization, leaders, and members. An organizational base—including the Black churches, the center of Black political life in the South; existing civil rights organizations, such as the NAACP, the Congress of Racial Equality (CORE), the Southern Christian Leadership Conference (SCLC), as well as other activist groups; and local Black colleges—already existed. These organizations had already tried out many legal and political strategies, often with great success. Public opinion, especially in the North, was ready. Boycotts and sit-ins appeared to be the most rational way of challenging local segregation laws. These tactics did not represent a radical break away from existing social organization, but, rather, were built upon it. The first boycott, for instance— of the Montgomery, Alabama, bus system in 1955—was "mass-based, nonbureaucratic, Southern-led, and was able to transform preexisting church resources into political power" (Morris, 1984).

These preexisting structures were waiting for effective leadership—for someone to organize the organizations. Beginning in 1958, in Oklahoma City, the sit-ins spread through established organizations, community linkages, and overlapping personal networks. They were led by established leaders of established organizations, supported by their memberships. The conclusion is clear: "Collective action is dependent on internal organization" (Morris, 1984). In the case of the Black sit-ins and boycotts, the organizational problem was linking the movement's overall leaders, such as Dr. Martin Luther King, Jr., to the rank and file of many grass-roots organizations. The genius of this movement was its ability to set up multiple linkages between the various local leaders, on the one hand, and the overall leaders, on the other. Because there were many leaders, many sponsoring organizations, and many linkages among them, the removal of a single leader would not have destroyed the movement altogether (as it had the Italian-American Civil Rights League).

A Synthesis. Clearly, different theories must account for different social movements. No single explanation can ever be concocted for the emergence of every one of them, because they are so diverse. Some leaders mobilize public discontent against serious social injustices; others are little more than money-grubbing, publicity-mad "entrepreneurs." Some movements, too, emerge more spontaneously, on a more grass-roots level, out of deeply felt grievances. Some movements do not require intense commitment or participation by their followers; members may be people who just feel some sympathy for the group's goals and pay nominal dues. Other movements demand constant participation and commitment—even to the point of death—for example, a revolution. A single person may join only one social movement or dozens of them; contradictions among their goals and ideologies may be easily shrugged off. Some other movements seek to monopolize their followers' loyalties and to eliminate the ideological influence of all other movements. Some movements have religious foundations; others seek to nullify religion's influence altogether. Some seek to revolutionize society; others to prevent revolution (and to prevent it in many different ways). No single theory can explain the social conditions that lead men and women to participate in social movements. Only a multitude of partial theories, perspectives, and explanations can account for their almost infinite variety.

Some social movements have had a profound impact on our society. The civil rights movement has stirred the nation's conscience, generated legislation in a number of areas of life, multiplied Black participation in the political process many times over, and given hope to millions of poor and mistreated people. Here, Dr. Martin Luther King delivers his "I Have a Dream" speech in Washington in 1963.

UPI

527

SUMMARY

1. Collective behavior and social movements are dynamic phenomena that take place when conventional norms are set aside and the traditional order breaks down.

2. Sociologists define collective behavior as the spontaneous, unstructured actions of a fairly large number of people responding to a given stimulus.

3. Sociologists define social movements as organized efforts by a large number of people to change or preserve some major aspect of society.

4. Collective behavior arises, according to one argument (the value-added theory), as a result of the conjunction of six factors. If all of these are present, collective behavior will take place; the absence of any one of these factors decreases its likelihood. Other theories attempting to explain collective behavior include contagion, convergence, and emergent-norm theories.

5. There are two principal types of collective behavior; crowd behavior takes place when participants are in one another's physical presence, and mass behavior occurs when people are physically dispersed.

6. Crowds have several distinct features: They are anonymous, suggestible, and spontaneous, and members feel invulnerable and strong in them.

7. There are four basic types of crowds: "casual," "conventional," "expressive," and "acting."

8. Mass delusion is a common type of collective behavior that takes place not in face-to-face crowds, but among people in many places; the mass panic following Orson Welles's radio broadcast *The War of the Worlds* provides an example of this phenomenon.

9. Mass delusions are not isolated events; they grow out of the social circumstances of people's lives and reveal fundamental social processes at work.

10. Fads and fashions make up another type of mass collective behavior. They typically serve as mechanisms for social identification and differentiation.

11. Crazes generally arise as a result of the need for a solution to certain problems in some people's lives; the "pyramid game" is a classic example of a craze.

12. Rumors generally arise about topics that are important to people who tell and listen to them when valid information is lacking.

13. Social movements share some similarities with collective behavior, but they are strikingly different in significant ways, as well.

14. Social movements are of several varieties. One typology lists six basic types of social movements: reactionary, conservative, reformist or revisionary, revolutionary, escapist or retreatist, and expressive.

15. Three conditions must exist to create a social movement: certain undesirable objective conditions; a subjective awareness of their

undesirability and the feeling that something can and should be done about them; and a means of coordinating or organizing this discontent.

16. Different theories rely more heavily on one or another of these three factors.

17. One theory of the genesis of social movements is the relative-deprivation explanation—a feeling of discontent generated by comparing one's lot in life with that of others.

18. The theory of rising expectations holds that social movements arise because objective conditions cannot improve as fast as the rise in people's expectations of how conditions ought to improve.

19. A third explanation for participation in social movements emphasizes the role of leadership in mobilizing discontent—the resource-mobilization theory.

20. No single theory can account for all social movements, or even all aspects of one social movement. There is a wide range of different social movements, and only a synthesis of parts of these theories can account for their existence.

SUGGESTED READINGS

Jan Harold Brunvand, *The Vanishing Hitchhiker: American Urban Legends and their Meanings.* New York: Norton, 1981; *The Choking Doberman and Other "New" Urban Legends.* New York: Norton, 1984; *The Mexican Pet: More "New" Urban Legends and Some Old Favorites.* New York: Norton, 1986.
Fascinating descriptions and analyses of dozens of "urban legends"—folktale-like rumors purported to be true that are told and retold by individuals who haven't bothered to check out their validity. All are, of course, false. Did you hear the one about "the hairy-armed hitchhiker?" "The death of little Mikey?" "The jogger's billfold?" "Burt Reynolds's telephone credit card number?" "The solid cement Cadillac?" They're all here—and dozens more. Entertaining as well as informative and theoretically relevant.

Robert Curvin and Bruce Porter, *Blackout Looting!* New York: Gardner, 1979.
A study of the widespread looting that took place following New York City's power failure on July 13, 1977. This book is insightful and demolishes sterotypes that are commonly held about the typical looter.

J. Craig Jenkins, *The Politics of Insurgency: The Farm Worker Movement in the 1960s.* New York: Columbia University Press, 1985.
An analysis of the rise and decline of a political movement made up of poor, marginal, politically weak agricultural farm workers—the United Farm Workers (UFW). Tests the resource-mobilization theory. This book is characteristic of the newer approach in the field, which attempts to disassociate the phenomenon of social movements from the collective behavior approach and to locate it within the context of political sociology.

Doug McAdam, *Political Process and the Development of Black Insurgency, 1930–1970.* Chicago: University of Chicago Press, 1982.
A study of the Black civil rights movement, designed to test the adequacy of the "classical" model of social movements: that social movements emerge as a response to strain, individual discontent, and an effort to ease psychological tension. The author finds the classical model faulty. A major alternative, resource-mobilization

theory, likewise, is deficient, according to McAdam. He proposes an alternative model: Social movements are the outcome of a combination of expanding political opportunities as well as factors relating to indigenous organization, "as mediated through a crucial process of collective attribution."

David L. Miller, *Introduction to Collective Behavior.* Belmont, California: Wadsworth, 1985.
A basic textbook in the field. Introduces the social behaviorist/interactionist (SBI) perspective. Stresses the continuities between collective behavior and social movements rather than their disjunctions.

Aldon Morris, *The Origins of the Civil Rights Movement: Black Communities Organizing for Change.* New York: Free Press, 1984.
Morris emphasizes the rational, deliberate, and concerted organizing efforts of civil rights organizations and the strength of local networks in their success. Offers a critique of traditional views, especially classic collective behavior approaches, resource-mobilization theory—with its emphasis on external support—and the role of Weber's concept of charisma. A truly path-blazing study.

Hal Morgan and Kerry Tucker, *More Rumor!* New York: Viking Penguin, 1987.

Frances Fox Piven and Richard A. Cloward, *Poor People's Movements: Why They Succeed, How They Fail.* New York: Pantheon, 1977.
Not all social movements achieve their goals. Two sociologists analyze the conditions that make for success or failure in four representative "poor people's movements."

Ralph L. Rosnow and Gary Alan Fine, *Rumor and Gossip: The Social Psychology of Hearsay.* New York: Elsevier, 1976.
How and why does a rumor arise? What sustains it? Why does it die out? Intriguing analysis of hearsay. Integrates the authors' approach with specific examples, such as the 1969 rumor that Paul McCartney had died. Emphasizes multiple networks in the transmission of rumor and gossip.

chapter 20

SOCIAL CHANGE

Visiting an old friend, you walk toward the neighborhood you lived in as a child. You turn a corner, and suddenly you feel disoriented, out of place. The local grocery store is gone, replaced by a giant supermarket. A row of two-family houses has been torn down, and a twenty-story apartment complex towers above the site where it once stood. A superhighway knifes through the neighborhood. You are reminded how dramatically the modern world changes.

You are not the only person to make this discovery. A once-rural county in California is now a center of the computer industry. In once-booming Midwestern cities, corporations cut back on automobile production, factories lie idle, and tens of thousands of workers are laid off. In small Middle Eastern countries, the discovery of oil causes buildings to sprout in the desert, automobiles to replace camels, and families to own such modern luxuries as television sets and computers; one oil-rich nation, the United Arab Emirates, boasts a strikingly higher per capita income (nearly $24,000) than the United States ($14,000). In Africa, the Sahara Desert creeps southward, destroying once-fertile lands; millions of people in tribal villages are turned into starving refugees. In South America, multinational corporations purchase vast tracts of land in the Amazon jungle, cut down millions of trees, and deprive Indian tribes of their ancestral land.

Social change is everywhere. Practically nothing in the world remains the same year after year, decade after decade. In the 1930s, television sets did not exist; by the 1980s, almost every family in America owned at least one. In 1870, automobiles did not exist; less than a century later, almost every family in America owned one. In 1930, driving cross-country was a slow, dangerous adventure along small, local roads. Today, it can be done almost entirely on major four- or six-lane superhighways. Early in the nineteenth century, three-quarters of all employed Americans worked on farms; today, less than 3 percent do so. At the end of World War II, the very few electronic computers then in existence filled several large rooms and could perform only fairly simple operations; today's computers fit easily on desk tops and perform calculations quite unknown, even to mathematicians, only decades ago.

Changes in material objects are apparent to all of us. It is easy to tell the difference between an automobile and a horse, smoke signals and a telephone, a Florentine palace and a steel-and-glass skyscraper. Changes in culture and social structure are no less momentous, although often they are less obvious. Not too long ago, married women were rarely employed; now, a majority hold jobs. Premarital intercourse was once considered shameful and even deviant; today, it is widely accepted and widely practiced. At the turn of the nineteenth century, only a tiny minority of American teenagers even attended high school; currently, fewer than one student in ten fails to reach high school. As material objects change, so does society; likewise, as society changes, material objects do, too.

WHAT IS SOCIAL CHANGE?

Social change The transformation of major aspects of a culture and society.

Social change means the transformation of major aspects of a culture and society—changes in beliefs, values, customs, behavior, social relations, material culture, stratification, and anything else of importance. In previous chapers, we have encountered specific social changes in several areas of life—population shifts, urban growth, and technological change, to name just three. In this chapter, we examine social change in general: how and why it takes place, and what happens when it does.

Of course, social change takes place everywhere and at all times (Moore, 1974, pp. 12–22). If we gaze at the sweep of the last few hundred thousand years, we are struck by how much human life has changed. Small tribal villages become absorbed into empires; empires rise, become great, and fall; monarchies yield to democracies; democracies are replaced by fascist dictatorships. In some places, religion's influence in public affairs has plummeted; in other countries, religious leaders overthrow secular ones. Hunters become farmers; farmers become factory workers; factory workers become bureaucrats and civil servants. In one generation, practically no people in a rural village ever traveled more than a dozen miles from the place of their birth; in the next generation, everyone has visited cities hundreds of miles away. Within the span of a couple of decades, some countries where people have lived in age-old poverty suddenly grow rich on oil revenues and then, just as suddenly, become poor again. New inventions create new industries and kill off old ones.

An ancient Greek philosopher, Heraclitus, made the now famous observation that no one can step into the same river twice, because the river is always changing. His point was that reality—especially human reality—is impermanent, shifting. Indeed, the only reality is eternal change. On reflection, we may well decide that Heraclitus was wrong, or at least half-wrong. Naturally, the river changes from moment to moment—but how much does it change? Has the water changed into mercury? Has the river's current halted? Has the temperature of the water risen from 36°F to 200°F? No. As with the river, so with human beings. Did anyone ever change from a wise man to a fool in two minutes flat? Or from an honest person to a thief or a liar? Of course, the world is eternally changing, even from moment to moment, but the important questions are: how much, and in what way? Change is a question of degree; sometimes a change is so small as to be almost nonexistent.

The Tasaday, discovered in the 1970s in a Philippine rain forest, are a tiny band of people with a Stone-Age culture. Until they came into contact with other cultures, these people were almost untouched by social change.

Toby Bankett/Pyle/Photo Researchers

Some kinds of trivial change are indeed universal, but major changes take place only at certain times and under certain conditions.

For hundreds of thousands of years, social change took place far more slowly than it does today. Societies and cultures tended to be far more stable. For instance, in the early 1970s, a tiny band of people called the Tasaday was discovered in the Philippine rain forest, following a way of life similar to that of Stone-Age peoples who lived hundreds of thousands of years ago. Until the Tasaday came into contact with other cultures, they were practically untouched by social change. Preindustrial societies were not always stagnant, but before the advent of industrialization, the pace of change was much slower than it became afterwards.

KINDS OF SOCIAL CHANGE

So far we've used social change as a catch-all term to refer to very different kinds of transformations. Few doubt that contemporary society is different from the society of a decade ago, let alone a century or a thousand years ago. But exactly how is society different? Rarely do societies change in all respects, from top to bottom. Typically, change chips away at a society piecemeal, and some aspects change more drastically or more quickly than others.

Change takes place on two levels: the individual, or micro, level and the social, or macro, level (Lauer, 1977, p. 5). Let's examine each in turn.

The Micro Level

Micro level of social change
Change that takes place on the individual, person-to-person level.

The **micro level of social change** is change at the level of individuals, by themselves and also interacting with other individuals.

1. *Individual attitudes.* In any society, certain beliefs are shared more or less widely. Certain other beliefs are held rarely or not at all. Such beliefs change over time. For instance, according to a series of Gallup polls, in 1966, only a minority (42 percent) of all Americans favored the death penalty for certain crimes. By 1981, this figure had reached a clear-cut majority—67 percent. Few Americans now believe in witchcraft, however though, in the 1600s and the 1700s, many did.

2. *Individual behavior.* Just as certain beliefs may be more or less common or uncommon, so, too, may certain kinds of behavior. Behavior also changes over time. For instance, in the 1930s and 1940s, only 3 percent of all girls had engaged in sexual intercourse by age 15, and 19 percent had by age 19 (Kinsey, Pomeroy, Martin, and Gebhard, 1953, pp. 286, 333). By 1979, 22.5 percent of 15-year-old girls had had at least one sexual experience, as had 69 percent of those who were 19 (Zelnick and Kanter, 1980, p. 231.)

3. *Interaction patterns.* Like attitudes and individual behavior, the way people relate to one another, or interact, changes over time. For instance, as the telephone became widely adopted, in the 1920s, it produced at least two changes in social interaction. In towns and cities, telephone calls diminished the frequency of "face-to-face neighboring," because friends called rather than visited one another. Yet in rural areas, telephones made voice-to-voice contact possible between people who had previously been inaccessible to each other (Lynd and Lynd, 1929, p. 275; Ball, 1968, p. 63; Aronson, 1971).

The Macro Level

Macro level of social change
Change that takes place on the institutional, structural, and society-wide level.

The **macro level of social change** is change at the level of institutions, and it, too, is engulfed by changes.

1. *Technology.* In the 1700s, hand- or animal-powered engines were replaced by inanimate sources of power, such as coal, and many human skills were replaced by machines.

2. *Economic base.* In 1958, Cuba's economy was privately owned—in part, by foreigners. After Fidel Castro took power in 1959, Cuba's industry was nationalized and run by the state. A capitalist economy was transformed into a socialist one.

3. *Political system.* From 1933 to 1945, Germany was ruled by a Nazi dictatorship that systematically rejected and trampled upon human rights. Today, Germany is two countries: East Germany, a communist state, and West Germany. The latter is a democracy

with an elected government and full protection of civil rights and civil liberties.

4. *Religion.* In the A.D., 570s, when the Prophet Muhammed was born, most of the peoples of the Middle East practiced some form of polytheism. Over the next few decades, the Islamic religion propounded by the Prophet converted almost all of these peoples (and many Jews and Christians, as well) to a rigid form of monotheism.

5. *Education.* In 1800, most schools in the United States were private, although some were supported by local governments. The federal government did not support local education in any way. By the early twentieth century, nearly all American children of school age were exposed to some form of tax-supported education.

6. *Family.* Before 1890, the Mormons (an American religious group that settled Utah) practiced polygamy, and the United States refused to grant statehood to the Utah Territory. Not until the Mormons agreed to give up polygamy was statehood granted, in 1896.

7. *Stratification.* In medieval Europe, almost the only criterion of a person's social rank was ancestry. Today, social rank depends largely on occupation and income.

8. *Community-level demographic characteristics.* In 1950, the population of Albuquerque, New Mexico, was less than 100,000; that of Cleveland, close to a million. By 1984, Albuquerque's population had more than tripled, to well over 350,000, while Cleveland's shrank by nearly half, to just over half a million.

9. *Society-wide demographic characteristics.* Our population is getting older over time (see Chapters 12 and 18): In 1970, the median age was 28; in 1980, 30. By 2000, if present trends continue, it will be 36, and it will rise to 38 plus in the year 2010, and to over 41 in 2050.

10. *World-wide political change.* Last, many nations that were, until recently, colonial dependencies of Europe have achieved independence. These and other nations are participants in multinational and even global organizations like the North Atlantic Treaty Organization (NATO) and the United Nations, respectively—themselves, quite a new thing under the sun. So, too, are the multinational corporations whose economic tentacles reach into almost all countries.

SOURCES OF SOCIAL CHANGE

Where does social change come from? What are the mechanisms or sources of social change? Do some of them, like technology, influence or cause others, like individual beliefs and behavior? Are some more basic and influential than others?

Of course, the causes of social change need not be the same everywhere. Ancient Rome's decline and fall had one set of causes, the industrialization of Western Europe and North America, quite another.

Social Conflict

The Marxist perspective emphasizes conflict among social categories—especially classes—as the major source of large-scale social change. Class conflict, Marx wrote, is the "locomotive" of historical change. It leads to revolution, and only revolutions can overturn the old order and usher in the new. Yesterday, the bourgeois revolution overturned feudalism; tomorrow, the socialist revolution will overturn capitalism, Marx believed. Everywhere in the world, some groups or classes control more of a society's resources: more land, a higher income, profits, more power, more of the good things of life. At the same time, other groups or classes have less, and come to resent the injustice. Although inequality in the distribution of a society's resources does not inevitably or always result in social conflict, it does create the potential for conflict. Marx emphasized that **class consciousness**—the awareness that the members of a deprived, exploited class have of their deprivation and exploitation, of what their class interests are, and of what they need to sweep away the bases of their deprivation and exploitation—sharpens conflict, generates revolution, and brings about social change.

Non-Marxist sociologists emphasize social conflict, too, but they argue that class conflict is only one of a number of different kinds of social conflict (Coser, 1956; Dahrendorf, 1959). In fact, conflicts among religious, racial, ethnic, national, age, sexual, and regional categories and groups have all generated large-scale social change the world over. Not all or even most of these conflicts have been over the distribution of material resources, although many of them have. Some are "symbolic" in nature: the attempt by one group to have its own views translated into the law of the land to enhance its respectability and lower that of other groups (Gusfield, 1967). Some entail the desire by one group to engage in certain practices that another wishes to outlaw, such as abortion and pornography today, or the sale of alcohol after the turn of the nineteenth century. Whatever the source, there can be no doubt that intergroup conflict is a major motivator of social change. When the members of one social category or group believe that society should be arranged quite differently from the way it is now, and press to bring this about, the stage is set for some sort of social transformation. Indeed, it is possible that group conflict is the most important source of social change.

Technological Innovation

Technology—the application of scientific knowledge to practical ends—is one among the most important sources of social change. In the Middle Ages, the invention of the stirrup, the ring that riders use to mount horses, strengthened the power of cavalry and of the knightly class that dominated it (White, 1962). More recently, in the Arctic, snowmobiles have multiplied the social interaction among individuals living at great distances from one another (Pelto and Müller-Wille, 1972). Many such technological revolutions change society in unanticipated and even undesired ways.

Perhaps the most fundamental of all these technological revolutions was the development of agriculture (see Chapters 4 and 17), which utterly transformed nearly all major aspects of every society that adopted it. Moreover, agriculture in turn speeded up the pace of further change because it created an economic surplus that supported people who did not gather food. It also promoted the growth of armies and thus more

Class consciousness The shared, mutual awareness of members of a social class of their own class interests.

frequent warfare among societies; the rise of monarchies, despotism, and more rigid forms of social stratification; the blossoming of formal art; and the emergence of settled communities, as well as an increase in their size and complexity, and in the size and complexity of their architecture.

The other momentous technological innovation was, of course, industrialization (see Chapter 17). The factory system was not simply a new and more efficient way of manufacturing material goods but also a way of life. For instance, preindustrial societies took a casual attitude toward the passage of time. They had little need to measure it precisely, by hours and minutes.

> A few years ago in Kabul [Afghanistan] a man appeared, looking for his brother. He asked all the merchants of the marketplace if they had seen his brother and told them where he was staying in case his brother arrived and wanted to find him. The next year he was back and repeated the performance. By this time one of the members of the American embassy had heard about his inquiries and asked him if he had found his brother. The man answered that he and his brother had agreed to meet in Kabul, but neither of them had said what year (Hall, 1959, p. 29).

Industrialization made hours and minutes vitally important. To hold a job, workers had to arrive at work at a fairly precise hour; to arrange deals, factory owners had to meet, at agreed-upon times, with buyers and sellers.

Even specific technological innovations can affect societies profoundly. Consider the automobile. It has affected the courtship and dating patterns of adolescents and young adults, the growth of the suburbs, the decline of public transportation, the economic development of isolated and inaccessible areas, and the growth of related industries (like steel, glass, and oil). Indeed, it has created a "car culture" among many young people, who spend much of their time "hanging out" in or around cars, and just "driving around."

Ideas

Another kind of innovation changes the way people in one society—or in many—see the world, or one aspect of it. Like technological change, new ideas often have a profound impact on the way we live; in fact, many sociologists argue that ideas affect material culture as much as material culture affects ideas. For instance, in *The Protestant Ethic and the Spirit of Capitalism*, Max Weber (see Chapters 1, 9, and 16) argued that religious ideas can influence economic development. Weber believed that the ideas of Calvinism, a major branch of Protestantism, had helped capitalism to emerge by giving religious value to hard work, self-denial, and commitment to a profession. Conversely, the failure of Catholicism to grant *religious* importance to these virtues was an obstacle to industrial capitalism in Catholic societies.

This "Protestant-ethic" theory has stimulated much debate—indeed, many dozens of books and perhaps thousands of articles, have been devoted to it. Marxists particularly reject the idea that ideas can be a primary cause of material conditions; it is precisely the other way around, they assert. Weber, however, presents an elusive target for attack, because he explicitly admits that material conditions influence ideas; he is arguing against "monocausal" materialism, not against materialism itself. Whatever the merits of Weber's Protestant-ethic theory, it does seem clear that ideas can be a major source of social change.

Ideas about justice and injustice have helped inspire many revolutions, and without such ideas, revolutions do not occur. The ideas of Christianity and Islam have led to invasions, wars, conquests, alliances, mass conversion, and large-scale cultural diffusion on every continent of the globe.

Cultural Diffusion

Cultural diffusion The spread of cultural items from one society to another.

We can see evidence of **cultural diffusion** all around us. Archaeological evidence suggests that even in very remote times, long chains of traders moved goods from Scandinavia and Africa to the Mediterranean, and from China to the West. Evidence for the diffusion of ideas (as opposed to material objects) fills every church, to say nothing of every school. War, trade, exploration, and colonization gave Europe horses and the concept of zero in mathematics (from the Arabs), gunpowder and silk (from China), tobacco and corn (from the American Indians). The latter took guns from Europe; the Chinese learned how to build the pagoda as a result of contacts with India; and Arabic architecture was influenced by such trade partners as the Greeks, the Romans, and the Byzantine Christians.

In fact, many cultural items have spread world-wide from a common source, creating some similarities among very different societies. Some anthropologists argue that the overwhelming majority of all cultural phenomena in all societies have been imported from other societies (Murdock, 1934). Even cultural items we associate with particular societies or nations may have originated elsewhere. For instance, spaghetti had its origins not in Italy but in China and was not adopted by Italians until Marco Polo's travels, in the thirteenth century. Likewise, many foods associated with the American South, like the sweet potato, had their origin in Africa. Glass was invented by the ancient Egyptians; cotton was first domesticated in ancient India; the toilet was devised in Rome; coffee was discovered by the Arabs; towels were first manufactured by the Turks; rubber was discovered by the ancient Mexicans; the printing press was invented in Germany; and the decimal system was devised by the ancient Hindus. People who regard themselves as "100 percent American" are unaware that most of our culture comes from other societies, all over the globe (Linton, 1937).

Population

If a country's population increases enough, food supplies become insufficient and people may starve (see Chapter 18). Overpopulation in one part of the Earth often leads to mass migration, colonization, and war in less populated areas. A substantial increase in one part of our population, the elderly, is undermining the Social Security system. The post-World War II "baby boom" contributed to severe economic competition, slow career growth, and unemployment for the generation whose members are now in their 30s. A decline in the birth rate has closed schools and maternity hospitals all over the United States. As our people move from the Northeast and Midwest to the South and West, old towns die, and new ones appear and expand. The increasing size of the minority electorate in the United States has given Blacks and Hispanics control over many big city governments. Country people, Black and white, move to large cities, where their traditions disintegrate and their family structures weaken. Their adolescent boys run afoul of the law. In short, changes in the size and composition of the population are a major source of social change.

Overview

We have by no means exhausted all the sources of social change. Natural catastrophes—earthquakes, volcanoes, droughts, and floods—have weakened and destroyed or otherwise transformed many civilizations; in fact, much of the preindustrial world's history consisted of an ongoing struggle against such catastrophes. As though they were not enough, we must also struggle against catastrophes of human origin, notably war and invasion, which have also been major factors in promoting social and cultural change. When one society invaded another, defeated it, annexed it, and imposed new customs and foreign rule upon it, large-scale change was inevitable. Social movements and revolutions have overturned traditional social, political, and economic structures and introduced new ones, transforming societies in nearly every detail. Even seemingly random events often lead to drastic social change. In 1914, the assassination of an Austrian archduke by a Slavic nationalist triggered World War I. A nightwatchman's accidental discovery of a 1972 burglary eventually resulted in the resignation of President Richard Nixon and his most powerful advisers.

Social change is perhaps the most complex of all sociological phenomena and the most difficult to explain. No single factor causes all major social change, or even many single social changes. And all these factors are interconnected. Typically, each factor is contingent—dependent—upon others. Revolutions, for instance, almost never take place solely as a result of material injustices, nor solely because revolutionary ideas have been spread among the masses; to get a revolution, we must have both these factors. In combination, these different factors usually exert a mutual influence on one another. Industrialization, for instance, has transformed the family, and certain family systems, in turn, tend to promote industrialization more than others do (W. J. Goode, 1963). Social change reflects the great complexity of social life in general.

MODELS OF SOCIAL CHANGE

Sociologists and historians have been writing about social change for more than a century and a half. Why do societies change? Over the long run, what is the general direction of change? What does the future hold for us?

There are four basic perspectives on social change: the evolutionary model, the cyclical model, the functionalist model, and the conflict model. These four theories are not different in every detail, but they are competitive: Sociologists who accept one generally reject the others.

The Evolutionary Model

In the nineteenth century, evolution was the most popular model, or theory, of social change. In this view, human society moved "up and up and up, and on and on and on"—in an inevitable process of improve-

Evolutionary model of social change The view that societies grow in an inevitable process of improvement: from less developed to more fully developed, from simple to complex. These changes are usually steady and gradual.

Unilinear model of social change The now-obsolete view that all societies progress through the same pattern of development.

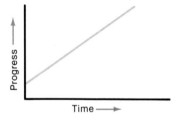

The Unilinear Evolutionary Model of Social Change

Progress ⟶

Time ⟶

Multilinear model of social change The view that social change does not follow a single line of development, but takes place along different lines and at different rates, from one society to another.

ment. This **evolutionary model of social change** received a strong push from Charles Darwin's *On the Origin of the Species* (1859). Certain social thinkers, notably Herbert Spencer (see Chapter 1), believed that Darwin's ideas on biological evolution could be applied to social evolution as well. To most Europeans, it was evident that their society was more complex, more advanced, and more wonderful than the societies of the East and the South. To these early observers, it seemed obvious that European society had itself evolved, over centuries, from simpler to more complex forms. Non-Western societies, they reasoned, were simply stuck at an earlier stage of this evolutionary process. This view is called the simple or **unilinear** (one-directional) **model of social change** (see accompanying figure).

Today, this perspective is regarded as not only ethnocentric (culturally biased), but wrong as well. To early observers, "different" meant "inferior." Contemporary social scientists are much more cautious about making claims of superiority or inferiority. Besides, in many ways even apparently primitive societies are much more complex than ours: For instance, the kinship system of the Australian Aborigines is far more complex than ours. West African art is now regarded by experts as technically and artistically equal to comparable works produced in the West. And when Marco Polo visited China in the thirteenth century, he was awed by the magnificence of the civilization he encountered there.

A second problem with the unilinear evolutionary model is its assumption that all societies evolve in the same way, along a single line. In fact, each society evolves in its own way, at its own pace, in its own direction. Social evolution is not a mechanical, standardized process; rather, it is caused by many factors, and some may be present in one society but not in others. Even thousands of years ago, Western societies differed from those of the non-Western world. Each society and culture has its own, to some degree unique, history and pattern of social change.

Consider a few examples. Christianity played one role in the social development of Europe; Islam, quite a different role in the Middle East. Norway's predominantly rural population is different from Belgium's, which is far more urban. Some societies have a long history of warfare with their neighbors; others have benefited from many centuries of peace. One society has an extremely patriarchal family structure; another, one that is far more egalitarian. Each feature of every society can influence social change. This process cannot possibly be uniform or unilinear, because so many factors interact within it—factors set in a different "mix" in every society.

The nineteenth century unilinear evolutionary model is surely dead. However, more sophisticated derivatives of it still have believers. The **multilinear model of social change** is one such derivative. It states that social change does not follow a single line of development but takes place along different lines and at different rates, from one society to another. Contemporary evolutionists recognize that all features of a society need not be at the same level of development; a society may be extremely complex in one area of life and quite simple in another. They recognize, too, that "complex" does not always mean "better." Some simpler societies promote the security and happiness of their members better than modern societies do. Still, contemporary evolutionist thinkers do emphasize that over time societies have a general tendency to change from simple to complex; from small to large; from rural to urban; and from relatively homogeneous to increasingly heterogeneous. These changes have a momentous though not always predictable impact on all features of every society that undergoes them (Lenski, 1966; Parsons, 1966, 1977; Lenski and Lenski, 1987).

The Cyclical Model

Early evolutionary theorists believed in the inevitability of progress—"things are getting better and better, every day in every way." The advocates of the **cyclical model of social change** were more pessimistic. Industrialization, they thought, was a mixed blessing that often produced as much misery as wealth. Studies of the great civilizations of the past—ancient Greece, and Rome, Egypt, Babylonia, and Assyria—led some observers to conclude that societies go through a cycle of growth and decay, not a straight line "onward and upward." In other words, cyclical theorists argued for an "up and down" pattern of social change (see accompanying figures).

The most prominent of these theorists, Oswald Spengler (1928), compared society to a biological organism: Both undergo a process of birth, growth, maturity, decay, and death. A civilization blossoms in its youth, when its creativity in art, science, philosophy, and social organization unfolds. After this "golden age," the cyclical theorists argued, all societies decline. Their members become cynical, selfish, rigid, and materialistic; they lose their youthful creativity and idealism. The society disintegrates into warfare and internal strife. This process, Spengler declared, is inevitable, the "destiny" of every civilization. Western society, he wrote during World War I, stood poised on the brink, about to slide into the downhill phase of its cycle. Spengler is no longer taken very seriously. Societies are not even remotely comparable to organisms, and decline is no more inevitable than progress.

Another variety of the cyclical model views social change as a process of repetition, alternating continuously from one type of society to another. Some cyclical theorists argue that this repetitive pattern involves a "back and forth" model: One stage is followed by another stage, which in turn gives way to the first, and the pattern endlessly repeats itself through time. Vilfredo Pareto (1848–1923), an Italian sociologist and economist, held such a view of social change. He argued that society's leaders shift back and forth between two types: "lions," who use force to rule, and "foxes," who rely mainly on cunning, fraud, corruption, and "diplomacy." Society has no overall tendency to be ruled by one or the other type—they simply alternate in power over time (Pareto, 1935, pp. 1516–1518; 1968).

Another cyclical theory of social change was offered by Pitirim Sorokin (1889–1968), a Russian-American sociologist, who argued that cultures alternate among three different orientations. "Ideational" cultures are those whose members view truth and reality as eternal, God-given, final, absolute, and beyond the here and now. The members of such cultures regard morality as "imperative, everlasting, and unchanging" (Cuzzort and King, 1980, p. 136) and devalue the physical and sensual side of life. By contrast, "sensate" cultures anchor reality, not in the great beyond, but in the here and now—in the senses of sight, hearing, taste, smell, and touch. Sensate cultures have relativistic, not absolute, codes of morality: They see right and wrong as subject to interpretation and change. Members of a sensate culture believe in indulging themselves physically and sensually. "Idealistic" cultures blend these two extremes, the ideational and the sensate.

Sorokin regarded modern Western society as sensate, the Middle Ages as ideational, and ancient Greek society as idealistic. Cultures shift from

Cyclical model of social change The view that societies tend to go through an "up and down" pattern of social change.

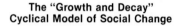

The "Growth and Decay" Cyclical Model of Social Change

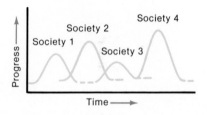

The "Continuous Alteration" Cyclical Model of Social Change

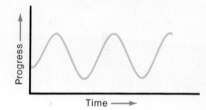

one culture orientation to another, back and forth, without any apparent progression or development (Sorokin, 1941). One problem with Sorokin's theory is its failure to provide any explanation for the repetitive pattern he regarded as inevitable. Because explanation is usually regarded as the primary ingredient of any adequate theory, today's sociologists regard Sorokin's cyclical model as inadequate. Moreover, it is very difficult to force an entire society (as opposed to any one part of it) into a simple scheme of classification. When we look closely at the Middle Ages, we see many sensate elements, just as we can see many ideational elements in our own society. Sorokin classified societies chiefly by examining their works of art, and even here the complexity of life often defeats the classifier. Is *The Canterbury Tales*, for instance, an ideational work or a sensate one? It depends on which page you read, and also on your own outlook.

The Functionalist Model

Functionalism, of course, attempts to show how the many elements of each society combine to create and preserve social order. To the functionalists, an institution that survives is by definition "functional." Institutions harmful (or dysfunctional) to society as a whole will not survive. All classes within a society normally share certain core values, which hold that society together, and each class makes a contribution to the society as a whole. Each class plays a part in maintaining the society's functioning. Society's institutions are consistent with one another: Essentially consistent values are promoted by the family, the educational system, the state, and all other institutions. In short, the functionalists stress social harmony, consensus, and cohesion.

Functionalists do not argue that the many parts of a society are always perfectly integrated. Sometimes, they are not. When basic institutions conflict, the strain spreads throughout society, because all these institutions are interconnected. Although society's normal condition, as the functionalists see it, is "balanced equilibrium," conflict among social institutions may at times upset this balance and create pressure for social change. Temporary disharmony sets the stage for the creation of a new harmony. For instance, agricultural societies tend to have close-knit families, because men, women, and children often work together in the fields. Industrialization physically separated the members of the family and thus made it harder for them to fulfill traditional roles (Parsons, 1951, p. 510). At that point, the functionalists argue, old institutions must change or new ones must be created to relieve this temporary state of disharmony, or disequilibrium. Industrial societies, for instance, created elementary schools and day-care centers to fill roles that preindustrial mothers had performed themselves. In addition, fathers increasingly take care of their children, and the birth rate among employed couples has dropped drastically. A temporary condition of strain was resolved by reintegrating somewhat changed social institutions.

Although functionalism and the evolutionary models are not inconsistent, the functionalist model of social change stresses stability, not change. Perhaps, too, it overemphasizes consensus and the impact of an institution on society as a whole, rather than its various parts. Some sociologists prefer to focus on processes of social conflict.

The Conflict Model

Conflict theorists emphasize antagonism and conflict rather than harmony; disagreement rather than consensus; and violent rather than peaceful change. Karl Marx (see Chapter 1), the founder of conflict theory, argued that until communism is instituted, no society can be in true equilibrium. In all class societies, one class exploits the others. Exploitation creates conflict and violence and, eventually, social change. Such revolutionary violence propels society to a new and higher stage, creating new social classes, new antagonisms, and new sources of conflict. These "contradictions" set the stage for yet another revolution and a higher stage of history. This process, according to Marx, is characteristic of a **dialectical model of social change**. It is revolutionary, not strictly evolutionary; sudden, not gradual; and marked by distinct stages, not a "seamless" development. Overwhelming, irresolvable, conflicting forces explode and propel society to a new and higher level of history. The final stage of history, communism, represents a kind of social plateau, a point where all conflicts have been resolved and social change and revolution are no longer needed (see accompanying figure).

In capitalist society, these conflicts and contradictions reach their final stage. The antagonism that lies at the heart of all social relations now comes into the open. Factory owners adopt self-interest as their battle cry and seek to pay their workers as little as they possibly can. The workers, for the first time united in factories, become aware of their collective exploitation. At this point, no compromise is possible, Marx believed. Revolution is inevitable; the question is "when," not "if." A system based on exploitation was inherently unstable and ultimately only a communist revolution could resolve that instability (Marx, 1906; Marx and Engels, 1968).

Marx has had an enormous influence on contemporary conflict theorists, but many of them nonetheless recognize his limitations. Most of today's sociologists believe that Marx exaggerated the importance of the economic factor and of class conflict (Dahrendorf, 1959). There are other kinds of conflict, too, including conflict among nations; between men and women; and among racial, religious, and tribal groups. Not all these conflicts are economic in origin.

Moreover, Marx failed to predict which societies would initiate a communist revolution. His theory focuses on the advanced industrial societies, such as England and Germany, because factory workers in these nations would have the greatest opportunity to become aware of their collective exploitation. He was wrong. The development of a working-class consciousness in those countries produced labor unions and socialist political parties, not revolutions. If anything, there may be less economic conflict today than there was earlier in this century. Communist revolutions broke out in agricultural, not industrial, nations: Russia in 1917 and China from 1945 to 1949. Apparently, Marx failed to identify the mechanism of these revolutions—why they took place—so his theory of social change is flawed.

Marx failed, as well, to recognize that meaningful social change can be peaceful. In most of the older industrialized countries, the workers have peacefully won such gains as legally enforced vacations, minimum wages, unemployment insurance, free education, socialized medicine—in short, the welfare state. Here in the United States, peaceful methods dismantled the structure of legally enforced segregation, and forced the United States government to withdraw its troops from Vietnam. These powerful and meaningful changes were no less important because they were not won through revolution.

Even so, no sociologist today would doubt the importance of conflict in social change. In every society, social groups and classes compete with one another for scarce resources, often economic ones. Sometimes this competition breaks out into overt violence. Most conflict, however, is relatively peaceful—demonstrations and protests, debates in the mass

Dialectical model of social change According to this model, change occurs abruptly, proceeds in distinct stages, and happens as a result of conflicts in society.

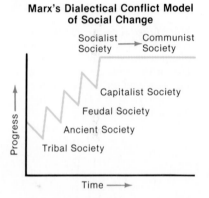

Marx's Dialectical Conflict Model of Social Change

Marx failed to recognize that a great deal of social change comes about without overt violence. Demonstrations against the war in Vietnam had an impact on the U.S. government's decision to withdraw its troops.

Susan McCartney/Photo Researchers

media, elections and political appointments, the passage of laws, hiring and firing in the marketplace. Today's conflict theorists must try to understand why, how, and to what effect social change takes place. Such an understanding requires a grasp of all facets of society, not just one. What makes social change such an exciting field of study is its complexity, not its simplicity.

MIND OR MATTER?

Although we should certainly avoid "the myth of a singular theory of change" (Moore, 1974, pp. 24–25)—"monocausal," or one-factor, explanations of it—different perspectives necessarily stress certain factors more than others. Certain theories of social change view material culture as its source and engine. Certain other theories stress "ideal," or intellectual factors, like beliefs, attitudes, and ideas. Materialists admit that ideas are important but contend that they reflect material culture, to them the ultimate cause of all change in human history. Idealists insist that material factors are important but, ultimately, less important than ideas, which make us accept or resist change in all its forms (Lauer, 1977, pp. 151–201). The sociological thinker most closely identified with materialism is Karl Marx (see Chapter 1). The idealistic tradition is usually associated with Max Weber (see Chapter 1). (In truth, Weber stressed the material factors as much as he did ideas as agents of social change.) Of course, many sociologists attempt to blend these two traditions and stress both factors equally. They do not fall clearly into either camp.

The Protestant Ethic

Just after the turn of the present century, Max Weber published one of the most controversial sociological works ever written, *The Protestant Ethic and the Spirit of Capitalism* (Weber, 1930). As we saw earlier, Weber argued that the theology of a particular kind of Protestantism strongly promoted the Industrial Revolution and helped account for the fact that Protestant countries industrialized earlier than Catholic countries did. In other words, industrialization came about largely as a result of religious ideas, or so Weber argued.

According to Weber, many societies, not just Protestant ones, had the material means to create true industrial economies—India, for instance, China, and parts of the Middle East. Yet the Industrial Revolution began in Protestant England, not in these other areas. Why? Weber argued that the influence of Calvinism was the key factor. Calvinism was strongly "ascetic": It rejected sensuousness, self-indulgence, luxury, and frivolous time wasting. But its asceticism was "inner worldly"—not "other wordly"—focused on the life to come, in heaven. To a Calvinist, the battle of good and evil had to be waged in the here and now. Why? Because the Calvinists believed that only a small number would be among God's "Elect"—those who would receive eternal salvation—and they believed that God had chosen the Elect at the moment of creation. No human being could hope to change God's judgment. This doctrine of "predestination" created the most acute anxieties among the Calvinists. To calm these anxieties, individual Calvinists looked for indications that they, too, might be numbered among the Lord's Elect. One such indication, they believed, was worldly success. Therefore, "intense worldly activity is recommended [by the Calvinists] as the most suitable means [of reducing religious doubts]. It and it alone gives the certainty of grace [salvation]" (Weber, 1930, p. 112). Activity in this world, in the here and now, is not a means of *attaining* salvation but a sign of it. The Calvinistic branches of Protestantism thus insisted on "the necessity of proving one's faith in the worldly activity" (Weber, 1930, p. 121). But this worldly activity was conceived by them in a new way: Not as a mere means for earning a living, but as a sign of salvation.

Work was not a mere job but a "calling." Because there was religious value in hard work—the "surest and most evident proof of . . . genuine faith"—Calvinists took a greater interest in it, but not in order to live more lavishly. They worked in order to fulfill God's will, and because God (as they saw it) did not approve of what we now call "conspicuous consumption," they reinvested more of their earnings than Catholics did. Capitalism required such "accumulation." Therefore, the Protestant ethic was "the most powerful lever for the expression of that attitude toward life" called "the spirit of capitalism" (Weber, 1930, p. 172). In brief, Weber argued that the puritan outlook of early Protestantism "favored the development of a rational bourgeois economic life . . . It stood at the cradle of modern economic man."

Although Weber's name is associated with the **idealistic view of social change,** only in contrast to the Marxists can Weber be called an idealist. In reality, Weber did not wish "to substitute for a one-sided materialistic an equally one-sided spiritualistic causal interpretation of culture and history" (Weber, 1930, p. 183). "Each," Weber wrote, "is equally possible." In fact, in other writings, Weber stressed material factors. Ideas do not by themselves create social change, he argued; material conditions must permit us to accept them.

Idealistic view of social change The perspective that views ideas as the main agent of social change.

Marxism: A Materialist View of Social Change

Marx, the founder of the **materialist view of social change,** argued that society's "mode of production of material life determines the general characteristics of the social, political, and spiritual processes of life," including the processes of change. Social change is the product of certain inherent flaws, or "contradictions," in a society's economic system. In a capitalist society, one such contradiction is that between the interests of the workers and those of their employers. This contradiction creates a class struggle, which generates a socialist revolution. Another contradiction of capitalism was the irrationality (as Marx saw it) of linking the inherently collective industrial modes of production to an individualistic "mode of appropriation," private profit. This contradiction is manifested in so-called crises of overproduction, in which consumers do not have enough income to purchase the goods industry produces and industry, therefore, comes to a halt. It is this *reality*, in Marx's view, that would give rise to the *idea* that capitalism must be replaced. In short, a society's material conditions shape its ideas and generate social change.

Materialist view of social change The perspective that holds that material conditions and phenomena determine social change, not ideas.

A Synthesis

Do material conditions provide the "locomotive" for change—or do ideas? Which precedes and therefore causes the other: technology or "ideal" culture?

Most sociologists believe that the material and the ideal realms influence each other. Technology, the economy, and the other material aspects of culture influence the ideas and beliefs and behavior of its members in certain ways, under certain circumstances, and to varying degrees. Let's look at a few examples.

The introduction of the rifle (and the horse) into the Plains Indian culture transformed its attitudes toward warfare. Before the coming of these material innovations, the Plains Indians carried on their wars chiefly by hurling spears across vast distances. Rarely was anyone killed. The gun and the horse produced new attitudes toward war: Combat became quite violent, and fierceness and bravery, and even cruelty to the enemy, were highly valued. Yet the introduction of exactly the same material object, the rifle, produced no such change among the Eskimo; it simply made hunting more efficient and less dangerous.

What about the influence of industrialization on the family? It is beyond all doubt that this influence was profound, yet it appears, as well, that changes in the family facilitated the process of industrialization (W. J. Goode, 1963, p. 370).

Consider another case: bicycles. No doubt, bicycles have recently been catching on among adults in the United States. Yet even now, they are significantly less common here than they are in Europe. Even when distances are short, Americans still prefer to drive. The technical object is just as available to us as it is to Europeans, but we have certain values and beliefs—ideas—that make bicycles less acceptable to us than they are to people in Europe. Different ideal cultures influence the rate at which each culture adopts and uses a material object.

Not all technological innovations "catch on" in a society. Ideal culture—ideas—may not be receptive to some of them. The Yir Yoront, an Australian tribe, refused to accept, use, or build canoes, whose existence and usefulness they understood (Sharpe, 1952). The Mayans of ancient Mexico invented the wheel but used it only as a children's toy. Other societies invented the wheel with momentous results. As anthropologist W. H. R. Rivers pointed out some seventy-five years ago, bows and arrows, pottery, and canoes have been invented, used, proved to be useful and effective, and then simply abandoned by some societies—seemingly without reason. What happened? Certain ideas held by their members made these material and technical innovations unacceptable, unwelcome, objectionable, or irrelevant.

The plain and simple truth is this: Neither ideas nor material culture rule society in a consistently unidirectional fashion. For a material item to be influential and generate social change, the members of the society must hold beliefs that give that item a meaningful place in their lives. Likewise, ideas often grow out of certain material circumstances—or, to be more specific, out of people who live in those circumstances—and not others. Ideas act as a precondition for material culture, and material culture acts as a precondition for ideas. We need both to generate social change. Only a meaningless system of measurement can make one more influential than the other.

THE PROCESS OF INDUSTRIALIZATION

Once the Industrial Revolution, regardless of its causes, was under way, irreversible social and cultural consequences flowed from it. The fact that the world will never be as it was before industrialization makes cyclical theories of social change quite suspect.

Before the 1700s, fragile economic ties linked distant societies and nations. England obtained tea from India and China; China and India, in turn, bought tools from England; America sold tobacco, sugar and cotton to Europe, and it purchased cloth and machinery from Europe, and so on. But this international commerce did not create an organized international economic system. One country might trade with another, but this two- (or sometimes three-) way trade did not unite the nations of the world in a unified world-wide market.

Industrialization changed all that. Since the 1700s, a world economy has gradually taken shape (Wallerstein, 1974). The world's largest corporations are no longer confined to one city or even one country; they are multinational in scope, with branches everywhere on Earth (see Chapter 17). Nearly all nations are linked in a continuous economic system, buying and selling to one another, providing raw materials, labor, or a purchasing market for one another. Say, for example, that a large oil company wants to drill for oil in an Asian country. Large oil companies are multinational, with subsidiaries all over the world. The money for investment might come from the London money market. The drilling equipment might come from Houston, Texas. Other equipment might come from other parts of the United States, from Europe, and from Japan. The workers might come from just about anywhere. In today's economic environment, any large deal is a veritable United Nations of commerce. "In this sense, and only in this sense, the unification of the world is nearly complete" (Moore, 1974, p. 94).

The world's largest companies are not only organized on a global scale but also sell their products globally. Corporations in the economically developed countries no longer use less developed nations (LDCs) solely to extract raw materials. The people of the LDCs make up a sizable part of these companies' market. Products such as Coca-Cola, Honda motorcycles, and Texas Instruments calculators are sold in practically every country of the world. Hollywood films earn more than half their total profits overseas. The companies that manufacture and distribute these products influence lives all over the globe, both directly and indirectly.

Diffusion and Convergence

It was once believed that most nations would eventually imitate Western Europe and North America by industrializing. This so-called **diffusion theory** recognized that the values and culture of particular societies might affect the pace of industrialization—but not the fact of its inevitability.

Diffusion, moreover, assumed that cultural differences among industrialized societies would gradually diminish, a prediction called the **convergence hypothesis.** Because an industrial economy requires a high average level of education, and because most industrial work is performed in factories, schools and factories would everywhere act as agents of socialization, "rationalizing" the people of the world—in other words, getting them to accept a "modern" view of the world and the behavior that goes with modernity. The mass media also act as agents of industrial socialization. Moreover, the champions of the convergence hypothesis believed that the LDCs would go through the process of industrialization, and therefore of modernization, much faster than the Western nations had done—in only a few decades, perhaps, not in centuries (Lerner, 1958; Inkeles, 1969; Inkeles and Smith, 1974).

Diffusion theory The view that industrialization will follow the same path everywhere as was true of Western society in the eighteenth and nineteenth centuries, and that the same cultural transformation that the West experienced will also mark social change elsewhere. See also **Convergence hypothesis.**

Convergence hypothesis The view that cultural differences among industrialized societies will gradually diminish.

Modernization

Industrialization and modernization, and the attitudes and beliefs that go with them, are tightly intertwined. On the one hand, no society can industrialize unless its members have somewhat modern attitudes, because no economic system can be imposed upon people who are not willing to work within it. On the other hand, industrialization, once accomplished, further modernizes attitudes and behavior. The two have a mutual influence.

What are "modern" attitudes and beliefs? What sort of mental changes would take place in an industrializing, modernizing society? Let's look at a few that the diffusionists predicted.

1. *A growing acceptance of change.* People in a modernizing country are no longer willing to follow traditional customs "because we've always done it that way." They become much more open to innovation and much more oriented to the future, less so to the past.

2. *A belief in the power of individual effort.* In "modern" societies people no longer accept fate, or inevitability. They believe that individual effort can move the world.

3. *High personal aspirations.* In a modern, industrial society, people are more ambitious than the people of traditional societies. "Modern" men—and now women—want to attain prestigious positions, rewarding work, high salaries, and material goods.

4. *A cosmopolitan outlook.* Modern people no longer regard their relatives, tribe members, fellow villagers, or neighbors as their sole reference group, the group within which they interact. Modern societies socialize their citizens to seek and maintain wider social relations, stretching out across limited social and physical boundaries.

5. *The desire for education.* Modern technologies demand highly educated workers and even consumers. These people get accustomed to the idea that education is the route to self-advancement. Industrialization thus provides both the incentive and the opportunity for people to seek higher education.

6. *Loyalty to the central government.* Modern people, first and foremost, regard themselves as citizens of nation-states, not as mem-

Societies in much of the world are industrializing. This process is having a profound, though sometimes unpredictable, impact on their cultures as well. Modernization means a growing acceptance of change and a declining importance of traditional beliefs and values.

Mehmet Biber/Photo Researchers

bers of tribes, ethnic groups, or races, or as speakers of one language or another. They have a strong national identity, which transcends local bonds.

7. *Growth of the nuclear family*. With modernization, the extended family—especially households with many generations and relatives living under the same roof—becomes less important and less common. Young men and women fall in love, marry people of their own choosing, and establish independent households relatively free from parental influence. Their children in turn form equally independent family units.

8. *A decline in the importance of ancestry*. In traditional societies, almost all people inherited the social status of their ancestors, especially of their parents. We can never change our ancestry, so in traditional societies, few people changed their social status. In modern societies, social rank is achieved through personal accomplishments, not bestowed by inheritance. Social mobility permits people to rise and fall in socioeconomic status.

9. *Secularization*. The importance of religion declines in modern, industrial societies. Religious beliefs and practices become irrelevant or burdensome to many people. The state ceases to enforce religious doctrines. The clergy has less and less power over the lives of the people. No one religion dominates society; religious diversity and freedom become the rule.

10. *A decline in male domination*. Industrial societies need as much talent and ability as they can get. Systematically denying women access to the workplace is inefficient, a waste of human resources. More and more women leave the domain of the home and family and work for a living. Their sex slowly—very slowly—becomes an irrelevant issue on the job, and their achievements and pay gradually—very gradually—equal those of men. Women struggle for and approach equal political power and equal status in personal relations.

This account of modernization is a "model," not an empirical description of any particular industrialized society. Each of these changes has occurred during the past two or three centuries, but the pace of change has been very uneven. Some of these trends—women's liberation, for instance—everywhere occurred more slowly than the other trends—social mobility, for instance. And each trend took hold more strongly in some places than in others. None of these trends is complete anywhere. Still, they embody—in a simple, broad, and crude and exaggerated way—the effects of industrialization and modernization as they took place in Europe and North America from the 1700s on. Who can doubt that more people want and get education today than did so in 1700? Or that religion has less power than it did in the Middle Ages? Or that social mobility is greater in the modern West than it was anywhere in 1600?

The Limits of Industrialization

The diffusionist-convergence pattern suggests that these trends must transform the LDCs, much as they transformed the West, though perhaps more unevenly. That expectation has not been fulfilled. To begin with, the LDCs have not industrialized as quickly or as evenly as the classic theory of economic development had predicted. The economies of most

Industrialization around the world has been proceeding unevenly. The economies of many less industrialized nations stagnate, while other nations are booming. Even within the same country, significant sectors retain a traditional economy alongside highly industrialized sectors.

Joseph Nettis/Photo Researchers

LDCs are stagnating, not growing. The gap between average income in the fully industrialized nations and in the LDCs is increasing, not decreasing (Portes, 1976). (Average income in the LDCs is only $500 a year—one-tenth the average income of developed countries.) The LDCs' infant mortality rate is more than five times higher than that of developed countries—120 per 1,000 births and twenty per 1,000, respectively. The number of people for every doctor is five times as high in the LDCs—3,500, as opposed to 680 in the developed countries. And the LDCs' rate of literacy, 43 percent, is less than half the rate in the developed countries, 97 percent.

Population.   There are many reasons for the stagnating economies of the LDCs. High birth rates are one (see Chapter 18). Britain, during its Industrial Revolution, never had a rate of population growth higher than 1.4 percent a year, so population growth was not an obstacle to economic expansion (Hunter, 1969, p. 6). The birth rate of the LDCs is higher than 2.5 percent, and in some, higher than 3 percent. This means that the economy must increase its agricultural productivity at that rate merely to keep its population alive at the present level of near-starvation. Many countries do not achieve even that.

Dependency theory The view that less economically developed societies stagnate because they are kept in a state of dependency by multinational corporations.

Dual-sector economies Economic systems prevalent in less fully industrialized societies, in which a high proportion of the work force is outside the industrial sector—in effect, outside the economy altogether—working in subsistence, survival activities.

Economic Dependency.   The **dependency theory** (Frank, 1969; Wallerstein, 1974) provides a second account of stagnation in the LDCs. According to it, many LDCs stagnate because they provide raw materials and cheap labor for multinational corporations, whose home bases are located in the economically developed nations and which seek to keep the LDCs poor and exploitable. True industrialization, this theory suggests, requires that corporate profits stay in the countries where they are earned, so they can be invested and consumed there.

Dual-Sector Economies.   A third explanation of stagnation in the LDCs is the existence in many of these countries of **dual-sector economies:** traditional and modern. The two sectors exist side by side without intermingling or influencing one another. Visitors to the largest cities in a number of these countries will see modern factories and office buildings, bustling streets, rush-hour traffic, well-equipped hospitals, efficient airports, and swanky apartment buildings and hotels. But a closer look reveals fringe areas densely populated by people living in squalor. A few miles outside these cities, the majority of the population often lives in feudal subjection, and in poverty even greater than that of the cities.

In dual-sector economies, a sizable part of the work force, typically a majority, is outside the economy altogether. These people have no full-time, year-round jobs with stable incomes. They sit by roadsides and sell mangoes; they walk the streets collecting bottles and discarded papers; they live in makeshift shacks on empty lots; they sell chewing gum; they do odd jobs; they do whatever they have to do to survive. The industrialized sector of the economy does not touch their lives at all. The wealth generated by partial industrialization does not "trickle down" to them. A comparable dual sector exists in highly industrialized economies, but it comprises a fraction of the proportion that it does in LDCs.

Some observers claim that these dual economies are a direct product of capitalism, another mechanism of keeping less developed nations economically dependent (Frank, 1969). In any case, the LDCs have clearly not followed the classic Western pattern of industrialization.

The Limits of Convergence. Modernization, like industrialization, is taking place around the world very unevenly. In some ways, in a number of places, the very process of industrialization has produced a reaction *against* modernization. Consider the case of Iran. This was a country where oil wealth created a fairly large modern sector. Yet the oil wealth did not trickle down to the masses. It benefited only a small elite, which attempted to introduce modern social and cultural innovations, such as coeducation. The result was a fundamentalist Muslim revolt that eventually overthrew a pro-Western government and created an "Islamic" state.

Many nations of the world have what economists call a "dual sector" economy. One sector is highly industrialized and modern. The second sector lacks industry, its people are poor, and it is essentially outside the economy altogether. Here, the slums of Rio de Janeiro in the foreground contrast with modern apartment buildings in the background.

United Nations

WHAT DO YOU THINK?

America in the 1990s and Beyond

In the 1980s, three major United States corporations—American Express, Bristol-Myers, and Sun Oil—approached Oxford Analytica, an interdisciplinary commercial "think tank," to size up, describe, evaluate, and analyze current and future social, political, and economic trends in the United States. Oxford Analytica assembled a team of sociologists, demographers, political scientists, and economists to gather the relevant information, draw the indicated conclusions, and write up the final report. The book *America in Perspective* (1986) is that report.

What will the 1990s and later decades look like? In what specific area of life will social change take place—and exactly what will the nature of this change be? The Oxford Analytica group found that, in the United States over the coming decades, the following changes would take place:

In the area of *population*:

More couples will have only two children. Sterilization after two children will become increasingly common. There will be no further "baby booms."

People will live longer lives; the old will be a greater proportion of the total population, and they will increase in absolute number, as well.

Large numbers of both legal and illegal immigrants will continue to enter the United States. Population growth will come mainly from immigration, and not as a result of births within the United States itself.

Women will form an increasingly larger share of the work force.

"Nonfamily" households—the widowed and the divorced without children—will form an increasing number and proportion of all households in the United States.

Hispanics will increase faster than Blacks and whites in the population, and early in the twenty-first century, they will outnumber Blacks.

The process of suburbanization will continue, and large cities will continue to lose population. Migration from the "Frost Belt" to the "Sun Belt" will continue, although at a slower rate.

The proportion that retirees form of the total population will rise, although this will be modified by the fact that the size of each age cohort, as it moved into old age, will vary somewhat, owing to the birth rate the year or decade that each cohort was born.

In the area of *life chances* (see Chapter 9):

Family income will cease to grow at past rates.

Differences in income between rich and poor will remain very large, and they will not diminish.

Downward mobility and upward mobility will counterbalance one another.

Racial and ethnic discrimination will decline.

As race becomes less important, social and economic class will become more so.

Only among Hispanics will social class not become more rigid.

"Getting ahead" economically will diminish as a realistic expectation; "holding one's own" will replace it.

In the area of *lifestyle*:

Family life and values will continue to be stressed.

While the proportion of married women who work will rise, the proportion of men who work will decline.

Men will share domestic chores and responsibilities with their working wives more than they do today.

Although divorce and cohabitation will be widespread, marriage will continue to be popular, especially if children are desired. At

---

That state—like a number of others in the LDCs—did not benefit from a greater sense of national unity or identity, convergence theory notwithstanding. If anything, the industrialization of the LDCs may be sharpening ethnic divisions. Within Iran, the Kurds are currently fighting to secede and form a separate state, as they are in Turkey and Iraq, two other partly industrialized countries in which they are a minority.

the same time, the number of out-of-wedlock children among teenagers will increase.

Rural America will become increasingly suburban in its lifestyle, and less distinctively rural.

In the realm of *politics*:

In national politics, the South and West will gain some political clout, while the Northeast and Midwest will weaken somewhat.

The political strength of Hispanics will increase.

The established political parties will diminish in strength and in voter identification.

Interest groups will increase in importance and in bargaining power in American politics.

The conservative mood set in the 1980s will continue for the foreseeable future.

Voter apathy will continue.

The dilemma between a continued high level of government assistance financed by higher taxes versus a lower level of government assistance combined with lower taxes will become increasingly painful in the years to come.

The Oxford Analytica team isolated eight basic *themes* or concepts that will continue to be important in American social and cultural life. These themes are:

The Importance of the "American Dream." Although upward mobility in the years to come will decline somewhat, it will remain high relative to that in other countries; in addition, the American standard of living will continue to remain high in comparison with that in industrialized countries.

Diffusion. The political, economic, and social system of the United States will continue to be decentralized, diffuse, dispersed, and complex.

Conservativism. Though America's social and political conservatism is broad, it is not deep, and major conflicts divide groups and categories on the ideological right.

"Europeanization." Major social and political characteristics once thought to characterize Europe will come to typify the United States, as well. America will become more "Balkanized," more diverse and less homogeneous, and different regions of the country will become more distinct and divergent. The class system will become more rigid and hierarchical, less fluid, and less socially mobile; in addition, class consciousness will increase. The blue-collar segment of the economy will decline in power, relative income, and social status. The gap between rich and poor will increase.

The Household Frontier. Social life will become more "home-centered" in the years to come, more inward-looking and private. (Because of the continuing high level of divorce, however, this may encompass several households simultaneously.) People will rely on the family to make life work and reaffirm basic values.

A High-Risk and High-Stress Society. Americans will face even more momentous choices in the years to come than they have in the past; this will result in more stress, anxiety, and conflict. Social and economic life will become riskier and more filled with tension.

Limits of Technological Life. Technology, thought to be a cure for all of society's ills, will be widely recognized to have distinct limitations—indeed, negative repercussions on society, as well.

Testing Confidence. Confidence in the United States, which eroded in the past, will undergo a resurgence.

Will these changes come about? What do you think?

Source: Oxford Analytica, 1986.

Oil-rich Nigeria fought a war to prevent the establishment of a separate nation, Biafra, formed by one of its ethnic minorities, the Ibo. Mineral-rich Katanga Province (now Shaba) tried to break away from Zaire (then the Congo) and only a long, bloody conflict brought it under central control. Tribalism and secessionist movements clearly are stronger today than they were a generation ago. Some observers believe that they have been promoted by the impact of economic development—by the clash of traditionalism and modernity, tensions that have created a greater need for an intimate, secure sense of identity (Marris, 1975).

The strength of religion, tribalism, and regionalism in so many LDCs argues strongly against the diffusionist and convergence hypotheses. The LDCs do not appear to be following the Western pattern of industrial and social development; nor does modernization appear to be an automatic by-product of industrialization. In part, as the Marxists point out, the LDCs may be economically stagnant because they—unlike the first countries to industrialize—are surrounded by highly industrialized nations, which try to dominate and exploit them. Even from an idealist point of view, the diffusionist and convergence hypotheses are inadequate, because they assume that the process of industrialization permits only minor variation from society to society. Idealists point out that cultural, religious, and moral attitudes might very well retard, prevent, or control economic development. Consider, for instance, the Indian caste system, which though officially illegal is still strong enough to prevent many people from working alongside people of other castes. Such an institution is a serious obstacle to any large-scale undertaking. Moreover, many people in LDCs believe that the capitalist mentality is cold, ruthless, and exploitive. As one LDC political leader put it. "There are certain things which we shall refuse to do or accept, whether as individuals or as a nation, even if the result of accepting them would give a surge forward in our economic development" (quoted in Hunter, 1969, p. 17).

POSTINDUSTRIAL SOCIETY

As we saw in Chapter 17, the American economy can be categorized as postindustrial. The majority of our people work in the service sector, for instance. Unlike industrial economies, postindustrial economies need manufactured goods, and also food. But those sectors take a back seat, while the service sector becomes increasingly important. Physical labor in all its forms becomes less important. In an industrial economy, labor power is the most important commodity; in a postindustrial economy, knowledge is. The machine is the most important tool in the industrial economy; in the postindustrial economy, the computer is.

In many ways, **postindustrial society** will be as different from industrial society as industrial society was from agricultural society. But how? Sociologist Daniel Bell (1976) has outlined some of the most significant of these changes, all of which were revolutionary in their impact.

Postindustrial society A society whose work force is located mainly in the service sector of the economy.

1. *The shift to people-oriented economic activity.* In an agricultural economy, "work" is the struggle of human beings to extract a livelihood from nature. In an industrial economy, work is a struggle with machines to create material objects. In a postindustrial economy, work is primarily an exchange among people—doctor and patient, scientist and manager, writer and editor, teacher and student. Interpersonal contact and interpersonal skills assume an unprecedented importance.

2. *The centrality of knowledge and the spread of a "knowledge class."*

While American society is postindustrialist, with a majority of its work force in the tertiary, or service sector, it also represents the most productive agricultural economy in the world. This is partly because agriculture here is highly mechanized.

Roger Foley/Photo Researchers

Science has become the foundation of the economy to a degree that is also unprecedented. Science-based industries—computers, electronics, optics, and polymers—in which major innovations take place yearly, even monthly, come to dominate the economy. The research-and-development departments of such companies have higher and higher proportions of their total budgets. "Knowledge workers" come to play so central a role they may share in the corporate profits, a trend already evident in the computer industry. As scientific knowledge and technology become more important to the economy, so does the technical and professional class that generates this knowledge.

3. *The "routinization" of science.* From the seventeenth century to well into the second half of the twentieth, scientific inquiry had a romantic, adventurous image in the public mind. Scientists were seen as pioneers, idealists, free of the contaminating forces of political and economic bias. Although an exaggeration, this image had some basis in truth. In a postindustrial society, science will become increasingly bureaucratized, more of a captive of economics. Business will sponsor applied research, drawing scientists away from "pure" research. The military, too, will hire more scientists. Fewer scientists will be free to follow the spirit of free inquiry.

4. *The rise of meritocracy.* The more profitable knowledge becomes, the more costly it is to exclude people with marketable talents and skills. Achievement, therefore, assumes increasing importance in a postindustrial society. Rewards will tend to be distributed according to ability and performance, not on the basis of ascribed characteristics. Background and inheritance will gradually lose out to education, ability, skill, and effort. Women, in particular, will come to compete on an equal basis with men.

The author of the most influential analysis of postindustrial society (Bell, 1976, p. 14) emphasizes that these changes are tendencies rather than things that have already happened or will definitely happen everywhere in the future. The analysis provides a model, an "ideal type." And although this model has its critics, these changes are undeniably taking place.

The crucial question is: How will a postindustrial economy influence a postindustrial society? Suppose that workers do shift from the manufacturing sector to the service sector. What does this mean for the rest of society? How will the rise of meritocracy affect other classes? Will a postindustrial society educate its children more effectively than we do at present and thereby make social mobility more common than it is today? Or will the stress on technical knowledge create a rigid two-class system, with those who have it on one side and those who don't on the other? Perhaps, if so, postindustrial society will be more, not less, stratified than the industrial economy was. Clearly, with an unemployment rate of 6 percent in 1987, it would seem that a dominant service sector is no guarantee of overall economic vitality. In fact, the shift to postindustrialism leaves in its wake a multitude of dying industries.

Just as the transition from an agricultural to an industrial economy generated social changes that were both beneficial and, at first, disastrous, likewise, the transition from an industrial to a postindustrial economy will no doubt hurt significant segments of our society. Nonetheless, these changes have to be faced, understood, and dealt with. Although we need not enthusiastically welcome the arrival of our future, it would be fatal to ignore it.

SUMMARY

1. Social change may be defined as the transformation of major aspects of culture and society.

2. Social change is practically universal.

3. Social change takes place in different societies at different rates; it is more rapid and extensive today than it was in the past.

4. Some aspects of society may change more than others; it is necessary, therefore, to specify different kinds of change. Individual behavior and attitudes, technology, stratification, religion, and population characteristics are some examples of the different ways that societies change.

5. The mechanisms or sources of social change include conflict, technological innovation, ideas, cultural diffusion, and changes in population.

6. Four basic models have been used to describe the process of social change: the evolutionary (both unilinear and multilinear), the cyclical, the functionalist, and the conflict or dialectical model.

7. Some theorists have emphasized ideas as the primary agent of social change; some argue, in opposition, that material conditions are more influential. Clearly, a synthesis of the idealist and the materialist views is necessary, because each is crucial.

8. Industrialization has probably been the most momentous of all processes of social change in the history of humankind.

9. The diffusionist school argues that non-Western nations will experience much the same process of industrialization that Western societies did centuries ago. As a result, industrializing societies and cultures all over the world will become more like one another. This is called the convergence hypothesis.

10. The sorts of mental changes that convergence theorists believe would take place in an industrializing, modernizing society include: a growing acceptance of change, a belief in the power of individual effort, the desire to attain a high educational level, a decline in patriarchy.

11. Industrialization is taking place very unevenly around the world; it has happened in some countries, but not others.

12. High birth rates in third-world nations, the dependency of these nations on foreign multinational corporations, and the maintenance of dual economies are the three major reasons why industrial "take-off" has not occurred in these lesser developed countries.

13. Modernization, like industrialization, is taking place around the world very unevenly. Traditional values have not disappeared or even weakened in many industrializing countries.

14. A postindustrial economy has most of its workers in the tertiary or service sector. Some social scientists believe that the transition from an industrial to a postindustrial economy will profoundly affect the other sectors of the economy and society generally.

SUGGESTED READINGS

Daniel Bell, *The Coming of Post-Industrial Society: A Venture in Social Forecasting*. New York: Harper Colophon, 1976.
Social change has transformed American society from an industrial to a postindustrial society. What are its basic characteristics? How did it happen? What are some consequences of this transformation? This book provides some answers.

Eva Etzioni-Halevy, *Social Change: The Advent and Maturation of Modern Society*. Boston: Routledge & Kegan Paul, 1981.
A basic overview of the subject.

Gerhard Lenski and Jean Lenski, *Human Societies* (5th ed.). New York: McGraw-Hill, 1987.
A textbook adopting the multilinear model.

Wilbert E. Moore, *Social Change* (2nd ed.). Englewood Cliffs, New Jersey: Prentice-Hall, 1974.
A brief introduction to the subject. It emphasizes the functionalist orientation.

John Naisbitt, *Megatrends: Ten New Directions Transforming Our Lives*. New York: Warner Books, 1982, 1984.
Like Toffler, Naisbitt has written a bestseller and an enormously controversial book, both praised and damned, sometimes by the same reviewer. And also like Toffler, Naisbitt is a "bluebird of happiness," arguing from a point of view of "irrepressible optimism." This book has been termed by *The New York Times* "the literary equivalent of a good after-dinner speech." At the same time, *Megatrends*, like *The Third Wave*, deserves to be read, and its central theses, to be thought about and debated.

Alvin Toffler, *The Third Wave*. New York: William Morrow, 1980; New York: Bantam Books, 1981.
A broad, sweeping examination of virtually all of the history of social change, especially what the author dubs "The Third Wave"—the current transition in the United States from an industrial to an information- or computer-based economy. Toffler argues that the world is on the threshold of a new and superior age, based on a technology that will solve almost all our problems. Almost no one will remain untouched by the changes sweeping over us at this very moment. This book, an instant bestseller when it was published, has been praised and criticized in nearly every corner of the globe. On the one hand, called "titillating but slipshod," "less than systematic or convincing," and, on the other, described as "magnificent," "superb," and "astonishing," this book deserves to be read by anyone interested in social change.

GLOSSARY

"Acceptable" death The modern practice of dying quietly, even though intense anxiety is associated with the event for all concerned. "Acceptable" death reduces social disruption.

Achieved status A position that is acquired or attained through one's own efforts.

Acquired status See **Achieved status.**

Activity theory The theory that people who kept active are those who age the most successfully.

Actor Someone who engages in behavior.

Advanced horticultural society An agricultural society that uses the hoe as the farming implement.

Affirmative action The practice of favoring minority-group members in hiring, promotion, and other economic, political, educational, or housing decisions.

Age cohort A group of people of roughly the same age who move through the life course together.

Ageism The prejudice and discrimination that aged persons face because their role in society is not valued.

Agents of socialization Individuals or institutions that teach the culture of a society—including its attitudes, values, and norms.

Age-sex pyramid A figure demographers use to portray the age and sex distribution of a population; the sexes are divided into each half of the figure, and age groupings are arrayed horizontally from top to bottom.

Age stratification theory The theory that allows us to analyze the people who belong to age cohorts that have different characteristics. These differences explain why people of different generations hold attitudes particular to that cohort and dissimilar to other cohorts.

Aggregate A bunch of people who happen to be in the same place at the same time, but who share no special social bond.

Agrarian society An agricultural society in which the primary method of production is the plow.

Altercasting In social interaction, as a result of our own needs, our creating identities for or assigning roles to others who do not acknowledge these roles or regard them as important.

Anomie A social condition of normlessness, where traditional values have lost their hold on people.

Anomie theory An explanation that locates the cause of deviance in the discrepancy between the cultural goal of material success and the means society provides to achieve that goal.

Apartheid The policy of rigid racial separation that prevails in South Africa.

Ascribed status A position to which one is assigned through no effort of one's own.

Assimilation The absorption of a racial or ethnic minority into the social and cultural life of the majority such that it disappears as a distinct and identifiable group.

Audience Individuals with whom an individual, or a group of individuals, interact, and who witness or react to their behavior.

Audience cult A loosely structured, diffuse religious entity which has no formal organization and whose adherents rarely meet.

Authoritarianism A rigid, hierarchical view of social life and human relations, usually accompanied by intolerance for a diversity of views and the belief that rules should be strictly obeyed.

Authority The exercise of legitimate power.

Background understandings In ethnomethodology, assumptions we make about social rules that are rarely spelled out explicitly.

Back region An area where role performance is hidden from the view of a given audience.

Backstage See **Back region.**

Behaviorism A theory in psychology that argues that learning or socialization, through the mechanism of reinforcement (a system of rewards and punishment), accounts for nearly all animal and human behavior.

Beliefs Cultural conventions about what is true or false.

Biased sample A sample of a population drawn in such a way that every individual does not have an equal chance of appearing in the sample.

Birth rate A measure of how many children the women of a given society or social category bear: annual number of births per 1,000 in the population. (See crude birth rate.)

Body language A type of nonverbal communication that conveys messages by means of our facial expressions and how we stand, walk, or gesticulate with our hands.

Bourgeoisie In Marxism, the factory owners, the capitalist class.

Bureaucracy A type of formal organization that is large and hierarchical and that forms the basis of an occupation and career for its employees.

Bureaucratic authority Authority that emanates from the public's faith in the rules and regulations governing a particular office.

Bureaucratic personality An individual who emphasizes rules for their own sake and forgets about the goals that the rules were designed to promote.

Capital Any resource or asset that can be used to make a profit, such as money, a factory, or property.

Capitalism An economic system in which the means of production and the ownership of wealth are in private hands.

Case study The observation of a single individual, group, organization, community, and so on, to highlight general features of social life.

Caste system A system of stratification in which social position is nearly entirely ascribed, or inherited.

Charisma An exceptional power or quality attributed to certain leaders.

Charismatic authority Authority that emanates from leaders who inspire allegiance because of the special, purely personal qualities they are thought to possess, independent of any office.

Chromosomes Material in cells that determines hereditary characteristics.

Church An established religious body that has a rigid hierarchy, an extensive bureaucracy, and a powerful influence over secular society, especially the government, and that claims universalism in a society—that is, it claims all the members of a society as members of the church. As a general rule, the church is conservative: It compromises with and supports existing social values and social structures, especially the stratification and political systems.

Civil liberties Rules that exist in democracies, spelling out rights that citizens have regarding free speech, protection against arbitrary or unwarranted arrest, surveillance, and so on.

Civil religion The belief that one's country and political system are special and "chosen" in the view of the deity; turns nationalism, patriotism, and ethnocentrism into a kind of religion.

Class A layer or stratum of people with the same socioeconomic status.

Class consciousness The shared, mutual awareness of members of a social class of its own class interests.

Class system A stratification system in which social position is largely achieved through individual effort.

Client cult A cult based on giving and receiving specific services, such as therapy, success, and peace of mind.

Collective behavior The relatively spontaneous, unstructured actions of a fairly large number of people responding to a given stimulus.

Communism According to Marx, the ultimate and highest stage of historical development: a stateless society in which the means of production are owned and run collectively. The term's current, popular, and somewhat erroneous meaning refers to the nations and ideologies aligned with the Soviet Union.

Compositional theory A perspective urban sociologists use to explain why city life is different from life in less settled areas; it argues that the social characteristics of people in cities generally, and in certain cities specifically, give them their distinctive flavor—and not the qualities that all cities share (size, density, and heterogeneity).

Concentric-zone model In urban ecology, the view (now obsolete) that cities develop into a series of concentric zones, much like an archery target, each with its own specialized function, people, and institutions.

Concrete operational stage In Piaget's theory of cognitive development, the period of life from age 7 to about 12, when concepts like speed, volume, number, and weight are understood, and the child can take the role of the other; abstract concepts, like love and death, are grasped only by means of specific references to the concrete world.

Conditioning Learning as a result of reward and punishment.

Confidentiality The principle that certain information given to a researcher should not be revealed, especially if it is likely to harm the informant in any way. It applies most directly and specifically to ensuring the informant's anonymity and protecting his or her identity—that is, making sure that no one can link up any of the behavior described or opinions expressed in a published work with a specific individual.

Conflict perspective of education The view that education is an arena for a power struggle among different social and economic groups in a society, the result of which is the imposition of the most powerful group's ideology on everyone else.

Conflict theory A sociological perspective arguing that exploitation and coercion dominate social relations among groups in society.

Conjugal family A family unit that is made up only of parents and their children; also called nuclear family.

Consensus perspective The view that most members of society agree on the most important values and issues; it is regarded as an aspect of functionalism.

Conservativism The political view that the economy should be regulated by the government very little, that welfare and other programs designed to assist the poor should be kept to a minimum, that the military should be strongly supported, and that communism should be contained abroad, even at the cost of supporting extremely undemocratic regimes.

Contagion theory The theory that argues that the moods, attitudes, and behavior of individuals in a collectivity are generated, communicated, and intensified by the presence of others; hence, contagion causes collective behavior.

Content analysis The systematic examination of cultural material that already exists in a physical, often documentary, form—such as photographs, short stories, news, advertising, love letters, comic books, even garbage—to draw conclusions about social life.

Contingency A seemingly irrelevant or incidental feature of an act that actually influences the labeling process—that is, whether it or its actor is condemned or not.

Continued subjugation The exploitation of minority groups by the majority group, accompanied by discrimination and racism.

Continuity theory The theory that people have a basic core personality and that their behavior thus continues more or less unchanged as they age.

Control A relevant variable in a study that is held constant to determine causal relationships between other variables.

Control group A category of individuals in an experiment who do not receive the experimental treatment, but who are exactly like the "experimental group" in every other crucial respect.

Convergence hypothesis The view that cultural differences among industrialized societies will gradually diminish.

Convergence theory The theory that argues that people who share certain predispositions come together and act out those predispositions; hence, individual characteristics, not the presence of others, cause collective behavior.

Cooptation The process of absorbing able sons and daughters of the working classes into the ranks of the affluent so that they won't threaten the *status quo*; this helps solidify the rule of the elite.

Corporate crime Illegal actions enacted by representatives of large companies on behalf of the interests of those companies.

Corporate interlocking A situation brought about by individuals who sit on the boards of directors, and who therefore presumably help control, two or more large corporations.

Correlates of socioeconomic status Aspects of people's lives that are related to their social-class positions.

Correlation A formal, statistical way of measuring the strength of the relationship between two variables. A **positive correlation** exists when a variable moves in one direction and the other variable moves the same way; a **negative correlation** means that as one variable increases, the other decreases.

Counterculture Groups that have made a conscious effort to reject some of the basic beliefs, values, and norms of the majority.

Crazes Short-lived activities, usually in fairly superficial areas of life, in which a large number of people engage for a short period of time. Some of these people are obsessive and fanatical about the activities in question.

Credentialism Setting up arbitrary, formal educational requirements for elite, high-paying jobs that bear little connection to the actual job requirements. Its unstated purpose is two-fold: first, to exclude children from less privileged families from these jobs and to give a competitive advantage to those with upper-middle-class backgrounds; and second, to socialize future occupants of these high-paying positions into conservative, *status quo* accepting values and norms.

Critical mass The size a community must reach to support a certain type of institution, group, or organization. See **Subcultural theory.**

Crowd A gathering of people physically assembled at the same place at the same time, focused on the same stimulus.

Crude birth rate The number of children born each year per 1,000 people in the total population.

Crude death rate The annual number of deaths per 1,000 people in the total population.

Cult A religious body that is novel in a society, strikingly different from the religious mainstream, and that does not arise from existing religious bodies.

Cult movement A full-fledged religious organization that attempts to satisfy its members' religious needs in their entirety.

Cultural diffusion The spread of cultural items from one society to another.

Cultural integration The consistency of the various aspects of a culture.

Cultural relativism Viewing cultures on the basis of their own beliefs and assumptions.

Cultural universal A custom or practice that is common to all societies.

Culture All of the learned and shared products of a society.

Culture-transmission theory A perspective that explains deviant behavior in terms of learning unconventional values in a straightforward fashion.

Cyclical model of social change The view that societies

tend to go through an "up and down" pattern of social change.

Deindustrialization The process and period of transition between a manufacturing and a service economy. During deindustrialization, industrial firms earn a declining share of a nation's total profits, and lay off workers; many go out of business altogether.

Democracy A form of government in which a majority rule the electoral system and the citizens enjoy civil liberties.

Democratic socialist Someone who believes that the transition to socialism can take place democratically, through the electoral process, and that socialist governments should be run on a democratic basis, with civil liberties, a toleration of dissenting views, the consent of the governed, and open elections. (See also **socialism** and **democracy**.)

Demographic transition The pattern a society exhibits in population change as a result of industrialization, from having a high birth rate and a high death rate, through having a high birth rate and a falling death rate, to having a low birth rate and a low death rate.

Demography The systematic study of the size, composition, and spatial distribution of human populations, as well as changes in all three, and the causes and consequences of such changes.

Demonic possession Being possessed by spirits and being forced to do evil things; a popular explanation for deviance in the Middle Ages.

Denomination A religious organization that accepts the validity of other religions, is fairly secularized, and generates a fairly mild religious commitment.

Dependency theory The view that less economically developed societies stagnate because they are kept in a state of dependency by multinational corporations.

Dependent variable The factor on which an effect is posited or may be observed; in the design or analysis of a study, the variable that is a candidate for a given effect.

Determinist theory A perspective urban sociologists use to explain why city life is different from life in less settled areas; it argues that the general characteristics of cities—specifically, size, density, and heterogeneity—determine what social life in urban areas will be.

Deterrence One goal or function of punishment: discouraging people from committing crimes.

Deviance Behavior that offends some people in a society and that moves them to disapproval, condemnation, or punishment of the actor.

Deviant Having the characteristics of violating the norms of a culture.

Deviant subculture A subculture based on unconventional and widely condemned behavior and beliefs.

Dialectical model of social change According to this model, change occurs abruptly, proceeds in distinct stages, and happens as a result of conflicts in society.

Diffusion theory The view that industrialization will follow the same path everywhere as was true of Western society in the eighteenth and nineteenth centuries, and that the same cultural transformation that the West experienced will also mark social change elsewhere. See also **Convergence hypothesis.**

Direct labeling Being caught and condemned as a deviant for engaging in deviant behavior.

Direct legal discrimination Discrimination that is supported by law. This form of discrimination no longer exists in the United States.

Direct nonlegal discrimination Discrimination that is not embodied in law, but that results from actions by individuals.

Discrimination Treating racial, ethnic, and other minorities unfairly and unjustly, judging them according to irrelevant criteria.

Disengagement theory The theory that people disengage from society because their social roles require it once they reach a certain age. Disengagement is thought to be beneficial for society because it allows younger people to assume the vacant roles, and older people to withdraw to enjoy the benefits of retirement.

Disinvestment The withdrawal of capital from one industry or sector and its investment in another one.

Division of labor The specialization of roles, activities, and work functions involved in production within a society or a bureaucracy.

Duel-sector economies Economic systems prevalent in less fully industrialized societies, in which a high proportion of the work force is outside the industrial sector—in effect, outside the economy altogether—working in subsistence, economic activities.

Dyad A two-person group.

Dysfunction Something that has a detrimental effect on society as a whole.

Ecclesia See **Church.**

Ecology The study of physical and geographical interrelationships among groups, neighborhoods, and social categories in a given environment, such as a city.

Economic determinism A perspective that argues that material factors play the central role in influencing social phenomena, especially social change.

Economy The production and distribution of scarce goods and services.

Ectomorph A thin, frail individual.

Ecumenical Practicing cooperation among a number of religious bodies.

Education The institution devoted to the transmission of knowledge, beliefs, and values by individuals occupying formal instructional positions ("teachers") to individuals occupying learning positions ("students").

Ego Freud's term for that part of the personality that tries to reconcile our selfish, destructive side with our conscience, or socialized side.

Emergent status A position that grows spontaneously out of the special relations that some people have with one another.

Emergent-norm theory The perspective that holds that many onlookers to collective behavior are initially ambivalent, indifferent, amused, or even quietly unfriendly toward that behavior, thus lending an illusory unanimity of support for it.

Empathy The ability to understand or interpret how another person thinks or feels.

Empirical Pertaining to the five senses: something that can be seen, heard, felt, tasted, or smelled, and that can likewise be verified independently by others' senses.

Enculturation The process by which a minority group or member is absorbed into the majority group and loses its subcultural distinctiveness.

Endogamy Marrying within one's own group or category.

Endomorph A plump individual.

Established sect A sect that rejects the secular world and the general society, but whose membership relies less on conversion than on natural reproduction.

Estate system A partly closed system of stratification, in which ascription, or birth, is the main criterion of rank, although some movement up or down is possible.

Ethnic group A collectivity of people who share a common subculture that is passed down from generation to generation, and who are usually regarded, and regard themselves, as sharing a common ancestry, as well.

Ethnocentrism Viewing another culture from the perspective of one's own. In the area of sex roles, the belief that men and women in all societies should act as they do in one's own society.

Ethnomethodology A perspective within sociology that investigates how interacting parties come to share definitions of reality in everyday life.

Evolutionary model of social change The view that societies grow in an inevitable process of improvement; from less developed to more fully developed, from simple to complex. These changes are usually steady and gradual.

Exogamy Marrying outside one's own group or category.

Experiment A research method that puts randomly assigned subjects into carefully designed situations, studies their reactions, and determines the impact of specific variables on their behavior.

Experimental group A category of individuals in an experiment who receive an experimental condition or treatment so that its effect may be observed.

Explanation An account for why things are the way they are, or something is the way it is, that shows why something occurs or what causes it.

Exploratory gesture An action that individuals enact in order to determine others' reactions to it, to test whether they may move even further in a particular direction.

Expressive leader Someone who leads by generating and sustaining a sense of solidarity, togetherness, and harmony.

Extended family A family unit made up of more than parents and their children.

Extermination The physical destruction of a minority group by the majority group.

Fads Activities, usually in fairly superficial areas of life, in which a large number of people engage for a short period of time; followers do not become obsessive or fanatical about fads.

Falsifiability A quality that all scientific statements must have: the capability of being disconfirmed or disproved if relevant data are collected.

Falsifiable Capable of being supported or disproven by using the appropriate evidence. Falsifiable statements permit meaningful answers to two questions: "What facts would show that this assertion is true?" and "What facts would show that it is false?"

Family The social institution that assigns responsibility for the physical survival, upbringing, and socialization of children.

The far right See **Reactionary**.

Fashions Fluctuating styles in appearance and behavior.

Fertility The number of children born to women in the population.

Folkways Norms that are not strongly held, are regarded as almost optional, and call for only mild chastisement of the transgressor.

Formal operational stage In Piaget's theory of cognitive development, the period of life after the age of 12, when the adolescent begins to think abstractly, without specific references to the concrete world.

Formal organization A group that has been deliberately created to achieve specific sets of goals and whose members' activities are systematically integrated to achieve them.

Formal social control The imposition of sanctions on offenders by agents and agencies that have been empowered by society to enforce the law; includes the police, the courts, and the prisons.

Front region An area where the role performance of an individual or a performance team is visible to a given audience.

Functionalism A sociological perspective that stresses

stability, cohesion, consensus, and the impact of behavior and custom on society as a whole.

Functionalist perspective of education The view that the educational system acts to contribute to the stability, cohesion, and consensus prevailing in a society.

Fundamentalism In Christianity, belief in the literal and infallible truth of the Bible; more generally, adhering to an orthodox doctrine and practice.

Game stage In George Herbert Mead's theory, the period of life when children learn to integrate their actions into a network of organized activities (such as in a baseball game), and they adopt the view of how all the parts relate to the whole.

Gemeinschaft A type of society or social setting characterized by intimacy, informality, closeness, strong emotion, cooperation, and common values and goals.

Gender The culturally determined traits associated with, and roles played by, males and females.

Gender identity The conception that one has of one's self as a male or female.

Generalization A statement with broad application or relevance to phenomena that exist in a wide range of different times and places.

Generalized other The perspective of the many individuals in the community, taken as a whole.

Genetic abnormality Pathological chromosomes; one theory of why some people commit crimes.

Gesellschaft A type of society or social setting characterized by formality, emotional reserve, superficial, segmental relations between individuals, and an indifference to community values and goals.

Hawthorne effect The impact research has on the people studied, resulting from their awareness of being studied; it is usually regarded as a distortion of experimental findings.

Hermaphrodite An individual who possesses some biological characteristics of both sexes.

Heterosocial Sex-integrated; a quality that characterizes marriages that are egalitarian, companionate, and sexually integrated.

Homogamy The tendency for people with similar characteristics to marry one another.

Homosocial Sex-segregated.

Hormones Chemicals secreted into the bloodstream by specific organs called glands which stimulate or inhibit certain biochemical processes.

Horticultural society A society whose economy is based primarily on using the hoe or the digging stick as an agricultural method.

Hunting and gathering society A society that feeds its members primarily by foraging for food in the wild.

Hypothesis A statement set forth in advance of a study predicting the occurrence of a set of phenomena or proposing an explanation for facts that should be observed.

Id In Freud's theory of psychoanalysis, the aggressive, sexual side of the personality that demands gratification, often at the expense of others.

Ideal type The characterization of a phenomenon in a slightly exaggerated form to highlight its distinctive features.

Idealistic view of social change The perspective that views ideas as the main agent of social change.

Illegitimate power Power exercised by individuals against those who reject their right to rule.

Impression management Presenting an image of oneself to others, often one that is more favorable than others would think in the absence of creating a public image.

Incarceration Imprisonment.

Incest taboo A rule prohibiting family members from marrying or having sex with one another.

Income The money or other gain received by an individual for labor or services or from property.

Independent variable One factor that influences or has an effect on a second factor (the "dependent" variable).

In-depth qualitative interview See **Unstructured interview.**

Index crimes Crimes used by the FBI to measure or indicate the nation's overall crime rate: murder, rape, robbery, aggravated assault, burglary, motor vehicle theft, and larceny-theft.

Indirect discrimination See **Institutional racism.**

Indirect labeling Being aware that one's behavior and identity are strongly condemned, or widely regarded as deviant, without actually being caught or condemned for engaging in it.

Industrialization The transition to an economic system based on the use of inanimate power sources, such as coal or oil, the invention of machines to replace animal or physical human power, and the organization of workers into large productive units.

Infant mortality The number of deaths of babies, before they reach the age of 1, per 1,000 births in a given year.

Infant mortality rate The number of babies who die each year before their first birthday per 1,000 total births.

Infantilization The period of helpless dependency of infants on their parents.

Informant In participant-observation or field methods, an individual who supplies information to the researcher, an insider in the social setting that is being observed.

Information control Manipulating the presentation of facts about oneself to others to one's own advantage.

In-group A collectivity of people whose members feel themselves to be separate from, even in opposition to, other groups.

Inner-directed Being strongly governed or motivated by one's own values and standards, rather than by those of other people.

Interactionism See **Symbolic interactionism.**

Interactionist theory See **Labeling theory.**

Institution All the norms, statuses, and roles centered around a particular need, theme, or activity.

Institutional racism A pattern of treating minority groups that results in continuing existing racial inequality, even without formal discrimination.

Instrumental leader Someone who leads by coordinating the activities of group members so they can rationally pursue specific goals.

Intergenerational mobility The amount of movement from one socioeconomic status level, or social class, to another, from one generation to the next.

Interval sampling Selecting individuals to study on the basis of their appearance in a sequence—for instance, choosing every tenth name in a telephone book or interviewing every twentieth person entering a building.

Intragenerational mobility The amount of movement from one socioeconomic status level, or social class, to another within an individual's lifetime.

Labeling theory A perspective within sociology that focuses on the impact of being caught and stigmatized as a deviant. (Also called **interactionist theory.**)

Latent function Consequences of social actions or customs that the members of a society are unaware of and may not desire.

Latent goal An unacknowledged end toward which a group, an organization, a society, or any social arrangement is directed or that it manages to achieve.

Legitimate power Authority. Power that exists when those subject to it accept the right of others to exercise it.

Less developed countries (LDCs) The poorer, less industrialized countries of the world.

Liberalism The political view that the government should fund programs to assist the poor, that civil liberties should be strictly observed, and that a rapprochement should be reached with communist regimes abroad.

Life chances Anything that can be purchased: material goods, medical care, food, shelter, clothing, transportation.

Life expectancy The average number of years individuals living in a given country or social category live, on the average.

Linguistic relativity hypothesis See **Sapir-Whorf hypothesis.**

Lobby A certain kind of highly organized interest group, with an office, a staff, and access to legislators and politicians.

Looking-glass self The term Cooley used to explain the images we have of ourselves through the eyes of others.

Macro level of social change Change that takes place on the institutional, structural, and society-wide level.

Macro level of social structure The organization of society at the organizational and institutional level, above the level of interacting individuals.

Macro-level theory A perspective that examines the "big picture," society on a structural and institutional level, rather than at the individual level.

Majority group The racial or ethnic segment of a society's population that holds the dominant power.

Manifest function Consequences of social actions or customs the members of a society know about and usually desire.

Manifest goal The stated, widely recognized purpose for a group, organization, social institution, or action.

Marxism A sociological perspective arguing that economic conflict between social classes is the most important dimension or factor to examine in capitalist society.

Mass Individuals who are physically dispersed but who share a common attitude or belief and act upon it, sometimes alone, sometimes with others.

Mass delusion A mistaken notion, often one that is acted upon, that takes place, not among face-to-face crowds, but among people who are scattered in many places.

Mass media The means of communication that are one-sided and reach very large numbers of the public.

Master status The position that is central to an individual's life and that determines or influences other positions and statuses.

Material artifacts Physical objects created and shared by the members of a society.

Materialist view of social change The perspective that holds that material conditions and phenomena determine social change, not ideas.

Means of production Anything that is capable of producing goods and services, especially for a profit and on a large scale. Examples are a gold mine, a large tract of farm land, a large sum of money, or a factory.

Megalopolis A huge "super city" created by the urbanization and suburbanization of previously rural areas between contiguous cities.

Merchant Someone who buys and sells goods or commodities for a profit as an occupation or profession.

Mesomorph A muscular, athletic individual.

Methodology A systematic, scientific research technique that is used to study a phenomenon.

Micro level of social change Change that takes place on the individual, person-to-person level.

Micro level of social structure The organization of society at the interpersonal level at which individuals, occupying specific positions, interact with one another.

Micro-level theory A perspective that examines social relations on a small scale, at the level of person-to-person encounters.

Middle-range theory The view that constructing grand, all-inclusive abstract theories is not productive, and that studying delimited or specific aspects and issues in society is.

Migration rate The number of people entering or leaving a country for each 1,000 people in its total population.

Minority group A segment of a society's population that is deprived of power and economic resources because of racial or ethnic characteristics; members of such a group are a target of prejudice, discrimination, or institutional racism.

Mode of production The way a society generates food and other economic goods.

Model See **Ideal type.**

Monotheism Belief in the existence of only one God.

Morality of constraint In Piaget's theory of the moral development of the child, the view of rules as absolutes, imposed from above, to be rigidly obeyed; takes place between the ages of 2 and 7.

More developed countries (MDCs) The more affluent, more industrialized countries of the world.

Mores The norms that are regarded as important, the violation of which brings strong punishment to the offender.

Multilinear model of social change The view that social change does not follow a single line of development, but takes place along different lines and at different rates, from one society to another.

Multinational corporation A large company that has subsidiary offices, and does substantial business, in a number of different countries.

Multiple-nuclei model In urban ecology, the theory that cities develop minor, specialized, geographically scattered centers, rather than a single downtown area.

Natural selection The survival and perpetuation of favorable characteristics in biological organisms.

Nature versus nurture The debate between the view that biology determines human behavior and the view that environment largely does.

Negative correlation See **Correlation.**

Nomadic Having no fixed residence; moving around from time to time.

Nonprobability sampling A technique of selecting individuals to study that does not use a random device.

Nonverbal communication Conveying messages through means other than words.

Norms Instructions telling the members of a society what is correct and incorrect behavior; rules about what people should and should not do.

Nuclear family See **Conjugal family.**

Object permanence The realization that things still exist even when they are not in sight.

Offices Full-time positions that confer prestige and power on their incumbents.

Open-ended question A question that does not require that the respondent choose among forced alternatives, but that can be answered in a free-flowing, detailed fashion.

Operationalization The process of measuring a concept with a specific indicator.

Other-directed Being influenced or motivated primarily by the values and standards of one's peers, rather than one's own.

Out-group A collectivity of individuals (not necessarily a true sociological group) to whom in-group members feel themselves to be opposed.

Oversocialized conception of man and woman The view that human beings are wholly a product of socialization and that they believe everything they have been taught.

Paradigm A model of how the world works; a theory or perspective.

Participant-observer A sociological researcher who studies human behavior either by taking part in the activities of the informants or subjects under study or by witnessing those activities in a naturalistic way.

Performance team A group of individuals engaged in a collective presentation of self.

Performed role What someone who occupies a specific position actually does; may conflict with the expectations or demands of the role itself.

Play stage In George Herbert Mead's theory, the period during which children act out imaginary roles, one at a time; facilitates taking the role of the other.

Plea bargaining "Negotiated justice," whereby a defendant gives up the right to a trial and, in exchange, is convicted on a lesser charge, which draws a lighter sentence.

Pluralism A condition of racial and ethnic diversity in a society in which groups retain their distinctive characteristics and customs, and economic and political differences among them are minimal or practically nonexistent.

Pluralism theory The school of thought that argues

that power is dispersed rather than centralized, contingent rather than general, and exercised with the consent of the governed rather than in an unchecked fashion.

Political action committee (PAC) An organization that attempts to further its own interests by influencing the political process; a well-organized interest group.

Politics The exercise of power. Sometimes defined as the pursuit of power.

Polyandry A marital arrangement whereby one woman is permitted to marry more than one man.

Polygamy Marriages that involve one individual married to more than one partner.

Polygyny A marital arrangement whereby one man may be married to more than one woman.

Polytheism Belief in the existence of a number of gods.

Population transfer The forced movement of a racial or ethnic minority by the majority group from one geographic area to another, where it will be less troublesome to the majority.

Positive correlation See **Correlation.**

Postindustrial economy An economic system with a highly efficient, productive industry and a sizable and growing tertiary sector.

Postindustrial society A society whose work force is located mainly in the service sector of the economy.

Potential group A collectivity of people who possess characteristics that might serve as the basis for future group formation.

Power The ability to get one's way, despite the resistance of others.

Power-elite theory The perspective that holds that the most important decisions in American politics are made by a small, highly cohesive group of individuals at the top of major institutions.

Prejudice A preconceived, unfavorable opinion of a social category based on racial, ethnic, religious, or other characteristics.

Preoperational stage In Piaget's theory of the cognitive development of the child, the period lasting from about 18 months to 7 years old, when children grasp the idea of objective permanence, and cause and effect, but remain egocentric, unable to adopt the perspectives of others.

Prescriptive norms Rules telling the members of a culture what they *should* do.

Presentation of self Conveying a certain image of ourselves to others in a conscious, intentional fashion.

Prestige Positive evaluation or social honor bestowed by others; often used in evaluating an occupation.

Preverbal stage The period during which children do not yet talk.

Primary deviation The simple commission of a deviant act. See **Secondary deviation.**

Primary group Group based on informal, intimate, personal social relationships.

Primary sector That segment of the economy that extracts natural resources directly from the land—such as mining, fishing, and farming.

Primary sex characteristics Physical characteristics of the body that pertain specifically to reproduction, such as the genitals.

Privileged communication See **Confidentiality.**

Probability sampling A technique of choosing individuals to study by using a random device. In order to generate a true probability sample, each person in the targeted universe must have an equal chance of being selected.

Proletariat According to Marxist theory, the working class in a capitalist economy; those who must sell their labor to live.

Proscriptive norms Rules telling members of a culture what they should *not* do.

Proxemics The use of social physical space to communicate social messages.

Psychoanalysis A theory in psychology, originated by Sigmund Freud, which holds that repressed childhood experiences and sexual drives largely shape each individual's personality and behavior.

Qualitative Having the characteristic of being inexact, and thus relying on information that is subjective and illustrative rather than definitive; being incapable of being measured precisely.

Quantitative Capable of being measured or expressed in precise, statistical terms, such as in the form of a percentage or an arithmetic ratio.

Quota sampling A sampling technique based on achieving a certain percentage of respondents with certain characteristics in the sample—for instance, half women and half men.

Race According to the dictionary, a group of persons related by common ancestry or heredity; according to sociologists, a category of persons believed, by themselves or others, to share a common ancestry.

Racism A negative, hostile attitude toward members of a minority group. See **Prejudice.**

Radicalism The political ideology that is most closely associated with the ideas of Karl Marx; radicals believe that the capitalist economy is exploitative and oppressive by its very nature, and must be overthrown for socialism.

Rationality The deliberate setting of goals and the development of means designed to achieve them.

Reactionary Someone whose beliefs are consistent with the extreme right wing of the political spectrum; reactionaries wish to do away with the electoral process, civil rights, and civil liberties.

Reference group A collectivity of individuals to which

we may or may not belong, but which we use as a standard to evaluate ourselves.

Reflexivity The condition or process of seeing ourselves through the eyes of others—at least, as we think others see us.

Registration A continuous, official record of social facts.

Rehabilitation One goal or function of punishment: conducting programs that turn the miscreant away from a life of crime.

Relative deprivation, theory of An explanation of how protest movements, particularly revolutions, emerge that attempts to use the objective and subjective factors behind these social movements.

Relativity Variation in judgments by different cultures, subcultures, or historical time periods about whether a given act is good or bad.

Religion A system of beliefs and practices relative to sacred things that unite adherents into a kind of moral community.

Representative sample A group of individuals chosen to be studied who reflect the characteristics of the population from which they were drawn.

Resocialization The process of "forgetting" what we have learned earlier and learning new attitudes, values, and behaviors.

Resource-mobilization theory The perspective that holds that discontent in a population does not explain social movements, because discontent exists virtually everywhere. The key factor explaining social movements is the ability of leadership to mobilize that discontent.

Respondent The individual who is interviewed or who fills out a questionnaire in a survey.

Retribution One goal or function of punishment: revenge.

Revolutionary Someone who believes that governments in capitalist states should be overthrown, violently if necessary, and replaced with socialist or communist governments in which the means of production are controlled by the public, not the private, sector.

Rising expectations, theory of A theory maintaining that dissatisfaction often rises as conditions improve, because expectations rise faster than conditions improve—thereby setting the stage for social movements and even revolution.

Role The normative expectations attached to a specific position.

Role conflict A contradiction between the demands of two different positions that someone occupies at the same time.

Role distance Enacting the demands of a role with distance and detachment.

Role set All of the normative expectations attached to a position whose occupant interacts with a number of complementary statuses.

Role strain Contradictions among the many demands attached to a single status.

Sample A group of individuals chosen from a population to be studied in social research.

Sapir-Whorf hypothesis The theory that language profoundly shapes thought and action.

Secondary analysis The use of material or information that was not collected by the researcher originally, such as census data.

Secondary deviation The attempt by deviants to deal with the problems created by labeling.

Secondary group Collectivity whose members relate to one another formally and impersonally.

Secondary sector That segment of the economy that transforms natural resources into products—such as turning iron ore into steel or wood pulp into cardboard boxes; most of this sector is the industrial sector, or manufacturing.

Secondary sex characteristics Physical characteristics that develop during adolescence as a result of the action of hormones, such as facial hair on males and breasts on females.

Sect A schismatic religious body that broke off from a parent church, and possesses a strong sense of its own righteousness and of the error of other religious bodies and that remains somewhat aloof from secular society, which it views as corrupt.

Sector model In urban ecology, the view that cities generate "sectors," or wedge-shaped areas that grow out from their central core, usually along transportation lines.

Secularization A process of becoming influenced by nonreligious forces and losing a more intense and "purer" religious orientation.

Self The notion that each individual has of his or her own identity.

Sensorimotor stage In Piaget's theory of the cognitive development of the child, beginning at birth and lasting until the age of 18 months to 2 years, when the child's central and overwhelming concern is making physical contact with the world and navigating through it.

Service sector of the economy Economic activities that use products to perform a service—like teaching, flying an airplane, banking, providing legal assistance, and so on. Service activities do *not* involve extracting raw materials from the earth (like fishing, farming, and mining), which is called the primary sector, and they do *not* involve manufacturing or turning raw materials into products, which is called the secondary sector.

SES Abbreviation for "socioeconomic status."

Sex The condition of being a biological male or female.

Sexism The ideology or behavior that supports gender inequality.

Sexual funnel A situation that exists whereby the

higher the stratificational position, the smaller the proportion of women there are.

Sign One thing that stands for another, the meaning of which is direct, obvious, and nonsymbolic.

Significant others Those individuals who are emotionally important to a person.

Simple horticultural society An agricultural society whose principal implement for growing food is the digging stick.

Snowball sampling A technique of selecting respondents by beginning with a few individuals that the researcher knows to possess a certain characteristic (for instance, vegetarians); then, after interviewing them, asking each to supply a few names of others with the same characteristic; and, finally, continuing this process until the sample has "snowballed" into an acceptable size.

Social change The transformation of major aspects of a culture and society.

Social control All of the social efforts to discourage deviant behavior and the mechanisms designed to ensure conformity to norms, rules, and laws.

Social group A collectivity of people who interact with one another, share a common identity, and adhere to a special and distinct set of norms.

Social interaction The process of individuals' acting toward, responding to, or taking into account other people.

Social mobility Movement up or down the class structure.

Social movements Organized efforts by a large number of people to change or preserve some major aspects of society.

Social sanctions Rewards or punishments called for in a culture for engaging, or not engaging, in certain actions.

Social structure A network of interconnected, normatively governed, social relationships in a society.

Socialism State ownership of the means of production. As it is widely used today, the term refers to a "mixed" economy—that is, one partly in state hands and partly in private hands.

Socialization the process of learning; especially refers to acquiring the values, attitudes, roles, and identities taught by our culture.

Society The people who live in a given area and share a common culture.

Sociobiology The theory that human behavior, like physical characteristics and animal behavior, is acquired through biological inheritance, as a result of natural selection.

Socioeconomic status A position along a continuum of income, prestige, power, or education, or a combination of them.

Sociological imagination The ability to link specific details of individual lives with general structures of social life, to see where individuals fit into the "big picture."

Sociology The systematic study of social life.

Somatotype Body type or physical characteristics; one theory of why some people commit crime and deviant behavior.

Special-interest group An organization or a group that has a fairly specific goal or purpose and that attempts to influence the political process to achieve that goal.

Standardized interview schedule See **Structured interview.**

State A political entity characterized by centralized, institutionalized rule and a sense of common identity among the population.

Statistical category A collectivity of individuals who share a given characteristic, regardless of whether it creates a true group out of those who share it.

Status A normatively governed position in a society.

Status set All of the positions occupied by a single individual.

Stereotype A simple, rigid, and often negative image held about the members of a group without regard for the facts.

Stickiness of labels The fact that because deviant labels are difficult to shed, they often "stick" to us for a long time.

Stigma The public scorn or condemnation that deviant behavior attracts to the perpetrator.

Stratification A system or means of ranking people in a hierarchy according to whether or not they possess things that are valued, such as wealth, prestige, and power; distribution of social rewards.

Structural mobility Movement up or down the class ladder that is caused by the opening up or the shrinking of positions in a given economic system or structure.

Structured interview An interview in which the interviewer asks specific questions, with a limited number of possible answers, in a predetermined order.

Subcultural theory A perspective urban sociologists use to explain why city life is different from life in less settled areas; it argues that cities sustain groups, institutions, and organizations that are not viable in smaller communities because of the sizes of their populations. See **Critical mass.**

Subculture Groups or categories of people whose beliefs, norms, and values differ somewhat from those of the majority.

Subjects Individuals in an experiment whose behavior is studied.

Superego In Freud's theory of psychoanalysis, that part of the personality that represents the conscience, or society's view of right and wrong.

Survey A set of research techniques that entails drawing a fairly large sample, asking specific questions, and analyzing the data obtained in a rigorous, quantitative fashion.

Symbol One thing that stands for another, whose meaning is arbitrary and imposed by the human mind.

Symbolic interactionism A perspective within sociology that stresses the meaning phenomena have for individuals and groups, the interaction that takes place among individuals, and the ways in which people interpret things in the world.

Systematic Methodical, based on a plan, set up in such a way that valid comparisons can be made.

Tabula rasa The obsolete view that, at birth, human beings are a "blank slate" onto which anything may be written; usually associated with the extreme "nurture" position of early behaviorists.

Taking the role of the other Seeing the world through the eyes of another person.

Teleological fallacy The mistaken view that everything exists, including natural phenomena, for a specific purpose.

Tertiary sector The "service" sector of the economy, which uses manufactured products to perform services—a teacher uses chalk, a bus driver uses a bus, and so on.

Theory A general approach, a perspective, a paradigm; an explanation for a general class of phenomena, such as Darwin's theory of natural selection.

Tokenism With regard to the sexes (and races), granting a few women (or Blacks) high-level positions to indicate that the system operates fairly and without respect to sexual (or racial) status.

Totalitarian state A state that is extremely repressive. Its citizens have neither majority rule nor civil liberties.

Traditional authority Authority based on custom; rulers wield legitimate power because their subjects believe them to possess a sacred right to rule.

Traditionalism A wish to preserve tradition and resist change.

Tradition-directed Governed by centuries-old customs and a rigid social structure.

Triad A three-person group.

Triangulation A method of confirmation using several research methods to get a "fix" on social reality.

Unbiased sample A sample that was drawn in such a way that every individual or unit in the population has an equal chance of appearing in it. As a result of such a selection technique, it is to be expected that these individuals reflect the characteristics of the population from which they were drawn.

Unconscious According to psychoanalytic theory, the repressed, submerged portion of mental life of which one is not aware, but which determines behavior nonetheless.

Underemployed Working at a job requiring less education, training, or skill than one has.

Unilinear model of social change The now-obsolete view that all societies progress through the same pattern of development.

Unrepresentative sample A group of individuals selected for study whose characteristics do not reflect those of the population from which they were drawn.

Unstandardized interview schedule See **Unstructured interview.**

Unstructured interview An interview that is open-ended and free-flowing and that permits the respondent flexibility and detail in his or her answers.

Urban ecology The study of spatial relationships among people and institutions in cities.

Urbanization The emergence of cities and their growth over many centuries.

Urban legends Contemporary, more or less spontaneously generated stories with certain stereotypical features; they are told and believed as true, even though they are, in fact, quite fanciful.

Value-added theory The perspective that isolates six preconditions for collective behavior: structural conduciveness, structural strain, generalized beliefs, precipitating factors, mobilization for action, and operation of social control.

Value-free Free of bias, value judgments, or personal opinions. Some sociologists argue that this stance is necessary to engage in any science, whereas others argue that all approaches to studying the world are inevitably based on values.

Values Notions of what is regarded as good or bad, desirable or undesirable.

Variable The operationalization of a concept that varies or changes from one person, time, situation, or society to another.

Verbal stage In George Herbert Mead's theory, the period of childhood that begins with speech.

Victimless crime An illegal action that is voluntarily engaged in by the participants, the consequences of which, with respect to harm, are debatable.

Wealth Significant economic assets.

White-collar crime Illegal actions committed by affluent individuals of high socioeconomic status in the course of their occupational activities; typically refers to corporate crime.

Xenophobia Extreme hostility toward foreigners and anything foreign.

REFERENCES

Adler, Freda. 1975. *Sisters in Crime: The Rise of the New Female Criminal*. New York: McGraw-Hill.

Adler, Jerry, et al. 1984. "The Year of the Yuppie." *Newsweek*, December 31, pp.14–24.

Adorno, Theodore W., et al. 1950. *The Authoritarian Personality*. New York: Norton.

Ager, Susan. 1980. "What's Beneath the Pyramids: Fear and Fantasy, Greed and Giddy Glee." *Gambling Times*, June, pp. 3, 4, 9.

Alba, Richard D. 1985a. "Interethnic and Interracial Marriage in the 1980s Census." Albany, N.Y.: Center for Social and Demographic Analysis. Unpublished paper.

Alba, Richard D. 1985b. *Italian Americans: Into the Twilight of Ethnicity*. Englewood Cliffs, N.J.: Prentice-Hall.

Albrecht, Stan L., Darwin L. Thomas, and Bruce A. Chadwick. 1980. *Social Psychology*. Englewood Cliffs, N.J.: Prentice-Hall.

Alexander, Jeffrey (ed.). 1985. *Neofunctionalism*. Beverly Hills, Calif.: Sage.

Allan, Carol, and Herman Brotman. 1982. *Chartbook on Aging*. Washington, D.C.: The White House Conference on Aging.

Allon, Natalie, and Diane Fichel. 1977. "Urban Courting Patterns: Singles Bars." In Arthur B. Shostak (ed.), *Our Sociological Eye: Personal Essays on Society and Culture*. Port Washington, N.Y.: Alfred, pp.8–26.

Allon, Natalie, and Diane Fichel. 1979. "Singles Bars." In Natalie Allon, *Urban Lifestyles*. Dubuque, Iowa: William C. Brown, pp.128–179.

Allport, Floyd. 1924. *Social Psychology*. Boston: Houghton.

Allport, Gordon, and Leo Postman. 1947. *The Psychology of Rumor*. New York: Holt.

Alperovitz, Gar, and Jeff Faux. 1984. *Rebuilding America*. New York: Pantheon Books.

Alston, Jon P. 1971. "Religious Mobility and Socioeconomic Status." *Sociological Analysis*, 32 (Summer): 140–148.

American Sociological Association. 1977. *Careers in Sociology*. Washington, D.C.: American Sociological Association.

Amir, Menachem. 1971. *Patterns of Forcible Rape*. Chicago: University of Chicago Press.

Anderson, Charles H., and Jeffrey Royle Gibson. 1978. *Toward a New Sociology* (3rd ed.). Homewood, Ill.: Dorsey Press.

Argyle, Michael. 1981. "The Laws of Looking." In Ian Robertson (ed.), *The Social World*. New York: Worth, pp.95–99.

Aries, Phillipe. 1974. *Western Attitudes Toward Death* (P. M. Ranum, trans.). Baltimore: Johns Hopkins University Press.

Aronson, Sidney. 1971. "The Sociology of the Telephone." *International Journal of Comparative Sociology*, 12 (3): 153–167.

Armor, David T., T. Michael Polich, and Harriet Stambul. 1976. *Alcoholism and Treatment*. Santa Monica, Calif.: Rand Corporation.

Asch, Solomon E. 1951. "Effects of Group Pressure Upon the Modification and Distortion of Judgment." In Harold S. Guetzkow (ed.), *Groups, Leadership and Men*. Pittsburgh: Carnegie Press, pp.177–190.

Asch, Solomon E. 1955. "Opinions and Social Pressure." *Scientific American*, 193 (November): 31–35.

Asch, Solomon E. 1956. "Studies of Independence and Conformity I: A Minority of One Against a Unanimous Majority." *Psychological Monographs*, 70 (9): 1–70.

Atchley, Robert C. 1978. "Aging as a Social Problem: An Overview." In M. Seltzer, S. Corbett, and R. Atchley (eds.), *Social Problems of the Aged*. Belmont, Calif.: Wadsworth, pp.4–21.

Austin, Charles. 1982. "Marriage Seen as Godly Duty." *The New York Times*, July 2, pp. B1, B4.

Axelrod, Morris, Floyd J. Fowler, and Arnold Gurin. 1967. *A Community Survey for Long Range Planning—A Study of the Jewish Population*. Boston: Combined Jewish Philanthropies of Greater Boston.

Babbie, Earl. 1980. *Sociology: An Introduction* (2nd ed.). Belmont, Calif.: Wadsworth.

Bainbridge, William Sims, and Rodney Stark. 1980. "Client and Audience Cults in America." *Sociological Analysis*, 41 (Fall): 199–214.

Bakal, Carl. 1979. *Charity U.S.A.: Investigation into the Hidden World of the Multi-Billion Dollar Charity Industry*. New York: Times Books.

Ball, Donald W. 1968. "Toward a Sociology of Telephone and Telephoners." In Marcello Truzzi (ed.), *Sociology and Everyday Life*. Englewood Cliffs, N.J.: Prentice-Hall, pp.59–75.

Baltzell, E. Digby. 1958. *Philadelphia Gentlemen*. New York: Free Press.

Baltzell, E. Digby. 1966. *'Who's Who in America* and *The Social Register*: Elite and upper Class Indexes in Metropolitan America." In Reinhard Bendix and Seymour Martin Lipset (eds.), Class, Status and Power (2nd ed.). New York: Free Press, pp.266–275.

Barlow, Hugh D. 1987. *Introduction to Criminology* (4th ed.). Boston: Little, Brown.

Baumeister, Roy F. 1985. "The Championship Choke." *Psychology Today*, April, pp.48–52.

Baumgold, Julie. 1982. "Childrearing: Oldthink, Newthink." *New York*, October 4, pp.34–38.

Becker, Ernest. 1962. *The Birth and Death of Meaning*. New York: Free Press.

Becker, Howard S. 1963. *Outsiders: Studies in the Sociology of Deviance*. New York: Free Press.

Becker, Howard S. 1967. "Whose Side Are We On?" *Social Problems*, 14 (Winter): 239–247.

Becker, Howard S. 1970. *Sociological Work: Method and Substance*. Chicago: Aldine.

Becker, Howard S. 1973. "Labelling Theory Reconsidered." In *Outsiders* (rev. ed.). New York: Free Press, pp.177–212.

Becker, Howard S., Blanche Geer, Everett C. Hughes, and Anselm L. Strauss. 1961. *Boys in White: Student Culture in Medical School*. Chicago: University of Chicago Press.

Beeghley, Leonard. 1978. *Social Stratification in America: A Critical Analysis of Theory and Research*. Santa Monica, Calif.: Goodyear.

Bell, Alan P., and Martin S. Weinberg. 1978. *Homosexualities: A Study of Diversity Among Men and Women*. New York: Simon & Schuster.

Bell, Daniel. 1976. *The Coming of Postindustrial Society: A Venture into Social Forecasting*. New York: Harper & Row.

Bell, Robert R. 1971. "Female Sexual Satisfaction as Related to Levels of Education." *Sexual Behavior*, 1 (November): 9–14.

Bellah, Robert N. 1970. "Civil Religion in America." In *Beyond Belief: Essays on Religion in a Post-Industrial World*. New York: Harper & Row, pp.168–215.

Bellah, Robert N. 1974. "American Civil Religion in the 1970s." In Russell E. Richey and Donald G. Jones (eds.), *American Civil Religion*. New York: Harper & Row, pp.255–272.

Bellah, Robert N. 1975. *The Broken Covenant: American Civil Religion in Time of Trial*. New York: Seabury Press.

Benedict, Ruth. 1934. *Patterns of Culture*. Boston: Houghton Mifflin.

Bendix, Reinhard. 1960. *Max Weber: An Intellectual Portrait*. Garden City, N.Y.: Doubleday.

Bem, Sandra L., and Daryl J. Bem. 1970. "Training the Woman to Know Her Place: The Power of Nonconscious Ideology." In Daryl J. Bem (ed.), *Beliefs, Attitudes and Human Affairs*. Monterey, Calif.: Brooks-Cole.

Berg, Ivar. 1970. *Education and Jobs: The Great Training Robbery*. New York: Praeger.

Berger, Peter L. 1963. *Invitation to Sociology*. Garden City, N.Y.: Doubleday.

Berger, Peter L. 1967. *The Sacred Canopy: Elements of a Sociological Theory of Religion*. Garden City, N.Y.: Doubleday.

Berger, Peter L., and Brigitte Berger. 1972. *Sociology: A Biographical Approach*. New York: Basic Books.

Bernard, Cheryl, and Edit Schlaffer. 1983. "'The Man in the Street': Why He Harasses." In Laurel Richard and Vera Taylor (eds.), *Feminist Frontiers: Rethinking Sex, Gender, and Society*. Reading, Mass.: Addison-Wesley, pp.172–175.

Bernard, Jesse. 1972. *The Future of Marriage*. New York: World.

Bernard, Jesse. 1983. *The Future of Marriage* (rev. ed.). New Haven, Conn.: Yale University Press.

Berry, Brian J., and John D. Kasarda. 1977. *Contemporary Urban Ecology*. New York: Macmillan.

Berscheid, Ellen, Karen Dion, Elaine Walster, and G. William Walster. 1971. "Physical Attractiveness and Dating Choice: A Test of the Matching Hypothesis." *Journal of Experimental Social Psychology*, 7 (March): 173–189.

Bieber, Irving, et al. 1962. *Homosexuality: A Psychoanalytic Study of Male Homosexuals*. New York: Basic Books.

Binder, David. 1985. "Bulgarians Harvesting Incentives." *The New York Times*, June 29, p.2.

Binyon, Michael. 1985. *Life in Russia*. New York: Berkeley Books.

Bird, Caroline. 1979. *The Two-Paycheck Marriage*. New York: Rawson Wade.

Bird, Caroline, with Sara Welles Briller. 1970. *Born Female: The High Cost of Keeping Women Down* (rev. ed.). New York: McKay.

Birmingham, Stephen. 1967. *Our Crowd: The Great Jewish Families of New York*. New York: Harper & Row.

Birmingham, Stephen. 1971. *The Grandees: America's Sephardic Elite*. New York: Harper & Row.

Birnbaum, Judith Ablew. 1975. "Life Patterns and Self-Esteem in Gifted Family-Oriented and Career-Committed Women." In Martha T. Shuck Mednick, Sandra Schwartz Tangri, and Lois Wladis Hoffman (eds.), *Women and Achievement: Social and Motivational Analyses*. New York: Halsted Press, pp.396–419.

Blake, Judith. 1979. "Is Zero Preferred? American Attitudes Toward Childlessness in the 1970s." *Journal of Marriage and the Family*, 41 (May): 245–257.

Blau, Francine D. 1979. "Women in the Labor Force: An Overview." In Jo Freeman (ed.), *Women: A Feminist Perspective*. Palo Alto, Calif.: Mayfield, pp.265–289.

Blau, Peter M. 1964. *Exchange and Power in Social Life*. New York: John Wiley.

Blau, Peter M., and Otis Dudley Duncan. 1967. *The American Occupational Structure*. New York: John Wiley.

Bluestone, Barry, and Bennett Harrison. 1982. *The Deindustrialization of America: Plant Closings, Community Abandonment, and the Dismantling of Basic Industry*. New York: Basic Books.

Blumer, Herbert. 1969a. "Collective Behavior." In Alfred McClung Lee (ed.), *Principles of Sociology* (3rd ed.). New York: Barnes & Noble.

Blumer, Herbert. 1969b. *Symbolic Interactionism*. Englewood Cliffs, N.J.: Prentice-Hall.

Blumstein, Philip, and Pepper Schwartz. 1983. *American Couples: Money, Work, Sex*. New York: William Morrow.

Bogue, Donald J. 1985. *The Population of the United States: Historical Trends and Future Predictions*. New York: Free Press.

Boocock, Sarane Spence. 1980. *Sociology of Education: An Introduction* (2nd ed.). Boston: Houghton Mifflin.

Bookbinder, Bernie. 1980. "Measuring the Political Spectrum." *LI Magazine*, November 2, p.17.

Boserup, Ester. 1965. *The Conditions of Economic Growth*. Chicago: Aldine.

Bowles, Samuel. 1978. "Schooling and the Reproduction of Inequality." In Richard C. Edwards, et al., *The Capitalist System*. Englewood Cliffs, N.J.: Prentice-Hall, pp.317–329.

Bowles, Samuel, and Herbert Gintis. 1976. *Schooling in America: Educational Reform and the Contradictions of Economic Life*. New York: Basic Books.

Boyer, Ernest L. 1983. *High School: A Report of the Carnegie Foundation for the Advancement of Teaching*. New York: Harper & Row.

Braidwood, Robert John. 1975. *Prehistoric Men*. Glenview, Ill.: Scott, Foresman.

Brajuha, Mario. 1983. "Slinging Hash Is No Way to Make a Living." *Newsday*, June 3, p.79.

Brajuha, Mario, and Lyle Hallowell. 1986. "Legal Intrusion and the Politics of Fieldwork: The Impact of the Brajuha Case." *Urban Life*, 14 (January): 454–478.

Braidwood, Robert John. 1975. *Prehistoric Men*. Glenview, Ill.: Scott, Foresman.

Bredemeier, Harry C., and Richard M. Stephenson. 1964. *The Analysis of Social Systems*. New York: Holt, Rinehart & Winston.

Breines, Wini. 1981. "The Politics of Sex and the Family." In Scott G. McNall (ed.), *Political Economy: A Critique of American Society*. Glenview, Ill.: Scott, Foresman, pp.24–46.

Brenner, M. Harvey. 1984. *Estimating the Effects of Economic Change on National Health and Social Well-Being: A Study*. Washington, D.C.: U.S. Government Printing Office.

Brim, Orville G., Jr. 1966. "Socialization Through the Life Cycle." In Orville G. Brim and Stanton Wheeler, *Socialization After Childhood: Two Essays*. New York: John Wiley, pp.1–49.

Bronfenbrenner, Urie. 1970. *Two Worlds of Childhood*. New York: Russell Sage.

Brookings, H. Hartford. 1980. "Permanent Underclass Is in Fact Increasing." *The New York Times*, July 6, p.E5.

Brownmiller, Susan. 1975. *Against Our Will: Men, Women, and Rape*. New York: Simon & Schuster.

Brownstein, Ronald, and Nina Easton. 1983. *Reagan's Ruling Class: Portraits of the President's Top One Hundred Officials*. New York: Pantheon.

Brunvand, Jan Harold. 1980. "Urban Legends: Folklore for Today." *Psychology Today*, June, pp.50–62.

Brunvand, Jan Harold. 1981. *The Vanishing Hitchhiker: American Urban Legends and Their Meanings*. New York: Norton.

Brunvand, Jan Harold. 1984. *The Choking Doberman and Other "New" Urban Legends*. New York: Norton.

Buckner, H. Taylor. 1971. *Deviance, Reality, and Change*. New York: Random House.

Burns, John F. 1985a. "The Kim Dynasty's North Korea: A Nation Centered on One Family." *The New York Times*, July 9, pp.A1, A8.

Burns, John F. 1985b. "For North Koreans, Spontaneity Is in Short Supply." *The New York Times*, July 10, p.A8.

Busby, Linda T. 1975, "Sex-Role Research on the Mass Media." *Journal of Communication*, 25 (Autumn): 107–131.

Buss, Terry F., and F. Stevens Radburn. 1983. *Mass Unemployment: Plant Closings and Community Health*. Beverly Hills, Calif.: Sage.

Camerini, Ingrid. 1976. "The Ideal and the Reality: Women in Sweden." In Joan I. Roberts (ed.), *Beyond Intellectual Sexism: A New Woman, A New Reality*. New York: McKay, pp.277–285.

Cameron, William Bruce. 1966. *Modern Social Movements: A Sociological Outline*. New York: Random House.

Campbell, Angus. 1975. "The American Way of Mating." *Psychology Today*, 8 (May): 37–43.

Cantril, Hadley. 1966. *The Psychology of Social Movements*. New York: Wiley.

Caplow, Theodore, Howard M. Bahr, and Bruce A. Chadwick. 1981. "Piety in Middletown." *Society*, 18 (January/February): 34–37.

Caplow, Theodore, Howard M. Bahr, and Bruce A. Chadwick, et al. 1983. *All Faithful People: Change and Continuity in Middletown's Religion*. Minneapolis: University of Minnesota Press.

Carey, James T. 1969. "Changing Courtship Patterns in the Popular Song." *American Journal of Sociology*, 74 (May): 720–731.

Carmichael, Stokely, and Charles V. Hamilton. 1967. *Black Power: The Politics of Liberation in America*. New York: Random House.

Chadwick, Bruce A., Howard M. Bahr, and Stan L. Albrecht. 1984. *Social Science Research Methods*. Englewood Cliffs, N.J.: Prentice-Hall.

Chambliss, William J. 1973a. *Functional and Conflict Theories of Crime*. New York: MSS Modular Publications.

Chambliss, William J. 1973b. "The Saints and the Roughnecks." *Society*, 11 (December): 24–31.

Chavez, Lydia. 1987. "Poll Gauges White Protestants' Views of Jews." *The New York Times*, January 8, p.A22.

Chaze, William L., Gordon M. Bock, Sarah Peterson, George White, and Juanita R. Hogue. 1983. "English Sometimes Spoken Here: Our Big Cities Go Ethnic." *U.S. News and World Report*, March 21, pp.49–53.

Cherlin, Andrew. 1981. *Marriage, Divorce, Remarriage*. Cambridge, Mass.: Harvard University Press.

Choldin, Harvey M. 1985. *Cities and Suburbs: An Introduction to Urban Society*. New York: McGraw-Hill.

Cialdini, Robert B. 1984. *Influence: How and Why People Agree to Things*. New York: William Morrow.

Clark, Kenneth B. 1980. "The Role of Race." *The New York Times Magazine*, October 5, pp.25–33ff.

Clinard, Marshall B., and Robert F. Meier. 1985. *Sociology of Deviant Behavior* (6th ed.). New York: Holt, Rinehart & Winston.

Clinard, Marshall B., and Peter C. Yeager. 1980. *Corporate Crime*. New York: Free Press.

Clymer, Adam. 1983a. "Campaign Costs Soar as Median Spending for Senate Seat Hits $1.7 Million." *The New York Times*, April 3, p.20.

Clymer, Adam. 1983b. "Joblessness Causing Stress and Gloom About Nation." *The New York Times*, February 2, p.A19.

Clymer, Adam. 1984. "Cost of Winning a House Seat Rose in '84, But at a Slower Rate." *The New York Times*, December 4, p.A29.

Clymer, Adam. 1985. " '84 PAC's Gave More to Senate Winners." *The New York Times*, January 6, p.20.

Cohen, Albert K. 1955. *Delinquent Boys: The Culture of the Gang*. New York: Free Press.

Cohen, Albert K., and Harold M. Hodges. 1963. "Lower-Blue-Collar Class Characteristics." *Social Problems*, 10 (Spring): 303–334.

Cohen, Daniel. 1975. *The New Believers: Young Religion in America*. New York: M. Evans.

Cohen, Mark Nathan. 1977. *The Food Crisis in Prehistory: Overpopulation and the Origins of Agriculture*. New Haven, Conn.: Yale University Press.

Cohen, M., and N. Davis. 1981. *Medication Errors: Causes and Prevention*. Philadelphia: G. F. Stickley.

Cohn, Richard M. 1982. "Economic Development and Status Change of the Aged." *American Journal of Sociology*, 87 (March): 1150–1161.

Cole, Stephen. 1980. *The Sociological Method: An Introduction to the Science of Sociology* (3rd ed.). Chicago: Rand McNally.

Cole, Stephen. 1983. "Crime as the Cost of American Creativity," *Newsday*, August 24, p.56.

Coleman, James S. 1961. *The Adolescent Society*. New York: Free Press.

Coleman, James S. 1968. Review of Harold Garfinkel's *Studies in Ethnomethodology*, Englewood Cliffs, N.J.: Prentice-Hall, 1967, in *American Sociological Review*, 33 (February): 126–133.

Coleman, James S., et al., 1966. *Equality of Educational Opportunity*. Washington, D.C.: U.S. Government Printing Office.

Coleman, James W. 1985. *The Criminal Elite: The Sociology of White Collar Crime*. New York: St. Martin's Press.

Collins, Jean E. 1978. "Publishers Depict Women in New Ways." *The New York Times*, April 30.

Collins, Glenn. 1983. "Stranger's Stare: Baleful or Beckoning?" *The New York Times*, April 11, p.A22.

Collins, Glenn. 1985. "A New Look at Intermarriage in the U.S." *The New York Times*, February 11, p.C13.

Collins, Randall. 1971. "Functional and Conflict Theories of Educational Stratification." *American Sociological Review*, 36 (December): 1002–1019.

Collins, Randall. 1975. *Conflict Sociology: Toward an Explanatory Science*. New York: Academic Press.

Collins, Randall. 1979. *The Credentialist Society: An Historical Sociology of Education and Stratification*. New York: Academic Press.

Collins, Randall. 1985a. *Sociology of Marriage and the Family: Gender, Love, and Property*. Chicago: Nelson Hall.

Collins, Randall. 1985b. *Three Sociological Traditions*. New York: Oxford University Press.

Collins, Randall (ed.). 1985c. *Three Sociological Traditions: Selected Readings*. New York: Oxford University Press.

Collins, Randall, and Michael Makowsky. 1984. *The Discovery of Society* (3rd ed.). New York: Random House.

Committee for Economic Development. 1981. *Transnational Corporations and Developing Countries: New Policies for a Changing World Economy*. New York: Committee for Economic Development.

Cornelison, Ann. 1977. *Women of the Shadows*. Boston: Little Brown.

Coser, Lewis. 1956. *The Functions of Social Conflict*. New York: Free Press.

Coser, Lewis. 1977. *Masters of Sociological Thought* (2nd ed.). New York: Harcourt Brace Jovanovich.

Cousins, Albert N., and Hans Nagpaul. 1979. *Urban Life: The Sociology of Cities and Urban Society*. New York: John Wiley.

Cowell, Alan. 1981. "U.N. Predicts World Population Will Level at 10.5 Billion in 2110." *The New York Times*, June 15.

Cowell, Alan. 1985. "Defiance in South Africa." *The New York Times Magazine*, April 14, pp.30–49.

Cowgill, Donald. 1974. "Aging and Modernization: A Revision of the Theory." In Jaber F. Gubrium (ed.), *Late Life, Communities, and Environmental Policy*. Springfield, Ill.: Charles C Thomas, pp.123–146.

Cox, Harold. 1984. *Later Life: The Realities of Aging*. Englewood Cliffs, N.J.: Prentice-Hall.

Cressey, Donald R. 1953. *Other People's Money*. New York: Free Press.

Crittenden, Ann. 1981. "World Hunger Is Exacting High Human Toll." *The New York Times*, August 17, pp.A1, D10.

Cross, K. Patricia. 1971. *Beyond the Open Door: New Students to Higher Education*. San Francisco: Jossey-Bass.

Crowley, Joan E., Teresa E. Levitin, and Robert P. Quinn. 1973. "Seven Deadly Half Truths About Women." *Psychology Today*, March pp.94–96.

Crudele, John. 1986. "After the Cabbage Patch Kids." *The New York Times*, August 23, pp.29, 41.

Csikszentmihalyi, Mihaly, Reed Larsen, and Suzanne Prescott. 1977. "The Ecology of Adolescent Activity and Experience." *Journal of Youth and Adolescence*, 6 (September): 281–294.

Cummings, Judith. 1982. "Bakke Graduating as Debate Over Case Goes On." *The New York Times*, June 4, p.A14.

Cummings, Judith. 1983. "Breakup of Black Family Imperils Gains of Decades." *The New York Times*, November 20, pp.1, 56.

Currie, Elliot P. 1968. "Crimes Without Criminals: Witchcraft and Its Control in Renaissance Europe." *Law and Society Review*, 3 (August): 7–32.

Curtis, James. 1971. "Voluntary Association Joining: A Cross-National Comparative Note." *American Sociological Review*, 36 (October): 872–880.

Curtiss, Susan. 1977. *Genie: A Psycholinguistic Study of a Modern-Day "Wild Child."* New York: Academic Press.

Curvin, Robert, and Bruce Porter. 1979. *Blackout Looting! New York City, July 13, 1977*. New York: Gardner Press.

Cuzzort, Ray P., and Edith W. King. 1980. *20th Century Thought* (3rd ed.). New York: Holt, Rinehart & Winston.

Dahl, Robert. 1982. *Dilemmas of Pluralist Democracy: Autonomy vs. Control*. New Haven, Conn.: Yale University Press.

Dahrendorf, Ralf. 1959. *Class and Class Conflict in Industrial Society*. Stanford, Calif.: Stanford University Press.

Da Matta, Roberto. 1981. *Universo do Carnaval: Imagens e Reflexões*. Rio de Janeiro: Edições Pinakotheke.

Da Matta, Roberto. 1984. "Carnival in Multiple Planes." In John J. MacAloon (ed.), *Rite, Drama, Festival, Spectacle*. Philadelphia: ISHI, pp.210–258.

Davidowitz, Steven. 1980. "Can Women and Men Compete?" *The New York Times*, August 3.

Davies, James C. 1962. "A Theory of Revolution." *American Sociological Review*, 27 (February): 5–19.

Davies, James C. 1969. "The J-Curve of Rising and Declining Satisfaction as a Cause of Some Great Revolutions and a Contained Rebellion." In Hugh Davies Graham and Ted Robert Gurr (eds.), *Violence in America: Historical and Comparative Perspectives*. New York: Bantam Books, pp.690–730.

Davis, Alan J. "Sexual Assaults in the Philadelphia Prison System." *Trans-action*, 6 (December): 8–16.

Davis, Kingsley. 1937. "The Sociology of Prostitution." *American Sociological Review*, 2 (October): 744–755.

Davis, Kingsley, and Wilbert Moore. 1945. "Some Principles of Stratification." *American Sociological Review*, 10 (April): 242–249.

Dawson, Richard E., and Kenneth Prewitt. 1969. *Political Socialization*. Boston: Little, Brown.

Days, Drew S., III. 1983. "The Courts Have Affirmed Race-Conscious Approaches." *The New York Times*, December 11, p.4E.

Decter, Midge. 1974. *The New Chastity and Other Arguments Against Women's Liberation*. New York: Capricorn Books.

Degler, Carl N. 1980. *At Odds: Women and the Family in America From the Revolution to the Present*. New York: Oxford University Press.

Delaney, Paul. 1980. "Some Blacks Get Ahead But More Getting Left Behind." *The New York Times*, July 6, p.E5.

Deloria, Vine, Jr. 1981. "Native Americans: The American Indians Today." *Annals of the American Academy of Political and Social Science*, 455 (March): 139–149.

Delph, Edward William. 1978. *The Silent Community*: *Public Homosexual Encounters*. Beverly Hills, Calif.: Sage.

Denisoff, R. Serge, and Ralph Wahrman. 1979. *An Introduction to Sociology* (2nd ed.). New York: Macmillan.

Deutsch, Morton, and Harold B. Gerard. 1955. "A Study of Normative and Informational Social Influences Upon Individual Judgment." *Journal of Abnormal and Social Psychology*, 51 (November): 629–636.

Deutscher, Irwin. 1973. *What We Say/What We Do*: *Sentiments and Acts*. Glenview, Ill.: Scott, Foresman.

Dickson, Paul, and Joseph C. Goulden. 1983. *There Are Alligators in Our Sewers and Other American Credos*. New York: Delacorte Press.

Dion, Karen, Ellen Berscheid, and Elaine Walster. 1972. "What Is Beautiful Is Good." *Journal of Personality and Social Psychology*, 24 (3): 285–290.

Doll, R. C. 1969. *Variations Among Inner City Elementary Schools*. Kansas City, Mo.: University of Missouri, Kansas City Center for the Study of Metropolitan Problems.

Dollard, John, et al. 1939. *Frustration and Aggression*. New Haven, Conn.: Yale University Press.

Domhoff, G. William. 1967. *Who Rules America*? Englewood Cliffs, N.J.: Prentice-Hall/Spectrum.

Domhoff, G. William. 1979. *The Powers That Be*: *Processes of Ruling Class Domination in America*. New York: Vintage.

Domhoff, G. William. 1983. *Who Rules America Now*? *A View for the '80s*. Englewood Cliffs, N.J.: Prentice-Hall/Spectrum.

Domhoff, G. William, and Hoyt B. Ballard (eds.). 1968. *C. Wright Mills and the Power Elite*. Boston: Beacon.

Dominick, Joseph R., and Gail E. Rauch. 1972. "The Image of Women in Network TV Commercials." *Journal of Broadcasting*, 16 (3): 259–264.

Douglas, Jack D., and Paul K. Rasmussen, with Carol Ann Flanagan. 1977. *The Nude Beach*, Beverly Hills, Calif.: Sage.

Dowd, Maureen. 1985. "Retreat of the Yuppies: The Tide Now Turns Amid 'Guilt' and 'Denial.'" *The New York Times*, June 28, pp.B1, B4.

Drevenstedt, Jean. 1976. "Perceptions of Onsets of Young Adulthood, Middle Age, and Old Age." *Journal of Gerontology*, 31: 53–57.

Drosnin, Michael. 1986. *Citizen Hughes*. New York: Bantam Books.

Dullea, Georgia. 1981a. "On Ladder to the Top, A Mentor Is Key Step." *The New York Times*, January 26, p.B6.

Dullea, Georgia. 1981b. "When Motherhood Doesn't Mean Marriage." *The New York Times*, November 30, p.B16.

Duncan, Otis Dudley, David L. Featherman, and Beverly Duncan. 1972. *Socioeconomic Background and Achievement*. New York: Seminar Press.

Durkheim, Emile. 1915. *The Elementary Forms of the Religious Life* (Joseph Ward Swain, trans.). London: George Allen & Unwin.

Durkheim, Emile. 1951. *Suicide*: *A Study in Sociology* (John A. Spaulding, trans., and George Simpson, trans. and ed.). New York: Free Press (originally published in 1897).

Eckholm, Erik. 1984. "As Ancient Ways Slide Into Oblivion, Hunter Tribes Face Painful Choices." *The New York Times*, October 9, pp.C1, C9.

Edgerton, Robert B. 1976. *Deviance*: *A Cross-Cultural Perspective*. Menlo Park, Calif.: Cummings.

Edwards, John N. 1969. "Familial Behavior as Social Exchange." *Journal of Marriage and the Family*, 31 (August): 518–526.

Edwards, Richard C. 1984. "Work Incentives and Worker Responses in Bureaucratic Enterprises: An Empirical Study." In Donald R. Treiman and Robert V. Robinson (eds.), *Research in Social Stratification and Mobility*. Greenwich, Conn.: JAI Press, pp.3–26.

Edwards, Richard C., Michael Reich, and Thomas E. Weiskopf. 1986. *The Capitalist System* (3rd ed.). Englewood Cliffs, N.J.: Prentice-Hall.

Eels, Richard. 1976. *Global Corporations*: *The Emerging System of World Economic Power* (rev. ed.). New York: Free Press.

Ehrenhalt, Samuel M. 1986. "Economic Scene: Work-Force Shifts in 80's." *The New York Times*, August 15, p.D2.

Eibl-Eibesfeldt, Irenaus. 1972. "Similarities and Differences Between Cultures in Expressive Movements." In R. A. Hinde (ed.), *Non-Verbal Communication*. Hillsdale, N.J.: Lawrence Erlbaum, pp.97–116.

Ekman, Paul. 1978. "Facial Expressions." In Aron W. Siegman and Stanley Feldstein (eds.), *Nonverbal Behavior and Communication*. Hillsdale, N.J.: Lawrence Erlbaum, pp.97–116.

Ekman, Paul. 1985. *Telling Lies*: *Clues to Deceit in the Marketplace, Politics and Marriage*. New York: Norton.

Ellis, Godfrey T., Gary R. Lee, and Larry R. Peterson. 1978. "Supervi-

sion and Conformity: A Cross-Cultural Analysis of Parental Socialization Values." *American Journal of Sociology*, 84 (September): 386–403.

Engels, Friedrich. 1969. "The Origin of the Family, Private Property and the State." In Karl Marx and Friedrich Engels, *Selected Works*. Moscow: Progress Publishers, vol.3, pp.191–334 (originally published 1884).

Epstein, Cynthia Fuchs. 1970. *Women's Place*. Berkeley: University of California Press.

Erikson, Robert S., Norman R. Luttbeg, and Kent L. Tedin. 1980. *American Public Opinion*: *Its Origins, Content and Impact* (2nd ed.). New York: John Wiley.

Eshleman, J. Ross. 1985. *The Family*: *An Introduction* (4th ed.). Boston: Allyn & Bacon.

Evans, Robert R., and Jerry L. L. Miller. 1975. "The Peaking of Streaking." In Robert R. Evans (ed.), *Readings in Collective Behavior* (2nd ed.). Chicago: Rand McNally, pp.401–417.

Fallows, James. 1985. "America's Changing Landscape." *The Atlantic*, March, pp.47–68.

Family Service America. 1984. *The State of Families, 1984–85*. New York: Family Service America.

Farb, Peter. 1980. *Humankind*. New York: Bantam.

Farley, Reynolds. 1984. *Blacks and Whites*: *Narrowing the Gap*? Cambridge, Mass.: Harvard University Press.

Farmer, Val. 1986. "Broken Heartland." *Psychology Today*, April, pp.54–62.

Farnsworth, Clyde H. 1984. "A Doubling of the World's People to 10 Billion in 2050 Is Predicted." *The New York Times*, July 11, pp.A1, A4.

Fast, Julius. 1970. *Body Language*. New York: Evans.

Feagin, Joe R. 1984. *Racial and Ethnic Relations* (2nd ed.). Englewood Cliffs, N.J.: Prentice-Hall.

Federal Bureau of Investigation (FBI), U.S. Department of Justice. 1986. *Uniform Crime Reports*: *Crime in the United States*. Washington, D.C.: U.S. Government Printing Office.

Feldman, Kenneth A., and Theodore M. Newcomb. 1969. *The Impact of College on Students*. San Francisco: Jossey-Bass.

Felipe, Nancy J., and Robert Sommer. 1969. "Invasions of Personal Space." *Social Problems*, 14 (Fall): 206–214.

Fenstermaker, Sarah Berk. 1984. *The Gender Factory*: *The Apportionment of Work in American Households*. New York: Plenum Press.

Ferree, Myra Marx. 1976. "The Confused American Housewife." *Psychology Today*, September, pp.76–80.

Ferretti, Fred. 1980. "He Works; She Works; *She* Does the Housework." *The New York Times*, May 31.

Firestone, Shulamith. 1970. *The Dialectic of Sex*: *The Case for Feminist Revolution*. New York: William Morrow.

Fischer, Claude S. 1984. *The Urban Experience* (2nd ed.). San Diego: Harcourt Brace Jovanovich.

Fischer, David. 1977. *Growing Old in America*. New York: Oxford University Press.

Fishman, Pamela M. 1978. "Interaction: The Work Women Do." *Social Problems*, 25 (April): 397–406.

Fiske, Edward B. 1982. "Fewer Blacks Enter Universities; Recession and Aid Cuts Are Cited." *The New York Times*, November 28, pp.1, 32.

Fiske, Edward B. 1983a. "Commission on Education Warns 'Tide of Mediocrity' Imperils U.S." *The New York Times*, April 27, pp.A1, B6.

Fiske, Edward B. 1983b. "Study Asks Tighter Curriculums." *The New York Times*, September 16, pp.A1, A13.

Fiske, Edward B. 1984a. "U.S. Pupils Lag From Grade 1, Study Finds." *The New York Times*, June 17, pp.1, 30.

Fiske, Edward B. 1984b. "Last June's High School Seniors Had 4-Point Rise on College Test." *The New York Times*, September 20, pp.A1, B17.

Fiske, Edward B. 1984c. "American Students Score Average or Below in International Math Exams." *The New York Times*, September 23, p.30.

Fitzpatrick, Joseph P., and Lourdes Traviesco Parker. 1981. "Hispanic-Americans in the Eastern United States." *Annals of the American Academy of Political and Social Science*, 455 (March): 98–110.

Fleischmann, Manly. 1973. *The Fleischmann Report on the Quality, Cost, and Financing of Elementary and Secondary Education in New York State*. New York: Viking Press.

Fortes, Meyer. 1963. "Time and Social Structure: An Ashanti Case

Study." In Meyer Fortes (ed.), *Social Structure: Studies Presented to A. R. Radcliffe-Brown*. New York: Russell & Russell, pp.54–84.

Fox, Mary Frank, and Sharlene Hesse-Biber. 1984. *Women at Work*. Palo Alto, Calif.: Mayfield.

Frank, Andre Gunder. 1969. *Latin America: Underdevelopment of Revolution*. New York: Monthly Review Press.

Frank, Isaiah. 1980. *Foreign Enterprise in Developing Countries*. Baltimore: Johns Hopkins University Press.

Freedman, Jonathan L., T. Merrill Carlsmith, and David O. Sears. 1970. *Social Psychology*. Englewood Cliffs, N.J.: Prentice-Hall.

Freedman, Jonathan L., and Scott C. Fraser. 1966. "Compliance without Pressure: The Foot-in-the-Door Technique." *Journal of Personality and Social Psychology*, 4 (August): 195–203.

Freeman, Derek. 1983. *Margaret Mead and Samoa: The Making and Unmaking of an Anthropological Myth*. Cambridge, Mass.: Harvard University Press.

Freeman, Richard B. 1976. *Black Elite: The New Market for Highly Educated Black Americans*. New York: McGraw-Hill.

Gagnon, John H. 1977. *Human Sexualities*. Glenview, Ill.: Scott, Foresman.

Gagnon, John H., and Cathy S. Greenblat. 1978. *Life Designs: Individuals, Marriages, and Families*. Glenview, Ill.: Scott, Foresman.

Gailey, Phil. 1982. "Portrait of the U.S. Electorate in 1982: Older, Mobile, and Ethnically Diverse." *The New York Times*, November 3, p.A23.

Galbraith, John Kenneth. 1969. *How to Control the Military*. New York: Doubleday.

Galbraith, John Kenneth. 1984. "The Heartless Society." *The New York Times Magazine*, September 2, pp.20, 21, 40, 44.

Gallup, George H. 1972. *The Gallup Poll: Public Opinion, 1935–1971*. New York: Random House.

Gallup, George H. 1978. *The Gallup Poll: Public Opinion, 1972–1977*. Wilmington, Del.: Scholarly Resources.

Gallup, George H. 1979. *The Gallup Poll: Public Opinion, 1978*. Wilmington, Del.: Scholarly Resources.

Gallup, George H. 1982. *The Gallup Poll: Public Opinion, 1981*. Wilmington, Del.: Scholarly Resources.

Gallup, George H. 1984. *The Gallup Poll: Public Opinion, 1983*. Wilmington, Del.: Scholarly Resources.

Gallup, George H. 1985. *The Gallup Poll: Public Opinion, 1984*. Wilmington, Del.: Scholarly Resources.

Gallup, George, Jr., and David Poling. 1980. *The Search for America's Faith*. Nashville, Tenn.: Abigdon.

Gans, Bruce Michael, and Walter L. Lowe. 1980. "The Islam Connection." *Playboy*, May, pp.119–120ff.

Gans, Herbert J. 1962. *The Urban Villagers*. New York: Free Press.

Gans, Herbert J. 1973. *More Equality*. New York: Pantheon.

Gardner, Carol Brooks. 1980. "Passing By: Street Remarks, Address Rights, and the Urban Female." *Sociological Inquiry*, 50: 328–356.

Garfinkel, Harold. 1967. *Studies in Ethnomethodology*. Englewood Cliffs, N.J.: Prentice-Hall.

Geertz, Clifford. 1973. *The Interpretation of Cultures*. New York: Basic Books.

Geertz, Clifford. 1983. *Local Knowledge*. New York: Basic Books.

Gerbner, George. 1980. "TV: The New Religion Controlling Us." *Newsday*, Ideas Section, November 9, pp.1, 6–7.

Gerth, Hans, and C. Wright Mills. 1953. *Character and Social Structure: The Psychology of Social Institutions*. New York: Harcourt, Brace & World.

Gibbons, Don C. 1982. *Society, Crime, and Criminal Careers* (4th ed.). Englewood Cliffs, N.J.: Prentice-Hall.

Gilder, George. 1974. *Naked Nomads: Unmarried Men in America*. New York: Quadrangle.

Gilder, George. 1975. *Sexual Suicide*. New York: Bantam Books.

Gilder, George. 1982. *Wealth and Poverty*. New York: Bantam Books.

Glaser, Daniel. 1978. *Crime in Our Changing Society*. New York: Holt, Rinehart & Winston.

Glassner, Barry. 1982. "Labeling Theory." In M. Michael Rosenberg, Robert A. Stebbins, and Allan Turowetz (eds.), *The Sociology of Deviance*, New York: St. Martin's Press, pp.21–41.

Glassner, Barry, and Julia Loughlin. 1986. *Drugs in Adolescent Worlds: Burnouts to Straights*. New York: Macmillan.

Glazer, Nathan. 1957. *American Judaism*. Chicago: University of Chicago Press.

Glazer, Nathan. 1972. *American Judaism* (2nd ed.). Chicago: University of Chicago Press.

Glick, Paul C. 1975. "A Demographer Looks at American Families." *Journal of Marriage and the Family*, 37 (February): 15–26.

Glick, Paul C., and Arthur T. Norton. 1977. "Marrying, Divorcing and Living Together in the U.S." *Population Bulletin*, 32 (October): 1–39.

Glock, Charles Y., and Rodney Stark. 1965. *Religion and Society in Tension*. Chicago: Rand McNally.

Glock, Charles Y., and Rodney Stark. 1966. *Christian Beliefs and Anti-Semitism*. Harper & Row.

Goffman, Erving. 1959. *The Presentation of Self in Everyday Life*. Garden City, N.Y.: Doubleday Anchor.

Goffman, Erving. 1961a. *Asylums*. Garden City, N.Y.: Doubleday Anchor.

Goffman, Erving. 1961b. *Encounters: Two Studies in the Social Organization of Gatherings*. Indianapolis, Ind.: Bobbs-Merrill.

Goffman, Erving. 1963a. *Stigma: Notes on the Management of Spoiled Identity*. Englewood Cliffs, N.J.: Prentice-Hall/Spectrum.

Goffman, Erving. 1963b. *Behavior in Public Places: Notes on the Social Organization of Gatherings*. New York: Free Press.

Goffman, Erving. 1971. *Relations in Public: Micro-Studies of the Public Order*. New York: Basic Books.

Goffman, Erving. 1974. *Frame Analysis*. New York: Harper & Row.

Goffman, Erving. 1976. *Gender Advertisements*. New York: Harper Colophon.

Goffman, Erving. 1981. *Forms of Talk*. Philadelphia: University of Pennsylvania Press.

Goldfield, David R., and Blaine A. Brownell. 1979. *Urban America: From Downtown to No Town*. Boston: Houghton Mifflin.

Goldfarb, Ronald L. 1975. *Jails: The Ultimate Ghetto of the Criminal Justice System*. Garden City, N.Y.: Doubleday.

Goldfarb, Ronald L., and Linda R. Singer. 1973. *After Conviction*. New York: Simon & Schuster.

Goldman, Ari. 1985. "New Directory Finds Decline in Number of U.S. Catholics." *The New York Times*, May 23, p.A24.

Goldman, Merle, and Marshall I. Goldman. 1984. "In China, Islets of Capitalism." *The New York Times*, July 24, p.A21.

Goldstein, Sidney. 1974. "American Jewry, 1970: A Demographic Profile." In Marshall Sklare (ed.), *The Jew in American Society*. New York: Behrman House, pp.93–162.

Goode, Erich. 1966. "Social Class and Church Participation." *American Journal of Sociology*, 72 (July): 102–111.

Goode, Erich. 1980. *Social Class and Church Participation*. New York: Arno Press.

Goode, Erich. 1984. *Deviant Behavior* (2nd ed.). Englewood Cliffs, N.J.: Prentice-Hall.

Goode, William J. 1959. "The Theoretical Importance of Love." *American Sociological Review*, 24 (February): 38–47.

Goode, William J. 1960a. "Illegitimacy in the Caribbean Social Structure." *American Sociological Review*, 25 (February): 21–30.

Goode, William J. 1960b. "Norm Commitment and Conformity to Role-Status Obligations." *American Journal of Sociology*, 66 (November): 246–258.

Goode, William J. 1963. *World Revolution and Family Patterns*. New York: Free Press.

Goode, William J. 1964. *The Family*. Englewood Cliffs, N.J.: Prentice-Hall.

Goode, William J. 1972. "The Place of Force in Human Society." *American Sociological Review*, 37 (October): 507–519.

Goode, William J. 1973. "Functionalism: The Empty Castle." In Goode, *Explorations in Social Theory*. New York: Oxford University Press, pp.64–94.

Goode, William J. 1977. *Principles of Sociology*. New York: McGraw-Hill.

Goode, William J. 1978. *The Celebration of Heroes: Prestige as a Control System*. Berkeley: University of California Press.

Goode, William J. 1982. *The Family* (2nd ed.). Englewood Cliffs, N.J.: Prentice-Hall.

Goode, William J., and Paul K. Hatt. 1952. *Methods in Social Research*. New York: McGraw-Hill.

Goodman, Norman. 1985. "Socialization I: A Sociological Overview," and "Socialization II: A Developmental View," In Harvey A. Farberman and R. S. Perinbanayagam (eds.), *Foundations of Interpretive Sociology: Original Essays in Symbolic Interaction*. Greenwich, Conn.: JAI Press, pp. 73–116.

Goodman, Walter. 1984. "Scholars Debate Affirmative Action." *The New York Times*, May 22, p.B2.

Goring, Charles. 1913. *The English Convict*. London: His Majesty's Stationery Office.

Gornick, Vivian. 1979. "Introduction." In Erving Goffman, *Gender Advertisements*. New York: Harper Colophon, pp.vii–ix.

Gortmaker, Steven L. 1979. "Poverty and Infant Mortality in the United States." *American Sociological Review*, 44 (April): 280–292.

Goslin, David. 1965. *The School in Contemporary Society*. Glenview, Ill.: Scott, Foresman.

Gough, Kathleen. 1964. "The Nayars and the Definition of Marriage." In P. B. Hammond (ed.), *Cultural and Social Anthropology*. New York: Macmillan, pp.167–180.

Gove, Walter R. 1972. "The Relationship Between Sex Roles, Mental Illness, and Marital Status." *Social Forces*, 51 (September): 34–44.

Gove, Walter R., and Jeanette F. Tudor. 1973. "Adult Roles and Mental Illness." *American Journal of Sociology*, 78 (January): 812–832.

Granovetter, Mark. 1979. "The Idea of Advancement in Theories of Social Evolution and Development." *American Journal of Sociology*, 85 (November): 489–515.

Granovetter, Mark. 1982. "Reply to Nolan." *American Journal of Sociology*, 87 (January): 947–950.

Greer, Germaine. 1971. *The Female Eunuch*. New York: McGraw-Hill.

Greer, Germaine. 1980. *The Obstacle Race*. New York: Farrar, Straus & Giroux.

Greer, William. 1987. "Companies and Social Conscience." *The New York Times*, January 17, p.52.

Griffin, Susan. 1971. "Rape: The All-American Crime." *Ramparts*, September, pp.26–35.

Griffin, Susan. 1986. *Rape: The Politics of Consciousness* (3rd ed.). Harper & Row.

Gross, Kenneth. 1984. "The Carmichaels: Cultivating a Family Empire." *Newsday Magazine*, June 17, pp.8–12, 26–30.

Gruson, Lindsey. 1983. "Survey Finds 73% Oppose Racial Quotas in Hiring." *The New York Times*, September 25, p.29.

Gunn, Tony. 1977. "A False Identity: Getting an Alias Isn't Very Difficult." *The Daily Tar Heel*, April 12, pp.1, 4.

Gurr, Ted Robert. *Why Men Rebel*. Princeton, N.J.: Princeton University Press.

Gusfield, Joseph R. 1967. "Moral Passage: The Symbolic Process in Public Designations of Deviance." *Social Problems*, 15 (Fall): 175–188.

Haavio-Mannila, Elina. 1975. "Convergences Between East and West: Tradition and Modernity in Sex Roles in Sweden, Finland, and the Soviet Union." In Martha T. Shuh Mednick et al. (eds.), *Women and Achievement: Social and Motivational Analyses*. New York: Halsted Press, pp.71–84.

Hacker, Andrew. 1984. "Women vs. Men in the Work Force." *The New York Times Magazine*, December 9, pp.124–129.

Hacker, Andrew (ed.). 1983. *U/S: A Statistical Portrait of the American People*. New York: Viking Press & Penguin Books.

Hacker, Helen. 1951. "Women as a Minority Group." *Social Forces*, 30 (October): 60–69.

Hall, Edward T. 1959. *The Silent Language*. Greenwich, Conn.: Fawcett.

Hall, Edward T. 1969. *The Hidden Dimension*. Garden City, N.Y.: Doubleday Anchor.

Hall, Edward T. 1977. *Beyond Culture*. Garden City, N.Y.: Anchor Books.

Hall, Francine, and Douglas T. Hall. 1979. *The Two-Career Couple*. Reading, Mass.: Addison-Wesley.

Hamilton, Charles V. 1972. *The Black Preacher in America*. New York: William Morrow.

Hare, Bruce R. 1983. "How Education in City and Suburbs Is Failing Blacks." *Newsday*, February 27, Ideas Section, p.5.

Harlow, Harry F. 1958. "The Nature of Love." *American Psychologist*, 13 (December): 673–685.

Harlow, Harry F., and Margaret K. Harlow. 1965. "The Affectional Systems." In Allan Martin Schreier et al. (eds.), *Behavior of Nonhuman Primates: Modern Research Trends*. New York: Academic Press, pp.287–334.

Harris, Chauncey D., and Edward L. Ullman. 1945. "The Nature of Cities." *Annals of the American Academy of Political and Social Science*, 242 (November): 7–17.

Harris, Louis, and Associates. *The Myth and Reality of Aging in America*. Washington, D.C.: Prepared for the National Council of Aging.

Harris, Marvin, 1974. *Cows, Pigs, Wars, and Witches: The Riddles of Culture*. New York: Random House.

Harris, Marvin. 1975. "Male Supremacy Is on the Way Out: It Was Just a Phase in the Evolution of Our Culture." *Psychology Today*, January, pp.61–69.

Hauser, Robert M., and Thomas N. Daymont. 1977. "Schooling, Ability, and Earnings: Cross-Sectional Findings 8 to 14 Years After High School Graduation." *Sociology of Education*, 50 (July): 182–206.

Harvey, John H., and Gifford Weary (eds.). 1985. *Attribution: Basic Issues and Applications*. Orlando, Fla.: Academic Press.

Haveman, Ernest, and Patricia Salter West. 1952. *They Went to College: The College Graduate in America Today*. New York: Harcourt, Brace.

Havighurst, Robert J. 1963. "Successful Aging." In R. Williams, C. Havighurst, and W. Donahue (eds.), *Processes of Aging*. New York: Atheron, pp.299–320.

Havighurst, Robert J. 1964. *The Public Schools of Chicago: A Survey for the Board of Education for the City of Chicago*. Chicago: The Board of Education of the City of Chicago.

Havighurst, Robert J., and Daniel V. Levine. 1979. *Society and Education* (5th ed.). Boston: Allyn and Bacon.

Havighurst, Robert J., and Bernice L. Neugarten. 1975. *Society and Education* (5th ed.). Boston: Allyn & Bacon.

Hawley, Amos. 1981. *Urban Society* (2nd ed.). New York: John Wiley.

Hayano, David M. 1979. "Poker Lies and Tells." *Human Behavior*, 8 (March): 18–22.

Hayano, David M. 1980. "Communicative Competency Among Poker Players." *Journal of Communication*, 30 (Spring): 113–120.

Hayano, David M. 1982. *Poker Faces: The Life and Work of Professional Poker Players*. Berkeley: University of California Press.

Hayano, David M. 1984. "Foreword." In Mike Caro, *Book of Tells: The Body Language of Poker*. Secaucus, N.J.: Lyle Stuart, pp.xiii–xvi.

Hayes, Rose Oldfield. 1975. "Female Genital Mutilation, Fertility Control, Women's Roles, and the Patrilineage in Modern Sudan: A Fundamental Analysis." *American Ethnologist*, 2 (November): 617–633.

Hechinger, Fred M. 1985a. "Students Are Mirrors of Society." *The New York Times*, January 22, p.C11.

Hechinger, Fred M. 1985b. "An Inside Look at High Schools." *The New York Times*, September 3, pp.C1, C7.

Heider, Eleanor Rosch, and D. C. Oliver. 1972. "The Structure of the Color Space in Naming and Memory for Two Languages." *Cognitive Psychology*, 3 (April): 337–354.

Heilbroner, Robert L. 1980. *The Making of Economic Society* (6th ed.). Englewood Cliffs, N.J.: Prentice-Hall.

Hendin, Herbert. 1975. *The Age of Sensation*. New York: Norton.

Hennessee, Judith Adler, and Joan Nicholson. 1972. "NOW Says: TV Commercials Insult Women." *The New York Times Magazine*, May 28, pp.12–13, 48–51.

Hennig, Margaret, and Anne Jardim. 1977. *The Managerial Woman*. Garden City, N.Y.: Doubleday.

Hentoff, Nat. 1981. "What If the Front Page Were Made Up By Blacks?" *The Village Voice*, April 8–14, p.4.

Herberg, Will. 1974. "America's Civil Religion: What It Is and Whence It Comes." In Russell E. Richet and Donald G. Jones (eds.), *American Civil Religion*. New York: Harper & Row.

Herbers, John. 1981. "Census Finds Blacks Gaining Majorities in Big Cities." *The New York Times*, April 16, pp.A1, B14.

Hershey, Robert D., Jr. 1985. "U.S. Expected to Report Creation of 10 Million Jobs Since '82." *The New York Times*, December 6, p.B28.

Heyns, Barbara. 1978. "Review Essay: Schooling in Capitalist America, by Samuel Bowles and Herbert Gintis." *American Journal of Sociology*, 83 (January): 999–1006.

Hightower, Jim. 1980. "Food Monopoly." In Mark Green and Robert Massie, Jr. (eds.), *The Big Business Reader: Essays on Corporate America*. New York: Pilgrim Press, pp.9–18.

Hildebrand, John. 1983. "For This I Went to College?" *Newsday*, May 4, Part II, p.3.

Hildebrand, John. 1985. "The Gimmie Generation." *Newsday*, March 19, Part II, pp.4–5.

Hill, Robert B. 1979. "The Illusion of Black Progress: A Statement of the Facts." In Charles V. Willie, *The Caste and Class Controversy*. Bayside, N.Y.: General Hall, pp.76–79.

Hill, Robert B. 1981. *Economic Policies and Black Progress: Myths and Realities*. Washington, D.C.: National Urban League.

Hills, Stuart L. 1980. *Demystifying Deviance*. New York: McGraw-Hill.

Hindelang, Michael J. 1978. "Race and Involvement in Common Law Personal Crimes." *American Sociological Review*, 43 (February): 93–109.

Hochschild, Arlie Russell. 1973. *The Unexpected Community*. Englewood Cliffs, N.J.: Prentice-Hall.

Hollingshead, August B. 1949. *Elmtown's Youth*. New York: John Wiley.

Holmes, Lowell D. 1986. *Quest for the Real Samoa: The Mead/Freeman Controversy and Beyond*. South Hadley, Mass.: Bergin & Garvey.

Homans, George Caspar. 1950. *The Human Group*. New York: Harcourt, Brace.

Homans, George Caspar. 1961. *Social Behavior: Its Elementary Forms*. New York: Harcourt, Brace & World.

Hoover, Kenneth R. 1984. *The Elements of Social Scientific Thinking* (3rd ed.). New York: St. Martin's Press.

Hopwood, Daniel R. 1983. "Learning Crime by the Book." *Police Product News*, October, pp.55–56.

Hornstein, Harvey A., Elisha Fisch, and Michael Holmes. 1968. "Influence of a Model's Feeling About His Behavior and His Relevance as a Comparison Other on Observers' Helping Behavior." *Journal of Personality and Social Psychology*, 10 (3): 222–226.

Horowitz, Irving Louis. 1967. *The Rise and Fall of Project Camelot*. Cambridge, Mass.: MIT Press.

Hoyt, Homer. 1939. *The Structure and Growth of Residential Neighborhoods in American Cities*. Washington, D.C.: U.S. Government Printing Office.

Hughes, Langston. 1953. *The Langston Hughes Reader*. New York: Brazillier.

Humphreys, Laud. 1970. *Tearoom Trade: Impersonal Sex in Public Places*. Chicago: Aldine.

Humphreys, Laud. 1975. "Retrospect: Ethical Issues in Social Research." In Humphreys, *Tearoom Trade* (enlarged ed.). Chicago: Aldine, pp.223–232.

Hunt, Morton. 1975. *Sexual Behavior in the 1970s*. New York: Dell.

Hunter, Guy. 1969. *Modernizing Peasant Societies: A Comparative Study in Asia and Africa*. New York: Oxford University Press.

Huron, Douglas B. 1984. "Hiring Quotas Are Unfashionable, But Effective." *Newsday*, August 19, Ideas Section, p.5.

Hurn, Christopher J. 1978. *The Limits and Possibilities of Schooling: An Introduction to the Sociology of Education*. Boston: Allyn & Bacon.

Ianni, Francis A. J., with Elizabeth Reus-Ianni. 1973. *A Family Business: Kinship and Control in Organized Crime*. New York: New American Library.

Ibrahim, Youssef M. 1980. "World Fertility in Rapid Decline, According to Vast New Study." *The New York Times*, July 15, pp.C1, C2.

Inkeles, Alex. 1969. "Making Men Modern: On the Causes and Consequences of Individual Change in Six Developing Countries." *American Journal of Sociology*, 75 (September): 208–225.

Inkeles, Alex, and David H. Smith. 1974. *Becoming Modern: Individual Changes in Six Developing Countries*. Cambridge, Mass.: Harvard University Press.

Irish, Marian D., James W. Prothero, and Richard J. Richardson. 1981. *The Politics of American Democracy* (7th ed.). Englewood Cliffs, N.J.: Prentice-Hall.

Irwin, John. 1980. *Prisons in Turmoil*. Boston: Little, Brown.

Itard, Jean-Marc-Gaspar. 1962. *The Wild Boy of Aveyron*. New York: Appleton-Century-Crofts (originally published 1801 and 1806).

Jacobs, Jerry. 1970. "A Phenomenology of Suicide Notes." *Social Problems*, 15 (Summer): 60–72.

Jacoby, Susan. 1974. *Inside Soviet Schools*. New York: Hill & Wang.

Jacquet, Constant H., Jr. (ed.). 1986. *Yearbook of American and Canadian Churches*. Nashville, Tenn.: Abigdon Press.

Jain, Shail. 1975. *Size Distribution of Income: A Compliation of Data*. Washington, D.C.: World Bank.

Jencks, Christopher, et al. 1979. *Who Gets Ahead? The Determination of Economic Success in America*. New York: Basic Books.

Jencks, Christopher. 1983. "Discrimination and Thomas Sowell." *New York Review of Books*, March 3, pp. 33–38.

Jenkins, J. Craig. 1985. *The Politics of Insurgency: the Farm Worker Movement in the 1960s*. New York: Columbia University Press.

Jenkins, J. Craig. 1986. "Stirring the Masses: Indigenous Roots of the Civil Rights Movement," review essay of Aldon Morris, *The Origins of the Civil Rights Movement: Black Communities Organizing for Change*. New York: Free Press, 1984, in *Contemporary Sociology*, 15 (May): 354–357.

Johnson, Bruce D. 1972. *Marihuana Users and Drug Subcultures*. New York: John Wiley.

Johnson, Harry M. 1960. *Sociology: A Systematic Introduction*. New York: Harcourt Brace.

Johnston, Lloyd D., Patrick M. O'Malley, and Jerald G. Bachman. 1985. *Use of Licit and Illicit Drugs by America's High School Students, 1975–1984*. Washington, D.C.: U.S. Government Printing Office.

Johnstone, Ronald L. 1983. *Religion in Society: A Sociology of Religion*. Englewood Cliffs, N.J.: Prentice-Hall.

Jones, Edward E. "Interpreting Interpersonal Behavior: The Effects of Expectancy." *Science*, 234 (October 3): 41–46.

Kanter, Rosabeth Moss. 1976a. "Why Bosses Turn Bitchy." *Psychology Today*, 9 (May): 56–59.

Kanter, Rosabeth Moss. 1976b. "Women in Organizations." In Alice Sargent (ed.), *Beyond Sex Roles*. St. Paul, Minn.: West, pp.371–387.

Kaplan, Charles P., Thomas Van Valey, and Associates. 1980. *Census '80: Continuing the Pathfinder Tradition*. Washington, D.C.: U.S. Bureau of the Census.

Karlins, Marvin, Thomas Coffman, and Gary Walters. 1969. "On the Fading of Social Stereotypes: Studies in Three Generations of College Students." *Journal of Personality and Social Psychology*, 13 (September): 1–16.

Kawai, Masao. 1965. "Newly-Acquired Precultural Behavior of the Natural Troop of Japanese Monkeys on Koshima Inlet." *Primates*, 6 (August): 1–30.

Kelley, Dean M. 1977. *Why Conservative Churches Are Growing: A Study in the Sociology of Religion* (2nd ed.). New York: Harper & Row.

Kenji, Ima. 1976. "Japanese-Americans: The Making of a 'Good' People." In Anthony Gary Dworkin and Rosalind T. Dworkin (eds.), *The Minority Report: An Introduction to Racial, Ethnic and Gender Relations*. New York: Praeger, pp.256–262.

Kephart, William M. 1987. *Extraordinary Groups: The Sociology of Unconventional Life-styles* (3rd ed.). New York: St. Martin's Press.

Kerckhoff, Alan, and Kurt W. Back. 1968. *The June Bug: A Study of Hysterical Contagion*. New York: Appleton-Century-Crofts.

Kessler, Suzanne J., and Wendy McKenna. 1978. *Gender: An Ethnomethodological Approach*. New York: Wiley-Interscience.

Kilborn, Peter T. 1984. "4 Years Later: Who in U.S. Is Better Off?" *The New York Times*, October 9, p.A31.

Kilborn, Peter T. 1986. "Whites Own 10 Times the Assets Blacks Have, Census Study Finds." *The New York Times*, July 19, pp.1, 46.

Kilduff, Marshall, and Ron Javers. 1978. *The Suicide Cult*. New York: Bantam Books.

Kinsey, Alfred C., Wardell B. Pomeroy, and Clyde E. Martin. 1948. *Sexual Behavior in the Human Male*. Philadelphia: W. B. Saunders.

Kinsey, Alfred C., Wardell B. Pomeroy, Clyde E. Martin, and Paul H. Gebhard. 1953. *Sexual Behavior in the Human Female*. Philadelphia: W. B. Saunders.

Kitagawa, Evlyn M., and Philip M. Hauser. 1973. *Differential Mortality in the United States: A Study in Socioeconomic Epidemiology*. Cambridge, Mass.: Harvard University Press.

Kitano, Harry L. 1976. *Japanese Americans: The Evolution of a Subculture* (2nd ed.). Englewood Cliffs, N.J.: Prentice-Hall.

Kitano, Harry L. 1985. *Race Relations* (3rd ed.). Englewood Cliffs, N.J.: Prentice-Hall.

Kitsuse, John I. 1962. "Societal Reactions to Deviant Behavior: Problems of Theory and Method." *Social Problems*, 9 (Winter): 247–257.

Kitsuse, John I. 1972. "Deviance, Deviant Behavior, and Deviants: Some Conceptual Problems." In William J. Filstead (ed.), *An Introduction to Deviance: Readings in the Process of Making Deviants*. Chicago: Markham, pp.233–243.

Kitsuse, John I. 1980. "The New Conception of Deviance and Its Critics." In Walter R. Gove (ed.), *The Labelling of Deviance: Evaluating a Perspective*. Beverly Hills, Calif.: Sage, pp.381–392.

Knowles, Louis L., Kenneth Prewitt, et al. 1969. *Institutional Racism in America*. Englewood Cliffs, N.J.: Prentice-Hall.

Knox, Robert A., and James A. Inkster. 1968. "Postdecisional Dissonance at Post Time." *Journal of Personality and Social Psychology*, 8 (April): 319–323.

Knupfer, Genevieve. 1947. "Portrait of the Underdog." *Public Opinion Quarterly*, 11 (Spring): 103–114.

Knupfer, Genevieve. 1953. "Portrait of the Underdog." In Reinhard Bendix and Seymour Martin Lipset (eds.), *Class, Status and Power: A Reader in Social Stratification*. New York: Free Press, pp.255–263.

Knupfer, Genevieve, Walter Clark, and Robin Room. 1966. "The Mental Health of the Unmarried." *American Journal of Psychiatry*, 122 (February): 842–844.

Kohn, Melvin L. 1969. *Class and Conformity: A Study in Values*. Homewood, Ill.: Dorsey.

Kohn, Melvin L. 1981. "Personality, Occupation and Social Stratification: A Frame of Reference." In Donald T. Treiman and Robert V. Robinson (eds.), *Research in Social Stratification and Mobility*, vol. 1. Greenwich, Conn.: JAI Press, vol. 1, pp.267–297.

Kohn, Melvin L., and Carmi Schooler. 1982. "Job Conditions and Personality: A Longitudinal Assessment of Their Reciprocal Effects." *American Journal of Sociology*, 87 (May): 1257–1286.

Koller, Marvin R. 1962. "Residential and Occupational Propinquity." In Robert F. Winch et al. (eds.), *Selected Studies in Marriage and the Family*. New York: Holt, Rinehart & Winston, pp.472–477.

Komarovsky, Mirra. 1967. *Blue Collar Marriage*. New York: Vintage.

Kranczer, Stanley. 1984. "United States Population Outlook." *Statistical Bulletin*, January-March, pp.16–19.

Krause, Charles A., et al. 1978. *Guyana Massacre: The Eyewitness Account*. New York: Berkeley Books.

Krauss, Irving. 1976. *Stratification Class and Conflict*. New York: Free Press.

Kurian, George Thomas. 1979. *The Book of World Ranking*. New York: Facts on File.

Labov, William, and Wendell A. Harris. 1983. "De Facto Segregation of Black and White Vernaculars." Unpublished paper given at the 12th meeting on New Ways to Analyze Variation in Language, Montreal, October 27.

Ladd, Everett Carl, Jr., and Seymour Martin Lipset. 1975. *The Divided Academy: Professors and Politics*. New York: McGraw-Hill.

Lang, Gladys Engel. 1972. "Sociologists Look at Crowd and Mass Behavior." In Helen MacGill Hughes (ed.), *Crowd and Mass Behavior*. Boston: Holbrook Press, pp.1–8.

Lang, Kurt, and Gladys Engel Lang. 1961. *Collective Dynamics*. New York: Crowell.

Lang, Kurt, and Gladys Engel Lang. 1968. "Collective Behavior." In *International Encyclopedia of the Social Sciences*. New York: Macmillan, pp.556–565.

Langer, Ellen J. 1978. "Rethinking the Role of Thought in Social Interaction." In John H. Harvey, William John Ickes, and Robert F. Kidd (eds.), *New Directions in Attribution Research*, vol. 2, Hinsdale, N.J.: Lawrence Erlbaum, pp.36–58.

LaPierre, Richard T. 1934. "Attitudes vs. Actions." *Social Forces*, 13 (December): 230–237.

LaPierre, Richard T. 1938. *Collective Behavior*. New York: McGraw-Hill.

Larkin, Ralph W. 1979. *Suburban Youth in Cultural Crisis*. New York: Oxford University Press.

Larson, Reed. 1978. "Thirty Years of Research on the Subjective Well-Being of Older Americans." *Journal of Gerontology*, 33: 109–125.

Lasswell, Harold D. 1936. *Politics: Who Gets What, When, and How*. New York: McGraw-Hill.

Lauer, Robert H. 1977. *Perspectives on Social Change*. Boston: Allyn & Bacon.

Lawrence, Robert Z. 1984. *Can America Compete?* Washington, D.C.: Brookings Institute.

Laws, Judith Long, and Pepper Schwartz. 1977. *Sexual Scripts: The Social Construction of Female Sexuality*. Hinsdale, Ill.: Dryden.

Lee, Alfred McClung, and N. D. Humphrey. 1943. *Race Riot*. New York: Dryden.

Lee, Richard B. 1968. "What Hunters Do For a Living, or, How to Make Out on Scarce Resources." In Richard B. Lee and Irven DeVore (eds.), *Man the Hunter*. Chicago: Aldine.

Lee, Richard B. 1979. *The !Kung San: Men, Women, and Work in a Foraging Society*. Cambridge, England: Cambridge University Press.

Lee, Richard B., and Irven DeVore (eds.). 1968. *Man the Hunter*. Chicago: Aldine.

Lefkowitz, Monroe, Robert R. Blake, and Jane Srygley Mouton. 1955. "Status Factors in Pedestrian Violation of Traffic Signals." *Journal of Abnormal and Social Psychology*, 51 (November): 704–706.

Leibowitz, Lila. 1978. *Females, Males, Families: A Biosocial Approach*. North Scituate, Mass.: Duxbury Press.

Lekachman, Robert. 1977. "The Specter of Full Employment." *Harper's*, February, pp.35–40.

Lemert, Edwin M. 1951. *Social Pathology*. New York: McGraw-Hill.

Lemert, Edwin M. 1972. *Human Deviance, Social Problems, and Social Control* (2nd ed.). Englewood Cliffs, N.J.: Prentice-Hall.

Lenski, Gerhard E. 1963. *The Religious Factor*. Garden City, N.Y.: Doubleday.

Lenski, Gerhard E. 1966. *Power and Privilege: A Theory of Social Stratification*. New York: McGraw-Hill.

Lenski, Gerhard E., and Jean Lenski. 1987. *Human Societies* (5th ed.). New York: McGraw-Hill.

Lerner, Daniel. 1958. *The Passing of Traditional Society*. New York: Free Press.

Levine, Robert, and Ellen Wolff. 1985. "Social Time: The Heartbeat of Culture." *Psychology Today*, 19 (March): 28–35.

Lewis, Paul. 1986. "In Wages, Sexes May Be Forever Unequal." *The New York Times*, December 21, p.20E.

Lincoln, C. Eric. 1973. *The Black Muslims in America* (rev. ed). Boston: Beacon Press.

Lindsey, Robert. 1979. "Hispanics Lead U.S. Minorities in Growth Rate." *The New York Times*, February 18, pp.1, 16.

Lindsey, Robert. 1982. "The New Asian Immigrants." *The New York Times Magazine*, May 9. pp.22ff.

Linton, Ralph. 1936. *The Study of Man*. New York: Appleton-Century-Crofts.

Linton, Ralph. 1937. "One Hundred Percent American." *The American Mercury*, 40 (April): 427–429.

Lipman-Blumen, Jean. 1984. *Gender Roles and Power*. Englewood Cliffs, N.J.: Prentice-Hall.

Lipset, Seymour Martin. 1963. *Political Man: The Social Bases of Politics*. Garden City, N.Y.: Doubleday Anchor.

Lipset, Seymour Martin. 1982. "The Academic Mind at the Top: The Political Behavior and Values of Faculty Elites." In *Public Opinion Quarterly*, 46 (Summer): 143–168.

Lipset, Seymour Martin, and Reinhard Bendix. 1959. *Social Mobility in Industrial Society*. Berkeley: University of California Press.

Lofland, John. 1966. *Doomsday Cult*. Englewood Cliffs, N.J.: Prentice-Hall.

Lofland, Lyn H. 1973. *A World of Strangers: Order and Action in Urban Spaces*. New York: Basic Books.

Lopreato, Joseph, and Lawrence E. Hazelrigg. 1972. *Class, Conflict, and Mobility: Theories and Studies of Class Structure*. San Francisco: Chandler.

Lott, Albert J., and Bernice E. Lott. 1965. "Group Cohesiveness as Interpersonal Attraction: A Review of Relationships with Antecedent and Consequent Variables." *Psychological Bulletin*, 64 (4): 259–309.

Louv, Richard. 1985. *America II*. New York: Penguin Books.

Lowenthal, Leo. 1961. *Literature, Popular Culture and Society*. Englewood Cliffs, N.J.: Prentice-Hall/Spectrum.

Luckmann, Thomas. 1967. *The Invisible Religion*. New York: Macmillan.

Lyndenberg, Stephen, Alice Tepper Marlin, and Sean O'Brien Strub. 1987. *Rating America's Corporate Conscience*. Reading, Mass.: Addison-Wesley.

Lynch, Allen. 1984. "We Must Drop Quotas In Affirmative Action as Unhelpful, Unfair." *Newsday*, May 21, p.46.

Lynd, Robert, and Helen Merrill Lynd. 1929. *Middletown: A Study in American Culture*. New York: Harcourt and Brace.

Lynd, Robert, and Helen Merrill Lynd. 1937. *Middletown in Transition: A Study in Cultural Conflicts*. New York: Harcourt and Brace.

Lyons, Richard D. 1980. "Living Underground Presents No Identity Crisis." *The New York Times*, December 14, p.8E.

Maas, Peter. 1976. *King of the Gypsies*. New York: Bantam Books.

Mace, Miles. 1971. *Directors: Myth and Reality*. Cambridge, Mass.: Harvard University Press.

Mack, John. 1983. "Inside Sing Sing: An Inmate Chronicles the Revolt." *The Village Voice*, February 8, pp.1, 9–11.

Madsen, Axel. 1980. *Private Power: Multinational Corporations for the Survival of Our Planet*. New York: William Morrow.

Malcom, Andrew H. 1985. "Deaths on the Iowa Prairie: 4 Victims of Economy." *The New York Times*, December 11, pp.A1, A22.

Malinowski, Bronislaw. 1930. "Parenthood, the Basis of Social Structure." In V. F. Calverton and Samuel D. Schmalhausen (eds.), *The New Generation*. New York: Macaulay, pp.113–168.

Mamay, Patricia, and Richard L. Simpson. 1981. "Three Female Roles in Television Commercials." *Sex Roles*, 7 (December): 1223–1232.

Mandel, William M. 1975. *Soviet Women*. Garden City, N.Y.: Doubleday Anchor.

Manderscheid, Ronald W., and Mathew Greenwald. 1983. "Trends in Employment of Sociologists." In Howard S. Freeman et al. (eds.), *Applied Sociology*. San Francisco: Jossey-Bass, pp.51–63.

Mangione, Thomas W., Ralph Hingson, and Jane Barrett. 1982. "Collecting Sensitive Data." *Sociological Methods and Research*, 10 (3): 337–346.

Marcus, Francis Frank. 1983. "Louisiana Repeals Black Blood Law." *The New York Times*, July 16, p.A10.

Mariolis, Peter. 1975. "Interlocking Directorates and Control of Corporations: The Theory of Bank Control." *Social Science Quarterly*, 56 (3): 426–439.

Marris, Peter. 1975. *Loss and Change*. Garden City, N.Y.: Doubleday.

Marshall, Donald S. 1971. "Sexual Behavior on Mangaia." In Donald S. Marshall and Robert C. Suggs (eds.), *Human Sexual Behavior*:

Variations in the Ethnographic Spectrum. New York: Basic Books, pp.103–162.

Martin, Kay, and Barbara Voorhies. 1975. *Female of the Species.* New York: Columbia University Press.

Martin, Susan E. 1978. "Sexual Politics in the Workplace: The Interactional World of Policewomen." *Symbolic Interaction,* 1 (Spring): 44–60.

Martin, Susan E. 1980. *Breaking and Entering: Policewomen on Patrol.* Berkeley: University of California Press.

Marty, Martin E. 1976. *A Nation of Believers.* Chicago: University of Chicago Press.

Marum, Andrew, and Frank Parise. 1984. *Follies and Foibles: A View of 20th Century Fads.* New York: Facts on File.

Marx, Gary T. 1967. "Religion: Opiate or Inspiration of Civil Rights Among Negroes?" *American Sociological Review,* 32 (February): 64–72.

Marx, Karl. 1906. *Capital: A Critique of Political Economy* (Samuel Moore and Edward Aveling, trans.). New York: Charles H. Kerr (originally published in 1867).

Marx, Karl. 1968. "Wage Labour and Capital." In *Karl Marx and Friedrich Engels, Selected Works in One Volume.* New York: International Publishers, pp.64–94.

Marx, Karl, and Friedrich Engels. 1947. *The German Ideology.* New York: International Publishers (originally written in 1846).

Marx, Leo. 1974. "The Uncivil Response of American Writers to Civil Religion in America." In Russell E. Richey and Donald G. Jones (eds.), *American Civil Religion.* New York: Harper & Row, pp.222–251.

Massey, Grace Carroll, Mona Scott Vaughn, and Sanford M. Dornbusch. 1975. "Racism Without Racists: Institutional Reform in Urban Schools." *The Black Scholar,* 7 (March): 3–11.

Matras, Judah. 1975. *Social Inequality, Stratification and Mobility.* Englewood Cliffs, N.J.: Prentice-Hall.

Matras, Judah. 1984. *Social Inequality, Stratification and Mobility* (2nd ed.). Englewood Cliffs, N.J.: Prentice-Hall.

McAdam, Doug. 1982. *Political Processes and the Development of Black Insurgency, 1930–1970.* Chicago: University of Chicago Press.

McCaghy, Charles H. 1967. "Child Molesters: A Study of Their Careers as Deviants." In Marshall B. Clinard and Richard Quinney (eds.), *Criminal Behavior Systems: A Typology.* New York: Holt, Rinehart & Winston.

McCaghy, Charles H. 1985. *Deviant Behavior: Crime, Conflict, and Interest Groups* (2nd ed.). New York: Macmillan.

McNeely, R. L., and Carl E. Pope (eds.). 1981. *Race, Crime, and Criminal Justice.* Beverly Hills, Calif.: Sage.

McTavish, Donald. 1971. "Perceptions of Old People: A Review of Research Methodologies and Findings." *Gerontologist,* 11: 90–101.

Mead, Margaret. 1928. *The Coming of Age in Samoa.* New York: William Morrow.

Mead, Margaret. 1935. *Sex and Temperament in Three Primitive Societies.* New York: William Morrow.

Mechanic, David. 1980. *Mental Health and Social Policy* (2nd ed.). Englewood Cliffs, N.J.: Prentice-Hall.

Medalia, Nahum, and Otto N. Larsen. 1958. "Diffusion and Belief in a Collective Delusion: The Seattle Windshield Pitting Epidemic." *American Sociological Review,* 23 (April): 180–186.

Meislin, Richard T. 1977. "Poll Finds More Liberal Beliefs on Marriage and Sex Roles, Especially Among the Young." *The New York Times,* November 27.

Menzel, Emil W., Jr. 1966. "Responsiveness in Free-Ranging Japanese Monkeys." *Behaviour,* 26:130–149.

Merton, Robert K. 1949. "Discrimination and the American Creed." In Robert M. MacIver (ed.), *Discrimination and National Welfare.* New York: Harper & Row, pp.99–126.

Merton, Robert K. 1957. *Social Theory and Social Structure* (rev. ed.). New York: Free Press.

Merton, Robert K. 1968. *Social Theory and Social Structure* (enlarged ed.). New York: Free Press.

Merton, Robert K. 1972. "Insiders and Outsiders: A Chapter in the Sociology of Knowledge." *American Journal of Sociology,* 77 (July): 9–47.

Merton, Robert K., George G. Reader, and Patricia Kendall (eds.). 1957. *The Student-Physician: Introductory Studies in the Sociology of Medical Education.* Cambridge, Mass.: Harvard University Press.

Milgram, Stanley. 1974. *Obedience to Authority: An Experimental View.* New York: Harper & Row.

Miller, David L. 1985. *Introduction to Collective Behavior.* Belmont, Calif.: Wadsworth.

Miller, Judith. 1983. "Wartime Internment of Japanese Was 'Grave Injustice,' Panel Says." *The New York Times,* February 25, pp.A1, A12.

Miller, S. M. 1960. "Comparative Social Mobility." *Current Sociology,* 9 (1): 1–89.

Miller, Walter B. 1958. "Lower Class Culture as a Generating Milieu of Gang Delinquency." *Journal of Social Issues,* 14 (3): 5–19.

Millett, Kate. 1970. *Sexual Politics.* Garden City, N.Y.: Doubleday.

Mills, C. Wright. 1956. *The Power Elite.* New York: Oxford University Press.

Mills, C. Wright. 1957. "The Power Elite: Comment on Criticism." *Dissent,* 5 (Winter): 22–34.

Mills, C. Wright. 1959. *The Sociological Imagination.* New York: Oxford University Press.

Mills, Jeannie. 1979. *Six Years With God: Life Inside Jim Jones' Peoples Temple.* New York: A&W Publishers.

Minerip, Michael. 1985. "Asian-Americans Question Ivy League's Entry Policies." *The New York Times,* May 30, pp.B1, B4.

Mintz, Beth, and Michael Schwartz. 1985. *The Power Structure of American Business.* Chicago: University of Chicago Press.

Molotsky, Irving. 1984. "31 States Gain in College Test Scores." *The New York Times,* December 19, p.B6.

Montgomery, Paul L. 1982. "4,000 Followers of Moon Wed at the Garden." *The New York Times,* July 2, pp.B1, B4.

Moore, Wilbert E. 1974. *Social Change* (2nd ed.). Englewood Cliffs, N.J.: Prentice-Hall.

Morgan, Hal, and Kerry Tucker. 1984. *Rumor!* New York: Penguin Books.

Morgan, Hal, and Kerry Tucker. 1987. *More Rumor!* New York: Penguin Books.

Morgan, Richard E., John C. Donovan, and Christine P. Potholm. 1979. *American Politics: Directions of Change, Dynamics of Choice.* Reading, Mass.: Addison-Wesley.

Morgan, Robin, and Gloria Steinem. 1980. "The International Crime of Genital Mutilation." *Ms.* March, pp.65–67, 98, 100.

Morgan, S. Philip, and Kiyosi Hiroshima. 1983. "The Persistence of Extended Family Residence in Japan: Anacronism or Alternative Strategy?" *American Sociological Review,* 48 (April): 269–286.

Morganthau, Tom, et al. 1980. "A One-Man Crime Wave." *Newsweek,* December 22, p.30.

Morris, Aldon. 1984. *The Origins of the Civil Rights Movement: Black Communities Organizing for Change.* New York: Free Press.

Morris, Desmond. 1969. *The Naked Ape.* New York: Dell.

Morris, Desmond. 1977. *Manwatching: A Field Guide to Human Behavior.* New York: Abrams.

Mosteller, Frederick, and Daniel Patrick Moynihan (eds.). 1972. *Equality of Educational Opportunity: Papers Deriving from the Harvard University Faculty Seminar on the Coleman Report.* New York: Random House.

Muhammad, Larry. 1980. "The Muslims Five Years After Elijah." *Sepia,* 29 (March): 31–37.

Mullins, Nicholas C, with Carolyn J. Mullins. 1973. *Theories and Theory Groups in Contemporary Sociology.* New York: Harper & Row.

Murdock, George Peter. 1935. "Comparative Data on the Division of Labor by Sex." *Social Forces,* 15 (May): 551–553.

Murdock, George Peter. 1949. *Social Structure.* New York: Macmillan.

Murdock, George Peter, and Caterina Provost. 1973. "Factors in the Division of Labor by Sex." *Ethnology,* 12 (April): 203–225.

Nagel, Stuart S. 1966. "The Tipped Scales of American Justice." *Transaction,* 3 (May-June): 3–9.

Naisbitt, John. 1984. *Megatrends: Ten New Directions Transforming Our Lives* (rev. ed.). New York: Warner Books.

Nam, Charles B., and Susan Gustavus Philliber. 1984. *Population: A Basic Orientation* (2nd ed.). Englewood Cliffs, N.J.: Prentice-Hall.

Nance, John. 1975. *The Gentle Tasaday.* New York: Harcourt Brace Jovanovich.

National Commission on Excellence in Education. 1983. *A Nation at Risk.* Washington, D.C.: U.S. Government Printing Office.

Needleman, Jacob. 1970. *The New Religions.* Garden City, N.Y.: Doubleday.

Nelson, Bryce. 1983. "Despair among Jobless Is on Rise, Studies Find." *The New York Times,* April 2, p.25.

Nettler, Gwynn. 1978. *Explaining Crime* (2nd ed.). New York: McGraw-Hill.

Neugarten, Bernice. 1964. *Personality in Middle Later Life*. New York: Atherton.

Neugarten, Bernice. 1971. "Grow Old with Me. The Best Is Yet to Be." *Psychology Today*, (December, pp.45–48, 79, 81.

Newton, Esther. 1972. *Mother Camp: Female Impersonators in America*. Englewood Cliffs, N.J.: Prentice-Hall.

Nicholaus, Martin. 1969. "The Professional Organization of Sociology: A View From Below." *Antioch Review*, 29 (Fall): 375–387.

Niebuhr, Richard. 1929. *The Social Sources of Denominationalism*. New York: Holt.

Niemi, Richard G. 1973. "Political Socialization." In Jeanne N. Knutson (ed.), *Handbook of Political Socialization*. San Francisco: Jossey-Bass, pp.117–138.

Nierenberg, Gerard I., and Henry H. Calero. 1971. *How to Read a Person Like a Book*. New York: Hawthorn.

Noble, Kenneth B. 1984. "Plight of Black Family is Studied Anew." *The New York Times*, January 29, p.E20.

Nordheimer, Jon. 1977. "The Family in Transition: A Challenge From Within." *The New York Times*, November 27, pp.1, 74.

Norman, Michael. 1980. "The New Extended Family: Divorce Reshapes the American Household." *The New York Times Magazine*, November 23, pp.27–28, 44, 46, 53.

Norton, Eleanor Holmes. 1985. "Restoring the Traditional Black Family." *The New York Times Magazine*, June 2, pp.43, 79, 93–98.

Nossiter, Bernard D. "World Population Is Slowing, U.N. Finds." *The New York Times*, June 15, p.10.

Nugent, John Peter. *White Nights*. New York: Rawson, Wade.

Oakes, John B. 1984. "The PAC-Man's Game: Eating Legislators." *The New York Times*, September 6, p.A23.

O'Dea, Thomas F. 1957. *The Mormons*. Chicago: University of Chicago Press.

O'Dea, Thomas, and Janet O'Dea Aviad. 1983. *The Sociology of Religion* (2nd ed.). Englewood Cliffs, N.J.: Prentice-Hall.

Ofshe, Richard. 1980. "The Social Development of the Synanon Cult: The Managerial Strategy of Organizational Transformation." *Sociological Analysis*, 41 (Summer): 109–127.

Olson, Helen. 1980. "How to Make $16,000 Building Pyramids in your Spare Time." *Gambling Scene*, 3 (June): 30–32.

Orne, Martin T., and Frederick J. Evans. 1965. "Social Control in the Psychological Experiment: Anti-Social Behavior and Hypnosis." *Journal of Personality and Social Psychology*, 1 (3): 189–200.

Osherow, Neal. 1984. "Making Sense of the Nonsensical: An Analysis of Jonestown." In Elliot Aronson (ed.), *Readings About the Social Animal* (4th ed.). New York: W. H. Freeman, pp.68–86.

O'Toole, Patricia. 1981. "Hers." *The New York Times*, May 21, p.C2.

Ouchi, William. 1981. *Theory Z: How American Business Can Meet the Japanese Challenge*. Reading, Mass.: Addison-Wesley.

Oxford Analytica. 1986. *America in Perspective*. Boston: Houghton Mifflin.

Pachon, Harry P., and Joan W. Moore. 1981. "Mexican Americans." *Annals of the American Academy of Political and Social Science*, 455 (March): 111–124.

Palmore, Erdman. 1969. "Sociological Aspects of Aging." In E. Busse and E. Pfeiffer (eds.), *Behavior and Adaptation in Later Life*. Boston: Little, Brown, pp.33–69.

Parelius, Ann Parker, and Robert J. Parelius. 1978. *The Sociology of Education*. Englewood Cliffs, N.J.: Prentice-Hall.

Pareto, Vilfredo. 1935. *The Mind and Society: A Treatise on General Society* (Andrew Bongiorno and Arthur Livingston, trans.). New York: Harcourt Brace.

Pareto, Vilfredo. 1968. *The Rise and Fall of Elites: An Application of Theoretical Sociology*. Totowa, N.J.: Bedminster Press (originally published in 1901).

Park, Robert E., Ernest W. Burgess, and Roderick D. McKenzie (eds.). 1925. *The City*. Chicago: University of Chicago Press.

Parnes, Herbert S. 1981. *A Longitudinal Study of Men, Work, and Retirement*. Cambridge, Mass.: MIT Press.

Parsons, Talcott. 1951. *The Social System*. New York: Free Press.

Parsons, Talcott. 1959. "The School Class as a Social System: Some of its Functions." *Harvard Educational Review*, 29 (Fall): 297–318.

Parsons, Talcott. 1966. *Societies: Evolutionary and Comparative Perspectives*. Englewood Cliffs, N.J.: Prentice-Hall.

Parsons, Talcott. 1977. *The Evolution of Society* (Jackson Toby ed.). Englewood Cliffs, N.J.: Prentice-Hall.

Parsons, Talcott, and Robert F. Bales. 1955. *Family*, Socialization and Interaction Process. New York: Free Press.

Patterson, Miles L. 1978. "The Role of Space in Social Interaction." In Aron W. Siegman and Stanley Feldstein (eds.), *Nonverbal Behavior and Communication*. Hillsdale, N.J.: Lawrence Erlbaum, pp.265–290.

Pear, Robert. 1981. "Will Voting Rights Survive If Voting Rights Act Doesn't?" *The New York Times*, May 3, p.2E.

Pear, Robert. 1985a. "Gain Made by Blacks as Mayors." *The New York Times*, June 22, p.A10.

Pear, Robert. 1985b. "Low Number Given for Illegal Aliens." *The New York Times*, June 25, p. A14.

Pelto, Pertti J., and Ludger Müller-Wille. 1972. "Snowmobiles: Technological Revolution in the Arctic. In Russell Bernard and Pertti J. Pelto (eds.), *Technology and Social Change*. New York: Macmillan, pp.166–199.

Pennock, Roland J. 1979. *Democratic Political Theory*. Princeton, N.J.: Princeton University Press.

Phillips, J. L., Jr. 1969. *The Origins of the Intellect: Piaget's Theory*. San Francisco: Freeman.

Pfohl, Stephen J. 1985. *Images of Deviance and Social Control*. New York: McGraw-Hill.

Piaget, Jean. 1954. *The Construction of Reality of the Child*. New York: Basic Books.

Piaget, Jean. 1960. *The Child's Conception of Physical Causality*. Totowa, N.J.: Littlefield Adams.

Piaget, Jean. 1965a. *The Moral Judgment of the Child*. New York: Free Press.

Piaget, Jean. 1965b. *The Child's Conception of Number*. New York: Norton.

Piaget, Jean. 1970. *The Child's Conception of Movement and Speed*. New York: Basic Books.

Pileggi, Nicholas. 1981. "Inside Riker's Island." *New York*, June 8, pp.24–29.

Pines, Maya. 1982. "Recession Linked to Far-Reaching Psychological Harm." *The New York Times*, April 6, pp.C1, C2.

Pinkney, Alphonso. 1985. *The Myth of Black Progress*. New York: Oxford University Press.

Piven, Frances Fox, and Richard A. Cloward. 1977. *Poor People's Movements: Why They Succeed, How They Fail*. New York: Pantheon.

Piven, Frances Fox, and Richard A. Cloward. 1982. *The New Class War: Reagan's Attack on the Welfare State and Its Consequences*. New York: Pantheon.

Pollack, Andrew. 1986. "Video Games, Once Zapped, in Comeback." *The New York Times*, September 27, pp.1, 39.

Portes, Alejandro. 1976. "On the Sociology of National Development." *American Journal of Sociology*, 82 (July): 55–85.

Prial, Frank T. 1982. "More Women Work at Traditional Male Jobs." *The New York Times*, November 15, pp.A1, C20.

Proximire, William. 1970. *America's Military-Industrial Complex*. New York: Praeger.

Purnids, Joyce. 1981. "New York Blacks Say They've Lost Political Power." *The New York Times*, March 29, pp.1, 42.

Quindlen, Anna. 1977. "Relationships: Independence vs. Intimacy." *The New York Times*, November 28, pp.1, 36.

Rainwater, Lee. 1966. "Some Aspects of Lower Class Sexual Behavior." *Journal of Social Issues*, 22 (April): 96–108.

Rappaport, Rhona, and Robert Rappaport. 1976. *Dual Career Families Re-Examined*. New York: Harper & Row.

Rash, Chester Leon. 1980. *The Coleman Report: A Case Study of the Linkage Between Social Science Research and Public Policy*. PhD dissertation, Department of Sociology, State University of New York at Stony Brook.

Ravitch, Diane. 1978. "Back to Basics," *The Public Interest*, 50 (Winter): 119–123.

Reckless, Walter R. 1973. *The Crime Problem* (5th ed.). New York: Appleton-Century-Crofts.

Redman, Charles L. 1978. *The Rise of Civilization: From Early Farmers to the Ancient Near East*. San Francisco: Freeman.

Reich, Michael. 1981. *Racial Inequality: A Political-Economic Analysis*. Princeton, N.J.: Princeton University Press.

Reinhold, Robert. 1978. "World Population Slows." *The New York Times*, November 20, pp.A1, A32.

Reiss, Ira L. 1980. *Family Systems in America* (3rd ed.). New York: Holt, Rinehart & Winston.

Reynolds, William Bradford. 1983. "The Use of Discrimination to Cure Discrimination." *The New York Times*, December 11, p.4E.

Riesman, David, in collaboration with Reuel Denny and Nathan Glazer. 1950. *The Lonely Crowd: A Study of the Changing American Character*. New Haven: Yale University Press.

Riesman, David, Nathan Glazer, and Reuel Denny. 1953. *The Lonely Crowd: A Study of the Changing American Character.* Garden City, N.Y.: Doubleday-Anchor.

Ritzer, George. 1975. *Sociology: A Multiple Paradigm Science.* Boston: Allyn & Bacon.

Robbins, William. 1985. "Despair Wrenches Farmers' Lives as Debts Mount and Land Is Lost." *The New York Times,* February 10, pp.1, 30.

Roberts, Keith A. 1984. *Religion in Sociological Perspective.* Homewood, Ill.: Dorsey Press.

Roberts, Sam. 1985. "Poll Finds Minority Groups Critical of New York Schools." *The New York Times,* May 16, pp.A1, B9.

Robinson, Robert V. 1984. "Reproducing Class Relations in Industrial Capitalism." *American Sociological Review,* 49 (April): 182–196.

Rodseth, Bob. 1980. "Pyramid Players: Exponents of the Exponent." *Gambling Scene,* 3 (June): 14–16.

Roethelsberger, Fritz, and William T. Dickson. 1939. *Management and the Worker.* Cambridge, Mass.: Harvard University Press.

Rohter, Larry. 1987. "Women Gain Degrees, But Not Tenure." *The New York Times,* January 4, p.E9.

Rorvik, David. 1980. "Cattle Mutilations: The Truth at Last." *Penthouse,* September, pp.121–122, 142–143.

Rose, Arnold. 1967. *The Power Structure.* New York: Oxford University Press.

Rose, Jerry. 1982. *Outbreaks: The Sociology of Collective Behavior.* New York: Free Press.

Rose, Peter I. 1974. *We and They: Racial and Ethnic Relations in the United States* (2nd ed.). New York: Random House.

Rosenbaum, David E. 1980. "Working Women Still Seek Man-Sized Wages." *The New York Times,* July 27, p.E3.

Rosenhan, D. L. 1973. "On Being Sane in Insane Places." *Science,* 179 (19 January): 250–258.

Rosenthal, Robert, and Lenore Jacobson. 1968. *Pygmalion in the Classroom.* New York: Holt.

Rosnow, Ralph L., and Gary Alan Fine. 1976. *Rumor and Gossip: The Social Psychology of Hearsay.* New York: Elsevier.

Rosnow, Ralph L., and Allan J. Kimmel. 1979. "Lives of a Rumor." *Psychology Today,* June, pp.88–92.

Roos, Patricia A. 1985. *Gender and Work: A Comparative Analysis of Industrial Societies.* Albany, N.Y.: State University of New York Press.

Rossi, Alice S. 1968, "Transition to Parenthood." *Journal of Marriage and the Family,* 30 (February): 26–39.

Rossides, Daniel W. 1976. *The American Class System.* Boston: Houghton Mifflin.

Roth, Philip. 1963. "Defender of the Faith." In *Goodbye Columbus and Five Short Stories.* New York: Bantam Books, pp.115–143.

Rubin, Lillian Breslow. 1976. *Worlds of Pain: Life in the Working-Class Family.* New York: Basic Books.

Rudolph, Barbara. 1986. "Singing the Shutdown Blues." *Time,* June 23, pp.58–60.

Russell, George, et al. 1984. "People, People, People." *Time,* August 6, pp.24–25.

Rutter, Michael, Barbara Maughan, Peter Mortimore, and Janet Ouston, with Alan Smith. 1979. *Fifteen Thousand Hours: Secondary Schools and Their Effects on Children.* Cambridge, Mass.: Harvard University Press.

Ryan, William. 1976. *Blaming the Victim* (2nd ed.). New York: Vintage.

Ryan, William. 1981. *Equality.* New York: Pantheon Books.

Rytina, Joan Huber, William H. Form, and John Pease. 1970. "Income and Stratification Ideology." *American Journal of Sociology,* 75 (January): 703–716.

Saghir, Marcel T., and Eli Robins. 1973. *Male and Female Homosexuality: A Comprehensive Investigation.* Baltimore: Williams & Wilkins.

Sanders, Ed. 1977. "The Cattle Mutilations, Part II: On the Trail of the Night Surgeons." *Oui,* May, pp.79–80, 121ff.

Sapir, Edward. 1929. "The Status of Linguistics as a Science." *Language,* 5 (4): 207–214.

Sapir, Edward. 1949. *Selected Writings in Language, Culture, and Personality.* Berkeley: University of California Press.

Schmalz, Jeffrey. 1984. "Strange Sights Brighten The Night Skies Upstate." *The New York Times,* August 25, pp.25, 42.

Schrier, Arnold. 1970. *Ireland and the American Emigration.* New York: Russell & Russell.

Schultz, James. *The Economics of Aging.* Belmont, Calif.: Wadsworth.

Schumer, Fran. 1982. "Downward Mobility." *New York,* August 16, pp.20–26.

Schur, Edwin. 1965. *Crimes Without Victims.* Englewood Cliffs, N.J.: Prentice-Hall.

Schwartz, Barry, and Stephen Barsky. 1977. "The Home Advantage." *Social Forces,* 55 (March): 641–651.

Scott, Hilda. 1984. *Working Your Way to the Bottom: The Feminization of Poverty.* Boston: Pandora Press.

Scully, Diana, and Joseph Marolla. 1985. "Riding the Bull at Gilley's: Convicted Rapists Describe the Rewards of Rape." *Social Problems,* 32 (February): 251–263.

Seligsohn, Leo. 1981. "The Jerry Falwell Force." *LI Magazine,* March 22, pp.14–20, 38ff.

Serrill, Michael S., et al. 1985. "The New Black Police Chiefs." *Time,* February 18, pp.84–85.

Serrin, William. 1984. "Experts Say Job Bias Against Women Persists." *The New York Times,* November 25m pp.1, 32.

Severo, Richard. 1982. "Poll Finds Americans Split on Creation Idea." *The New York Times,* August 29, p.22.

Sexton, William. 1983. "Breaking the Birthrate." *Newsday,* March 28, Part II, pp.4–5.

Sewell, William H., Robert M. Hauser, and David L. Featherman. 1976. *Schooling and Achievement in American Society.* New York: Academic Press.

Sewell, William H., and Vimal P. Shah. 1967. "Socioeconomic Status, Intelligence, and the Attainment of Higher Education." *Sociology of Education,* 40 (Winter): 1–23.

Sexton, William. 1981. "China to Phase Out Communes: A Utopian Plan Fails Its Promise." *Newsday,* September 13, pp.5, 13.

Sharp, Lauriston. 1952. "Steel Axes for Stone Age Australians." *Human Organization,* 11 (Summer): 17–22.

Shaver, Philip, and Jonathan Freedman. 1976. "Your Pursuit of Happiness." *Psychology Today,* August, pp.26–32, 75.

Sheehy, Gail. 1976. "The Mentor Connection: The Secret Link in the Successful Woman's Life." *New York,* April 5, pp.33–39.

Sheils, Merrill, Diane Weathers, Lucy Howard, and Ron Given. 1983. "A Portrait of America." *Newsweek,* January 17, pp.20–33.

Sheldon, William H. 1940. *The Varieties of Human Physique.* New York: Harper.

Sheldon, William H., et al. 1949. *Varieties of Delinquent Youth.* New York: Harper & Row.

Sherif, Muzafer. 1936. *The Psychology of Social Norms.* New York: Harper.

Sherman, Howard T., and James L. Wood. 1979. *Sociology: Traditional and Radical Perspectives.* New York: Harper & Row.

Shibutani, Tamotsu. 1966. *Improvised News: A Sociological Study of Rumor.* Indianapolis, Ind.: Bobbs-Merrill.

Shibutani, Tamotsu. 1986. *Social Processes: An Introduction to Sociology.* Berkeley: University of California Press.

Shibutani, Tamotsu, and Kian M. Kwan. 1965. *Ethnic Stratification: A Comparative Approach.* New York: Macmillan.

Shinnar, Shlomo, and Ruel Shinnar. 1975. "The Effects of the Criminal Justice System on the Control of Crime." *Law and Society Review,* 9 (Summer): 581–611.

Shipp, E. R., and Joseph P. Fried. 1981. "99% of Felony Arrests in City Fail to Bring Terms in State Prison." *The New York Times,* January 4, pp.1, 28.

Silverman, Irwin. 1971. "Physical Attractiveness and Courtship." *Sexual Behavior,* 1 (September): 22–25.

Simmel, Georg. 1950. *The Sociology of Georg Simmel* (Kurt Wolf, trans. and ed.). New York: Free Press (originally published in 1903).

Simmons, J. L. 1969. *Deviants.* Santa Barbara, Calif.: Glendessary Press.

Simon, David R., and D. Stanley Eitzen. 1982. *Elite Deviance.* Boston: Allyn & Bacon.

Simpson, George Eaton, and J. Milton Yinger. 1972. *Racial and Cultural Minorities: An Analysis of Prejudice and Discrimination* (4th ed.). New York: Harper & Row.

Simpson, George Eaton, and J. Milton Yinger. 1985. *Racial and Cultural Minorities: An Analysis of Prejudice and Discrimination* (5th ed.). New York: Plenum Press.

Singh, Harjinder. 1977. *Caste Among Non-Hindus in India.* New Delhi: National Publishing House.

Sjoberg, Gideon. 1960. *The Preindustrial City.* New York: Free Press.

Skinner, B. F. 1971. *Beyond Freedom and Dignity.* New York: Alfred Knopf.

Skogan, Wesley G. 1977. "Dimensions of the Dark Figure of Unreported Crime." *Crime and Delinquency,* 23 (January): 41–50.

Skolnick, Arlene. 1987. *The Intimate Environment: Exploring Marriage and the Family* (4th ed.). Boston: Little, Brown.

Smelser, Neil. 1962. *Theory of Collective Behavior*. New York: Free Press.

"Adam Smith" (George J. W. Goodman). 1982. *Paper Money*. New York: Dell.

Smith, Hedrick. 1984. *The Russians* (rev. ed.). New York: Ballantine Books.

Snyder, Mark, Elizabeth Decker Tanke, and Ellen Berscheid. 1977. "Social Perception and Interpersonal Behavior: On the Self-Fulfilling Nature of Social Stereotypes." *Journal of Personality and Social Psychology*, 35 (9): 656–666.

Socarides, Charles W. 1975. *Beyond Sexual Freedom*. New York: Quadrangle.

Socarides, Charles W. 1978. *Homosexuality*. New York: Jason Aronson.

Solomon, Lewis D. 1978. *Multinational Corporations and the Emerging World Orders*. Port Washington, N.Y.: Kenikat Press.

Sorokin, Pitirim A. 1941. *Social and Cultural Dynamics*. New York: American Book Company.

Sowell, Thomas. 1981a. *Ethnic America*. New York: Basic Books.

Sowell, Thomas. 1981b. *Markets and Minorities*. New York: Basic Books.

Span, Paula. 1981. "Madison Ave Chases the Baby Boom." *The New York Times Magazine*, May 31, pp.55–57.

Spengler, Oswald. 1928. *The Decline of the West* (Charles Francis Atkinson, trans.) New York: Alfred Knopf.

Spradley, James T., and David W. McCurdy (eds.). 1977. *Conformity and Conflict: Readings in Cultural Anthropology* (3rd ed.). Boston: Little, Brown.

Srinivas, Mysore Narasimhachar. 1962. *Caste in Modern India and Other Essays*. Bombay: Asia Publishing House.

Srole, Leo, et al. 1962. *Mental Health in the Metropolis: The Midtown Manhattan Study*. New York: McGraw-Hill.

Stark, Rodney, and William Sims Bainbridge. 1980. "Secularization, Revival, and Cult Formation." *The Annual Review of the Social Sciences of Religion*, 4: 85–119.

Stark, Rodney, and William Sims Bainbridge. 1985. *The Future of Religion: Secularization, Revival and Cult Formation*. Berkeley: University of California Press.

Stark, Rodney, and Charles Y. Glock. 1968. *American Piety: The Nature of Religious Commitment*. Berkeley: University of California Press.

Steffensmeier, Darrell T., and Robert M. Terry. 1973. "Deviance and Respectability: An Observational Study of Reactions to Shoplifting." *Social Forces*, 51 (June): 417–426.

Stephan, Walter G., and David Rosenfield. 1982. "Racial and Ethnic Stereotypes." In Arthur G. Miller (ed.), *In the Eye of the Beholder: Contemporary Issues in Stereotyping*. New York: Praeger, pp.92–136.

Stevens, William K. 1985. "Black and Standard English Held Diverging More." *The New York Times*, March 15, p.A14.

Stewart, James R. 1980. "Collective Delusion: A Comparison of Believers and Skeptics." Unpublished paper delivered before the Midwest Sociological Society, Milwaukee, April 3.

Stockton, William. 1981. "The Technology Race." *The New York Times Magazine*, June 28, pp.14–18, 49ff.

Stone, Philip J. 1972. "Child Care in Twelve Countries." In Alexander Szala (ed.), *The Use of Time*. The Hague, The Netherlands: Mouton, pp.249–264.

Stouffer, Samuel A. 1955. *Communism, Conformity, and Civil Liberties*. Garden City, N.Y.: Doubleday.

Stouffer, Samuel A., Edward A. Suchman, Leland C. DeVinney, Shirley A. Star, and Robin Williams, Jr. 1949. *The American Soldier*, vol.1. Princeton, N.J.: Princeton University Press.

Stuart, Reginald. 1982. "Job Losses End Prosperity for More Families." *The New York Times*, October 10, pp.1, 40.

Sudman, Seymour, and Norman M. Bradburn. 1982. *Asking Questions: A Practical Guide to Questionnaire Design*. San Francisco: Jossey-Bass.

Suelzle, Marijean. 1970. "Women in Labor." *Trans-action*, 8 (November/December): 50–58.

Sutherland, Edwin H. 1949. *White Collar Crime*. New York: Dryden.

Sutherland, Edwin H., and Donald R. Cressey. 1978. *Criminology* (10th ed.). Philadelphia: Lippencott.

Sweeney, John. 1982. "Long Marriages: Good and Bad," *Newsday*, August 23, Part II, p.2.

Swinton, David H. 1985. "A Color-Conscious Means to an End." *The New York Times*, March 10, p.24E.

Sykes, Gresham M. 1978. *Criminology*. New York: Harcourt, Brace Jovanovich.

Szasz, Thomas S. 1961. *The Myth of Mental Illness*. New York: Harper & Row.

Szymanski, Albert T., and Ted George Goertzel. 1979. *Sociology: Class, Consciousness, and Contradictions*. New York: Van Nostrand.

Tavris, Carol, and Susan Sadd. 1977. *The Redbook Report on Female Sexuality*. New York: Delacorte Press.

Tavris, Carol, and Carole Offir. 1977. *The Longest War: Sex Differences in Perspective*. New York: Harcourt Brace Jovanovich.

Tavris, Carol, and Carole Wade. 1984. *The Longest War: Sex Differences in Perspective* (2nd ed.). San Diego: Harcourt Brace Jovanovich.

Tannenbaum, Frank. 1938. *Crime and the Community*, New York: Ginn.

Taylor, Charles Lewis, and Michael Hudson. 1972. *World Handbook of Political and Social Indicators* (2nd ed.). New Haven, Conn.: Yale University Press.

Terkel, Studs. 1975. *Working*. New York: Avon.

Thompson, Hunter S. *Hell's Angels*. New York: Ballantine Books.

Toffler, Alvin. 1981. *The Third Wave*. New York: Bantam Books.

Tolchin, Martin. 1985. "More Cities Paying Industry to Provide Public Services." *The New York Times*, May 28, 1985, pp.A1, D17.

Tolchin, Martin, and Susan Tolchin. 1983a. "The Rush to Deregulate." *The New York Times Magazine*, August 21, pp.34–38, 70ff.

Tolchin, Martin, and Susan Tolchin. 1983b. *Dismantling America—The Rush to Deregulate*. New York: Houghton Mifflin.

Tönnies, Ferdinand. 1957. *Community and Society* (Charles Loomis, trans.). East Lansing: Michigan State University Press (originally published in 1887).

Tower, Samuel A. 1981. "Commemorative Pair Marks Royal Wedding." *The New York Times*, July 26.

Traub, Stuart H., and Craig B. Little (eds.). 1985. *Theories of Deviance* (3rd ed.). Itasca, Ill.: Peacock.

Treaster, Joseph B. 1985. "Cuba Is Ending State's Ownership of Homes." *The New York Times*, June 30, p.4.

Treiman, Donald J. 1977. *Occupational Prestige in Comparative Perspective*. New York: Academic Press.

Trow, Martin. 1973. "The Second Transformation of American Secondary Education." In Sam D. Sieber and David E. Wilder (eds.), *The School in Society*. New York: Free Press, pp.45–61.

Tumin, Melvin M. 1953. "Some Principles of Stratification: A Critical Review." *American Sociological Review*, 18 (August): 387–394.

Tumin, Melvin M. 1973. *Patterns of Society: Identities, Roles, Resources*. Boston: Little, Brown.

Tumin, Melvin M. 1985. *Social Stratification: The Forms and Functions of Inequality* (2nd ed.). Englewood Cliffs, N.J.: Prentice-Hall.

Turnbull, Colin. 1962. *The Forest People*. New York: Simon & Schuster.

Turner, Jonathan H. 1981. *Sociology: Studying the Human System* (2nd ed.). Santa Monica, Calif.: Goodyear.

Turner, Jonathan H. 1985. *Sociology: A Student Handbook*. New York: Random House.

Turner, Ralph H. 1964. "Collective Behavior." in Robert E. L. Faris (ed.), *Handbook of Modern Sociology*. Chicago: Rand McNally, pp.382–425.

Turner, Ralph H., and Lewis M. Killian. 1986. *Collective Behavior* (3rd ed.). Englewood Cliffs, N.J.: Prentice-Hall.

Tyler, Gus. 1972. "The Multinations: A Social Menace." *The American Federationist*, 79 (7): 1–7.

Tyree, Andrea, Moshe Semyonov, and Robert W. Hodge. 1979. "Gaps and Glissandos: Inequality, Economic Development, and Social Mobility in 24 Countries." *American Sociological Review*. 44 (June): 410–424.

United States Commission on Civil Rights. 1978. *Social Indicators of Equality for Minorities and Women*. Washington: U.S. Government Printing Office.

United States Bureau of the Census. 1979. *Current Housing Reports, Series H-150-77, Financial Characteristics by Individual Indicators of Housing and Neighborhood Quality for the United States and Regions, Annual Housing Survey: 1977, Part F*. Washington, D.C.: U.S. Government Printing Office.

United States Department of Commerce, U.S. Bureau of the Census. 1975. *Historical Statistics of the United States, Colonial Times to 1970*. Washington, D.C.: U.S. Government Printing Office.

United States Department of Commerce, U.S. Bureau of the Census. 1979. *Current Population Reports, Series P-23*. Washington, D.C.: U.S. Government Printing Office.

United States Department of Commerce, U.S. Bureau of the Census. 1982. *Current Population Reports, Series P-20 No. 372. Marital Status and Living Arrangements: March 1981*. Washington, D.C.: U.S. Government Printing Office.

United States Department of Commerce, U.S. Bureau of the Census. 1983. *Current Population Reports, Series P-60, No. 139. Lifetime Earn-*

ings for Men and Women in the United States: 1979. Washington, D.C.: U.S. Government Printing Office.

United States Department of Commerce, U.S. Bureau of the Census. 1983. *Current Population Reports, Series P-60. Money Income of Families and Persons in the United States: 1981*. Washington, D.C.: U.S. Government Printing Office.

United States Department of Commerce, U.S. Bureau of the Census. 1985. *Current Population Reports, Series P-20, No. 397. Advance Report, Voting and Registration in the Election of November, 1984*. Washington, D.C.: U.S. Government Printing Office.

United States Department of Health and Human Services. 1981. *Income and Resources of the Aged, 1978*. Washington, D.C.: U.S. Government Printing Office.

Useem, Michael. 1975. *Protest Movements in America*. Indianapolis, Ind.: Bobbs-Merrill.

Useem, Michael. 1980. "Corporations and the Corporate Elite." *Annual Review of Sociology*, 6: 41–77.

Useem, Michael. 1984. *The Inner Circle: Large Corporations and the Rise of Business Political Activity in the U.S. and U.K*. New York: Oxford University Press.

van den Berghe, Pierre. 1978. *Man in Society: A Biosocial View* (2nd ed.). New York: Elsevier.

Van Stolk, Mary. 1972. *The Battered Child in Canada*. Toronto: McClelland & Stewart.

Vaughn, Mary K. 1978. "Multinational Corporations: The World as a Company Town." In Ahmed Idris-Sovin, et al. (eds.), *The World as a Company Town: Multinational Corporations and Social Change*. The Hague: Mouton, pp.15–35.

Viorst, Judith. 1981. "Some Good Things to Know." *Redbook*, February, pp.16, 124.

Vital Statistics. 1979. "Advance Report: Final Marriage Statistics, 1977 from the National Center for Health Statistics." *Monthly Vital Statistics Report*, Department of Health, Education and Welfare Publication, U.S. Public Health Service, 20 (Supplement July 20) (4): 79–112.

Vogel, Ezra. 1979. *Japan as Number One: Lessons for America*. Cambridge, Mass.: Harvard University Press.

Voorhies, Barbara. 1972. "Supernumerary Sexes." Unpublished paper presented at the 71st Meeting of the American Anthropological Association, November, Toronto.

Waller, Willard W. 1937. "The Rating and Dating Complex." *American Sociological Review*, 2 (October): 727–734.

Waller, Willard W. 1970. *On the Family, Education, and War: Selected Writings* (William J. Goode, Frank F. Furstenberg, and Larry Mitchell, eds.). Chicago: University of Chicago Press.

Wallerstein, Immanuel. 1974. *The Modern World-System*. New York: Academic Press.

Ward, Russell A. 1979. *The Aging Experience: An Introduction to Social Gerontology*. New York: J. B. Lippencott.

Washington, Joseph R., Jr. 1972. *Black Sects and Cults*. Garden City, N.Y.: Doubleday.

Watkins, Mel. 1978. "Why N.B.A. Teams Succeed at Home." *The New York Times*, January 9, p.C23.

Watson, John. *Behaviorism*. 1925. New York: The People's Institute Publishing.

Wattenberg, Ben T., and Richard M. Scammon. 1973. "Black Progress and Liberal Rhetoric." *Commentary*, 55 (April): 35–44.

Webb, Eugene T., Donald T. Campbell, Richard D. Schwartz, and Lee Sechrest. 1966. *Unobtrusive Measures: Non-Reactive Research in the Social Sciences*. Chicago: Rand McNally.

Weber, Max. 1930. *The Protestant Ethic and the Spirit of Capitalism* (Talcott Parsons, trans.). New York: Scribner's (originally published in 1905).

Weber, Max. 1946. *From Max Weber: Essays in Sociology* (Hans H. Gerth and C. Wright Mills trans. and ed.). New York: Oxford University Press.

Weber, Max. 1947. *The Theory of Social and Economic Organization* (Talcott Parsons, ed., A. M. Henderson and Talcott Parsons trans.). New York: Oxford University Press.

Weber, Max. 1963. *The Sociology of Religion* (Ephraim Fischoff trans.). Boston: Beacon Press.

Weber, Max. 1968. *Economy and Society: An Outline of Interpretive Sociology* (Guenther Roth and Claus Wittich, ed., Ephraim Fischoff et al. trans.). New York: Bedminster Press.

Weeks, John. 1986. *Population: An Introduction to Concepts and Issues*. Belmont, Calif.: Wadsworth.

Weinberg, Martin S. 1970. "The Nudist Management of Respectability." In Jack D. Douglas (ed.), *Deviance and Respectability: The Social Construction of Moral Meanings*. New York: Basic Books, pp.375–403.

Weinstein, Eugene A., and Paul Deutschenberger. 1963. "Some Dimensions of Altercasting." *Sociometry*, 26 (December): 454–466.

Weisskopf, Michael. 1985. "Rationed Babies." *Newsday*, February 12, Part II, pp.4, 5, 16.

Weitzman, Lenore J. 1970. *Social Suicide: A Study of Missing Persons*. PhD Dissertation, Department of Sociology, Columbia University.

Weitzman, Lenore J. 1981. "Social Suicide." In Samuel E. Wallace and Albin Eser (eds.), *Suicide and Euthanasia: The Rights of Personhood*. Knoxville: University of Tennessee, pp.10–23.

Weitzman, Lenore J., Deborah Eifler, Elizabeth Hodaka, and Catherine Ross. 1972. "Sex Role Socialization in Picture Books for Pre-School Children." *American Journal of Sociology*, 77 (May): 1125–1149.

West, Hollie I. 1979. "Getting Ahead: And the Man Behind the Class-Race Furor." *The Washington Post*, January 1, pp.C1, C13.

Westoff, Charles F. 1974. "Coital Frequency and Contraception." *Family Planning Perspectives*, 6 (Summer): 136–141.

White, Lynn, Jr. 1962. *Medieval Technology and Social Change*. New York: Oxford University Press.

Whiting, J. W. M. 1977. "Cross-Cultural Perspectives on Parenthood." Unpublished paper presented at the Grover Conference on Marriage and the Family, May.

Whorf, Benjamin Lee. 1956. *Language, Thought and Reality*. Cambridge, Mass.: MIT Press.

Wickman, Peter, and Phillip Whitten. 1980. *Criminology: Perspectives on Crime and Criminality*. Lexington, Mass.: D. C. Heath.

Williams, Dennis A., et al. 1981a. "Why Public Schools Fail." *Newsweek*, April 20, pp.62–73.

Williams, Dennis A., et al. 1981b. "Teachers Are in Trouble." *Newsweek*, April 27, pp.78–84.

Williams, Dennis A., et al. 1981c. "Hope for the Schools." *Newsweek*, May 4. pp.66–72.

Williams, Robin, Jr. 1970. *American Society: A Sociological Interpretation* (3rd ed.). New York: Alfred Knopf.

Willie, Charles V. 1978. "The Inclining Significance of Race." *Society*, 15 (July/August): 10, 12–15.

Willie, Charles V. 1979. *Caste and Class Controversy*. New York: General Hall.

Wilson, Bryan. 1982. *Religion in Sociological Perspective*. Oxford, England: Oxford University Press.

Wilson, Everett K., and Hanan Selvin. 1980. *Why Study Sociology? A Note to Undergraduates*. Belmont, Calif.: Wadsworth.

Wilson, James Q., and Richard J. Herrnstein. 1985. *Crime and Human Nature*. New York: Simon & Schuster.

Wilson, John. 1973. *Introduction to Social Movements*. New York: Basic Books.

Wilson, John. 1978. *Religion in American Society: The Effective Presence*. Englewood Cliffs, N.J.: Prentice-Hall.

Wilson, Robert A., and Bill Hosokawa. 1980. *East to America: A History of the Japanese in the United States*. New York: William Morrow.

Wilson, William Julius. 1980. *The Declining Significance of Race* (2nd ed.) Chicago: University of Chicago Press.

Wilson, William Julius. 1984. "The Urban Underclass." In Leslie W. Dunbar (ed.), *Minority Report*. New York: Pantheon Books, pp.75–117.

Wimberly, Ronald C. 1976. "Testing the Civil Religion Hypothesis." *Sociological Analysis*, 37 (Winter): 341–352.

Wimberly, Ronald C., and James A. Christenson. 1981. "Civil Religion and Other Religious Identities." *Sociological Analysis*, 42 (Summer): 91–100.

Wimberly, Ronald C., Donald A. Clelland, and Thomas C. Hood. 1976. "The Civil Religious Dimension: Is It There?" *Social Forces*, 54 (June): 890–900.

Winch, Robert F. 1962. "The Functions of Dating in Middle-Class America." In Winch et al. (eds.), *Selected Studies in Marriage and the Family*. New York: Holt, Rinehart & Winston, pp.506–509.

Winer, Michael. 1985. "Asian-Americans Question Ivy League's Entry Policies." *The New York Times*, May 30, pp.B1, B4.

Wirth, Louis. 1938. "Urbanism as a Way of Life." *American Journal of Sociology*, 44 (July): 3–24.

Wiseman, Frederick. 1972. "Methodological Bias in Public Opinion Surveys." *Public Opinion Quarterly*, 36 (Spring): 105–108.

Wiseman, Jacqueline P. 1970. *Stations of the Lost: The Treatment of Skid Row Alcoholics*. Englewood Cliffs, N.J.: Prentice-Hall.

Woods, Donald J. 1987. "Recall the Days of 'We Shall Overcome.'" *The New York Times*, January 18, pp.H1, H27.

Worchel, Stephen, Jerry Lee, and Akanabi Adewole. 1975. "Effects of Supply and Demand on Ratings of Object Value." *Journal of Personality and Social Psychology*, 32 (5): 906–914.

Wrong, Dennis H. 1961. "The Oversocialized Conception of Man in Modern Sociology." *American Sociological Review*, 26 (April): 183–193.

Wuthnow, Robert. 1976. "The New Religions in Social Context." In Charles Y. Glock and Robert N. Bellah (eds.), *The New Religious Consciousness*. Berkeley: University of California Press, pp.267–293.

Wuthnow, Robert (ed.). 1979. *The Religious Dimensions: New Directions in Quantitative Research*. New York: Academic Press.

Yaukey, David. 1985. *Demography: The Study of Human Population*. New York: St. Martin's Press.

Yinger, J. Milton. 1960. "Contraculture and Subculture." *American Sociological Review*, 25 (October): 625–635.

Yinger, J. Milton. 1970. *The Scientific Study of Religion*. New York: Macmillan.

Yinger, J. Milton. 1982. *Countercultures*. New York: Free Press.

Zelnick, Melvin, and John F. Kantner. 1980. "Sexual Activity, Contraceptive Use, and Pregnancy Among Metropolitan-Area Teenagers." *Family Planning Perspectives*, 12 (September-October): 230–237.

Zetterberg, Hans L. 1966. *On Theory and Verification in Sociology* (3rd ed.). Totowa, N.J.: Bedminster Press.

Zimmerman, Don H., and Candace West. 1975. "Sex Roles, Interruptions, and Silences in Conversations." In Barrie Thorne and Nancy Henley (eds.), *Language and Sex: Differences and Dominance*. Rowley, Mass.: Newbury House, pp.105–129.

Zinn, Maxine Baca. 1985. "Sex Roles and Sex Stratification." In D. Stanley Eitzen, *Conflict and Order: Understanding Society*. Boston: Allyn & Bacon, pp.353–397.

Zopf, Paul E., Jr. 1984. *Population: An Introduction to Social Demography*. Palo Alto, Calif.: Mayfield.

Zuckerman, Harriet. 1977. *Scientific Elite: Nobel Laureates in the United States*. New York: Free Press.

NAME INDEX

SUBJECT INDEX